Realizing 3D Animation in Blender

Master the fundamentals of 3D animation in Blender, from keyframing to character movement

Sam Brubaker

<packt>

Realizing 3D Animation in Blender

Copyright © 2024 Packt Publishing

All rights reserved. No part of this book may be reproduced, stored in a retrieval system, or transmitted in any form or by any means, without the prior written permission of the publisher, except in the case of brief quotations embedded in critical articles or reviews.

Every effort has been made in the preparation of this book to ensure the accuracy of the information presented. However, the information contained in this book is sold without warranty, either express or implied. Neither the author(s), nor Packt Publishing or its dealers and distributors, will be held liable for any damages caused or alleged to have been caused directly or indirectly by this book.

Packt Publishing has endeavored to provide trademark information about all of the companies and products mentioned in this book by the appropriate use of capitals. However, Packt Publishing cannot guarantee the accuracy of this information.

Group Product Manager: Rohit Rajkumar

Publishing Product Manager: Kaustubh Manglurkar

Book Project Manager: Aishwarya Mohan

Senior Editor: Debolina Acharyya

Technical Editor: Reenish Kulshrestha

Copy Editor: Safis Editing

Indexer: Manju Arasan

Production Designer: Joshua Misquitta

DevRel Marketing Coordinator: Anamika Singh and Nivedita Pandey

First published: July 2024

Production reference: 1140624

Published by Packt Publishing Ltd.

Grosvenor House

11 St Paul's Square

Birmingham

B3 1RB, UK

ISBN 978-1-80107-721-7

www.packtpub.com

This book is dedicated to my wife, Elina, my parents, Mike and Charlotte, and the many members of the Blender community who have taught me, inspired me, and involved me in their wonderful artistic endeavors over the years.

– Sam Brubaker

Contributors

About the author

Sam Brubaker is an artist, 3D animator, and Blender expert. After stumbling upon Blender by chance in 2004, Sam was determined to be an animator, and in 2006 his short film won the Blender Foundation's Suzanne Award for best animation. In 2012, Sam graduated from North Carolina State University with a bachelor's in art and design and immediately started a career as a freelance animator, followed by a stint as a Blender instructor. He has since been a freelancer and educator living on both coasts of the United States. He now resides in the Midwest with his wife, Dr. Elina Thomas.

About the reviewer

Daniele Daldoss is a creative designer who finds his focus in turning classic design into motion graphics and 3D animation. His work ranges from one-off artwork projects to full-scale branding development with the extra mile of including digital technologies in the process. His clients are a mix of small businesses as well as large-scale international corporations.

One year ago, he was hired as a Motion Graphics Team Leader by an international company.

He's been doing 3D design since 2005, his first year at the Academy of Fine Arts. In 2014, he switched to Blender after a colleague suggested it as software more in line with his way of working. He immediately fell in love with it. Today, he works full-time With Blender and couldn't be happier.

Jonathan Daniel has been using Blender for over 6 years at this point and is an avid aircraft and tank enthusiast, often modeling these military vehicles in Blender as a hobby.

Table of Contents

Preface   xv

Part 1: Introduction to Blender and the Fundamentals of Animation

1

Basic Keyframes in the Timeline   3

Technical requirements	4	Editing keyframes in the Timeline	13
Navigating the Timeline	4	Basic keyframe editing	13
Moving through time	5	Duplicating keyframes	14
Setting the frame range	6	Holding a position	14
Adjusting the Timeline view	6	Editing the timing of your animation	15
Animation playback	7	Animating nearly any property in Blender	16
Creating simple movement with keyframes	8	Other keying methods	17
Keying the initial location	8	Keying the material color	17
The keyed property	10	Summary	18
Keying the second location	11	Questions	19
Principles of keying	12		
Keying rotation	12		

2

The Graph Editor   21

Technical requirements	22	Navigating the Graph Editor	23
Getting the ball rolling	22	Bringing up the Graph Editor	23

The X and Y axes in the Graph Editor	24	Adding bouncing keyframes in the Graph Editor	37
Animation channels	25		
Adjusting the Graph Editor view	28	**F-curve extrapolation**	**43**
Interpolation and easing	**32**	Linear extrapolation	43
Setting the interpolation mode	32	Cyclic extrapolation	44
Setting the easing type	34	**Summary**	**47**
Making the ball bounce	**36**	**Questions**	**47**
Linear interpolation for objects in mid-air	36		

3

Bezier Keyframes 49

Technical requirements	**50**	Bounces with Free handles	68
One tired animator	**50**	**Heading, weight, and balance**	**70**
The connected parts of our unicycle	51	Motion paths as a visual guide	71
keying the course checkpoints	51	Tilting while turning	74
A novel method for inserting keyframes in the Graph Editor	55	Leaning into it	77
Bezier handle types	**57**	**Copying keyframes to another channel**	**80**
Exposing keyframe handles	58	Copying keyframes	81
Overview of Bezier handle types	59	Keying a single property	81
Automatic and Auto Clamped Bezier handles	60	Pasting keyframes	82
Vector and Aligned handles	63	Scaling keyframe values	83
Combining Vector and Aligned handles	64	**Summary**	**84**
Editing Bezier handles	**65**	**Questions**	**85**
Smooth movement with Aligned handles	66		

4

Looking into Object Relationships 87

Technical requirements	**88**	Centering the origin	91
Understanding object origins	**88**	Grabbing the origin	92
The truth about objects and origins	90	**Parenting objects**	**94**

The parent/child relationship	95	Animating the path	106
Understanding constraints	**97**	**Drivers**	**109**
Adding a constraint	98	Adding a driver	110
World space versus local space	99	Editing a driver	110
Copying constraints	101	Driver F-curves	115
Following a path	**101**	The final chart of object relationships	118
Editing the animation path	102	**Summary**	**118**
Adding a Follow Path constraint	104	**Questions**	**119**

5

Rendering an Animation 121

Technical requirements	**122**	Why output an image sequence and not a video?	139
Setting up the camera	**122**	Output settings	140
Adding a camera to the scene	123	Pre-render checklist	143
Camera view-finding	124	Rendering the animation	144
The animated camera	127	Viewing the rendered frames	145
Rendering basics	**127**	**Converting an image sequence to a video**	**145**
What is rendering, really?	127	The Video Sequence Editor	146
Controls for rendering	130	Output settings for video export	149
Setting up our scene for rendering	133	Outputting a video	151
Predicting and managing render performance	138	**Summary**	**151**
Rendering an image sequence	**139**	**Questions**	**151**

Part 2: Character Animation

6

Linking and Posing a Character 155

Technical requirements	**156**	Linked libraries	157
Linking a character in a new scene	**157**	Making a library override	162
		Understanding Rain's armature	**164**

The art of rigging Rain	165	**Creating a library of poses**	**195**
The CloudRig interface	168	The Asset Browser	195
Posing an armature	**172**	Creating a pose asset	196
Pose mode	173	Practicing poses	197
IK bones	177	**Summary**	**200**
FK bones	181	**Questions**	**201**
Fingers, faces, and other accessories	186		

7

Basic Character Animation — 203

Technical requirements	**203**	Organizing the Dope Sheet	224
Preparing Rain in a new scene	**204**	**Going further into animating this character**	**230**
A brief recap on linking Rain into a new project	204	Two more in-between poses	230
Using a pose asset	205	In-between operators for posing	235
Setting bone relationships for an animation	207	Waving	236
Hiding bones	211	**Polishing the animation**	**238**
Keying pose bones	**212**	Using the Graph Editor on bones	239
Blocking or roughing the animation	212	Animating Rain's accessories	242
Reviewing our key poses	217	**Summary**	**243**
The Dope Sheet	**218**	**Questions**	**244**
Introduction to the Dope Sheet	219		

8

The Walk Cycle — 245

Technical requirements	**245**	Moving forward on the Y axis	253
Preparing the walk cycle scene	**246**	Establishing the stride length	254
The timeline of a walk cycle	246	Looping the animation	258
Timeline markers	248	Putting Rain on a treadmill	262
Getting Rain ready to walk	250	Using a preview playback range	266

Adding more periodic motion	267	Copying animation from the left foot to the right foot	283
Torso movement	268		
Swaying from side to side	269	Finishing the walk cycle	286
The Action Editor	269	FK toes	286
More torso animation with sine waves	272	FK arms	288
		Final touches?	289
Advanced footwork	276	Summary	291
Rolling the foot	276	Questions	291
Picking up the feet	278		
Correcting the motion of the legs	279		

9

Sound and Lip-Syncing 293

Technical requirements	293	Key facial expressions	299
Using sound in Blender	294	Automatic keyframing and keying sets	301
Importing audio files into the Video Sequencer	294	The science of lip-syncing	303
Using sound strips	296	Phonetics for animators	303
Timeline settings for working with sound	298	Animating the mouth	308
		Summary	309
Acting without speaking	299	Questions	309

10

Prop Interaction with Dynamic Constraints 311

Technical requirements	312	Constraints with animated influence	329
Touching the object	312		
Setting up the shot	312	Keying the influence of a constraint	329
Reaching for an object	316	Releasing the ball	330
Setting up an object-to-bone relationship	319	Animating a throwing/tossing motion	330
		Animating the ball being thrown	336
Dummy bones – a smarter way to rig	320	Summary	342
The Copy Transforms constraint	323	Questions	342

Part 3: Advanced Tools and Techniques

11

F-Curve Modifiers — 345

Technical requirements	345	Adding the Noise modifier	354
Where to find F-curve modifiers	346	Copying modifiers	356
Adding our first F-curve modifier	347	**More fun with Noise modifiers**	**358**
Getting fancy with F-curve modifiers	**349**	Using a Noise modifier to simulate an explosion	358
The Stepped Interpolation modifier	349	Restricting the frame range of a modifier	359
The Built-In Function modifier	350	**Summary**	**360**
Setting the clock with math	352	**Questions**	**361**
Using the Noise modifier	**354**		

12

Rigid Body Physics — 363

Technical requirements	363	Selecting rigid body collision shapes	377
Creating a rigid body world	364	**Destroying a wall**	**378**
Our first rigid body simulation	364	Building a wall	378
Active and passive rigid bodies	368	Destroying the wall	381
Rigid body collision	**371**	Baking the simulation	385
The smashing-junk-together algorithm	373	**Summary**	**386**
Collision shapes	373	**Questions**	**386**

13

Animating with Multiple Cameras — 387

Technical requirements	387	The active camera	389
Ready camera two	388	Switching cameras in the Timeline	391
Setting up multiple cameras	388	**Camera overrides**	**393**

Viewing with a local camera	393	**Summary**	**398**
Using multiple cameras in the Video Sequencer	394	**Questions**	**399**

14

Nonlinear Animation   401

Technical requirements	402	Actions in the NLA	408
Reusing actions	402	Layering actions	412
Appending the walk cycle	403	Appending the second action	413
Assigning an action in the Action Editor	403	Animated Strip Time	414
A hard lesson in forgotten settings	405	The Strip Time property	415
The action strip	406	Summary	417
Introduction to the Nonlinear Animation editor	406	Questions	418

Index   419

Other Books You May Enjoy   430

Preface

When someone takes an interest in learning 3D animation, the first question they usually ask is, "What program should I use?"

The answer, according to the smartest and most experienced animators, is that it's a waste of time to argue about this. An app is merely a tool, not what makes you an animator. What matters are an animator's ideas, patience, and willingness to learn. Every minute spent mulling over "which app is best" is a distraction from actually animating, so just pick one and get started!

I like that answer, don't you? Anyway, the correct answer is Blender.

It's not Blender's excellent features and competitive price ($0) that make it the best. This quirky free program has changed dramatically since the version I downloaded as a teenager in 2004. Its suitability as an industry tool for animators is no longer disputed like it once was. But the thing that makes it the best 3D program hasn't changed a bit – Blender is licensed under the GNU General Public License as free software. Not just free as in $0, but *really* free. The program – along with its source code – is free to download, modify, and share by anyone, and is legally stipulated to remain so in perpetuity. It cannot be acquired by another company. It will never charge you a subscription fee. If you expect to spend hours and hours of your time and creativity in a single program, that "feature" should matter to you most of all.

Another thing that hasn't changed about Blender is how much fun it is to teach. Blender has always been full of features that users find accidentally. The community shares these "secrets" with one another like scholars sharing esoteric knowledge. With this book, I hope to share a little of that magic with you.

Who this book is for

If you're new to 3D animation and would like to get started with the best 3D animation program out there, this book is for you. With my experience training 3D animators of all ages and skill levels, I'll transform you from a novice tinkerer into a real animator from as early as *Chapter 1*. Only the most basic starting familiarity with Blender is required.

Perhaps you're already a competent Blender user who has yet to really break into animation, an experienced animator who's looking to switch to an open source pipeline, or someone who just finished *Part 1* of this book. If that sounds like you, you'll find helpful exercises, tips, and commentary in the character animation chapters and chapters on advanced topics.

What you need to get started

This book does not come with a computer! To follow the exercises and make your own 3D animations, you'll need Blender, a suitable computer on which to run it, and an internet connection.

Software/hardware covered in the book	Operating system requirements
Blender	Windows, macOS, or Linux

Let's look at this in a bit more detail.

Your animation workstation

The minimum and recommended system requirements to run Blender can be found on the official Blender website:

`https://www.blender.org/download/requirements/`

Nearly all new laptops and desktop computers will meet these criteria. Even if your machine is no longer the latest model, there's a good chance it can run Blender perfectly fine as well.

Hardware

If you're shopping for a new computer or an upgrade specifically geared toward 3D animation, I recommend putting your money toward a dedicated NVIDIA or AMD graphics card. A high-performance GPU is the most crucial computer part to help ensure your animations play back smoothly in Blender.

You will also need a mouse and keyboard. Blender makes use of practically every key on your keyboard as a hotkey, so a full-size keyboard with all the functions and number pad keys will be the most helpful. As for the mouse, that's non-negotiable. You need a mouse with a left button, a right button, and a clickable scroll wheel in the middle. A touchpad will not do!

Operating system

Blender runs on Windows, macOS, and Linux. If you have a choice and you're curious about Linux, that happens to be the best operating system for Blender. Now would be an excellent time to try it out!

Put simply, Blender has all the technical requirements of a 3D video game. If you've got a computer that can play the latest games, an internet connection that can download them, and a mouse that's fast enough to beat them, you've probably got all the hardware you need to make 3D animations.

Prerequisite knowledge

Though this book is written with the novice reader in mind, we're going to skip the most elementary essentials and get straight to animating in *Chapter 1*. That means you'll need some starting familiarity with Blender and computers.

Computer literacy

You must know what a file is, because we will be saving files to folders. Later, we will need to click on those folders and find the files we saved there earlier.

Basic controls in Blender

You can be a Blender novice, just not a Blender never-seen-it-before. Do you know how to navigate 3D space in Blender and look at the default cube from all sides? How about selecting that cube and moving it to a different location on a particular axis? Can you delete the cube and replace it with a sphere? If these tasks don't sound too hard, you already have what it takes to tackle this book.

Finally, you must be able to download and install Blender on your own.

Blender

Blender is free to download and easy to install. The latest version can be downloaded from the official site `blender.org`, but every previous version is available as well.

For this book, I recommend downloading and installing version 4.0.2 here:

`https://download.blender.org/release/Blender4.0/`

Download the package that matches your operating system and install it. Using this version will ensure that what you see on your screen will be consistent with the instructions and screenshots of Blender in this book.

Blender is well maintained by developers at the Blender Foundation and in the worldwide community. Though updates to the software are frequent, the foundation keeps every previous version available online. Blender's backward/forward compatibility is quite good, so later versions of Blender, such as 4.1, 4.2, and so on, may also work with the exercises in this book. This will gradually change as time goes on.

What this book covers

Chapter 1, *Basic Keyframes in the Timeline*, to ease ourselves into the subject of keyframes, will cover how to create a rudimentary animation in Blender using the default cube and Blender's most basic animation editor, the Timeline.

Chapter 2, *The Graph Editor*, discusses Blender's graph editor, which is indispensable for creating more complex motion. To realize the usefulness and importance of this tool, we will use it to animate a bouncing ball.

Chapter 3, *Bezier Keyframes*, discusses Bezier keyframes. These versatile keyframes offer direct control over the shape of the F-Curve, allowing the animator to directly "draw" the animation. This will be useful for our third exercise: animating a unicycle!

Chapter 4, *Looking into Object Relationships*, by examining the ways objects can be parented, constrained, and driven by other objects, teaches us how objects can be made to move in precise ways without being directly animated.

Chapter 5, *Rendering an Animation*, discusses rendering. Your animation can't just live inside a `.blend` file forever. You'll want to render it as a sequence of still frames and export those frames to a video file that can be shared with others.

Chapter 6, *Linking and Posing a Character*, looks at linking and posing a character. An aspiring animator should become familiar with character animation using a professional-quality rig. In this chapter, you'll be introduced to *Rain*, an excellent rig provided for free by the Blender Foundation.

Chapter 7, *Basic Character Animation*, discusses character animation, which requires managing hundreds or sometimes thousands of keyframes for a single scene. Two new areas in Blender are needed to do so effectively: the Dope Sheet and the Action Editor.

Chapter 8, *The Walk Cycle*, explores making a character walk, which is essential but tricky! We'll have to use the tools and techniques from previous chapters with even greater care and precision. Along the way, we'll learn some additional techniques for ensuring symmetrical animation and smooth footwork.

Chapter 9, *Sound and Lip-Syncing*, will guide you through the process of importing a voiceover audio file and animating Rain's mouth to match the spoken words.

Chapter 10, *Prop Interaction with Dynamic Constraints*, covers proper interaction. Picking up an object and throwing it is one of many acts that are simple to do in real life but not so simple to animate. We'll need to add our own constraints, apply their effect at precise times, and even animate their influence.

Chapter 11, *F-Curve Modifiers*, returns to the Graph Editor. There's still more to the Graph Editor than meets the eye! F-Curve modifiers allow an animator to generate endless motion without endless keying! Animating a clock will be our exercise for applying this useful feature.

Chapter 12, *Rigid Body Physics*, explores the physics of rigid bodies. Why animate lots of objects by hand when the computer can do the work? In this chapter, we'll animate a wrecking ball destroying a wall – a perfect opportunity to use Blender's rigid-body simulation features.

Chapter 13, *Animating with Multiple Cameras*, covers various methods for using multiple camera objects in one animation. Most films and television shows are shot with more than one camera. There's no reason 3D animation can't be the same way.

Chapter 14, *Nonlinear Animation*, explores what is possibly Blender's most mysterious and esoteric feature, the Nonlinear Animation Editor, which allows you to *animate your animation*.

Getting the most out of this book

Each chapter in this book consists of an animation exercise with guided instructions. I recommend you read it while seated at your computer and follow along in Blender! That's the idea, anyway – maybe you'll decide to read the chapters out of order or disobey the instructions at your own peril. It's a book, not a schoolmaster.

The *Technical requirements* section in each chapter will tell you what additional things you need to follow along. Some chapters require that you download a specific file prepared specifically for this book by yours truly. Other chapters may require using an asset you created earlier, so always remember to save your work at the end of the exercise!

Finally, there is a *Questions* section at the end of every chapter that will challenge you on what you've learned. These are not ordinary quizzes! Some questions are straightforward and have answers given in the preceding pages. Other questions are intended to make you think critically or do your own exploration in Blender. A few are jokes or trick questions, but the hardest questions of all are the ones that only sound like tricks… if you can answer any of those, you get an A+.

Share your thoughts

Once you've read *Realizing 3D Animation in Blender*, we'd love to hear your thoughts! Scan the QR code below to go straight to the Amazon review page for this book and share your feedback.

```
https://packt.link/r/1801077215
```

Your review is important to us and the tech community and will help us make sure we're delivering excellent quality content.

Download a free PDF copy of this book

Thanks for purchasing this book!

Do you like to read on the go but are unable to carry your print books everywhere?

Is your eBook purchase not compatible with the device of your choice?

Don't worry, now with every Packt book you get a DRM-free PDF version of that book at no cost.

Read anywhere, any place, on any device. Search, copy, and paste code from your favorite technical books directly into your application.

The perks don't stop there, you can get exclusive access to discounts, newsletters, and great free content in your inbox daily

Follow these simple steps to get the benefits:

1. Scan the QR code or visit the link below

`https://packt.link/free-ebook/9781801077217`

2. Submit your proof of purchase
3. That's it! We'll send your free PDF and other benefits to your email directly

Part 1: Introduction to Blender and the Fundamentals of Animation

Math is all about numbers, modeling is all about vertices, gravel is all about very small rocks, and animation is all about keyframes. These are all boring but essential facts, which is why we begin this book with three whole chapters that – though they have different names to hold your attention – are solely about keyframes. First, we'll learn how to create them and move them left and right. Then, in the second chapter, we'll move them up and down, and, in the third chapter, we'll learn what makes them move by themselves when no one is looking.

By the time we get to the fourth chapter, we will have grown so sick of keyframes we'll want to learn how to animate using as few of them as possible. Finally, the fifth chapter is about frames, of which keyframes are not a type. What is a keyframe, you ask? Let's not get ahead of ourselves.

If you've never animated anything in Blender before, this is the place to start.

This part contains the following chapters:

- *Chapter 1, Basic Keyframes in the Timeline*
- *Chapter 2, The Graph Editor*
- *Chapter 3, Bezier Keyframes*
- *Chapter 4, Looking into Object Relationships*
- *Chapter 5, Rendering an Animation*

1
Basic Keyframes in the Timeline

For our first animation in Blender, we will animate the default cube. It has to be good for something! This may seem painfully boring, but we must keep things simple at first, and even simple objects can tell a story. Ours will be a 5-second epic about a young cube that ventures eastward into the unknown, then turns around, returns home, and rests in the end, wizened by many frames of traveling.

This exercise will serve as an introduction to Blender's **Timeline**, as well as **keyframes**, the building blocks of any animation. We'll use keyframes to determine the location, rotation, and color of the cube at various points in time.

Whereas this chapter is intended for readers with zero knowledge of Blender's animation system, you will need to have a little experience in Blender's basic functionality. This includes navigating the 3D Viewport, editing numeric values, and selecting and moving objects in 3D space.

In this chapter, we're going to cover the following main topics:

- Navigating the Timeline
- Creating simple movement with keyframes
- Editing keyframes in the Timeline
- Animating nearly any property in Blender

Technical requirements

To follow along, all you will need is Blender 4.0 running on a computer that meets the minimum system requirements. Later versions of Blender will probably be suitable for this book as well, with only minor changes, though this can't be guaranteed.

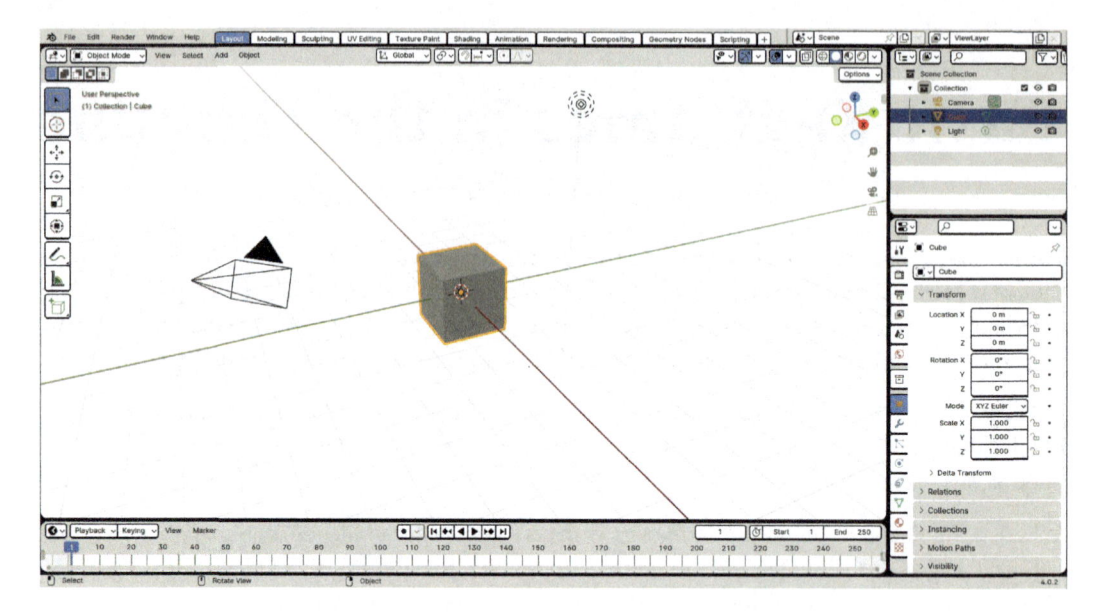

Figure 1.1: The default scene in Blender 4.0, shown here in the "Print Friendly" theme

If you have already made significant changes to your user preferences or startup file, go to **File | Defaults | Load Factory Settings** to restore the same environment as the one shown in *Figure 1.1*.

> **Tip**
>
> For the time being, there's no need to click on the **Animation** tab at the top of the screen or to switch to any other **workspace**. Everything in this chapter can be done in the default **Layout** workspace. Remember that workspaces are just preset window configurations for your convenience. They are not essential to each task for which they are labeled. Since Blender's interface is so flexible, I usually ignore them or make my own.

Navigating the Timeline

Open a new file in Blender and take a look at the numbered area at the bottom of the screen just below the 3D Viewport. This area is called the Timeline, the most basic editor for animation work:

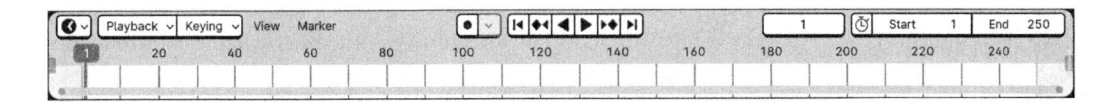

Figure 1.2: The Timeline

The Timeline displays your keyframes and contains controls for playback and basic keyframe editing. Much of the work of animating will involve this window and/or one of Blender's several other animation editors.

Moving through time

The first thing you probably learned in Blender was how to navigate the 3D Viewport, moving your viewing angle around in 3D space using the middle mouse button and various keyboard shortcuts. For the same reason that you needed to learn this before actually modeling anything, you must learn how to *navigate in time* before animating anything.

In the **header** (the part with menus) of the Timeline, you'll see some menus, playback controls, and finally some integer properties:

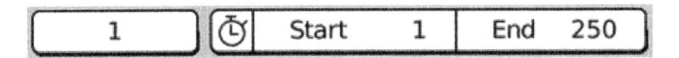

Figure 1.3: From left to right – the Current Frame, Start Frame, and End Frame properties

These are the **Current Frame**, **Start Frame**, and **End Frame** properties of your scene. The most crucial of these properties is the **Current Frame**.

Current Frame is a very special property that determines the frame, or point in time, in which the scene is displayed. Just as you must view a 3D model from many different angles, as an animator, you must move through time, viewing your animated scene at many different frames as you work.

Changing the **Current Frame** value moves backward and forward through time in your animation. There are a variety of ways to do this:

- Directly editing the **Current Frame** value in the header of the Timeline
- Clicking anywhere along the Timeline's row of frame numbers
- Tapping the left and right arrow keys on your keyboard
- Holding *Alt* while scrolling with the mouse wheel

> **Tip**
> The vertical blue line in the Timeline which marks the current frame is called the *playhead*. Dragging the playhead left and right is a technique called *scrubbing*, which is indispensable for reviewing and inspecting your animation.

Give these methods a try. As you adjust the **Current Frame** value, the horizontal position of the playhead in the Timeline will move with it. Keep in mind that, because we have not yet animated anything, nothing else in Blender will move.

Setting the frame range

The default scene in Blender has a **Start Frame** value of 1 and an **End Frame** value of 250. This means that the animation will begin at frame 1 and end at frame 250, for a total duration of 250 frames. At the default frame rate of 24 **frames per second** (**FPS**), this will yield an animation just over 10 seconds long.

> **Tip**
> The **Frame Rate** setting of your animation can be found in the **Dimension** panel of the **Output Properties** in the Properties Editor. For the remainder of this book, however, we'll stick with 24 frames per second, a nice divisible number and a rate commonly associated with a film-like or "cinematic" look.

250 frames is an awful lot for our first animation, so let's shorten the range we have to work with. Dial down the **End Frame** property from 250 to 120:

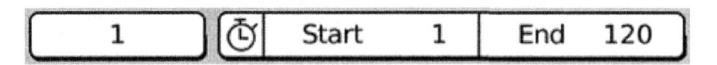

Figure 1.4: End Frame set to 120

This shortens the duration of the animation to 120 frames, exactly 5 seconds. Just enough time for our epic 3-part adventure!

Adjusting the Timeline view

Although we've set our animation to end at frame 120 and not at frame 250, the Timeline is still displaying a range of frame numbers from 0 to 250. We're no longer interested in any frames past 120, so let's adjust our view to use the horizontal span of this area more effectively:

1. Middle-click and drag rightward in the Timeline to move the frame range 0 to 120 into roughly the center of the area.
2. Use your scroll wheel or *Ctrl* and middle-click to zoom in so that the Timeline displays only the desired range of interest, 0 to 120.

As you can see, the controls for changing the Timeline view are pretty much the same as any other area in Blender:

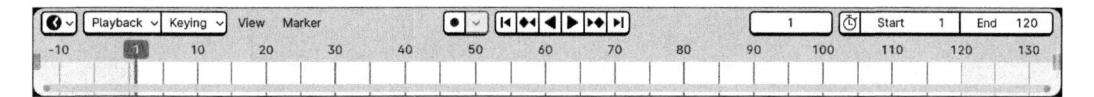

Figure 1.5: The Timeline, adjusted to show only frames 0 to 120

> **Tip**
> If you lose your way in the Timeline (or almost any other editor, for that matter), press the *Home* key or go to **View | Frame All**. This has the same result as what we just did, restoring the editor's view so that all visible content is nicely centered.

In later chapters, it will be necessary to scroll around, zooming in and out at different keyframes as our animations become more complex. For the rest of this chapter, however, we can leave the Timeline view where it is.

Animation playback

Controls for **playback** and for jumping to specific frames are in the center of the Timeline header:

Figure 1.6: Timeline playback buttons

Hitting the spacebar or clicking the **Play** button will play your (presently very boring) animation, rapidly incrementing the **Current Frame** value at the established frame rate. Hitting *Ctrl + Shift + Spacebar* or clicking the backward **Play** button plays your animation backward. Until stopped, the animation will play on repeat, looping back to the **Start Frame** after the **End Frame** has been reached.

You can **stop** the animation immediately at the current frame by hitting the spacebar again or by pressing the **Pause** button in the Timeline. Hitting *Esc* will stop the animation and also return to the original frame at which playback began. Remember to stop the animation before attempting to edit anything.

> **Tip**
> Playing and stopping animations is such a frequent action that I almost always use keyboard shortcuts instead of clicking on these buttons. The hotkeys for playback work in every editor, so you won't always have to have the Timeline open.

We've gone long enough without animating anything – let's now make the cube move!

Creating simple movement with keyframes

In the first act, our hero `Cube` will stride fearlessly from west to east. We'll achieve this using keyframes, a technique inherited from the traditional hand-drawn animation process.

In hand-drawn animation, a lead animator draws the most important frames in a shot, or "keyframes," which determine the positions and expressions of characters and objects in the shot at key points in time. These keyframes are then passed to the "in-betweener," who draws the rest of the frames in between to create a smooth appearance of movement.

In Blender and other animation apps, keyframes play a similar, though much simpler role: *determining what the value of a property will be at a given frame*. It's easier to see for yourself than read about it, so let's jump right in!

Keying the initial location

To begin, we'll give our main character, `Cube`, a suitable starting position:

1. Go to frame `10`.
2. Select the `Cube`.
3. Move the `Cube` up `1` unit on the *Z* axis so that it rests on the "floor" in the 3D Viewport.
4. Move the `Cube` `-5` units leftward on the *X* axis.
5. Now, let's insert our first keyframe! With the `Cube` still selected and your mouse cursor in the 3D Viewport, press the *I* key.

This brings up the **Insert Keyframe** menu, one of several ways to insert a location keyframe:

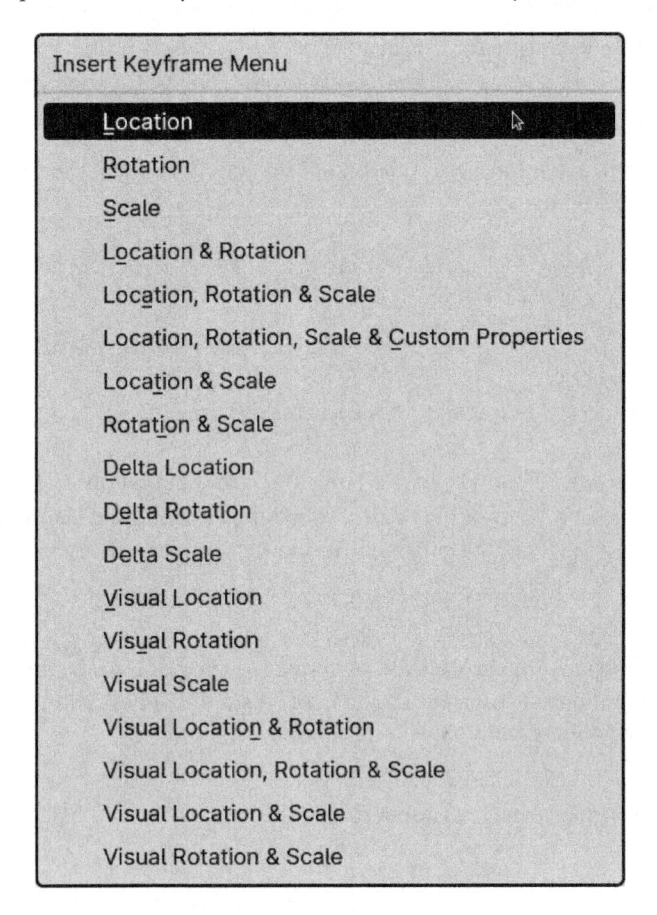

Figure 1.7: The Insert Keyframe menu

What you see here is a list of some (but not all) of the selected object's properties that can be keyed. Click **Location** to insert a location keyframe.

> **Important note**
> From this point onward, always be aware of what you have selected and what frame you are on, especially when inserting keyframes.

The keyed property

We have just inserted a keyframe for the location of the Cube on frame 10. This is huge! In the future, we will insert and edit dozens of these things at once, but for the moment, let's dwell on what has changed.

Firstly, a small diamond shape has appeared in the Timeline. If you don't see it at first, scroll up or press *Home*; it might be hiding:

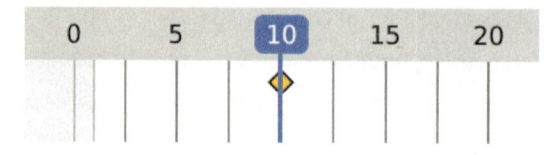

Figure 1.8: New keyframe on frame 10

That's our keyframe, insofar as it exists in the Timeline. Its horizontal position marks the frame on which you have "*keyed*" a property of the Cube. Although you can't see it yet in the Timeline, it also contains the **X**, **Y**, and **Z** values of the cube's **Location** property when it was keyed.

> **Tip**
> By default, the Timeline only displays the keyframes of selected objects; they will hide when you select a different object. In later chapters, we'll examine other editors better suited for displaying the keyframes of multiple objects at once.

Secondly, take a look at the cube's **Transform** properties:

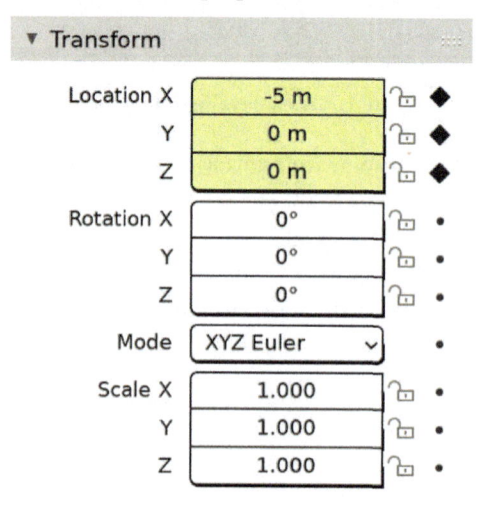

Figure 1.9: The keyed Location property

The **Location** values are now highlighted and distinguished by a small set of keyframe-shaped icons to the right. This indicates that they are "keyed."

> **Tip**
> Animated properties are highlighted yellow when there is a keyframe for that property on the current frame, green on every other frame, and orange when manually changed.

Try moving the Cube again, and then change frames. The Cube will immediately "snap" back to its keyed location. The property has been "taken over" by its keyframes. From now on, any manual change you make to the cube's location can only be temporary unless you insert another keyframe for it.

> **Important note**
> A single property cannot have two keyframes on the same frame. If you insert a keyframe where one already exists, the new keyframe will simply replace the old one.

Keying the second location

Play the animation and look closely at what happens to the Cube. Nothing! Now, play the animation backward. What happens then? Again, nothing – but now it's happening backward.

Our one keyframe simply determines that the Cube must be at a certain location on frame 10, but one keyframe isn't enough to create movement. Until we add a second location keyframe, our Cube will remain at just one location – not only on frame 10 but on every other frame as well.

Let's add that second keyframe:

1. Go to frame 40.
2. Move the Cube 10 units rightward on the *X* axis.
3. Press *I* and insert another **Location** keyframe:

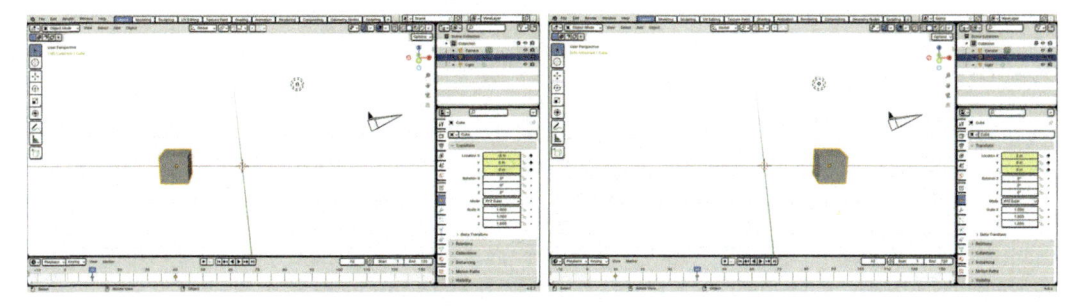

Figure 1.10: The Cube on frames 10 and 40

Now, play the animation. The `Cube` moves! Two keyframes were all we needed to create motion. Now let's take a closer look at what happens between those two keyframes.

Principles of keying

Note that we never issued any "commands" to the `Cube` in order to make it move. We did not, for instance, encode any events like "begin moving at frame `10`," or "stop moving after frame `40`." This is a misapprehension that novice animators often have. By inserting these keyframes, we simply declared that on frame `10`, the `Cube` shall be in one specific place, and on frame `40`, it shall be in another.

Also, watch what happens to the **X Location** value of the `Cube` as you change frames:

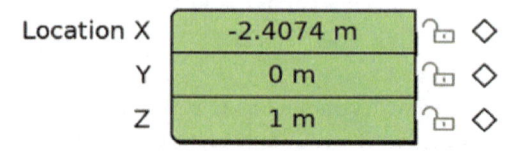

Location X	-2.4074 m
Y	0 m
Z	1 m

Figure 1.11: The Location property on frame 20

Although we might say we have "animated the `Cube`", it is more accurate to say that we have animated just one property of the `Cube` (**Location**), and even then, only one of the three components of that property actually changes (the **X Location**). For now, everything else about the `Cube` (for example, its **Rotation** and **Scale**) remains unaffected.

Finally, note that we didn't need to interfere in the 29 other frames between frame `10` and frame `40` in order to make the `Cube` move smoothly from one place to another. Blender handled that automatically, playing the role of in-betweener for us. This is arguably the greatest advantage that digital animation offers over traditional animation.

> **Tip**
> The method by which one value transitions to another is called **interpolation**. We'll explore some different interpolation modes in the next chapter.

Keying rotation

In the second act of our epic 120-frame animation, the `Cube` gets homesick and *turns around*, in preparation for the long journey back to its birthplace. We'll animate this part by keying not the **Location** property but the **Rotation** property.

As you might expect, we can follow the same process as before, using the **Insert Keyframe** (*I*) menu. Since you've already had some practice, we can cover this part more quickly:

1. Go to frame `45`.
2. Ensure the `Cube` is still selected.

3. Press *I* to bring up the **Insert Keyframe** menu and click **Rotation**.
4. Go to frame 55.
5. Rotate the Cube 180 degrees on the *Z* axis (clockwise or counterclockwise – your choice).
6. Repeat *step 3* to insert the second rotation keyframe.

There should now appear to be four keyframes in the Timeline: two for the cube's location and two for its rotation. For the moment, we cannot tell just from looking at the Timeline which are which but rest assured that they are distinct. We will learn how to look at their contents more closely in the next chapter.

When you playback your animation now, the Cube will move from west to east, wait 5 frames, then briskly spin around for 10 frames to face the opposite direction.

Editing keyframes in the Timeline

We're ready to animate the dramatic third-act finale! Having turned its back on the frontier to the east, our hero Cube will head back home, weary from its sojourn, to rest at the very same spot where its life began.

To animate this last part, we could continue with the same technique we've been practicing – going to a new frame, moving the object, inserting the keyframe, and so on – but there are other ways of animating at our disposal you need to be aware of.

As it happens, the Timeline is not just a window for displaying keyframes. We can also use it to edit them! In this section, we're going to set aside what we've learned about inserting new keyframes using the **Insert Keyframe** (*I*) menu and instead use the Timeline to take advantage of the ones we've already made.

Basic keyframe editing

How does one edit keyframes? Here are the only actions you need to know for now:

- To select a keyframe in the Timeline, click on it using whichever mouse button you've been using to select things. Hold *Shift* and click to select multiple keyframes.
- Use **Grab** (*G*) to move selected keyframes through time. You can also click and drag keyframes using the same mouse button you use for selecting.
- To **duplicate** keyframes, use **Duplicate** (*Shift* + *D*). Duplicated keyframes will be "stuck" to your cursor as if you had used **Grab** (*G*) on them.

If you're thinking this is just a list of controls you already know about, you're absolutely right! If you know how to select, move, and duplicate objects in the 3D Viewport, then you already know how to select, move, and duplicate keyframes in the Timeline. *The controls are exactly the same.*

This is the case for many other operations and control schemes. If it works in the 3D Viewport, chances are it will work in the Timeline and other animation editors.

> **Tip**
> Selected keyframes are highlighted in yellow. Newly inserted keyframes will be automatically selected. Before doing things like duplicating keyframes, make sure there aren't any unwanted keyframes in your selection. You can quickly make a mess of things by operating on more keyframes than you mean to!

Duplicating keyframes

A common use for editing keyframes directly is to duplicate certain segments of an animation to save time. To make the `Cube` return to its original location, we don't have to move it back ourselves; all we need to do is duplicate one of the keyframes we made earlier:

1. Select the keyframe we created on frame `10`.
2. Press *Shift + D* to duplicate it.
3. Move the duplicate keyframe to frame `90`.

> **Tip**
> The control schemes for editing keyframes are really quite similar to the ones you're used to in Blender's 3D Viewport. For instance: in *step 3* here, you can enter the value `80`, moving the duplicated keyframe exactly 80 frames from frame `10` to frame `90`.

We've keyed the `Cube`'s final resting place! Now, it will be in the same location on frame `90` as it was on frame `10`, but now our animation looks a little strange…

Holding a position

Watch how the `Cube` moves back to its starting point. How slow and clumsy looking! Right after frame `40`, it begins to move westward; it doesn't even get the chance to turn around before doing so.

This is a frequent mistake and/or a sign of an incomplete animation. The last location keyframe we made was on frame `40`. Then, we put the next one all the way over on frame `90` without considering how that would affect everything prior.

After frame 40, we want the Cube to hold still for a bit like it was doing before. This does not require any special "hold-still-type" keyframe. Instead, all we need to do is duplicate the other location keyframe from frame 40:

1. Select the Cube object's location keyframe on frame 40.
2. Press *Shift + D* to duplicate it.
3. Move the duplicate keyframe to frame 60.

Now that there is a location keyframe on frame 60 identical to the one on frame 40, there will be no change in location between those frames. Because we only edited location keyframes, the animation of the cube's rotation was not affected:

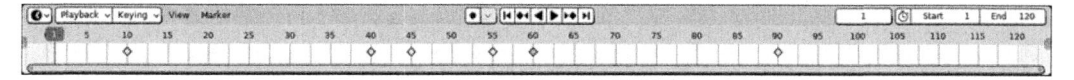

Figure 1.12: The Timeline with six keyframes

Editing the timing of your animation

Inserting keyframes according to these step-by-step instructions might have given you the impression that we're supposed to know ahead of time when and where to insert keyframes. On the contrary – animators rarely insert all their keyframes on the right frame on the very first try. When animating on your own, you will assuredly need to adjust the timing of keyframes after they have been added.

Take our current animation, for example. After the last keyframe on frame 90, we've still got 30 motionless frames before the scene ends. Why not slow things down and give our animation a little more breathing room so that we can use the full duration of our scene's frame range?

This next step will be more open-ended so that you can experiment and see how different placements of keyframes affect the animated result:

1. Go to any frame between the first and last keyframes.
2. Select only the keyframes that come after the **Current Frame**.
3. Grab the selected keyframes and move them 20 frames to the right.

> Tip
> Try hitting *]* (the closing bracket key) for *step 2*. Respectively, *[* and *]* are the shortcuts for **Before Current Frame** and **After Current Frame**, which are helpful for quickly selecting all keyframes that come either before or after the current frame.

If you haven't figured it out already, moving keyframes to the right delays them, widening the gap in time between those keyframes and keyframes left behind, and slowing down a part of the animation. Which part of the animation will be slowed down depends on where that extra gap between keyframes was made.

For example, moving the last two keyframes makes the Cube seem to hesitate before its return to the west:

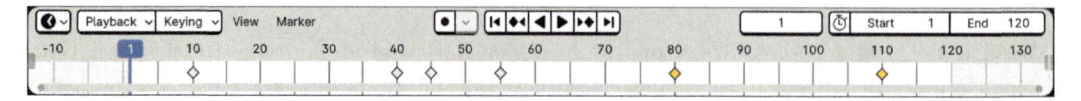

Figure 1.13: The Timeline with the last two keyframes moved

Moving the last three keyframes makes the cube's 180° rotation take longer:

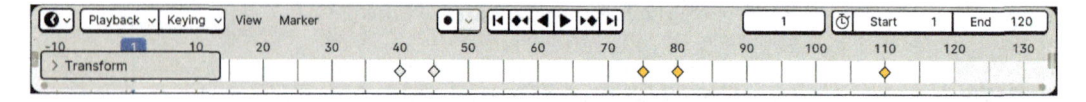

Figure 1.14: The Timeline with the last three keyframes moved

Also, moving all but the first keyframe makes the cube's initial embarkation a bit slower than its return trip:

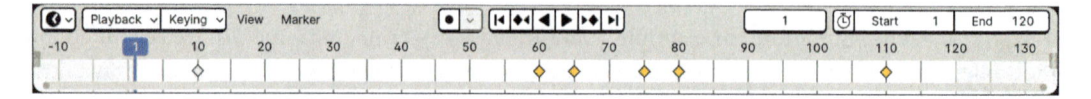

Figure 1.15: The Timeline with the last five keyframes moved

Without changing the order of these keyframes, feel free to continue experimenting with their timing.

Having finished giving movement to the Cube, we're nearly done with this chapter! We've brought a life of adventure to a simple object by causing just two of its properties to change over time.

The three spatial properties of a 3D object – location, rotation, and scale – might be the three most common properties you'll typically work with, in a 3D animation, but that's not all there is to animation. As we'll see in the next section, keyframes can be used to affect almost any property.

Animating nearly any property in Blender

Our odyssey concludes with the main character at rest, finally home from its harrowing adventure abroad. Is our hero triumphant, or sorrowful and full of regret? Hard to say (it's a cube), but one thing's for sure: things will never be the same again. Is it the world that has changed? Quite the contrary; no hero's journey is complete unless it is the hero who is changed by the world. One cube leaves, and a different cube (metaphorically speaking) returns.

In this section, we'll key one more property of the `Cube`, its color, to demonstrate how almost anything in Blender can be animated.

Other keying methods

So far, we've been using the **Insert Keyframe** menu to insert our initial keyframes, but this menu is purely a convenience, not a complete list of every keyable property in Blender. For one thing, it doesn't contain **Color**.

Fortunately, we don't need that menu. When you find a property you want to animate, Blender's interface offers a number of ways to key it right there on the spot:

- Right-click on the property and click **Insert Keyframe** from the context menu.
- Hover the mouse cursor directly over the property and press *I*.
- Click on the small dot to the right of the property (note that this dot is just for one-click convenience; a property without one may still be keyable).

Each of these methods accomplishes exactly the same result.

> **Tip**
> For every method that inserts a keyframe, you'll find a similar way to delete it. Try pressing *Alt + I* instead of *I*, for example.

Keying the material color

Let's try out keying the color of the `Cube`:

1. Select the `Cube` and go to **Material Properties** to edit the cube's default material, `Material`.
2. Find the **Base Color** property:

Figure 1.16: The Base Color property

3. Go to frame `1`.
4. Pick any color you like for the starting **Base Color**.
5. Key the **Base Color** using any one of the methods mentioned earlier.
6. Go to frame `120`.
7. Pick a different color for the ending **Base Color**.

8. Key the **Base Color** once more.
9. Switch the **Viewport Shading** mode to **Rendered** or **Material Preview** to see the result in the 3D Viewport:

Figure 1.17: Viewport Shading set to Material Preview mode

In addition to moving, the Cube will now gradually change from one color to another over the course of its journey. Personally, I've made mine change from a cheery green to a deep and woeful purple:

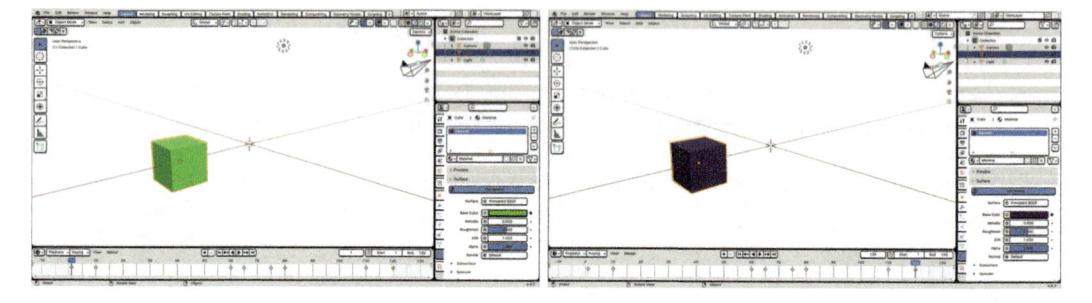

Figure 1.18: The Cube on frames 1 and 120

> **Tip**
> Numeric values aren't the only type of property that can be keyed. Checkboxes and on/off buttons, otherwise known as *Boolean* properties, can be keyed to turn on and off as well. Among other things, this can be helpful for making objects appear and disappear.

Summary

If you've made it this far, congratulations – you're an animator. Surprised? You shouldn't be – an animator is someone who makes animations, and what did you just do? With just the Timeline, the default cube, and fewer than a dozen keyframes, you animated an epic adventure!

Alright, I'll admit it – maybe our first animation wasn't that epic, but it was important! We took something boring and found the potential in it for something exciting. Sure, a cube is just a mesh with some faces and vertices, but then so are the characters and objects in your favorite 3D animated film. And all those fancy characters and objects were brought to life with a bunch of keyframes like the ones you just made.

The only difference? Mainly the amount of keyframes. We're going to need *a lot* more keyframes in the future. We'll also need to know a bit more about the true nature of those keyframes, which, for the sake of brevity in this chapter, has been kept secret. The Timeline, as it happens, is not the ideal tool for advanced keyframe editing. In the next chapter, we're going to need a completely different editor to crack those keyframes open and poke around inside…

Questions

1. Which two properties of the scene determine the length, in frames, of our animation?
2. How many seconds long would our animation be if our frame rate had been 30 frames per second?
3. What's a frame? What does it mean to *go to* a certain frame?
4. In traditional hand-drawn animation, a keyframe is a specific type of frame. Is this true of keyframes in 3D animation as well? How are they different?
5. Is it more accurate to say that a location keyframe makes an object *go* somewhere, or that it makes an object *be* somewhere?
6. What can you tell about a keyframe just by looking at it in the Timeline?
7. Does one need to key everything in order, from beginning to end?
8. How might one tell if a given property is animated?
9. Pick a random property in Blender and see if it can be animated. If so, how might that property be useful or interesting to animate?
10. What is a property? To what thing or things in Blender do properties belong?

2
The Graph Editor

In the previous chapter, we created a rudimentary animation while limiting our keyframe editing to Blender's Timeline. While this was necessary to keep things simple at first, we concealed some important animation workflows for the sake of brevity. For most animations, using only the Timeline would be very frustrating!

The next most important tool for 3D animation in Blender is the **Graph Editor**. In addition to doing almost anything the Timeline can do, the Graph Editor displays both the time and value of keyframes, along with the resulting animated property they affect, on a 2D graph.

To learn about the Graph Editor and what makes it so useful, we'll put it to practice in this chapter by animating one of the most popular case studies in the animation industry – a bouncing ball.

For nearly a hundred years, the bouncing ball has been a well-known learning exercise in both 2D and 3D animation. If we want our bouncing ball to look realistic, we'll need to pay close attention to its *velocity* and *acceleration* – things for which the Graph Editor is an indispensable tool.

In this chapter, we're going to cover the following main topics:

- Animating a rolling ball
- Navigating the Graph Editor
- Setting interpolation and easing types
- Animating a bouncing motion
- Setting extrapolation modes

Technical requirements

To follow along with this chapter, you'll need Blender, along with a suitable model of a regulation-sized football (otherwise known as a soccer ball).

You can download such a model here:

`https://github.com/PacktPublishing/Realizing-3D-Animation-in-Blender`

You can open the downloaded file and immediately begin working, or you can model your own football if you prefer:

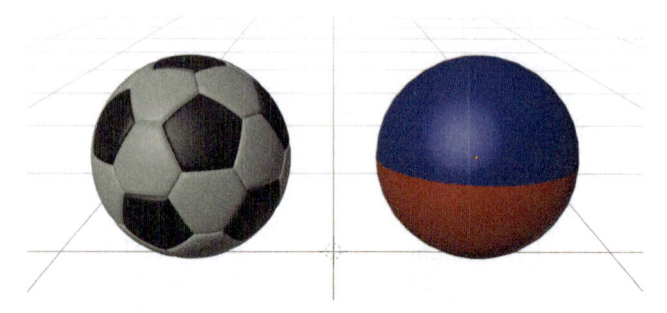

Figure 2.1: Left – the football model, and right – an acceptable ball that I modeled in one minute

Any sphere will do, as long as it is 0.7 meters in diameter, rests on the grid floor of the scene, and is multicolored so that you can easily see it roll.

Getting the ball rolling

Before we get into the Graph Editor, we'll need to insert some initial keyframes as we did in the previous chapter. As a general rule, it's better to *block out* the most important positions of an object before adding details, so our first two keyframes will simply make the ball roll from left to right.

Rolling is just rotation in perfect sync with location. All we need to do is key the location and rotation of the ball on the same frames, making sure that we rotate the ball according to a precise mathematical formula based on how far it moves. After we get the ball rolling, we'll use the Graph Editor to make it bounce.

Let's key the initial placement of the ball. To save time, we can key the location and rotation of the ball at once:

1. Go to frame `10`.
2. Select the ball and move it `-5` units leftward on the *X* axis.
3. Press *I* to bring up the **Insert Keyframe** menu and choose **Location & Rotation**.

    This inserts both rotation and location keyframes without requiring us to bring up the menu twice.

Next, let's get ready to insert a second set of location and rotation keyframes:

4. Go to frame `90`.
5. Move the ball 10 units rightward on the *X* axis.

    Now that we've determined how far the ball will move in the span of 80 frames, we just need to figure out how much it should rotate in order to roll realistically. If we key too much or too little rotation, the ball will appear to slide along the ground.

    So, how many degrees should we rotate the ball, and on what axis? Although there are some nice formulas to figure this out, that's a bit advanced for this chapter. For now, let's cheat a little and just enter some magic numbers:

6. Rotate the ball `1164` degrees on the *Y* axis.
7. Insert location and rotation keyframes, as we did in *step 3*.

When you play your animation, the ball should now roll smoothly from left to right without appearing to slide or skid. This simple motion will accompany the bouncing keyframes that we will add later.

Navigating the Graph Editor

While following along with the previous chapter, you may have wondered how an animator is supposed to recognize all those identical-looking keyframes in the timeline. Do we always have to remember which ones are for location and which ones are for rotation? What if the rotation and location keyframes exist on the same frame, as they do in our present animation? How can you edit them separately?

For that matter, how can you discern *any* of the values inside a keyframe? In the Timeline, a keyframe that makes something move a few inches down looks no different from one that takes it a hundred miles up into outer space.

The Timeline, then, is an insufficient tool to edit an entire animation. That's where tools such as the Graph Editor come in.

Bringing up the Graph Editor

One convenient way to get to the Graph Editor is to use the interface area where the Timeline currently is. The Graph editor will need more vertical space than the Timeline to be useful, so we just need to drag up the border between the Timeline and the 3D Viewport in order to make the area taller. After that, it's easy to switch out the Timeline for the Graph Editor:

1. Find the border between the 3D Viewport and the Timeline (your cursor will change to arrows when you hover the mouse over it).
2. Drag the border upward, resizing the lower area to roughly half the height of the whole screen.
3. Use *Ctrl + Tab* or the **Editor Type** menu to switch the area to the Graph Editor.

Now we're ready to begin working in the Graph Editor!

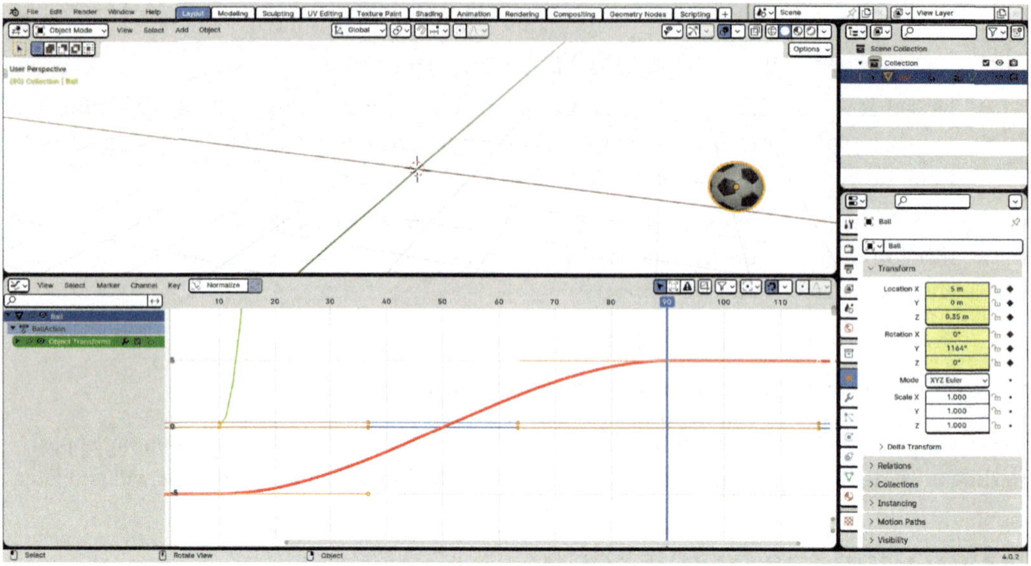

Figure 2.2: The user interface with the Graph Editor

This editor displays animated properties as lines in a 2D graph and displays keyframes as points along those lines, allowing you to intuitively edit both the timing and value of keyframes.

> **Important note**
>
> Like the Timeline, the Graph Editor's default setting is to only display the keyframes of selected objects. Make sure the ball is selected or the Graph Editor will appear blank.

This editor can be perplexing for those who've never seen it before, so let's take a moment to consider just what we're looking at.

> **Tip**
>
> In my examples, I've disabled **View | Show Cursor** to stop displaying an additional horizontal line in the Graph Editor, which is of limited usefulness.

The X and Y axes in the Graph Editor

Keyframes in the Timeline can only be moved left and right – that is, backward and forward through time. Whereas this makes the Timeline essentially a one-dimensional editor, you can think of the Graph Editor as a *two-dimensional Timeline*.

Just like in the Timeline, you'll see a row of frame numbers along the top of the Graph Editor, which – just like in the Timeline – may also be clicked on to scrub and move through time. Moving keyframes left and right along the *X* axis in the Graph Editor moves them backward and forward in time, just like in the Timeline. We can take it for granted, then, that the *X* axis in the Graph Editor represents time in frames... just like in the Timeline.

Unlike the Timeline, however, we now have a vertical axis, along which keyframes may be moved up and down. This *Y* axis represents the numeric value of each individual property. Depending on the property, this can be any kind of unit – meters, degrees, watts, whatever. If it's animated, the Graph Editor will display it.

> **Important note**
>
> Don't confuse the *X* and *Y* axes in the Graph Editor with the *X*, *Y*, and *Z* axes in the 3D Viewport. Properties of 3D objects such as **Location**, **Rotation**, and **Scale** all have *X*, *Y*, and *Z* components that relate to the *X*, *Y*, and *Z* axes in your 3D scene, respectively. When viewed in the Graph Editor, however, these components are all just numbers that map to the same *Y* axis like everything else.

Take a look at the red line in your Graph Editor that curves smoothly upward from left to right. By examining this curve against the numbers indicated on the X and Y axes, you might be able to guess which animated property it represents. What about the other lines? Don't worry if you aren't certain; we're about to take the guesswork out of which lines represent which properties.

Animation channels

On the left side of the Graph Editor, you'll see a panel with three nested lists:

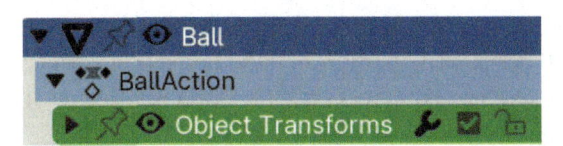

Figure 2.3: Fields for the object, action, and channel group

The `Ball` object contains the `BallAction` action, which in turn contains the **Object Transforms** channel group.

Click the small triangle to the left of the **Object Transforms** row to expand it. This reveals a list of all the **animation channels** we've just created:

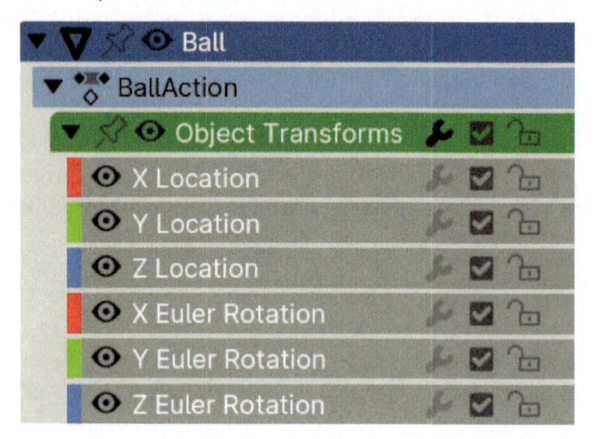

Figure 2.4: Animation channels

These animation channels comprise all the properties of the selected object that have keyframes, organized into a vertical list. Each independent channel contains all the keyframes for its assigned property.

> **Tip**
> Actions and channel groups are created automatically when you insert keyframes for the first time. You can think of these as nested "folders" for an object's animation channels. Ignore them for now. Unless you're doing advanced character animation, you will usually never need to reorganize your channel groups, or use more than one action for each animated object.

For each animation channel, there's a corresponding line graph displayed in the main section of the Graph Editor, called an **F-curve**. You can think of these F-curves as stock market graphs; each one is a line that represents the value of a property over time. Clicking a channel name in the left-side panel will select that channel and highlight its F-curve.

> **Important note**
> The terms *curve*, *F-curve*, and *channel* are used interchangeably in the Graph Editor. They essentially mean the same thing.

Six keyframes in one

Currently, our animation has six channels. If six channels seems like a lot, remember that spatial properties such as location and rotation are each a set of three numeric values – one for each axis in 3D space (*X*, *Y*, and *Z*).

When you clicked **Location & Rotation** in the **Insert Keyframe** menu, you actually inserted not one but six keyframes at once! Having done this twice, you now have a total of 12 keyframes, even though the Timeline appeared to show only 2:

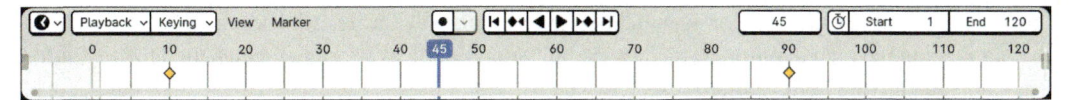

Figure 2.5: The timeline with two keyframes

In truth, there is no such thing as a single **Location & Rotation** keyframe. These **summary keys** are actually groupings of all the keyframes on the same frame, which can be selected in the Timeline and edited as though they were all one keyframe. That's how we edited our animation in the previous chapter. In this chapter, however, we'll need to be specific about exactly which channel's keyframes we want to edit.

> **Tip**
> Individual animation channels may also be accessed in the Timeline by dragging open the left-side panel, which is hidden by default. This allows you to edit individual channels without switching to another editor. The Timeline, however, still isn't the ideal tool to edit keyframes this way; that honor is reserved for the Dope Sheet, which we will cover in *Chapter 6*.

Hiding, locking, and deleting F-curves

Let's run through each animation channel for the ball and think about which ones are relevant for our bouncing ball animation:

- **X Location**: This one is what moves the ball from left to right. The F-curve for this channel is clearly visible in the graph editor; it's the red line that goes from a value of -5 on frame 10 to a value of 5 on frame 90.

- **Y Location**: We won't need to move the ball on the *Y* axis, so this channel can be discarded.

- **Z Location**: Adding more keyframes to this channel will make the ball move up and down. We'll definitely need this one to make the ball bounce!

- **X Euler Rotation**: The ball would look a bit odd if we animated this one. Given the direction that the ball is currently traveling, it only needs to rotate on its *Y* axis in order to look like it's rolling. If it spun in any other direction, that would ruin the effect!

- **Y Euler Rotation**: We animated this value to make the ball appear to roll convincingly as it moves along the *X* axis. You can see the F-curve for this one turn sharply upward at frame 10 before it disappears above the viewing boundary of the Graph Editor.

- **Z Euler Rotation**: We also do not need to animate this value.

Already, these are a lot of channels and keyframes to keep up with! If we're not careful, we might lose track of which channels are which, or accidentally edit the wrong keyframe. This is especially easy to do when many of our keyframes overlap.

Fortunately, we can hide, lock, or even delete the channels we don't want to see or edit. Each channel has an eye-shaped toggle button to turn its visibility on and off, as well as a lock-shaped toggle button that prevents it from being edited.

A channel can also simply be deleted if we don't plan on using it ever. Let's try it now on the animation channels we won't be needing:

1. Select the **Y Location**, **X Euler Rotation**, and **Z Euler Rotation** channels by left-clicking one channel name, then holding *Shift*, and clicking the other two.
2. Delete the selected channels by pressing *X* or going to **Channel | Delete Channels**. This also deletes all the keyframes for the channel.
3. Hide or lock the **Z Location** F-curve by clicking either the "eye" or "lock" toggle buttons. We'll return to this one shortly.

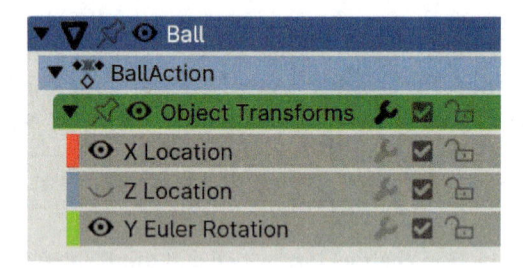

Figure 2.6: The three remaining animation channels

That's much better! Now we don't have any superfluous F-curves getting in the way of our work.

> **Tip**
> Locked or hidden F-curves will continue to affect the animated result as usual. If you want to disable an F-curve without deleting it, try out the checkmark-shaped toggle button, which "mutes" the F-curve. A muted F-curve may still be visible in the Graph Editor but will have no effect on anything.

Adjusting the Graph Editor view

Take a look at the remaining F-curves in the Graph Editor. Can you see everything? While the red line of the **X Location** F-curve happens to be nicely centered in your view, the **Y Euler Rotation** F-curve is still mostly outside the viewing area. The value of this property starts at 0 on frame 10 and goes all the way up to 1164 on frame 90, so you can see one of its keyframes but not the other.

Most Blender experts agree that it's helpful to look at things before you edit them. Just as we need to move around in the 3D Viewport to manipulate 3D elements, we'll need to move around in the Graph Editor as well, viewing different keyframes at various points in time and at various scales.

Panning and zooming in the Graph Editor

You'll quickly discover that the navigation controls you've used in other areas of Blender work in the Graph Editor as well. Dragging with the middle mouse button pans your view in all four directions, while scrolling zooms in and out. However, you also soon notice that zooming with just the scroll wheel won't suffice when it comes to the Graph Editor.

Let's give it a try. Zoom out in the Graph Editor using the scroll wheel so that the whole curve of the **Y Euler Rotation** F-curve is visible. Now we can see the whole F-curve… sort of:

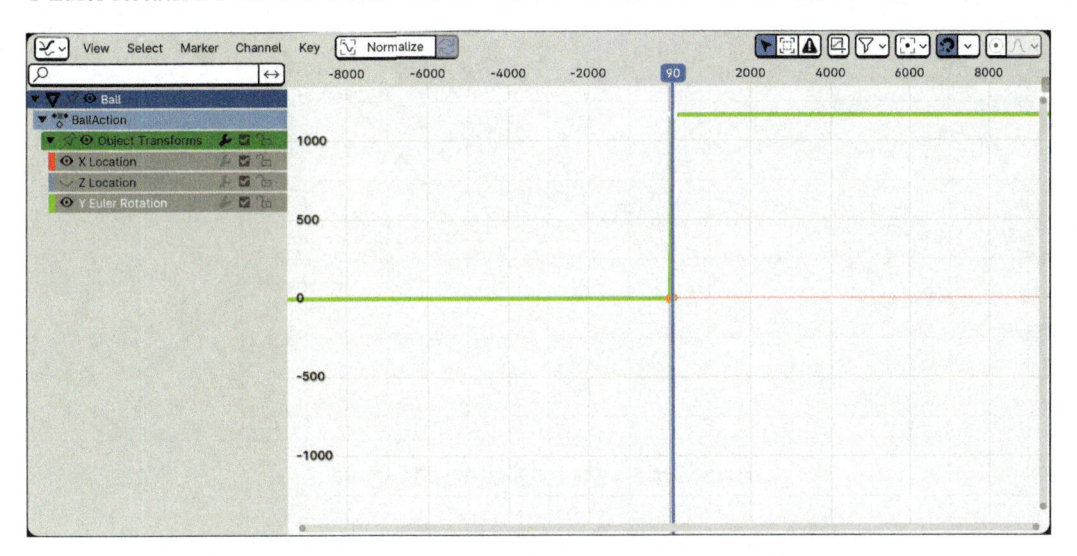

Figure 2.7: A zoomed-out view of the Y Euler Rotation F-curve

We've zoomed out enough so that the vertical range of the curve is visible, but in doing so, we've also zoomed out to a completely useless frame range on the graph's horizontal axis. The frame range of our whole animation is so narrow, the playhead nearly covers it up!

When we zoom with the scroll wheel in a 2D editor, we cause our view to be scaled in equal proportion horizontally and vertically. This is fine for zooming in and out on, say, an image texture, but it's not what we need in the Graph Editor.

Scaling the X and Y axes

What we need to be able to do here is "zoom" on the X axis differently than on the Y axis. Try this:

1. While holding *Ctrl*, carefully click and drag the middle mouse button rightward in the Graph Editor, until the horizontal range of the Graph Editor is mostly limited to the "curvy" part of the **Y Euler Rotation** F-curve.

2. Use the middle mouse button to pan the view so that the curve stays centered in the Graph Editor.

3. Repeat as needed until the **Y Euler Rotation** F-curve fills the whole display range, like so:

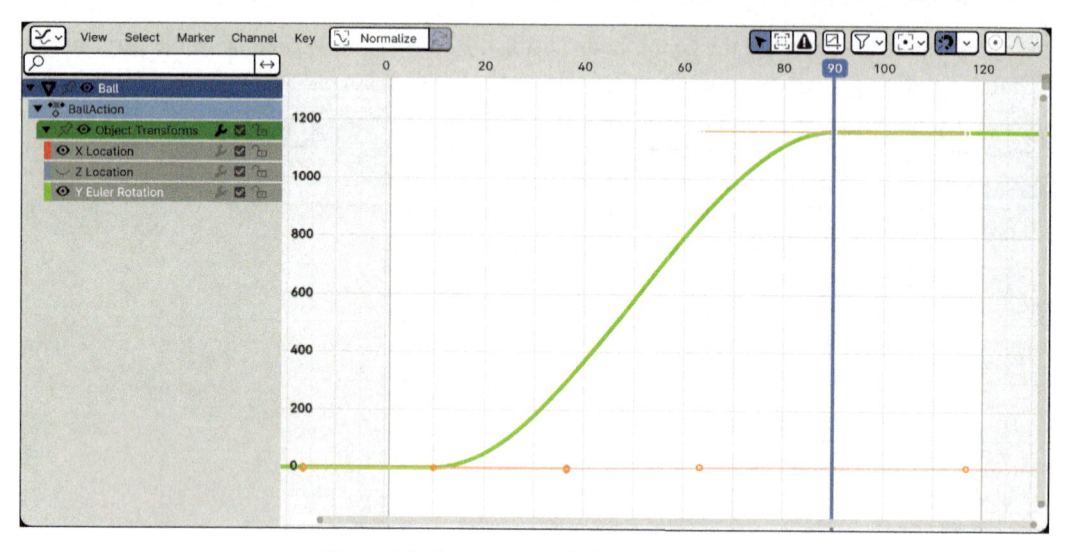

Figure 2.8: A more suitably framed F-curve

Using *Ctrl* and the middle mouse scales the X and Y axes of the Graph Editor independently, scaling the Y axis when you move the cursor up and down, and scaling the X axis when you move it left and right. This operation may take some getting used to. Keep in mind that this does not affect the animation; we're still just altering the ranges displayed by the Graph Editor.

This is an indispensable thing to know how to do, as the X and Y axes of the Graph Editor do not proportionately relate to one another as they do in other editors in Blender. Animated properties may be expressed in all kinds of units, some negative, some positive, some very big, and others very small, all of which are mapped to the same Y axis in the Graph Editor. Some values in your animations will rise and fall a great amount over a very short amount of time, whereas other values will take a long time to move only a tiny bit. For each case, you'll need to adjust your view in the Graph Editor accordingly.

So, now that you can clearly see both **Y Euler Rotation** keyframes, are we going to edit them specifically? Nah, this was all just practice for later, but look – now there's another problem we can practice fixing!

The normalized F-curve view

Look at what appears to have happened to the **X Location** F-curve. It looks nearly flat now! By adjusting the view to accommodate one F-curve, we've made it very difficult to discern the shape of the other one.

By default, location is expressed as a certain number of meters, whereas rotation is expressed as a certain number of degrees, both of which are mapped to the *Y* axis of the Graph Editor. Our ball must rotate `1164` degrees just to roll `10` meters, so a simple rolling animation will make the **Y Euler Rotation** F-curve go way higher than the **X Location** F-curve. This is inconvenient for us if we want to keep track of both F-curves at once. That's where the **Normalize** feature comes in.

When enabled, **Normalize** will "squeeze" all the F-curves on the *Y* axis so that they're all displayed within the same value range of `-1` to `1`. This is helpful when multiple F-curves with wildly different ranges all need to be edited together, although it can also make it harder to read their actual values.

Go ahead and enable **Normalize** in the header of the Graph Editor:

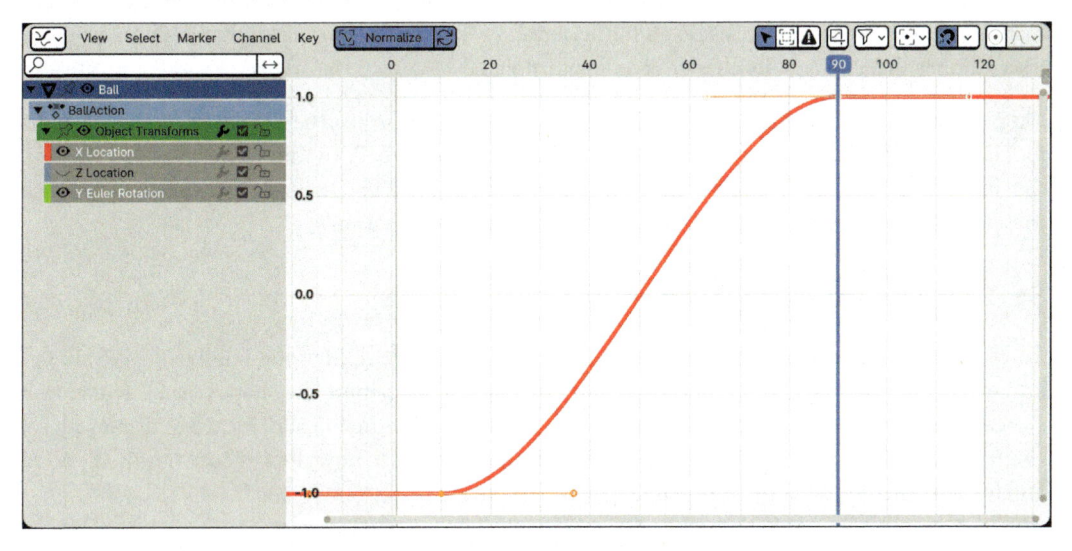

Figure 2.9: The normalized view in the Graph Editor

Much better! Note that the **X Location** and **Y Euler Rotation** F-curves now look identical, so one F-curve will hide behind the other. This might be a problem if we need to select a keyframe for one F-curve and not the other, but it's also a blessing in disguise; we can now check to make sure these two properties remain perfectly synchronized. Remember, however, that the values shown in the Graph Editor's *Y* axis no longer directly correspond to the true values of the animated property; the lowest and highest points of each F-curve now just map to `-1` and `1`.

Now that you've removed all the unnecessary F-curves and know the basics of navigating the Graph Editor, you're just about ready to begin editing keyframes!

Interpolation and easing

Take a close look at the **X Location** and **Y Euler Rotation** F-curves and note what happens to the segment between the keyframes on frames 10 and 90. The line gently begins to rise, reaches its steepest point at frame 50 as it continues to rise, then gently rolls off at the top.

Each keyframe dictates that a certain property equals a certain value at a certain time. When that keyframe is followed by another keyframe of a different value, the property's value must change from one to the other as the animation plays forward through time. On all the frames in between, we can think of the property itself as "moving" from one value to the next.

The way by which one value transitions to another is called **interpolation**. It was mentioned briefly in the previous chapter; it's the reason we can make just two keyframes on two different frames and get smooth-looking motion along all the frames in between. Whereas animation techniques such as stop-motion require the animator to increment things manually on each individual frame, digital animation tools employ interpolation algorithms that do a lot of the work for us. Interpolation is a mathematical process that works on all numeric values. Blender doesn't care what the property is; if it's a number that changes, its change can be interpolated.

There are various types of interpolation. What we see currently is just the default. It's a simple, nice-looking curve, but it isn't suitable for the motion of a bouncing ball. In this section, we'll explore all the different interpolation modes that are available to us in Blender. Once you've experimented with these, you'll have a better idea of which ones to use for this animation.

Setting the interpolation mode

There are multiple types – or modes – of interpolation available in Blender. For every keyframe in an F-curve, you can specify an interpolation mode that will determine the shape of the F-curve that comes after. Now that we have our Graph Editor open and only the relevant F-curves displayed, we can try out all the interpolation modes on the rolling ball and see how they affect both the F-curve and the animated result at the same time.

> **Tip**
> As in the Timeline, you don't need to be reminded of most of the controls to select and edit keyframes in the Graph Editor. Just pretend you're selecting and editing the vertices of a mesh!

Let's play around with interpolation now:

1. Select the first two keyframes (the ones on frame 10) for the ball's **X Location** and **Y Euler Rotation** animation channels.

2. Press *T* or go to **Key | Interpolation Mode** to **Set Keyframe Interpolation**.

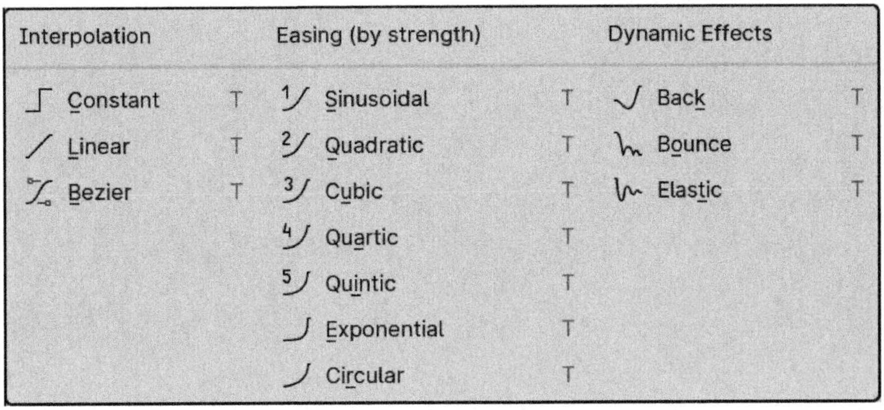

Interpolation		Easing (by strength)		Dynamic Effects	
Constant	T	1. Sinusoidal	T	Back	T
Linear	T	2. Quadratic	T	Bounce	T
Bezier	T	3. Cubic	T	Elastic	T
		4. Quartic	T		
		5. Quintic	T		
		Exponential	T		
		Circular	T		

Figure 2.10: The menu of available interpolation modes

3. Select an interpolation mode and play the animation to review the result!

Interesting, right? These are a lot of fun to play with. Although we can set the interpolation mode of selected keyframes in any animation editor in Blender, the Graph Editor is the only one that displays the shape of that interpolation.

Here's a brief overview of the different interpolation modes:

- **Constant**: This interpolation mode is really no interpolation at all; the value remains constant and simply "jumps" or "snaps" to the value of the subsequent keyframe.
- **Linear**: This is the simplest type of interpolation; this one draws a straight line between keyframes. The result is motion at a single speed, without any acceleration or deceleration.
- **Bezier**: The default mode of interpolation, this mode turns the keyframe into a Bezier node with editable handles that influence the trajectory of the F-curve before and after the keyframe. You may have seen nodes like these in curve objects and many vector graphics applications. Bezier keyframes are powerful but tricky; we'll learn more about them in the next chapter.
- **Easing (by strength)**: Make no mistake – these are also interpolation types, but special ones that must be set to either *ease in*, *ease out*, or both. We'll learn what that means momentarily.
- **Dynamic Effects**: These are unique modes that make the F-curve go in alternating directions; this is nice for when you want a simple bounce or elastic motion but don't need much precise control. They are also set to ease in or out.

Keep trying out different interpolation modes until you've watched at least one example of each.

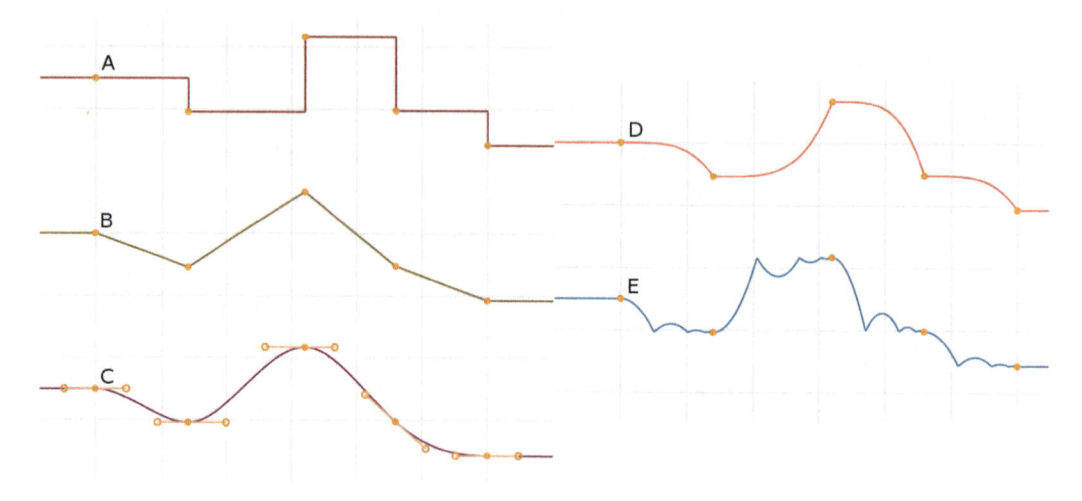

Figure 2.11: Constant, Linear, Bezier, Easing, and Dynamic interpolation

As you try out the different interpolation modes on your animation, pay close attention to how the shape of the F-curves relates to the motion of the ball. Note how the slope or steepness of an F-curve expresses the rate of change of the property value, which in turn determines the speed of the object.

Setting the easing type

If you try out a couple of the Easing interpolation modes, you'll notice the same behavior in all of them – they start slow, accelerate steadily, then abruptly stop at the end keyframe. What if we want the object to decelerate instead of accelerate? That's where **easing types** come in. Easing can be thought of as a subtype of interpolation that determines whether the interpolation function will ease in, ease out, or both. We can see what that means by trying it out ourselves.

Setting the Easing Type is as just easy as setting interpolation:

1. Using the steps described before, choose an interpolation mode under **the Easing** or **Dynamic Effects** column.

2. Use *Ctrl + E* or go to **Key | Easing Type** to set the easing type of the selected keyframes.

```
┌─────────────────────────────────┐
│  ∫  Automatic Easing    Ctrl E  │
│  ∫  Ease In             Ctrl E  │
│  ∫  Ease Out            Ctrl E  │
│  ∫  Ease In and Out     Ctrl E  │
└─────────────────────────────────┘
```

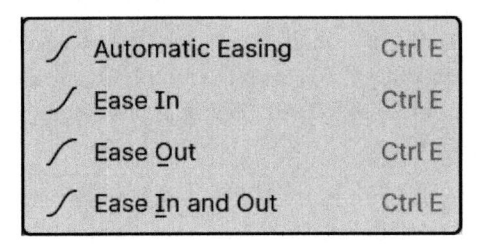

Figure 2.12: The Easing Type menu

3. Select an easing type from the menu and see its result.

Here's a rundown of available easing types and what they do:

- **Automatic Easing**: Largely pointless, this one just means **Ease In** for all the **Easing** interpolation modes and **Ease Out** for **Dynamic Effects** modes.
- **Ease In**: The F-curve begins slowly and accelerates, stopping abruptly at the end keyframe.
- **Ease Out**: The opposite of **Ease In**, this one starts fast and decelerates, leveling out at the end.
- **Ease In and Out**: The F-curve levels out smoothly at both ends, reaching its fastest point at the middle frame between the two keyframes.

You can skip **Automatic Easing**, but do take a look at the other three easing types in this list.

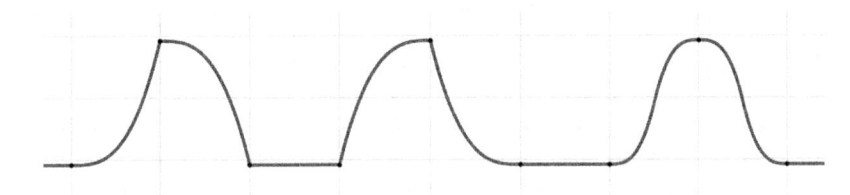

Figure 2.13: Ease In, Ease Out, and Ease In and Out

> **Important note**
> **Interpolation Mode** and **Easing Type** are properties of keyframes, even though the effect appears on the rest of the F-curve and not the keyframe itself. For each segment of an F-curve between two keyframes, *it is the keyframe at the beginning that determines the interpolation and easing.*

Pretty neat, but what is all this for? You're about to find out; now that you know what interpolation and easing are and how to set them, you're ready to make the ball bounce!

Making the ball bounce

How should a ball bounce? Unlike the magical color-changing cube we animated in the previous chapter, a bouncing ball is something you've seen in real life. This makes it a bit more challenging – we already have an idea in our mind as to what a bouncing ball ought to look like, so there are right and wrong ways to achieve this effect.

For guidance, we'll look to the laws of physics, which preside over the motion of things such as bouncing balls. Since we're animators and not physicists, these laws are just guidelines we can take or leave – this particular ball, for instance, will eventually be made to bounce and roll forever. Nevertheless, knowing a little physics will help us anticipate the forces at play and determine the best interpolation modes for our F-curves.

According to Newton's first law, *an object in motion shall remain in motion unless acted upon by an external force*. What this means is that force is required to change the direction or velocity of an object. So, what are the forces at work in a bouncing ball?

The most obvious force we want to simulate is gravity, which pulls things down. The second, less obvious force is that of our imaginary floor that (if we assume it's level) will force the ball back upward each time there's an impact. So, one force for down, and another for up. Up and down – hey, those are both on one axis. How convenient! To simulate these two forces acting on the ball, we'll do our fanciest keying on the **Z Location** F-curve. What about the other two F-curves, then?

Linear interpolation for objects in mid-air

If you've played or watched any sport with a ball in it, you'll notice that a kicked or thrown ball will have a constant rate of rotation and horizontal movement while it remains in mid-air. Besides a bird or a strong gust of wind, nothing in the air is going to significantly change how fast the ball spins or travels in a horizontal direction. What this means for us is that the **X Location** and **Y Euler Rotation** F-curves of our ball should show linear movement, without any change in speed.

The ideal interpolation mode for this is, of course, **Linear**:

1. Select both keyframes on frame `10` for the ball's **X Location** and **Y Euler Rotation** animation channels.
2. Set the keyframe interpolation to **Linear**.

This might be one of the least exciting interpolation modes to use, but it's the one that makes the most sense for these particular F-curves.

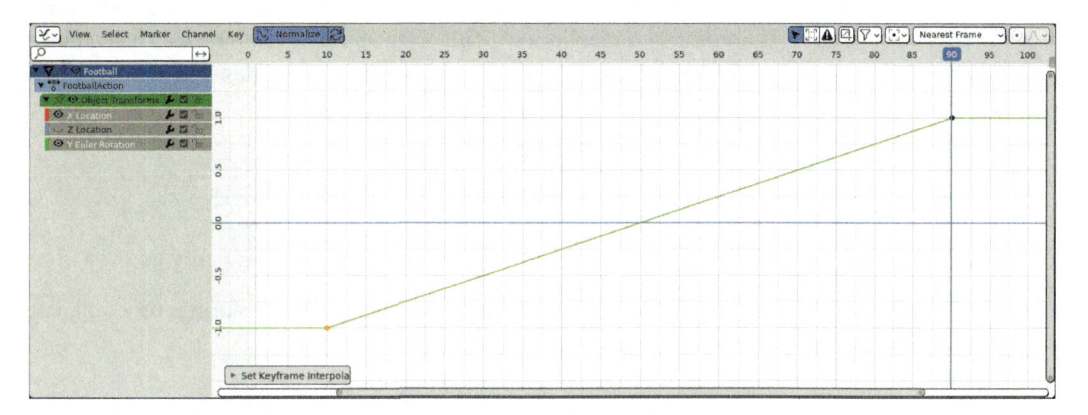

Figure 2.14: A Linear F-curve segment

Our animation still has those sudden changes in speed at frames 10 and 90, but we'll address that at the end. Let's get to the bouncing!

Adding bouncing keyframes in the Graph Editor

Whereas keying the **X Location** and **Y Euler Rotation** animation channels of the ball was straightforward (no pun intended), our **Z Location** F-curve is going to look completely different. We'll also need to carefully select some different modes of interpolation to simulate the physical forces at play.

As if there weren't enough methods in Blender for inserting keyframes already, we're also going to use this section as an example of how we can animate using only the Graph Editor. Without leaving this editor, we'll add the keyframes needed for a single bounce and then determine their interpolation.

> **Important note**
>
> You'll need to ensure that **Z Location** is unlocked and unhidden for this next part. Remember how to toggle the visibility and edit-protection of F-curves? You might also want to hide or lock the other two channels and maybe disable **Normalize**, but that's up to you. From here on out, you're in charge of your view and the display settings in the Graph Editor that we've learned so far.

Inserting keyframes within the Graph Editor

A single bounce will require three key values on the **Z Location** F-curve – the ball's low point on the grid floor, the high point of its bounce, and then its low point on the floor once more. This will require three keyframes (two if you use Bezier handles, but you don't know that yet). These keyframes will go on frames 10, 20, and 30, giving us a nice 20-frame bounce.

We've already got our first **Z Location** keyframe; let's add the second one now:

1. Select the **Z Location** channel.
2. Go to frame 20.
3. With your mouse cursor in the Graph Editor, press the *I* key. Note that this brings up a different menu than the one we used in the previous chapter:

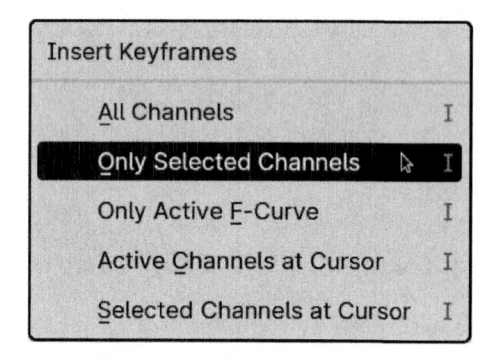

Figure 2.15: The menu to insert keyframes in the Graph Editor

4. From the menu, choose **Only Selected Channels**.

By using this menu to insert a keyframe on just the **Z Location** F-curve, we've added just one single keyframe, not a set of three or six as we had been doing before. This has zero effect on our other two F-curves. Why bother inserting extra keyframes where we don't need them?

This second keyframe can be used to determine the high point of the ball's bounce. Right now, of course, it's still on the floor...

Editing the value of keyframes

We're going to use this opportunity to move up the keyframe we've just made so that you can experience editing the value of a keyframe directly in the Graph Editor. We're going to move our second keyframe up by 1 meter, which just happens to be a nice-looking height for a 20-frame bounce.

Let's do it now:

1. Select the **Z Location** keyframe on frame 20.
2. Press *G* and *Y* and move it up by approximately 1 unit.

As you move that keyframe up on the Graph Editor's *Y* axis, pay attention to what happens in the 3D Viewport:

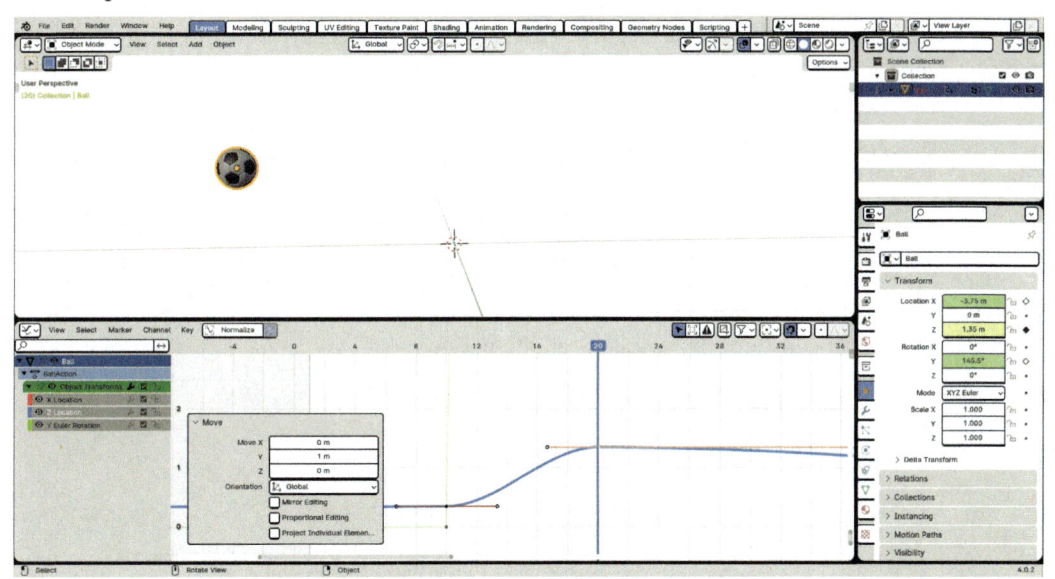

Figure 2.16: Moving the keyframe up on frame 20

If you're still on frame 20, you can see the ball move upward! By editing the value of the **Z Location** keyframe, we're affecting the ball's location on the *Z* axis from within the Graph Editor!

> **Tip**
> Changes made in the Graph Editor are immediately reflected in other areas according to how they affect the F-curve at the current frame. You don't have to go to the same frame as a keyframe to edit it, but it's often a good idea.

We're halfway to completing our bounce, now that we have a **Z Location** F-curve that shows a definite change. The ball starts on the floor, and then it goes up – next, we just need to get the ball back down.

Duplicating keyframes in the Graph Editor

Anything that goes up will have to come down. Making that happen to the ball will be the job of our third **Z Location** keyframe in this sequence, which we are presently to add.

What should the value (i.e., the *Y* axis position) of this keyframe be? The answer is the same value as the first keyframe, whereupon the ball is touching the floor. Our imaginary floor is flat and hasn't gone anywhere since the ball left it after frame `10`. The value for that keyframe happens to be `0.35`. That was easy. Figuring out the time (i.e., the *X* axis position) of this keyframe isn't hard either. If it took 10 frames for the ball to bounce up 1 meter, it should take another 10 frames to fall back down to its original height. 10 frames after frame 20 would put our keyframe on frame `30`.

We know exactly where our third keyframe needs to go, and there are plenty of ways to put it there in Blender. We could, for instance, simply insert another keyframe on frame `10` and move it down. Nothing wrong with that, but there's another way that's even faster – we can simply duplicate the keyframe on frame `10` and move it over to frame `30`. It's already at exactly the right height!

You already know how to move and duplicate keyframes in the Timeline. The method for doing so in the Graph Editor is the same, but with one additional step:

1. Select the **Z Location** keyframe on frame `10`.
2. Press *Shift* + *D* to duplicate the selected keyframe.
3. Press *X*.
4. Move the duplicate keyframe to frame `30`.

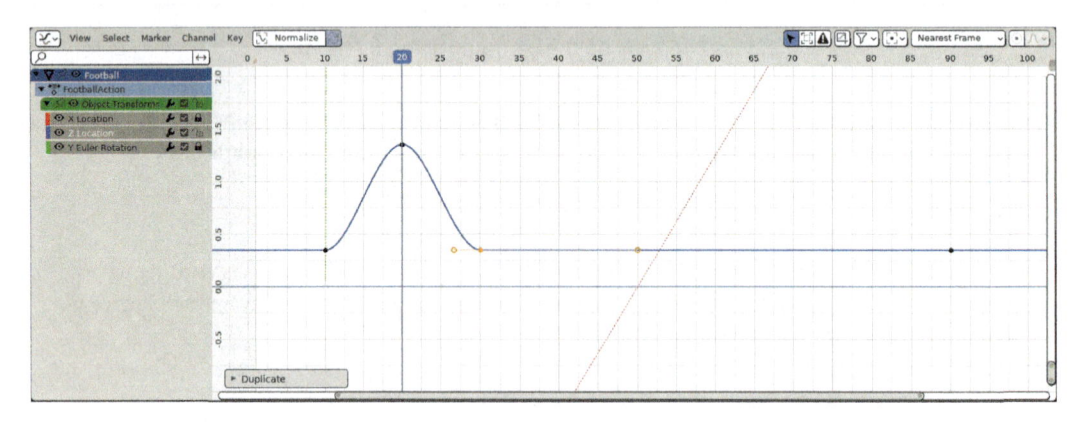

Figure 2.17: Three keyframes forming a "hump" in the Z Location F-curve

Did you catch that extra step I mentioned? We had to press *X*. This was for the same reason we had to press *Y* after grabbing a keyframe to move it up. Keyframes in the Graph Editor can be moved along two axes instead of just one – axes which map to completely different things. When we move keyframes left and right without locking them on the *X* axis, they can move up or down just a little, changing their value. Even a small difference in the value of this third keyframe could give us a strange result later on.

> **Important note**
> For the example in the previous paragraph, we will often want to lock our transformations to either the *X* or *Y* axis when moving keyframes in the Graph Editor. Just remember to press *X* or *Y*!

The first three keyframes on the **Z Location** channel now make the ball go up and come back down. Take a look at the shape of the F-curve, though – does this "hump" count as a bounce? Play the animation and see for yourself.

> **Tip**
> If you view your animation in the 3D Viewport from the front, you can watch how the ball's path perfectly mimics the shape of the **Z Location** F-curve as it moves from left to right.

If you think that's good enough, you must live underwater. Here on dry land, a ball does not bounce in a sine-wave motion. It does not steadily accelerate upward after leaving the floor, nor does it slow down right before touching it again. To complete this bounce, we're going to need to use what we learned earlier about interpolation and easing.

Proper interpolation and easing for a bouncing ball

How can we improve the motion of this "bounce"? The issue can't be the position of our three **Z Location** keyframes in the Graph Editor; we know that the ball has to start on the floor, we know it needs to reach a high point, and then we know it should come back down in the same amount of time. The frames and values of these keyframes are fine. What's wrong is the shape of the F-curve between those keyframes. We simply can't ignore interpolation!

So, what kind of interpolation do we need here? Can you pick it out from the **Set Keyframe Interpolation** menu? Don't say **Bounce** – that's cheating, and besides, you'll see it gives us little control over things such as the height, rate, and number of bounces.

Remember, we're trying to simulate gravity here! Gravity is observed as a constant downward acceleration, acceleration is the rate of change of velocity, and velocity is the rate of change of displacement (i.e., location). The kind of line we need to create, then, has *a rate of change which itself has a constant rate of change*.

I'll spare you the rest of this physics lesson. What this essentially means is that we need a slope with a quadratic function. Let's find that interpolation mode now:

1. Select the first two **Z Location** keyframes on frames `10` and `20`.
2. **Set Keyframe Interpolation** to **Quadratic**.

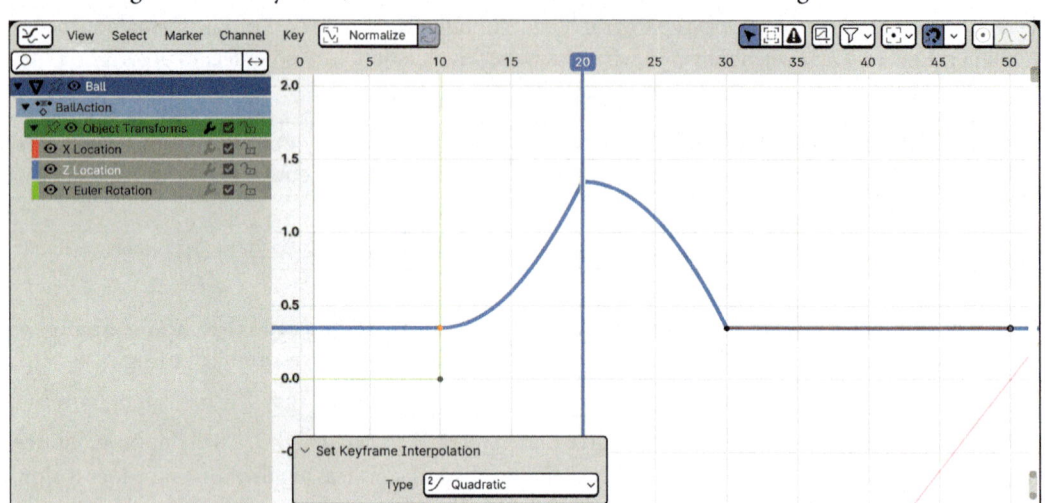

This gets us halfway there, but the first half of the bounce is still wrong:

Figure 2.18: A less-than-ideal, shark-fin-shaped F-curve segment

It *eases in*, and we need the segment to do the opposite of that. Good thing we know how to change easing types:

3. Select the first **Z Location** keyframe on frame `10`.
4. **Set Keyframe Easing Type** to **Ease Out**.

Now we have a bounce!

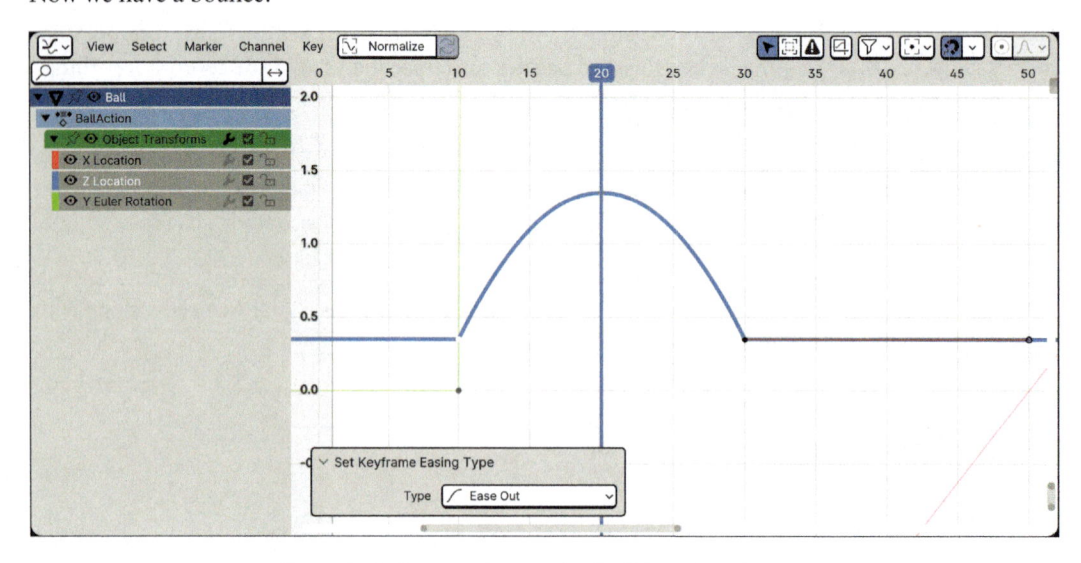

Figure 2.19: A proper bounce in the Z Location F-curve

There's just one small matter left – the ball only bounces once.

F-curve extrapolation

Presently, the ball bounces exactly once, which is not very exciting. It also stands still before frame `10` and after frame `90`, which is not a good look either. To fix this, we could simply duplicate the bouncing keyframes a few more times and shorten our scene frame range. There's a better way, though – one that will keep our ball bouncing and rolling... forever. We can accomplish this quite easily using a feature called **extrapolation**.

To understand extrapolation, imagine that the F-curve has a finite "main" segment between its first and last keyframes. Now, try to look at the rest of it, where it ends. You'll be zooming out for a long while. The F-curve is eternal; *it has no beginning or end*. It can't disappear just because there are no keyframes left! It must always have a definite value, even before the animation begins, and long after it has ended. Extrapolation is our word for what an F-curve should do for the rest of time.

By default, all F-curves have **Constant Extrapolation**, which simply extends them flatly, causing the value to stop changing. This is fine for most things but not for our present F-curves. After selecting different extrapolation modes for these, you'll be able to drag out the **End Frame** value and make the scene last an hour if you like, letting the ball bounce miles and miles off into the horizon.

Linear extrapolation

Let's address the first two F-curves that make the ball roll – **X Location** and **Y Euler Rotation**. Instead of adding the keyframes for these at the start and end frames of the scene, I asked you to add them on frames `10` and `90` so that the issue would be easier to see.

What if we wanted the ball to keep rolling? We'd have to extend these F-curves with keyframes that go further up and out. How much further out? This can get unruly if you're not sure exactly when the animation should end. Fortunately, those keyframes are fine exactly where they are.

All we need to do is set a different mode of extrapolation:

1. Select the **X Location** and **Y Euler Rotation** animation channels.
2. Press *Shift + E* or go to **Channel | Extrapolation Mode**.
3. Choose **Linear Extrapolation**.

Linear Extrapolation makes the F-curve continue on a linear slope, which is derived from the first two and last two keyframes. Since there are only two keyframes on each of these F-curves, and they both already use **Linear** interpolation, the F-curves will appear as perfectly straight lines when extrapolated this way:

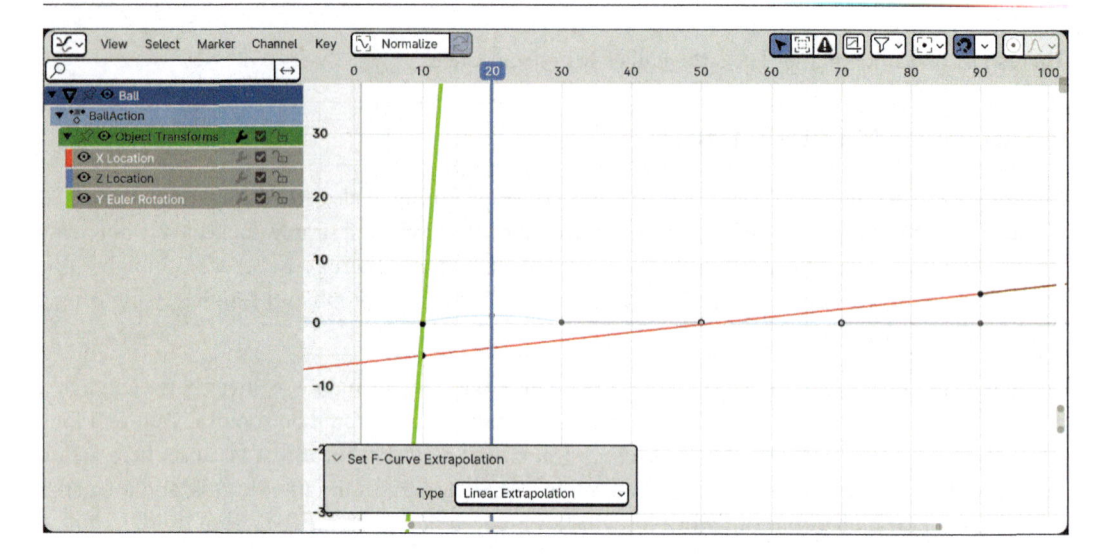

Figure 2.20: Linear extrapolation for the X Location and Y Euler Rotation F-curves

Note what this does to our animation. Not only does the ball keep on rolling, *it now always has been rolling*.

Cyclic extrapolation

Let's now turn to the **Z Location** F-curve. To make the ball bounce repeatedly, we could use what we already know and duplicate the three bouncing keyframes a hundred times or so… but let's not. There's another extrapolation mode available that can do all the work for us much more cleanly.

Let's look at it now:

1. Select the **Z Location** animation channel.
2. Press *Shift + E* or go to **Channel | Extrapolation Mode**.
3. Choose **Make Cyclic (F Modifier)**.

The F-curve now has what's called cyclic extrapolation. The keyed segment of the F-curve will now repeat indefinitely. Wait, though! Something's not right:

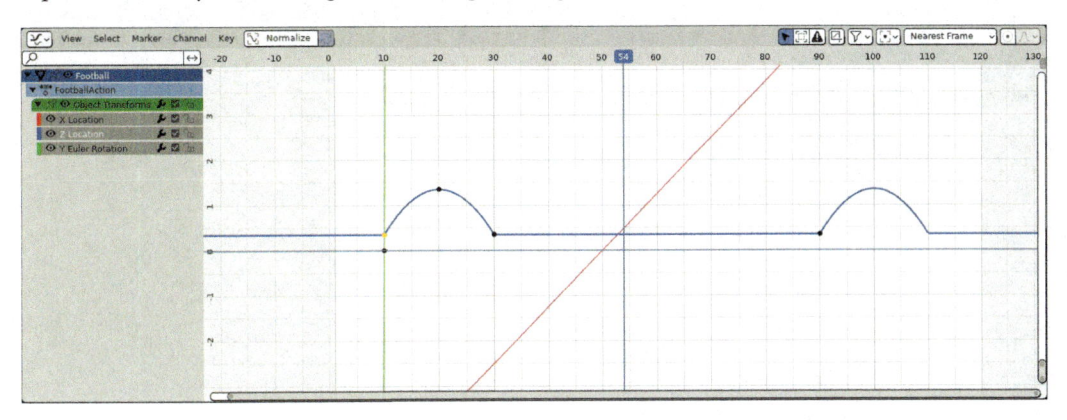

Figure 2.21: A bounce-and-roll kind of F-curve

That's an odd pattern. What's going on here?

Remember, cyclic extrapolation repeats the entire keyed segment of the F-curve – that is, everything between the first and last keyframes. Where is the last keyframe on this curve? All the way over on frame 90! We added it at the very beginning of this chapter and forgot about it. This sort of thing happens to animators all the time.

We want to repeat a 20-frame bounce, not an 80-frame bounce-and-roll. That pesky keyframe is messing up the cyclic period of our F-curve! Let's send it to Hell:

1. Select the **Z Location** keyframe on frame 90.
2. Press *X* to delete it.

Ah, that's much better.

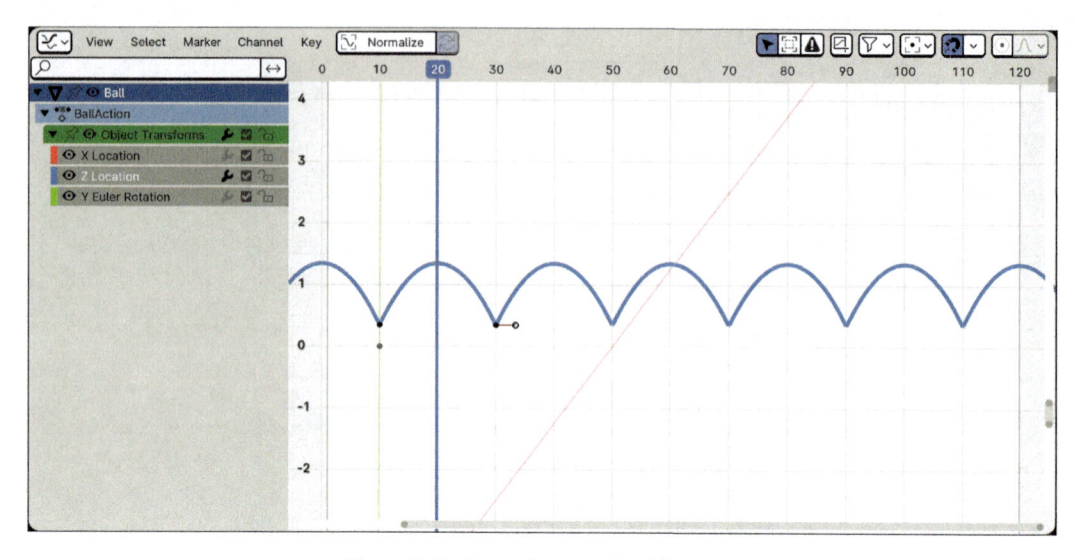

Figure 2.22: Properly repeating bounces

Now that only our three bouncing keyframes remain, the next bounce happens immediately after the previous one, giving us crisp, clean bounces.

You're finished with the bouncing ball animation! Continue playing around with it if you like – maybe set your **End Frame** to 10,000 and watch your creation go out into the world:

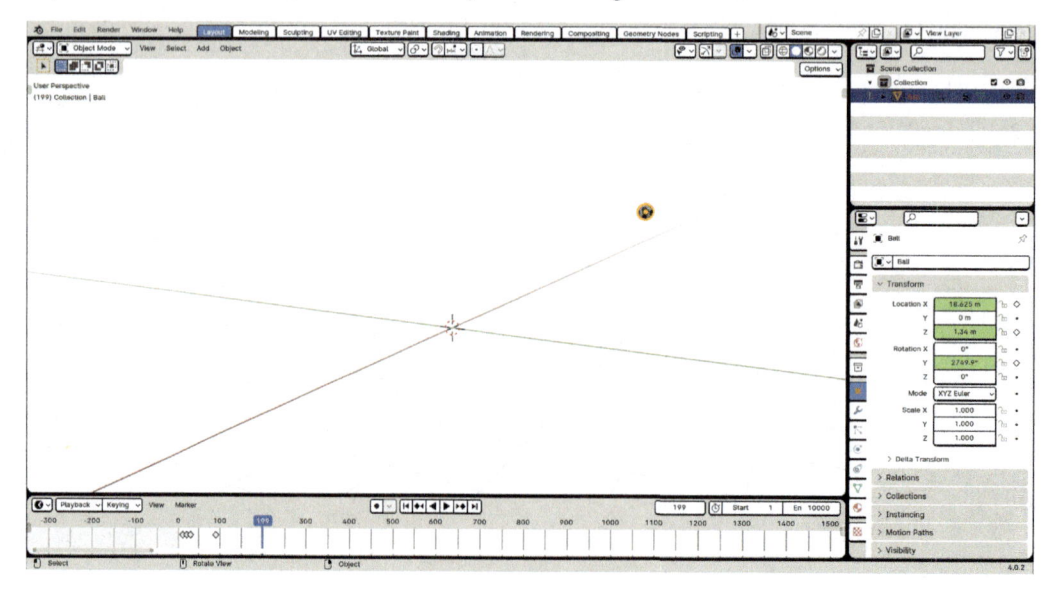

Figure 2.23: Come back!

And we're done!

Summary

By displaying all our animated properties as line graphs, the Graph Editor exposes the truth about 3D animation – it's all just a bunch of numbers. All the parameters in your scene and all the properties of every 3D object – they're all numbers that change over time. You make some numbers be one thing on one frame, and then you make those same numbers be something else on another frame. Keep going until it doesn't look terrible.

That's it. That's 3D animation. The end.

Well, maybe not exactly. We still have a whole book to fill on all those wonderful numbers, what they are, why we need them, where to find them, and how to make them do exactly what we want.

We've only just scratched the surface of what can be done with the Graph Editor. Those Bezier keyframes you saw, for instance... what might those be good for? Read on to see how we can directly sculpt the F-curves in our animations!

Questions

1. When you select **Location** from the **Insert Keyframe** menu, how many individual keyframes does that really insert? What about **Location & Rotation**? **Location, Rotation, & Scale**?
2. When you delete an animation channel, what happens to its keyframes? What if you delete all the keyframes on an F-curve?
3. In the Graph Editor, the *X* and *Y* axes are different. In the 3D Viewport, the *X* and *Y* axes are also different. How are these differences different, though?
4. What do directions such as up, down, left, and right mean when moving keyframes in the Graph Editor?
5. When **Normalize** is enabled, what does -1 on the *Y* axis of the Graph Editor mean?
6. Why is it generally a good idea to press *X* after duplicating keyframes in the Graph Editor?
7. What can you discern about an F-curve that is perfectly flat?
8. Does an F-curve segment with **Linear** interpolation show any speed? What about acceleration?
9. What parts of an F-curve are affected by extrapolation?
10. What specific operations did we learn in the Graph Editor that would not have worked in the Timeline?

3
Bezier Keyframes

At this point, it should go without saying that a keyframe is a kind of frame in the same way that an address is a kind of dress... that is to say, it isn't. In Blender, a keyframe is more like a little object that influences some property of something in your 3D scene. It exists outside the 3D Viewport in multiple areas; it takes the appearance of a point along a curve in the Graph Editor and a diamond-like shape in the Timeline and other editors. Its main attributes are value and time, which determine the value of an assigned property at a given frame, but it also possesses attributes such as interpolation and easing, which help determine the interpolated values between two keyframes.

There remains one special category of keyframe with its own particular attributes, which we left unexplored in the previous chapter: **Bezier keyframes**.

These keyframes are so powerful and potentially baffling that they deserve their own chapter in this book. Technically, **Bezier** is an interpolation mode found in the **Set Keyframe Interpolation** (*T*) menu, but it almost feels wrong to place this type of keyframe among a set of mere interpolation modes. Bezier keyframes are a game-changer. Before, we shaped the F-curve by just picking different interpolation modes and easing types from a menu; using Bezier keyframes, we can model it directly to create F-curves which are not possible with any other interpolation mode.

In this chapter, you'll learn about the following:

- A method for freely inserting keyframes in the Graph Editor
- Bezier keyframe handle types and how to set them
- How to edit "manual" keyframe handles
- The significance of points of inflection in an F-curve
- How (and why) to copy keyframes from one channel to another

Technical requirements

For this chapter, you'll need a unicycle scene, which may be downloaded here:

`https://github.com/PacktPublishing/Realizing-3D-Animation-in-Blender`

This unicycle has been specifically set up for this exercise, and the scene includes a short obstacle course to make things interesting. Open the `Unicycle.blend` file in Blender and let's get started!

One tired animator

Oh, yeah – we're animating a unicycle, by the way.

Figure 3.1: The unicycle

Animating a unicycle will be more challenging than the ball we animated in the previous chapter. It can bounce and roll but it will also need to steer and lean in the direction of its movement. It is also made up of multiple movable parts, so you'll need to pay closer attention to what you have selected.

This particular unicycle will move down the provided course sans rider. Imagine that it has come to life on its own, or perhaps there's an invisible person sitting on the saddle. Even without a rider, a unicycle can still be thought of as a character by itself!

The connected parts of our unicycle

Our unicycle model comprises four objects. These objects are "connected" via the use of **parenting** and **constraints**, a topic we shall cover in greater detail in the next chapter. For now, all you need to know is that the objects `Left Pedal` and `Right Pedal` are both parented to the object `Wheel`, which itself is constrained to the object `Seat`.

Wherever the seat goes, the wheel and its pedals will follow. This makes it our *root* object. For all intents and purposes, in this chapter, moving this object counts as moving the unicycle, even though there is no one object called "the unicycle." We will spend most of our time animating `Seat`. Afterward, we'll animate the rotation of `Wheel` so that it rolls properly. The two pedals can be left alone.

keying the course checkpoints

This chapter's animation will be more flexible than before. To get started, I'll give you some precise instructions on inserting the first few keyframes, which will serve as the foundation for the rest of your animation. Many more keyframes will be placed by yourself later on.

> **Tip**
> The scene and following keyframes are set up so that you may hold *Ctrl* while moving the object `Seat` to the indicated positions. This snaps your movements to 1-meter increments, helping keep things quick and exact. In other chapters, "meters" may be referred to simply as "units," which are effectively the same thing in Blender.

Get ready to add more location and rotation keyframes!

1. Go to frame 1.
2. Select the object `Seat`.
3. Move the unicycle up, back, and to the left, so that it stands at the starting line on top of the course.
4. Rotate it 90 degrees on the *Z* axis so that it faces toward the bridge of the course.

5. Key location and rotation with **Insert Keyframe** (*I*) | **Location & Rotation**.

Figure 3.2: The unicycle at frame 1

That was a lot of steps just for one frame! Let's speed things up to get through the next couple of keyframes.

6. The unicycle has 5 seconds to cross the first checkpoint. On frame 120, move the unicycle to the right on the *X* axis so that it lines up with the safety cone. Key location and rotation.

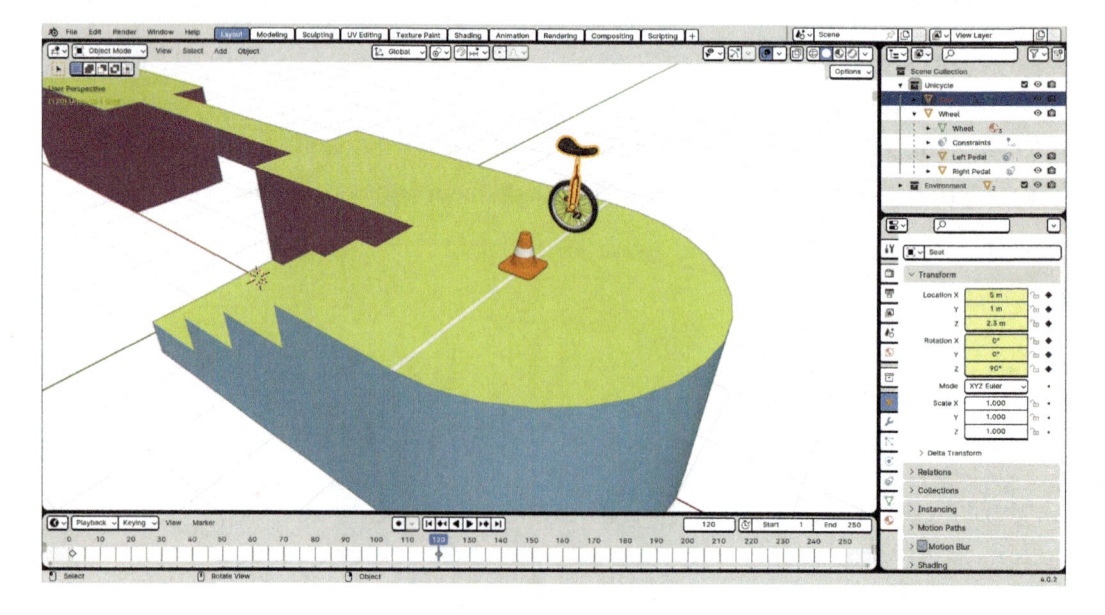

Figure 3.3: The unicycle at frame 120

7. Now the unicycle must turn right around the safety cone. On frame `150`, bring it forward on the *Y* axis to the other side of the cone. Rotate it `-180` degrees to the right on the *Z* axis so that it faces the steps. Key location and rotation.

Figure 3.4: The unicycle at frame 150

8. On frame `160`, move the unicycle `-1` meter on the *X* axis to the head of the steps. This will be its first jumping point. Key location and rotation.

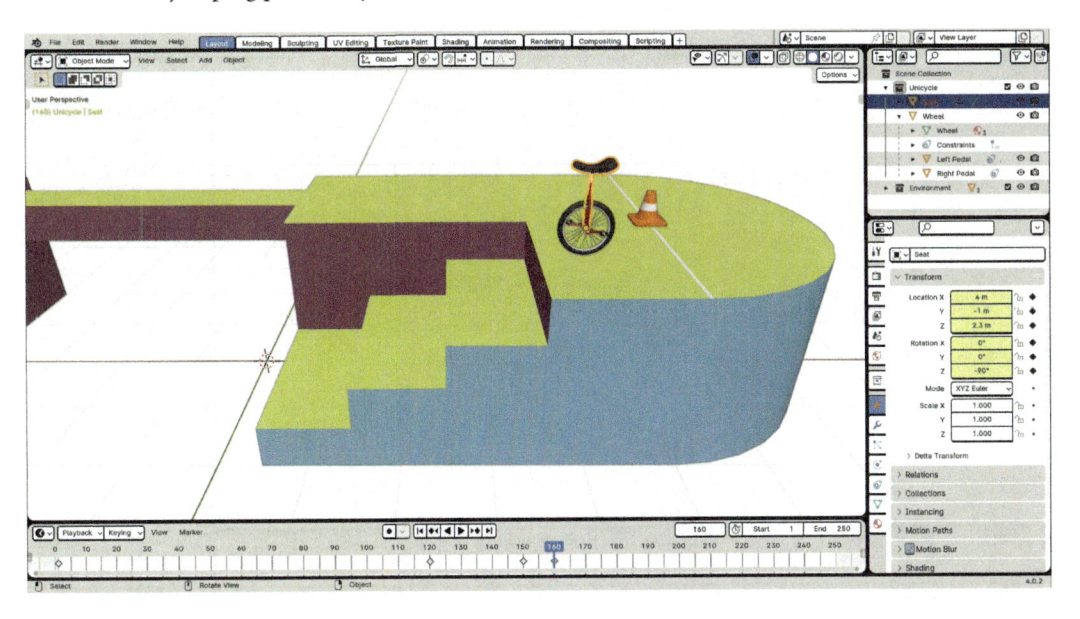

Figure 3.5: The unicycle at frame 160

9. On frame 200, bring the unicycle back down to the "ground" level of the scene at the foot of the steps. It should appear to rest on the Y axis grid line. Key location and rotation.

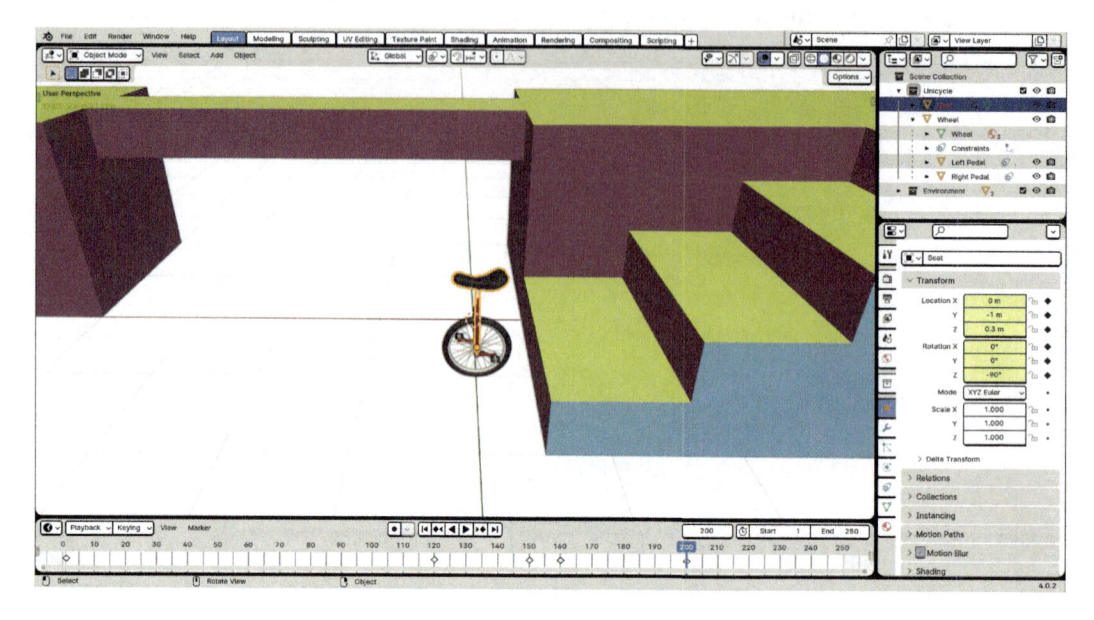

Figure 3.6: The unicycle at frame 200

10. Now for the final stretch! Go to frame 250 and move the unicycle about -15 meters to the left on the X axis. Key location and rotation.

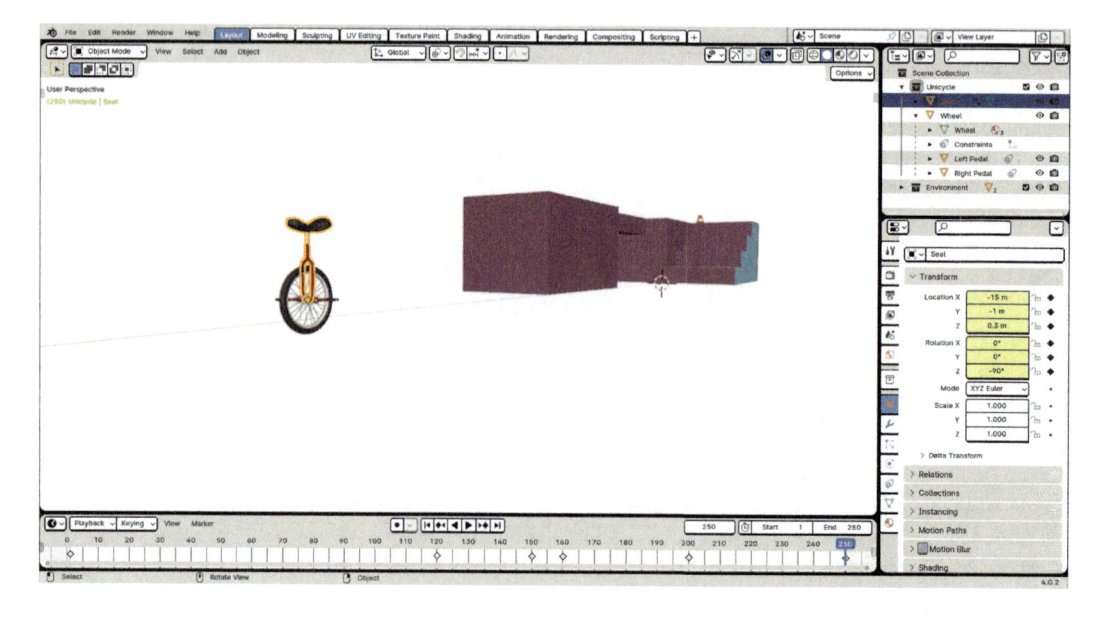

Figure 3.7: The unicycle at frame 250

> **Tip**
> After inserting these keyframes, use the *up* and *down* arrow keys on your keyboard to quickly review the positions of the unicycle at various keyframes. If you feel you have made a mistake at any one of these steps, don't be afraid to delete or overwrite an existing keyframe and try again.

That concludes the "paint-by-numbers" section of this chapter. Don't be discouraged that the animation doesn't look so great at this stage. The important thing is that our main positions have been blocked out, making it easier for us to continue our work on the animation by adding and editing more keyframes within the Graph Editor.

A novel method for inserting keyframes in the Graph Editor

Speaking of the Graph Editor, why don't we bring it up:

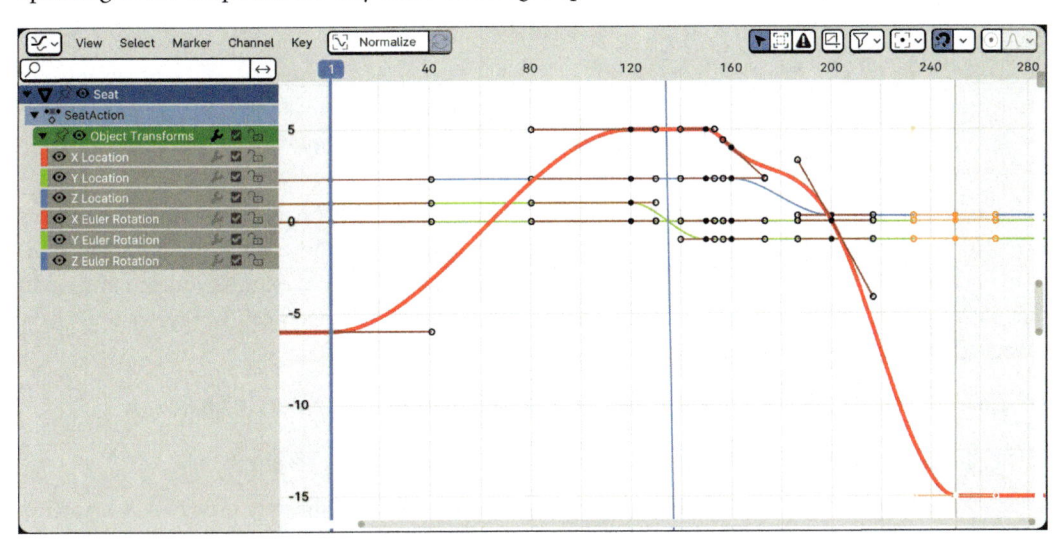

Figure 3.8: The Graph Editor at first glance

Goodness! Quite the leap from what we worked with in the previous chapter. You may wish to hide some channels here, but don't delete any of them. We will need all six animation channels for this object. How quaint that bouncing ball must seem in retrospect!

> **Important note**
> You will be shown a lot of pictures of F-curves in this chapter. Because this is a book with still images, it's up to you to watch the animated result on your own screen. Remember to keep a 3D Viewport open along with the Graph Editor, and always play back and scrub your animation after making changes to review what you've created.

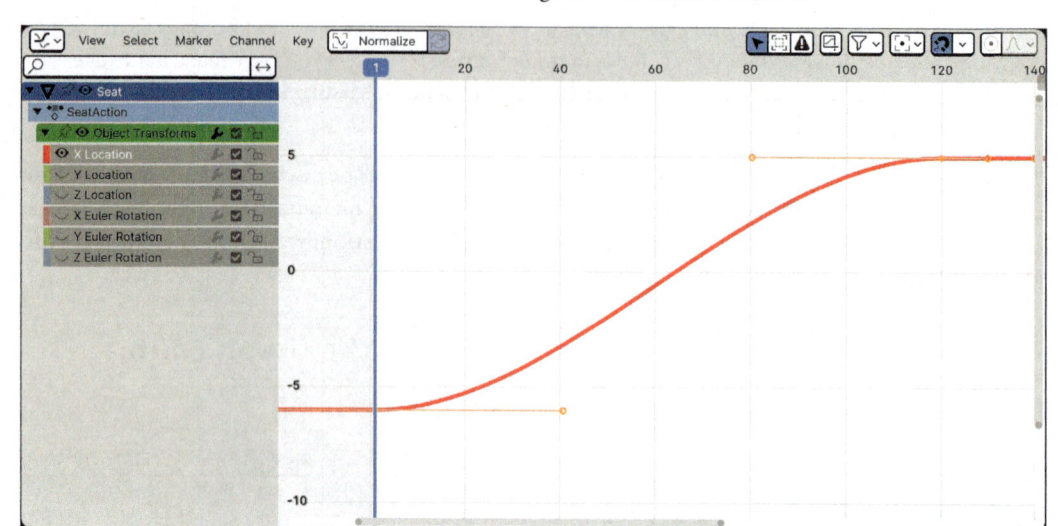

Let's turn our attention to the first 120 frames along the **X Location** channel:

Figure 3.9: The first part of the X Location F-curve

Kind of boring, right? We're going to spice up the motion along the **X Location** F-curve by inserting a few more keyframes along this section. And where, exactly, should those keyframes go? Why don't you decide? Why don't we use this section as an opportunity for you to express yourself and add a couple keyframes wherever you like? Yes, let's take those training wheels off! Unicycles don't have training wheels anyway.

While we're at it, we'll learn a fun way to insert keyframes arbitrarily in the Graph Editor:

1. In the Graph Editor, Select the **X Location** channel of the object `Seat`.
2. Hold *Ctrl* and click with the non-selecting mouse button to directly insert an **X Location** keyframe at the mouse cursor location.
3. Repeat until you have added 3 or 4 new **X Location** keyframes between frames `1` and `120`.
4. Adjust these new keyframes to your liking by selecting and grabbing them with G. The result should smoothly vary the speed and direction of your unicycle. Avoid making outrageous slopes and peaks which would cause the unicycle to move jarringly fast or go off the course.

> **Important note**
>
> When you wish to select and grab a Bezier keyframe, make sure you grab the keyframe itself (the dot in the middle), and not just one of its handles (those two little antennae sticking out on either side). We'll learn about handles in the next section.

I've chosen to add four keyframes that cause the unicycle to go backward, once at the very beginning, and again later on:

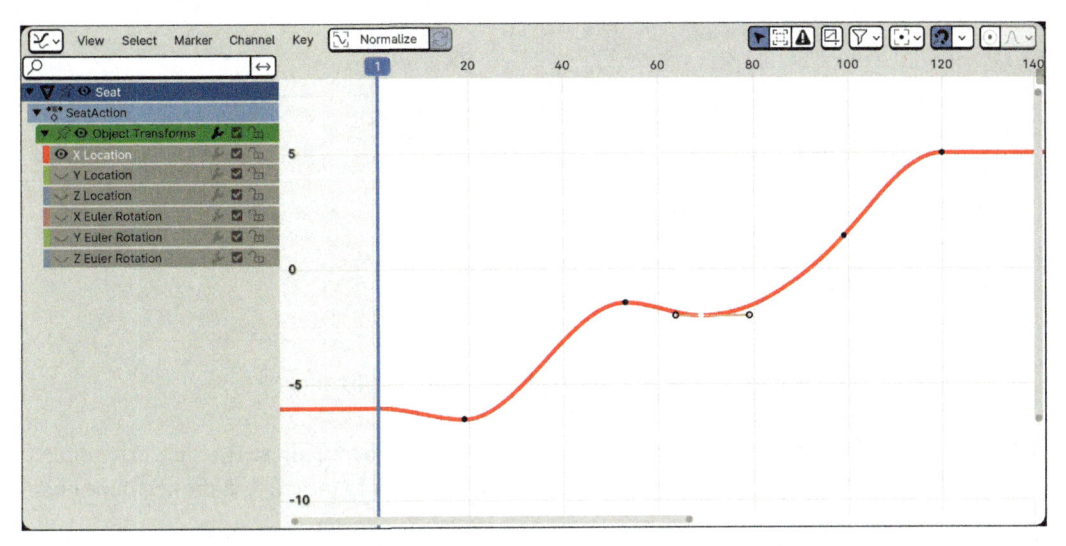

Figure 3.10: An example X Location F-curve

Your F-curve may look different. That's fine! It wouldn't be your animation if you simply copied what you see in my Graph Editor.

Now that we've added our own personal flair to our blocked-out animation, it looks... still pretty bad. Not to worry; we're about to improve things using the magic of Bezier handles.

Bezier handle types

In Blender's Graph Editor, **Bezier** is categorized as a keyframe interpolation mode. This mode may be found in the **Set Keyframe Interpolation** (*T*) menu, but there's no need to bring up that menu for this exercise, as **Bezier** is the default interpolation mode. All your keyframes are already Bezier keyframes!

It's easy to tell the difference between a Bezier keyframe and any other type of keyframe. Bezier keyframes have **handles**:

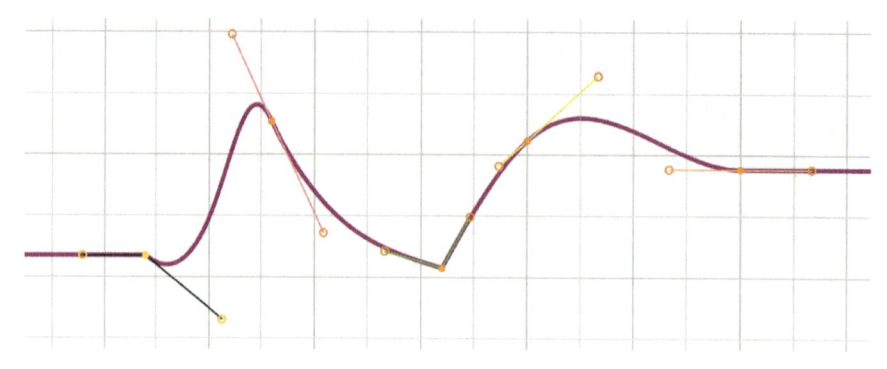

Figure 3.11: Bezier-type keyframes with visible handles

The keyframe itself is the middle dot along the F-curve. The handles are those two dots extending to the left and right of the keyframe, connected by lines that lie *tangent* to the curve at the keyframe point.

If you've used any kind of vector graphics application, you'll recognize what these are and their functionality will not surprise you. Bezier handles bend a curve, pushing its trajectory in the direction of the handle. The longer the handle, the stronger its influence on that segment of the curve. In Blender's Graph Editor, we can edit these handles directly or take advantage of the automatic behavior of certain handle types to create F-curve shapes which are not possible with any other interpolation mode.

Before we go any further, there's one important step we must take to help make these handles easier to see and select.

Exposing keyframe handles

You may have noticed that only your selected keyframes appear to have handles. By default, a keyframe must be selected before its Bezier handles will appear in the Graph Editor. What an inconvenient way to work! For this exercise, we'll want to be able to see and select all those handles without having to select the keyframe first:

1. Go to the **View** menu of the Graph Editor.
2. Disable **Only Selected Keyframes Handles**.

Now we can see all our handles! Much better.

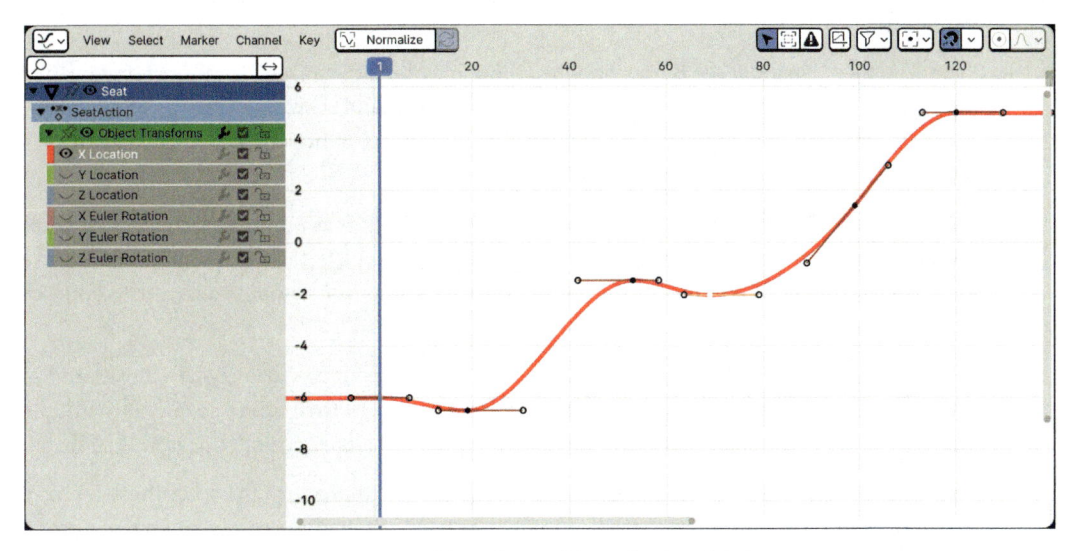

Figure 3.12: All handles visible in the Graph Editor

> **Tip**
> There are a few other handy features hiding in the **View** menu of the Graph Editor. Another helpful one you might consider enabling is **Show Sliders**, which displays the current value of each animated property directly in the animation channel list. Editing these sliders in the Graph Editor is yet another way of inserting keyframes!

Overview of Bezier handle types

In the previous chapter, we selected different easing types from the **Set Keyframe Easing Type** (*Ctrl + E*) menu, which is necessary when using any of the **Easing** or **Dynamic Effects** interpolation modes. In contrast, Bezier keyframes do not have an easing type. They instead have handle types, which are set using the **Set Keyframe Handle Type** (*V*) menu:

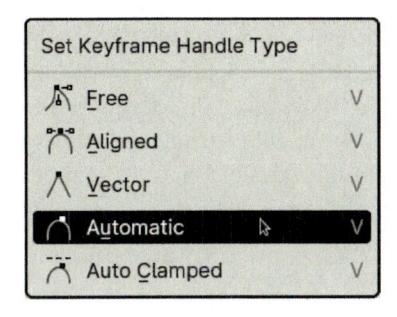

Figure 3.13: The Set Keyframe Handle Type menu

These types determine what kind of automatic behavior the handle should have, if any. Here's a rundown of all of them:

- **Free**: The most "manual" of Bezier handles, these may be moved freely and independently of each other. This can produce a sharp angle in the F-curve, and therefore a sharp change in the speed or direction of an object. **Free** handles remain faithful to how they are adjusted and are not affected by adjacent keyframes.
- **Aligned**: This type of handle may be moved almost freely. It does not react to anything except for its "sibling" on the opposite side of the keyframe, with which it must be aligned. Use these for manual control where you still want the F-curve to retain its smoothness at the point of the keyframe.
- **Vector**: A somewhat misleading name (technically all Bezier handles are vectors), these handles automatically point toward adjacent keyframes or the apex of their curve segments. Multiple **Vector** handles in a row will create an F-curve that looks just like one with linear interpolation.
- **Automatic**: These handles rotate and scale automatically to produce the smoothest F-curve possible. **Automatic** handles are terrific for loose and natural-looking movement but are prone to "drifting" and "overshooting," making a mess if used carelessly.
- **Auto Clamped**: The default handle type, and by far the most practical and common. Like **Automatic** handles, they also try to make a smooth curve, but like to remain flat wherever possible so as to avoid undesirable movement.

> **Important note**
> Using **Set Keyframe Handle Type** (*V*) isn't the only way to change the handle type of a Bezier keyframe. Manually editing any handle will cause its type to change to **Free** or **Aligned**. For this reason, it is easy to alter handle types in Blender by accident!

We'll get a chance to take advantage of each one of these handle types in our animation. Let's start with the easiest one!

Automatic and Auto Clamped Bezier handles

As you moved around your Bezier keyframes with **Auto Clamped** handles, you may have noticed the handles moving automatically in relation to neighboring keyframes. **Auto Clamped** and **Automatic** keyframe handles are similar in that they are not directly controlled by the animator. These so-called "handles" aren't meant to be handled at all! Instead, the handles react automatically based on the position and trajectory of neighboring keyframes, in order to produce an optimally smooth F-curve. This feature is indispensable in animations with thousands of keyframes, where we don't want to have to edit the handles of every single one.

Let's return to the first part of our **X Location** F-curve, between frames 1 and 120, along which we just added a few random keyframes to make it more interesting. The result should look fairly smooth, but it could be smoother.

Let's try out the **Automatic** handle type:

1. Select all the **X Location** keyframes before frame 120.
2. Press *V* to bring up the **Set Keyframe Handle Type** menu. Select **Automatic**.
3. Having done this, you may wish to further tweak the position of these keyframes in order to accommodate their curious new behavior.

The **X Location** F-curve and the resulting animation should now look a bit smoother than before:

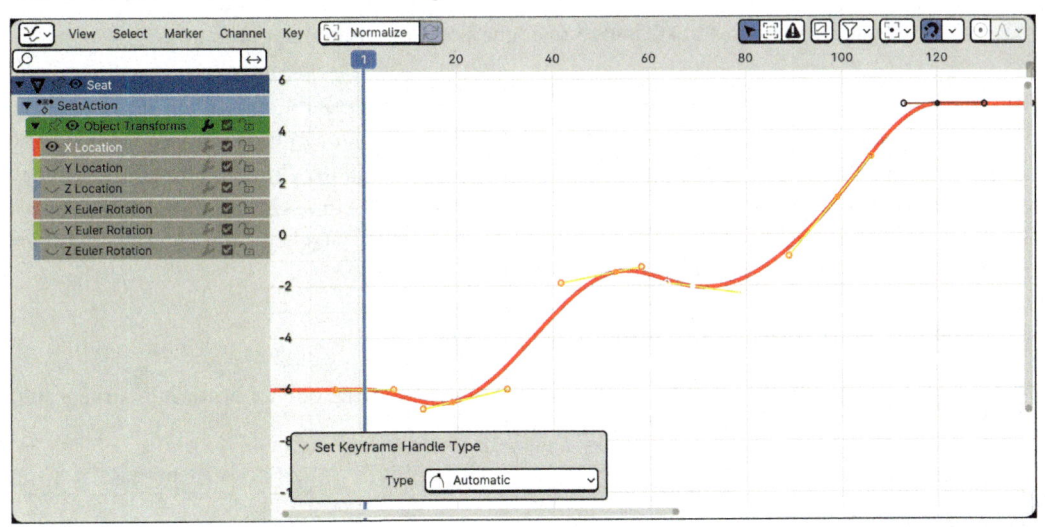

Figure 3.14: F-curve with "fully automatic" keyframes

Compare your new **Automatic** keyframe handles to the **Auto Clamped** ones you had before. **Auto Clamped** handles are more modest; they like to remain as flat as possible, keeping the value range of the F-curve constrained between each pair of adjacent keyframes.

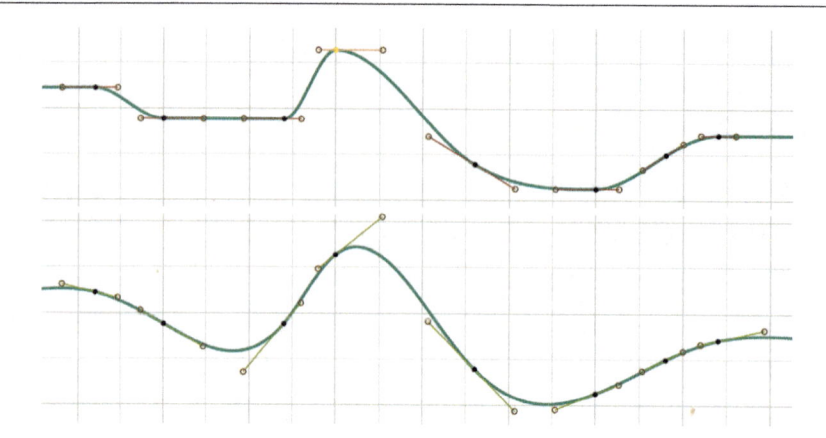

Figure 3.15: Top – Auto Clamped keyframes; bottom – Automatic keyframes

Automatic handles, on the other hand, are wild and have no such reservations. They let the F-curve flow like a winding river, giving themselves whatever direction and magnitude is needed to make the curve along the points as smooth as possible. When moving them in the Graph Editor, one has to pay less attention to their precise *XY* position, and more to whatever F-curve gets produced. The effect of this behavior makes **Automatic** handles ideal for weighty, wobbly, wiggly movements, where things stay animated and less precision is required.

Why not use Automatic keyframes everywhere?

There's a reason why **Auto Clamped** is the default. Take a look at what our **Y Location** F-curve would look like if we gave the keyframes all **Automatic** handles:

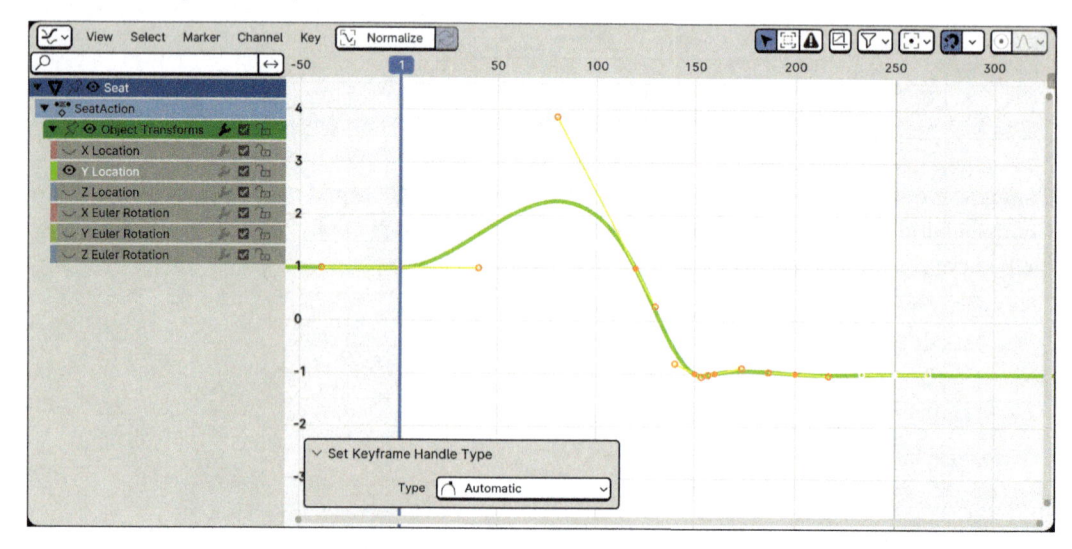

Figure 3.16: Y Location F-curve with all Automatic keyframes

This is a good example of that *drift* effect mentioned earlier. Here, the unicycle would drift off the whole course! We never wanted it to move that much on the *Y* axis.

Automatic handles are so wild that it's hard to make them stay flat where you might want them to. This same effect also causes "overshoot," leading to unpredictable extremes, or "peaks" along the F-curve that do not lie at the keyframes and making the F-curve harder to control.

In contrast, **Auto Clamped** keyframe handles are more sensible. Wherever there are two such keyframes along an F-curve, you can be sure that the value along that F-curve segment will stay within the range of values between those keyframes and will not change direction. Flat sections of the curve will stay flat, and peaks will always stick to the time and value of the keyframe. For the remainder of our exercises, we'll keep using **Auto Clamped** keyframe handles as the default, choosing carefully and deliberately which handles to change to another.

We've learned enough about the distinction between **Automatic** and **Auto Clamped**. Let's move on to two other handle types.

Vector and Aligned handles

There's still a lot of work to do! For the moment, we'll set aside our unicycle's feeble "turn" between frames `120` and `150`, where the unicycle does not yet "go around" anything, and focus on another section of the **X Location** F-curve that needs our attention.

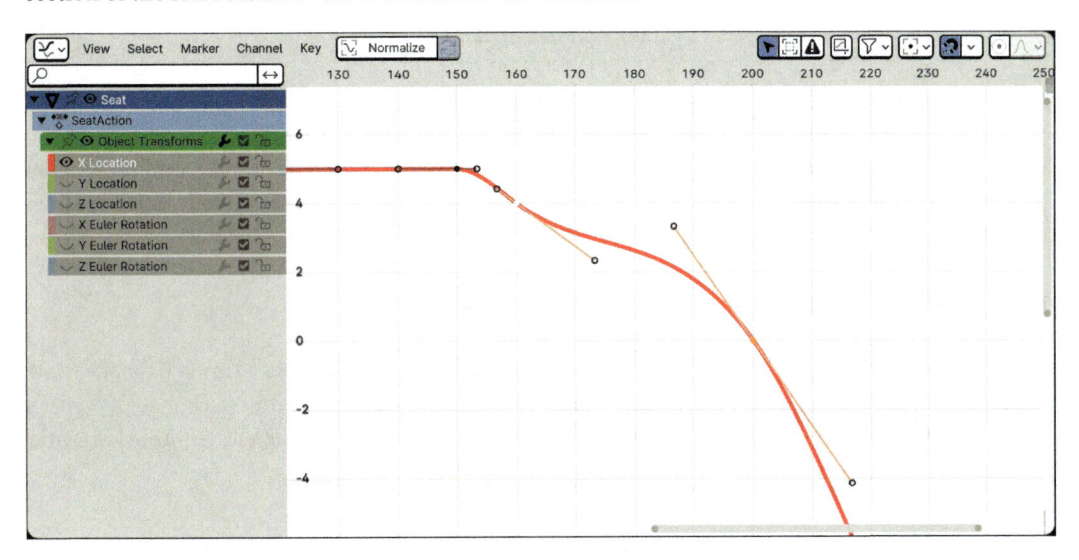

Figure 3.17: X Location F-curve from frame 160 to 200

Between frames `160` and `200`, we want our unicycle to "hop" from step to step as it moves downstairs. Just like in our exercise with the bouncing ball, this means that the unicycle will spend most of its time not touching the floor in this part, so it ought to have a constant horizontal speed – that is, linear interpolation on the **X Location** F-curve.

We could do this using the **Linear** interpolation mode, but let's try using **Vector** handles instead:

1. Select the two **X Location** keyframes of `Seat` on frames `160` and `200`.
2. Press *V* and **Set Keyframe Handle Type** to **Vector**.

Now the opposing handles of the two keyframes point directly at each other, creating a perfectly straight line segment:

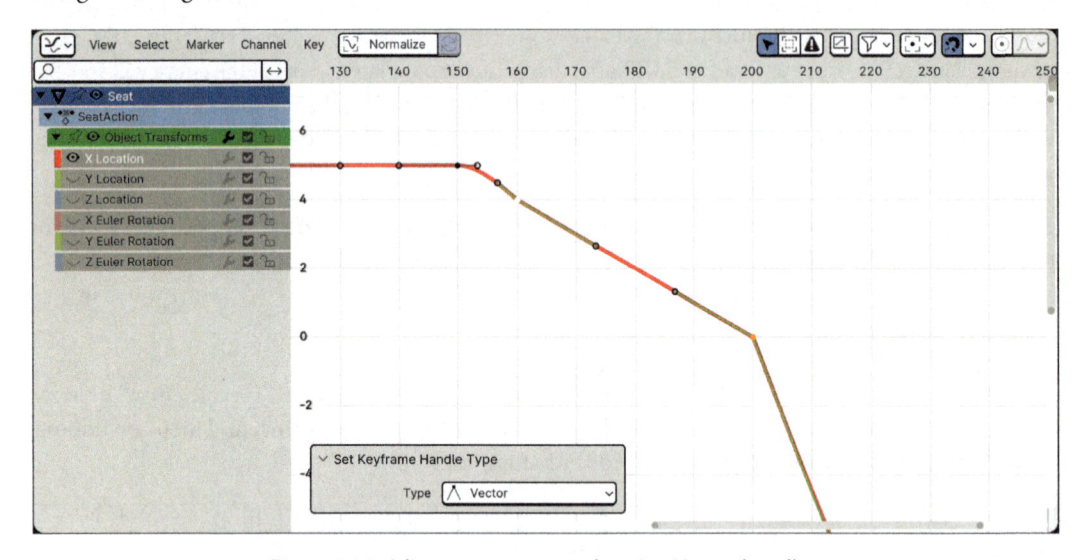

Figure 3.18: A linear segment made using Vector handles

If you think this is identical to the **Linear** interpolation mode, you're correct! These **Vector** handles have limited usefulness compared to the other handle types. There is, however, one small trick we can use them for…

Combining Vector and Aligned handles

Did you know a single Bezier keyframe can have two different handle types? This is true of certain handle combinations and may be useful in cases such as the following. In order to change the type of one handle instead of both, all you need to do is select a single handle instead of the whole keyframe.

Let's try this out with the keyframes we just edited:

1. Select the left handle of the **X Location** keyframe on frame `160`.
2. Hold *Shift* and select the right handle of the **X Location** keyframe on frame `200`.
3. Set both keyframes' handles to **Aligned**.

Notice how the **Aligned** handles are now rigidly aligned with their sibling **Vector** handles. They can be scaled if you try to grab them but they cannot change direction on their own:

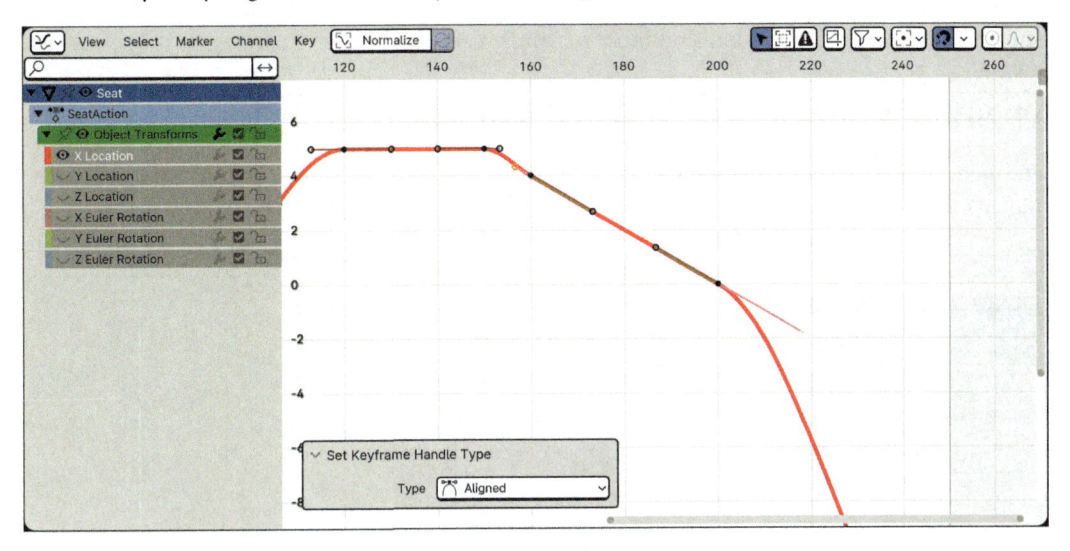

Figure 3.19: Bezier keyframes with a combination of Vector and Aligned handles

By using **Aligned** handles with **Vector** handles, we're able to eliminate those sharp corners we initially had and maintain a smooth F-curve while keeping the linear section unaffected. The result eases in to – and out from – the constant speed between frames `160` and `200`.

Although clever, this example is one of the rarer use-cases for **Aligned** handles. In the next section, why don't we get more practice with them by editing some directly?

Editing Bezier handles

In the previous section, we tried out all the Bezier handle types not directly controlled by the animator: **Auto Clamped**, **Automatic**, and **Vector**. These types all have a sort of "automatic" behavior, which is influenced by neighboring keyframes.

The remaining types, **Aligned** and **Free**, have no such automatic behavior. They remain fixed to the keyframe's center point and don't go anywhere unless edited directly. We can't move forward unless we learn how to do that, then!

Editing Bezier handles in Blender is hardly different from other elements. Here are the main operators:

- **Rotate** (*R*): This changes the direction of the selected handle, and therefore the trajectory of the curve at the point of the keyframe.
- **Scale** (*S*): This changes the magnitude of the handle, and therefore the strength of the effect of its direction.
- **Grab** (*G*): Grabbing the handle moves it freely, affecting both its direction and magnitude.

No surprises here! Don't worry too much about selecting or rotating; in most cases you can just use **Grab** (G). Clicking and dragging works too.

Knowing what we know now, let's continue working on our **X Location** F-curve.

Smooth movement with Aligned handles

One more section of the **X Location** F-curve desperately needs our attention: the turn-around between frames 120 and 150:

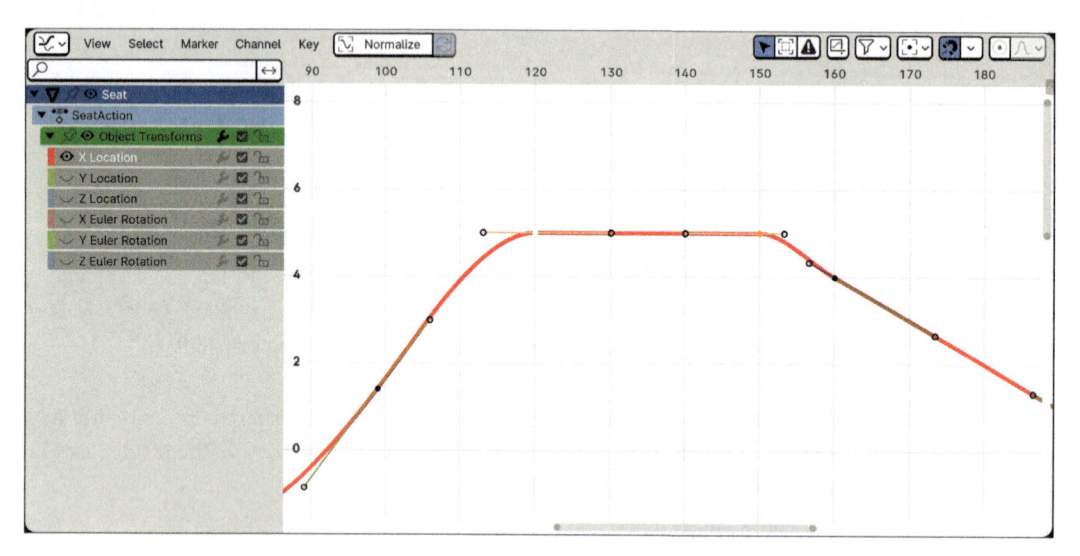

Figure 3.20: Undesirably flat section of the X Location F-curve

In order to make the unicycle actually go around the safety cone, we'll need to do something to push this part of the curve upward so that, by frame 135, the unicycle is beyond the safety cone instead of passing through it. We don't need to insert a keyframe at frame 135 to accomplish this, though. Instead, we can edit the handles of the keyframes we already have. We don't need to change the handle types to **Aligned** this time. That will happen automatically when we edit the handles:

1. Select the *right* handle of the **X Location** keyframe for Seat on frame 120.
2. Use **Grab** (G) to move it upward.
3. Do the same for the *left* handle of the **X Location** keyframe on frame 150.

4. Continue editing these two keyframes until you get a nice, symmetrical, arch-like shape between frames `120` and `150`, with minimal "wrinkles" on either side:

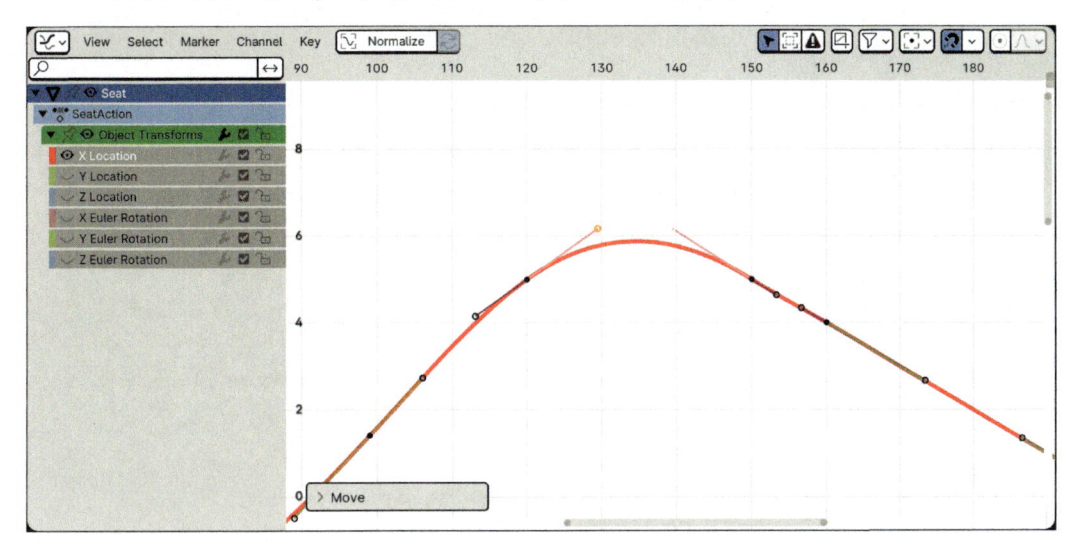

Figure 3.21: The improved X Location F-curve

We aren't just avoiding adding extra keyframes out of stubbornness. Sometimes it really does help to use as few keyframes as possible to achieve smooth motion. The result should make the unicycle go clear around the safety cone in a somewhat elliptical path.

We're nearly finished with this F-curve! Let's wrap things up with one final adjustment. Why should the unicycle slow down to a standstill at frame `250`? It'd be less dull if it appeared as though it were going to keep cruising after the end of the animation.

Let's adjust that last keyframe so the unicycle accelerates (and maintains) a cruising speed until the very last frame:

1. Select and **Grab** (*G*) the *left* handle of the keyframe on frame `250`, moving it upward.
2. You might also **Scale** (*S*) the **Aligned** *right* keyframe handle on frame `200`.

3. Repeat until the unicycle reaches a satisfactory speed in a satisfactory manner.

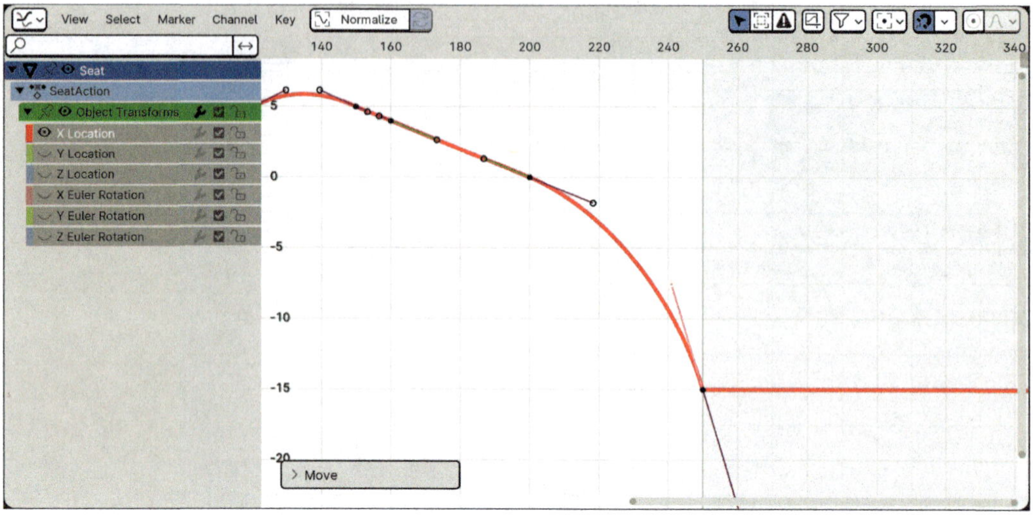

Figure 3.22: Final part of the X Location F-curve

Our work on the **X Location** F-curve is now complete. Bear in mind that not all (or even most) of your animations will be made this way (i.e., one F-curve at a time) but for now, it's nice to have finished an entire F-curve. Now on to the next one!

Bounces with Free handles

Moving down our list of animation channels for the `Seat` object, we can now turn our attention to **Z Location**. **Y Location**, as it happens, may be left the way it is.

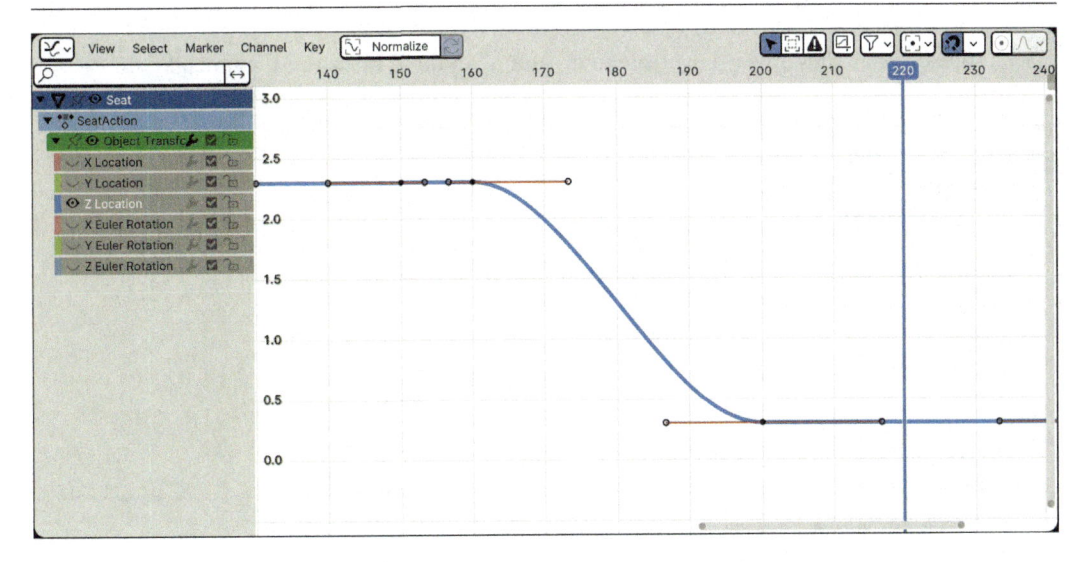

Figure 3.23: The current Z Location F-curve

Our chief concern here is the part of the F-curve between frames 160 and 200. During this 40-frame interval, we want the unicycle to hop down that short flight of steps. If we use keyframes with **Free** handles, we can achieve this with a minimal number of additional keyframes.

Our course just happens to have 4 steps to traverse within these 40 frames, so the unicycle must jump 4 times – that's 10 frames per jump. By inserting keyframes on frames 170, 180, and 190, we'll have divided the F-curve into 4 segments, each 10 frames long. We can then edit the handles of all the keyframes to manually create each upward bounce.

This time, you may use whatever method you like to insert keyframes:

1. Insert **Z Location** keyframes for Seat on frames 170, 180, and 190.
2. Adjust the value of each new keyframe so that the unicycle touches one of the steps at each one (hint: the steps descend at increments of half a meter).
3. Select all the **Z Location** keyframes from frames 160 to 200 (including the ones on frames 160 and 200).
4. Convert the selected keyframes to the **Free** handle type.

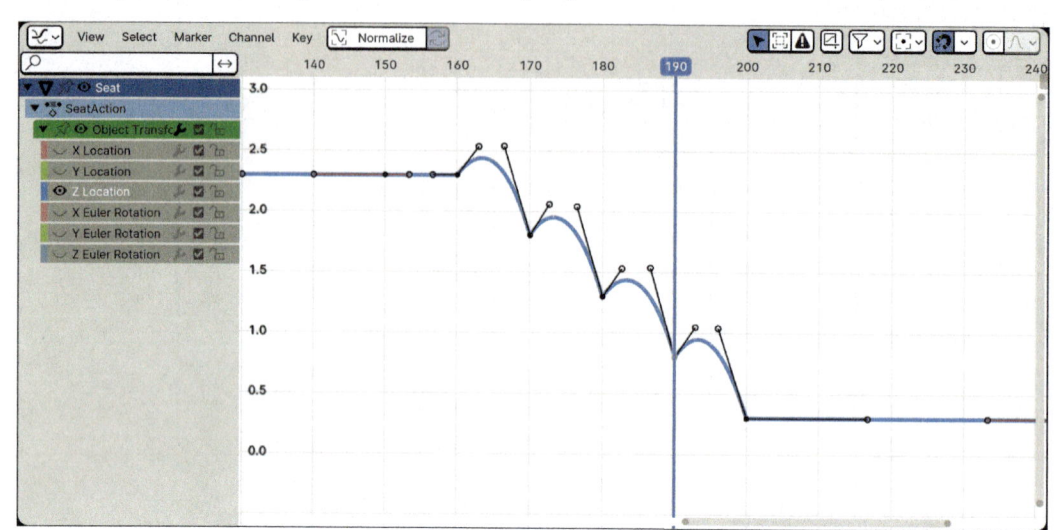

5. Adjust the handles upward to create four "jumps" in the **Z Location** F-curve, like so:

Figure 3.24: Downstairs-hopping motion along the Z Location F-curve

Free handles can be independently moved like the antennae of an old television set, making them ideal for this type of action. Note that we don't actually need keyframes at the top of the arc; the opposing handles of two keyframes are all we need to create motion.

Review the state of your animation thus far and make any other tweaks you like to the **Location** F-curves of `Seat`. When you're satisfied, we'll use what we have as the basis for animating the rotation of the seat and the wheel in the following sections.

Heading, weight, and balance

Let's review the remaining animation channels for `Seat` that need our attention:

- **X Euler Rotation** makes the unicycle seat unicycle rock back and forth, which is necessary for conveying weight and balance as the unicycle moves backward and forward.

- **Y Euler Rotation** makes the unicycle lean left and right. As the unicycle turns right from frame `120` to `150`, we want it to lean rightward.

- **Z Euler Rotation** turns the unicycle, determining its heading (or at least what ought to be its heading). We animated this one a bit already from frame `120` to `150` but it needs adjustment.

For our unicycle to show convincing balance, weight, and direction, all of these channels will need to be animated and/or have their animation corrected in the Graph Editor. Exactly how we animate them will depend on a careful study of the existing motion that we've already created.

Motion paths as a visual guide

How much our unicycle ought to lean in any direction on its *X* or *Y* axis is somewhat subjective. On the other hand, where it should point on the *Z* axis is not a matter of taste; it might be a magic unicycle, but it must point in the direction of its movement! So, rather than moving down the list of rotational components in alphabetical order, we're going to take care of the **Z Euler Rotation** F-curve first. We're nearly finished with it anyway since it only needs to change between frames `120` and `150`.

Watch closely at what happens between those frames, however. There are frames where the unicycle's apparent heading does not quite point in the direction of its actual movement. Its orientation is slightly askew, causing it to appear to slide diagonally. This is easier to see if you view the unicycle from above and scrub between the frames.

> **Tip**
> You have been scrubbing, haven't you? You must scrub! For good, precise animations, it's essential that you review your animation by looking at the action in the 3D Viewport from various angles while scrubbing through frames in your animation editor. Just click and drag along the row of frame numbers at the top of any animation editor. This helps reveal issues in your animation that might be harder to diagnose in realtime.

If you still don't believe me, there's a way to make the error much easier to see and then fix using a **motion path**:

1. With `Seat` selected, go to the **Object Properties** tab in the **Properties** area.
2. Locate and open the **Motion Paths** panel.

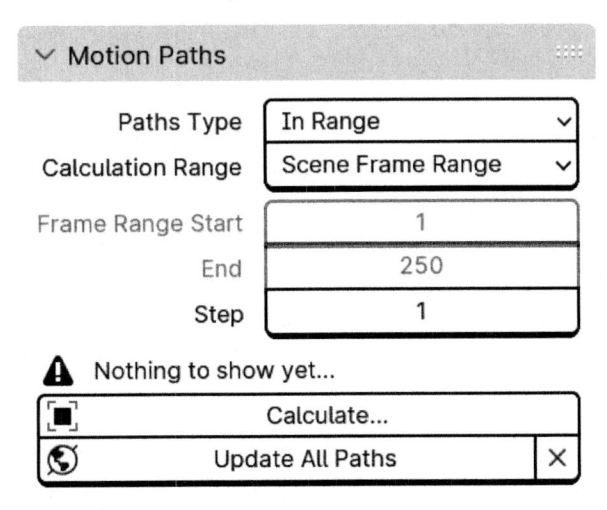

Figure 3.25: The Motion Paths panel

3. Click **Calculate**, followed by **OK** (the default settings here are fine).

Now you can really see the path of the unicycle:

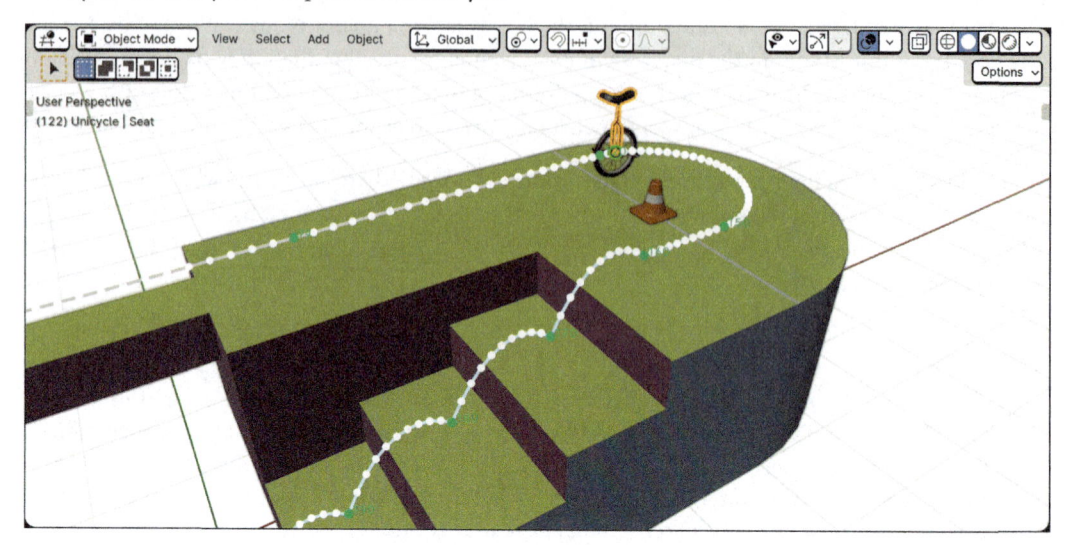

Figure 3.26: Motion path of the unicycle

> **Important note**
>
> This motion path is purely a visual reference and cannot be edited directly. It only shows the location of the object's origin at each frame. If you make changes to your animation that would affect the path, you must click **Update Paths** to see those changes reflected.

The issue is now obvious when viewed from above. Even a still image reveals that the unicycle doesn't quite point where it ought to point:

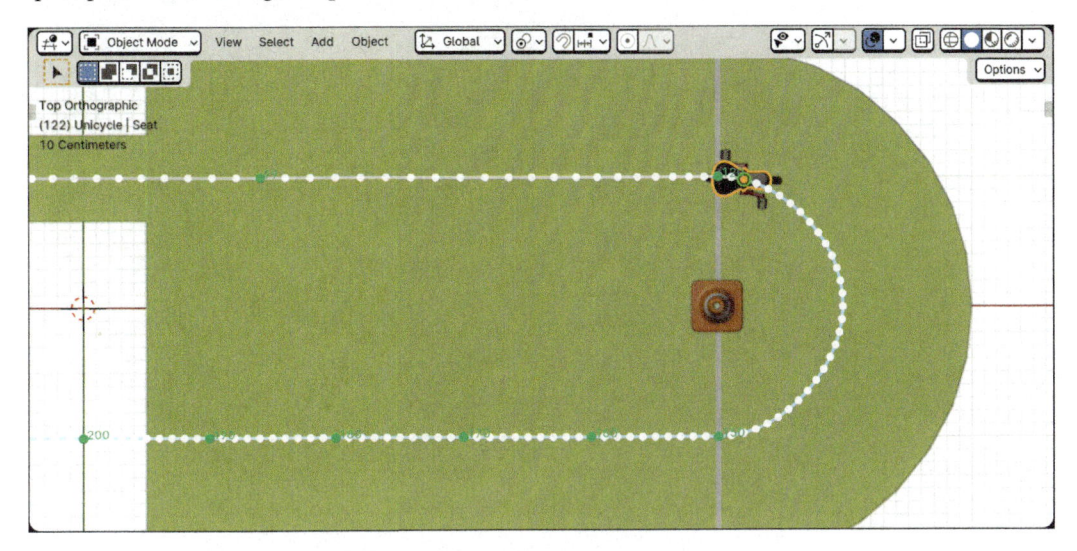

Figure 3.27: The motion path viewed from above

Having this visual aid, we can fix the **Z Euler Rotation** F-curve with greater confidence:

1. Find the **Z Euler Rotation** F-curve for `Seat`.
2. Using as few keyframes as possible, edit the F-curve so that the unicycle points in the direction of its movement on each frame between `120` and `150`.

Your own solution will depend on how you animated the **X Location** and **Y Location** of `Seat` in the previous sections. In my case, I found that I was able to get a decent result simply by scaling down the keyframe handles to get an almost linear shape:

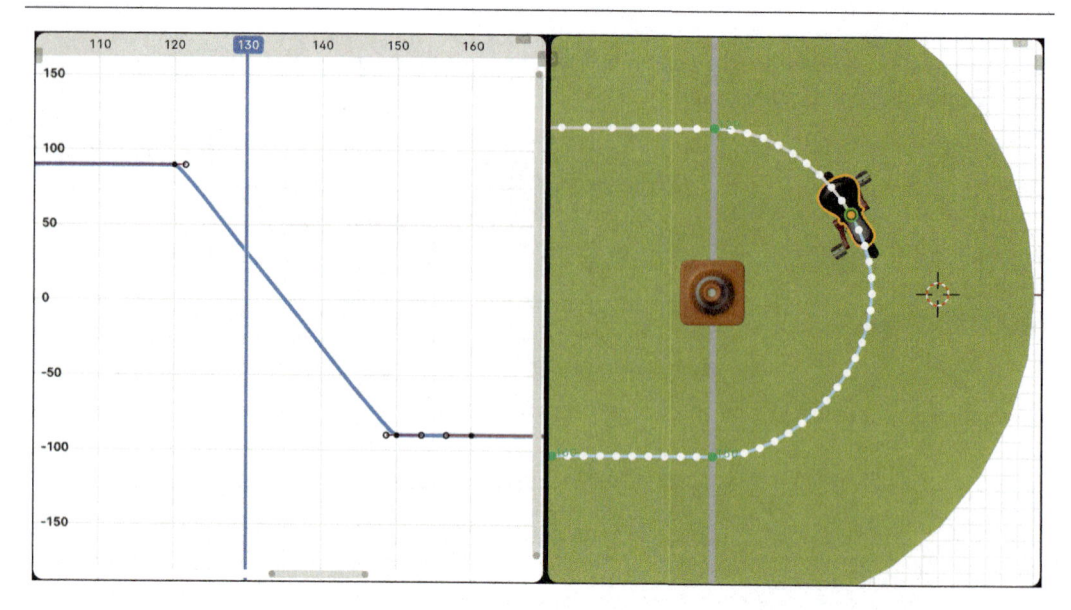

Figure 3.28: Example corrected Z Euler Rotation F-curve and its result

Once you're satisfied with your unicycle's steering, we can move on to the next channel needed to make the turn look complete.

> **Tip**
>
> Motion paths can be a helpful reference at times but can also be distracting at other times, cluttering the 3D Viewport. When you're done with this section, you can hide the motion path you created for `Seat` by disabling **Motion Paths** in your 3D Viewport's **Viewport Overlay** settings, or remove it completely by clicking the **X** button in the **Motion Paths** panel of the object's **Object Properties** tab.

Tilting while turning

If you can ride a bicycle, you'll know you need to lean in the direction of your steering or you'll quickly fall over. A unicycle is no different. In this section, we'll edit the **Y Euler Rotation** F-curve to make the unicycle lean so that it turns more realistically.

How far should the unicycle lean, and how soon before it begins to turn? I'll say 20 degrees and 10 frames, but that's just my opinion. You're the animator – you decide what looks good. On that note, you can also decide what Bezier handle types to use here and how they should be edited.

Let's give it a try:

1. Insert a **Y Euler Rotation** keyframe for `Seat` at frame `110`, or roughly 10 frames before the turn at frame `120`.
2. Edit the value and handles of the existing **Y Euler Rotation** keyframes at frames `120` and `150` to make the unicycle lean in the direction of the turn before going upright again.

My attempt looks like this:

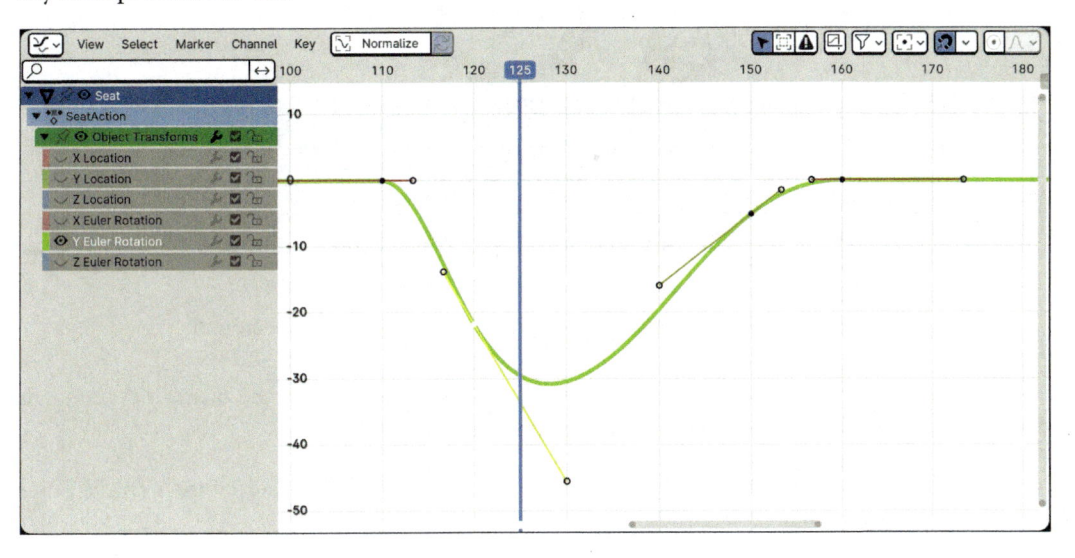

Figure 3.29: An example Y Euler Rotation F-curve

But wait – having leaned the unicycle for the first time, we now see that this causes the wheel to no longer touch the floor:

Figure 3.30: The rotated unicycle, now hovering slightly above ground

As the unicycle leans, we want it to stay on the floor. We'll have to edit the **Z Location** F-curve one more time, moving the whole unicycle down a tiny bit to compensate:

1. Insert a **Z Location** keyframe at frame `110` (or wherever you inserted the extra **Y Euler Rotation** keyframe).
2. Edit the **Z Location** keyframes so as to move the unicycle downward ever-so-slightly as it leans, to keep the wheel touching the surface of the course.

You may have guessed that this part of the **Z Location** F-curve ought to mimic the **Y Euler Rotation** F-curve. When zoomed in on the *Y* axis of the Graph Editor, one should look very much like the other:

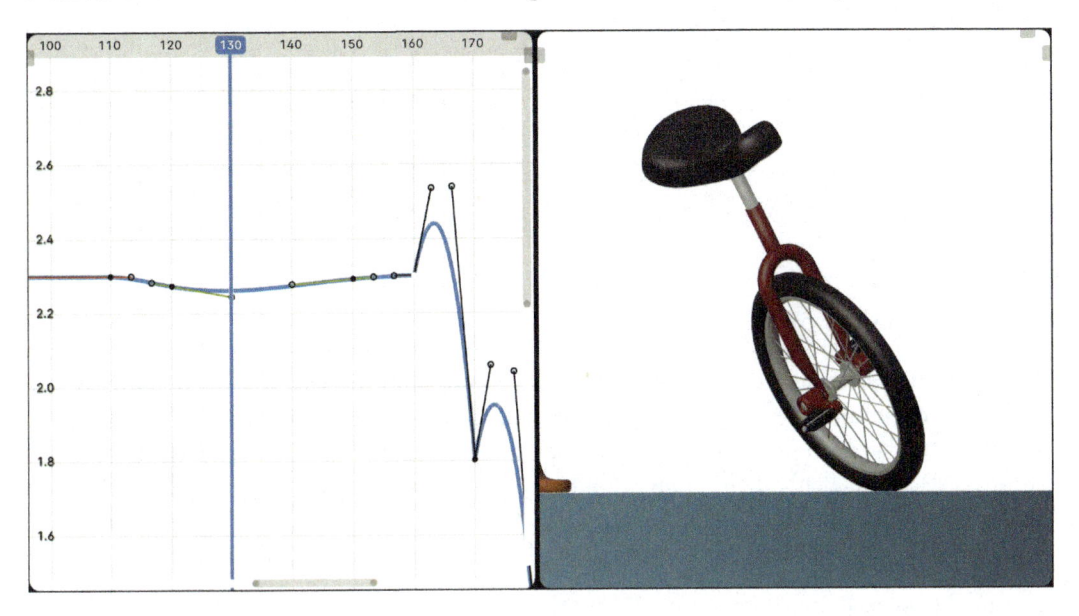

Figure 3.31: Example correction of the Z Location F-curve, with the result

This method is not (nor does it have to be) perfectly accurate, so don't worry about getting it exactly right.

Now that our unicycle tilts as it turns, it's beginning to look more like a real object and less like something held upright by a string from above. In order to complete this illusion of weight and balance, there's just one more channel left to animate.

Leaning into it

We've saved the **X Euler Rotation** channel for last. For the same reason that the unicycle needed to lean on its *Y* axis when turning, the seat will also need to lean on its *X* axis as it moves backward and forward. This is especially clear when you watch the unicycle move from left to right between frames `1` and `120`.

Whenever the **X Euler Rotation** of `Seat` is positive, the unicycle leans forward; whenever it is negative, the unicycle leans backward. When should the unicycle lean forward and when should it lean backward? *"Simple,"* you might think, *"it should lean forward when it moves forward, and lean backward when it moves backward. The faster it moves forward or backward, the more it should lean in that direction."* That's close, but not quite right.

Instead of looking at the direction of the unicycle's movement, we should instead look at the direction of its *acceleration*. As a general rule, the unicycle should lean forward when the unicycle accelerates forward, and backward when it accelerates backward. The harder it accelerates, the more it should lean in the direction of the acceleration so as to appear balanced.

> **Important note**
> Here, "accelerate" means "slow down" just as much as it means "speed up." When in mid-air, for instance, a bouncing ball is always accelerating downward due to gravity, even while it's still moving upward.

Identifying points of inflection

Most of our unicycle's horizontal movement occurs on the global X axis, so we can figure out the acceleration of our unicycle mainly by examining the **X Location** F-curve of `Seat`. Acceleration can be seen in the change in slope, or "bend," of an F-curve. Whenever the **X Location** F-curve shows forward acceleration, that's when **X Euler Rotation** should be positive, and whenever the **X Location** F-curve shows backward acceleration, that's when **X Euler Rotation** should be negative. Frames at which the bend of the **X Location** curve switches direction are called **points of inflection**.

Here are the points of inflection on my **X Location** F-curve. Note that they don't necessarily occur at keyframes:

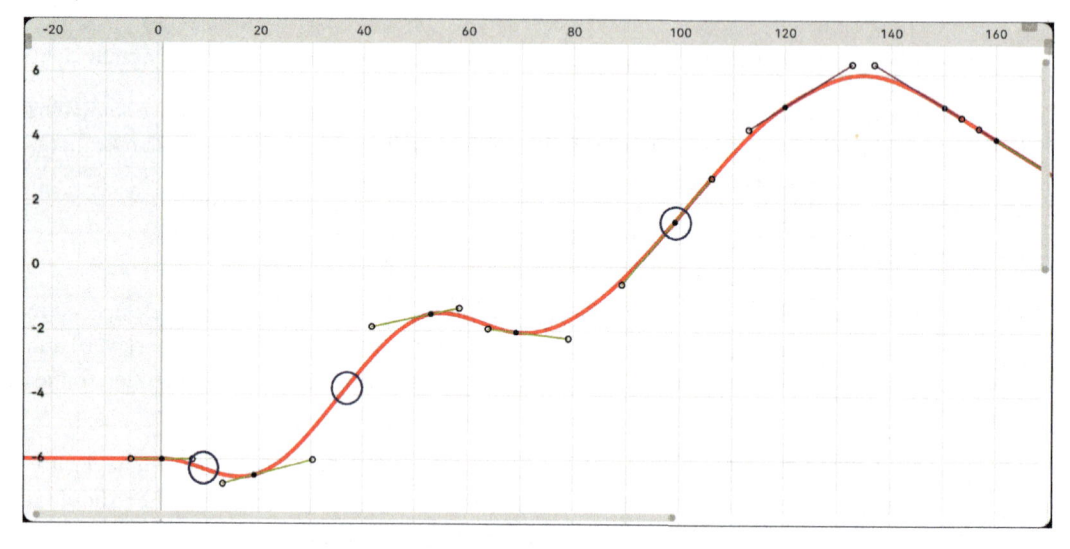

Figure 3.32: Each circle indicates an approximate point of inflection in the X Location F-curve

We're going to mark these points of inflection on one curve with keyframes on the other. At each frame where there is a point of inflection on the **X Location** F-curve, the **X Euler Rotation** should be zero, making `Seat` go upright for a frame as it switches between leaning backward or forward. This means that every point of inflection along the **X Location** F-curve will be accompanied by an **x-intercept** (i.e., a value of 0) along the **X Euler Rotation** F-curve.

Your **X Location** F-curve includes your own personal touch in which you added a few extra keyframes between frames `1` and `120` to vary the motion, so I can't tell you explicitly where to add the next few keyframes. Instead, you'll have to look carefully at your **X Location** F-curve to find the points of inflection yourself:

1. Adjust the channel visibility settings of your Graph Editor so that both the **X Location** and **X Euler Rotation** F-curves are visible.
2. Select the **X Euler Rotation** F-curve.
3. On each frame where there is a point of inflection along the **X Location** F-curve, use **Insert Keyframe** (*I*) | **Only Selected Channels** to insert an **X Euler Rotation** keyframe, leaving the value of **X Euler Rotation** at `0`.

Your **X Euler Rotation** F-curve will still be flat, of course, but now it has keyframes that will ensure that the F-curve has a value of `0` at all the right frames, regardless of what other keyframes we insert next.

Completing the illusion of balance

Having marked all the **X Location** points of inflection with **X Euler Rotation** keyframes, we can now add positive and negative keyframes along the F-curve:

1. From the start of the animation to frame `120`, insert non-zero **X Euler Rotation** keyframes (at least one between each old keyframe from the previous steps) to make `Seat` lean in the direction of its acceleration indicated by the bending of the **X Location** F-curve.
2. In the section between frames `120` and `160`, the unicycle spins on the *Z* axis and has some movement on both the *X* and *Y* axes. Keep this part of the F-curve relatively flat or go with whatever looks good using as few frames as possible.
3. Between frames `160` and `200`, the unicycle's **X Location** has a constant speed with no acceleration. Keep this part of the **X Euler Rotation** F-curve mostly flat.
4. Repeat *step 3* for the **X Euler Rotation** F-curve between frames `200` to the end. Note that the unicycle has turned around, so now downward on the **X Location** F-curve means forward instead of backward.
5. Make any further adjustments as desired to your **X Euler Rotation** F-curve until you're pleased with the result. You might consider using more **Automatic** keyframes, rotating some of the *x-intercept* keyframes, or varying how much the unicycle leans according to the amount of acceleration.

6. Here is my final **X Euler Rotation** F-curve, shown along with the **X Location** F-curve so you can see how the former is affected by the latter:

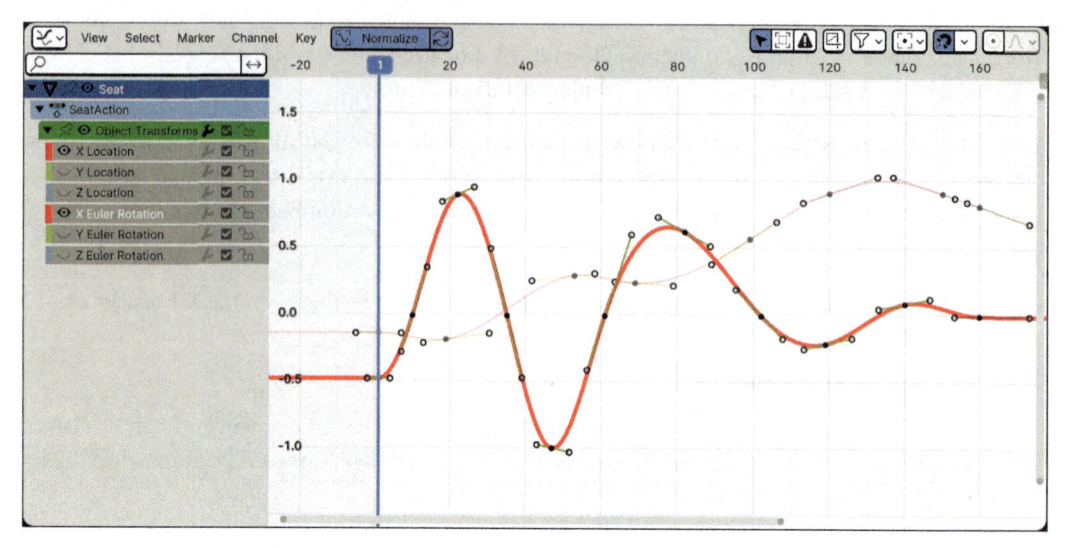

Figure 3.33: Example X Euler Rotation and X Location F-curves

That may have been our most difficult channel to animate so far! This technique, where we examine one F-curve while animating another, has use cases for all sorts of animated objects and characters.

The `Seat` object is now completely animated and the unicycle displays lifelike balance as it tilts, turns, and moves across the course. As for the remaining elements that comprise our unicycle, there's just one obvious object left that we still need to bring to life.

Copying keyframes to another channel

To ride a real unicycle, you have to pedal, rotating the wheel to make the unicycle move forward or backward. Ironically, in this exercise, we animated the rest of the unicycle first before figuring out how the wheel should rotate!

Our final task in this chapter is to animate the rotation of the `Wheel` object. Up to this point, `Wheel` has been dragged along by `Seat`. If we properly animate it rotating, it will appear to have friction with the floor and hopefully even look as though it's the thing that drives the rest of the unicycle. To appear correct, the rotation of `Wheel` must be closely related to the movement of `Seat` – so closely related, in fact, that we can **copy and paste** the keyframes.

Keyframes can be copied and pasted using the conventional and unsurprising **Copy Keyframes** (*Ctrl + C*) and **Paste Keyframes** (*Ctrl + V*) operators. This is a useful alternative to **Duplicate** (*Shift + D*), but with one special advantage: keyframes may be copied from one channel and pasted in another.

The process of copying and pasting keyframes in Blender is by no means exclusive to Bezier keyframes, but it is a useful technique in the Graph Editor and one that will save us a lot of time as we finish the animation for this chapter! I'll also show you a few other animation tricks that we missed earlier.

Copying keyframes

As you may have guessed, we're going to copy keyframes from the **X Location** F-curve of `Seat`, as almost all of our unicycle's horizontal movement occurs on the global *X* axis of our scene:

1. Find the **X Location** F-curve for `Seat` in the Graph Editor.
2. Select all (and only) the **X Location** keyframes.
3. Use **Copy Keyframes** (*Ctrl + C*).

> **Tip**
> You can quickly select all the keyframes in one channel by double-clicking the channel name, or by selecting one keyframe from the F-curve and using **Select Linked** (*L*). Be sure there aren't keyframes from other channels in your copied selection; it may cause issues when you try to paste them.

The selected keyframes have now been copied to the "clipboard," the invisible halfway house where copied data waits to be pasted. Next, we must create the channel that will be their permanent home.

Keying a single property

Only one single property belonging to `Wheel` will need to be animated: **X Euler Rotation**. Copied keyframes cannot be pasted into an F-curve that does not yet exist, so before we paste anything, we must key this property first. This will create an **X Euler Rotation** F-curve in the Graph Editor.

Here's a way to key just one spatial property instead of all three:

1. Select the `Wheel` object.
2. Find the **Rotation** property of `Wheel` in the **Transform** panel. This panel may be found in **Object Properties** in the **Properties** editor, or in the **Item** tab of the sidebar in the 3D Viewport.
3. Right-click on the **X** component of the **Rotation** property, and choose **Insert Single Keyframe** from the context menu.

This keys just one single property instead of all three for each axis:

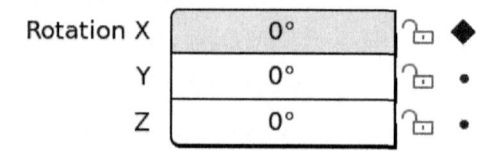

Figure 3.34: Keyed X Euler Rotation property

The **X Euler Rotation** channel for `Wheel` should now be visible in the Graph Editor, and we don't even have to delete any unnecessary channels. This one keyframe will serve as a temporary placeholder of sorts and will be replaced when we paste over it.

Pasting keyframes

We can now paste the copied keyframes to our new channel:

1. Select the **X Euler Rotation** channel of `Wheel`.
2. Use **Paste Keyframes** (*Ctrl + V*).

   Some operators, like the last one, have parameters that can be modified in the **operator** panel, which appears in the corner of the editor after the operator is executed. We need to tweak those parameters now.

3. Open up the **Paste Keyframes** operator panel in the bottom-left corner of the Graph Editor.
4. Change **Offset** to **No Offset** and **Type** to **Overwrite All**.

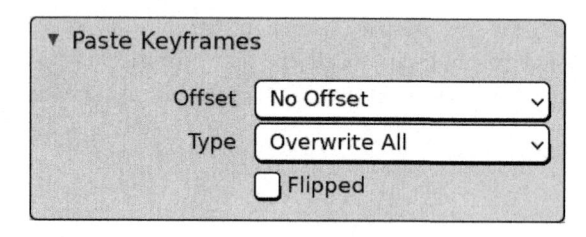

Figure 3.35: The Paste Keyframes operator panel

These new operator settings ensure that the pasted keyframes have the same timing as the original ones and that our one temporary keyframe from earlier is removed.

Notice that your pasted keyframes appear to be *amplified*, having a much greater value range than the original keyframes you copied. This is because rotation values in Blender are stored in radians but expressed as degrees. When location keyframes are copied and pasted to a rotation channel, the nominal values are effectively multiplied by *180/π*. In our case, this automatic *scaling up* of values actually puts them closer to where they need to be. We just need to scale them a bit more...

Scaling keyframe values

Can you see why we copied the keyframes we did? As long as the unicycle moves on just the *X* axis, the **X Euler Rotation** of `Wheel` can be considered a function of the **X Location** of `Seat`. It's not a complex function either, but a linear one; the wheel should roll one way as the unicycle goes forward, and the other way as the unicycle goes backward. That's why our keyframes could simply be copied from one channel to the other!

Inspect the effect of the **X Euler Rotation** F-curve of `Wheel` by viewing the unicycle closely as you scrub along frames `1` through `120`. Does it appear to roll on the floor? Sort of, but not quite. Having copied and pasted the right keyframes, we still have one variable that has not yet been taken into account: the degree (literally, the degrees) to which the wheel must spin with respect to the unicycle's location. This factor (literally, a factor) will depend on the diameter of the wheel. If the wheel were much smaller, it would need to spin more to keep up with the unicycle's movement; if it were many times larger, it might make it across the bridge without even doing a full rotation.

Our next task, then, is to multiply the wheel's **X Euler Rotation** values to account for the wheel's relative size. We can do so by scaling the keyframes on the *Y* axis of the Graph Editor:

1. Select all the **X Euler Rotation** keyframes of `Wheel`.
2. Hit **Scale** (*S*), press *Y*, and enter `3.33` to scale up the F-curve on the Graph Editor's *Y* axis by a factor of 3.33.

The wheel now has correct rotation – for the first 120 frames, at least:

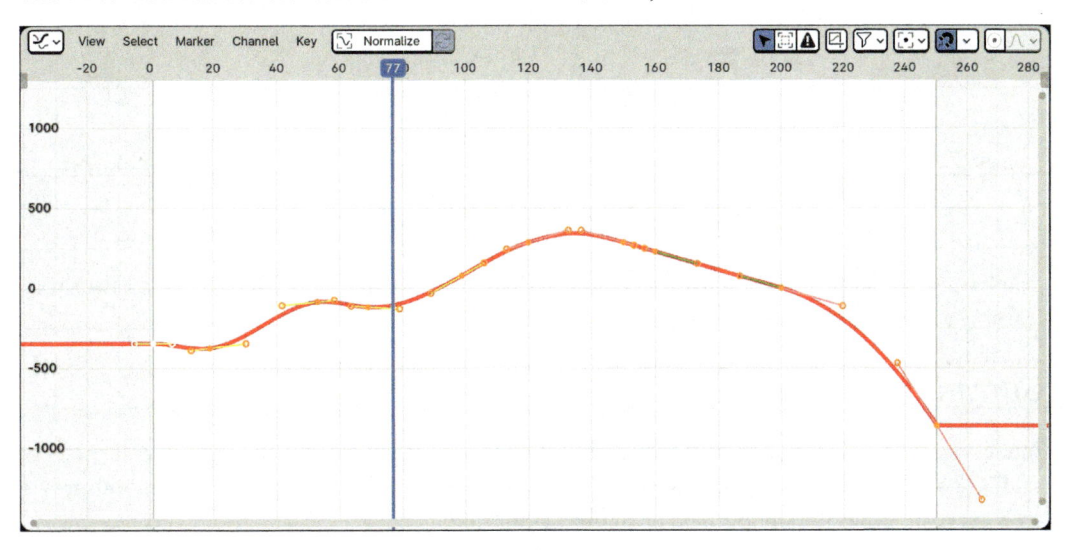

Figure 3.36: The X Euler Rotation F-curve for Wheel

After that, the unicycle turns 180° on the Z axis; backward becomes forward, and forward becomes backward. We'll need to "flip" the rotation keyframes in the second half to reflect this change.

Again, this can be done by scaling the keyframes on the Y axis of the Graph Editor:

1. Select all the **X Euler Rotation** keyframes of `Wheel` from frames `150` to `250`.
2. Hit **Scale** (*S*), press *Y*, and enter `-1` to invert the keyframe values.
3. Move the selection up on the Y axis to correct the F-curve between frames `120` and `150`.

That final step will require some guesswork and old-fashioned eyeballing to keep the rolling motion looking consistent as the unicycle turns and moves on the global Y axis for a brief period.

The final result should look something like this:

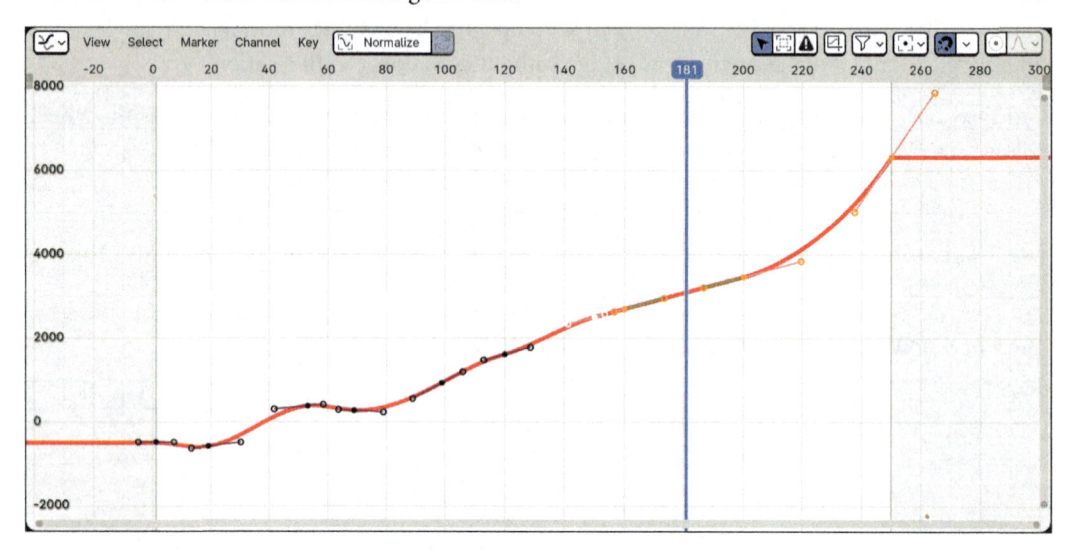

Figure 3.37: The final X Euler Rotation F-curve

You have finished the exercise for this chapter. Hopefully, animating a unicycle was easier than learning to ride one!

Summary

Interesting things happen when we rotate time and make it go left to right on a graph. A line can be said to "go" places, flatness becomes stillness, steepness becomes quickness, and the smoothness of an F-curve becomes the smoothness of an object's motion.

Did it feel odd interpreting animation from a bunch of line graphs? In a way, F-curves are a bit like sheet music; at first, it's difficult to see how the notes on a staff create a melody or how the keyframe handles of an F-curve create the movement of an object in space. Yet the information is there, and with some practice, it becomes easy to "sight-read," hearing music or seeing motion in one's mind just by looking at its image. Having completed two chapters on just the Graph Editor, you know enough to bend these lines to your will and get creative with your own compositions.

While working with Bezier keyframes, we also studied ways in which the location or rotation of one thing might be influenced by something else, such as how the rotation of the seat depended on its horizontal acceleration, or how the rotation of the wheel depended on the seat's horizontal movement. Consider how much harder the wheel would have been to animate if it weren't constrained to the seat, though; we'd have had to copy keyframes to a lot more than just one channel! As we'll see in the next chapter, these relationships between objects can be determined by more than just cleverly-crafted F-curves.

Questions

1. In what sense is Bezier a mode of interpolation?
2. What property do Bezier keyframes have instead of an easing type?
3. What do **Bezier** handles do to the F-curve?
4. When might it be useful to use **Vector** handles?
5. Why can't we make an F-curve go in a loop? What would happen if it did?
6. Are **Free** handles free to move by themselves, or free to be moved by the user? Whose definition of freedom is this? Are you free?
7. Fill in the blank: *slope* is to *velocity* as *bend* is to _____.
8. What is the difference between an x-intercept, a peak, and a point of inflection? How are they similar?
9. In the last section, we scaled up the **X Euler Rotation** F-curve of Wheel by 3.33 on the Graph Editor's *Y* axis. Where did that number come from? Hint: search for its reciprocal.
10. What would happen to the animation if we scaled an F-curve on the Graph Editor's *X* axis?

4
Looking into Object Relationships

It's easy to take for granted how the things in our universe relate to one another. Our Earth relates to the Sun, orbiting it in perpetuity, drawn inward by gravity. The Earth's own gravity pulls you toward its center while the solid ground pushes you, keeping your movements constrained to the planet's surface as it spins through the cosmos. Magnets relate by attracting and repelling each other. Your pants stay on your legs when you walk around.

In the world of 3D animation, we can't take such relationships for granted. If we don't do the work of nature ourselves, bodies in space will not interact, things will fall apart and pass through solid matter, and characters' pants will remain at a fixed point in space after their legs have walked away (this happens way more often than you'd think).

For this chapter, we will set aside most of what we've learned so far about animating objects directly with keyframes. Instead, we'll learn to animate objects indirectly using a variety of object relationships – settings that govern how one object's properties are determined by another. This is less like an animation lesson and more like a lesson in how to construct a scene so the objects in it can be animated effectively.

The following exercise will instruct you on how to animate a toy train with multiple moving parts along a track. After setting up the relationships between objects, you will only need a single F-curve to animate the whole thing!

In this chapter, you'll learn how to do the following:

- Move the origin of objects
- Attach objects to other objects
- Copy the rotation of an object
- Animate objects along a precise path
- Use drivers to control rotation

Technical requirements

The toy train scene for this chapter's exercise can be downloaded here:

https://github.com/PacktPublishing/Realizing-3D-Animation-in-Blender

Open the downloaded .blend file in Blender and get started:

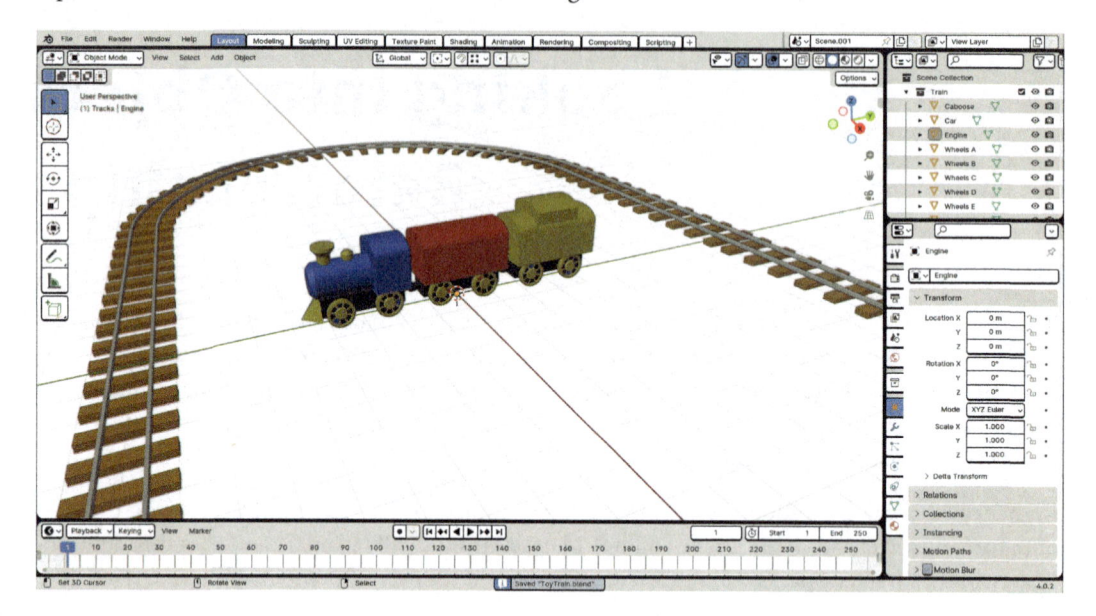

Figure 4.1: The toy train scene

Unlike the unicycle in the previous chapter, which was set up to be animated straight away, the objects that comprise the parts of the toy train have no relationships. No part of the train follows any other object... yet. That's what this exercise is all about!

Understanding object origins

Here's some advice – if you want to be in a healthy relationship, you first have to work on yourself. A relationship is a lot of commitment, so before we assign relationships between our objects, we need to make sure they're ready. If an object has unresolved issues, it's better to fix those issues now, before they become another object's problem.

The parts of our toy train have just one small issue in common. Select any object that is part of the train and see whether you can find its **origin**:

Figure 4.2: The wheel object's origin at the center of the scene

Every object in Blender appears to have an origin, a point in space that looks like a small orange dot in the 3D Viewport when the object is selected. It is often thought of as the object's "center," although it doesn't necessarily have to be at the center of anything.

In our case, it looks like the origin of every train part is at the global center of our scene. Why do object origins matter? Look what happens if we try to rotate any of the wheels:

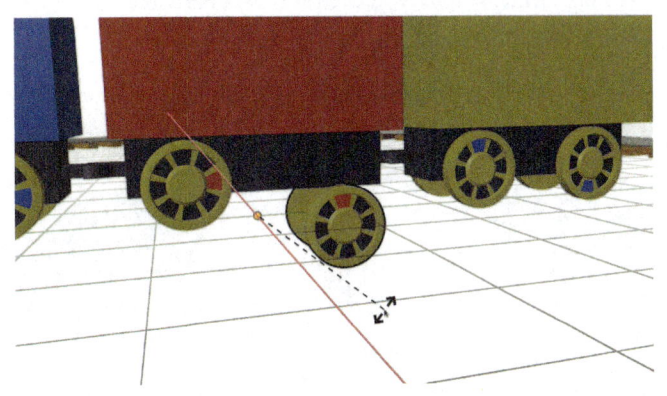

Figure 4.3: Rotating a wheel with an un-centered origin

Talk about out of true! Imagine trying to animate such a thing. The origin determines the point in space about which the mesh geometry rotates and scales. If the origin of any of our wheels is offset from where its center of rotation ought to be, it will not spin properly. In this case, the origin of the wheels is so far off that the wheels don't even rotate – they orbit!

I promise I didn't create this problem out of mischief; it's a common issue you may encounter when importing 3D models into Blender from another format, or when separating the pieces of a single mesh into multiple objects. The geometry appears to be in all the right places, but the origins are all in one location somewhere else.

To solve this issue, we simply need to move the origins, right?

The truth about objects and origins

So you want to "move the origin," do you? But not the object? If the location of the origin can differ from the location of the object, then what is the location of the object, exactly? Let's look at the location of one of the wheels:

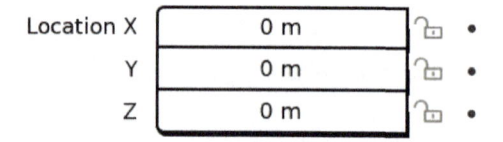

Location X	0 m
Y	0 m
Z	0 m

Figure 4.4: The location of one of the wheel objects

That can't be right, can it? [0.0, 0.0, 0.0] is the global center of the scene, where the origin is. So where's the object? What even is the difference between an object and an origin? We've been animating objects this whole time, but are you even sure what an object is?

Ready for the truth? Look at that orange dot again. *That's the object.*

Figure 4.5: The object

The origin and the object are essentially the same thing. An object in Blender is merely a point in space, with a name and basic properties such as location, rotation, and scale. These points are the only things that get considered in most object relationships. We've been moving origins since *Chapter 1*!

Whenever we refer to something called the origin, we're talking specifically about that point and nothing else. Everything else attached to that point is the object's data. In the case of mesh-type objects like our wheels and train cars, this means the mesh geometry (that is, all the vertices, edges, and faces exposed to you in **Edit Mode**).

> **Tip**
> An **empty** object is a special type of object in Blender that has no data. Like a mesh object with all of its vertices deleted, it is essentially nothing but an origin. "Empties" can be used in relationships just like any other object but are never rendered. You can add one by going to **Add | Empty**.

So, you can't move the origin separately from the object because the terms *object* and *origin* have no meaningful distinction. The task is null. Meaningless. Less than impossible.

Moving the object *inversely to its geometry*, however, is no problem at all.

Centering the origin

Blender offers a couple of operations and settings that refer to the origin as something distinct from the object, which can be moved "by itself." This is convenient for us, but it masks a more complex operation in which two things move simultaneously – the object in one direction and the mesh geometry in the other direction.

Let's get back to those wheels. There are 12 wheels but only 6 wheel objects. Each one is a pair of wheels with left/right symmetry. If each of these six wheel-pairs is to rotate properly about six imaginary axles, we must, in a manner of speaking, "move the origins" to where the centers of rotation ought to be.

This can be accomplished with a single operator:

1. Select all six wheel objects.
2. Click **Object | Set Origin | Origin to Geometry**.

Figure 4.6: Six centered origins for the wheel objects

Now each wheel object is in the right location, perfectly centered with its geometry. All the wheels can now rotate correctly on the *X* axis.

> **Tip**
> When calculating the center of a mesh, the operators **Origin to Center of Mass (Surface)** and **Origin to Center of Mass (Volume)** can sometimes yield more favorable results on complex models. In our case, it makes no difference for the wheels, which have simple geometry.

It looks like we "moved the origins" to the center of each pair of wheels, but we really didn't! Instead, for each pair of wheels, the global center of the mesh geometry was calculated, the object itself was moved to that point, and its mesh geometry was moved in the inverse direction. It's as if we moved the object in **Object Mode** and then went into **Edit Mode**, selected everything, and moved it back.

The effect makes it look as though only the origin has moved. However, we know better!

> **Tip**
> In addition to the technique in the following section, you can also relocate an origin anywhere by moving the 3D cursor to the desired spot and then using **Object | Set Origin | Origin to 3D Cursor**.

Grabbing the origin

The labeling of certain operations and settings in Blender's interface suggests that Blender really wants us to believe that objects possess an origin that can be moved by itself. Although we know better, we'll continue to indulge the developers in their fantasy and let them think they have us fooled. Sure, let's "move" some more "origins."

Let's turn our attention to the three main components of the train, which we will later constrain to the tracks – the `Engine` object at the front, `Car` in the middle, and `Caboose` at the back. Unlike the wheels, their origins do not have to be exactly at the centers of their geometry; in fact, it will make things easier for us if we keep them on the ground and space them exactly 3 meters apart. Using one of the **Set Origin** operators to center the origins would only complicate things, as each train car has different geometry.

The `Car` object is already exactly where it needs to be. We just need to move `Engine` and `Caboose` so that the origins are below the respective meshes in the same way. Doing so requires us to enable just one setting before grabbing the objects as we normally would:

1. In the header of the 3D Viewport, go to **Options | Transform | Affect Only** and enable **Origins**.

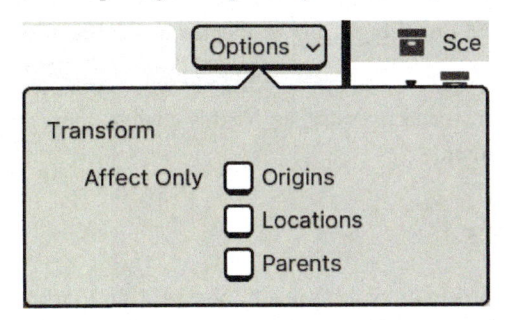

Figure 4.7: Affect Only | Origins enabled in the 3D Viewport

2. Select the object `Engine`.
3. Use **Grab** (*G*), press *Y*, and move the origin -3 units forward on the *Y* axis so that it rests below the train engine mesh.
4. Select the object `Caboose`.
5. Use **Grab** (*G*), press *Y*, and move the origin 3 units back so that it rests below the caboose mesh.
6. Remember to disable **Options |Transform | Affect Only | Origins** when you're finished.

The three objects are now evenly spaced 3 units apart:

Figure 4.8: Three train car origins

Remember, we haven't actually "moved only the origins" in the way that you might be led to believe. What we just did was move objects like we normally do, only this time, as we did so, the meshes of those train cars also got moved in the opposite direction. It's the same as walking on a treadmill – you're moving forward relative to the conveyor belt while remaining in the same location globally. When **Affect Only | Origins** is enabled, our transform operations affect both the object and the mesh data at once. We didn't affect "only" one thing at all; we affected more than what we would have otherwise!

We've corrected all the object origins – or, more accurately, we've corrected the locations of our objects and the relative offset of their respective meshes. Next, we will explore a way to – in a sense – make one object the origin of another.

Parenting objects

Whereas the term *origin* refers to an object's position in relation to its own data, in this section, we will learn the most basic relationship between two different objects – that of **parent** and **child**.

In Blender, parenting is when you "attach" one or more objects to another object, allowing the parent object and all its children to be moved and animated as one.

Objects can be parented to other objects using the **Set Parent To** menu (*Ctrl + P*):

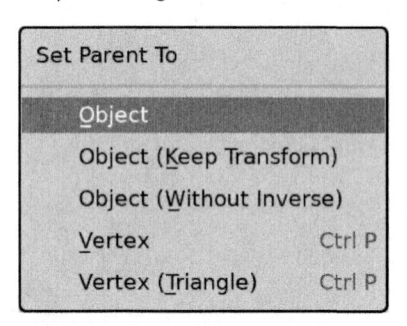

Figure 4.9: The Set Parent To menu

> **Important note**
> Before executing **Set Parent To** (*Ctrl + P*), you'll need to have multiple objects selected – at least one object to be the child and one object to be the parent. The active object (that is, the last object you selected) will become the parent. To avoid getting parent and child mixed up, remember that the object you want to be the parent must be selected last.

This will be perfect for attaching the wheels to the train cars:

1. Select both `Wheels A` and `Wheels B`.
2. Hold *Shift* and select `Engine` (selecting `Engine` last ensures it is the active object).
3. Use **Set Parent To** (*Ctrl + P*) | **Object**.

We've parented wheels to the train engine! Let's repeat this method for the wheels of the other two cars:

1. Parent `Wheels C` and `Wheels D` to `Car`.
2. Parent `Wheels E` and `Wheels F` to `Caboose`.

If you grab (*G*) any one of the train cars, you'll see that its wheels are now attached. You'll also see some thin dotted lines in the 3D Viewport connecting the origins of the children to the origin of the parent:

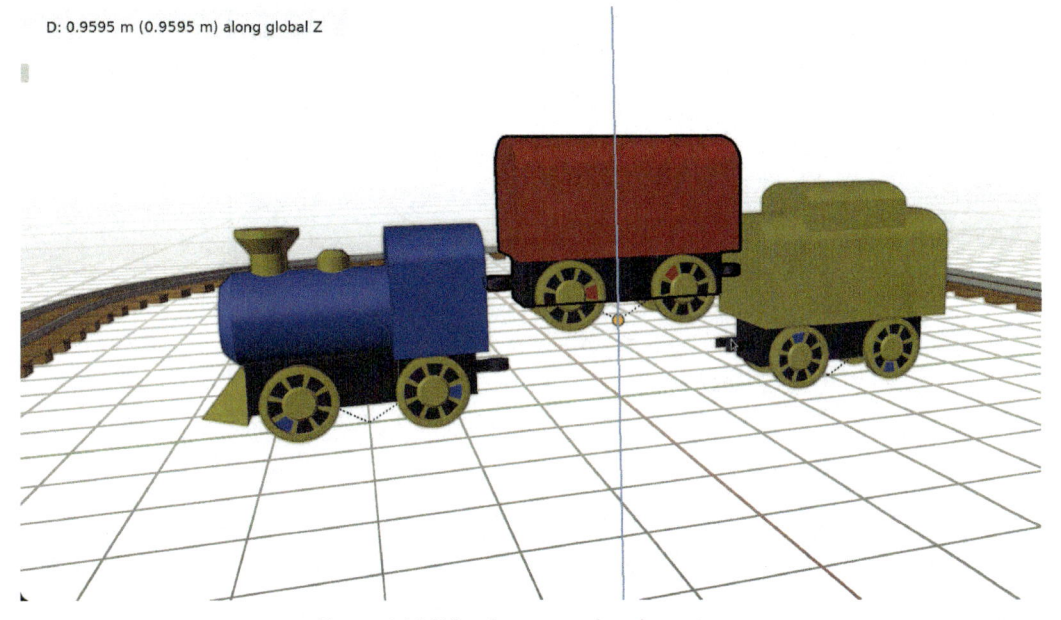

Figure 4.10: Wheels parented to the train car

> **Tip**
> You can grab (*G*), rotate (*R*), or scale (*S*) an object just to test its relationships. Don't be shy – pick things up and shake them around to see what's attached! You can always right-click to cancel the operation.

Each train car object is now the proud parent of two wheel objects. Imagine how much time this will save us, now that we can move the cars around without needing to worry about the location of the wheels!

The parent/child relationship

Any object in Blender can be a parent or child. An object can have an unlimited number of children, but it cannot have more than one parent.

You can see all the children of an object by inspecting it in the Outliner. The children appear as "files" in the "folder" of the parent:

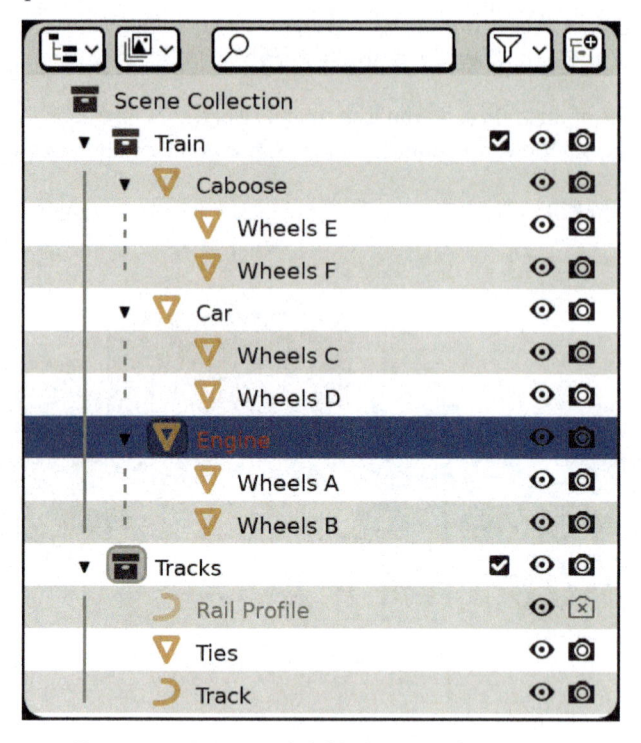

Figure 4.11: Parent and child objects in the Outliner

Likewise, you can also see what an object's parent is in the **Relations** panel, within **Object Properties**:

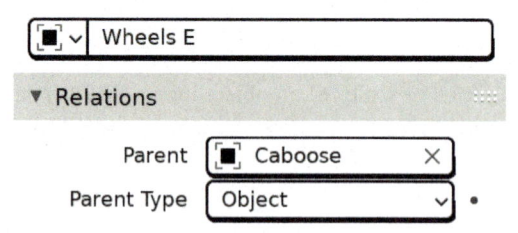

Figure 4.12: The Relations panel of one of the wheel objects

> **Important note**
>
> You can select a different parent for an object by editing its **Parent** field in the **Relations** panel, but this will not necessarily yield the same result as using the **Set Parent To** (*Ctrl + P*) | **Object** operator, which automatically performs additional transform offsets to maintain the global position of the child object.

Parenting is a feature with a wide number of applications, such as whenever you need to stick a thing onto another thing (it's really that useful). The practical result, in many cases, is the same as selecting multiple mesh objects and using **Join** (*Ctrl + J*), fusing everything into one single mesh.

Consider why we didn't do that for the wheel objects, though. Each one of them is still a discrete object that, even when parented, can still be animated. Preparing these wheel objects for animation will be the task of our next main section on constraints.

Dependencies

A parent/child relationship in Blender is a **dependency**; the global position of the child object depends on the position of its parent. These relationships may be *nested* so that a child of one object may itself be a parent of some other object. This is a strictly one-way relationship, however. The parent affects the child, but nothing the child does can ever affect the parent. In a sense, the parent doesn't even "know" that it has any children.

Here's a simple visualization of the relationships we've created so far, with gray arrows pointing from each child object to the parent it depends on:

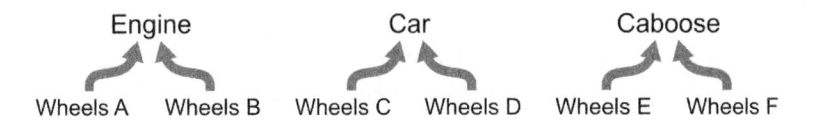

```
     Engine              Car              Caboose
     ↗   ↖              ↗   ↖              ↗   ↖
Wheels A  Wheels B  Wheels C  Wheels D  Wheels E  Wheels F
```

Figure 4.13: A visualization of the current parent/child dependencies

As we continue creating dependencies, this diagram will get increasingly complex...

Now, let's move on to the constraints.

Understanding constraints

Our toy train has 12 wheels that we want to spin as the train moves along the tracks. Because they're all part of one train on one set of tracks, these wheels may all rotate in sync. Each wheel on one side of the train is joined with the wheel on the opposite side for a total of six wheel objects. That's better than 12, but it's still a lot for us to animate. Using **constraints** will make our task much easier.

Constraints are a kind of object relationship, like parenting, but more advanced. An object can have multiple constraints, even if it already has a parent. There's a variety of constraint types to choose from:

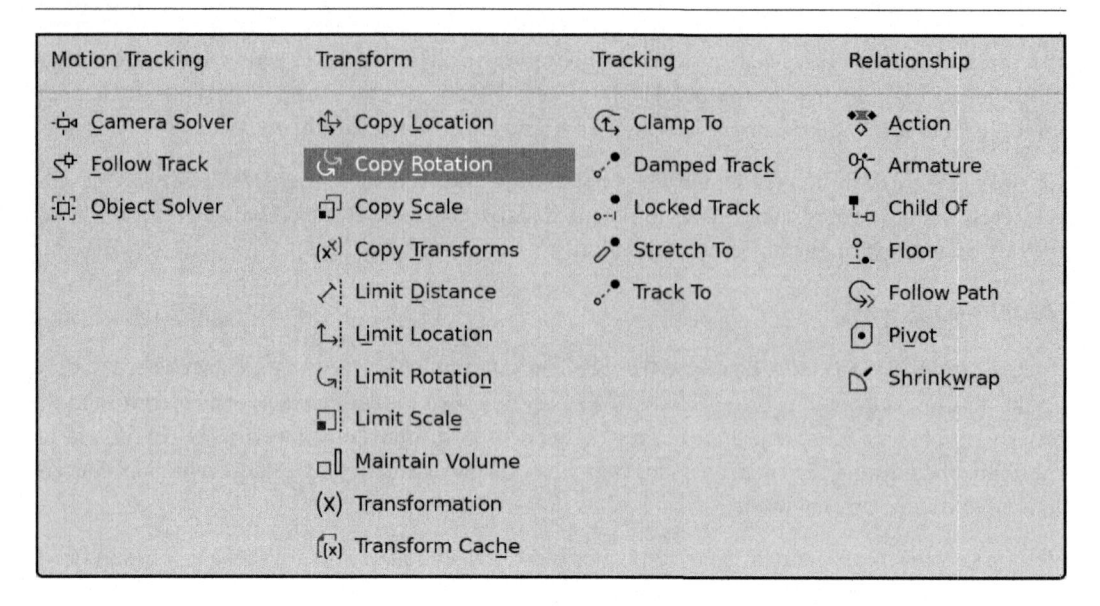

Motion Tracking	Transform	Tracking	Relationship
Camera Solver	Copy Location	Clamp To	Action
Follow Track	Copy Rotation	Damped Track	Armature
Object Solver	Copy Scale	Locked Track	Child Of
	Copy Transforms	Stretch To	Floor
	Limit Distance	Track To	Follow Path
	Limit Location		Pivot
	Limit Rotation		Shrinkwrap
	Limit Scale		
	Maintain Volume		
	Transformation		
	Transform Cache		

Figure 4.14: The Add Object Constraint menu

By using **Copy Rotation** constraints in this section, we can make five wheel objects copy the rotation of one – much easier than keying (or driving) the rotation of all six.

Adding a constraint

We'll start by adding a **Copy Rotation** constraint to the wheels at the back, using the front set of wheels as the **Target**:

1. Select `Wheels F`.
2. In the Properties Editor, go to the **Object Constraint Properties** tab.
3. Click **Add Object Constraint** and choose **Copy Rotation**.
4. In the settings of the new **Copy Rotation** constraint, choose the object `Wheels A` to be the **Target**.

`Wheels F` will now copy the rotation of the **Target** `Wheels A`. As `Wheels A` rotates, `Wheels F` will do the same.

> **Important note**
> Each constraint is "owned" by the object it directly affects. Most constraints require a second object to be the **Target**. This is another type of dependency, like a parent/child relationship. The constraint affects the owner and not the target.

Before we copy this constraint to every other wheel besides the target, we need to make sure that all of its settings are correct.

World space versus local space

The current constraint settings would seem to give us the result we want, if all we wanted to do was spin the wheels on the *X* axis. However, our system of interrelated objects will also follow some tracks, so our needs are more complex.

If we rotate the engine on the *Z* axis, for instance, we can preview what will happen when the train makes a turn:

Figure 4.15: Wheels F "breaking" when Engine is rotated

The **Copy Rotation** constraint seems to make `Wheels F` copy the rotation of `Wheels A` a little too faithfully, causing `Wheels F` to break free from its imaginary axle. This happens because the constraint is evaluating the rotation of both the target and owner in **World Space**, the absolute global coordinate space of your 3D scene. The constraint, in a sense, does not "care" whether either object has parents; it reads the global rotation of the target and uses it to override the global rotation of the owner.

A more sensible approach is to evaluate both objects in **Local Space**:

1. In the properties panel of the **Copy Rotation** constraint of `Wheels F`, find the **Target** and **Owner** evaluation space properties.
2. Change both **Target** and **Owner** from **World Space** to **Local Space**.

The final settings of the constraint should look like this:

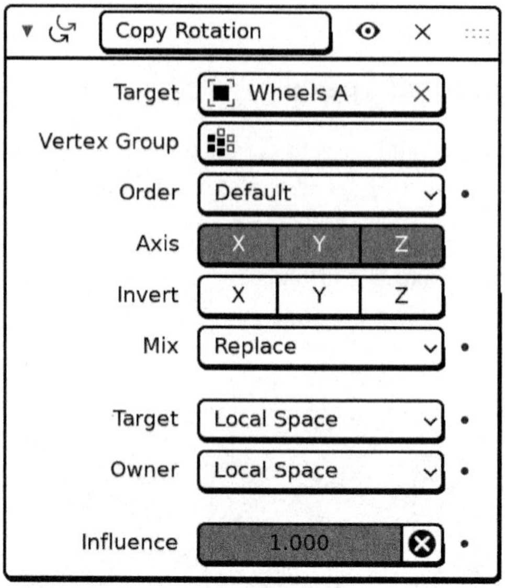

Figure 4.16: The correct settings for the Copy Rotation constraint

Now the wheels work as they should. One wheel still copies the rotation of the other but will not "break." What's going on here?

Imagine you are seated aboard a moving train. You are, in a sense, parented to the train car. In **World Space**, you're moving just as fast as the train car, turning as it turns, moving from station to station. In **Local Space**, however, you're sitting perfectly still, facing forward, not going anywhere. If you stand up and move about the train car, you'll be moving at a walking speed in **Local Space** while still moving at roughly the train's speed in **World Space**.

The wheels of our toy train are passengers in the same way; their rotations may be evaluated in the absolute domain of **World Space**, or the relative domain of their **Local Space**. By evaluating the rotation of the `Wheels A` **Target** object in **Local Space**, the constraint will only read its relative rotation with respect to its parent object, `Engine`. The rotation is then applied to the local space of the owner `Wheels F` with respect to its own parent, `Caboose`.

> **Important note**
>
> An object will always possess its own transform properties, but if it has a parent or a constraint, these properties may no longer directly relate to the object's position in **World Space**. They might only contribute to the final result, or may even cease to have any effect at all. For this reason, the values of these properties are often referred to as *nominal* transform values ("in name only").

This constraint now has all the correct settings and may be copied to the remaining four wheel objects.

Copying constraints

Having perfected the settings of the **Copy Rotation** constraint for `Wheels F`, we want `Wheels E`, `Wheels D`, `Wheels C`, and `Wheels B` to each have their own **Copy Rotation** constraint just like it.

Rather than adding and adjusting the same constraint four more times, Blender has an operator to quickly copy a constraint from one object to another:

1. Select `Wheels B`, `Wheels C`, `Wheels D`, and `Wheels E`.
2. Hold *Shift* and select `Wheels F`.
3. Use **Object | Constraints | Copy Constraints to Selected Objects**.

This copies the constraint owned by the active object to all of the other selected objects. Now all five wheel objects have identical constraints and can be rotated simply by rotating the remaining front pair, `Wheels A`.

> **Tip**
> Those dotted lines connecting all the objects to their parents and constraint targets can be distracting and sometimes even misleading. Consider hiding them by disabling **Relationship Lines** in the **Viewport Overlays** menu.

Here's an updated visualization of the relationships we've made so far. The thin gray lines represent constraints, which have the same one-way dependency that parent/child relationships do:

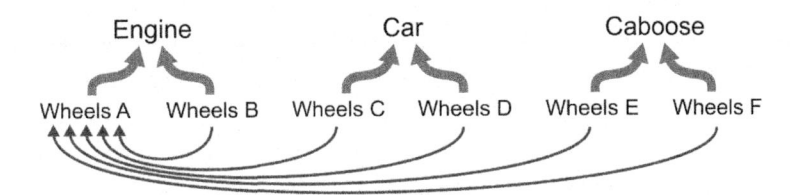

Figure 4.17: The dependency chart with lines for constraints

We've finished parenting the wheels to the train cars and giving them the appropriate constraints. This train is ready to hit the tracks!

Following a path

Our animation will look sloppy if any one of the train cars strays even slightly from the tracks as it moves. To animate the train using the methods we learned in previous chapters, we'll have to tweak all six location and rotation F-curves simultaneously for each train car to keep its wheels directly on the rails as the track bends.

Let's prepare ourselves for what will assuredly be the most tedious and frustrating task we've done yet and add those first **Location & Rotation** keyframes:

1. Actually, let's not.
2. Do not insert location or rotation keyframes.
3. That would be ridiculous.

Can you imagine how difficult that would have been? It was already enough trouble animating the unicycle in the last chapter, and that thing only had to turn once. The **Follow Path** constraint is a much better way of precisely animating objects along a path, especially when that path bends and twists along multiple axes in space.

The path we'll use in this section is nothing at all like the **Motion Path** feature we used in the previous chapter, which was merely a visual guide. Not only can this type of path be edited directly, it also already exists in your scene.

Editing the animation path

Inspect the object `Track` and you'll see that it is not a mesh object. It's a **curve** object, a versatile type of object useful in both modeling and animation. This one particular curve has been set to extrude the shape of `Rail Profile` along its length, creating two parallel rails. It is also the target of modifiers that duplicate and bend the object `Ties`, creating those wooden railroad ties that cross the rails. Elegantly, this same curve object that determines the path of the train tracks can just as well determine the path of objects constrained to it.

It gets even better – the specific type of curve is a Bezier spline, and you already know how to edit Bezier splines. The control points of this curve object are the same as the Bezier keyframes in an F-curve. It's like editing a three-dimensional F-curve!

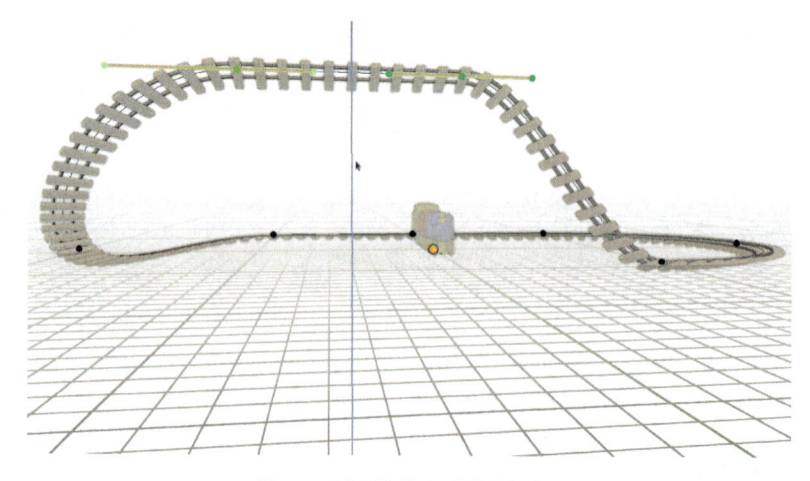

Figure 4.18: Rails in Edit Mode

It's more difficult to edit animation paths after objects have been constrained to them, so we'll take this opportunity to personalize the railroad and make the path of our train more interesting than the simple oval that it is now.

In addition to the standard controls and operators for selection and transform, there are a few others you ought to know about to edit 3D Bezier curves:

- **Segments | Subdivide** inserts control points between two or more selected adjacent control points.
- **Tilt** (*Ctrl + T*) twists the curve at selected control points, allowing you to put banking turns and corkscrews in the path.
- **Toggle Cyclic** (*Alt + C*) removes the segment joining the first and last control points, if you'd like to have a path that does not loop.
- **Set Handle Type** (*V*) sets the handle type, same as with Bezier keyframes!

Let's give these controls a try:

1. Select the object `Track` and go into **Edit Mode**.
2. Edit the path to your liking along any axis.
3. Use only **Automatic** and **Aligned** Bezier handle types, and ensure that there are no turns too sharp for the train cars. The train will follow the path no matter what, but we want it to look believable!

> **Important note**
> You can bend the curve object Rails to just about any shape you like in **Edit Mode**, but avoid transforming the object itself in **Object Mode**. This could make it more difficult to add constraints to the train cars.

I've decided to go wild with my own tracks and create a roller coaster of sorts:

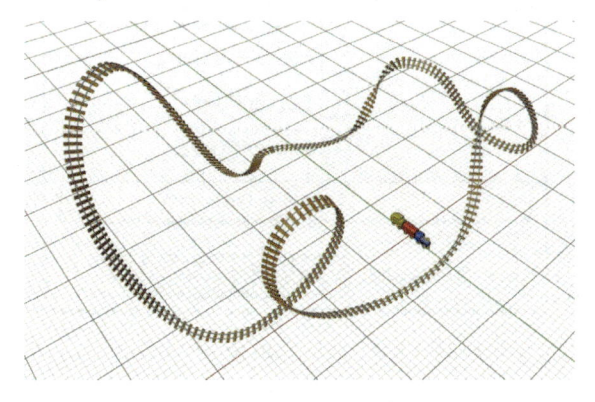

Figure 4.19: An example of an edited Rails object

Once you're satisfied with your railroad, you can leave **Edit Mode**. It's time to put the train on the tracks!

Adding a Follow Path constraint

The **Follow Path** constraint is one of a handful of constraints that evaluates more than just the transforms of the target object. The target has to be a curve-type object, and its data (i.e., the spline we just edited) will be evaluated so that the constraint owner is effectively parented to a point along the spline.

Interestingly, we don't need to manually move any of the train cars to the tracks. The **Follow Path** constraint will do most of the work for us when we add it:

1. Select any one of the train car objects `Engine`, `Car`, or `Caboose`.
2. Go to **Object Constraint Properties** and add a **Follow Path** constraint.
3. In the new constraint's properties, change **Target** to `Track`, change **Forward Axis** to **-Y**, and enable **Follow Curve**.
4. Copy the constraint to the remaining train car objects.

> **Important note**
> The **Animate Path** button is not as helpful as it sounds. Don't press it.

All three train cars should have a constraint that looks like this:

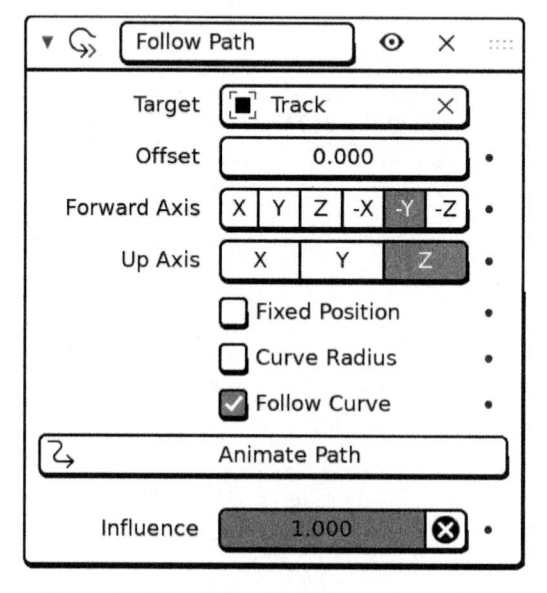

Figure 4.20: The Follow Path constraint settings

The cars themselves, meanwhile, are *almost* all on the rails.

Correcting path offsets

If your train cars happened to be placed onto a curved portion of the tracks after you added their constraints, only one of them, `Car`, will actually be on the tracks. The other two cars just seem to stick out from the middle one, as if the whole thing is one straight train car:

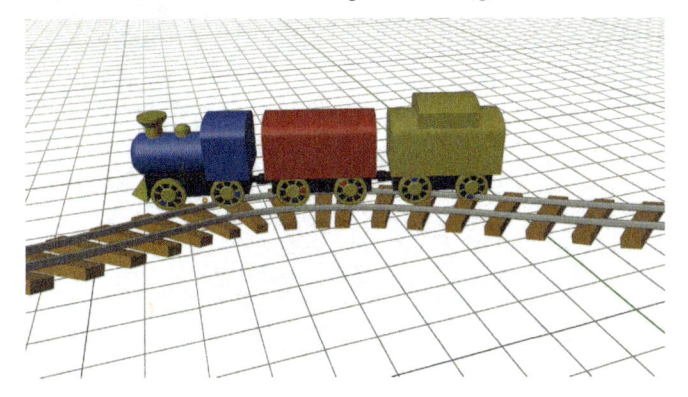

Figure 4.21: Train cars displaced from rails

In its current predicament, this train will not bend properly around the track. Why is this happening, and how can we fix it?

Consider what happened when you added the first **Follow Path** constraint. The train car seemed to automatically snap to a point somewhere along the spline of `Track`. Presently, this invisible point is at the starting position of the path (somewhat arbitrary if the curve is cyclic). This point's position along the curve can be animated (and will be, later), and the **Follow Path** constraint owner will effectively be parented to it. The offset of the constrained object from this point along the curve is equal to the transform difference between the constraint owner and the target curve object, evaluated before the effect of the constraint.

Now consider where the train cars were before you constrained them. `Engine`, `Car`, and `Caboose` have the nominal locations `[0, -3, 0]`, `[0, 0, 0]`, and `[0, 3, 0]`, respectively. The origin of the curve object Track is located at `[0, 0, 0]`. Therefore, only the origin of `Car` will be constrained correctly along the curve, whereas the other two train cars "stick out" on the local *Y* axis by 3 units, one forward and one backward.

Our solution is to "reset" the location values of those other two train cars and instead adjust their relative positions along the curve, using the offset value of their **Follow Path** constraints:

1. Select the object `Engine`.
2. Use **Object | Clear | Location** (*Alt* + *G*) to reset the object's nominal location to `[0, 0, 0]`.
3. Adjust the **Offset** value of the **Follow Path** constraint so that `Engine` is again coupled with `Car` at the appropriate distance. The exact value will vary depending on the total length of the path that you edited.

4. Repeat *steps 2* and *3* for `Caboose`. The correct **Offset** value will most likely be the exact inverse of the one for `Engine`.

Now every train car's origin lies precisely along the curve:

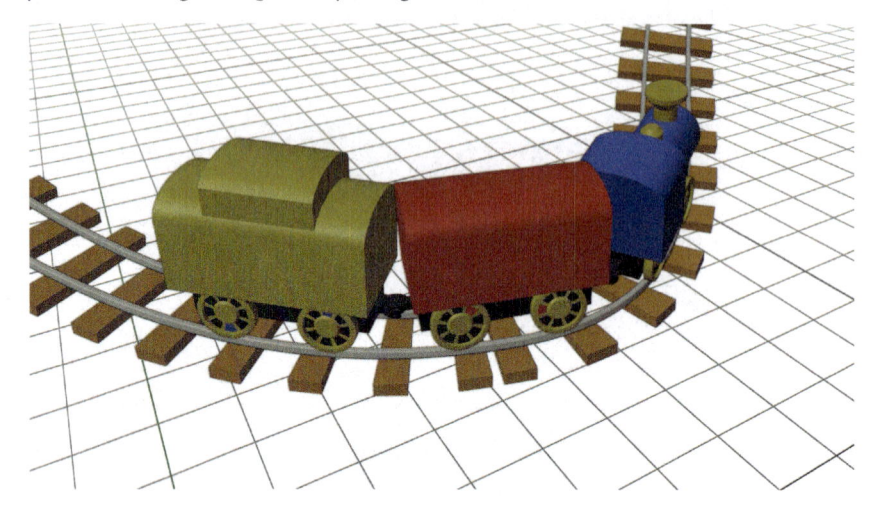

Figure 4.22: Correctly offset train cars

The train cars' position along the track can now be animated with a single property. That property, however, might not be where you expect...

Animating the path

You might have guessed that we would animate the object `Engine` and constrain the other two train cars behind it, similar to how a train works in real life. Nothing of the kind. Instead, the three train cars now each share a single constraint target, `Track`. We will animate the whole train by animating a single property of the target's data.

> **Important note**
> The term *data* in that last sentence is vital. An object and its data are two distinct datablocks with their own properties, which are found in separate tabs of the Properties Editor. The object `Track` is a user of curve data that is also named `Track`. These names are arbitrary and do not have to match.

After selecting the curve object `Track`, the property we're looking for can be found in the **Path Animation** panel of the **Object Data Properties** tab of the Properties Editor:

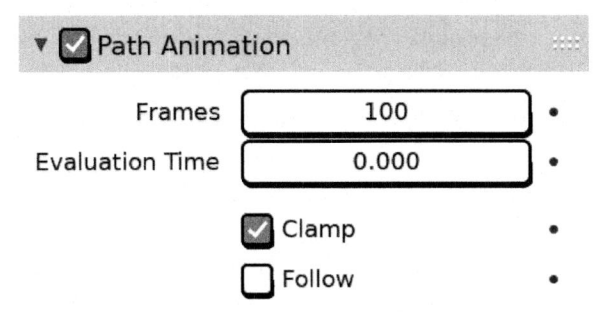

Figure 4.23: The Path Animation panel

These properties work in conjunction with any **Follow Path** constraints that use the curve as a target. The **Frames** property defines how many "frames" should pass for constrained objects to traverse the total length of the curve. "Frames" is in quotes here because, "frames" in this context refers to arbitrary units of the **Evaluation Time** property, which can be animated at any rate we like.

In truth, these properties have nothing necessarily to do with frames or time. **Evaluation Time** is a numerator, **Frames** is a denominator, and the divided result equals the relative position of constrained objects along the total length of the path. If we leave the value of **Frames** at `100`, we can think of **Evaluation Time** as a percentage!

Keying Evaluation Time

The functionality of these **Path Animation** properties is contrived and they're badly labeled. Even the tooltip text appears to be lying. Such is the delightful quirkiness of open-source projects.

Let's have ourselves a hearty chuckle and insert our two initial keyframes:

1. Select the object `Track` and find the **Path Animation** panel in the **Object Data Properties** tab of the Properties Editor.
2. Go to frame 0 (yes, frame 0) and insert a keyframe for **Evaluation Time**.
3. Go to frame `250` (the end frame), change **Evaluation Time** to `100`, and insert another keyframe.

You can now watch the train move along the total length of the track!

Refining the speed of the train

Depending on the length of your track, you may find that the default animation duration of 250 frames is not enough time for the train to cover the length of your track without moving too fast, or perhaps 250 frames is too long and the train moves too slowly.

If you're happy with the speed of your train and the duration of your animation, you can skip this step. Otherwise, let's adjust some things so that we get the general speed that we want:

1. Using either **Linear** interpolation or **Vector** Bezier handles, make the **Evaluation Time** F-curve linear. This lets us watch the train go by at its average speed.
2. Grab (*G*) the second **Evaluation Time** keyframe and move it to a new frame, giving the train a different speed.
3. Adjust the value of **End Frame** so that the animation ends on the same frame as the second keyframe you just moved.
4. Repeat *steps* 2 and 3 until you are happy with the average speed of the train.

Once we've determined the optimal duration of our animation and the train is moving at a decent average speed, it will be easier to insert more keyframes to vary its speed based on the shape of the path that it follows.

Points of inflection along peaks

If your track goes up and down at all, you may wish to vary the **Evaluation Time** F-curve to accordingly vary the speed of the train. We want the train to speed up as it goes downhill and slow down as it goes uphill. This means that each change in direction between uphill and downhill (i.e., a peak or trough) should be accompanied by a point of inflection in the F-curve.

Using keyframes with **Aligned** Bezier handles, we can create our own points of inflection, making the F-curve flatter at the peaks of the path:

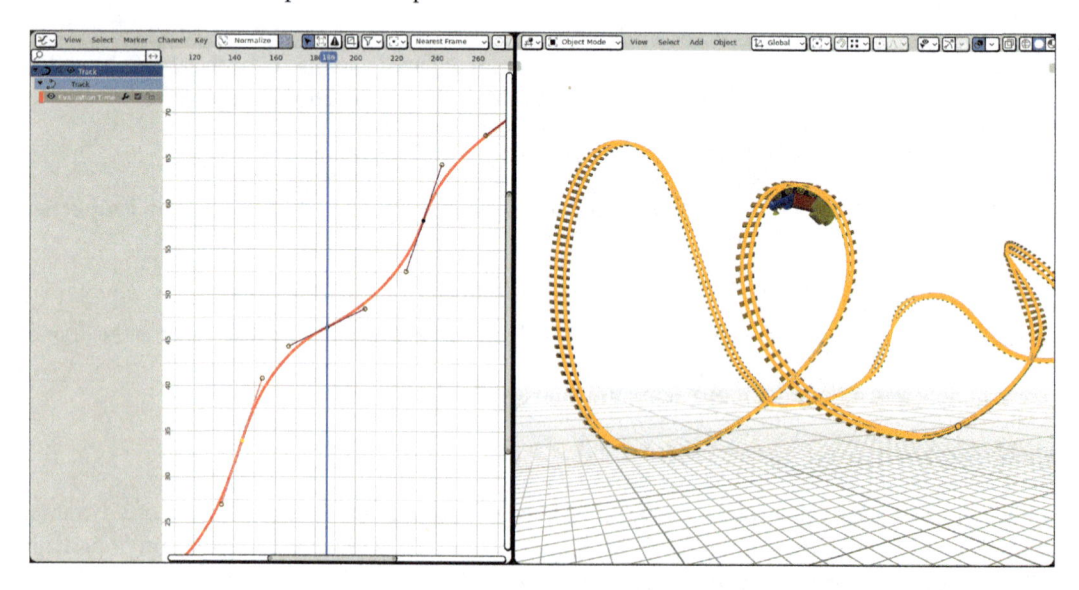

Figure 4.24: A keyframe at a high point in the example path

And we can make it faster at the troughs:

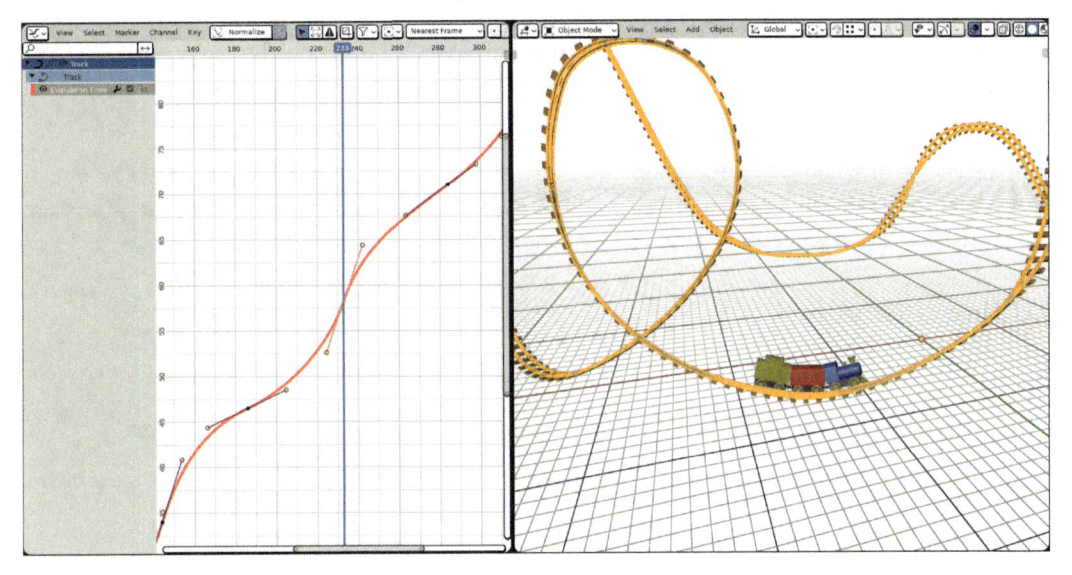

Figure 4.25: A keyframe at a low point in the example path

Now it's your turn:

1. Scrub through your animation in the Graph Editor.
2. Find each frame at which the train is at a peak or trough in the tracks, and mark it by inserting a keyframe on the **Evaluation Time** F-curve.
3. Convert all keyframes to **Aligned** Bezier keyframes.
4. Rotate (R) the keyframes according to the shape of the path, making them flatter at peaks and more vertical at troughs.
5. Continue adjusting the rotation and timing of keyframes until you are happy with the result. Try to have at least one small part of the animation where the train moves very slowly.

Look at all the motion we've created with just one F-curve! We're nearly finished with this animation. All that remains is to make the wheels spin!

Drivers

Because of the constraints we added to five of the six wheel objects, we need only concern ourselves with the remaining pair of wheels at the front of the train, `Wheels A`. However this wheel spins, the other wheels behind it will do so as well.

So how are we to make it spin? The **X Euler Rotation** value of `Wheels A` should be a simple multiplicative function of the **Evaluation Time** property of `Track`. This should remind you of our unicycle wheel in the previous chapter. This time, however, we don't need to copy and paste any keyframes. Doing so only suggests a relation between two properties. By using a **driver**, we can encode this relation so that it works automatically.

A driver is less of an object relationship and more of relationship between a property and one or more other properties. We'll use a driver on the **X Euler Rotation** property of `Wheels A` and use the **Evaluation Time** property of `Track` as the input variable that will drive it.

Adding a driver

Any property that can be keyed can be driven, and adding a driver to a property is easy:

1. Select the object `Wheels A` and find its **Transform** properties.
2. Right-click on the **X Rotation** property and select **Add Driver** (*Ctrl + D*) from the context menu.

The driven property will be highlighted in purple:

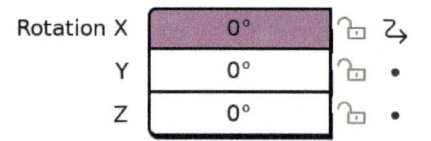

Figure 4.26: The driven X Euler Rotation property

As with keyed properties, the driver has "taken over" the **X Euler Rotation** property of `Wheels A`. The value of the property can no longer be directly edited, not even temporarily!

> **Important note**
> Keyed properties cannot be driven, and driven properties cannot be keyed.

The property is now driven. Great. Driven by what, though? Answering that means answering the riddle of that puzzle box that also popped up when we added the driver.

Editing a driver

The **Edit Driver** region appears when you add a new driver and disappears as soon as you move the mouse cursor away. It can be brought back at any time by right-clicking on the driven property and choosing **Edit Driver** from the context menu.

These driver settings determine the variables that will affect the driver value and how they will be evaluated:

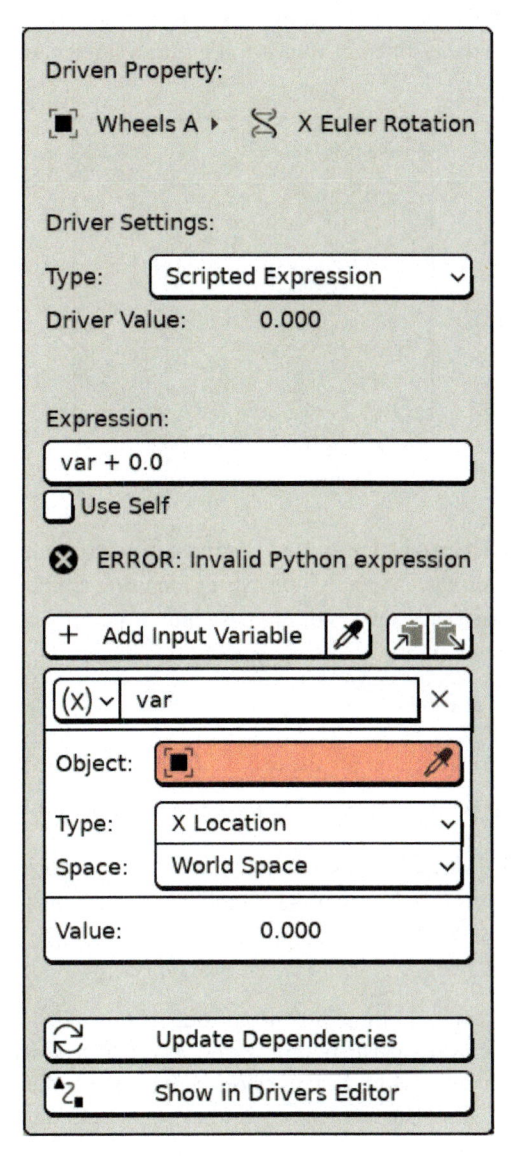

Figure 4.27: The Edit Driver region

If you see an error message here, it means you've made a mistake. Just kidding! Drivers are non-functional when initially added. Making our driver work will be a bit trickier than adding it.

Driver types

Each variable in a driver is a numeric value. Because a driver can use multiple variables, there are several methods to evaluate these different values and return a single number that will determine the driver value:

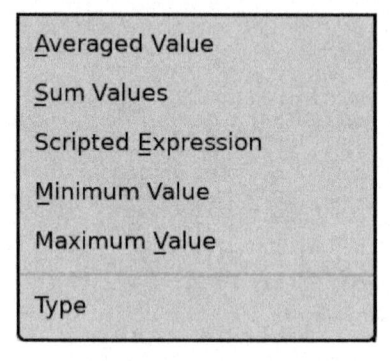

```
Averaged Value
Sum Values
Scripted Expression
Minimum Value
Maximum Value
─────────────────
Type
```

Figure 4.28: Driver types

The default driver type is **Scripted Expression**, the most powerful method. This type provides an **Expression** field, in which you can enter a Python expression using multiple input variables to calculate the driver value. For this particular driver, though, we only need one input variable, and it does not need to be used in an expression.

Let's use a more simple driver type:

1. Bring up the **Edit Driver** region for the driver of the **X Euler Rotation** of `Wheels A`.
2. Change the driver **Type** from **Scripted Expression** to **Averaged Value**.

Because we will only use one variable in this driver, it makes no difference whether we use the average, sum, minimum, or maximum. The **Name** of the variable itself no longer matters either.

> **Tip**
> Each scripted expression is a short line of Python code that must be repeatedly executed. This could potentially cause crashes, performance issues, and even security vulnerabilities, so it's a good practice to avoid using **Scripted Expression**-type drivers if they aren't necessary.

Driver variables

Now that we've simplified the driver a bit, we can turn our attention to the one variable, `var`, which alone will determine the driver value. A variable has to get its value from something else in the scene. This can be almost anything, ranging from the transform difference between two objects to nearly any numeric property of any data block in the current file.

We're looking to use a single property for our target. There's a lot of properties to choose from, so let's narrow down the possibilities:

1. Change the **Type** of the input variable `var` from **Transform Channel** to **Single Property**:

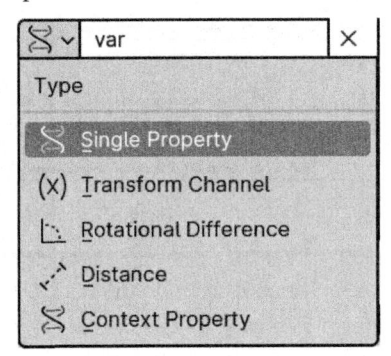

Figure 4.29: The input variable types

2. The property we're looking for technically belongs to a curve-data block, not an object. In the **Prop** row, change the **ID Type** from **Object** to **Curve**:

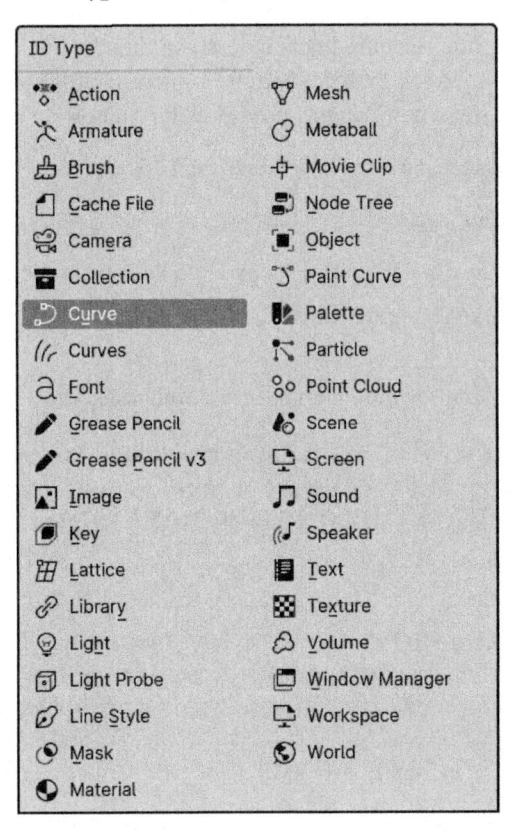

Figure 4.30: The available ID types

3. Now to select the curve we've been using to animate the train! Click on the ID field and select the `Track` curve.

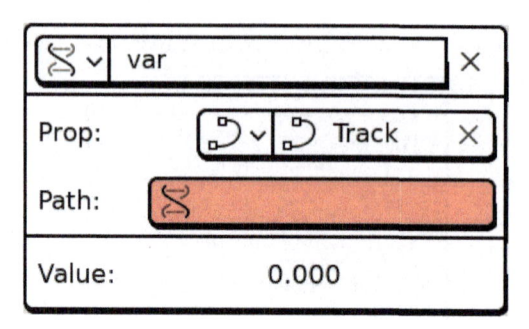

Figure 4.31: The variable using the Track ID block

We're now on track (so to speak) to drive the **X Euler Rotation** of `Wheels A` using a single property belonging to the curve datablock `Track`. There's just one more field we need to fill in – the one that determines which property that actually is!

Copying the data path

We have to enter something into the **Path** field of the driver input variable to specify that we want to use **Evaluation Time**, the property of `Track` which we animated in the previous section. It's just a text field, though. Clicking on it will not give us any kind of menu. So how do we know what to write in it?

The answer can be found by returning to the **Evaluation Time** property:

1. Find the **Evaluation Time** property of the curve data `Track` in the Properties Editor.
2. Right-click on the property and choose **Copy Data Path** from the context menu.
3. Return to the **Edit Driver** region for the driver of the **X Euler Rotation** property of object `Wheels A`.
4. Click on the **Path** field of the input variable `var` and paste (*Ctrl + V*) the copied text.

The string `eval_time` is the identifier of the **Evaluation Time** property within Blender's Python API. The full data path is `bpy.data.curves['Track'].eval_time`. You can think of these data paths as like web addresses, or URLs, of properties within Blender.

> **Tip**
>
> In your **User Preferences**, go to **Interface | Display | Tooltips** and enable **Python Tooltips**. Now you can see the Python data paths of any property by hovering the mouse cursor over it. This is helpful for creating drivers or any type of Python script in Blender.

Your settings for the driver should now look like this:

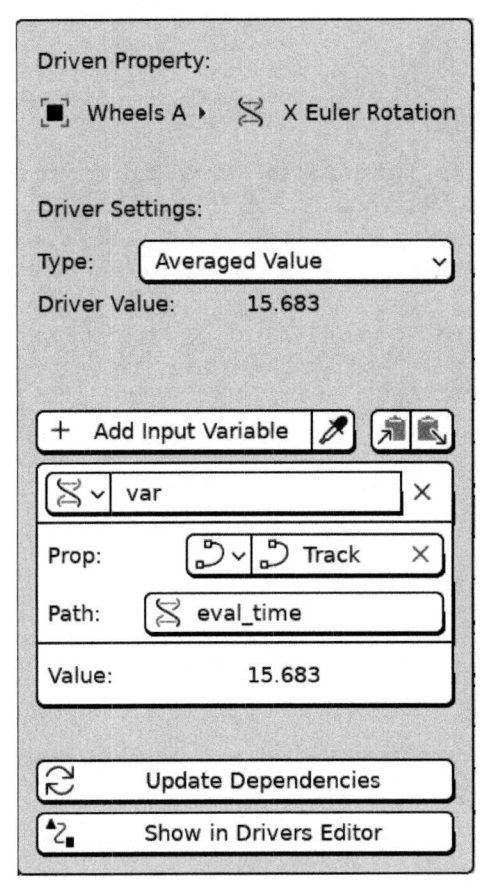

Figure 4.32: The final settings for the X Euler Rotation driver

Notice the error message is gone. Finally, a valid input variable for our driver! The driver value now equals the target property, and the wheels will rotate automatically as the train moves along the track. Are they rolling at the correct speed, though?

Driver F-curves

Like the wheel of the unicycle in the previous chapter, our train wheels' rate of rotation needs adjusting. Unless you happened to get very lucky, they probably roll a little too slowly or quickly in relation to the speed of the train along the track and have the perennial issue of looking like they're skidding. Our last step will be to correct this issue using the F-curve of the driver we made.

116 Looking into Object Relationships

That's right – our driver has its own special F-curve! You can't see it from the **Edit Driver** region we just used, but this last feature is of major importance to how the driver value ultimately affects the driven property value.

Displaying driver F-curves

Driver F-curves can be found by bringing up the **Drivers Editor** in an area of your user interface, or by right-clicking on a driven property and choosing **Open Drivers Editor** from the context menu. This area provides a complete overview of all the drivers in your scene. You can also find all of the parameters we just edited in the **Drivers** tab of the right-hand sidebar.

Here's our Drivers Editor:

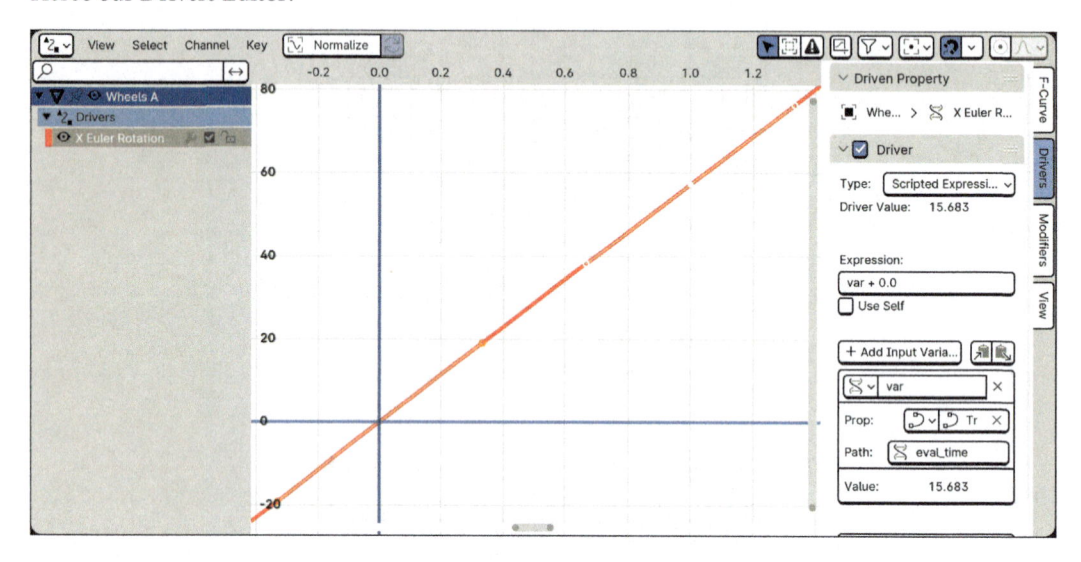

Figure 4.33: The Drivers Editor

It looks a lot like a Graph Editor, doesn't it? In most respects, it *is* a Graph Editor, but with one more essential difference – the X axis of this graph does not map to time. Instead, this X axis maps to the driver value of the driver, the number that is calculated based on the evaluated variables. The Y axis of the graph maps to the final value that will be passed to the driven property. Our driver's F-curve is itself a kind of function – the last thing that modulates how the target property **Evaluation Time** of `Track` will affect the driven property **X Euler Rotation** of `Wheels A`.

> **Tip**
>
> All the settings in **Edit Driver** can also be found in the Drivers Editor, in the **Drivers** tab of the right-hand sidebar (*N*).

The default driver F-curve is a diagonal line with linear extrapolation, making it a 1:1 function that effectively passes the driver value directly to the driven property. In many cases, you can ignore it. In our case, however, we must edit the slope of this F-curve to adjust the rate of our wheels' automatic rotation. Recall that rotational values are stored and evaluated as radians and only expressed/displayed as degrees, so the F-curve of our **X Euler Rotation** driver might already look like it has a steep slope. You'll likely need to make it even steeper still.

Editing the driver F-curve

The slope of the F-curve of the **X Euler Rotation** driver for `Wheels A` will depend on the total length of `Track`. I can't tell you the length of your own railroad, so you'll have to figure out the best slope for your driver F-curve using trial and error this time:

1. Find a frame range at which the train moves very slowly.
2. At one of those frames, zoom in closely at the wheels of your train in the 3D Viewport.
3. In a separate area of the interface, bring up the Drivers Editor.
4. Select either one of the keyframes of the **X Euler Rotation** driver F-curve.
5. Grab (*G*) the selected keyframe and move it to adjust the slope of the F-curve.
6. Scrub between frames to review the new effect of the driver in the 3D Viewport.
7. Keep adjusting until the wheels of your train appear to have traction on the rails of the track.

Once your train wheels spin correctly, you're done:

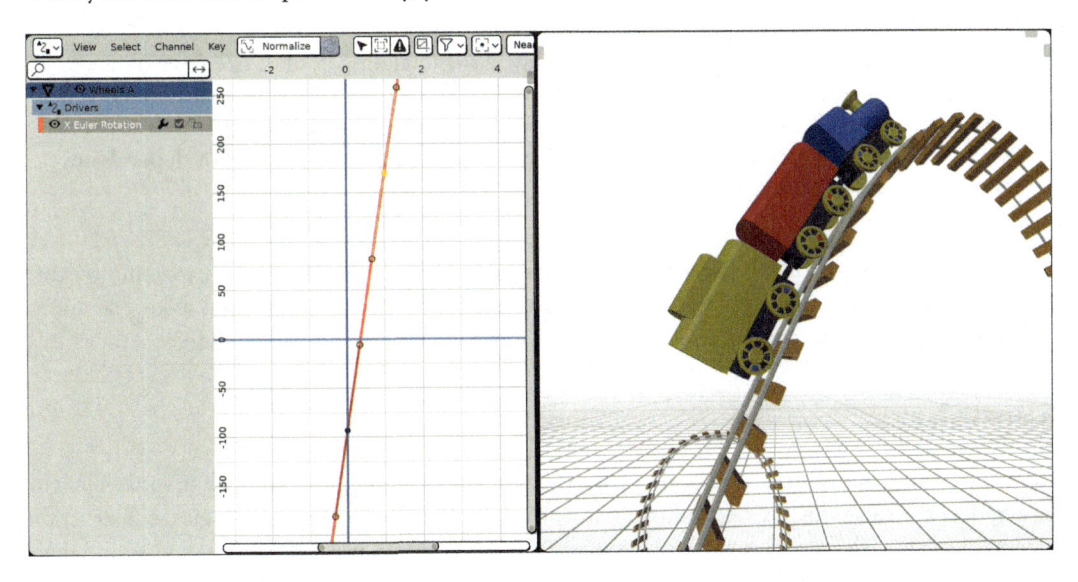

Figure 4.34: The corrected driver F-curve and animated train

Using a driver this way has a benefit in common with the other object relationships we've made – if we choose to go back and make changes to the animation of **Evaluation Time**, no keyframes will need to be copied and nothing else about the train will need to be adjusted. An elegant solution!

The final chart of object relationships

To clarify how we're able to animate so many things using so few animation channels, take a look at this chart showing all the complex network of relationships we've made:

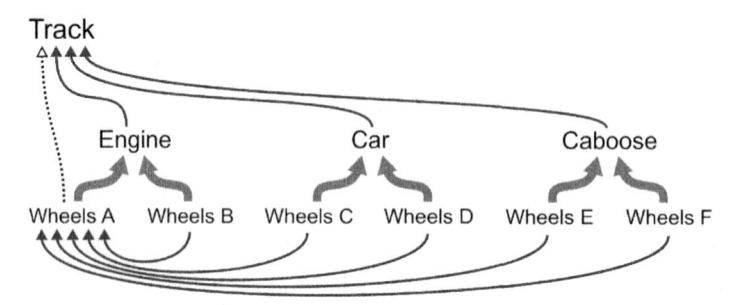

Figure 4.35: The final relationship chart – the dotted black line represents the driver

We've created quite the family tree of objects that affect other objects! Following the direction of the various dependencies, you can see how everything ultimately leads to the object `Track`.

> **Important note**
>
> In any system of related objects, imagine walking on the relationship chart from one object to the next in the direction of the arrows, never traveling backward. Eventually, you should reach an object which has no dependencies, after which you cannot proceed. Any part of the chart where you can circle back to the same place twice is called a **cyclic dependency** or **dependency loop**, which will usually cause an error.

I broke my promise – strictly speaking, we did have to edit more than one F-curve to complete this animation. Still, if we think of animation in a reductive sense, as the direct insertion of keyframes for each property, it's remarkable how much motion can come out of so little "animation"!

Summary

After completing this exercise and getting your train moving, you might feel more like a mechanic or an engineer than an animator, but animation is a broad category that includes the logical construction of whole systems. The way that you build your scene and the relationships between objects and their properties can be just as important as all the keyframes in your animation channels.

The subjects we covered here may have seemed complicated, but there's so much more to learn! All those different constraints, variable types, dependency chains, coordinate systems, Python expressions, driver F-curves... a mysterious cavern of logic and mathematics rumbles beneath all of these simple-looking "features." If we strayed too far into the topic of rotation alone, we'd never come back to finish the rest of this book.

We'll learn more about parents, constraints, and drivers when we put them to use in character animation in *Part 2* of this book. Before that, however, we'll take a brief diversion into something more urgent – how to convert all the work we've done into a video file!

Questions

1. What is an object origin? In what instances do we refer to origins as such?
2. Using **Affect Only | Origins**, are we in fact affecting less about an object than we normally would when we move its origin?
3. How might you tell whether an object is the parent of any other object? (There are at least three ways.)
4. In real life, most children have two parents. Can this be true of objects in Blender?
5. Can an object, practically speaking, be a grandparent?
6. What is the difference between the constraint owner and a constraint target? Which one is affected by the constraint?
7. Inspect the **Transform** properties of one of the rear wheels. It is moving and spinning, so why don't the values in these sliders appear to change?
8. What does the **Type** of the driver determine?
9. In what sense are the wheels of the train animated? In what sense are they *not* animated?

5
Rendering an Animation

Have we truly *finished* any of the animations in this book so far? All we have to show for our hard work are a couple of .blend files. Sure, we can open one in Blender, hit play, and watch our objects go, but is that the way animations are meant to be seen?

No, people expect to watch an animation as a **video**, a sequence of 2D images displayed in rapid succession, formatted as a digital file compatible with modern websites and media players. They will also expect each frame of that video to look nice, with lighting and shading and whatnot, and without any grid lines or cursors getting in the way. To produce such a video file, we must **render** the animation.

It's uncommon for a book on Blender to get this far without yet mentioning rendering. Rendering is the last step of 3D animation, which produces the finished image or frames of a work that will be seen by others. In this final and essential stage of 3D animation, we use the 3D data in our scene to output a sequence of 2D images, each one a "snapshot" of the scene at a given frame. The high-quality **image sequence** generated by rendering will then furnish the frames of a video which will be our final product.

In this chapter, we will cover the following topics:

- Setting up the camera
- Preparing an animated scene for rendering
- Rendering the animation to a sequence of image files
- Importing the images into Blender's **Video Sequencer** and rendering them to a video file

Technical requirements

The exercise for this chapter is more open-ended than the others. All you will need is a `.blend` file with complete animation. Any project from the previous four chapters will work. As an example, I choose to use my unicycle animation from *Chapter 3*:

Figure 5.1: Rendered frame of the unicycle animation, after treatment

Decide which chapter's exercise you'd like to render and open it up in Blender.

Rendering generates a sequence of high-quality image files, which can take up a lot of file space, so you'll also want to make sure you have adequate storage on your computer's file system. To render one of the animations from the previous chapters, 1 gigabyte of free space should be enough.

Setting up the camera

You can render a frame with **Render | Render Image** (*F12*), or you can render all of them with **Render | Render Animation** (*Ctrl + F12*).

Don't get ahead of yourself, though! Does your scene have a **camera**?

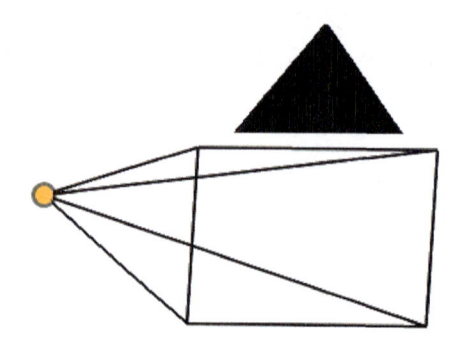

Figure 5.2: A camera object

If it doesn't, you'll get this error message when you try to render:

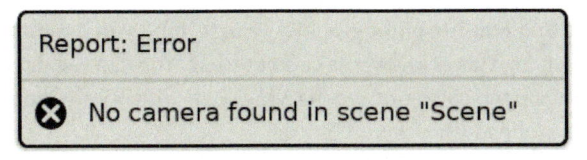

> Report: Error
>
> ❌ No camera found in scene "Scene"

Figure 5.3: Error message when trying to render without a camera

The camera is a critical object. If we think of our 3D scene as a movie set and our animated objects as actors, then our camera may be thought of as the camera. It's not a deep analogy. Just like a real-life camera, our scene will be captured through the "lens" of this virtual camera.

The scenes you downloaded for the exercises in part one of this book did not have a camera, which makes them incomplete for rendering. Let's add one and set it up now.

Adding a camera to the scene

You can add a camera object using **Add** (*Shift + A*) | **Camera** in the 3D Viewport.

> **Important note**
>
> A scene may have multiple cameras, but there may only be one **active camera** at any given point in time. This is the one through which the scene will be rendered and viewed. If there's only one camera object in the scene, it's usually the active camera.

When initially added, it's unlikely that your new camera will be in the right place:

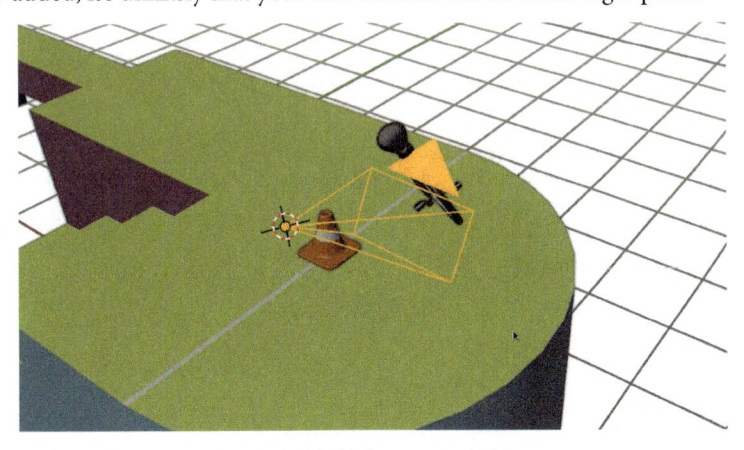

Figure 5.4: Initial camera position

Not to worry – cameras are objects that can be moved like any other, and they come with a few extra tricks we can use to quickly set them up.

Camera view-finding

As with both rendering and real-life photography, the first thing you'll want to do with your camera is look through it. In Blender, this is known as **camera view**. You can toggle camera view by clicking the camera widget in the upper-corner of the 3D Viewport, with **View Camera** (`, 1), or with **View | Viewpoint | Camera** (*numpad 0*):

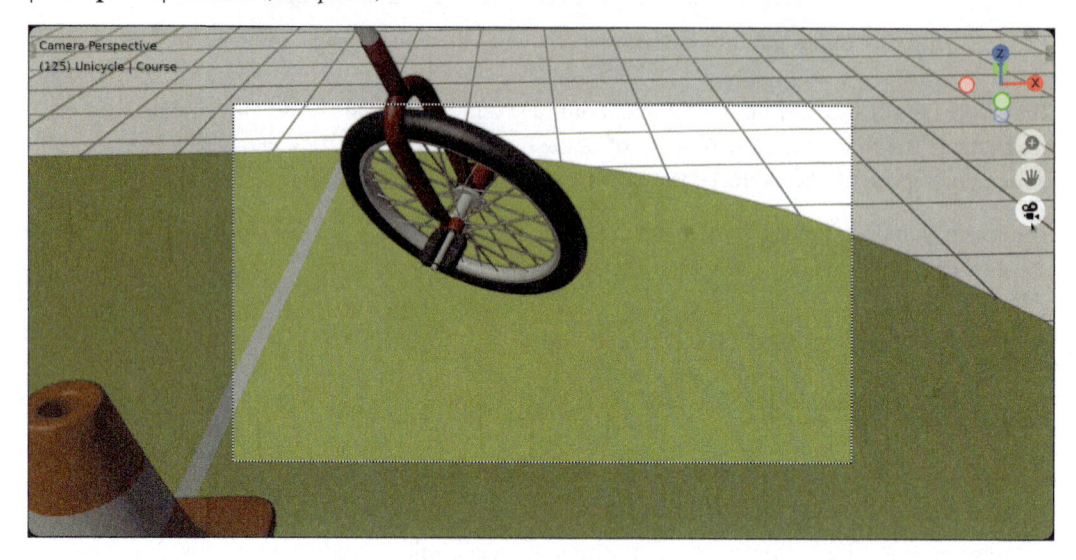

Figure 5.5: Camera view

Camera view gives us a vital preview of how our final product will look. Within the solid lines of that rectangle, we can see what our camera sees. Anything outside it will not be *directly* rendered, but may still emit light, cast shadows, or otherwise affect the result indirectly.

> **Tip**
>
> If you have room on your computer screen, you might consider splitting the interface into multiple 3D Viewports and keeping one of them in camera view. This enables you to work in one Viewport while previewing what the camera sees in the other at the same time.

Now that we can see through our camera, we can meaningfully adjust its position and other properties.

Positioning the camera

Most filmmakers will advise that you should have your camera pointed at what you want your viewers to see. In your case, unless you're ashamed of your work, that would mean the thing you animated. You'll want to re-position your new camera so that it properly frames the animated object in your scene.

Here are some ways of doing so:

- Just grab and rotate your camera like anything else! You can even select and move the camera while looking through it in camera view.
- Use the standard 3D Viewport navigation controls to find a viewing angle you like, then use **Align Active Camera to View** (*Ctrl + Alt + Numpad 0*). This snaps the active camera to match your view.
- By default, using the middle mouse button in the 3D Viewport will exit camera view, leaving the camera behind. If you like, however, you can go to the **View** tab of the sidebar (*N*) and enable **View Lock | Lock | Camera to View**. Now camera view – along with the camera – will follow you as you adjust your view with the middle mouse button.

Here's what my camera view looks like after a few clicks:

Figure 5.6: Adjusted camera view

These methods all exclusively affect the camera *object*, specifically its location and rotation. Those are definitely the most important properties, but there's another property belonging to the camera *data* (if you recall the distinction between objects and their data), which will also significantly affect the rendered result.

The camera lens

With our camera selected, we can go to the **Object Data Properties** tab in the **Properties** editor, which now has an icon that looks like a film camera. Arguably the most important camera data property is in the **Lens** panel:

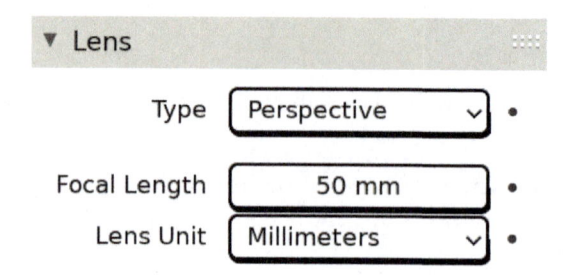

Figure 5.7: Lens properties of the Camera data

Adjusting the **Focal Length** has the effect of *zooming* in and out, with numeric values that correspond to those of a real camera zoom lens.

Figure 5.8: Zoomed-in camera view

To compensate for this effect, you might try *dollying* the camera by grabbing it on its local Z axis, pushing it closer or further away from the subject while keeping it centered. Here are three possible views, showing how zooming and dollying have a significant effect on the appearance of a shot:

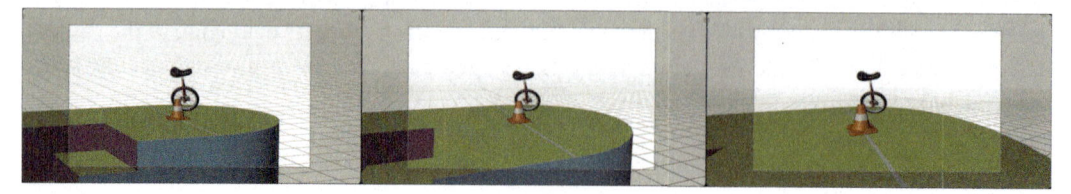

Figure 5.9: Distant and zoomed-in, normal, near and zoomed-out

When you've found a good position and focal length for your camera, don't forget to playback the animation in camera view. The shot might look good on one frame, but how does it look on every frame?

The animated camera

At the end of your animation, is the animated object still there in front of the camera where you left it?

Figure 5.10: Camera view on frame 125... and frame 250

Our animated objects are living things that will not necessarily stay in one place for us. Our camera, therefore, must become a living thing as well.

Animating the camera is as easy as anything else. I can make my camera follow the unicycle by keying its rotation and focal length:

Figure 5.11: The now-animated camera at different frames

When you're satisfied with how your animation looks in camera view, you may proceed to the next section, where we will begin to render it!

Rendering basics

Having set up a virtual camera in your virtual scene, you're ready to press the virtual shutter-release button on it and snap a virtual photo. In other words, you can render a frame!

What is rendering, really?

Rendering is a fundamental process in 3D graphics in which the artist lets the program do most of the work – simulating things like perspective, color, shadows, and reflections – the same phenomena that affect how light from the real world is sensed by our eyes or by a camera.

The rendered image should look nicer than what we see in the 3D Viewport (that's the idea, anyway). This added quality comes at a price, however: it can take a while.

Figure 5.12: The image on the right took 20 minutes to render

Rendering can be a time-consuming process, where the artist must sit and wait for the computer to process the data and spit out each image, not always knowing what the result will be. Depending on what's being rendered and on what hardware, a single image can take anywhere from a millisecond to a month to finish rendering. In the case of animation, this process must repeat for every single frame!

A short note on render engines

The specific part of a 3D application that performs rendering is called a **render engine**. Render engines are so advanced that they are sometimes packaged as applications in their own right. Upon starting a new project, it's common for 3D artists to select which engine they intend to use before beginning work in earnest.

Blender comes with multiple render engines of its own, which can be found at the very top of the **Render Properties** tab:

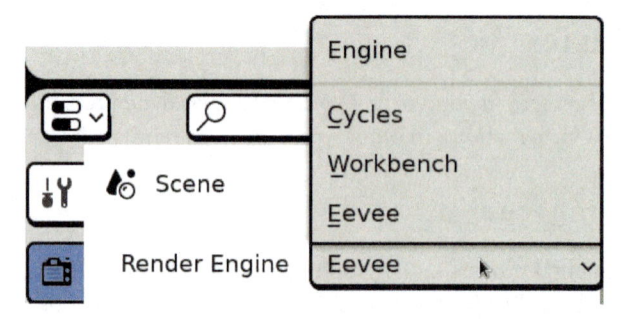

Figure 5.13: Render engines in Blender

Cycles and **Eevee** are the main engines used for rendering high-quality images. These two render engines are both robustly featured and complement each other nicely.

A quick summary of the difference between **Cycles** and **Eevee**: **Cycles** is realistic but not necessarily fast, and requires careful adjustment of settings to make it render more quickly without sacrificing quality. In contrast, **Eevee** is fast but not necessarily realistic, and requires extra work to improve image quality without sacrificing too much performance.

We'll stick with using the **Eevee** render engine for this chapter as it is much faster by default, making it more suitable for quickly rendering your first animation.

The Rendered Viewport Shading method

Render is a confusing term with multiple meanings. Strictly speaking, all 3D data must be rendered somehow if it is to be shown on the 2D pixel grid of a computer screen. The 3D Viewport renders our scene in realtime as we work, using various **Viewport Shading** (Z) methods optimized for performance. If it didn't, we wouldn't be able to see what we were working on!

This example shows three 3D Viewports, each using a different Viewport Shading method – **Wireframe**, **Solid**, and **Material Preview**:

Figure 5.14: Three realtime Viewport Shading methods

This brings us to the most important Viewport Shading method for this chapter. For the highest-quality interactive preview of the scene, check out the **Rendered** (Z, 8) Viewport Shading method in the 3D Viewport. This method renders the scene right in the 3D Viewport using the render engine we've selected:

Figure 5.15: 3D Viewport using the Rendered method

This method is the closest we can come to previewing the rendered result within the 3D Viewport. It is especially useful when combined with camera view. You can play the animation in this shading method too, though the result may not always play back at an acceptable frame rate.

Remember that **Rendered** is still a shading method, like **Wireframe**, **Solid**, or **Material**. It is not quite the same as executing a Render operation. In the case of properties that have one value for the Viewport and another for rendering, the viewport value will be used, which tends to be lower, favoring performance over quality like most other things in the 3D Viewport. It cannot preview any post-processing done with the Video Sequencer or the Compositing Nodes either.

This is all to say that what you see in **Rendered** is not necessarily the same as what you get when you *render*...

Controls for rendering

In most cases, to *render* means something more specific than a setting in the 3D Viewport: it is to perform an operation that renders the active scene from the perspective of the active camera, according to parameters determined by the **Render Properties** and **Output Properties**. This generates an image or sequence of images that may become the frames of a video.

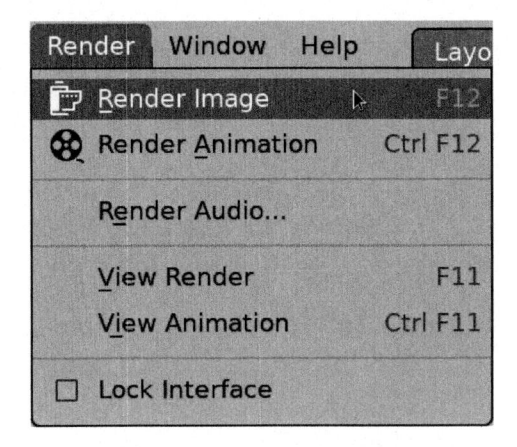

Figure 5.16: The Render menu

In animation projects, it's important to study individual rendered frames to assess their quality. Here are the main operators/controls for rendering one frame:

- **Render | Render Image** (*F12*) renders the scene at the current frame and displays the result in the Image Editor.
- **Image | Save** (*Alt + S*) may then be used in the Image Editor to save the image as a file.
- *Esc* may be pressed at any time to cancel a render in progress, and again to leave the Image Editor that was called at render time.
- **Render | View Render** (*F11*) returns to the Image Editor, displaying the last image that was rendered. It does not render anything new.

> **Important note**
> After pressing **Render Image** (*F12*) for the first time, novice users often ask, excitedly, how to play back or orbit around the result in the Image Editor. No such luck. Remember that the image in the Image Editor is just that – an *image*: a static 2D grid of colored pixels.

Finally, here are the operators for rendering an animation:

- **Render | Render Animation** (*Ctrl + F12*) renders and outputs an image for every frame in the animation in order from **Start Frame** to **End Frame**. Unless canceled with *Esc*, the process continues until the last frame is rendered.
- **Render | View Animation** (*Ctrl + F11*) searches the output path for the video or image sequence that ought to have been rendered, and attempts – with varying success – to play it back at the specified frame rate.

> **Important note**
>
> A frame rendered with **Render Image** (*F12*) is identical to that same frame rendered with **Render Animation** (*Ctrl + F12*). The only difference is whether Blender stops after rendering one frame!

Using **Render Animation** at this stage will not yield a good result. For one thing, we haven't checked our **Output Properties** yet. Furthermore, there's a broader reason why we shouldn't get ahead of ourselves.

Why shouldn't we render the whole animation right now?

Before we render all the frames, how about we render just one?

Here's my result when I use **Render Image** (*F12*):

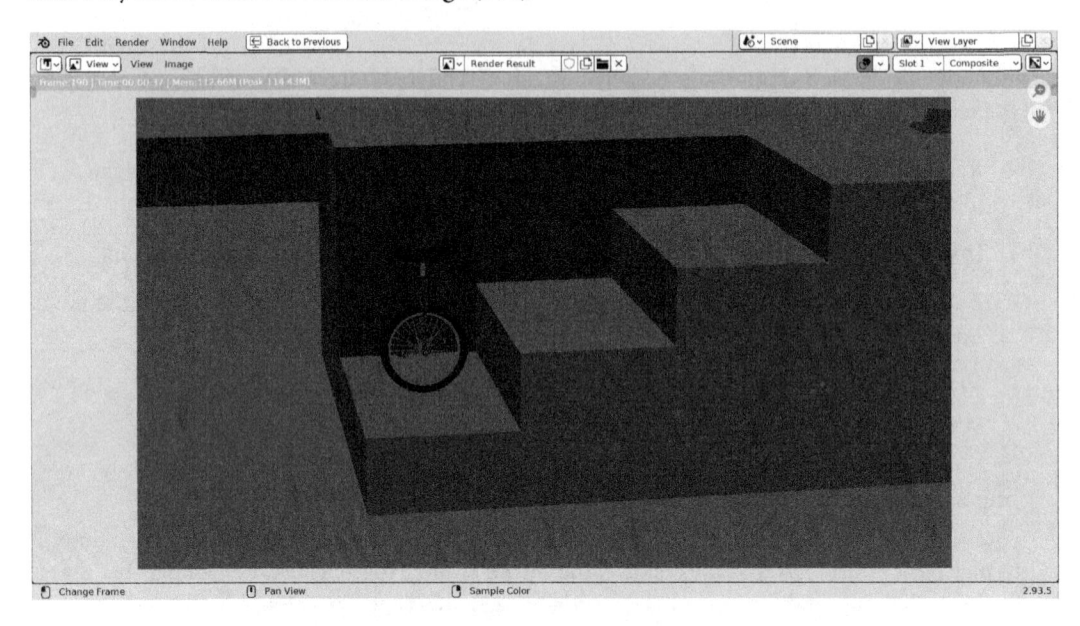

Figure 5.17: Rendered frame without lights, sky, or ground

By rendering just one frame, I can see my scene is missing some things, including proper lighting and the ground. If I had waited for the entire animation to finish rendering before checking what it looked like, I'd have discovered the same thing, but only after using up file space and wasting several minutes rendering.

Of course, this is just one frame. Maybe every other frame in the scene looks fine when rendered. I wouldn't bet on it, though. That's the thing about rendering: we can't be absolutely certain what the final product looks like until we've rendered it, but we can still make deductions based on what we see in the 3D Viewport and individual rendered frames.

As you proceed through the next section, remember to use both the **Rendered** (*Z, 8*) method in the 3D Viewport and **Render Image** (*F12*) at various frames to monitor how our changes to the scene and its properties affect the rendered result.

Setting up our scene for rendering

Everything we do in Blender is ultimately done with rendering in mind; that it will contribute, directly or indirectly, to the rendered product. Anything else is wasted labor. That means there aren't many topics in Blender about which we can say with finality, "this has nothing to do with a chapter on rendering."

Lighting, environments, shading: these are dense enough to fill several other books and are just as important to a 3D artist working on a still image as they are to a 3D animator. As animation is our chief concern, this section will sail past most of these topics, covering just enough to set up our scene so that it can be rendered passably.

Adding the sky and the ground

For the sake of simplicity, the `.blend` files you downloaded for the exercises in part 1 do not have any light objects. This lack of light makes the rendered scene suffer from a problem known among industry professionals as "too dark" for reasons too advanced to explain in this book. I'll just defer to another saying we have in the business: "Let's put a light in there so it's not as dark."

While we're at it, we might as well fix up our scene with a proper sky instead of the default gray background we have now. A complete scene should also have a ground so it doesn't look like everything else is floating in space: a simple grid object at the center of the scene should do nicely.

Let's throw in these essential elements now:

1. Add a sun to your scene with **Add** (*Shift + A*) | **Light** | **Sun**. Try rotating it a bit to cast longer shadows.
2. Go to the **World Properties** tab of the Properties editor. Give your scene's background a nice color, or perhaps even a **Sky Texture**:

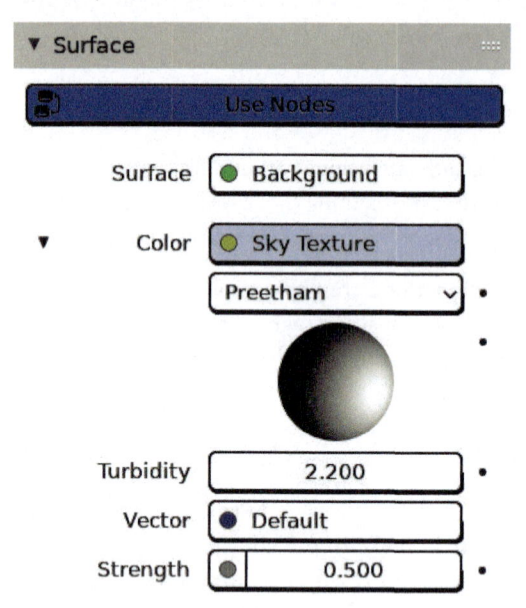

Figure 5.18: Example Sky Texture settings for the background

3. Use **Snap** (*Shift + S*) | **Cursor to World Origin** and **Add** (*Shift + A*) | **Mesh** | **Grid** to add a flat grid that will act as the floor or ground of your scene.
4. **Scale** (*S*) up your floor object by at least `100` times.

Now we've got a light, a sky, and a ground on which to cast shadows!

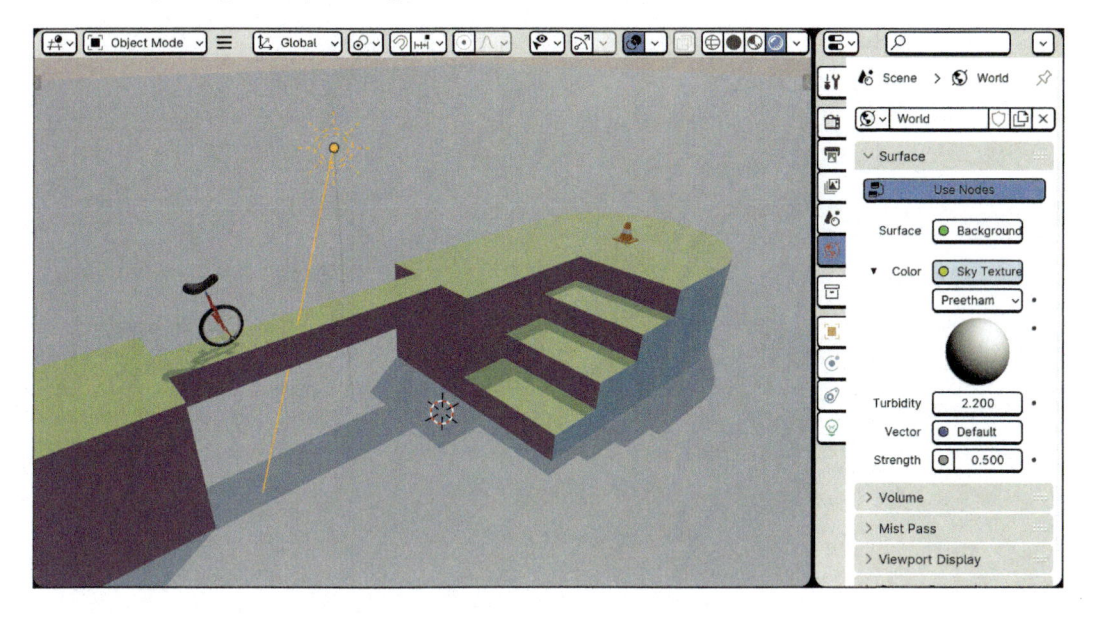

Figure 5.19: Scene with light, sky, and ground

Some quick and easy render settings

The **Render Properties** tab contains settings for various features in Eevee which, when enabled, may enhance the realism of your renders. Here are a few to consider.

Enabling **Ambient Occlusion** improves realism by darkening the crevices between geometry:

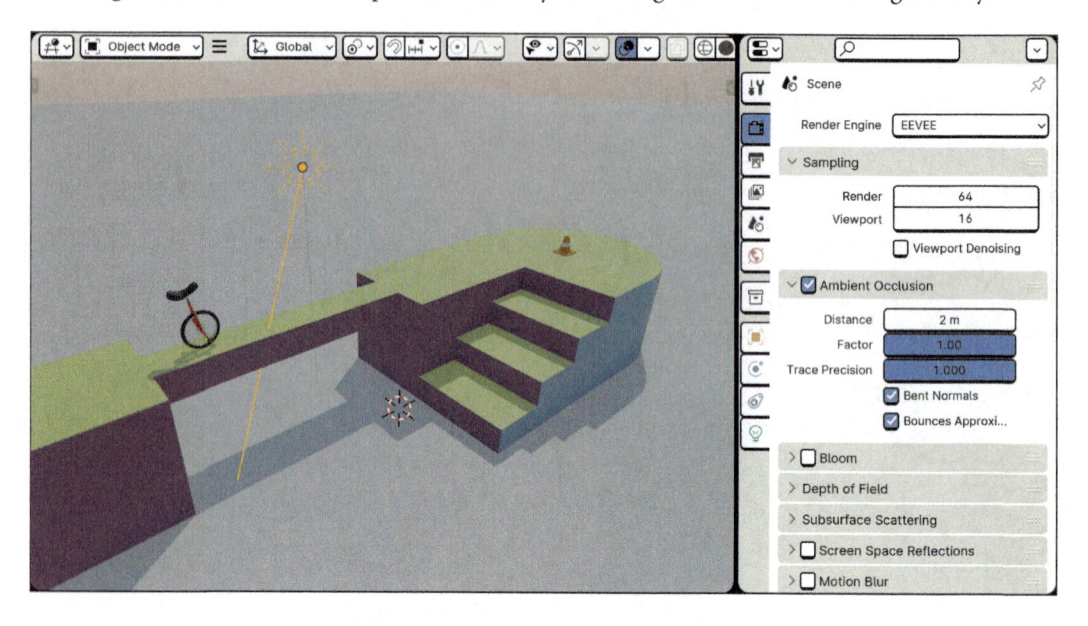

Figure 5.20: Scene with Ambient Occlusion

Shiny materials look nicer with **Screen Space Reflections** enabled:

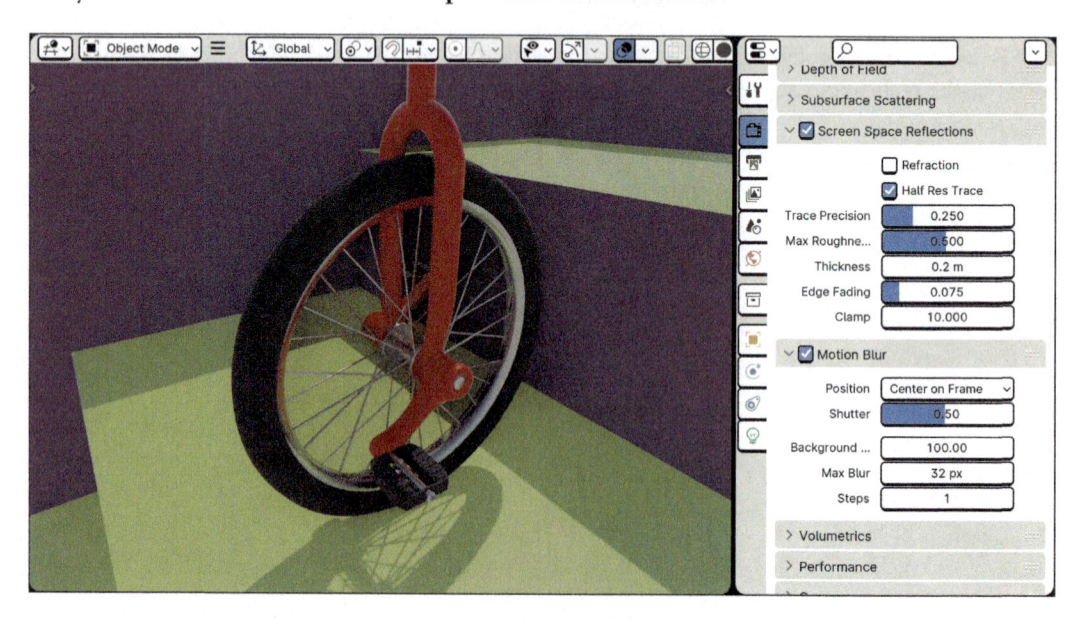

Figure 5.21: Close-up of the unicycle with Screen Space Reflections enabled

Finally, **Motion Blur** is an excellent feature for animations. When enabled, geometry is blurred in the direction of its movement, like with a real camera:

Figure 5.22: Rendered frame with Motion Blur enabled

That concludes our tutorial on lighting and render settings – less of a masterclass and more like fumbling in a dark bathroom for the light switch. What can I say? This is an animation book! As long as the animated objects are clearly visible when rendered, that's good enough.

As this is an open-ended exercise, you are encouraged to make as many additional improvements to your scene as you like. If it looks good in a still image, it will likely look just as good in animation, though it may take longer to render.

Render resolution

There's one remaining scene property that is crucial to rendering. Even if we don't need to edit it for the rest of the exercises in this book, you should still be aware of it, as it affects image quality, render time, and even the camera in your scene.

Resolution X, **Resolution Y**, and **Resolution %** can be found in the **Dimensions** panel in the **Output Properties**:

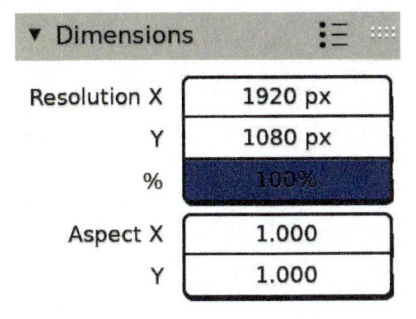

Figure 5.23: Resolution settings

These properties determine the pixel dimensions of the rendered image. Apply **Resolution %** to both **Resolution X** and **Resolution Y**, then multiply them: that's how many pixels Blender will render per frame.

It goes without saying that a higher-res image is considered higher quality. That improvement, however, comes with a commensurate increase in render time. Likewise, lower-resolution images will render more quickly.

> **Tip**
>
> **Resolution %** is provided as a convenient way of scaling down the render resolution without having to edit both **X** and **Y** values proportionately. A resolution of `1920 x 1080` at `50%` will render at 960 x 540, and in roughly 1/4 of the time! Rendering at a lower resolution is another technique artists have for previewing the rendered result more quickly.

As it happens, Blender's default resolution of `1920 x 1080` is just fine in most cases. This is a nice resolution with ubiquitous support among modern formats, websites, and media players. Should you choose to use something different, it's best to pick a standard resolution, such as the one for your computer monitor.

For more information, refer to a list of common resolutions here:

`http://en.wikipedia.org/wiki/List_of_common_resolutions`

Predicting and managing render performance

When viewing rendered images, pay attention to the string of information at the top left of the display region:

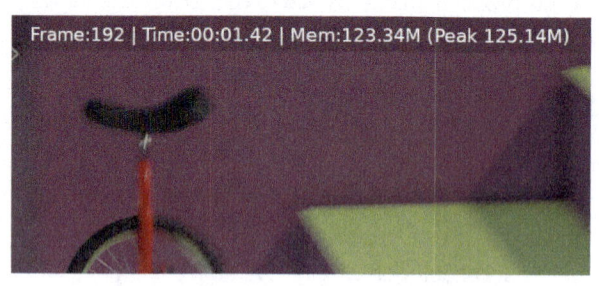

Figure 5.24: Information about the rendered frame

That value next to **Time** is how long the frame took to render. As we add objects and enable render features in our scene, this number will climb. Multiply the **Time** it takes to render one frame by the total number of frames in your animation, and you've got a rough estimate of how long the entire animation will take to render.

Does it matter if one frame takes 2 seconds to render instead of 1? It might, if the animation is 3,000 frames long and it's due in 1 hour! The 3D artist has a balancing act to perform when it comes to rendering complex scenes at high quality. Fill your scene with too many objects or crank up some settings too high, and Blender may take an unreasonably long time to finish rendering. It might even crash!

Your artistic tastes, your hardware specifications, and your patience are all your own, so you're the one who must decide how long you're willing to wait for rendering to finish.

> **Tip**
> Using the **Slot** feature in the header of the Image Viewer, you can store multiple rendered images for convenient comparison. Image slots also preserve the rendering info in the top bar, so you can compare image render times along with the images themselves.

It's always good practice to test your scene using **Render Image** (*F12*) at various frames. When you are confident that all the frames in your animation will look fine and render within an acceptable time frame, you're ready for the next big step!

Rendering an image sequence

As we get closer to viewing the final product, we've been previewing it in one of two ways: watching the animation playback in camera view, or rendering still images with **Render Image** (*F12*). This means we've had to watch our animation in low-quality and/or view some high-quality frames that don't move, and then use our imagination to fill in the gaps in anticipation of what the final video will look like. Well, anticipate no more! It's time to render your animation.

Rendering an animation is a lot like rendering a still image, only this time, *every* frame in the animation must be rendered. When **Render Animation** (*Ctrl + F12*) is called, Blender will render and automatically output (save) an image for every frame in the scene's frame range, beginning with the **Start Frame** and continuing all the way until the **End Frame** is saved.

The result of this operation will be an image sequence: a folder stored on your computer that contains every frame in your animation as an individual image file.

Why output an image sequence and not a video?

When we render an animation in Blender, we can choose, using the **Format** setting, to output a sequence of image files or just one video file. Since a video file is what we need, why not render directly to that?

Admittedly, we could! Practically speaking, the projects in this book are short and simple enough to output either way. However, this chapter aims to teach the best practice for rendering animations. That means rendering to an image sequence first, then converting that image sequence to a video, either in Blender or another application.

Here are our reasons:

- Any error that might occur while saving an image file in a sequence will be isolated to that one file, whereas a single corrupted frame in a video could affect the rest of the frames and ruin the whole thing.
- If you have a crash or power outage while rendering, or otherwise have to cancel a render in progress using *Esc*, an image sequence makes it much easier to resume rendering from the last completed frame.
- Along with Blender, most professional video editors and compositors handle image sequences quite well – sometimes better than video files.
- Depending on how the video will be published, it may need to be encoded in various formats, quality levels, and resolutions. In that case, you'll have to convert what you've rendered to another video anyway.

To summarize: video files are janky. If you render directly to video files, you'll someday regret it, so let's take this time to do things the right way.

Output settings

When you render an image using **Render Image** (*F12*), Blender holds it temporarily in the image editor, letting you decide whether to save it using **Image** | **Save** (*Alt + S*). On the other hand, Blender cannot hold every image in an entire animation, so **Render Animation** (*Ctrl + F12*) must automatically save each image somewhere after it is rendered. This means we have to establish suitable output settings before initiating a render.

These properties, which belong to the scene, may be found in the **Output** panel in the **Output Properties** tab of the Properties Editor:

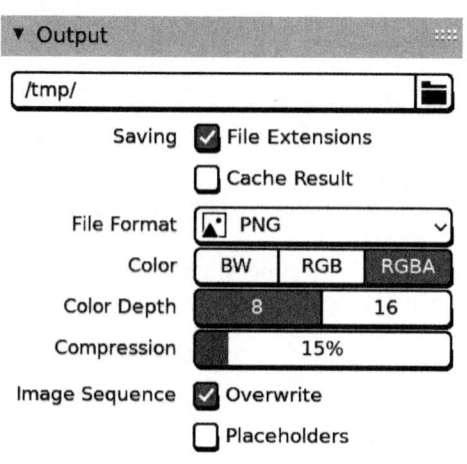

Figure 5.25: File output settings

Setting the Output Path

The very first property in the **Output** panel is the **Output Path**. This field determines the location on your computer to which rendered images will be automatically saved.

By default, images will be saved to a folder called `tmp`. That's a dumb place to save images! Let's find a better one:

1. Click on the small folder icon to the right of the **Output Path** field. This launches a file browser, which makes it easier to set the path.
2. Navigate to a location on your computer's filesystem which will be easy to find later. I recommend the same folder as the one that contains the `.blend` file you're working on.
3. Click the **Add New Directory** button to add a new folder. Give it a name you'll remember later.
4. Double-click on the new folder to enter it, and click **Accept**.

This fresh new folder will be the container for the several hundred image files we're about to generate. With that many files, it's important to keep them in their own container, or things could get messy!

> **Tip**
> In lieu of using the file browser, the Output Path text field can be edited directly. Any folder in the path that does not yet exist will be automatically created when the first frame is saved.

Output file formats

As with saving an image in any other program, we must select a particular format. Image formats are standards for encoding an image so that enough data is preserved without taking up too much bandwidth or file space.

Here are the main factors to consider when choosing an image format:

- The of size saved images
- Image quality and data retention
- The speed at which the images can be read and written
- Compatibility with other applications

Blender can read any image it can output, so that last factor doesn't concern us for this chapter. The other factors, however, still matter, especially when it comes to rendering an image sequence. All those frames add up quickly, so we'll need to select a format that performs well and preserves image quality while not taking up unnecessary space on our computer's filesystem.

Click on the **File Format** property to select from a list of supported image and video formats:

Image		Movie
BMP	Cineon	AVI JPEG
Iris	DPX	AVI Raw
PNG	OpenEXR MultiLayer	FFmpeg Video
JPEG	OpenEXR	
JPEG 2000	Radiance HDR	
Targa	TIFF	
Targa Raw	WebP	

Figure 5.26: Output file formats

Here's a brief rundown of supported image formats:

- **PNG** (`.png`) and **TIFF** (`.tif`) are both *lossless* image formats, meaning that they employ compression methods that keep file sizes down without degrading image quality. These formats are well supported in other applications.

- **OpenEXR** (`.exr`) is a **high dynamic range (HDR)** format that encodes 32-bit floating-point values for each channel (instead of the usual 8 or 16-bit integers). It is the only format that preserves all the color data in the rendered image, including highlights that exceed the brightness encoded by most other formats. **Multilayer EXR** is a type of `.exr` image that can encode multiple image layers. The `.exr` files are superb for advanced compositing pipelines, but more than what we'll need for this book.

- **JPEG** (`.jpg`) is a lossy image format that can effectively compress image data to conveniently small file sizes at the cost of quality. The **Quality** slider determines the degree to which image quality is favored over small file size. `.jpg` image files tend to be smaller than `.tif` or `.png`, but there is always some loss of data, even at 100% quality.

- **JPEG 2000** (`.jp2`) was developed as the successor to **JPEG**. It has many advantages over `.jpg`, `.tif`, and `.png`, but its read/write performance in Blender is less than ideal, and other applications have been slow to adopt it.

- **Radiance HDR** (`.hdr`) is another HDR format, but with less fidelity than OpenEXR. It is commonly used as a format for environment (sky) textures.

- **BMP**, **Iris**, **Targa**, **Targa Raw**, **Cineon**, and **DPX** are kept around for compatibility with older programs or specialized pipelines. Image files encoded in these formats don't offer notable benefits over the others listed, and will probably just be unnecessarily large.

- **WebP**: This is actually a really good format, but for some reason, everyone will hate you if you use it.

So, which format should we use? If there were a definite answer for all cases, Blender wouldn't offer us so many choices. For our purposes in this book, though, I recommend TIFF, as it is lossless, like PNG, but seems to output much more quickly in Blender.

After changing the **File Format** to **TIFF**, you can leave the rest of the settings to their defaults:

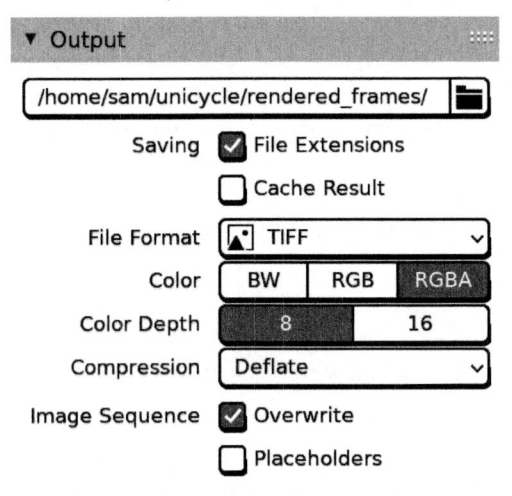

Figure 5.27: Example output settings

> **Tip**
> When **Overwrite** is disabled, Blender will skip rendering a frame if the file for it already exists in the **Output Path**. This is useful for resuming a partially completed rendering job.

Pre-render checklist

A common annoyance among 3D animators is to render something for hours, only to later discover that we made a mistake and have to render the whole thing over again – sort of like baking a cake with one missing ingredient. This happens to everyone eventually, but to avoid it as much as possible, here are some things we should verify before rendering an animation:

- We've watched the animation several times in camera view in the 3D Viewport
- At least one frame, when rendered with **Render Image** (*F12*), looks fine and did not take too long to render

- In the **Output Properties**, the Format is correct and the **Output Path** is one that we recognize and can find later
- The `.blend` file has been saved

If all of this is true, you're ready to render your animation!

> **Important note**
> Like flooring the gas pedal in a car, rendering is a resource-intensive process that pushes your computer's hardware to the limit of its capability. Make sure your computer is in a cool environment with good ventilation to avoid overheating. If you are rendering on a laptop, keep it plugged into a power source. Rendering will drain your laptop's battery like nothing else!

Rendering the animation

Ready? Press **Render Animation** (*F12*).

You are now rendering the animation. As mentioned before, this process takes some time. Since we're using Eevee, it shouldn't take forever, but it won't be instantaneous either.

> **Tip**
> Blender's interface does not "lock up" while rendering, so you can still click things and inspect settings in other windows. Always cancel or finish rendering before resuming normal work, though.

Using your operating system's file browser, you can navigate to the location set by **Output Path** and watch it slowly fill up with image files:

Figure 5.28: File Browser showing thumbnails of each image in sequence

Notice that each image file bears the frame number in its filename. This will be important later when we import the images back into Blender as a single sequence.

When the last frame in your animation has been saved, the render is finished.

Viewing the rendered frames

Blender comes with its own internal media player that can play back the image sequence that was just rendered. We can invoke it with **Render | View Animation** (*Ctrl + F11*). When called, this operation searches the Output Path for what ought to have been rendered. Of course, this only works if you've rendered something. If it finds what it's looking for, Blender's internal media player will attempt to play back the recently outputted video or image sequence.

Viewing the image sequence this way helps us quickly preview the rendered image sequence, to determine if it is acceptable before converting it to a video file. Do not be alarmed if the resulting video appears to lag or jitter, though – Blender's adorable little media player does not always playback everything at optimal performance. It doesn't even have a time bar, but it's trying its best!

> Tip
> After previewing the final product, it's common to want to make changes and render your animation again. Rendering a second time is as easy as rendering the first time, but consider setting a new Output Path if you don't want to overwrite the sequence in the old one.

Now that we've done the heavy lifting of rendering our scene to an image sequence, we can now convert those images to a single video.

Converting an image sequence to a video

If we can play back our image sequence with **View Animation** (*Ctrl + F11*), don't we already kind of have a video? Well, yes and no – a video may be little more than a sequence of images, but a sequence of image files alone will not be recognized by most media players, and is too large and unwieldy to be posted online or sent to anyone else. A proper video file contains all the frames in a single file and can apply both spatial and temporal compression methods to keep the video file down to a size much smaller than an image sequence.

Lots of professional video editing/encoding applications can convert an image sequence to a video file. For instance, I can use the video encoding utility *FFmpeg* to convert my sequence of `.tif` files to an `.mp4` file with a single command:

```
ffmpeg -r 24 -i render/%04d.tif my_video.mp4
```

You shouldn't need to download a new program or learn a whole new command-line syntax just to make your first video, though. This is a Blender book, and Blender already has everything we need!

The Video Sequence Editor

Blender comes with a **Video Sequencer**, which – compared to dedicated video editing applications – is both powerful and rudimentary (it can open multilayer EXR sequences, but it can't always play things back at full speed).

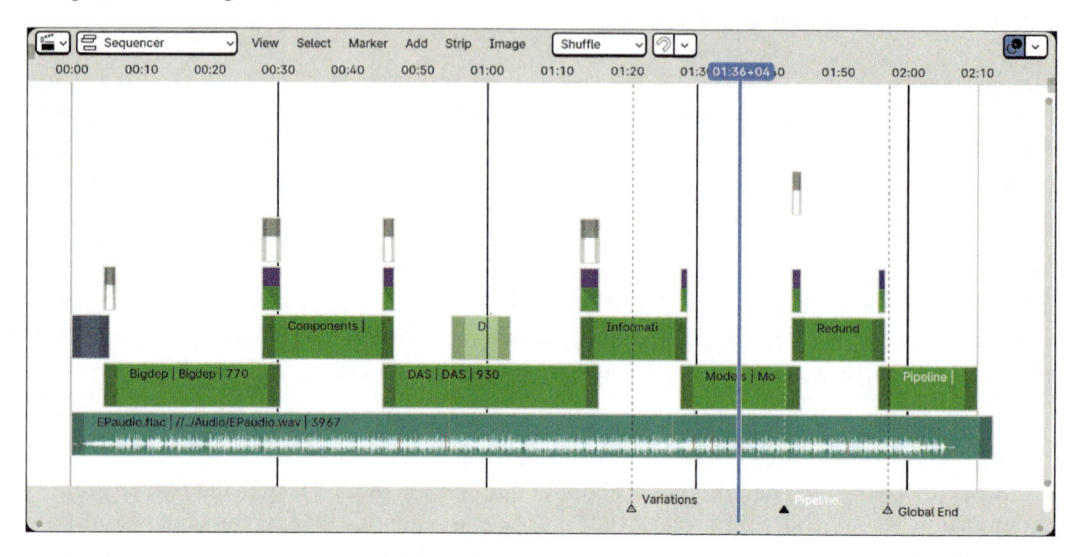

Figure 5.29: Example project in the Video Sequencer

You can access Blender's Video Sequencer by switching the **Editor Type** of an area in your screen to **Video Sequencer**. If you like, you can also add a **Video Editing** workspace by clicking the + tab at the top of your screen for **Add Workspace | Video Editing | Video Editing**.

We're going to dip our toe into this area so that we can import the image sequence we just rendered. After importing the image sequence as a strip in the Video Sequencer, we can then render to a video file, which will be our final product.

Creating a scene for video sequencing

In order not to get our image sequence mixed up with the 3D scene that generated it, we should use a separate scene in our `.blend` file for video sequencing. To make things easier, we can add a new scene that starts out with the same settings as the one we already have:

1. Find the **Scene** selector near the top-right corner of the screen.
2. Click the **New Scene** button and choose **Copy Settings**.
3. Instead of `Scene.001`, rename the new scene something that makes sense, like `Sequence`.

4. Bring up a Video Sequencer in the UI, if you haven't already.

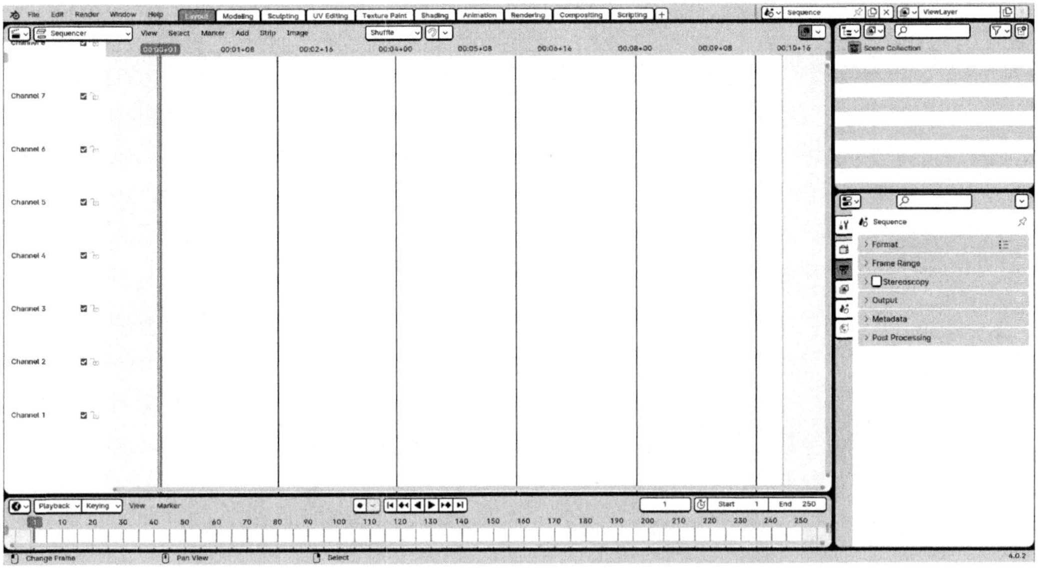

Figure 5.30: New scene with an empty Video Sequencer

Using **Copy Settings** gives our new scene identical **Output Properties** as the previous one – a quick way to ensure that both scenes have the same frame range and resolution. **Render Properties** will be the same as well, but as we'll soon see, those properties no longer concern us.

Importing the image sequence

Though we normally think of a scene in Blender as a 3D space with 3D objects viewable in the 3D Viewport, it can also merely serve as the container for a sequence in the Video Sequencer.

The elements in Blender's Video Sequencer are called strips. Let's add our image sequence **strip** now:

1. Go to the **Start Frame** (this should be frame 1). Doing this ensures that the strip, when added, will begin at frame 1, just like the animation in our original scene.
2. In the Video Sequencer, use **Add** (*Shift + A*) | **Image Sequence**.
3. Using the invoked file browser, navigate to the directory that contains your image sequence.
4. Select all the images in your sequence and click **Add Image Strip**.

> **Tip**
> Controls for navigating and moving strips in the Video Sequencer are largely identical to those of the Timeline.

Your Video Sequencer should now have an Image Sequence strip that takes up the duration of the scene's frame range:

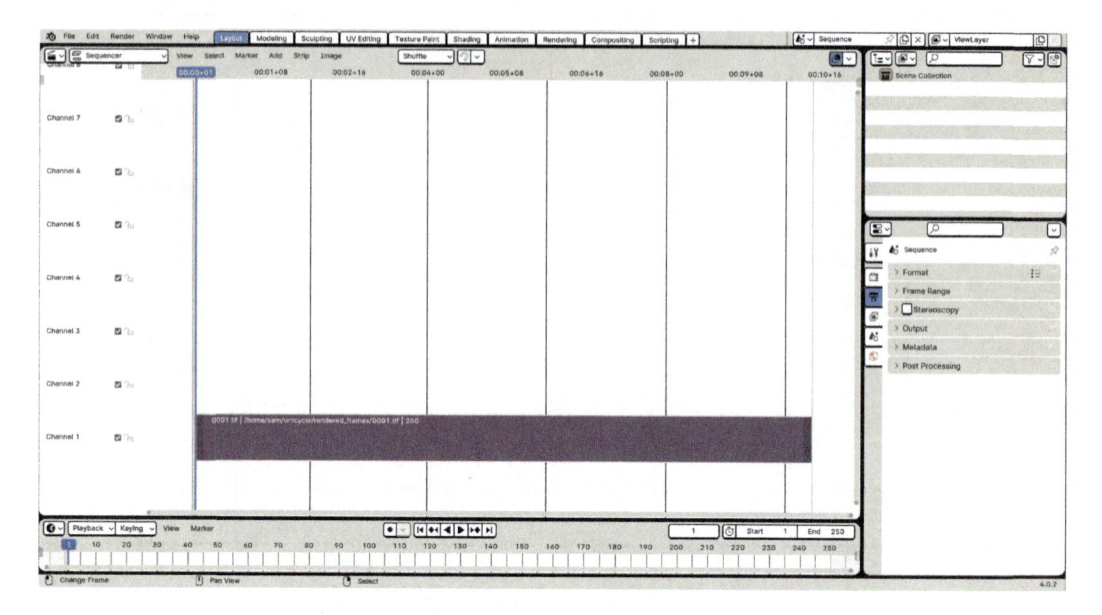

Figure 5.31: Image sequence strip in the Video Sequencer

That's all the sequencing we need to do for this chapter!

Rendering a frame from the Video Sequencer

So, how do we set Blender to use the image sequence in the Video Sequencer? Trick question – there's nothing more we need to do! Under **Post Processing** in your scene's **Output Properties**, use of the Video Sequencer is enabled by default:

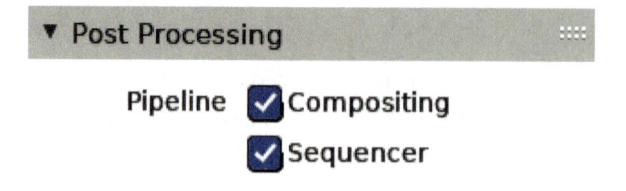

Figure 5.32: Post Processing settings

Sequencer has no effect when there's nothing in the Video Sequencer, but as soon as we add an image or video strip, Blender will bypass the 3D part of the active scene and instead render whatever is in the Video Sequencer.

You can try it yourself with **Render Image** (*F12*) now. These frames seem to render much faster than they did in the previous scene, don't they? That's because we're not really rendering in the way we've come to understand the word. Although we're technically using the same **Render Image** (*F12*) command, no 3D data is being evaluated this time. Because our current sequence is just one image sequence strip with no effects, Blender is pretty much just showing us the images we've already rendered.

> **Important note**
> Pay attention to which scene you are in, as it is easy to confuse a rendered frame in your initial scene with a "rendered" frame in your sequence scene.

Don't use **Render Animation** (*Ctrl + F12*) yet! Because our sequence scene still has the same **Output Path** and **Format** as our initial scene, doing so will overwrite the images with themselves. Not helpful at all! We'll need to establish a new **Output Path** and choose a proper video format.

Output settings for video export

Now that our Video Sequencer is ready to output the frames we want, let's return one more time to the **Output** panel in the **Output Properties** tab of the Properties Editor. This time, we'll adjust the settings to output a video file.

Setting the output path (again)

First, let's change this scene's **Output Path** so our video doesn't get buried with all those image files:

1. Click once more on the folder icon next to the **Output Path** to invoke a file browser.
2. Select a convenient location in your filesystem for the video file we're about to create.
3. Choose a file name for your video (anything will do) and click **Accept**.

I suggest using the parent directory (the folder that contains the folder that contains the image sequence). That way, the video file can live right next to the folder with the sequence that helped create it.

Now that our **Output Path** is out of the way, our final task is to choose the right video format.

Using built-in FFmpeg

At first glance, the **File Format** menu seems to offer few options for video formats, but the available settings expand when we select **FFmpeg Video**.

It's a bit of a misnomer to refer to FFmpeg as a format. FFmpeg is in fact a popular command-line utility for reading and writing a broad range of video formats. Don't worry – you won't have to learn any commands yourself; Blender's built-in implementation of FFmpeg handles that for us.

The parameters for FFmpeg are in the **Encoding** sub-panel:

1. In **Output Properties**, select **FFmpeg Video** as the **File Format**.
2. Open the **Encoding** sub-panel and set **Container** to **MPEG-4**.

The default values for all the other properties may be left as they are. These settings will create an .mp4 video, which will probably work on most websites and media players:

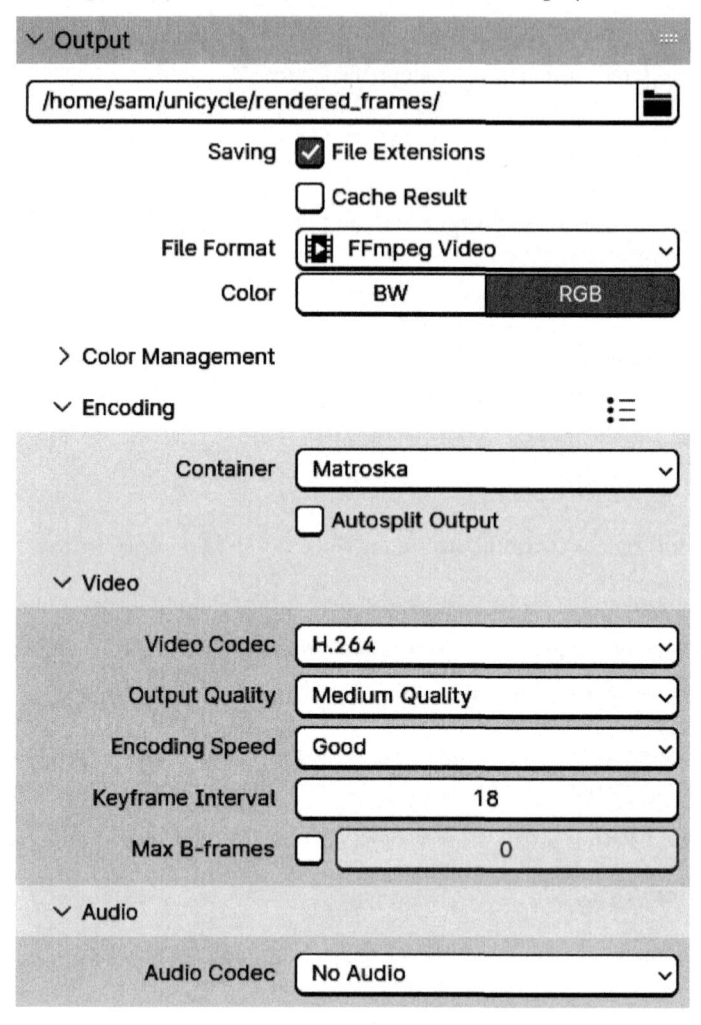

5.33: Output settings for video

Outputting a video

Press **Render** | **Render Animation** (*Ctrl + F12*).

That's all there is to it! Because we're "rendering" a pre-rendered image sequence this time, this job should not take more than a minute or two.

> **Tip**
> You can experiment with different containers, codecs, and quality settings to find the right combination of quality, file size, and support across different platforms and devices for your needs.

You're done! What you choose to do with your final video file is up to you, but I recommend letting other people watch it. That's usually the most satisfying way to view an animation. Otherwise, we wouldn't have bothered to render anything at all!

Summary

If you've rendered any still images in Blender before, much of what we covered in this chapter probably seemed redundant. It turns out that if you know how to render one frame in Blender and save it as an image, it's not much harder to render a few hundred more and convert them to a video. That's all a video is, really – just a bunch of frames displayed in rapid sequence to create the appearance of motion. Come to think of it, that's what an animation is, too.

In closing part one of this book, you have completed the technical essentials of making an animation in Blender and rendering the final product. By realizing the core concept of animation as mere numbers and images that change one frame at a time, you can animate anything you like… in theory. In practice, you'll probably want to read on to the next chapter, where we introduce a topic so dense it fills all of part two!

Questions

1. What makes the camera important for rendering?
2. Why do render engines have names? What's so special about them?
3. What are some ways of reducing the time it takes to render something?
4. Does Render Image (*F12*) produce different-looking images than Render Animation (*Ctrl + F12*)?
5. What does a lossy image format lose? Can we get it back?
6. What's the difference between an image and an image file? Where in Blender might we encounter an image, but not an image file?

7. Why would we take the extra step of outputting an image sequence before converting it to a video?
8. Earlier, we defined the word "render" to mean generating 2D images from 3D data. In what cases does it mean something else in Blender?
9. Which was it that we rendered in this chapter: the animation, the scene, the frames, the images, or the image sequence?

Part 2: Character Animation

Do you know how to walk? How to talk? Do you know how to stand, or sit, or pick something up with your hands? Do you know what face you're making at this very moment? Are you sure it's not weird?

If you answered "yes" to any of these questions, I don't believe you. Of course, I believe you can do these things. I'm sure you're very good at walking, talking, standing, sitting, picking things up, and making a not-weird face; you're so good you do it all without thinking, and that's the problem. You're not thinking. We do an awful lot of things without knowing how. Nowhere is this more apparent than in the field of character animation.

A 3D character is a complex system of interdependently moving parts, none of which move by anything such as instinct, reflex, or muscle memory. Every part must be positioned and keyed deliberately by the animator, just as we did with the objects we animated in Part One, only this time by the hundreds. If we do a good job, the character will look lifelike, as if her movement is just as spontaneous and natural as our own, but this requires that we think, really think, about how a body moves frame by frame. It means trying to animate a character walking... and realizing we don't know how to walk.

This part contains the following chapters:

- *Chapter 6, Linking and Posing a Character*
- *Chapter 7, Basic Character Animation*
- *Chapter 8, The Walk Cycle*
- *Chapter 9, Sound and Lip-Syncing*
- *Chapter 10, Prop Interaction with Dynamic Constraints*

6
Linking and Posing a Character

The preceding exercises in this book have all been leading up to this point. You are now prepared to learn how to animate a character!

What is a character? In literature, it's any person or being whose actions, thoughts, or words are expressed in the text. In filmmaking, a character is anyone portrayed by a cast member. In real life, it might be your uncle. He's such a character!

In 3D animation, a **character** has a more specific definition: a 3D model controlled by an **armature**. Bearing many analogs to an actual skeleton, an armature is a special object consisting of multiple **bones**, which, when moved, transform or deform the associated model. Together in one **collection**, the armature and all the objects it controls comprise the character or **character rig**. Character animation is the work of making the bones in a character's armature move in concert to make the character walk, jump, dance, or anything else we would have them do.

Creating a character for 3D animation is a separate project from animating one, and no less difficult! Character modeling is an advanced enough subject for a book on its own, another book could be written on building the armature, and attaching the said model to said armature might even merit a third book.

Luckily for us, we already have a character. Get ready to say hello to Rain...

In this chapter, you will learn how to do the following:

- Link a character into your scene
- Use the scripted interface for a character rig
- Pose a character
- Copy and save character poses

Technical requirements

There's no need to make a character from scratch – Blender Studio has provided a professionally-made character for anyone to download and use.

This character's name is **Rain**:

Figure 6.1: Rain

Rain comes ready to animate, with all of the features that professional animators expect in a human character rig but designed to be friendly to novice animators as well. Rain is licensed under a *Creative Commons CC-BY* license, which means that we can use her for any purpose in our works, so long as we give credit to the Blender Foundation, like so:

Rain Rig © Blender Foundation | `https://studio.blender.org/welcome/`

She can be downloaded for free here: `https://github.com/PacktPublishing/Realizing-3D-Animation-in-Blender`.

To get started, use the preceding URL to download the `.zip` file for Rain, and unpack the contents to a convenient place in your filesystem.

> **Important note**
> When unpacking the `.zip` file, make sure you unpack both the `maps` folder and `rain_v2_6_packt.blend` together to a single location. You can open `rain_v2_6_packt.blend` if you like, but do not save changes to it, as those changes may affect other files in the future!

Linking a character in a new scene

Before we jump into interacting with Rain's armature and sticking her in different poses, we must first explore some even more exciting topics: **linked libraries** and **file dependencies**. What fun!

Unlike previous chapters, where we opened a downloaded .blend file and immediately began working inside it, we won't be working directly on Rain's .blend file. If we did, we'd have to make a full copy of Rain – or her .blend file – for each animation she was used in. As we'll learn, this is bad practice for such a complex and valuable asset like Rain.

Instead, we'll create a new file that will reference the file containing Rain. This will make `rain_v2_6_packt.blend` a linked library.

Linked libraries

In Blender, the term *linked library* means a .blend file that contains data referenced by another .blend file, through the use of **File | Link**. The use of linked libraries is a technical process that professional studios (including the Blender Institute) apply in production whenever large or important assets like characters are used in an animation.

Every .blend file contains data, or **datablocks**, that can be linked or appended. These datablocks are organized into different categories for each type:

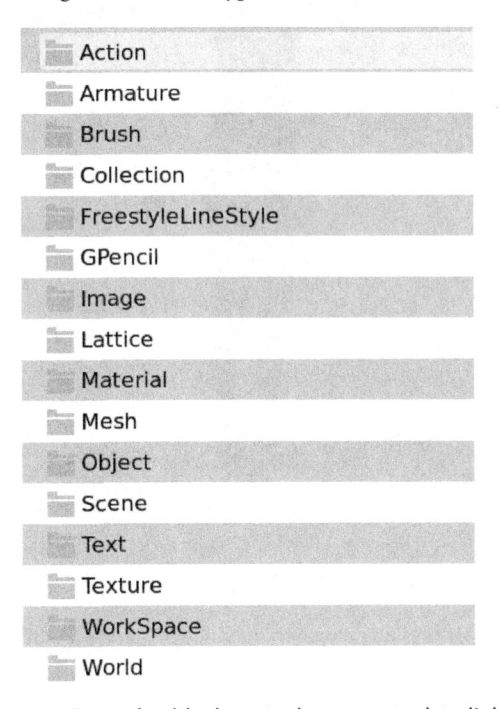

- Action
- Armature
- Brush
- Collection
- FreestyleLineStyle
- GPencil
- Image
- Lattice
- Material
- Mesh
- Object
- Scene
- Text
- Texture
- WorkSpace
- World

Figure 6.2: Some datablock types that appear when linking

Linking and Posing a Character

A character is comprised of multiple objects, which – if the character's creator has done a thorough job – exist in a single **collection** for easy linking. For Rain, that collection is called `CH-rain`.

Let's link that collection now:

1. Create a new file in Blender by going to **File** | **New** (*Ctrl + N*) | **General**.
2. Delete the object `Cube`.
3. Go to **File** | **Link**.
4. In the invoked file browser, find and select Rain's file, `rain_v2_6_packt.blend`.
5. Go to the folder labeled **Collection**.
6. Select and **Link** the collection `CH-rain`.

Under the default settings, this links the object collection `CH-rain` to our current file and automatically inserts a **collection instance**. Now Rain is in our scene!

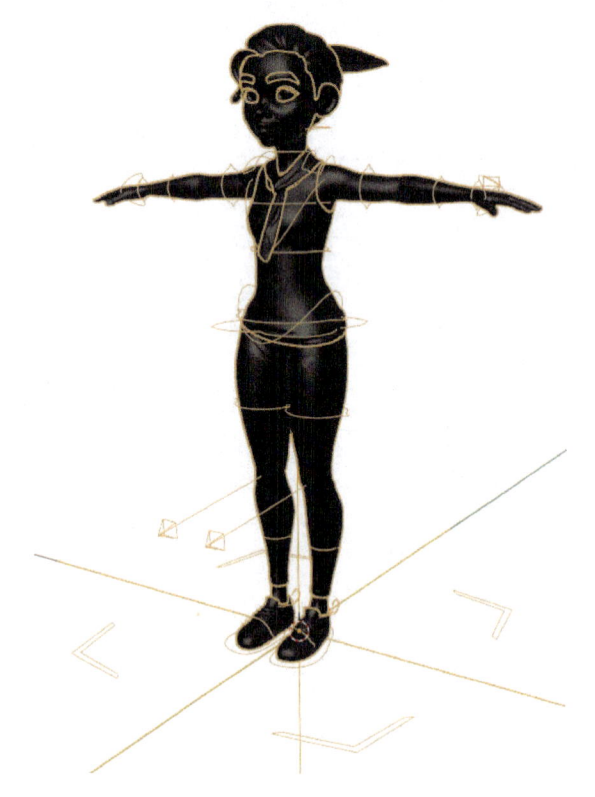

Figure 6.3: The linked collection instance of Rain in the 3D Viewport

Don't be worried if she looks a bit odd at first – we'll fix that later.

> **Important note**
>
> Collection instances are added at the 3D cursor like most other new objects. If your 3D cursor was not centered when you linked Rain, she won't be centered either. Use **Object | Clear | Location** (*Alt + G*) to center her.

Our current file is now using `rain_v2_6_packt.blend` as a linked library. Note that this does not directly affect the file `rain_v2_6_packt.blend`; it just means that we'll need to be a bit more careful with it than if we had appended the collection.

Linking versus appending

If you've ever used **File | Append** before, you know the other way of bringing something from one `.blend` file into another. At first glance, **Link** and **Append** may appear to have identical functions, but this isn't so. There's an essential distinction between the two that may catch an unwary user off guard: to **Link** is to create a dependency, whereas to **Append** is to create a redundant copy.

Appending is akin to duplicating. If we were to append Rain into our new scene instead of linking her, all of the data from `rain_v2_6_packt.blend` would be copied into our new file. This means duplicating every single datablock, right down to the material for Rain's shoelaces!

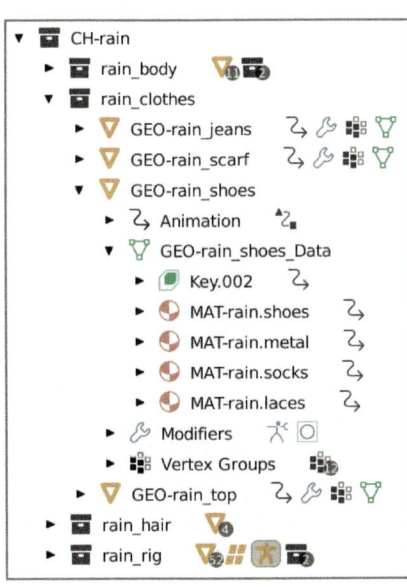

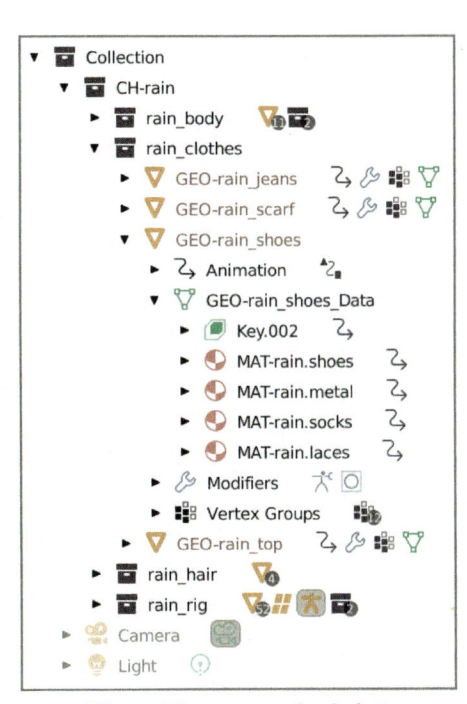

Figure 6.4: Visualization of data in both .blend files

Within our new file, we could modify any part of Rain however we liked (including her shoelaces) and forget about the original file from which she came. We'd effectively have two Rains instead of one.

On the other hand, by linking Rain, our new file depends on the old one. It must always reference Rain's data in `rain_v2_6_packt.blend`:

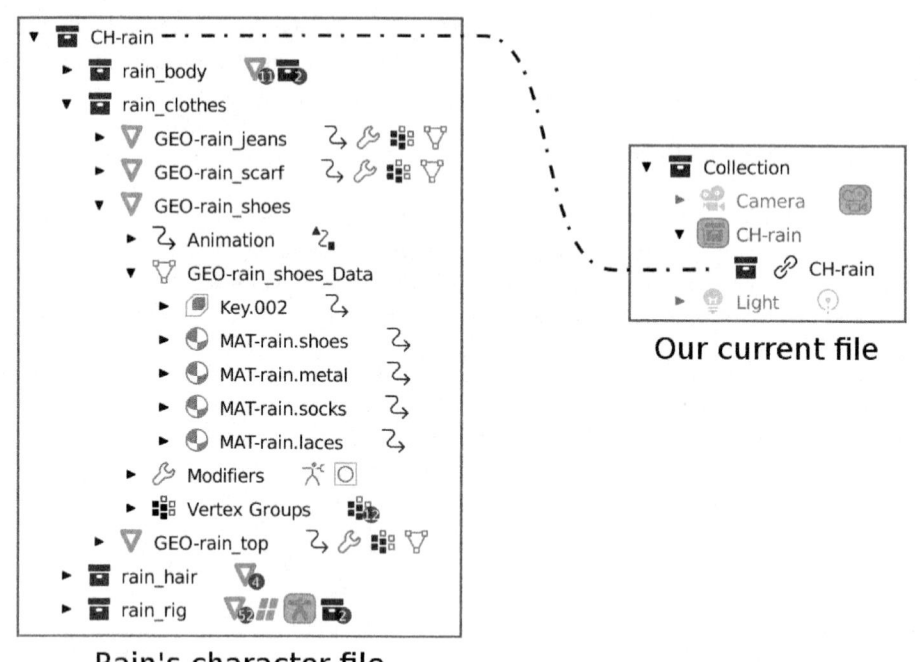

Figure 6.5: Visualization showing dependency between files

No permanent changes to Rain can be made unless we edit that original file. If the original file gets lost, Rain will disappear from our current scene as well.

It might seem like **Append** is a more convenient choice than **Link**, but appending is generally better for reusing minor assets from other projects, such as materials or simple models. For works as complex as Rain, appending is a cluttered way of working. The scenes we will create in *Part 2* need only to store the work we do on posing and keying; we don't need a unique version of Rain's shoelace material in every scene. At best, it would make our files larger than they need to be; at worst, it would expose all of Rain's data, making her vulnerable to errors that are difficult to repair. For our chapters on character animation, we'll stick to linking Rain instead of appending her.

Although it's often the most elegant solution, using a linked library does come with an important responsibility: to avoid breaking our new file's linked library, we need to make sure one file can always find the other using the **file path** it remembers.

> **Important note**
> File paths are much like web addresses, and they can break just as easily if you move or delete files recklessly. Whether it's an image, a sound, or a linked library, if a file path leads to a file that isn't there, its data will be lost from the `.blend` file that depends on it.

File paths – absolute versus relative

If the data in `rain_v2_6_packt.blend` is linked in our current file, but not stored within it, how will Blender go looking for the necessary data from within our current file?

The answer can be examined by going to **Blender File** in the Outliner:

Figure 6.6: The Outliner showing an absolute path to Rain's .blend file

Next to the chain-link icon indicating a linked library, you'll see the file path to `rain_v2_6_packt.blend` on your computer's filesystem. If you haven't saved the current file yet, this will be an **absolute file path** – a complete address that starts at the root directory of your computer's file system.

> **Tip**
> In Mac and Linux, the root directory is signified by a / at the beginning of a file path. In Windows, it will be a letter drive, such as C: or D:.

Absolute file paths can be quite long and contain the names of folders, which can vary between each user. On the other hand, a relative file path begins at the location of the file that refers to it. To load her image textures, for example, Rain uses relative file paths to image files in the `maps` folder.

> **Tip**
> Relative file paths in Blender begin with //, and may also include a ../ or two. The ../ makes the address go "out" one level into the parent folder. If you see too many ../ in a file path, it may indicate bad organization.

Blender prefers to use relative file paths by default, but they only work if the current file is saved. Let's save our current file to see the difference it makes:

1. Click **File** | **Save As** (*Shift + Ctrl + S*).
2. Save your current file in the same directory as `rain_v2_6_packt.blend`.

Now we're using a **relative file path** that is much shorter:

Figure 6.7: The same link but with a relative path

Because we saved our current file to the same directory as the library, the relative path only needs to contain the filename – that is, `rain_v2_6_packt.blend`. So long as we keep these files together in one folder, we don't have to worry about breaking such a simple path.

> **Tip**
> You can choose what type of file path to use by enabling or disabling **Relative Path** in the sidebar (*N*) of Blender's **File Browser**.

Now that we're aware of the explicit relationship between our current file and the file on which it depends, we can turn our attention solely to our current file.

Making a library override

Currently, Rain is a "black box". None of her linked data can be altered and her limbs cannot be moved. This is the default state of instances of linked object collections, which are essentially just Empty-type objects set to instantiate a collection. We can move her around like a chess piece, but if we want to pose and animate Rain as intended, we'll need to access her armature object, `RIG-rain`.

To access this object from within the collection instance, we must create something called a **library override**:

1. Select the object `CH-rain`.
2. Go to **Object** | **Library Override** | **Make**.

Note the distinct icon that appears next to the datablocks of overridden libraries:

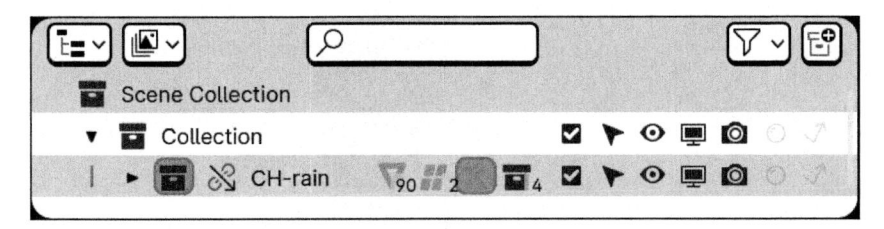

Figure 6.8: Library Override

Library Override allows us to select specific objects within a linked collection and manipulate their properties. We are now able to select Rain's armature object, `RIG-rain`. Rain was built to be controlled solely using `RIG-rain`, so we won't need to select any other object in her collection.

We're nearly ready to begin posing Rain, but she still looks a bit odd. Like many fully-featured character rigs, Rain has a couple of minor quirks that require a few more steps to fix.

Re-booting Rain

Because we just linked Rain, she doesn't look as good as she does in her original file. Depending on your 3D Viewport settings, her materials may look all black, or her eyes might look all glossy. Though her Python scripts were automatically linked with her, they were not automatically executed, so we don't see the helpful **CloudRig** interface for her armature yet, either.

After creating the library override Rain's collection, follow these steps to access Rain's Python-scripted interface and improve her appearance in the 3D Viewport:

1. **Save** (*Ctrl + S*) your `.blend` file.
2. Close and re-open your file or use **File** | **Revert**.

> **Important note**
> Python scripts might be blocked by Blender when you reload your file, which will cause a loss of functionality in Rain. To keep them running, click **Allow Execution** if prompted by Blender. Better yet, go to **User Preferences** and enable **Save & Load** | **Auto Run Python Scripts**.

This should be the only time you'll have to restart the file. Now Rain looks much nicer:

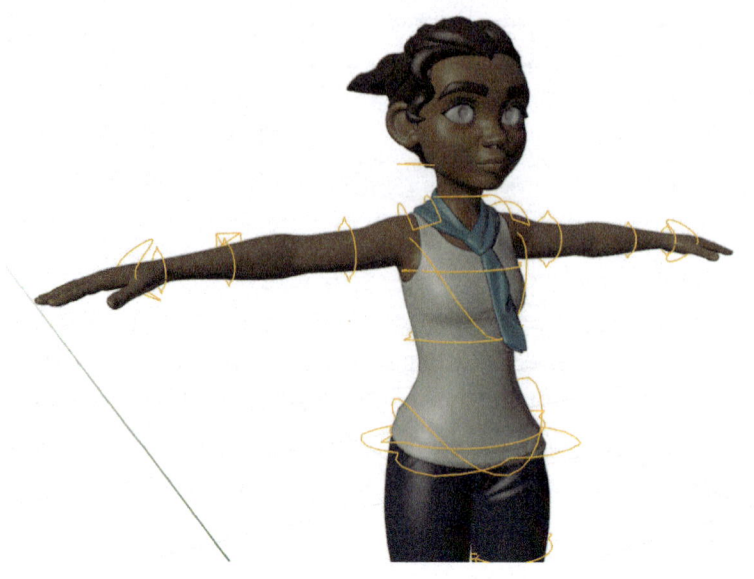

Figure 6.9: Rain in the 3D Viewport

> **Tip**
> Rain's eyes have a glossy layer of geometry, which makes them look odd with certain **Viewport Shading** settings. Switch to the **Material Preview** Viewport shading method for now or read onward to find the **Dummy Eyes** property in Rain's **Outfits** panel.

We're done with all the busy work of linking Rain; now she's fully ready to be used as a character in our scene!

Understanding Rain's armature

Having completed all the steps to link Rain into our scene, we now have access to her armature, which we can use to bend her limbs, apply expressions to her face, and otherwise move her around. An armature is a complex object – probably the most complex thing an animator has to work with. We'll need to understand just what an armature is, and where to find the Python-scripted interface that will help us simplify Rain before we begin working with her armature directly.

The art of rigging Rain

An armature may also be called a **rig**. The work of creating a rig for a character model is known as **rigging**, which is done by a **rigger**. A good rigger is an animator's best friend, as a good rig is more than just a skeleton that deforms a model – it's an entire interface for the animator.

Every character rig is different. Rigs vary in design and complexity depending on the style of the character, the type of creature it is, the personal choices of the rigger, and the needs of the animator who will be animating it:

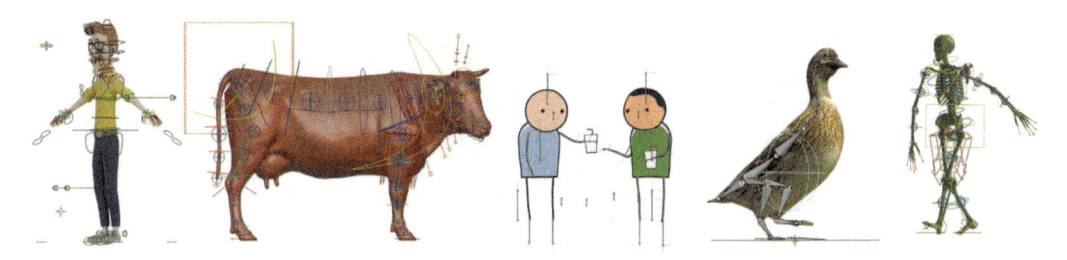

Figure 6.10: Some different character rigs in Blender

Nevertheless, there are some general conventions for rigging. Rain was chosen for this book not only because she makes it easy to get started with character animation, but also because her rig serves as a fairly typical example of other biped rigs you may come across.

> **Tip**
> There are tons of other character rigs available for Blender, created by individuals and published on various sites throughout the worldwide Blender community. Many of them, like Rain, are free to download and use. Beware, though – a character rigged by an amateur can be a nightmare to animate.

Everything is a bone

In Blender, the elements in an armature are all called **bones**, even if they don't look like bones. Rain's armature has over 2,000 bones; all organized in a complex system of parents, constraints, and drivers:

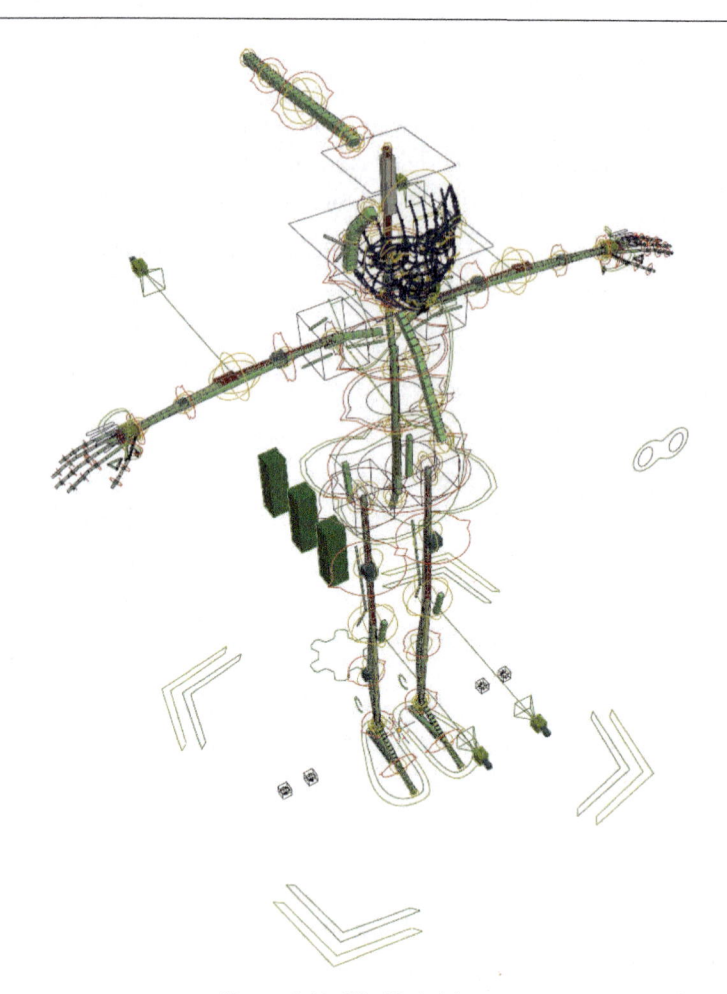

Figure 6.11: All of Rain's bones

That's 10 times as many bones as there are in a real human skeleton! Thankfully, most of these are hidden by the rigger; we're not meant to use all of them.

The bones intended for use by the animator have been modeled, colored, and organized into different categories for convenience. These are essentially control bones that move Rain indirectly, like sticks at the end of the strings on a puppet.

Understanding Rain's armature | 167

So, how many of those control bones are there? The answer is just shy of 400:

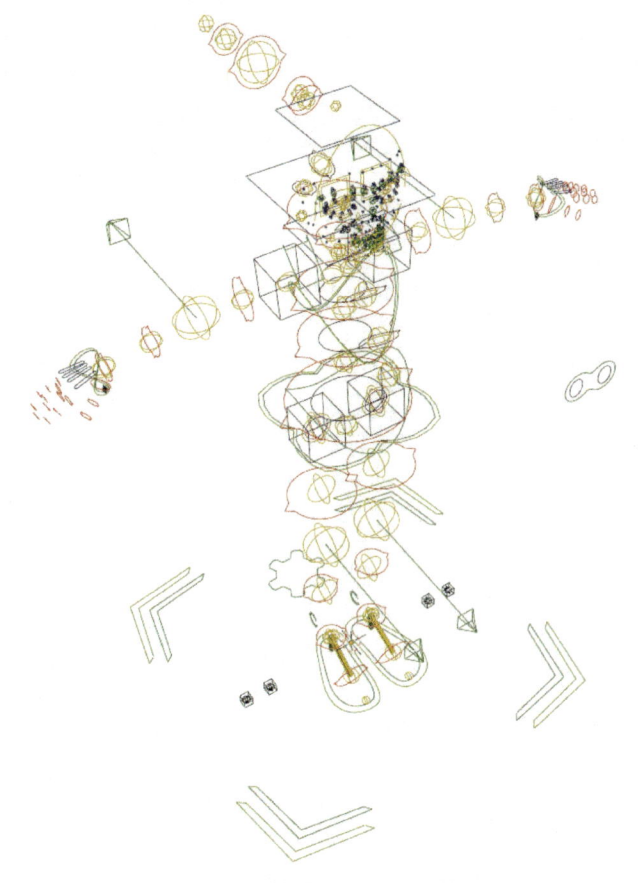

Figure 6.12: All of Rain's control bones

That's still a lot of bones! Even the few that are currently visible might be enough to seem overwhelming. We should simplify things a little. Read on to find out how you can reveal all of Rain's control bones, and then read a little further to find out how to hide them again.

168   Linking and Posing a Character

The CloudRig interface

Rain comes with a script called **CloudRig**, which provides a helpful control panel in the sidebar (*N*) of the 3D Viewport:

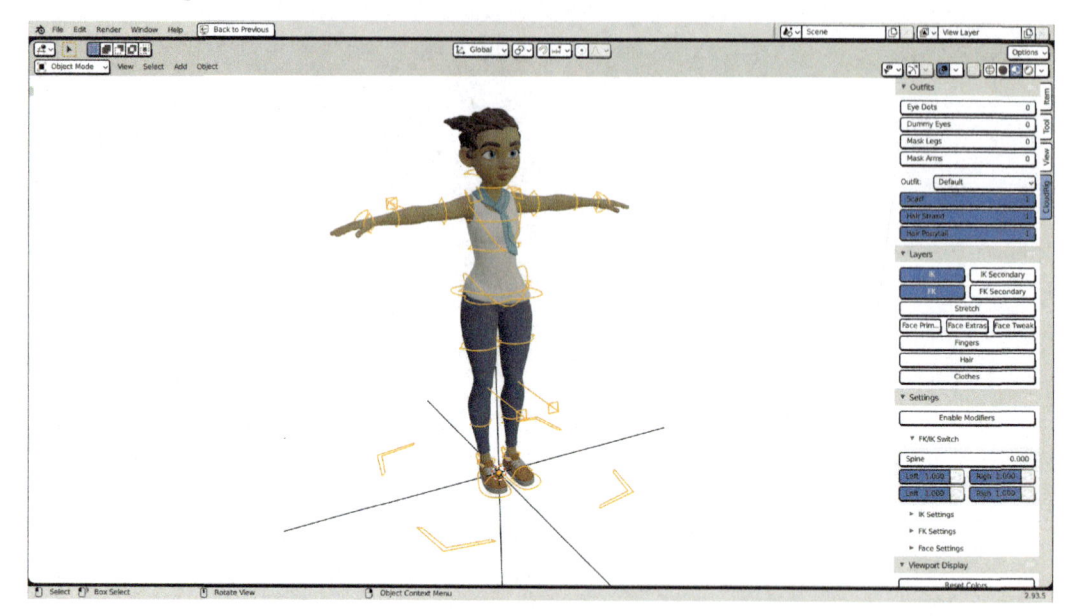

Figure 6.13: Rain with the CloudRig interface on the right

The tab for **CloudRig** is accessible whenever Rain's armature is the active object. All its available buttons, functions, and properties are visible regardless of which bone is selected.

Scripted control panels like these are often provided with advanced character rigs, and their layout and features are as varied as the rigs themselves. While not necessary for Rain to work, **CloudRig** conveniently organizes features and properties of Rain that would otherwise be scattered across various bones and areas of the interface.

> **Important note**
> **CloudRig** is not an add-on, and does not connect to any "cloud." It is executed from a text datablock that was linked along with the rest of Rain's collection.

Using the features in this panel, you can do the following:

- Toggle the visibility of parts of Rain's model
- Toggle the visibility of different groups of bones
- Alter the behavior of certain bones, their relationships, and the influence they have on Rain's model

Now, about those bones – we'll want to hide most of Rain's bones until we're ready to pose them, so we'll begin by doing that.

Armature layers

It bears repeating that Rain's armature has a lot of bones. For the sake of the animator's sanity, Rain's bones have been organized by category into different **armature layers**. As you work, you'll want to toggle the visibility of these different layers depending on what part of Rain you want to focus on.

Normally, to do this we'd have to go to the armature's **Object Data Properties** in the **Properties Editor** and click on a list of layers here:

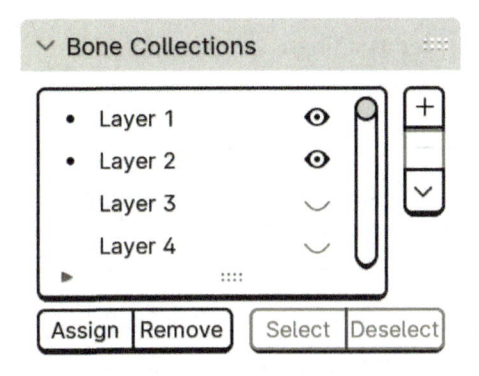

Figure 6.14: Rain's "Bone Collections"

> **Important note**
> As of Blender 4.0, armature layers are now called **Bone Collections**, but we will refer to them as layers for the rest of this book.

CloudRig gives us much easier access to the most important of these in the **Layers** panel:

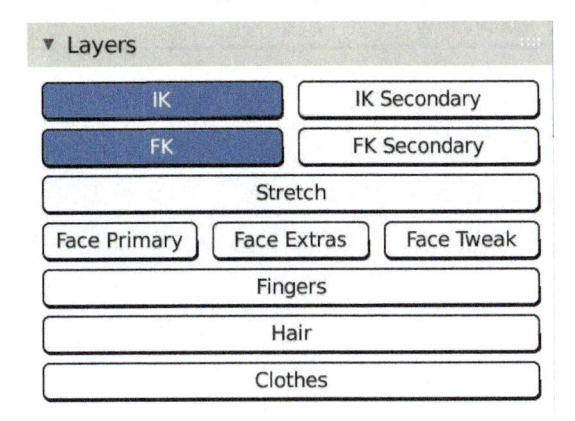

Figure 6.15: Rain's armature layers, labeled

That's not all the armature layers, of course – just the ones intended to be used by the animator. Every bone you will need to pose Rain (and a bunch more you may never need to touch) is in one of those layers. If you're looking for a bone that isn't here, either the rigger has failed or you're in over your head!

If you're curious as to what all of the bones in these layers look like, as shown in *Figure 6.12*, you may as well go ahead and click on all the layers in this panel. You'll quickly see why hiding armature layers is so helpful. It's *a lot* of bones. We'll address their functions and behaviors as we go along. Until then, let's hide all but the **IK** (short for **Inverse Kinetics**) layer for now:

1. Find the **Layers** panel in the **CloudRig** tab of the sidebar (*N*).
2. Disable all armature layers except **IK**.

That should make things easier for us at first as we start posing Rain.

> **Important note**
> Hiding/showing armature layers is done purely for our convenience as we work. Bones continue to affect the model whether they are hidden or not, but so long as they're visible, we can accidentally select them and potentially move the wrong thing.

To make things even easier, we're going to use another one of Rain's features to hide some of her geometry.

Preparing the appearance of Rain in the 3D Viewport

Take a look at **Outfits**, the first panel in **CloudRig**:

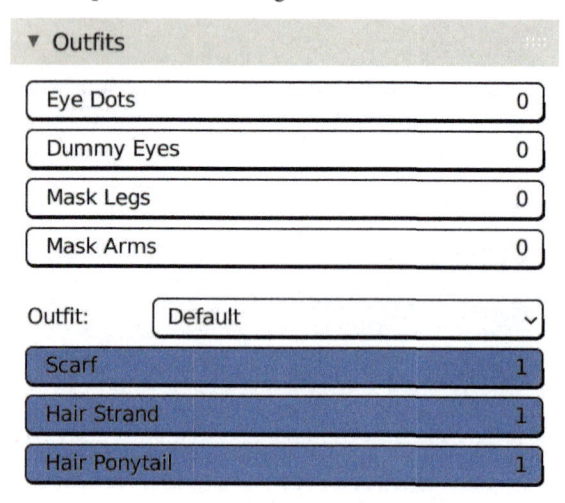

▼ Outfits	
Eye Dots	0
Dummy Eyes	0
Mask Legs	0
Mask Arms	0
Outfit:	Default
Scarf	1
Hair Strand	1
Hair Ponytail	1

Figure 6.16: The Outfits panel

This panel is less fun than it sounds; Rain doesn't currently have any outfits other than the one she's already wearing. Still, what we do have are some useful settings that determine the visibility of different parts of Rain.

In certain cases, hiding these parts of Rain can make it easier for us to pose and animate her. For instance, Rain's hair and scarf are poseable parts of her model, much like her arms and legs, but since clothes and hair don't do much except hang around, we typically pose and animate them last. Until that point, they're a visual distraction.

> **Important note**
> The properties in **Outfits**, though they appear to be expressed as *integers*, are essentially *Boolean*. Think of them as checkboxes; 1 means enabled and 0 means disabled.

Let's hide some things now:

1. Find the **CloudRig | Outfits** panel.
2. Disable **Scarf**, **Hair Strand**, and **Hair Ponytail**.

   Rain's new pixie cut and her lack of a scarf mean that she has fewer loose parts to worry about as we do initial work on her pose:

Figure 6.17: Rain with less hair and no scarf

3. We can go even further by enabling **Mask Arms**.

Now we've *really* simplified Rain's model:

Figure 6.18: They're gone!

The ability to hide the arms and/or legs might seem like an odd feature to have, but you'd be surprised how useful it can be to hide these parts until you're ready to pose them.

> **Tip**
>
> Consider enabling **Dummy Eyes** as well. These "fake" eyes don't look as nice as Rain's "real" eyes do when rendered, but they do make it easier to see the direction of her gaze in the **Solid** Viewport shading method as we work on her facial expressions.

We've simplified Rain as much as we need to. As for the rest of the **CloudRig** interface, it's easier to learn those functions as we put Rain into her first pose!

Posing an armature

Like the objects we animated in previous chapters, the bones in an armature all have location, rotation, and scale properties. Transforming one or more bones directly is called **posing**, the first step in character animation. Together, the given positions of the bones in an armature at a single point in time are referred to as a **pose**. As we animate Rain in later chapters, we'll put her in one pose, key the properties of those bones we just posed, then move on to the next pose at another frame, key the properties for those bones, and so on.

That's character animation. It's not all that different from animating objects! This time though, our objects are bones, there are hundreds of them, and they're connected in a complex system that may not seem intuitive at first. Easy, right? Maybe not. Before animating Rain, we'd better spend a section or two just on how to pose her.

Our first exercise will take Rain from a *T* pose to an idle, natural-looking standing position:

Figure 6.19: Resting "T pose" to idle standing pose

If we want it to look natural, even a simple standing pose requires manipulating a lot of bones.

Pose mode

To start posing Rain, select her armature and go to **Pose Mode** (*Ctrl + Tab*) within the 3D Viewport:

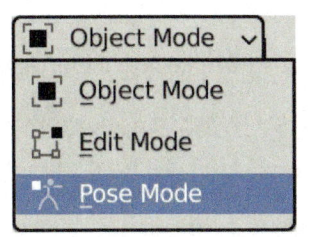

Figure 6.20: Pose Mode in the Interaction Mode menu

In **Pose Mode**, bones may be selected and transformed much like regular objects in **Object Mode**, using the same standard controls for **Move** (*G*), **Rotate** (*R*), and **Scale** (*S*).

Posing an armature in **Pose Mode** is technically distinct from editing an armature in **Edit Mode**, which is what the rigger does. We can't edit the bones in a linked armature object and we shouldn't ever need to while animating.

> **Important note**
> While in **Pose Mode**, you cannot add or select other objects; you must return to **Object Mode** to do so.

Because Rain's control bones have complex relationships and do not directly deform her mesh, the result of transforming a given bone is not always predictable. Though the shape of a given bone and its location on Rain's body offers clues as to that bone's function, the only sure way to know what a bone does is to see what happens when we move it.

> **Tip**
> Don't be afraid to move a given bone to see what it does. You can always **Undo** (*Ctrl + Z*), or use right-click or *Esc* to cancel the transformation before you confirm it. Additionally, in the next section, I'll show you how any change you make to a bone in **Pose Mode** can be reset.

Posing the torso and hips

Which bone do we start with? When initially posing a character, it's often best to start with the bone that controls the overall position of the torso. In Rain's case, this is `MSTR-Pelvis_Parent`. If you're having trouble finding it, it's the four-leaf-clover-shaped bone around Rain's hips.

> **Tip**
> To view the names of Rain's bones at a glance, go to the armature's **Object Data Properties** area, find the **Viewport Display** panel, and enable **Show | Names**. You'll probably want to disable this later when we un-hide more armature layers, though.

We're going to use `MSTR-Pelvis_Parent` to give Rain's legs a little room to bend:

1. Enter **Pose Mode** and select `MSTR-Pelvis_Parent`.
2. Move `MSTR-Pelvis_Parent` down about `-0.02` meters on the global *Z* axis.

Now let's swing Rain's hips to her right using the saddle-shaped bone known as `MSTR-Hips`:

1. Select `MSTR-Hips`.
2. Rotate `MSTR-Hips` about `10` degrees on the global *Y* axis.

Even with these subtle changes to just two bones, Rain appears more relaxed and natural. She's beginning to look less like a mannequin and more like a real person!

Figure 6.21: Subtle difference in pose

Note that both `MSTR-Pelvis` and `MSTR-Hips` move Rain's hips, but one is the child of the other and has a more localized effect. This extreme example shows the difference:

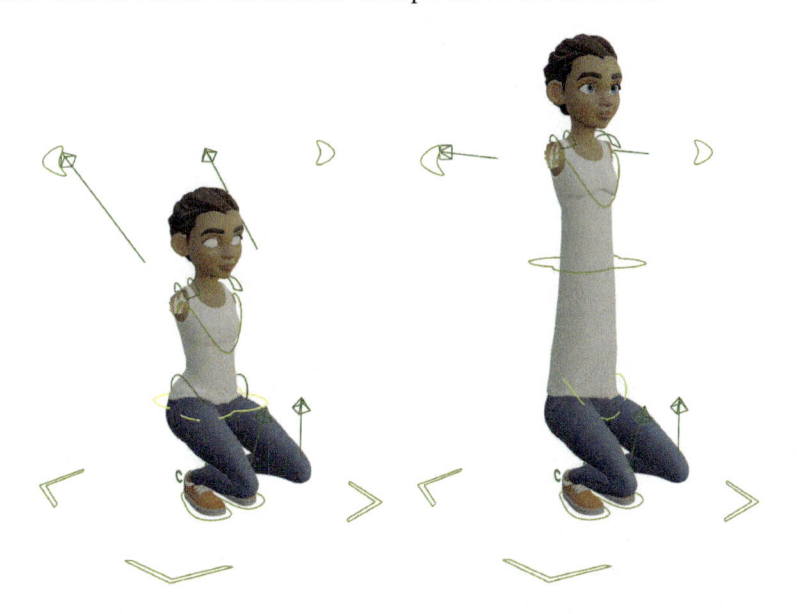

Figure 6.22: Making Rain squat with MSTR-Pelivs versus MSTR-Hips

Just because a bone can be moved doesn't always mean it ought to be! That said, you should feel free to experiment. In pose mode, all changes to bones are reversible, and there's no danger of accidentally deleting or breaking anything. If any bone gets bent too far out of shape, just remember the following operators to reset it…

"Un-posing" a posed bone

Every bone has a **rest position** – the initial position it starts with before we transform it in **Pose Mode**. After posing bones, we'll often want to reset them to their rest positions later. This is useful for "relaxing" a bone out of one pose before putting it in the next one, to make sure that Rain doesn't walk around with any slightly dislocated joints, or just to return to a state of sanity after getting silly…

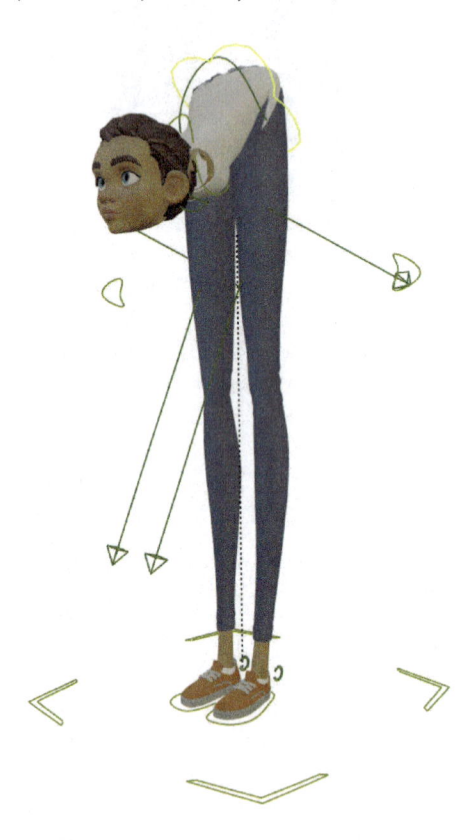

Figure 6.23: There's an easy way to fix this

In the preceding example, I've put `MSTR-Pelvis` in a ridiculous place. To fix this, there's no need to try and manually put `MSTR-Pelvis` back where it was, or to reset all its transform values numerically. All I need to do is select the offending bone and go to **Pose | Clear Transform**:

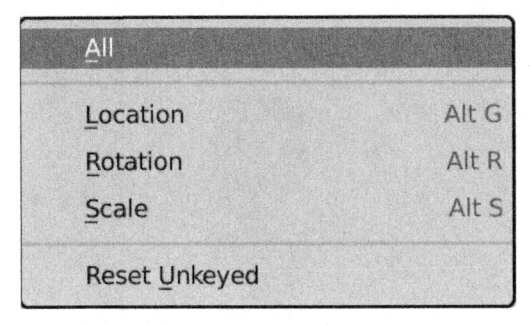

Figure 6.24: Clear Transform operators

Using **Pose** | **Clear Transform** | **All** puts `MSTR-Pelvis` back to where it started, a position from which it is easier to start posing again.

> **Tip**
>
> In addition to **Pose** | **Clear Transform** | **All**, the three main **Pose** | **Transform** operators (**Move** (*G*), **Rotate** (*R*), and **Scale** (*S*)) each have an associated **Pose** | **Clear** Transform operator: **Location** (*Alt + G*), **Rotation** (*Alt + R*), and **Scale** (*Alt + S*), respectively. These work the same as the **Object** | **Clear** operators in **Object Mode**, but they're especially useful in character animation.

If we know how to quickly reset any bone, we've nothing to fear when it comes to experimenting while posing. Any change we make in **Pose Mode**, no matter how absurd or distorted, can be reversed.

IK bones

Look at Rain's feet and notice how they remained stationary while we moved her hips and torso, causing her knees to bend. Currently, Rain's feet are controlled by the `MSTR-Foot_Parent.L` and `MSTR-Foot_Parent.R` bones, which move independently from the bones we just moved earlier by default.

> **Tip**
>
> Because people and creatures tend to be symmetrical on the *X* axis, a lot of armature bones come in mirrored pairs – one for the left-hand side and one for the right-hand side. The bones in these pairs will have identical names except for the suffix of *L* or *R*.

Let's see what happens when we move the bone for the left foot:

1. Select `MSTR-Foot_Parent.L` (this is the shoe-shaped bone around Rain's left shoe).
2. Rotate the bone out about 20 degrees on the global *Z* axis.
3. Move the bone to Rain's left, about 0.2 meters on the global *X* axis.
4. Move the bone back about 0.1 meters on the global *Y* axis.

A few more asymmetries contribute to the relaxed look of Rain's pose:

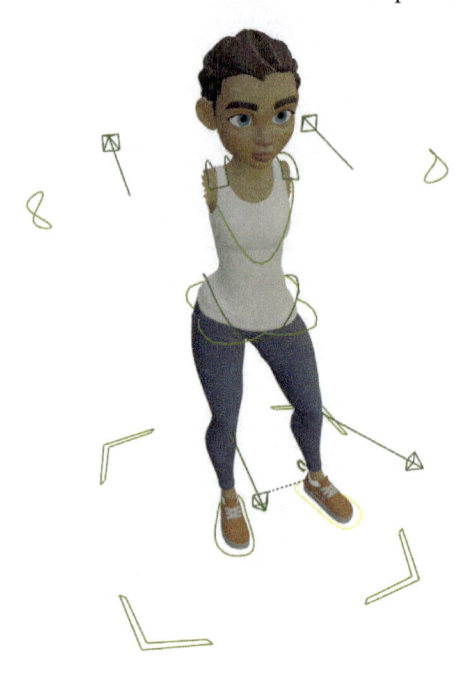

Figure 6.25: A casual, natural-looking leg stance

Have you noticed it, by the way? The small miracle that happens each time we move these bones? It's not about the bones we moved, but the bones we didn't have to directly move: namely, any bones in the legs themselves. With the help of a special type of constraint, a hidden chain of connected bones in each leg uses the relative position of the hips and feet to determine how the legs will stretch or bend at the knee.

This mechanic is known as **IK**, and without it, animating a "simple" action such as jumping or walking would be quite a headache. With *IK*, we can set the location of two bones acting as independent control points and let the rig automatically bend or stretch the bones in between. Imagine having to fine-tune the rotation of a thigh and a shin bone instead, just to keep the foot from shifting on the ground as the torso moved. It would be enough to make most animators quit!

IK hands

Rain's armature has five **IK chains** – that is, she has five main parts that can be controlled by an *IK* mechanism. The first two control her left and right legs; these are arguably the limbs that need *IK* the most. Another two are in her arms, bending the elbows to account for the relative positions of the hands and shoulders. Finally, a fifth can be used to bend or stretch the spine using the relative positions of the hips and chest.

Like the legs, the *IK* mechanics for Rain's arms are enabled by default. Her hands are exactly where we left them before we hid their geometry:

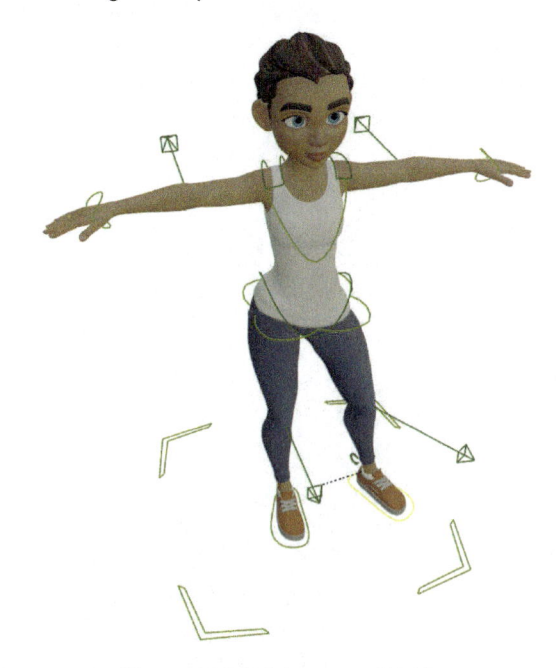

Figure 6.26: Rain's arms, unhidden

A bit distracting... now you see why it's helpful to keep parts hidden sometimes.

Let's unhide Rain's arms now and use another *IK* bone to rest her hand on her hip:

1. Go to the **Outfits** panel and disable **Mask Arms**.
2. Select `IK-Hand_Parent.R` (the saddle-shaped bone around Rain's right hand).
3. Move and rotate `IK-Hand_Parent.R` so that the back of Rain's right hand rests comfortably on her right hip.

Rain's right thumb should now be pointing behind her:

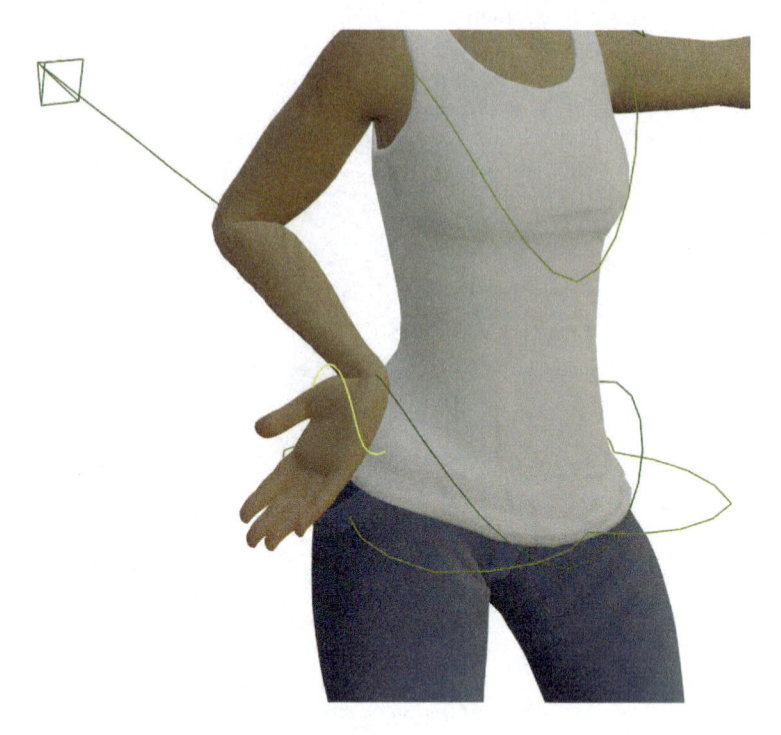

Figure 6.27: Rain's new hand pose

That's the beginning of a comfortable pose, but Rain's wrist, along with the rest of Rain's right arm, doesn't look very comfortable at all.

Ik pole targets

The algorithm that powers an *IK* constraint is referred to as an **IK solver**, in that the intermediate bones must offer a "solution" for how they ought to bend given the relative positions of the two independent target points at each end of the *IK* chain. After we moved Rain's hand, the *IK* solver gave us such a solution, though not a very good one this time. After bending the elbow just the right amount, the *IK* solver leaves one last thing ambiguous: in what direction should the elbow point?

That question can be answered using an **IK Pole Target**:

1. Select `IK-Pole_Forearm.R` (the bone at the end of a line that makes it appear to "pull" the right elbow).

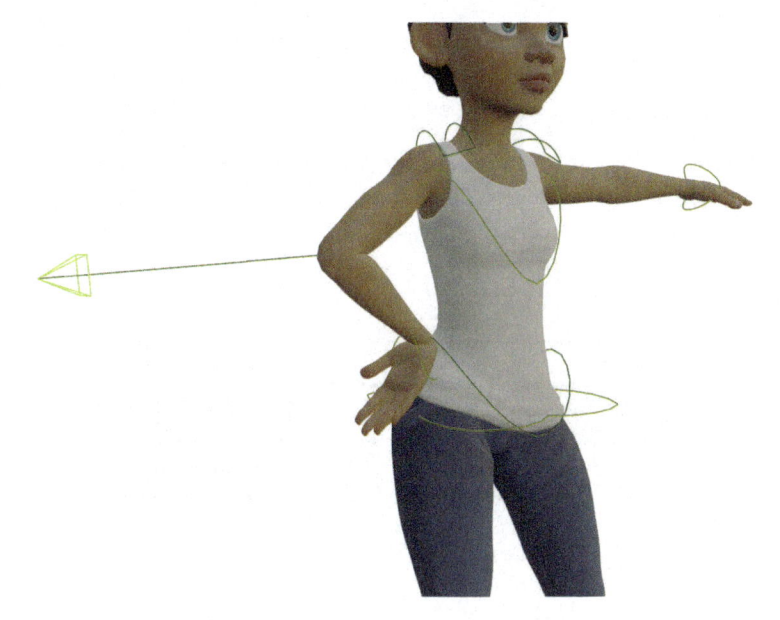

2. Move the bone outward and forward so that it makes Rain's elbow stick out toward her right:

Figure 6.28: A relaxed-looking elbow pose

That looks much better – more like what your arm does if you try to make the same pose yourself. In fact, why not try that right now as a reference?

Our idle pose is coming along, but the most glaring issue remaining is Rain's opposite arm. Next, we're going to make that arm hang naturally, but not with *IK* bones.

FK bones

We won't always want to use the bones in the *IK* layer to pose each of Rain's limbs. For every problem "solved" by an *IK* solver, there is often an equal drawback. What if, for instance, we want Rain's left arm to just hang straight down? An *IK* solver is unnecessary and cumbersome if we don't care about the exact location of Rain's left hand. All we want is for it to dangle at the end of Rain's left arm. We're more concerned about the angle of the left elbow than the position of the left hand; we want it to stay straight without bending or stretching – the opposite problem we had with the right arm!

As an advanced character rig, Rain has multiple ways in which her limbs can be posed. What we need is not *Inverse Kinematics*, but **Forward Kinematics**, or *FK*. For each of the five *IK* chains in Rain's rig, there's an *FK* chain of bones that may be used instead.

It will be easy to see the difference between *IK* and *FK* when we move our first *FK* bones, but we'll need to unhide them and enable their influence first. Let's turn our attention back to those bones in the *FK* layer that we initially hid.

Switching from IK to FK

When it comes to moving a chain of connected bones, *IK* and *FK* are opposite and irreconcilable methods with totally opposing logic. Both systems require separate chains of hidden bones. To give influence over a limb to one chain, we must take away influence from the other.

By default, Rain's arms and legs are controlled solely by *IK* bones, and her corresponding *FK* bones will have no effect. To determine whether a given limb is affected by its *FK* or *IK* bones, use the following properties in the **CloudRig** interface:

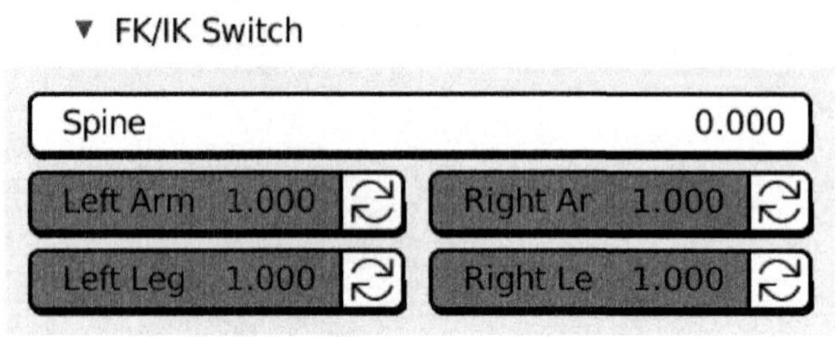

Figure 6.29: The FK/IK Switch panel

1. Enable the **FK** armature layer.
2. Find the **FK/IK** section in the **Settings** panel.
3. Set **FK/IK Switch | Left Arm** to 0.0.

You should see Rain's left arm shift from following one set of bones to following the other. This arm is now an *FK* arm, and we're ready to use its *FK* bones.

> **Tip**
> **FK/IK Switch** values tend to be either 0.0 for *FK* or 1.0 for *IK*. The values in between exist primarily for brief, smooth transitions between *FK* and *IK* when the property is animated. Rarely should you ever need to set a value of, say, 0.3.

Posing FK bones

Now, we can pose Rain's left arm using *FK*:

1. Select FK-Upperarm_Parent.L (the bone that looks like an armband around Rain's upper left arm).
2. Rotate FK-Upperarm_Parent.L down about 75 degrees on the global *Y* axis.

Rain's left hand should now touch or hover over her left thigh:

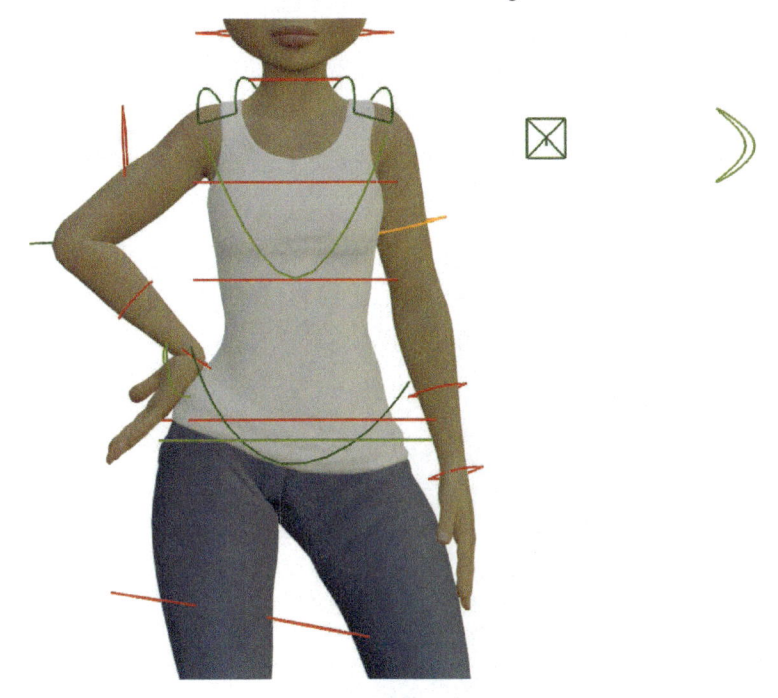

Figure 6.30: Left arm pose

That was easy! Using *FK* tends to be simpler than *IK*. *FK* bones give us direct control of joints and have straightforward relationships; `FK-Upperarm_Parent.L` is the parent of `FK-Forearm.L`, which is the parent of `FK-Hand.L`, and so on.

> **Tip**
> As opposed to *IK* bones, most of which are meant to be moved and rotated, the *FK* bones in Rain's rig are typically only meant to be rotated. Though they can sometimes be moved as well, we should generally do so only to make subtle corrections.

The FK spine

The *FK* bones that run along Rain's torso are enabled by default. Let's use them now to add some curvature to her spine, starting with the *FK* bone at the beginning of the chain and moving up:

1. Select `FK-Spine` (the belt around Rain's hips).
2. Rotate `FK-Spine` about 5 degrees on the global *Y* axis. This will make Rain lean to her left initially.

3. Select `FK-RibCage` (the next one up) and rotate it about -5 degrees, in the opposite direction on the global *Y* axis.
4. Continuing up the chain, rotate `FK-Chest` about -5 degrees on the global *Y* axis.
5. Rotate `FK-Neck` another -5 degrees on the global *Y* axis.
6. Finally, rotate `FK-Head` about 5 degrees on the global *Y* axis to tilt her head back to the left.

This gives a nice S-shaped curve to Rain's stance:

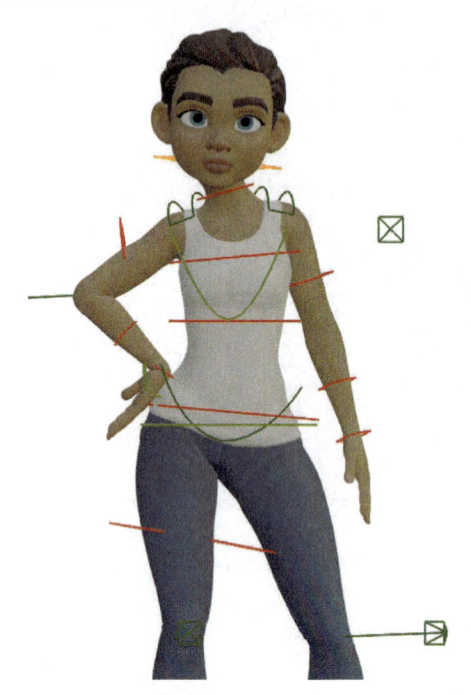

Figure 6.31: Effect of posing the spine

However, the work we put into posing Rain's left arm has been sullied – it no longer hangs like it used to. We can address this using another one of Rain's features.

Shoulders and FK Hinge

The elements in a parent/child relationship not only have dependencies – they also have **inheritance**; that is, the child inherits its transformation from its parent. This is true for bones and objects alike, but it's important for *FK* bones in cases such as ours.

When *FK* is used, the upper arm indirectly inherits its rotation from the shoulder. When we rotate Rain's left shoulder (or cause it to rotate), it rotates the left arm rigidly, as though it were part of the same *FK* chain. This is desirable in some cases and not in others, so the rigger has given us the ability to choose whether certain *FK* bones should inherit their rotation or not.

Using Hinge

When an *FK* bone doesn't inherit rotation from its parent further up the chain, the effect is referred to as **Hinge**. Try shrugging your own shoulders as a reference; even though you've just rotated your clavicles, your arms stayed hanging at roughly the same angle.

That's **FK Hinge**. Let's try it out on Rain:

1. Find the **FK Settings** section of the **Settings** panel in the **CloudRig** interface.
2. Set **FK Hinge | Left Arm** to `1.0`.

Rain's left arm is back to where it was (the right arm is still using *IK*, so it handled all our changes to the spine without a problem). **FK Hinge** is useful in that it allows us to adjust a character's spine and shoulders without affecting the rotation of their *FK* arms.

Shoulders – "the eyebrows of the body"

Now that neither arm inherits rotation from its shoulder, we can pose the shoulder bones more freely:

1. Rotate `MSTR-Clavicle.R` down and forward a bit to relax Rain's right shoulder.
2. Rotate `MSTR-Clavicle.L` up a smidge to balance out her right shoulder and accentuate the curvature in her stance.

Now Rain's overall pose is complete!

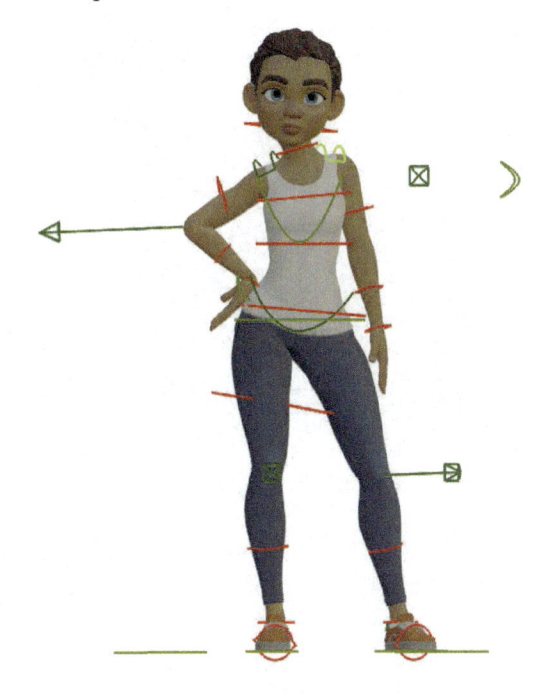

Figure 6.32: A nearly finished pose

The sheer number of bones and additional armature layers in Rain's rig can be daunting, but it turns out that just the *IK* and *FK* bones get us more than halfway to a finished pose.

Fingers, faces, and other accessories

When posing or animating a character, a general rule of thumb is to start from the center of the character and work outward. Anatomically, we understand this to mean starting from Rain's center of gravity at her pelvis, then posing the feet, hands, and head. Now, we're ready to pose details such as the fingers and facial expression, and then finally Rain's "inanimate" features – her hair and scarf.

> **Tip**
>
> Blender's **Object Gizmos** (particularly **Move** and **Rotate**) help take the guesswork out of which local axis to use when transforming a bone and are handy for quickly posing lots of little bones, which is what we'll be doing in this section. Consider going to your **Viewport Gizmos** menu in the **Header** area of the 3D Viewport and enabling them.

Fidgeting with digits

Let's move on to the bones in the **Fingers** layer:

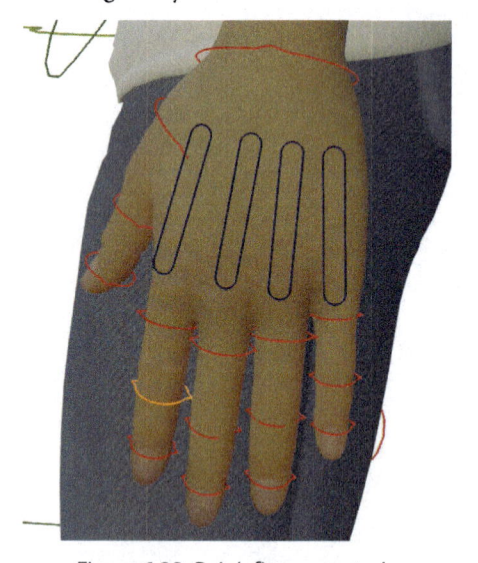

Figure 6.33: Rain's finger controls

Rain's finger controls are fairly simple; an *FK* chain for each digit, with bones for each phalanx and metacarpal. Though there may be 19 total bones for each hand, posing them isn't so hard if you know some shortcuts.

> **Important note**
> From this point onward, you're in charge of showing and hiding armature layers. Good thing the rigger has helpfully labeled them!

Using individual local axes

After unhiding the finger bones, let's enable a few settings that make it easy to pose multiple finger bones at once:

1. In the **Header** area of your 3D Viewport, change **Transform Orientation** to **Local**.
2. Change **Transform Pivot Point** to **Individual Origins**:

Figure 6.34: New transform settings in the 3D Viewport Header area

With these settings, we can rotate multiple phalanges at once on each one's local axis.

> **Important note**
> Pay close attention to whether you should transform something on a *global XYZ* axis or one of its *local XYZ* axes. Notice how Rain's finger bones are all misaligned from any global axis; little good would come of rotating them on all a single global axis now. This is the case with many other bones as well since we've rotated their parents further up the dependency chain.

Flexing the phalanges

With the settings we enabled, curling all the *FK* bones in Rain's fingers takes only two steps:

1. Select every bone in the **Fingers** layer (except for metacarpals in the palms – they shouldn't bend much).

2. Rotate the selection a little on the local X axis so that the fingers are relaxed, and not sticking straight out:

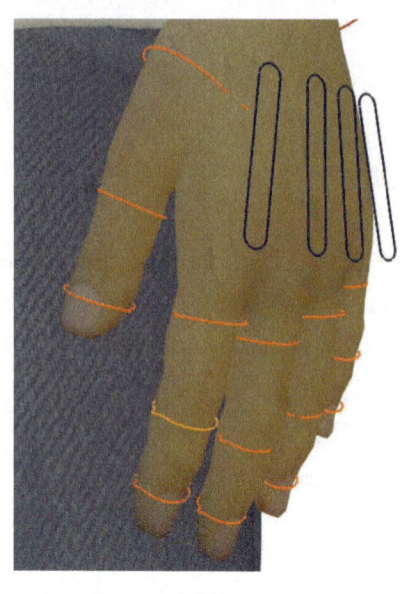

Figure 6.35: A casual hand pose

Not a bad method for posing 30 bones at once! If you like, try going back and tweaking a few individual bones to add flavor:

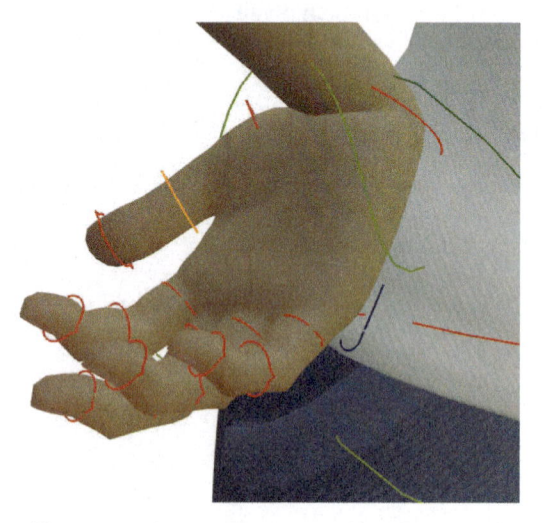

Figure 6.36: An even more casual hand pose

That's good enough for now; we'll have plenty more time to play with Rain's fingers when we give her an object to hold.

Facial expressions, or "posing the face bones"

When we enable the **Face Primary** layer, we're greeted by more bones than there were in the previous three armature layers combined:

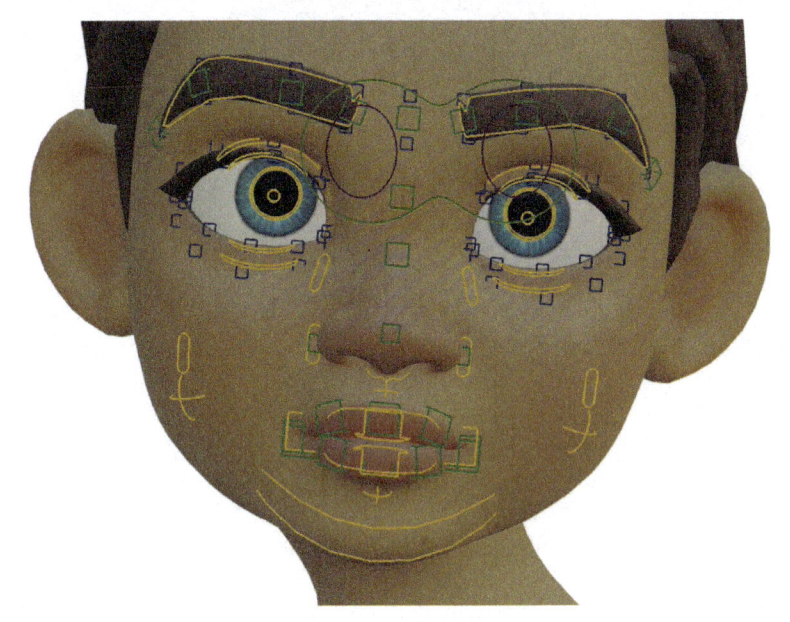

Figure 6.37: Rain's "face bones"

Just because a bone is there doesn't mean we have to pose it, so don't worry! Don't be sad! Smile! It takes fewer muscles to smile than to frown, and even fewer bones in Rain's facial rig to make Rain do the same.

Let's try posing a relaxed smile:

1. The two bones that control the corners of the mouth are the yellow boxes `ACT-Lips_Corner.L` and `ACT-Lips_Corner.R`. Select each one and move it a small amount toward Rain's ears.
2. Select both of Rain's upper eyelid bones `ACT-Eyelid_Upper.L` and `ACT-Eyelid_Upper.R` and move them down a tiny bit on their local Y axis.

> **Tip**
> A realistic smile pulls the corners of the mouth backwards toward the cheekbones, not directly upwards or outwards. A great big smile, if it's genuine, will also lift the cheeks and lower eyelids.

That's all it takes to go from a neutral face to a calm, happy one:

Figure 6.38: A gentle smile

> **Tip**
> Temporarily disable **Show Overlays** in the 3D Viewport to better see Rain without her bones.

Continue refining the expression if you like, starting with the main yellow bones and then tweaking the secondary green bones. A little more work on Rain's eyebrows seems to have piqued her curiosity:

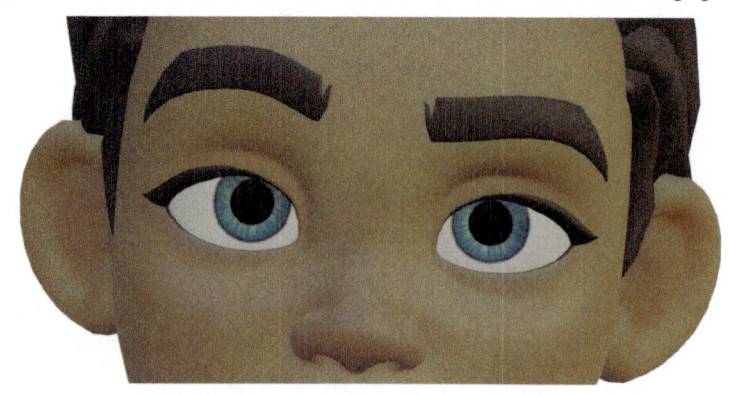

Figure 6.39: Further adjustment of the eyebrows

Some face bones, such as the ones for the eyelids, are constrained by the rigger so that they cannot be posed too "wrongly". Other bones, however, can be displaced freely, and being careless with them can cause nightmares:

Figure 6.40: Aaaaaagh!

The preceding example isn't even as bad as it gets! At least her eyes are pointing in the right direction… for now.

The eye target

The direction of a character's gaze (that is, what they're looking at) is of utmost importance in character animation. This is controlled by a couple of bones that you might not have noticed as they're floating at arms' length in front of Rain's face:

Figure 6.41: The eye target bones

Rather than directly rotating Rain's eyeballs, we can use the **eye target** to determine where they will point. This makes posing and animation easier in cases where Rain has something specific to look at.

To see how it works, let's return to a bone in the **FK** layer:

1. Find and select `FK-Head`.
2. Rotate `FK-Head` on the global Z axis to turn Rain's head a little to one side.

Note how Rain's gaze remains trained onto the eye target bones, causing her to give us the side-eye:

Figure 6.42: Rain stays looking at the eye target

With that, you know how the eye target bone works, and you don't even have to move it! Just make sure these bones stay in front of Rain's face; otherwise, she'll end up looking at the back of her skull.

> **Tip**
> If you don't want to have to think about Rain's eye target bones as her head moves, you can go to **Face Settings** and change **Eye Target Parent** to **Head**. This panel also lets you adjust the amount that Rain's eye rotation affects her eyelids and surrounding skin.

Rain's pose is nearly complete – all that's left to pose are those accessories we hid previously.

The final accessories

We can see that we've got a tiny bit more work to do when we unhide Rain's hair and scarf:

Figure 6.43: Rain's scarf and ponytail, un-posed

Things such as hair and loose clothing don't contribute to a character's pose the way other parts do. Without any muscles of their own, they just dangle there, reacting to gravity, Rain's movement, and maybe the wind. It's no wonder we would want to hide these parts until we finish posing everything else.

Let's give Rain her accessories back and make them dangle as they should:

1. Unhide the **Hair** and **Clothes** armature layers and enable **Scarf**, **Hair Strand**, and **Hair Ponytail** in the **Outfits** panel.
2. Pose Rain's ponytail so that it appears to hang down naturally. Start by rotating the red *FK* bones from the head outward, then use the spherical stretch bones to tweak the result.
3. Use the same method to pose Rain's scarf (the hair strand may be left alone in this case).

Now Rain's standing pose is finished. What an improvement on her original *T* pose!

Figure 6.44: The finished standing pose

Though our first pose was ostensibly a simple one, even this one took a while and required that we take advantage of many of Rain's features. With continued practice, posing a character gets easier with each pose!

That said, it would be a shame to let the work we already did go to waste. With that in mind, I'll show you how any pose we make can be saved and reused in later animations.

Creating a library of poses

Character animation is little more than a refined sequence of poses, so we can learn a lot by creating more of them as practice. Poses that convey things such as action, weight, force, tension, thought, and feeling are all part of what makes a compelling animation. And because it can take a while to make a single pose, you might want to reuse some of them in later animations!

Let's learn how to save poses so that we can keep the one we currently have for a later exercise.

The Asset Browser

In addition to models and materials, Blender's new **Asset Browser** can store the poses we make to our characters.

Let's bring it up now. To automatically create thumbnails for each pose, we'll need to add a camera to our scene as well:

1. Switch to **Object Mode** and **Add** (*Shift + A*) a **Camera** object to your scene.
2. Point the camera at Rain.
3. Bring up the **Asset Browser** area in a new area.
4. In the **Source List** (*T*) area to the left, change **Asset Library** from **All** to **Current File**.
5. Create a **New Asset Catalog** item by clicking +.
6. Name it `Rain Poses`.

Now we've got an empty catalog:

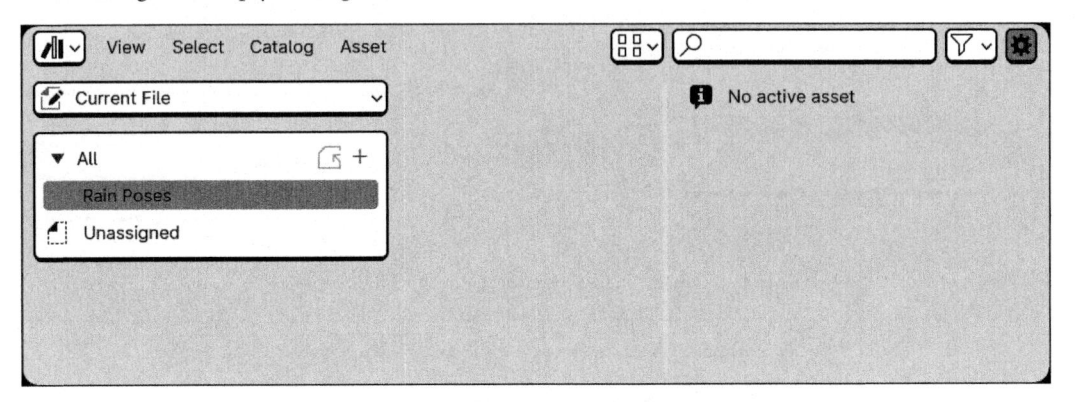

Figure 6.45: Catalog in the Asset Browser (currently empty)

Any pose we make that we like can be stored here. Let's start with the standing pose we've already made.

Creating a pose asset

To store a pose as an asset, follow these steps:

1. Select all the bones involved in the pose.
2. In the **Asset Browser** area, click **Asset | Create Pose Asset**.
3. Update the **Name** property in the right-hand sidebar (*N*) of the **Asset Browser** area to give the pose a more descriptive name.

Wherever the selected bones are when **Create Pose Asset** is clicked, that's the position they'll be in when the pose is applied later.

"All the bones involved in the pose" means all the bones we want to affect when we apply that pose to Rain in a new project. This includes all the bones we posed, but it may (or might as well) include some we didn't. For our current standing pose, we can go ahead and select all the bones in the layers we've used. For more localized poses, we can use a narrower selection of bones. This could mean selecting only the facial bones for an expression, or just the finger bones for a "hand pose" such as a clenched fist.

> **Important note**
> The bones that store **CloudRig** properties such as **IK/FK Switch** are not on a visible layer, so they won't be saved as part of the pose. We'll have to remember to adjust those settings ourselves.

Try it now. Here's our first pose in the **Asset Browser** area:

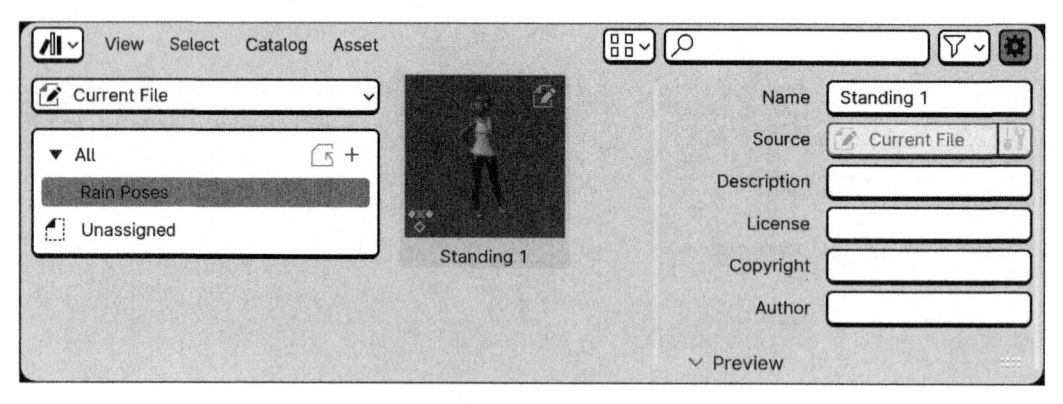

Figure 6.46: The standing pose saved as an asset

> **Tip**
> You can update the thumbnail of the asset at any time in the **Preview** panel in the right-hand sidebar (*N*).

Creating a library of poses 197

After saving our current pose, we're ready to make another one! You can select all the bones you posed and use **Pose | Clear Transform | All** to reset Rain to her original resting position, or, if you like, you can build off of this existing pose to make a new one in the following section.

Practicing poses

We're done posing by numbers; you now know enough about armature layers, **CloudRig** features, and manipulating bones in pose mode to make more poses on your own. Each time you create a pose you like, you can store it in the **Asset Browser** area with **Create Pose Asset**.

> **Tip**
> Use your own body as a reference when posing; move away from your computer and try doing the pose that you want to recreate! Sometimes a mirror is helpful for facial expressions.

Some more simple poses

Try making any number of common poses. If you save them, who knows – they might be useful later in an animation.

Standing

There's more than one way to stand. Building off of the existing pose we just made, we can explore alternative positions of the feet, arms, and spine:

Figure 6.47: Standing poses – leaning, arms crossed, hands folded

Next, we'll try something that's easy for Rain, but a bit more challenging for us: sitting!

Sitting and/or laying down

Try using cubes to serve as simple references for chairs and tables. For a fully reclined pose, you can use *FK* for all limbs:

Figure 6.48: Reclined poses

A sitting or sleeping character has more points of contact with the ground and/or furniture. So ironically the more relaxed a character gets the more work we have to do.

Now let's see how creative we can get with the face.

Facial expressions

Here are a few examples of facial expressions you can try. Remember to get as far as you can using the yellow bones in the **Face Primary** layer before moving on to other bones to tweak the expression:

Figure 6.49: Facial expressions

As always, it helps if you make the face the face yourself while working. Others might get concerned if you're in public though:

Figure 6.50: More facial expressions

Advanced poses

In truth, there's nothing "advanced" about these poses. Wild, dramatic poses can actually be easier than commonplace ones!

Figure 6.51: Some more advanced poses

How many other poses can you make? Keep practicing; posing requires a lot of work and practice, and we haven't even added any keyframes yet! Rain's rig is so advanced that we had to dedicate an entire chapter just to use her rig. This exercise will be the last one we do that isn't animated.

Remember to save this file so that we can reuse the standing pose later.

Summary

Other books and tutorials on character animation will attempt to pull you through a lengthy section on rigging your character before you learn to animate it. If you've taken a peek at Rain's hidden armature layers or looked at all her bones in the **Outliner** area, you can begin to appreciate why we skipped that particular task. In my opinion, learning to rig before learning to animate is like having to build a bicycle before learning to ride one – someone had to do it, but that person shouldn't have to be you. It took long enough to learn how to pose Rain without also having to name each bone ourselves!

Anatomy is a word with a twofold meaning when referring to a character rig. It could mean the shape and dimensions of the character, but it can also mean the invisible relationships between armature bones. An advanced character rig is an organism unto itself; a creature with its own hyper-anatomy, whose humanoid form is only a projection. What's inside of Rain isn't human; it's more like two spiders, one octopus, and the rigging of a 17th-century frigate. We love this monster; it makes animating fun!

Having learned how to pose Rain, we're ready to begin animating her. As mentioned previously, 3D character animation is essentially a process of posing, then keying, then posing again, and so forth. After a short while, this creates an animation with literally thousands of keyframes, but that's not a problem for a 3D animator. A thousand keyframes are as good as half a dozen if you know how to use them, something we'll cover in the next chapter.

Questions

1. Why should the objects that make up a character be organized into a collection?
2. If Rain is in our current .blend file, why is that file smaller than the one from which she came?
3. Why is an absolute file path like *FK*?
4. Where can you find the hidden bones we aren't supposed to animate?
5. What might "Inverse" in "Inverse Kinematics" mean?
6. Why would *IK* be more crucial for legs than arms?
7. Try rotating one of the small, circular *IK* bones behind Rain's ankles. What could that be useful for?
8. Why should we pose the hair and scarf last? Why would we hide these things in the first place?
9. Would it be easier to animate Rain if she had fewer bones?

7
Basic Character Animation

This is an animation book, and it's been two whole chapters since we inserted any keyframes! It's time to get back to work and animate this character we've spent so long learning how to pose.

If you know how to animate objects and how to pose a character, you pretty much already know how to animate a character as well. In pose mode, armature bones have the same keyable properties as objects (**Location**, **Rotation**, and **Scale**), and we will use the same methods for keying those properties as before.

Character animation isn't without its challenges, though! Our main challenges are two-fold: Firstly, our characters will look extra bad if animated poorly. Unconsciously, we know how people's bodies ought to move; the eye is a harsh judge of things it has seen a thousand times before.

Our second, more immediate challenge is that characters have a lot of bones. Was that not made clear in the previous chapter? Yes, characters have a lot of bones, and it's commonplace to key multiple bones at once as we animate, so our keyframes will number in the thousands after a short while. That's a lot of keyframes to manage and edit! Good thing we have the Dope Sheet.

In this chapter, you'll learn the following:

- How to apply a pose we created earlier
- What it means to "block out" the main poses in a character animation
- How to edit keyframes and organize animation channels in the Dope Sheet
- Dope Sheet techniques and operators for creating "Breakdown" poses
- Adding details and refining the character's motion

Technical requirements

As before, to complete this chapter's exercise, you'll of course need Blender (the free and open-source 3D application) and Rain (the free character rig for Blender). See the previous chapter for the link to download Rain and detailed instructions on how to link her into your scene.

In the previous chapter's exercise, we also created a standing pose, which we saved as an asset. We will reuse that pose for this chapter, but if you don't have it or can't append it, you can simply recreate it by posing Rain as usual.

Preparing Rain in a new scene

Our animation for this chapter will begin with Rain in the standing pose we made for her in *Chapter 6*. First, of course, we'll need to create a new scene with Rain in it. Do you remember how to do that?

A brief recap on linking Rain into a new project

This will be another 120-frame animation, with nothing in our scene besides Rain. In case you've forgotten what we did at the beginning of *Chapter 6* to bring Rain into a new project, here's a quick refresher. Remember these steps each time we start a new character animation with Rain:

1. Start a new file in Blender and go to **File | Link**.
2. Navigate to Rain's `.blend` file in the invoked file browser.
3. Go to the **Collection** folder and choose the collection `CH-rain` for linking.
4. With the collection instance `CH-rain` selected in your scene, go to **Object | Relations | Make Library Override**.
5. Save your file (*Ctrl + S*) and then restart it with **File | Revert**.
6. To start posing, select Rain's armature and go into **Pose Mode** (*Ctrl + Tab*).

Now we're ready to pose Rain once again:

Figure 7.1: Rain, freshly linked into a new scene

We've got a lot of posing ahead of us, but to save a little time on Rain's initial pose, we can fetch the one we made in the previous chapter.

Using a pose asset

Like Rain's object collection and most other forms of data in Blender, the pose we made earlier is an action **datablock** that can be linked or appended from one `.blend` file into another. We're going to append that pose so it can help us in our current animation.

> **Important note**
>
> Using our standing pose asset can save us some time, but not that much time. If for any reason you can't properly apply the pose we're looking for, it's not a showstopper. Just do the pose again manually, as we learned in *Chapter 6*, and continue to the next section.

Adding your poses to the asset browser

Follow these steps to retrieve the standing pose. This will also make available any other pose you saved as an asset from the previous exercise:

1. Go to **User Preferences | File Paths | Asset Libraries**.
2. Click the plus sign (+) for **Add Asset Library**.
3. Find the folder containing the file you created in the previous chapter.
4. Give the new asset library a better name.

Now we have a new asset library:

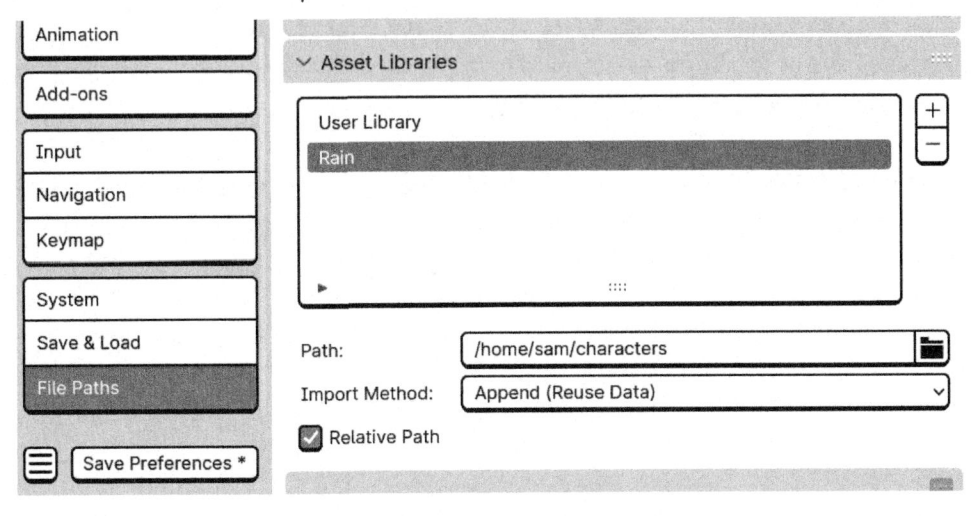

Figure 7.2: New Asset Library in User Preferences

For all `.blend` files in the chosen folder, anything marked as an asset will show up in the Asset Browser:

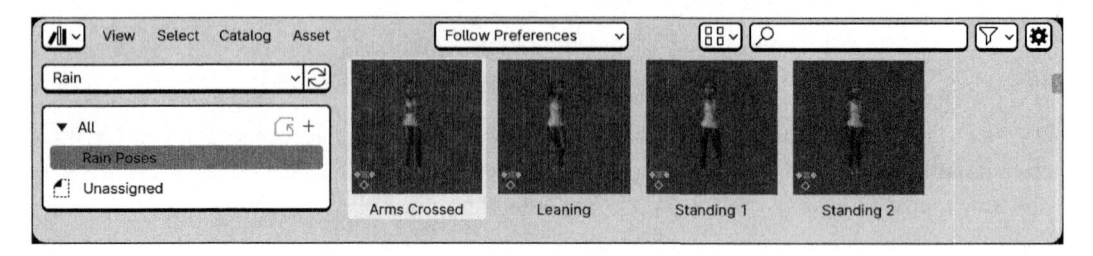

Figure 7.3: Poses in the Asset Browser

Let's get out of **User Preferences** and go there now.

Applying a pose from the Asset Browser

To apply the standing pose that we created in the previous chapter, do the following:

1. In the **Asset Browser**, find the **Asset Library** and **Catalog** containing the standing pose we created for Rain.
2. Make sure you are in **Pose Mode** for Rain's armature and that all bones are deselected.
3. Double-click the standing pose from the previous chapter to apply it.
4. To complete the pose, make any necessary adjustments to Rain's **CloudRig** properties that were lost from the original pose (such as her **FK/IK Switch** settings).

> **Important note**
>
> If any bones on the armature are selected when you apply a pose, all other bones will be ignored. To ensure that our standing pose is applied to the whole armature, including hidden bones, make sure all bones are deselected beforehand.

Using our pose from the pose library, we can quickly rid Rain of that boring T-pose and restore her to a relaxed, natural-looking standing position:

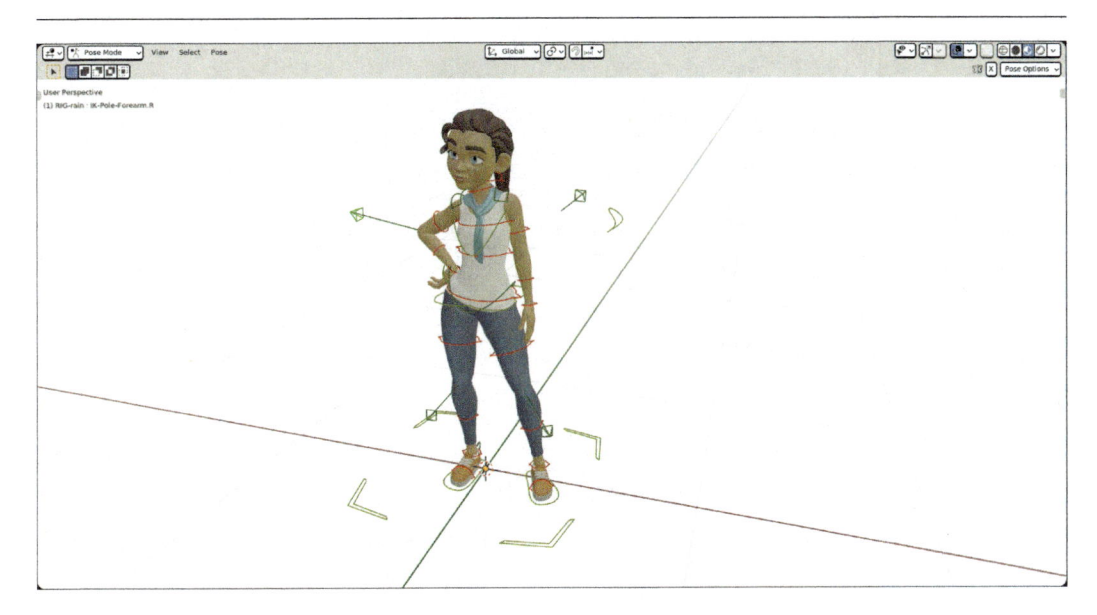

Figure 7.4: Rain's standing pose from the previous chapter

We didn't even have to select a single bone (not yet, at least)!

Are we animating a character yet? Technically, no. Poses applied from the Asset Browser are not integrated with the current animation; they just apply properties to many bones at once as though we just posed Rain ourselves.

Leaving the asset browser behind, we can continue to tweak the pose we see here as much as we like. With Rain in a good starting pose, we're nearly ready to insert our first set of keyframes. We just need to double-check a few more settings so that our first character animation experience goes smoothly.

Setting bone relationships for an animation

The static positions of Rain's bones look fine, but sometimes their relationships (or lack thereof) can create problems for us once those bones start to move around.

IK Parents

As mentioned before, you can test a bone by grabbing it and wiggling it around in the 3D Viewport. Look at what happens (or doesn't happen) when we move `MSTR-Pelvis_Parent`:

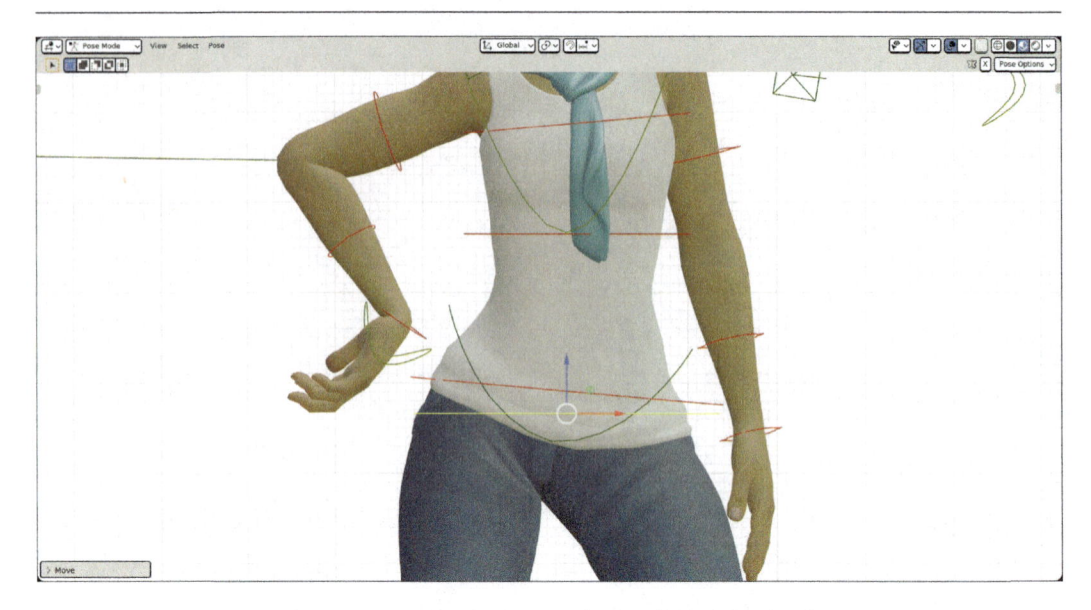

Figure 7.5: Moving Rain's torso leaves the hand behind

The `IK-Hand_Parent.R` bone remains fixed in space instead of sticking to her hip. This could cause us a headache once we start animating in earnest. We might be able to select, pose, and key both `MSTR-Pelvis_Parent` and `IK-Hand_Parent.R` together, but that method can be clunky, and any incidental shifting that occurs will be conspicuous.

What if one bone were parented to the other? As it happens, each of Rain's *IK* target bones is rigged with a limited number of bones that can act like their parents, should the animator require it.

You can find this feature under **IK Parents**, in the **IK Settings** panel of the CloudRig interface:

Figure 7.6: The Switch Parent feature in CloudRig

> **Important note**
> Using the **Switch Parent (Keep Transform)** operator is different from just changing the value of the **IK Parents** property. Using this operator changes the effective parent and also adjusts the bone's nominal transform values to compensate for the change so that it remains visually stationary. Similar to what happened when we set object origins in *Chapter 4*, this is another strange case of changing transforms in one sense in order to "keep" them in another!

It's better to make this change now, before inserting keyframes, rather than after:

1. In the **CloudRig** interface, find **IK Settings | IK Parents**.
2. Click the menu button next to the property **Right Arm**.
3. In the **Switch Parent (Keep Transform)** dialogue, select **Torso**.
4. For this animation, let's ensure that every other Parent setting in the CloudRig interface has a value of 0 (**Root**).

We're now free to pose and animate Rain's torso, and her hand will stay resting on her hip the whole time, even if her shoulder moves. Here's an extreme example:

Figure 7.7: The IK target helps keep Rain's hand where it should be

Such a prodigious use of bone constraints! What should we do if we want that hand to leave her side in the course of the animation, though?

Applying visual transforms

If you're looking for an extra challenge, you have the choice of making Rain use her right arm to wave in the next section, instead of using her left arm, which is already dangling freely.

It's better to do a waving motion with *FK* instead of *IK*, though, so this will require us to animate the **FK/IK Switch** settings for the right arm so that it changes from `1.0` (*IK*) to `0.0` (*FK*) during the course of our animation. That way, Rain's right arm will be controlled by its *FK* bones at the appropriate time.

Look at what happens when we change that property, though:

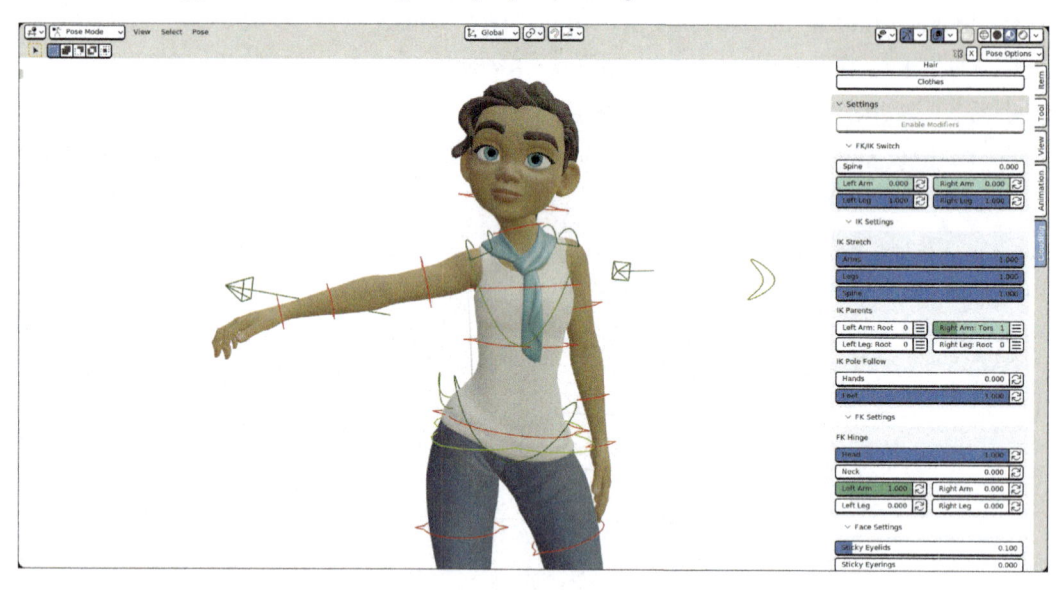

Figure 7.8: Switching from IK to FK

We didn't leave those *FK* bones in a very good place, did we?

The "hand-off" from *IK* to *FK*—and vice versa—is a delicate transfer of power between two rival parties, and should be handled subtly in a way that won't draw public attention. For the best results, we ought to move the *FK* bones to exactly the same place as the *IK* bones so they're ready to accept control over the arm ahead of time. That way, the change won't be so... violent.

To make this preparation quickly, we can apply the visual transform of the *FK* bones while they are still constrained to the *IK* chain:

1. Make sure **CloudRig | FK Settings | FK Hinge | Right Arm** is set to `1.0`.
2. Select the *FK* bones for the right arm: `FK-Upperarm_Parent.R`, `FK-Forearm.R`, and `FK-Hand.R`.
3. Use **Pose | Apply** (*Ctrl + A*) | **Apply Visual Transform to Pose**.

When used properly, the operator will have appeared to do nothing, but when you switch from *IK* to *FK* for the right arm, the right arm will still be in the same place!

Apply Visual Transform to Pose is a handy operator that automatically adjusts the selected bones' nominal transform values so that they affirm the visual effect of those bones' constraints. To put it another way, the bones now "want" to be in the same place their constraints are putting them in, so when the constraints are disabled later, the arm will stay put. The *FK* bones can then be animated from that starting position.

Now, our initial pose has all the correct parameters, including those transformations for which the effects are not yet visible, and it is nearly ready to be keyed for animation!

Hiding bones

Our initial animation pass will focus on the bones in Rain's two most important armature layers: **IK** and **FK**. We'll also enable the layers **Face Primary** and **Fingers** so that we can practice posing those parts as well.

That helps narrow down what bones we need to worry about, but we can go a bit further. These layers still contain a few bones that will definitely not need to be animated in this exercise. We won't need the bones on Rain's legs and feet, for instance; walking is too advanced for this chapter!

By hiding some bones now, we can pre-emptively clear up the clutter in both our 3D Viewport and the animation editors that display all our keyframes:

1. Enable the armature layers **IK**, **FK**, **Fingers**, and **Face Primary**. Disable all others.
2. Select all the visible bones on Rain's legs and feet.
3. Use **Pose | Show/Hide | Hide Selected** (*H*).
4. Repeat steps 2 and 3 for a few other bones that don't need to go anywhere in this animation: `ROOT`, `MSTR-Chest_Parent`, `IK-Hand_Parent.L`, `IK-Pole_Forearm.L`, `TGT-Eyes.L`, and `TGT-Eyes.R`.

> **Important note**
>
> Hidden bones can always be revealed later with **Reveal Selected** (*Alt + H*). Don't worry about why it's called "**Reveal Selected**" or how you would even select a hidden bone before revealing it.

Here's what Rain's rig looks like now. Note that I have also gone ahead and hidden Rain's hair and scarf objects using the **Outfits** feature we learned about in the previous chapter:

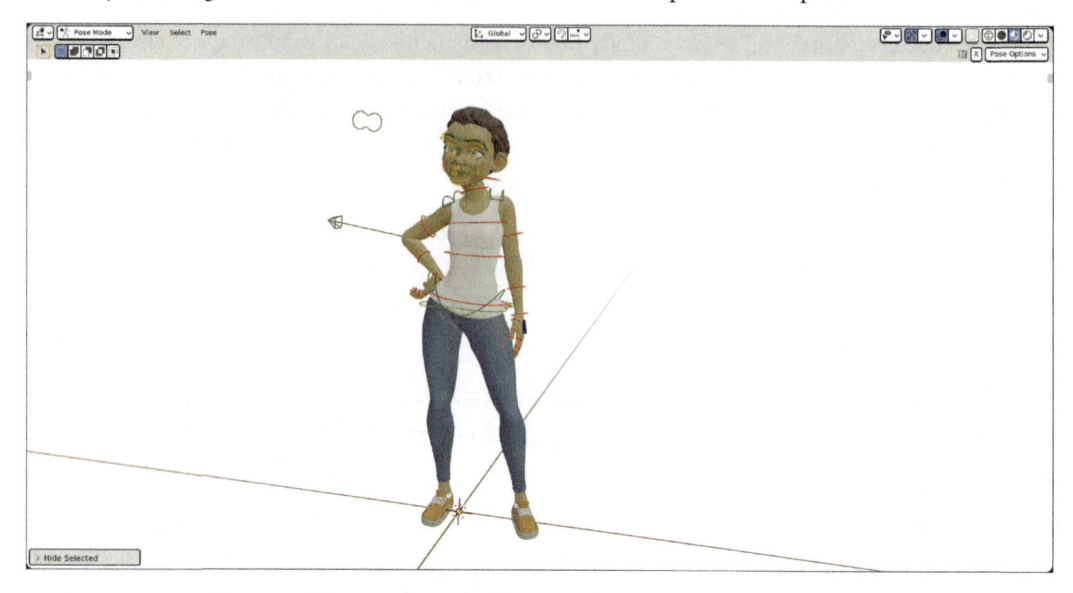

Figure 7.9: The remaining visible bones for our initial animation pass

The bones we just hid haven't gone anywhere, but they can no longer be seen or selected in the 3D Viewport. This is convenient for us, as we're about to key our first pose by selecting all the bones that remain!

Keying pose bones

For the 5-second animation in this exercise, Rain will begin by standing idle. A couple of seconds later, someone off-screen will catch her attention, and Rain will peer through the distance to identify the person. When she recognizes her friend, Rain will wave at them with excitement.

Exactly who Rain sees will be left to the imagination. Rain won't interact with anything or go anywhere. Her hands won't touch anything, and her feet will remain planted on the ground. It's not an ambitious scene, but even a short one like this requires careful attention.

So, where do we start? At the beginning? Perhaps, but not necessarily…

Blocking or roughing the animation

Throughout the character animation process, there are two guidelines we should keep in mind:

- Create and key the most important poses first. These are the "extreme" poses that, when seen by themselves, clearly convey the sequence of things our character feels and does. You won't always know exactly what frame each pose should be keyed on, but that's okay. After keying these poses, you can adjust their timing, edit their interpolation, and insert additional keyframes to refine the character's motion as she transitions from one pose to the next.

- Animate from the center of the character outward. This means establishing the position and motion of Rain's torso is more important than doing the same for her head, arms, and legs, which themselves should have greater priority than Rain's fingers and face. Finally, things such as hair and clothes should be animated last. Remember that you can use the CloudRig interface to temporarily hide some parts of Rain as you work so that they don't distract you.

In a way, these two guidelines are practical variations on the same idea; that is, we should complete a rough pass of the animation before going back and adding in any details, both in the anatomical and temporal sense. Note that "start at the beginning" is not one of the guidelines, though, in our case, there's no reason to start anywhere else.

With that in mind, let's have a look at the three main poses we'll be making for this exercise. We'll call these **idle**, **looking**, and **waving**:

Figure 7.10: Three key poses: idle, looking, and waving

We already finished that first pose. Let's go ahead and key it.

Keying the "idle" pose

We can key a whole pose by selecting all the remaining bones on our four most important layers and keying their transform properties all at once:

1. Go to Frame `1`.
2. Select all (*A*) of the visible bones.
3. Invoke the **Insert Keyframe Menu** (*I*) and choose **Location, Rotation, & Scale**.
4. If you plan on making Rain wave the hand that currently rests on her hip, it will need to switch from *IK* to *FK* later on. Go to the **CloudRig** interface and key the **Right Arm FK/IK Switch** value at `1.0` (**IK**).

With just a few clicks, we keyed the **Location**, **Rotation**, and **Scale** of every single bone on those four layers. You can't see them yet, but that's more keyframes than in all the other animations we've made in this book so far combined!

Why so many keyframes for so many bones at once? Hereafter, are we now obliged to consider the **Location**, **Rotation**, and **Scale** of each of those bones every time we insert a new keyframe? Not necessarily. Although it's true that we did key way more than we technically needed to, the tools in this chapter will allow us to view animation channels on a per-bone basis rather than for each animated property of that bone. More on that later.

> **Important note**
> Now that so many bones' positions are keyed, any change you make to them must be keyed as well; otherwise, the changes will be lost when you go to a different frame. Forgetting to insert keyframes for animated properties is a common cause of frustration, especially in character animation, where a great deal of time may be spent on just one pose. To prevent the accidental loss of work, there's no harm in "saving" your pose by inserting keyframes before you're finished with it.

Now that Rain's initial pose is keyed on frame `1`, we can move on to the next one.

The "looking" pose

Time to create a completely different pose! Before waving, Rain has to peer into the distance to see who or what has caught her attention.

One benefit of having already keyed so many bones at once is that we've taken the guesswork out of which bones to pose and key in this phase. The bulk of our attention for animating can be spent on just the **IK**, **FK**, **Fingers**, and **Face Primary** layers (and I don't mind if you're lazy with those last two).

Novice animators tend to be timid when creating the second pose in an animation, taking excessive care not to have it differ too much from the first one. Don't be shy; key poses are meant to look different!

If precise continuity between them mattered, they wouldn't be key poses. You are encouraged to reset and re-pose any bone you see. Focus on making this new pose look as good as possible by itself. We'll have plenty of time to obsess over the transition between poses later.

Let's get to work:

1. Go to frame 50 and begin posing.

   In the pose for this frame, Rain should look directly at some invisible person to one side and lean strongly toward them with her whole torso.

   Arms often counterbalance the movement of the torso. In this case, Rain's arms and shoulders should extend somewhat stiffly in the opposite direction of her lean.

2. Using the bones in the **Face Primary** layer, change Rain's facial expression to one of uncertainty, squinting her eyes as she struggles in this frame to recognize the person she sees. Find a good place for Rain's eye target, as this will mark the location of who she sees.

3. Key **Location**, **Rotation**, and **Scale** for all the same bones once again. Remember to key any other properties you've changed as well, such as **FK/IK Switch**.

Now we have two poses! Here they are together:

Figure 7.11: "Idle" and "Looking" poses, overlapped for contrast

The transition between these poses will look slow and awkward for now, but we'll work on that shortly. We've got one final key pose left.

The "waving" pose

Our third pose is Rain's elated reaction after she recognizes who she sees. As before, we want this key pose to look almost completely different, maintaining only the position of Rain's feet on the ground and the direction of her gaze. This means that the only visible bone you should leave in place is the eye target.

> **Important note**
>
> Try using the **Available** keying set from the **Insert Keyframe** menu (*I*), which only keys the properties of selected bones/objects that already have keyframes. This will be useful later on if you decide to delete some animation channels and don't want to accidentally key those properties again. Most properties you see in the CloudRig interface belong to hidden bones, so you'll still need to key those separately.

Don't be afraid to exaggerate here; it's easier to relax a pose later on than to intensify it. You may even go so far as to make Rain's limbs stretch just a tiny bit:

1. Go to frame 80.
2. For this pose, Rain should stand upright and raise one hand almost as high as she can with her fingers extended. Make sure the arm that does this is using *FK*.
3. Whichever arm you choose to raise, follow through with the shoulders and curve of the spine. In particular, the shoulder of the raised arm should itself be raised quite a bit.
4. After recognizing her friend, Rain's facial expression should be one of excitement.
5. Key everything the same as you've been doing.

Here's my final pose compared to the previous two:

Figure 7.12: Overlapping "idle", "looking", and "waving" poses

These key poses are awfully important, so let's make sure we get them right.

Reviewing our key poses

When you're finished, inspect your three key poses for errors. Let your judgment as an animator be your guide. If any bone's position in a pose looks "off" to you, fix it and re-insert the keyframes for it. It's easier to do this sooner rather than later when keyframes might get moved around. Just make sure you're on the same frame as the existing keyframe that you wish to overwrite; otherwise, you'll just add a new one next to it on the Timeline!

> **Tip**
> In addition to using the *Left* and *Right* arrow keys on your keyboard to increment the current frame, you can also jump between the keyframes of selected objects/bones using the *Up* and *Down* arrow keys. This is useful for focusing on key poses without being distracted by the frames in between.

Your work may look different than mine and perhaps even better! You may have Rain looking in a different direction, making a different face, or waving with a different hand. As long as the three poses make sense and look good to you, that's all that matters at this point.

As for the actual animation, that's a different story. It's time to refine Rain's motion using a new tool.

The Dope Sheet

Our three poses look fine, but the animation is nothing to write home about just yet. Rain doesn't "hold" her poses and it looks unnatural. At this stage, we can start adjusting our keyframes, duplicating them so as to determine how long each pose should be held before it transitions to the next one.

Let's bring up the whole thing in the **Graph Editor**:

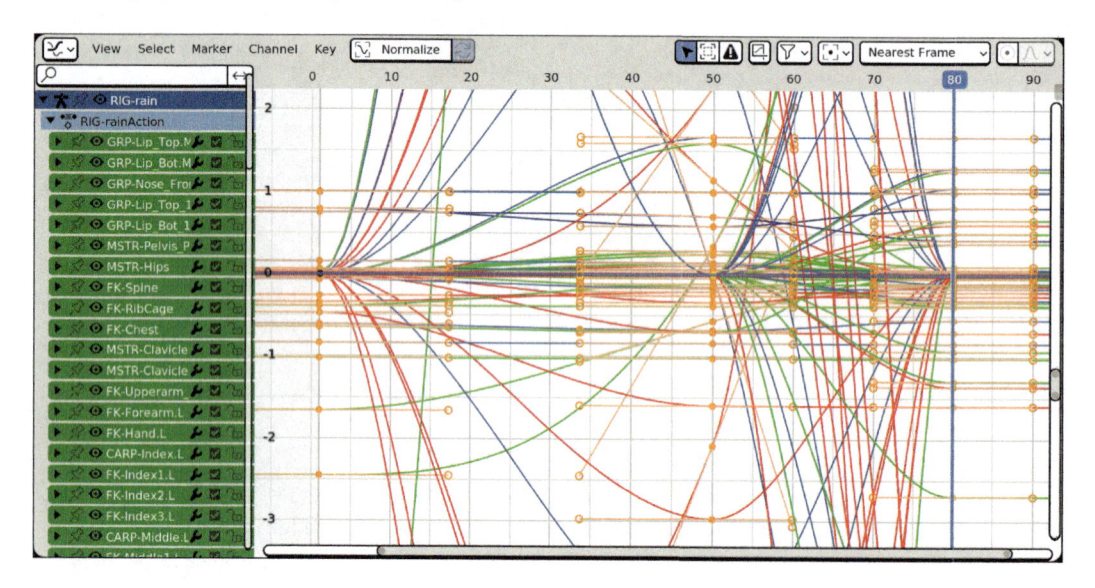

Figure 7.13: Graph Editor

This looks fine. Just kidding! Can you imagine? Character animation, along with other complex kinds of animation, yields too many F-curves for us to practically visualize in the graph editor all at once. Technically speaking, we could use it, but let's not.

For broad control over animations with a lot of animation channels, we have the Dope Sheet instead. Named after the spreadsheets used by traditional animators to plan the timing of their shots, a Dope Sheet can track the position (in time) of any/all keyframes in our animation.

Introduction to the Dope Sheet

You can get to the Dope Sheet by changing the editor type of an area in your interface or simply by switching to the **Animation** workspace tab at the top of the window.

Let's pull one up. In addition, we'll need to ensure that the Dope Sheet displays all our animation data, including the keyframes of the bones that might be hidden:

1. Bring up a **Dope Sheet** editor in your user interface.
2. In the header of the Dope Sheet, disable **Only Show Selected** and enable **Show Hidden**:

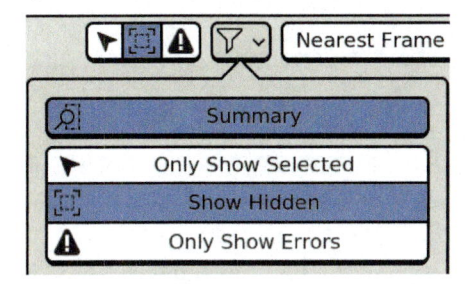

Figure 7.14: Visibility settings in the Dope Sheet

For bi-pedal characters with lots of animated bones, I find it's useful to put the 3D Viewport and Dope Sheet side-by-side. Here's what my interface looks like:

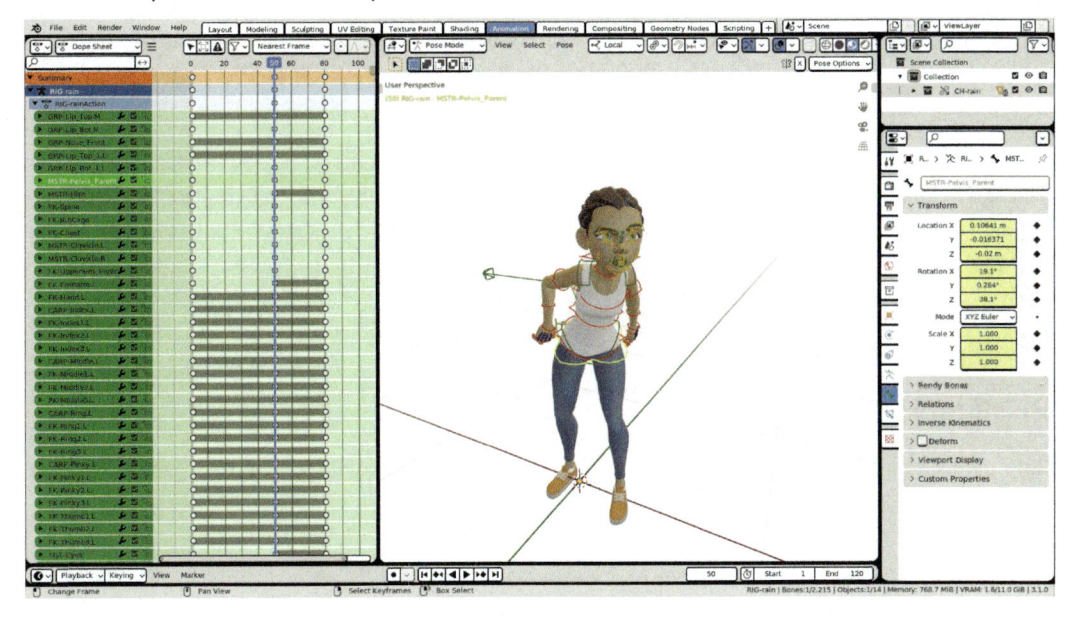

Figure 7.15: The Dope Sheet and 3D Viewport in "portrait" dimensions

With the Dope Sheet, we can see all the keyframes we inserted aligned nicely into rows for every channel. It's sort of like a Graph Editor without a Y axis; by sacrificing some information about keyframes and organizing them into rows, we can easily manage the keyframes for a larger number of animated properties at once.

Wait, isn't this just the Timeline?

Yes, they're practically the same editor with different headers:

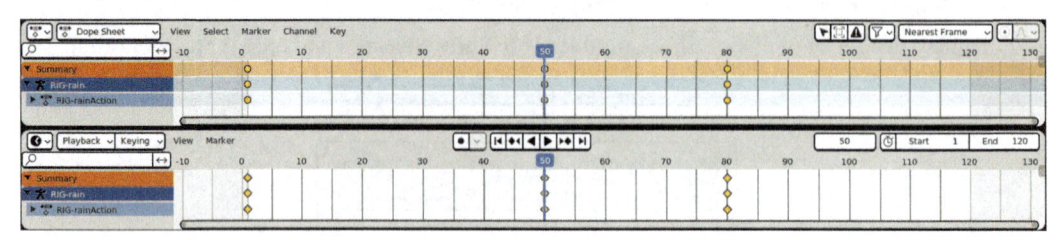

Figure 7.16: Dope Sheet placed above a Timeline

Originally, Blender's Timeline was only for playback and frame-seeking and could not be used to edit keyframes directly. Later on, some functionality was copied from the Dope Sheet to the Timeline for convenience. It sure made *Chapter 1* a lot easier!

Much of what we're about to do with the Dope Sheet will work in the Timeline as well. Don't get them mixed up, though; when it comes to editing keyframes, there's nothing the Timeline can do that the Dope Sheet can't do better. For one thing, the Timeline only displays the channels of selected objects and/or bones, whereas the Dope Sheet has the same flexibility as the Graph Editor when it comes to filtering the visibility of channels.

The Timeline's essential features (that is, everything the Dope Sheet can't do) are all located in its header, where we can find settings for playback, frame range, and the like. Everything below its header can be thought of as a "quick access" Dope Sheet. For this reason, you may wish to have both the Dope Sheet and the Timeline visible in your interface so that you'll have access to the features of both.

Now that we've cleared that up, we can return to what makes the Dope Sheet (and yes, the Timeline in some cases) so useful.

Animation channels (again)

Take a look at the contents of the left side panel of the Dope Sheet, which contains a nested list of all our animation channels:

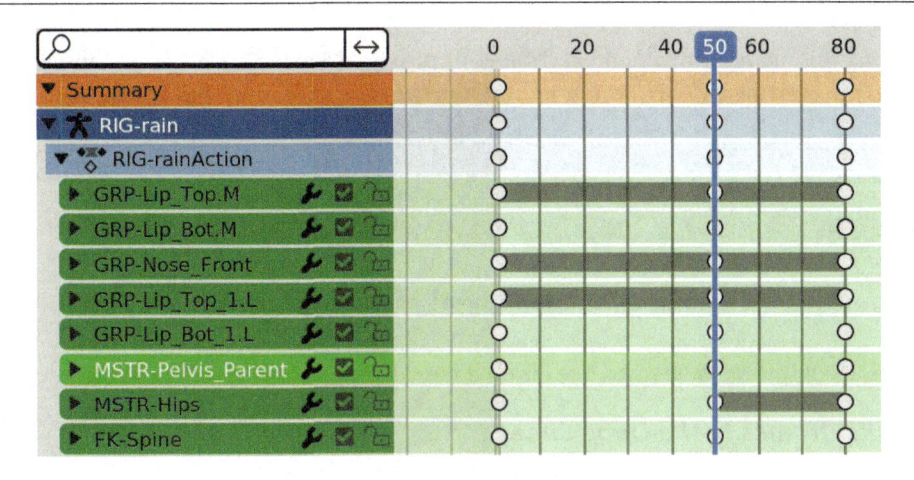

Figure 7.17: A list of channel groups named after each bone

At the very top, we have an item labeled **Summary**, which contains all the animated objects. This is followed by Rain's armature object and then the action. Our scene only has one animated object, which has just one action, so these first three channels at the top are redundant. You needn't bother making any distinction between them.

The animation channels within an action are automatically organized into channel groups. In the case of character animation, channel groups are automatically named after each bone. Whenever applicable, clicking on a channel group selects the bone that corresponds to it and vice-versa.

If you expand a channel group, you'll see the individual channels for each animated property of that bone:

Figure 7.18: Individual animation channels for one bone

This should all look familiar. It's just like what we saw before in the Graph Editor, and you can find it in the Timeline as well. This time, though, our animation has more channels and keyframes than ever before. Each time we inserted the **Location**, **Rotation**, and **Scale** keyframes for every bone in those first four layers, we created a whole column of keyframes, with over 1,000 for every pose.

Does having this many channels and keyframes disturb you? Me too! Let's use **Collapse Channels** (*Numpad -*) or click the little arrow next to the **Summary** row so we don't have to think about them:

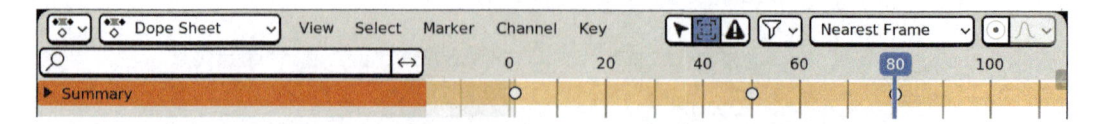

Figure 7.19: Collapsing the animation channels

Now there are only three keyframes, one for each pose! Not such a complex animation after all.

Editing keyframes in the Dope Sheet

Just because we can't see all that other data doesn't mean it isn't there; we just don't have to think about it until we're ready. For now, we can edit the timing of our three poses in the Dope Sheet as though they were three solitary keyframes.

> **Important note**
>
> The following operations need to affect all our keyframes. The Dope Sheet cannot edit the keyframes of hidden channels, so make sure that you disabled **Only Show Selected** and enabled **Show Hidden** before following the next steps.
>
> On the other hand, the channels within a collapsed channel-group do not count as being hidden. Whether a channel is collapsed or expanded does not matter in terms of its functionality.

The Dope Sheet holds no surprises when it comes to controls and keyboard shortcuts. Let's begin by using **Duplicate** (*Shift + D*) to make Rain hold her first two poses:

1. In the **Summary** row of the Dope Sheet, select the keyframe on frame 1.
2. Duplicate the selection, moving the new keyframe to frame 40.
3. Do the same for the keyframe on frame 50, moving the new one to frame 70.

We just refined the timing of our animation a little so that Rain holds each pose for a short while before transitioning to the next one. Duplicating keyframes is a common way of doing this, which is just like how we animated the cube in *Chapter 1*.

The shading between keyframes in the Dope Sheet gives us a visual clue as to where the action is happening. The long gray bars between identical keyframes indicate no change, whereas the non-grayed-out intervals between keyframes are where the motion is:

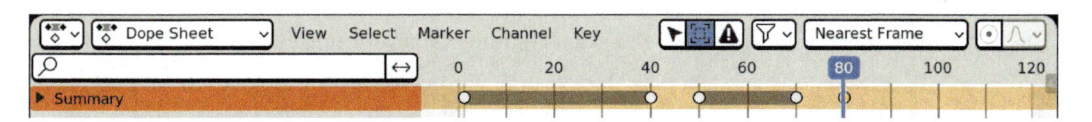

Figure 7.20: "Held" keyframes in the Summary row of the Dope Sheet

Much information is still hidden, though. Are these five keyframes, or more than 5,000? How many keyframes do we really have?

Summary or "grouped" keyframes

If we use **Expand Channels** (*Numpad +*), we can see how the keyframes in the **Summary** row actually work. Take a look at what happens when we select one:

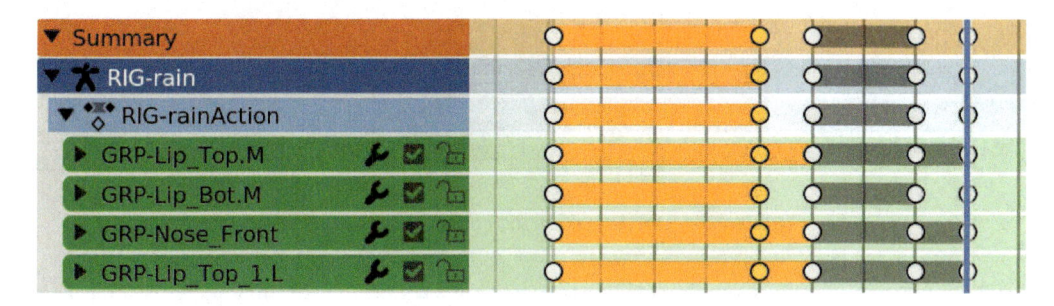

Figure 7.21: Selection of keyframes

Every keyframe that is visible (or would be visible if the channels were expanded) appears in the **Summary** row. The same is true for the next two rows, which are redundant for our purposes.

If two or more keyframes share the same frame, they get collapsed into one keyframe in the summary row which represents them all. I call these "summary keys", but you can call them "meta-keys", "grouped keys", or even "fool's keyframes"; there's no agreed-upon term for what they're called.

Let's move further down the hierarchy and select a summary key for one bone:

Figure 7.22: Selection of all the keyframes for one bone

Each bone's channel group is like its own summary channel, containing summary keys that effectively encode values for multiple channels. For many bones, we may never need to separately edit the keyframes for individual **Location**, **Rotation**, and **Scale** channels. Instead, we can work on a more abstract level, animating all those properties together for one whole "pose" at a time. With so many bones to worry about, we need all the abstraction we can get! We might even need more than what we already have.

Organizing the Dope Sheet

There's only so much we can accomplish by editing the keyframes for a whole character animation in just one row. As we work, we must insert and edit keyframes for particular bones instead of whole poses.

There is just one hurdle: expanding the action channel in the Dope Sheet feels more like an explosion than an expansion. There are simply too many bones in this list, even after having hidden a lot of other bones so that they wouldn't be keyed. Their order from top to bottom doesn't make much sense either.

Before we continue further with our animation, let's organize these channel groups. It'll make the rest of our work go more smoothly.

Re-grouping channels

Even when the channel groups are collapsed, there are a conspicuous number of rows in the Dope Sheet, enough to make our work harder than it needs to be. Take a look at these channel group names and consider the bones they correspond to:

Figure 7.23: Too long of a list

Look at how many channel groups there are for all the little bones in Rain's fingers and face! Some of these bones don't need to be animated, but a lot of them do, so we can't just delete this data. Do we really need to see the keyframes for each individual finger and face bone, though? Is it really that important to have separate channel groups for `FK-Pinky2.L` and `FK-Pinky3.L` so that we can distinguish the timing between the two distal phalanges in Rain's left pinky finger? Maybe later, but not for this animation.

Instead, we can use the **Channel |Group Channels** (*Ctrl* + *G*) operator to consolidate the many channels for Rain's finger and face bones into just a few channel groups.

To start, we should cull some visible bones and channels:

1. Hide the **IK** and **FK** armature layers, leaving only the **Fingers** and **Face Primary** layers visible.
2. Enable **Show Only Selected** in the Dope Sheet.

That should help reduce the danger of selecting the wrong bone or grouping a channel without meaning to.

> **Important note**
> Be sure of your selection before grouping channels in the Dope Sheet. If you accidentally group the wrong channels, there's no automatic way (besides **Undo** (*Ctrl* + *Z*)) to restore how they were grouped initially.

Grouping finger bone channels

Now it's easier to group the channels we want with **Channel | Group Channels** (*Ctrl + G*). Let's start with the fingers:

1. In the 3D Viewport, select the visible finger bones in Rain's left hand. This makes them visible in the Dope Sheet.
2. In the channel list of the Dope Sheet, make sure all the channel groups for the selected bones are themselves selected with *Select All* (*A*).
3. Use **Channel | Group Channels** (*Ctrl + G*), and name the new group `Fingers.L`.
4. Repeat steps 1–3 for the finger bones in the right hand and name the channel group `Fingers.R`.

Instead of 38 channel groups (one for each finger bone), we now have just two (one for each hand):

Figure 7.24: Two channel groups for the fingers

The summary keys in these channel groups will work as expected as well. If we keep the channel groups collapsed and continue keying the fingers all together, we can think of each hand as its own character, animated with summary "finger keyframes" that encode each "finger pose".

That's easier than dealing with the summary keys for 38 individual bones and much easier than dealing with the 342 individual **Location**, **Rotation**, and **Scale** channels for those bones (which, by the way, are still there):

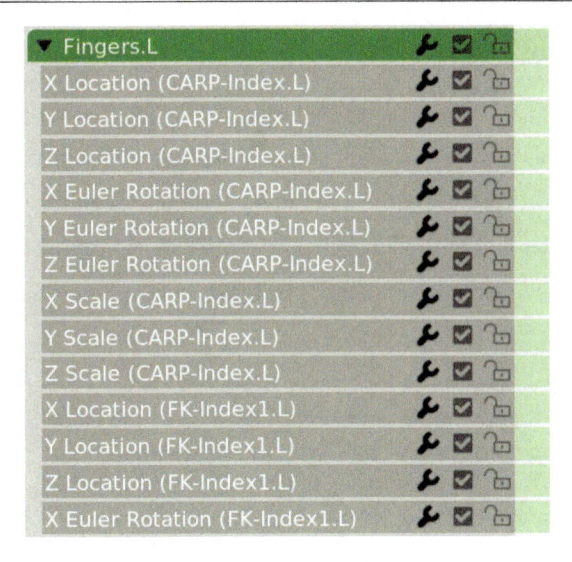

Figure 7.25: Aargh! Put it away!

As you can see, the channel groups can't be nested. I wish they could. Ask the developers about it. We can't put channel groups inside other channel groups; we can only empty them of their individual animation channels and put those channels into a new channel group.

> **Important note**
> Because channel groups for multiple bones can be so unruly when expanded, we'll avoid grouping channels unless we're certain we can keep them collapsed most of the time.

The display of channels in our Dope Sheet is getting more streamlined! Now, we're left with the animation channels for the face bones.

Grouping face bone channels

It would be tempting, but far too zealous, to group everything into one "face" channel. The upper half of the face will often move incongruously with the lower half during actions such as talking, and facial parts such as eyelids need to blink, moving separately from the eyebrows.

That doesn't mean each eyebrow bone needs to be animated separately, though! To collapse more channels while retaining some independence between parts of the face, we're going to organize all this clutter into four basic channel groups: Mouth, Nose, Eyebrows, and Eyes.

> **Important note**
> The names we give to channel groups are arbitrary, and do not change which bones or properties are affected. That is determined by the data path of each individual animation channel, which is immutable unless orphaned.

Nothing new to learn here. Just repeat what we already did, but for the face this time:

1. Select the bones along Rain's brow line, followed by their associated channels in the Dope Sheet.
2. Use **Group Channels** (*Ctrl + G*), and name the new group `Eyebrows`.
3. Repeat steps 1 and 2 for Rain's nose and inner cheekbones, naming the channel group `Nose`.
4. Do the same for Rain's mouth and the remaining cheekbones, naming the channel group `Mouth`.
5. Now, do the same for the bones that control Rain's eyes and eyelids but not the eye target. Name the new group `Eyes`.

After gathering all these animation channels into just a few channel groups, we can then re-enable the **FK** and **IK** armature layers and restore the filter settings of the Dope Sheet so that it displays all our animation data once again.

> **Tip**
> You can (and should) continue using Rain's armature layer settings and the filter settings in the Dope Sheet to limit the visibility of bones and their channels as you work on different areas of the animation. Work smarter, not harder; if you don't need to see it, find a way to hide it!

With any luck, the full list of channel groups will even fit on one screen! Now, if only their order made some sense…

Re-ordering channel groups

Most of our remaining channel groups are the default ones named after individual bones. There is nothing wrong with that, but the order in which they are listed from top to bottom has no logical order to it.

This makes no difference to the animated result, but it does make it needlessly difficult to find the channel for a given bone as we work. Every second we spend sorting through the clutter while trying to animate adds up and makes the process less enjoyable, so let's take advantage of these operators in **Channel | Move…**:

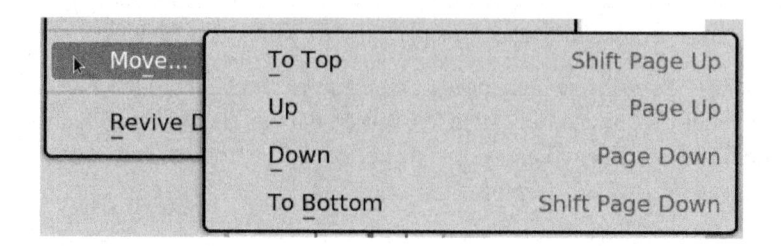

Figure 7.26: Operators for re-ordering selected channels

It's annoying to have to click through a menu hundreds of times, so definitely take advantage of the *Page Up* and *Page Down* hotkeys. Additionally, note that channel groups named after bones cannot be selected if those bones are hidden.

There's no strict convention on how channel groups should be ordered, but I recommend following these guidelines:

1. Keep channel groups together according to their prefixes. Put the MSTR- bones on top, followed by the IK- bones and FK- bones.
2. Within each "group" of channel groups with a common prefix, pay attention to what specific side of the rig each channel group's bone controls. Bones in the center of the rig should come first, then the left bones, and then the right ones.
3. For each limb, organize the channel groups for *FK* bones anatomically from proximal to distal (for example, FK-Upperarm_Parent.L, FK-Forearm.L, then FK-Hand.L).
4. Sort the remaining channel groups by anatomy, importance, or any other way that makes sense to you.

Here's my Dope Sheet after all the sorting:

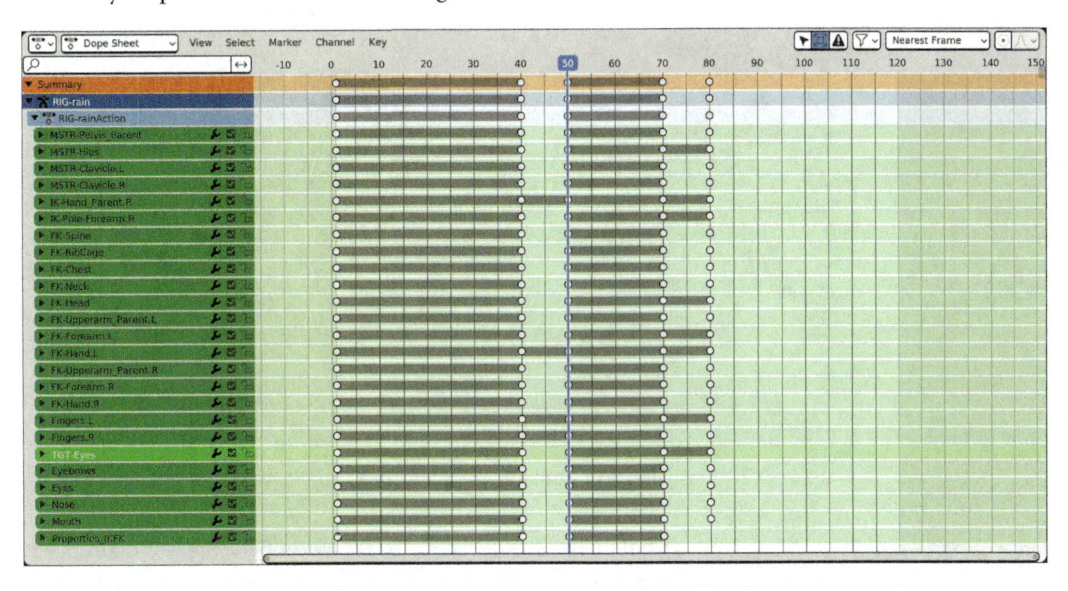

Figure 7.27: Fully re-organized Dope Sheet

Keep in mind that none of what we've just done affects the animation; it just affects how the animation data are organized when seen in the Dope Sheet. Properly sorted channel groups will make our job less frustrating once we get further into animating this character.

On that note, let's go further into animating this character!

Going further into animating this character

Animation can make seconds feel like days. During the frames when Rain holds her poses—not the intervals of movement between our key poses, but the long gray intervals between those intervals—Rain's body is statuesque. Our animation is still a simple sequence of discrete, whole-character poses, with each one encoded in a column of keyframes. As such, Rain's resulting motion is not yet very good, but we'll keep chipping away at it like a sculptor to stone. As we give form to our work, we'll get to witness Rain becoming all the more life-like.

Our next phase involves keying particular bones rather than the whole character all at once; carrying out the poses that require more attention as to how they relate to the poses that come before and after. This middle phase of animation is more detailed than blocking-out, but we're far from anything we'd call detailing. Some might call it the breakdown phase, but I like to call it, well, animating!

Two more in-between poses

In between the three poses we have, consider these two extra poses for Rain's head that we're about to add. We'll call them `Glancing` and `Recognizing`:

Figure 7.28: Idle, Glancing, Looking, Recognizing, and Waving

These poses will help improve and articulate the all-too-smooth transition between the main poses we currently have and make Rain's inner thought process more legible to the viewer.

Glancing

If you think about it, Rain shouldn't just go from standing idle to looking intently. For something to arouse Rain's attention, her eyes have to see it. Perception comes before reaction—not during it—and certainly not after.

We'll do the glancing pose by overwriting some keyframes on frame 40. Some posing can be performed just by duplicating one or more keyframes that already exist:

1. In the Dope Sheet, select the keyframe for **TGT-Eyes** on frame 50.
2. Duplicate (*Shift* + *D*) the selected keyframe to frame 40. This overwrites the existing keyframe.
3. Go to frame 40.

    Now, Rain's eyes are "glancing" at the same thing she will be "looking" at 10 frames later, although it doesn't look comfortable for the eyes to look that far ahead of time:

Figure 7.29: Ortho view of Rain's eyeballs turning a bit too much

Our empathy for our characters is important: if a pose looks like it hurts, it'll hurt to look at. Rain needs to turn more of her body, moving her head in the same direction so that her irises are still visible.

Let's continue posing:

4. **Rotate** (*R*) `FK-Head` in the direction of the eye target so that Rain's eyeballs don't look weird.
5. If you need to, rotate `FK-Neck` and `FK-Chest` a bit in the same direction to compensate for the head.

Don't leave frame 40 before keying your changes to Rain's head, or you'll lose them! With the Dope Sheet now at our disposal, we'll use this opportunity to introduce another method for inserting keyframes.

Inserting keyframes in the Dope Sheet

The Dope Sheet has its own **Insert Keyframes** (*I*) feature:

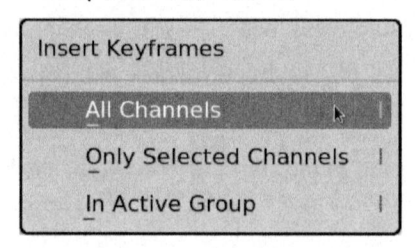

Figure 7.30: The Insert Keyframe menu

We've seen this menu before in the Graph Editor. This is useful for cases where you want to insert keyframes for existing animation channels without having to find and select their corresponding owners elsewhere in the interface.

Let's use it to key the changes we just made to the pose on frame 40:

1. In the Dope Sheet, use **Key** | **Insert Keyframes** (*I*).
2. Select **All Channels**. Note that there's no harm in keying "too much" on this frame since it already has keyframes for every bone.

    Now, the Dope Sheet makes it clear which channels were affected. Note the absence of gray bars for certain bones. This interval of motion between frames 1 and 40 is too slow, though, so let's tighten it up:

3. Select the changed keyframes for the "glancing" pose (these were the ones for `TGT-Eyes`, `FK-Head`, `FK-Neck`, and `FK-Chest` on frame 40).
4. Duplicate (*Shift + D*) the selection to frame 35.
5. Select the corresponding keyframes on frame 1 for the same bones.
6. Duplicate the selection to frame 30.

Now, Rain's head turn looks better and gives her an extra five frames to initially register what she sees before looking more closely:

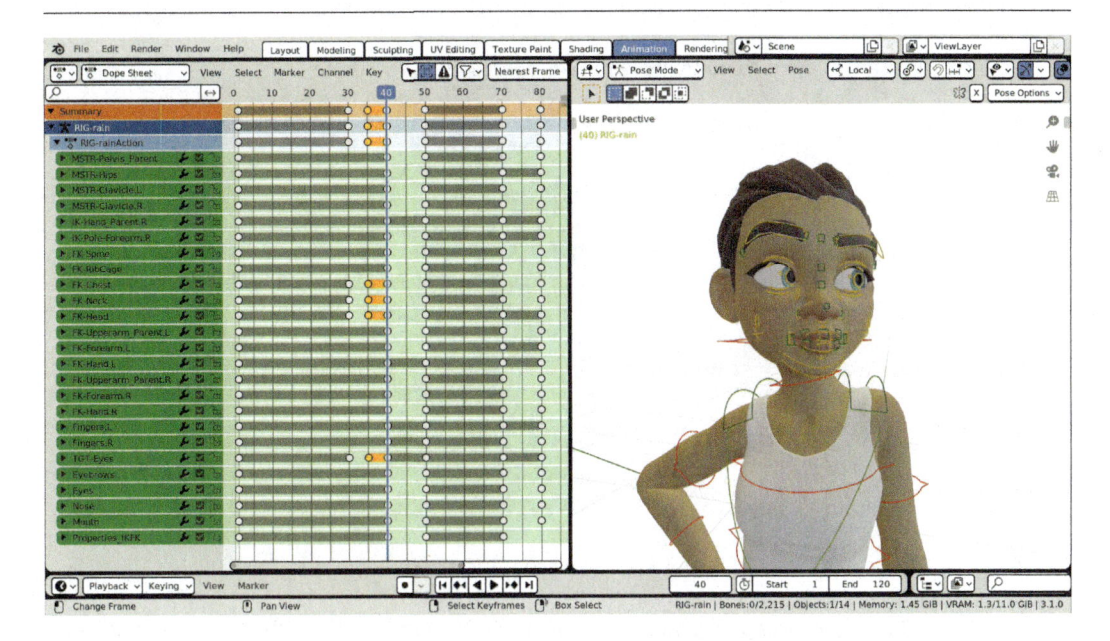

Figure 7.31: Rain's new pose, along with the Dope Sheet

This section of the animation looks okay for now. Let's add the next pose.

Recognizing

Similar to the glancing pose, we want to add another expression in between looking and waving: one of recognizing. This reflects Rain's thought process more articulately; a change in Rain's internal state precedes her decision to stand up and wave excitedly.

For this facial expression, we'll start just a tiny bit before frame 70:

1. Go to frame 68.
2. Create a new facial expression for Rain, one of surprised/delighted recognition.

This expression is open to many possibilities. Here's what I've done:

Figure 7.32: The recognizing pose

Now let's key the expression. Since we re-organized the channels for the face bones, it's easy to do this in the Dope Sheet:

3. Select the channel groups `Eyebrow`, `Eyes`, `Nose`, and `Mouth`.
4. Use **Key | Insert Keyframes** (*I*) **| Only Selected Channels**. This inserts new keyframes for the expression on frame 68.
5. We've no need for the old expression on frame 70 anymore, so let's overwrite it. Duplicate the keyframes on frame 68 to frame 70.
6. On frame 50, select the keyframes that precede the ones on frame 68 and duplicate them to frame 64.

Now, Rain holds her looking expression from frame 50 to frame 64. In contrast, her recognizing expression is relatively short-lived:

Figure 7.33: The sequence of keyframes for Rain's face

Why did we key things in a slightly different order this time? No reason; this was just to repeat the point that we can insert, duplicate, and overwrite keyframes in whatever order we find convenient.

In-between operators for posing

In the 3D Viewport, we have access to some special posing operators. Some of these appear as tools in the toolbar, but I prefer invoking them directly in **Pose | In-Betweens**:

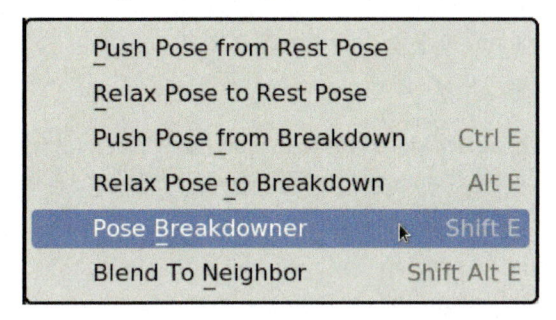

Figure 7.34: The in-between operators

Calling these operators **In-Betweens** makes them sound more important than they really are. We don't necessarily need them; they only work on bones in pose mode, and those last few only work on bones that are animated. Still, they have their uses; think of them as transform operators that take into account contexts such as the rest pose or the neighboring keyframes.

Pose Breakdowner (*Shift + E*), for instance, imagines a linear interpolation between the previous and following keyframes of selected bones. It then adjusts the pose somewhere in between depending on the factor, creating a breakdown pose:

Figure 7.35: The breakdown pose between two different poses at 0%, 50%, 80%, and 100%

Let's use it on Rain's *IK* and *FK* bones to create such a breakdown pose between frames 40 and 70:

1. Go to frame 50.
2. Select all the visible *IK* and *FK* bones (leave the face and fingers alone).
3. Use **Pose | In-Betweens | Pose Breakdowner** (*Shift + E*). Moving the mouse left or right interpolates the pose along the continuum of neighboring keyframes, visualized by a horizontal bar in the 3D Viewport header.
4. Choose a factor of about 90% and confirm.
5. Key your changes.

What we've done here is "relax" the pose a bit so that on frame 50, Rain is almost finished leaning in but keeps going until frame 70. Techniques such as this are subtle but useful for eliminating "stillness" in the early phases of an animation.

This is not unlike scrubbing to, say, frame 48, keying it, and moving those keyframes back to where we want them at frame 50. By using the operator, however, we can remain at the frame we want and get a breakdown pose that might not otherwise be readily available.

> **Tip**
>
> **Push Pose from Breakdown** (*Ctrl + E*) and **Relax Pose to Breakdown** (*Alt + E*) are helpful operators as well, but they will not have much effect unless the current pose is significantly different from what Blender thinks the breakdown pose should be.

Waving

One final part of Rain's animation remains conspicuously un-animated. Rain needs to actually wave her hand, not just hold it up! I'm going to show you a neat technique in the Dope Sheet for this kind of movement. Once you try it, you'll begin to see how it can be applied to all sorts of actions and body parts.

We'll start by thinking of Rain's raised arm as a character by itself with just three *FK* bones. For me, these are `FK-Upperarm_parent.R`, `FK-Forearm.R`, and `FK-Hand.R`. Here are their key poses:

Figure 7.36: Rain's arm waving to one side and to the other

Three bones and two poses; this should be a piece of cake:

1. On frame `83`, pose and key the raised arm inward over Rain's head. Make sure the upper arm, lower arm, and hand are all bent in the same direction.
2. On frame `86`, pose and key the arm to the other side, away from Rain's body. Have Rain straighten her elbow and bend her other joints in the opposite direction as before.

   This gives us all the keyframes we need to make a single "wave". Next, we duplicate them to repeat the motion.
3. Select the keyframes you just created on frames `83` and `86`.
4. Duplicate the selected keyframes, moving the new keyframes six frames forward.
5. Keep duplicating until you get past frame `120` (where we may end the animation).

Having duplicated this simple sequence of keyframes, we've got Rain doing a fairly basic waving motion using just the two alternating poses we made every six frames:

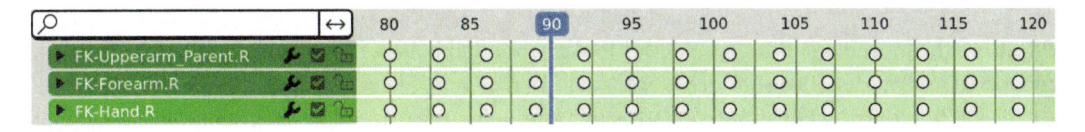

Figure 7.37: Repeating keyframes for Rain's arm

Watch it for yourself. I think it looks okay, but by using a simple trick in the Dope Sheet, we can make it look even better.

Staggering keyframes

Here comes the technique I've been waiting to show you. By offsetting the keyframes of the *FK* bones, we can create a more visually pleasing arc of motion in Rain's arm:

> **Tip**
> To select one long row of multiple keyframes, try **Box Select** (*B*). Take a look at the **Select** menu in the Dope Sheet for some other handy ways of selecting lots of keyframes at once.

1. Select all the waving keyframes for the *FK* forearm bone (either `FK-Forearm.L` or `FK-Forearm.R`) and **Move** (*G*) them one frame rightward.
2. Select all the waving keyframes for the *FK* hand bone (either `FK-Hand.L` or `FK-Hand.R`) and **Move** (*G*) them two frames rightward.

Now, the motion of the upper arm precedes the forearm, which precedes the wrist. Those initial two poses for the arm were convenient for keying the extreme positions of all three bones at once, but the final step was to break apart their keyframes.

Here's how the result will look in the Dope Sheet, assuming your channel groups are stacked like mine. If they are, you can see how helpful it is to have them ordered like this:

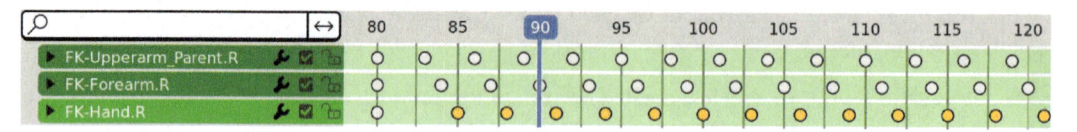

Figure 7.38: Staggered keyframes

What we've done here is create a delay in the movement of bones along the *FK* chain of the arm. Not only is Rain literally waving, the motion of her limbs is itself like a wave, traveling from the shoulder to the fingertips!

Offsetting the movement of bones like this looks better and helps sell the illusion of inertia between connected body parts. It's also much easier to do in the Dope Sheet than in the Graph Editor. We'll see this principle applied in all sorts of areas in Rain's animation, from her neck and limbs to her hair and scarf.

Polishing the animation

Figuring out the timing of thousands of keyframes is an iterative process with interrelating factors. At first, we keyed our initial poses based on broad, sometimes arbitrary decisions about what things ought to happen and when. Continuing with our work, the timing of additional keyframes was determined by the ones we had already made, and so forth.

Finally, we've reached a stage at which we can refine the motion of individual bones, smoothing-out their motion in some places and/or adding detail in others. We'll also key some bones that, as yet, have remained untouched.

> **Tip**
>
> Along with the other two guidelines we've learned, I've one remaining bit of advice for this part of the exercise: nothing is sacred! As you work, delete any unnecessary keyframes that seem to get in the way, and don't be afraid to edit any keyframe you want, even if it breaks apart those long columns for key poses.

Let's begin by paying a visit to our old friend the Graph Editor.

Using the Graph Editor on bones

We won't have a use for the Graph Editor for every individual bone, but if there's any bone that deserves this much attention, it's `MSTR-Pelvis_Parent`, the bone that moves all of Rain's torso. Think back to our guideline on animating from the center outward; if we get the motion of this bone right, the rest of Rain's animation will follow.

> **Tip**
>
> Use (*Ctrl* + *Tab*) to quickly alternate between the Dope Sheet and the Graph Editor.

Here's what my animation for `MSTR-Pelvis_parent` looks like in the Graph Editor:

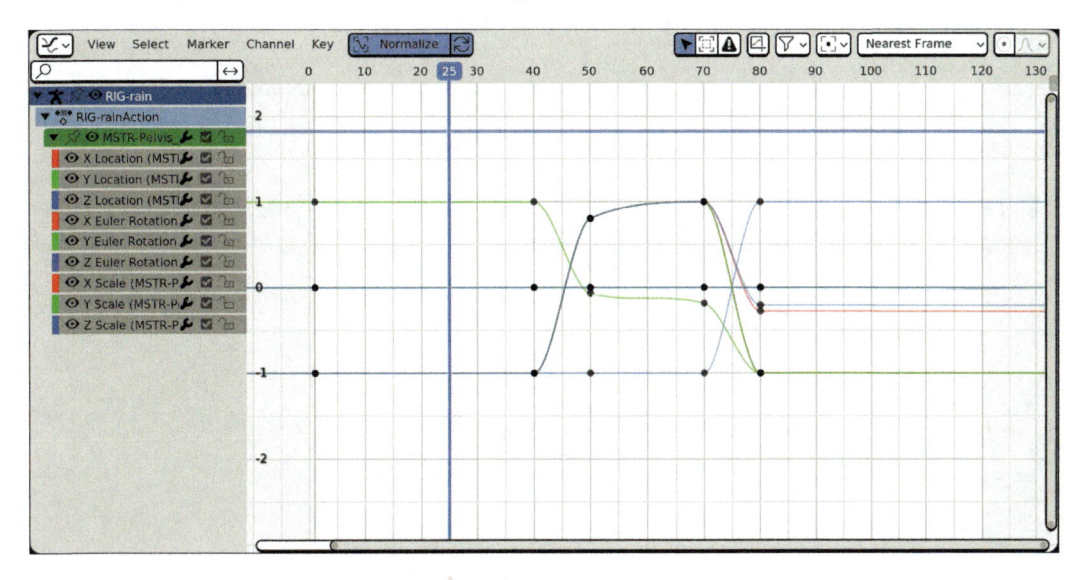

Figure 7.39: F-curves for pelvis bone (Normalize enabled)

Of course, these are all Bezier keyframes with Auto-Clamped handles. It's no wonder these are the default; they do such a good job on their own that we haven't had to think at all about keyframe handles and/or specific interpolation modes until now.

Finessing the motion of the torso

What can we do to improve the motion of this one bone? For one thing, a standing character's body should never hold perfectly still; like a living person, it should breathe and sway at least a little bit at all times. While all her F-curves are flat, Rain will look like a wax sculpture, even if it's just for a few frames.

In the following treatment, I've added a few random keyframes to address this stillness at the beginning and end, mostly in the **X Location** and **Y Location** F-curves:

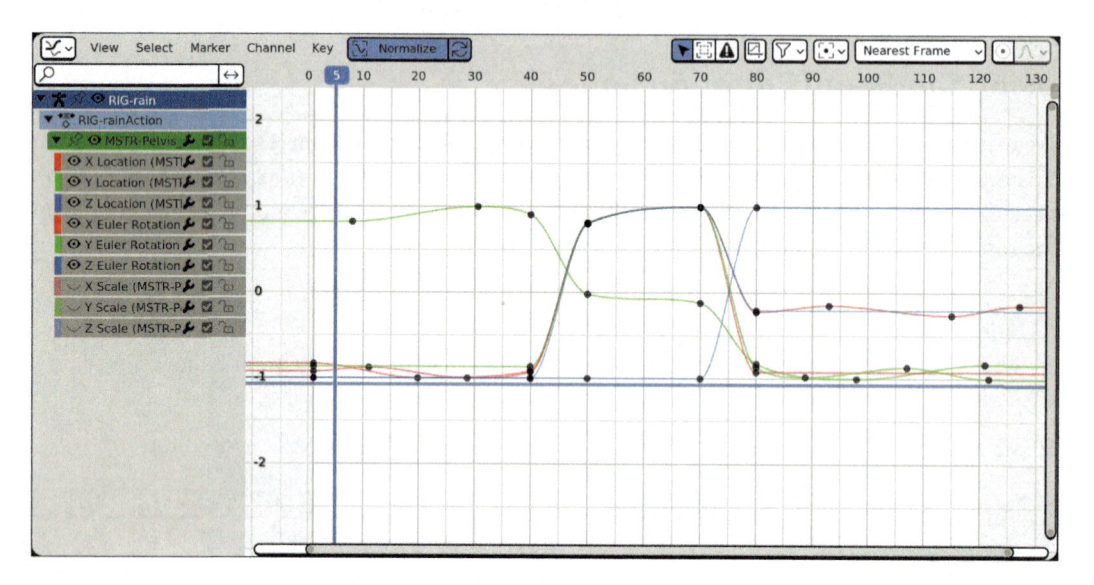

Figure 7.40: Some subtle variation added

This lazy technique feels less like animating than just "eliminating stillness", but even a tiny bit of extra movement can make all the difference between Rain the statue and Rain the believable human character.

The torso bone is also the "heaviest" bone in a sense; its movement should appear to carry a lot of momentum. This effect can be achieved by using **Key | Handle Type** (*V*) **| Automatic on all our keyframes**:

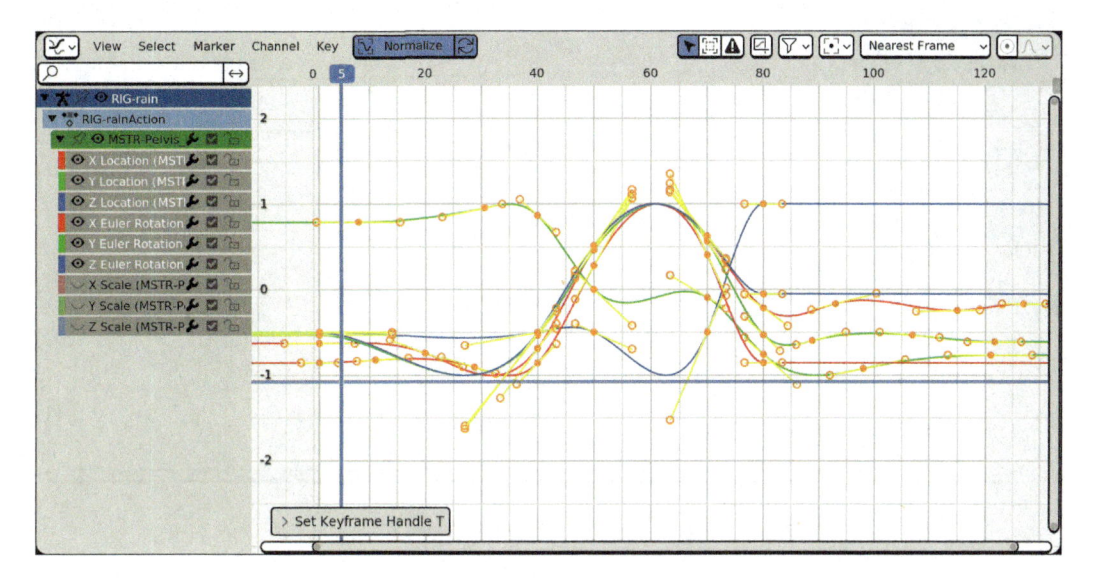

Figure 7.41: Automatic Bezier keyframes

Well, maybe not all of them... we'll need to be a bit more discriminating about which keyframes to let loose. We can also manually set some handles by using the **Aligned** type, throw in some more keyframes, and move them in any direction, whatever gives us the F-curves we want.

> **Tip**
>
> Interpolation works in both directions, so watch out for motion that begins too early. This is especially true for automatic keyframes. In the previous example, for instance, Rain's torso would "wind up" long before frame 40 in preparation for the next pose. This makes no sense; Rain's body shouldn't move in anticipation of something she doesn't yet know she's about to do.

Here's my final treatment:

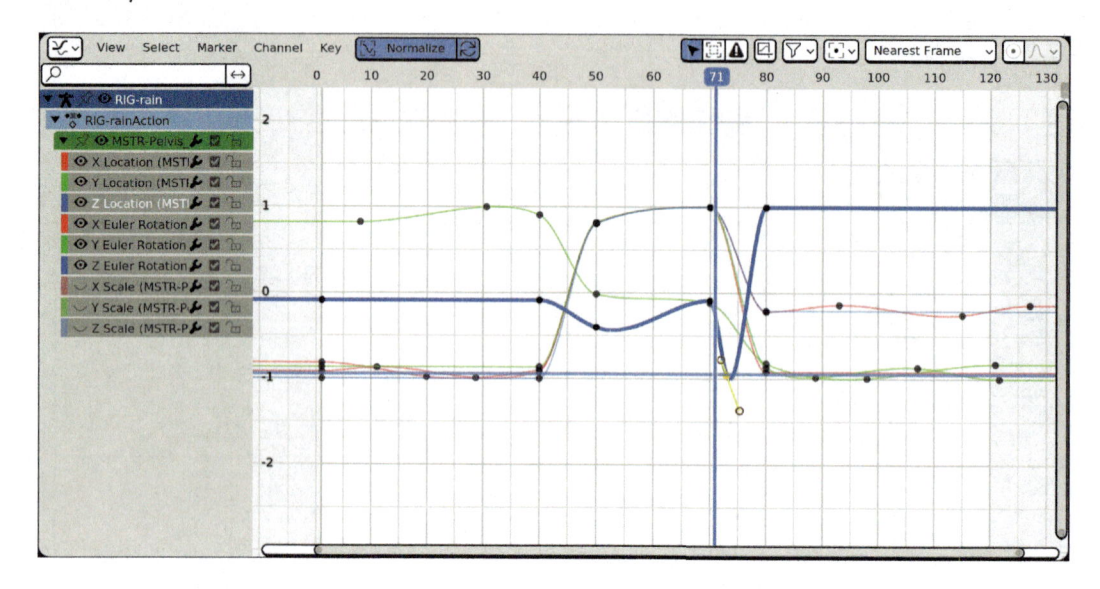

Figure 7.42: Final F-Curves for MSTR-Pelivs_Parent

Now it's your turn:

1. Select `MSTR-Pelvis_Parent` and find its keyframes in the Graph Editor.
2. Add some subtle movement to the flat sections of the F-curves; **X Location** and **Y Location** will benefit from this the most. You may ignore the rest.
3. Use Automatic Bezier handles on particular keyframes, along with anything else you like, until you're satisfied with the overall motion of Rain's torso.

We've gone over the animation for `MSTR-Pelvis_Parent` three times now, once during the blocking-out phase, again in the second animation phase, and one last time in the Graph Editor!

Animating Rain's accessories

We've come a long way just by animating the bones in the armature layers **IK**, **FK**, **Face Primary**, and **Fingers**, but there are a ton of bones in the other layers that are for animating as well. We're not obligated to animate everything, but some quick work in the **Hair** and **Clothes** layers is the next most obvious step. Just because we didn't key those bones earlier when we began animating doesn't mean we can't do it now. We can add animation to whatever we want whenever we decide it's convenient!

When we animate these last bits, Rain's remaining loose parts will come to life, and our animation will finally be complete:

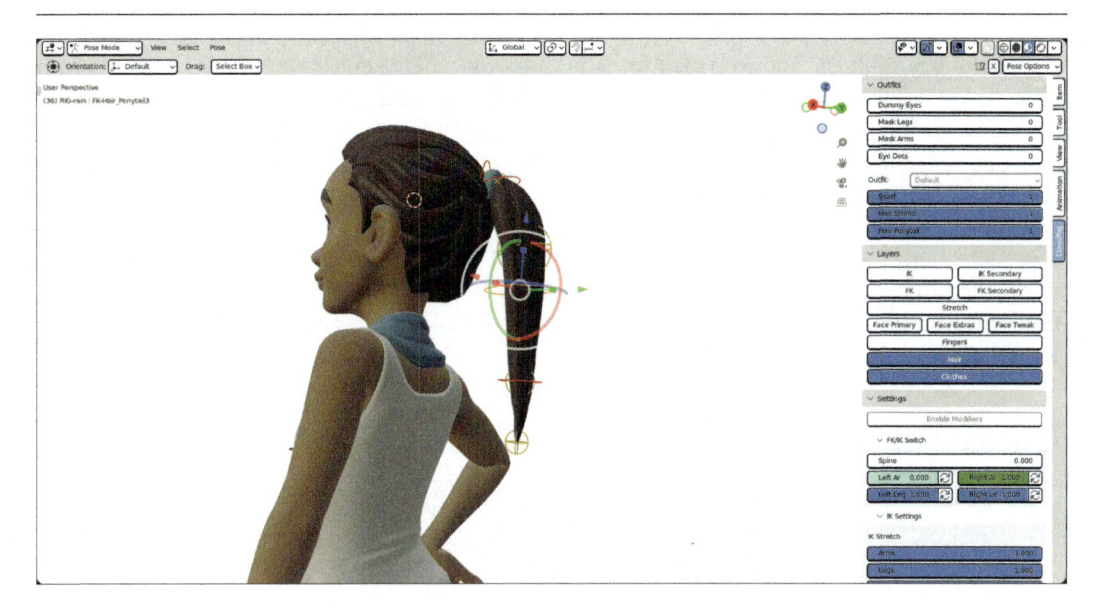

Figure 7.43: Animating Rain's hair and scarf bones

1. Enable the armature layers **Hair** and **Clothes** and disable the rest. Additionally, unhide Rain's **Hair** and **Scarf** meshes if you hid them earlier.
2. So that we don't get overwhelmed by all the new channels we're about to add, Disable **Show Hidden** in the Dope Sheet.
3. Find a frame where Rain is standing relatively still (frame 1, for instance) and pose her hair and scarf to ensure they appear to hang straight down according to the basic laws of gravity. Key the **location** and **rotation** of all the visible bones.
4. Scrub through your animation. Before and after each major change in Rain's pose, key the scarf and hair bones so they appear to point in the right direction (down).

What other details can you add? The blinking of eyelids, the twitching of fingers, or the swinging of arms and wrists; there are too many possibilities to cover in this chapter. That doesn't mean you have to stop, though!

Summary

Because they were so numerous, the keyframes we worked with in this exercise needed to be viewed in the Dope Sheet, where they took on a completely different appearance than in the Graph Editor. Moreover, while learning this new tool, we still had to simultaneously grapple with all the peculiarities of posing and keying the bones in a complex character rig. This might give someone the notion that character animation is an essentially different process from, say, cube animation, but this is an illusion. Keyframes are still keyframes, and bones are just weird little objects that pull on invisible puppet strings.

Another illusion I hope you won't fall for is to think that this exercise was a formal protocol for character animation instead of a crash course on the Dope Sheet and a handful of operators specific to pose bones. There are no hard rules in this chapter, only guidelines. Every character animation (and character) that you work on will be different and present unique and varied challenges for which you will discover your own solutions. Think freely, be creative, and don't forget to have fun!

Okay, now hurry up and finish having fun, because the next exercise **is** a formal protocol with hard rules! It is a singular, perennial challenge, and you may go mad trying to solve it on your own! Don't think freely; abandon all creativity and start panicking... because in the next chapter, we're doing a **walk cycle**.

Questions

1. How many bones are in a pose? Can one single bone have a pose?
2. Using Rain's **CloudRig** interface, what bones can act as the parents of our *IK* bones? In what cases might each bone be useful as a parent?
3. What are the differences between the Dope Sheet and the Timeline?
4. What can we do in the Graph Editor that we can't in the Dope Sheet?
5. Why use the Dope Sheet if the Graph Editor displays more information about keyframes?
6. Why did we edit/overwrite keyframes so much? Why not just get it right the first time?
7. For in-between operators such as **Push Pose from Breakdown** or **Relax Pose to Breakdown**, what does "Breakdown" mean?
8. Why should things like hair and clothing be animated last?

8
The Walk Cycle

Ah, yes... walking. Putting one foot in front of the other. That thing we all learn when we're small, and which comes naturally for the rest of our lives. *That thing which is very easy to do...*

Not so! Animators, babies, and the differently-abled alike know that walking is not to be taken for granted. If you want to know what it's like for an animator to attempt their first walking animation, picture a baby taking its first steps. They look ridiculous; they stumble, fall, get injured – sometimes it gets so frustrating that they even cry and soil themselves... and it's not so easy for the babies either.

Nevertheless, the characters in our animations can't just stand in one place forever, and that's why a whole chapter has been dedicated just to the peculiarities of getting a 3D character to move forward. We'll start by doing the hard part first...

In this chapter, you will learn the following:

- Labeling the steps in a walk cycle
- The correct way to make a character move forward
- Making F-curves cycle automatically
- How to make the *IK* feet "roll"
- Animating the toes and arms with *FK* bones

Technical requirements

To follow along with this chapter, you'll need a new scene open in Blender. This scene should contain Rain, the character rig we've been using. Follow the instructions at the beginning of *Chapter 6* if you need to download Rain or if you've forgotten how to link her into a new scene.

Preparing the walk cycle scene

Imagine walking alone down a straight, level hallway. With nothing to trip over or distract you, your walking movement will tend to repeat itself – left foot, right foot, left, right, left, right – until you reach your destination. It matters little whether the hallway is several meters or a mile long; your movement at a given segment of time would look like any other segment. For that matter, this would also be true of marching, jogging, running, skipping – any movement on two legs that repeats itself.

In the animation world, this sort of thing is called a **walk cycle** – a periodic walking animation that can repeat ad infinitum for as long as the animator needs. More than just a technical exercise, a walk cycle is a valuable asset that can be reused in any scene in which a character walks in a straight line.

To set up our scene for such an animation, we'll start by labeling some frames in the Timeline. Then we'll adjust some settings in Rain's rig so that she's prepared to walk forward continuously.

The timeline of a walk cycle

It is often said that a journey of a thousand miles begins with a single step, but let's not get ahead of ourselves – *a whole step?!* Animating our first step is a very big deal, and animating two steps is pretty much our whole journey. To realize such lofty ambitions, we must be patient and carefully plan ahead.

Walk cycle periodicity

How many frames should a single step take? This varies depending on the anatomy of the character and how fast you want them to go. For this exercise, I'll go ahead and select a number for us: 12 frames per step.

This means Rain will have 12 frames to put one foot forward like so:

Figure 8.1: Frames 0 and 12 of Rain's walk cycle

...and another 12 frames to put the opposite foot forward in the same way:

Figure 8.2: Frames 12 and 24 of Rain's walk cycle

The first 12 frames will be a left/right reflection of the subsequent 12 frames, so the entire walk cycle will have a **period** of 24 frames. If we key everything correctly, Rain's pose at frame 0 will look identical to frame 24 and the period will end exactly as it began (except, of course, that Rain will have moved one meter forward – more on that later).

The result will give Rain a nice, leisurely pace, not too fast or slow. More importantly, we love numbers like 12 and 24. Any number divisible by 4 is just fantastic.

We've established how many frames a single step should take, but a lot needs to happen in those frames! Again, we mustn't rush our first step, so let's break it down into smaller sections.

The phases of a walk cycle

While animators have many different names for the phases in a single step (and competing theories as to which one should come first), here are the ones we'll be using, starting with the left foot in front:

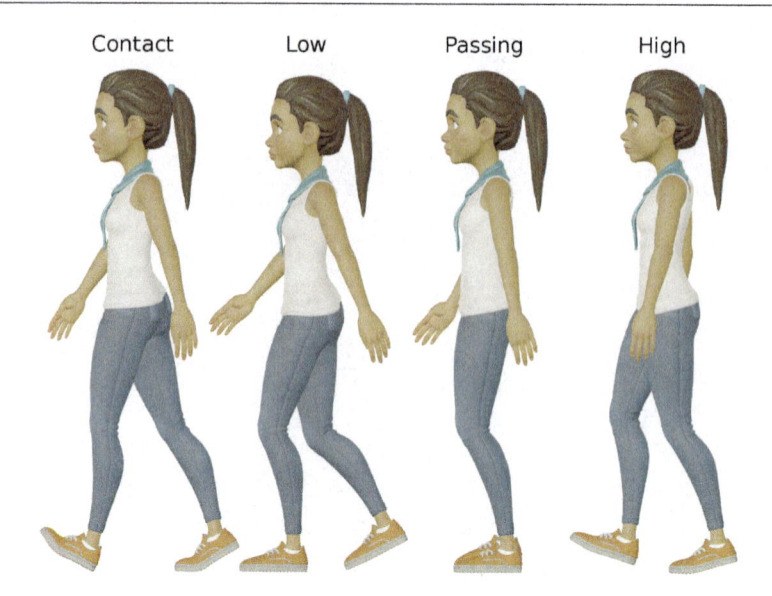

Figure 8.3: The key poses of our walk cycle, from left to right

Here's a pose-by-pose breakdown of what needs to happen:

- *Contact*: The front foot contacts the ground at the heel. The contacting foot will remain on the ground for the next 12 frames, carrying the character's weight until the subsequent contact phase.
- *Low*: Having downward momentum from earlier, the torso reaches its low point around this phase. The contacting foot now lies flat on the ground and the opposite foot gets lifted and carried forward.
- *Passing*: Swinging forward, the foot in the air passes the foot on the ground.
- *High*: The torso reaches its highest point here. The foot that was behind is now in front and will soon make touchdown for the next contact phase.

That's 4 poses on one foot, followed by the same 4 poses (reflected on the X axis) on the other foot, then back to the initial pose. 8 poses over a period of 24 frames means that each of these poses can be 3 frames apart, 24 being the nice divisible number that it is. Starting at 0, the most crucial frames in our walk cycle are therefore 0, 3, 6, 9, 12, 15, 19, 21, and 24.

As you might guess, a lot of our keyframes will live on these frames, so it will be helpful to have them labeled. That's where the next feature comes in.

Timeline markers

Markers are little triangles in an animation editor that allow us to label important frames, so we don't lose track of them. These will be especially helpful in complex work such as animating a walk cycle.

Adding markers

Let's insert markers now:

1. Go to frame 0 (yes, frame 0).
2. In the Timeline, use **Marker | Add Marker** (*M*).
3. Add a marker every 3 frames until you get to frame 24.

You should now have markers on frames 0, 3, 6, 9, 12, 15, 18, 21, and 24:

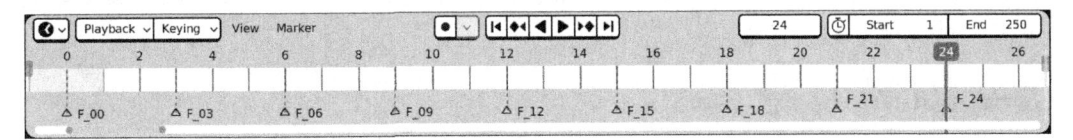

Figure 8.4: Markers in the Timeline

> **Tip**
> Markers can be selected, moved, duplicated, and deleted just like keyframes. Remember to keep your mouse cursor in the marker region when doing so, or you may accidentally operate on a keyframe instead.

New markers are automatically named according to the frame number at which they were added. This is not particularly helpful, and it can get confusing if you move the marker to a different frame. We had better give our markers some useful names.

Labeling markers

Let's rename our markers to correspond with the phases of our walk cycle:

1. Use **Marker | Rename Marker** (*F2*) to rename the markers at frames 0, 3, 9, and 12 `Left Contact`, `Left Low`, `Left Passing`, and `Left High`, respectively.
2. Repeat this for the markers at frames 12, 15, 18, and 21, naming them `Right Contact`, `Right Low`, `Right Passing`, and `Right High`.
3. The final marker on frame 24 should be named `Left Contact`, just like the one on frame 0.

Our markers now show more helpful labels:

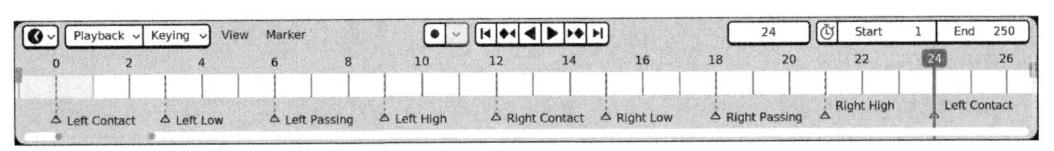

Figure 8.5: Renamed markers in the Timeline

> **Important note**
> It's no coincidence that the markers on frames 0 and 24 have the same name. These are two frames for what will appear to be one pose when we're finished. Any visual difference between them may indicate a glitch or stutter in the walk cycle.

The markers we just added will appear not only in the Timeline but in most other time-based editors, including the Graph Editor and Dope Sheet. While markers have some additional functions, such as switching the active camera, that's a topic for another chapter. For this exercise, our markers don't confer any functionality; they're just reference points to keep us from forgetting what ought to happen on a given frame.

Getting Rain ready to walk

As usual, an advanced character rig like Rain will have some parameters that need to be set in anticipation of the work we're about to do. We'll need to be very particular about which limbs use *IK* versus *FK*.

Focusing on the IK bones

Inverse kinematics is indispensable for any kind of walking animation. Without the *IK* bones for Rain's feet, animating a walk cycle would be intractably tedious.

Animating the *IK* bones for a walk cycle is hard enough as it is without those pesky other bones getting in our way, so let's isolate that layer and determine which additional parts of Rain should use *IK*:

1. If you haven't already, link Rain to the scene, just like we did in *Chapter 6* and *Chapter 7*.
2. In **CloudRig | Layers**, enable the **IK** armature layer and disable the rest.
3. Rain's feet are set to use *IK* by default, but let's also try using *IK* instead of *FK* for Rain's spine. Go to **CloudRig | Settings | FK/IK Switch** and set **Spine** to 1.0.

The choice to use *IK* instead of *FK* for the spine is not crucial for our walk cycle, but it will let us animate Rain's chest using only the `MSTR-Chest_Parent` bone. That way, we won't need to mess with *FK* bones until we get around to animating Rain's arms.

Figure 8.6: Rain with just her IK bones

We've isolated the *IK* armature layer for the time being, but this doesn't mean that all limbs should use *IK*.

No bones left behind

Rain is going to walk forward continuously on the *Y* axis. If a given bone is not animated to move forward, or if it is not parented directly or indirectly to another bone that moves forward, Rain will leave that bone behind. Any bone left behind had better not be one with a visible effect on Rain, or she might look catastrophically different after walking just a few paces!

As we learned earlier, it helps to preview what will happen when we animate a bone by simply moving it ourselves (without confirming the transformation, of course). Rain's main torso bone, `MSTR-Pelvis_Parent`, will certainly need to move forward if we expect her to walk anywhere, so let's grab it and run a rough diagnostic:

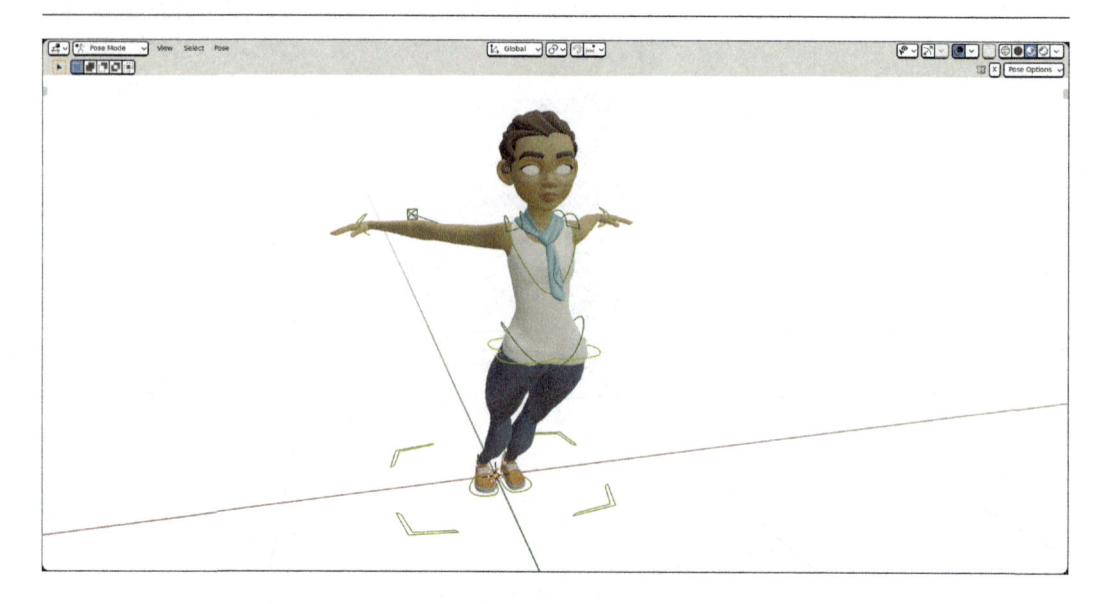

Figure 8.7: MSTR-Pelvis_Parent moving forward on the Y axis

From bottom to top, Rain's feet stick to the floor, but we want that. Using independent *IK* targets, the feet mustn't move forward until we want them to. Rain's hands, however, have nowhere important to be. All they need to do is swing from the shoulders, so they really ought to use *FK* instead of *IK*. We'll animate them last. Finally, Rain's eyeballs have rolled backward in her head.

Let's fix these issues now:

1. In the **FK/IK Switch** panel, set both **Left Arm** and **Right Arm** to 0.0.
2. Since we won't need them, you can hide the *IK* bones for Rain's arms. These are IK-Hand_Parent.L, IK-Hand_Parent.R, IK-Pole_Forearm.L, and IK-Pole_Forearm.R. Select them and use **Hide** (*H*).
3. Come to think of it, why don't we hide her arms altogether? Go to **CloudRig | Outfits** and set **Mask Arms** to 1 for now. Hiding Rain's hair and scarf like before would be a good idea too.
4. To prevent Rain's eyeballs from rolling back in their sockets, go to **CloudRig | Settings | Face Settings** and set **Eye Target Parent** to **Torso_Loc** (2). This will keep the bone TGT-Eyes in front of Rain as she walks away from the root bone.

If we didn't have these settings, the bones IK-Hand_Parent.L, IK-Hand_Parent.R, and TGT-Eyes would all have to be animated to move forward along with MSTR-Foot_Parent.L, MSTR-Foot_Parent.R, and MSTR-Pelvis. As we're about to see, any bone that must be animated to move continuously forward will require that we pay careful attention to its **Y Location** F-curve. Limiting the number of bones for which this is the case will make our job easier.

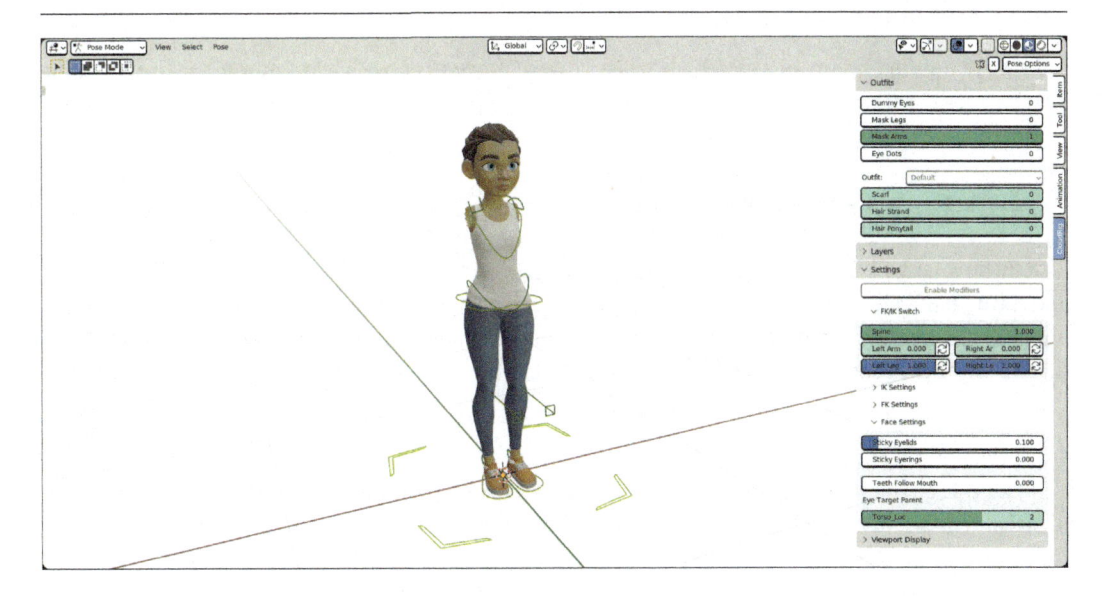

Figure 8.8: Rain simplified and ready to walk forward

We've avoided quite a few potential mishaps by planning ahead, marking our frames, and adjusting Rain's settings before inserting any keyframes. However, walking is such an involved animation that we'll still need to be cautious! Now that Rain is ready to start walking forward using only three bones, those three bones and their forward movement will be the sole focus of the next section.

Moving forward on the Y axis

Once again, it's time to start posing and inserting keyframes! In the previous chapter, we animated by keying major poses with many bones at once, but in this exercise, we'll begin by keying the locations of just three: MSTR-Foot_Parent.L, MSTR-Foot_Parent.R, and MSTR-Pelvis. After the adjustments we made to the properties in Rain's **CloudRig** interface, these three bones are all that will be responsible for Rain's forward movement on the Y axis. Special attention must be paid to their **Y Location** F-curves.

In fact, the forward movement of these bones along the Y axis is the only thing that concerns us for now! Forget about swinging the arms, turning the hips, or even picking up the feet; all that matters for now is moving one foot forward, then the other, then the rest of the body.

> **Important note**
> "Forward" in this chapter refers to forward from Rain's point of view, which requires negative numeric changes in our bones' **Y Location** values.

After we've finished keying our extremely basic forward movement, we'll learn how to make everything loop correctly. This requires that we resolve something of a paradox; Rain's walk cycle must end as it began, but she must also not be where she was...

Establishing the stride length

Exactly how far will Rain travel in 24 frames, and when will each foot swing forward while the other one stays planted to the ground? We can answer these questions by roughly keying the first *contact* poses. These are the crucial points at which the foot in front will contact the ground to support Rain's weight, while the foot behind prepares to lift up and swing forward.

> **Important note**
> I call these "rough" poses because we're only concerned with the bones' locations on the Y axis for now. Nevertheless, the Y locations of each bone must be entered precisely as written in the following instructions using numeric inputs. Even the tiniest discrepancy here, such as transforming one foot by -0.99 meters instead of -1.0, can compound over time, causing our independent bones to drift apart as the walk cycle repeats itself.

Keying the initial stride forward

For our first pose, I've prepared some magic numbers for posing Rain's feet in the *Left Contact* pose. Remember to enter them exactly:

1. Go to frame 0 (Left Contact).
2. Move MSTR-Foot_Parent.L exactly -0.2 m in front of Rain on the *Y* axis.
3. Move MSTR-Foot_Parent.R exactly 0.3 m behind Rain on the *Y* axis.
4. Key the location of MSTR-Foot_Parent.L, MSTR-Foot_Parent.R, and MSTR-Pelvis_Parent.

This is a far cry from the contact pose you saw earlier, but it'll do for now:

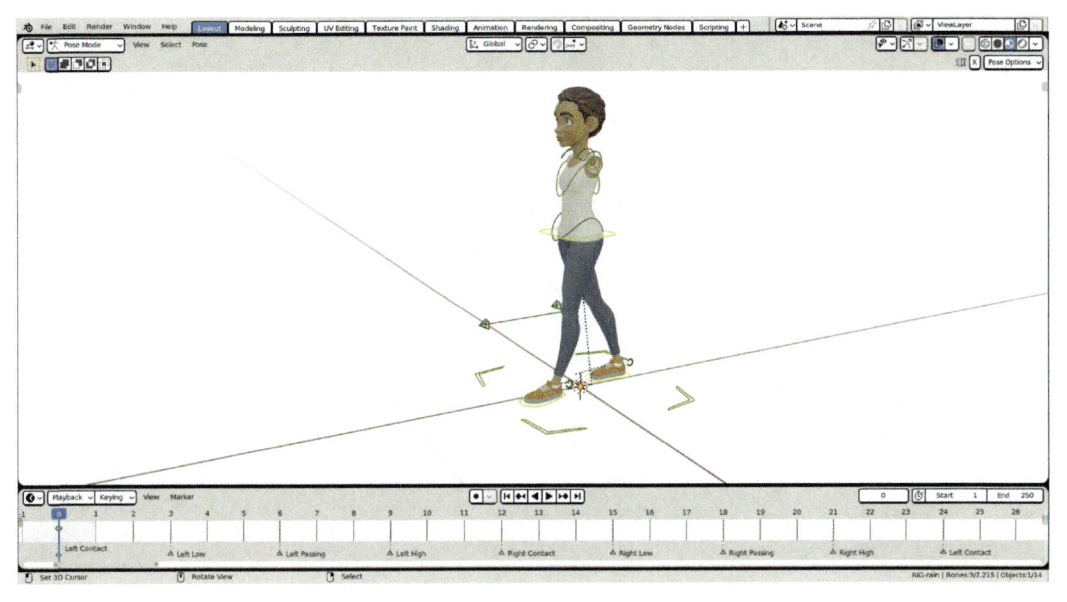

Figure 8.9: Rain putting one foot forward

The important thing is that we've established the distance between Rain's feet on the Y axis. If one foot is -0.2 meters ahead and the other is 0.3 meters behind, that gives us a total distance of half a meter. Double that and you've got the distance that the trailing foot must cover in order to get as far ahead of the opposite foot on the subsequent Contact pose.

This is known as the **stride length** of the walk cycle, a value that is no less critical than the walk cycle period. Together, the stride length and period determine the overall speed of a character's movement in world space. As it happens, our stride length is 1 meter, for a walking speed of 1 meter every 24 frames. Tidy, yes?

Two small steps for Rain

Now, to take our first real step forward! We'll skip ahead and key the Right Contact pose on frame 12:

1. Go to frame 12 (*Right Contact*).
2. Move `MSTR-Foot_Parent.R` exactly `-1.0` m forward on the *Y* axis.
3. Key the location of both *IK* foot bones (but not the torso).

There, our first step! Never mind how it looks right now:

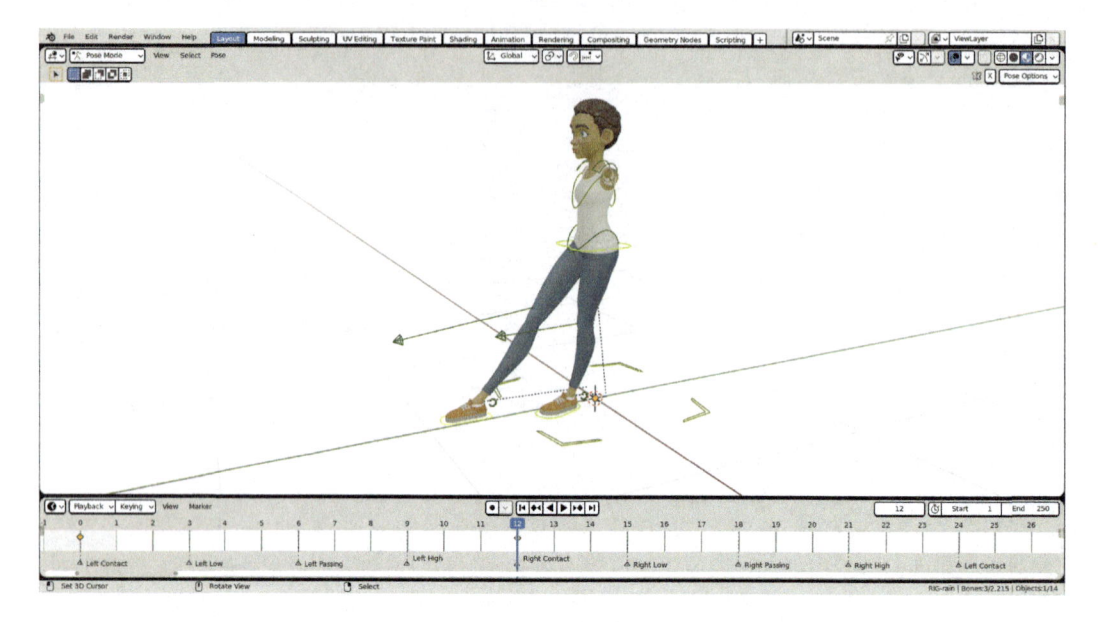

Figure 8.10: Right foot forward 1 meter

Now let's bring the left foot forward to key the final *Left Contact* pose. We will also need to move the torso one meter forward to catch up with everything else:

1. Go to frame 24 (the other *Left Contact*).

2. Move MSTR-Foot_Parent.L and MSTR-Pelvis_Parent exactly -1.0 m forward on the *Y* axis.

3. Key the location of all three bones.

With those last keyframes, we've ended the walk cycle on frame 24 exactly as it began on frame 0, but with one major change – each of the three bones has moved 1 meter forward:

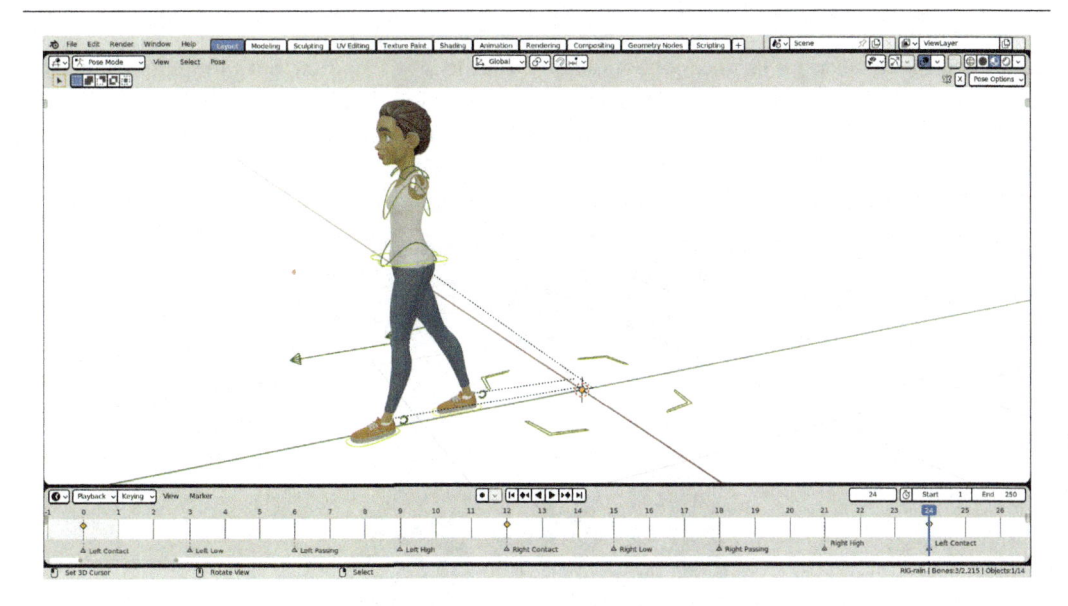

Figure 8.11: Rain on frame 24

Let's inspect our **Y Location** F-curves in the Graph Editor:

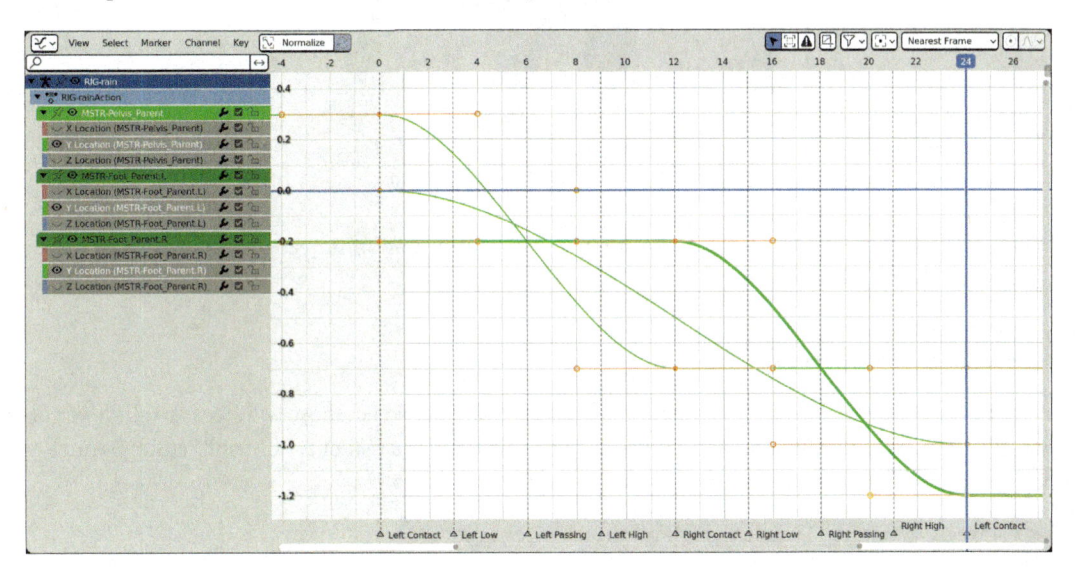

Figure 8.12: Y Location F-curves of forward-moving bones

The alternating flat sections for the foot bones represent the time that each foot will spend planted on the ground while the opposite foot swings ahead and the rest of the body moves forward. It's important that these flat sections stay flat, or the foot will slide while it's meant to stay in place.

Et voila, two steps – our walk cycle is practically finished!

Figure 8.13: Three initial key poses

What's that? I agree, it looks terr...ific! A terrific walking animation indeed. So terrific, in fact, that we're ready to make it loop forever.

Looping the animation

We need Rain to keep walking (okay, shuffling) continuously, but so far, those two steps are all we've got. For this to truly be a walk cycle, Rain must keep traveling for the rest of time, just like that bouncing ball we sent away in *Chapter 2*.

Let's start by making the movement of all three bones cyclic:

1. In the Graph Editor, Select all the F-curves for all three bones, `MSTR-Foot_Parent.L`, `MSTR-Foot_Parent.R`, and `MSTR-Pelvis_Parent`.
2. Use **Set Keyframe Extrapolation** (*Shift + E*) | **Make Cyclic**.

> **Important note**
> Though we are focused on **Y Location** channels for now, remember to make all the other F-curves cyclic as well.

We might be getting somewhere, but Rain is getting nowhere. Here are the resulting **Y Location** F-curves, zoomed out so we can see where this is all going beyond the first second of animation:

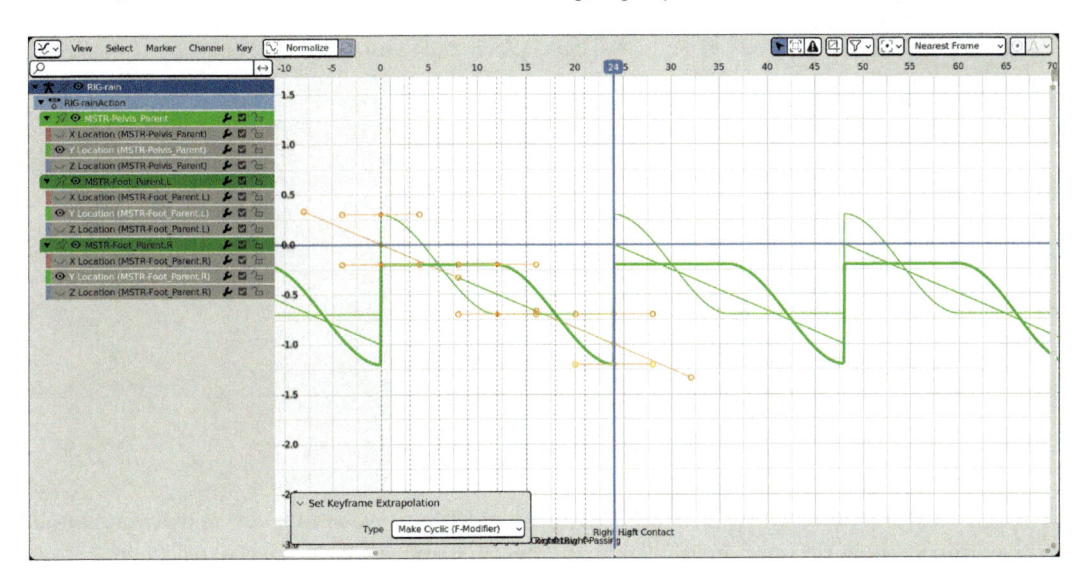

Figure 8.14: Cyclic F-curves

Ugh, how I hate those ugly vertical cliffs! They're rarely a good sign. This type of periodicity causes Rain's bones to snap back every 24 frames to their initial position – the result of cyclic F-curves with unequal first and last keyframes. It's technically repeating, but not the kind of repetition we're looking for. Rain goes nowhere, whereas we need her to have traveled 1 meter after 24 frames, 2 meters after 48, and so on.

Could **Linear Extrapolation** be the solution? That suffices for the torso, but it fails to repeat the motion of the feet:

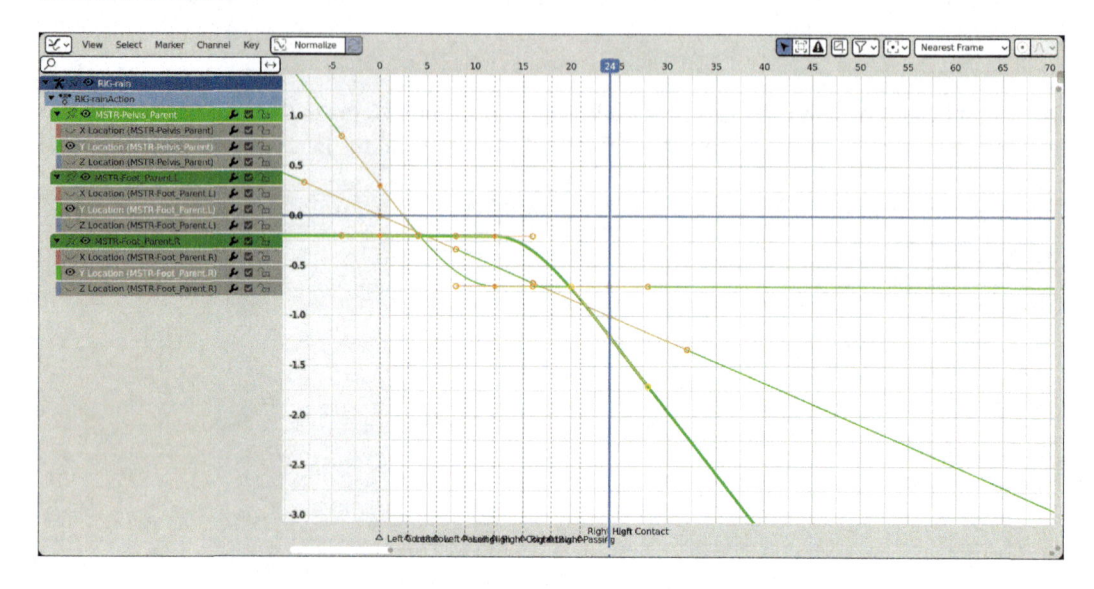

Figure 8.15: Extrapolated F-curves

What we need is a combination of extrapolation and repetition. We need F-curves that compound, with each repetition, the offset in value between their first and last keyframes; to *repeat with offset*, if you will.

Offsetting the loop

The property of being cyclical belongs to an F-curve as an **F-curve modifier**. F-curve modifiers work as non-destructive effects, much like the modifiers on a mesh object. The modifiers of the active F-curve can be found in the **Modifiers** tab, located in the right sidebar of the Graph Editor:

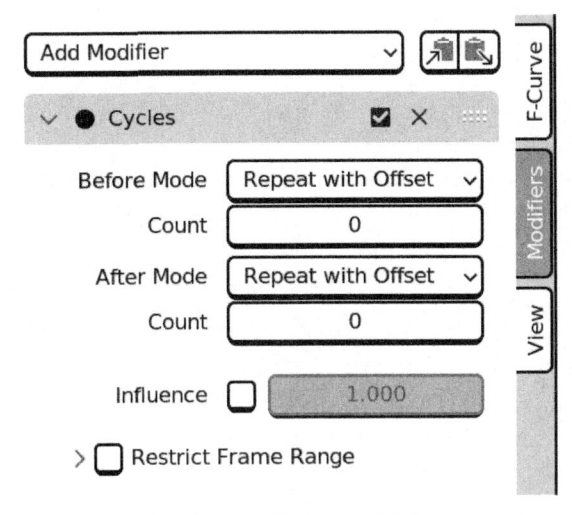

Figure 8.16: Cycles modifier

It turns out that the **Make Cyclic** operator simply adds a **Cycles** modifier to the selected F-curve!

> **Important note**
> "Cycles" in this context just means cyclic. The word has nothing to do with the Cycles renderer.

The **Cycles** modifier panel contains some additional settings we desperately need. You'll have to change them manually one modifier at a time, so it's a good thing there are only three F-curves that need this treatment:

1. Navigate to the **Modifiers** tab in the Graph Editor's right-hand sidebar (*N*).
2. For the **Cycles** modifier of each of the three **Y Location** F-curves, change both the **Before Mode** and **After Mode** to **Repeat with Offset**.

Here are our Y Location F-curves now:

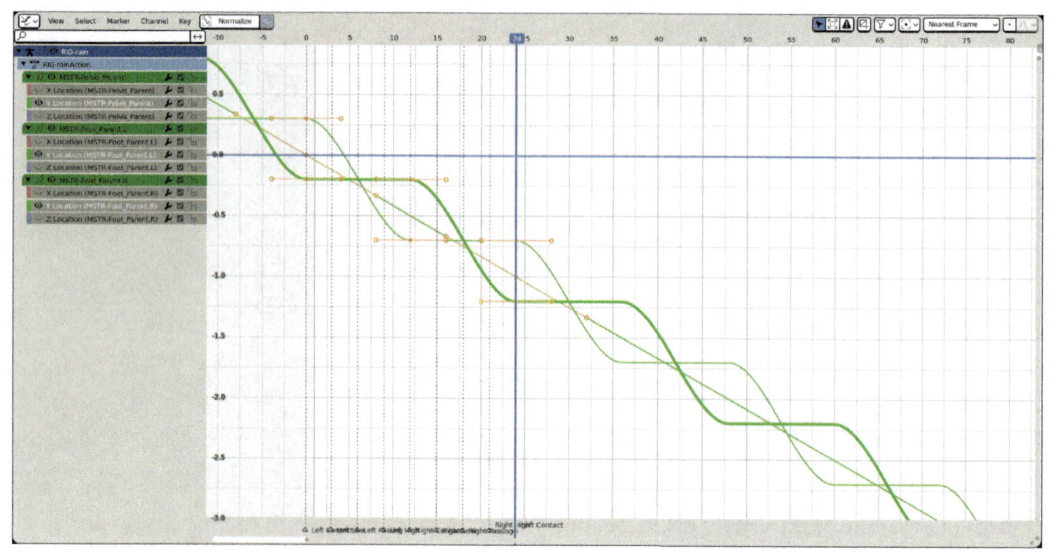

Figure 8.17: F-curves using Repeat with Offset

That's more like it. Now Rain keeps on shuffling forward like the marathon shuffler we always knew she could be.

> **Important note**
> Just as the period of a cyclic F-curve is determined by the total time between the first and last keyframes, the offset of a cyclic F-curve using **Repeat with Offset** is determined by the value change between those keyframes as well. In any case, the first and last keyframes are very important. Mind you don't move them accidentally!

Rain's walk cycle now goes for longer than 24 frames, but it goes without saying that it still needs work. We'll get to that, but there's one immediate problem with all this forward movement – it's hard to work on!

Putting Rain on a treadmill

During playback, it'll be irritating to try and work on our animation if Rain keeps walking away from us. Let the animation play for long enough, and Rain even leaves the screen:

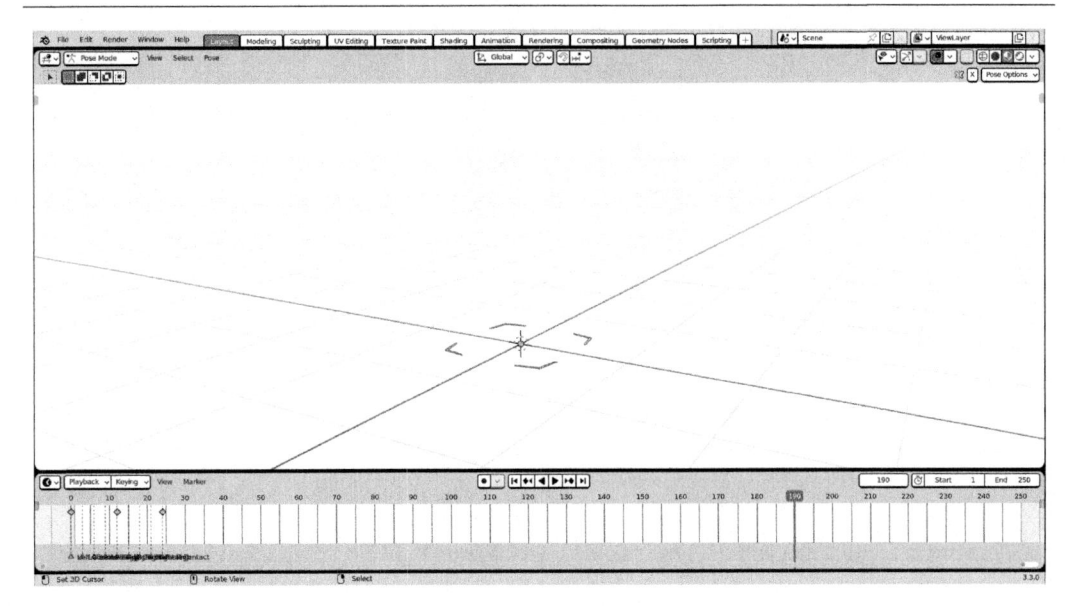

Figure 8.18: Hey, where'd you go?!

Recall the mantra of looping in 3D animation: *everything must return to where it began*. With an offset of -1.0 meters every 24 frames though, our walk cycle has one annoyingly non-cyclic aspect. Yes, we do want Rain to move forward, but not if this is how we have to work!

To fix this without undoing the work we've already done, we can choose a bone that acts as the parent of all three other bones, then animate it to move inversely to the direction of Rain's walking. This will have the effect of holding Rain in place while she walks, as though she were walking on a treadmill.

Inverting the stride offset

The most obvious bone to use for this purpose is the ROOT bone, to which every other bone is effectively parented. However, there's an even better choice hiding in Rain's *IK Secondary* armature layer – a bone called ROOT_Child:

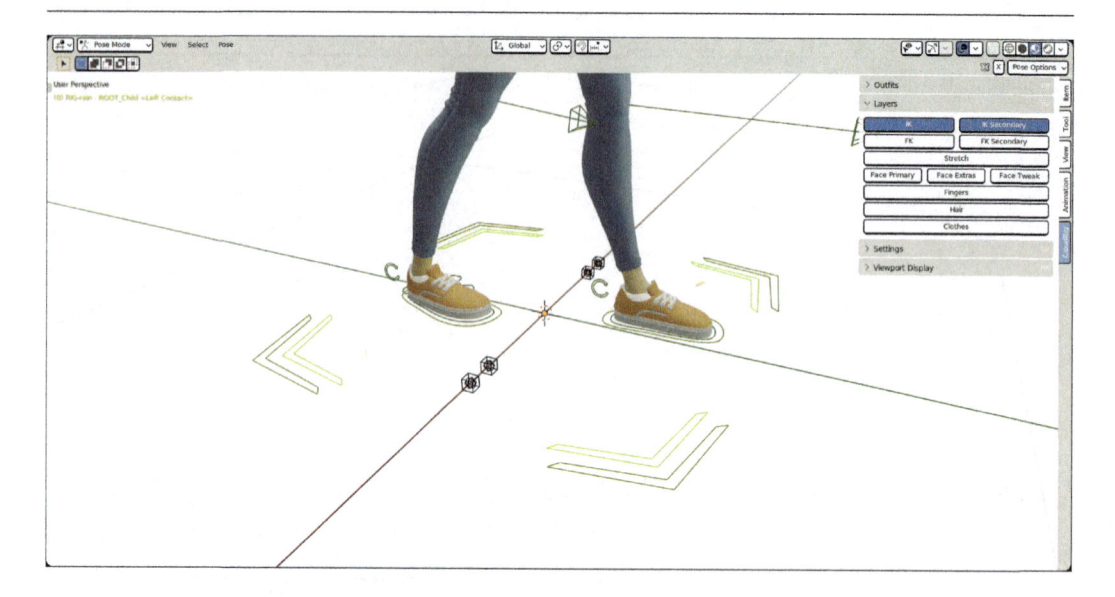

Figure 8.19: The ROOT_Child bone, slightly smaller than ROOT

`ROOT_Child` is the direct child of `ROOT` and acts as an intermediate parent between `ROOT` and most other bones.

Let's animate it now. I'll assume you know how to create a straight F-curve:

1. Enable the **IK Secondary** armature layer and find the bone `ROOT_Child`.
2. Animate `ROOT_Child` so that it moves continuously and inversely to Rain's stride. This will produce a linear **Y Location** F-curve with a slope of 1.0 meter every 24 frames.
3. You can disable the **IK Secondary** layer like it was before.

Rain's stride has been canceled out. Now she will stay in place as she walks, resulting in a perfect visual loop:

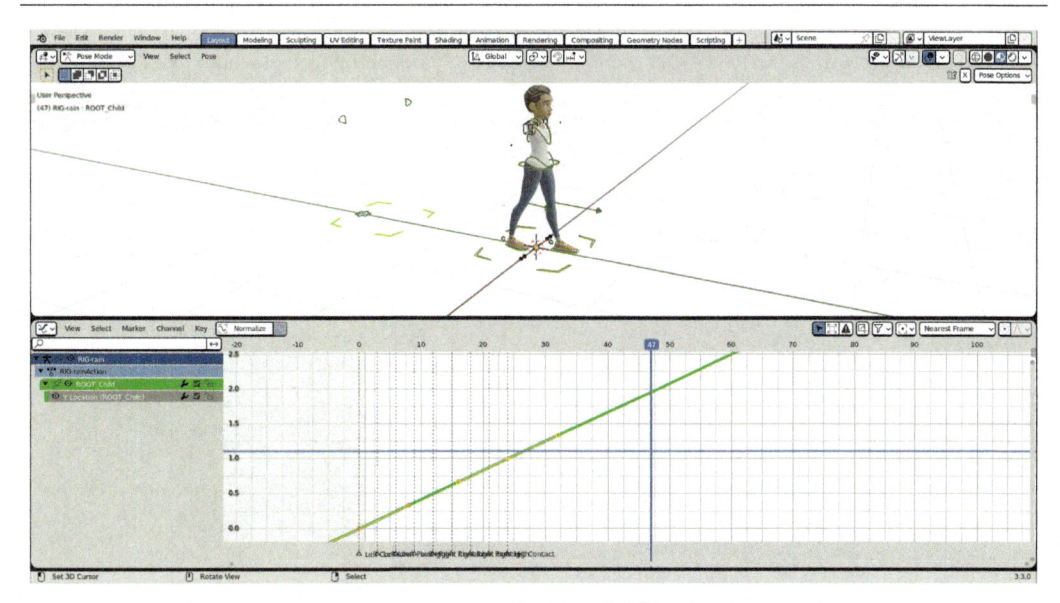

Figure 8.20: Linear animation of ROOT_Child holding Rain in place

If, later on, we wish to set Rain free and let her walk forward in world space like before, all we need to do is mute the **Y Location** F-curve of `ROOT_Child`.

This technique also works with `ROOT`, but using `ROOT_Child` instead confers some small advantages. Namely, it leaves the `ROOT` bone free to be used for other purposes in the future if we like.

Why go to all this trouble?

What's the point of having Rain move forward continuously by adding special cyclic modifiers to the **Y Location** F-curves, then canceling it all out? Could we not have simply keyed the contact poses without offsetting them by the stride length in the first place? Then, instead of animating the root bone going backward to cancel Rain's forward movement, we would just need to animate it forward.

That's all well and good, but let's see what the **Y Location** F-curves of the *IK* feet would need to look like:

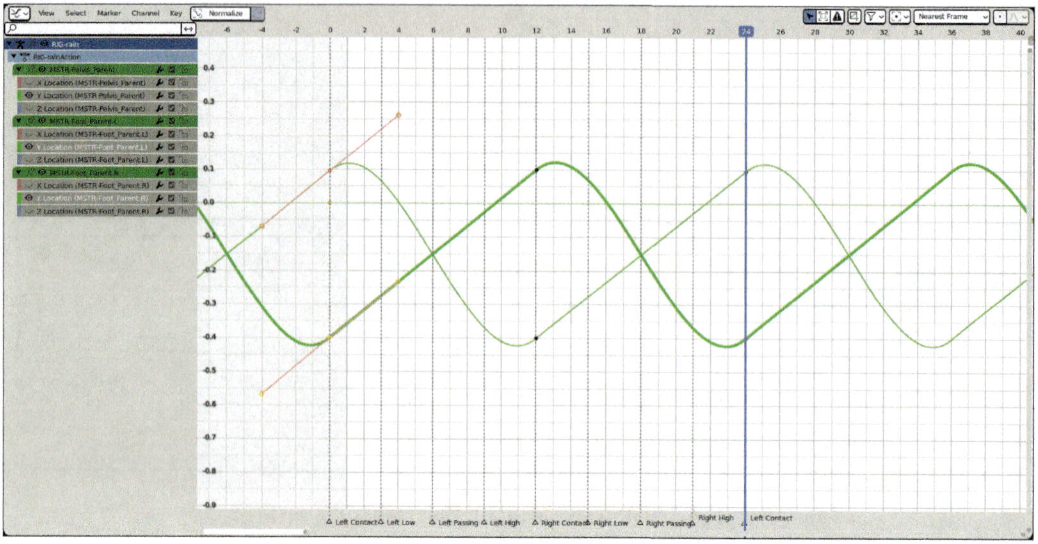

Figure 8.21: Alternate Y Location F-curves for walking IK feet

In this example, the treadmill effect is "baked in" to the movement of the *IK* feet. Those flat segments of each **Y Location** F-curve are instead diagonal, requiring specially edited Bezier keyframe handles. Were we to make edits to such an F-curve, we'd have to be extra careful to always preserve the slope of these diagonal segments or the feet would slide undesirably. Not a fun way to work.

Now Rain will walk in place no matter what our playback range is!

Using a preview playback range

If we let the animation play all the way to frame 250, we'll see a skip in the animation as the playhead jumps from frame 250 back to frame 1. For the animation to loop properly when played, our scene's end frame value ought to be some multiple of 24, like 240 or 120.

Really though, there's no need to let the animation play beyond frame 24. Once we've seen frames 1 through 24, we've seen them all, now that we've made sure our most important F-curves cycle properly. Shortening the working playback range will also help prevent the accidental insertion of keyframes beyond the range of the walk cycle, which could interfere with periodicity.

We already know how to set the playback range of our animation using the **Start** and **End** frame properties in the Timeline, but this time we'll use another little feature:

1. In the header of the Timeline, enable **Use Preview Range**. This is the button with the stopwatch icon next to the **Start** and **End** frame settings.

2. Using the alternate **Start** and **End** properties (exactly where the old ones were in the Timeline), set the scene's preview frame range to go from 1 to 24.

We are now working within a temporary, "preview" frame range:

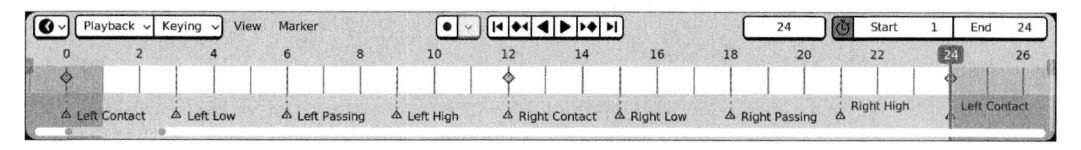

Figure 8.22: Alternative start and end frames

The new range affects only playback, and only for as long as **Use Preview Range** is enabled. The scene still retains its old **Start** and **End** frame numbers. This feature is useful for focusing on a small segment of frames in a longer animation without needing to change the "official" range of the whole scene.

> **Tip**
> You can toggle **Use Preview Range** on and off and should do so occasionally to inspect Rain's animation for errors past frame 24.

We can now play the animation and watch the walk cycle loop seamlessly for as long as we like.

It isn't much to look at now, but it is technically a walk cycle nonetheless! We did the hard part first and satisfied a very important technical requirement: establishing the cyclic forward movement of the independent bones in the *IK* chains for the legs. And the great thing about computer-assisted animation is that we can go back and improve things iteratively! In the next section, we'll do just that, starting with Rain's torso.

Adding more periodic motion

We're going to leave Rain's feet shuffling as they are and return our focus to the movement of `MSTR-Pelvis_Parent`. Working outward from the torso, we will then add some simple twisting using `MSTR-Hips` and `MSTR-Chest_Parent`, the bones for the hips and chest.

> **Important note**
> You no longer need to enter my exact values for this section, and you should feel free to experiment. The only hard rule is that you must be precise with your own values so that there's no asymmetry in the walk cycle.

When we're finished, Rain's walk cycle will start to look kind of believable (as long as you don't look at her arms or legs)!

Torso movement

Having completed the **Y Location** F-curve of `MSTR-Pelvis_Parent`, we can address the other two axes along which the torso should move. These F-curves will cycle normally without any offset, but as we'll see, some F-curves only require a half-length period.

Here's what my F-curves look like after the treatment:

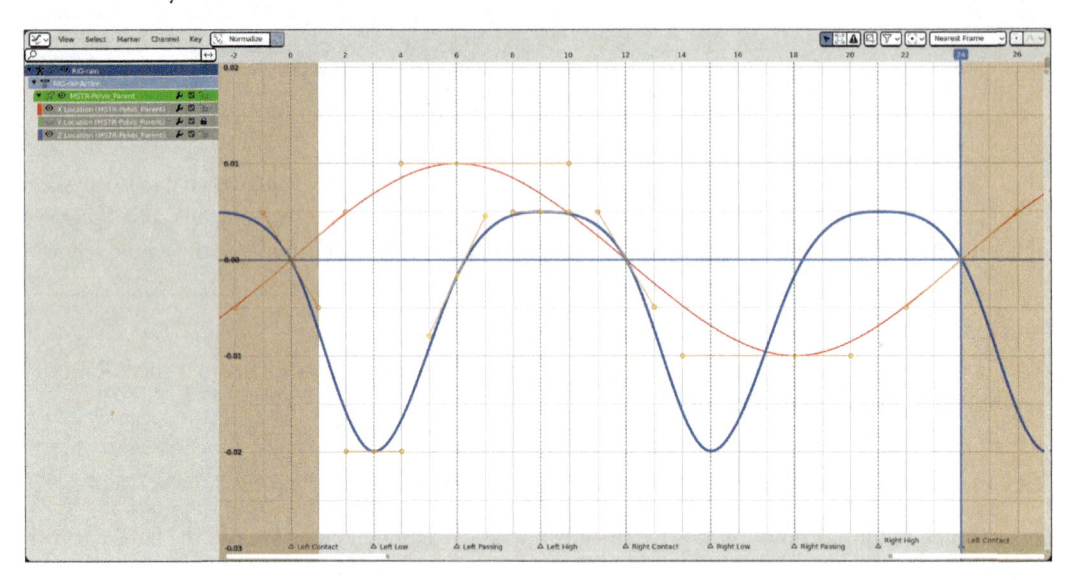

Figure 8.23: F-curves of MSTR-Pelvis_Parent

Now it's your turn.

Bouncing down and up

After **Y Location**, the next most important animation channel of `MSTR-Pelvis_Parent` is **Z Location**, which conducts the up-down motion of the body that everybody makes when they walk. This is what gives the `High` and `Low` walk cycle phases their names; the torso usually reaches its high point just before the front foot makes contact, and its low point right after.

Try it now:

1. Find the **Z Location** F-curve of `MSTR-Pelvis_Parent`.
2. Insert a keyframe at frame 3 (*Left Low*) so that Rain's torso reaches a low point, about -2 cm (`-0.02` meters).
3. Insert a keyframe at frame 9 (*Left High*) so that Rain's torso reaches a high point just above zero, about 0.5 cm (`0.005` meters).

4. To make Rain's low point a bit briefer, add a keyframe at frame 6 (*Left Passing*) that raises the torso just a little higher than it would've been otherwise.

5. Shorten the period of the F-curve by moving the last keyframe from frame 24 to frame 12.

Note that this up-down motion needs to happen twice in a period – once for each footstep. Instead of duplicating our keyframes, we simply made the period of this F-curve 12 frames instead of 24.

Swaying from side to side

In addition to up-down motion along the *Z* axis, a walking torso will also tend to sway side-to-side on the *X* axis, as the weight of the torso is held in alternating imbalance above one foot or the other.

> **Tip**
> The **Active Keyframe** panel, located in the right-hand sidebar of the Graph Editor, is handy for inspecting the exact values of keyframes.

Use any method you like to key this motion:

1. Find the **X Location** F-curve of `MSTR-Pelvis_Parent`.
2. Insert keyframes at both Passing frames, making Rain's whole torso sway to the left at *Left Passing* and to the right at *Right Passing*.

The amplitude of this wave should be subtle, about 1 cm (0.01 meters) in either direction. See the previous figure for reference.

Isn't it amazing how some subtle keying along two F-curves can bring our character to life? In fact, that last **X Location** F-curve is literally just a sine wave. Wait 'til you see what some more of these waves will do for Rain's hips and chest!

The Action Editor

From this point forward, literally every F-curve we add to our animation will need to be cyclic, but F-curves are not cyclic by default. One thing that could get annoying is having to perform **Make Cyclic** with each new F-curve that gets created.

Before we key any more bones, we'll address this issue in an editor that is way less exciting than it sounds: the **Action Editor**.

Intro to the Action Editor

Remember actions? They're the data blocks that contain multiple animation channels and channel groups for each animated object. Our whole walk cycle for Rain is contained within one of these actions; it was automatically created and given a generic name when we inserted our initial keyframes.

270   The Walk Cycle

Actions have some basic metadata that can be accessed through the Action Editor, which can be found by going to the Dope Sheet and changing the editing context:

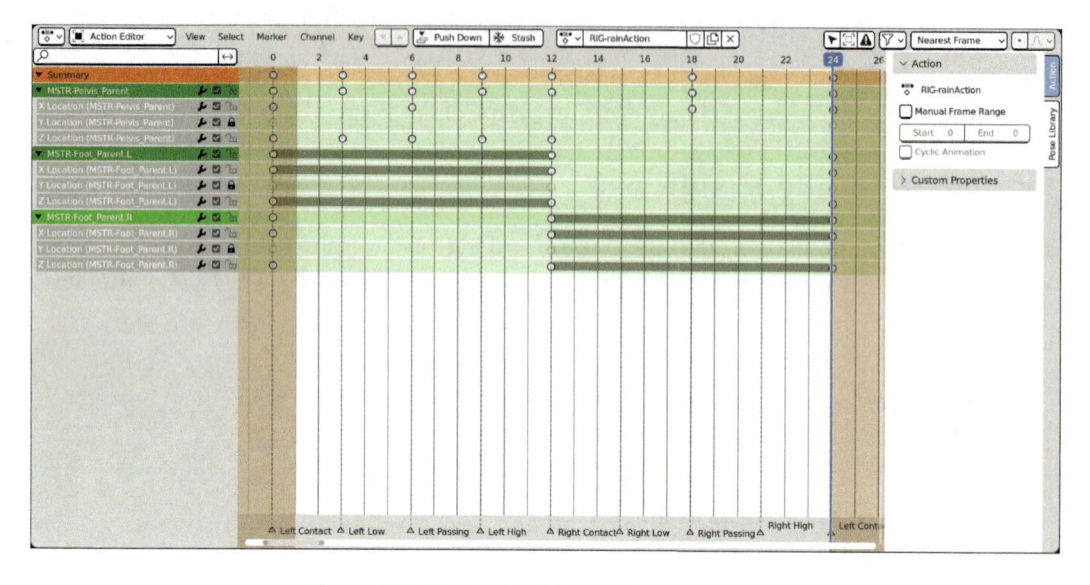

Figure 8.24: The Action Editor in the Dope Sheet

The Action Editor is nearly identical to the standard Dope Sheet. Its main difference is that it displays only one action at a time: the current action of the selected object. It also lets us edit some additional properties of the action, such as its name.

Renaming an action

First, let's use the Action Editor to rename Rain's current action:

1. Bring up the Dope Sheet.
2. Change the **Editing Context** of the **Dope Sheet** to **Action Editor**.
3. Rename the action to something you'll remember.

Renaming this action will make it easier to find so we can reuse it as an asset in future animations:

Figure 8.25: "Rain Walkcycle" is a perfect name

Adding more periodic motion

> **Tip**
> From here on out, you can keep the Action Editor open instead of the default Dope Sheet. It makes little difference since we won't be animating any other objects or working with any actions besides the current one for Rain's armature.

In addition to renaming actions, the Action Editor does another thing – maybe even two other things! Let's use it to enable some properties that establish the whole action as a cycle.

Establishing an action as cyclic

Some additional action metadata can be found in the right-hand sidebar of the Action Editor. Modifying some properties here will make our work easier:

1. Find the **Action** panel in the right-hand sidebar (*N*) of the Action Editor.
2. Enable **Manual Frame Range** and ensure that the **Start** and **End** frames of the action are 0 and 24.
3. Enable **Cyclic Animation**.

Note that these settings do not directly alter the F-curves or affect the animated result:

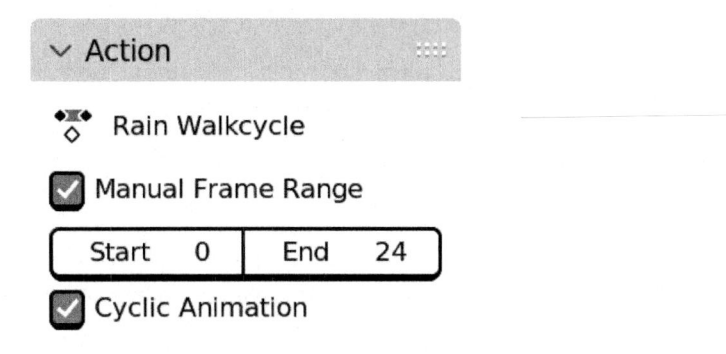

Figure 8.26: Cyclic Animation enabled for the action

All we did was to change some contextual information about the action so that some other features know it's supposed to be cyclic.

Enabling Cycle-Aware Keying

For the settings to have any effect, we'll need to enable **Cycle Aware Keying** in the Timeline like so:

1. Open the **Keying** popup in the header of the Timeline.
2. Enable **Cycle Aware Keying**.

Now, all future F-curves added to the `Rain Walkcycle` action will automatically be cyclic and have a period of 24 frames:

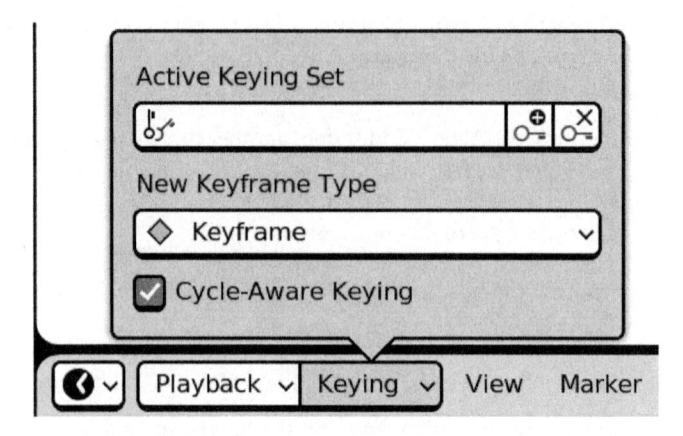

Figure 8.27: Cycle-Aware Keying enabled in the Timeline

Let's try it out on some more bones.

More torso animation with sine waves

The hips, chest, and shoulders are part of a walk cycle too. Some very simple keying work on these bones will go a long way to loosening up Rain's movement and making her walk cycle more believable.

Twisting the torso at the Contact poses

We'll begin with some rotation along the Z axis at the *Contact* poses. Because feet are typically farthest apart at the *Contact* phases of a walk cycle, the hips will rotate to help cover this distance (after all, they are directly connected to the legs). Consequently, the chest and shoulders should rotate inversely to counterbalance this motion:

Figure 8.28: Top view of Contact poses with rotating hips, chest, and shoulders

Give it a try:

1. Go to frame 0 (*Left Contact*).
2. Rotate `MSTR-Hips` about `-10` degrees on the *Z* axis in the direction of Rain's stride (left side goes forward, right goes back).
3. Rotate `MSTR-Chest_Parent` about 5 degrees on the *Z* axis in the opposite direction.
4. Continuing the gesture of the torso through to Rain's shoulders, rotate `MSTR-Clavicle.L` outward and `MSTR-Clavicle.R` inward a few degrees on the *Z* axis.
5. Insert rotation keyframes for these bones.

Notice that, with **Cycle-Aware Keying** enabled, keyframes have also been added at frame `24`. This saves us the trouble of keying the same thing at both *Left Contact* poses. The F-curve has also already been made cyclic for us.

Now we only need to insert keyframes for the *Right Contact* pose and we're done!

Mirroring the rotation of the torso

Paste Flipped Pose (*Ctrl* + *Shift* + *V*) doesn't just work for bones ending in `L` or `R`; it's also useful for mirroring the position of bones along the sagittal plane (the ones in the middle of the character that have no L/R suffix, such as the hips and chest)

Try it now to save a little time:

1. Select `MSTR-Hips`, `MSTR-Chest_Parent`, and both `MSTR-Clavicle` bones.
2. Copy the pose.
3. Go to the opposing passing frame (frame `12`) and paste the flipped pose.
4. Insert rotation keyframes for all four bones again.

Rain's walk cycle is looking better and better. It's even beginning to look – dare I say it – natural!

Phase shifting

Let's try another technique for making a sine wave, this time on the **Y Euler Rotation** F-curve of `MSTR-Hips`:

1. Find the **Y Euler Rotation** F-curve of the `MSTR-Hips` bone.
2. Select the keyframes at frames `0` and `24` and move them up by `5`.
3. Select the keyframe at frame `12` and move it down by `-5`.

   This makes Rain's hips swing on more than one axis. Not bad so far, but the peaks of this wave should really be at the Passing frames so that the hips help lift up each passing foot as it swings forward.

4. Select all keyframes of the **Y Euler Rotation** F-curve.
5. Move the selection to the right by `6` frames.

The resulting F-curve wave is not unlike the earlier one we made for the **X Location** of `MSTR-Pelvis_Parent`, but this time it only needed three keyframes:

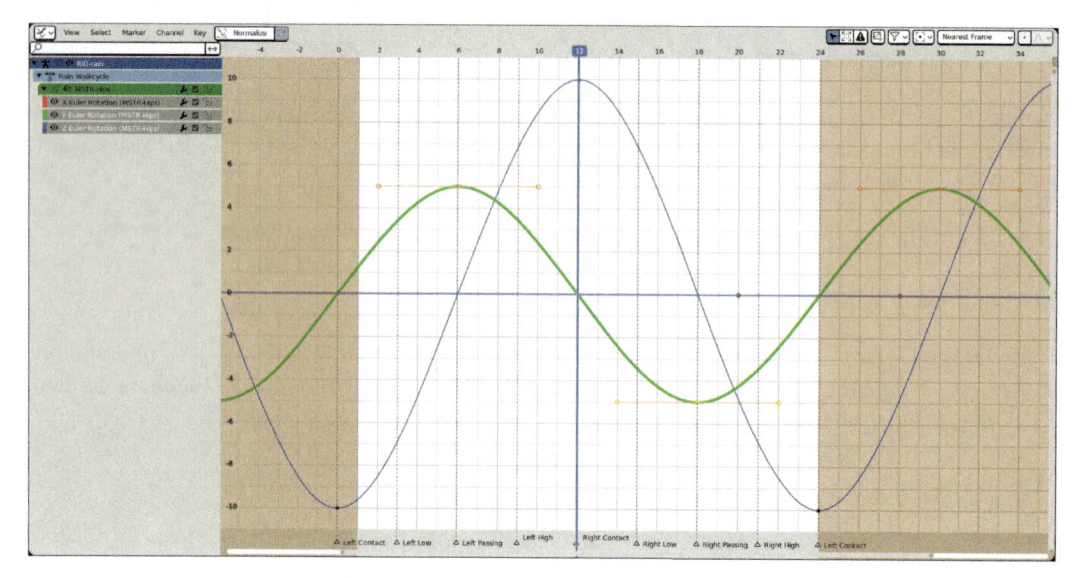

Figure 8.29: Rotation F-curves of MSTR-Hips

Moving all the keyframes of a cyclic F-curve one quarter of a period forward is what we'd call a *90° phase shift* if we wanted to get really technical. We don't, though, so I'll just say that keyframes in our walk cycle can be moved outside the initial frame range if we like.

> **Tip**
>
> Want to experiment with the walk cycle? While the animation is playing, you can move the keyframes of an F-curve along the *X* axis in the Graph Editor to alter the phase, or scale the keyframe values to enhance or reduce their intensity. This kind of experimentation can help you improve the result or come up with new ideas.

Look at how Rain walks now! Some very simple keying work was all it took to really sell the appearance of walking. We also saved ourselves some clicking by ensuring that all F-curves we add in the future will automatically be made cyclic as well.

If we were animating Rain for a waist-up shot, we could skip animating the feet and we'd nearly be done. This is often how 3D animators save time:

Figure 8.30: Example camera view above Rain's legs

Our objective is to make a complete walk cycle though, so let's turn our attention downward to Rain's feet.

Advanced footwork

We knew there was more to animating the feet than making them scoot forward – now comes the part where we make them really walk! A lot of animators run into trouble in this part, but by breaking the process down into logical steps as we've been doing, we can make things much less complicated.

We'll begin by animating the left foot over the whole period, from frame 0 to 24. Then, everything the left foot does, the right foot can do 12 frames later (or earlier). Since we've already keyed the **Y Location** F-curves of both feet, the trickiest part is taken care of.

> **Important note**
> Nearly all of the work in this section can (and should) be performed in orthographic side-view in the 3D Viewport. Numerical precision is no longer needed, but pay close attention to how posing the foot affects the knee.

Rolling the foot

For the first half of our walk cycle, the left foot stays in contact with the ground, but that doesn't mean it holds perfectly still. Here are the poses we're looking for:

Figure 8.31: The positions of the left foot at frames 0, 6, and 12

Initially, the left foot makes contact in front of Rain at the heel. The rest of the foot then quickly smacks the ground. After a few frames of lying flat, it will then begin to pivot forwards, but at a different point, this time flexing at the ball of the foot and bringing the whole ankle upwards.

These movements of the foot are known colloquially as heel roll and ball roll, or as foot roll altogether. You might suspect that this would be difficult to animate, and if Rain wasn't rigged with a roll bone on each foot, you'd be right!

Rain's roll bones are named `ROLL-Foot_Control.L` and `ROLL-Foot_Control.R`. These are the rotating-arrow-shaped bones that live behind Rain's ankles on the **IK** layer:

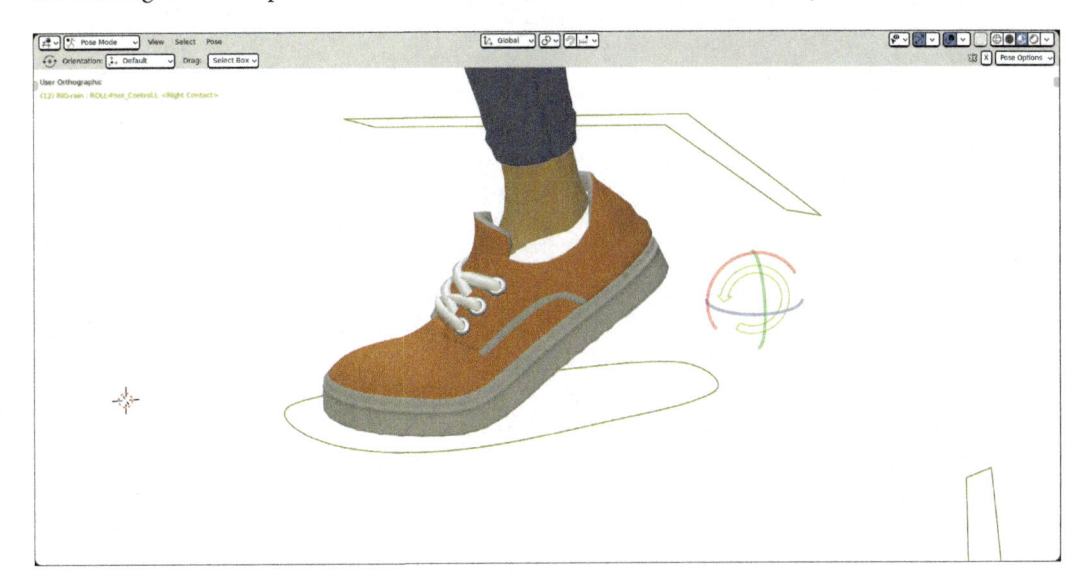

Figure 8.32: Roll bone of the left foot

Rotating one of these bones on its *X* axis activates a marvelous mechanism of invisible rigging in the foot, allowing the complex action of foot rolling to be achieved with a single control bone.

Keying the roll bone

Let's animate the roll bone for the left foot now:

1. Select `ROLL-Foot_Control.L`.
2. Key an **X Rotation** of about `-40` degrees at frame `0` (*Left Contact*).
3. Key an **X Rotation** of `0` at frames `3` (*Left Low*) and `6` (*Left Passing*).
4. Key an **X Rotation** of about `40` at frame `12` (*Right Contact*).

The Walk Cycle

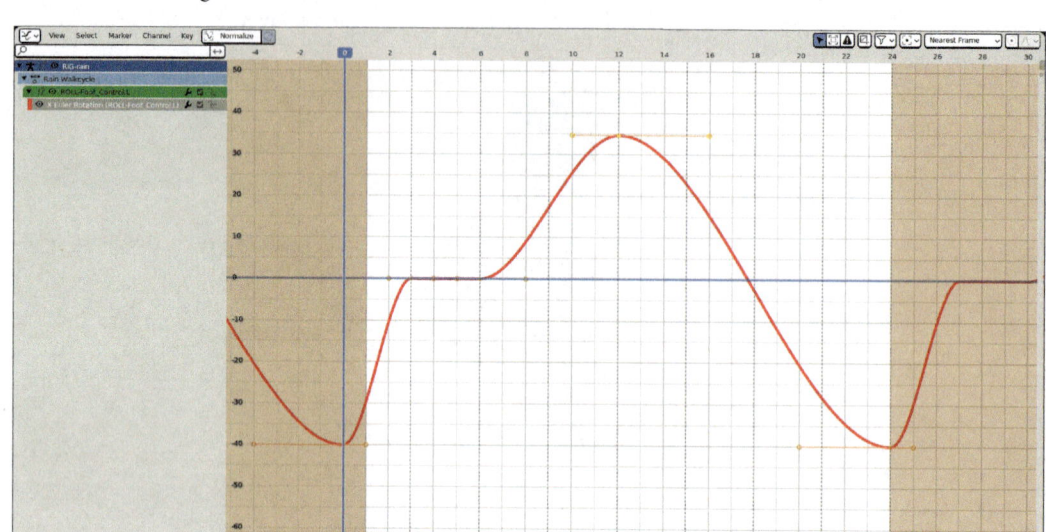

Here's the resulting F-curve. We'll tweak it a bit later:

Figure 8.33: X Euler Rotation F-curve of ROLL-Foot_Control.L

Isn't this bone great? We produced all that motion by keying just one property.

This concludes the first half of the left foot's 24-frame period. On frame 12, the right foot lands (or it will after we animate it) and the left foot is ready to take off!

Picking up the feet

For the first 12 frames of the walk cycle period, the left foot stays on the ground, holding up Rain's weight. For the following 12 frames, the left foot will no longer touch the ground in any meaningful way; instead, it must lift up so it can swing forward without scuffing the floor.

Lifting the foot completely off the ground can be accomplished by editing the **Z Location** F-curve of the foot's main *IK* bone.

1. Find the **Z Location** F-curve of MSTR-Foot_Parent.L.
2. On frames 15 and 21, add **Z Location** keyframes that lift up Rain's left foot.
3. Add a dip to the curve at frame 18 (*Right Passing*), lower than the neighboring keyframes, but still higher than 0.0, so the foot swings close to the ground as it passes.
4. Like the bouncing ball, the foot won't slow down before it strikes the ground, so make sure there's little to no easing out at frame 24.

The resulting F-curve looks a bit like a camel with two humps. You can tweak it a bit if you like:

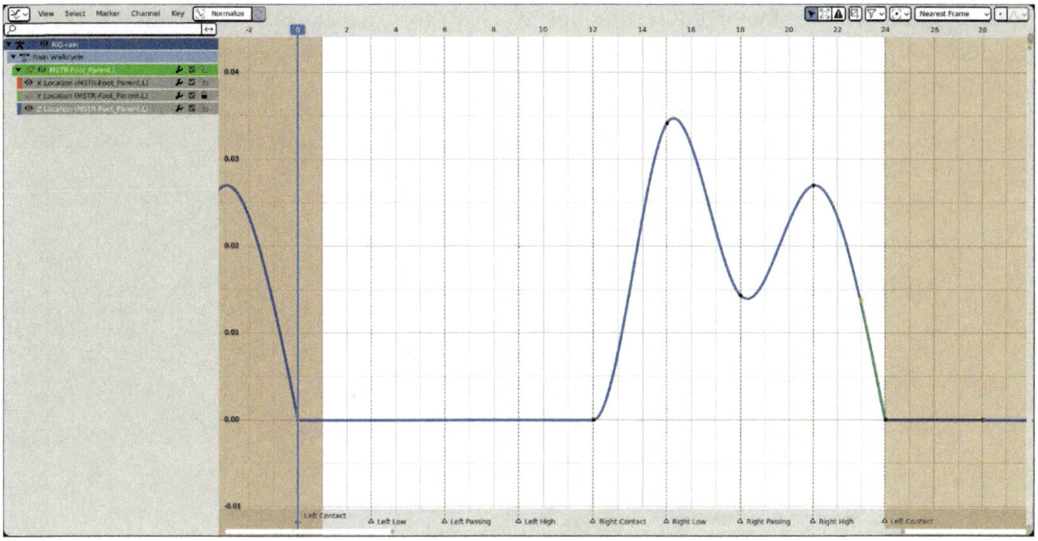

Figure 8.34: Z Location of MSTR-Foot_Parent.L

While the foot is in the air, the roll bone we animated earlier can do the work of rotating the foot steadily back, ready once again to strike the ground on frame 24.

Thus the animation cycle of a single foot is nearly complete! The movement still looks a bit wonky at the knees, however. Before we commit to copying the F-curves of the left foot to the right foot, we must perfect our work so that the whole leg moves smoothly.

Correcting the motion of the legs

Up until this point, we've been animating Rain's left foot as though it were its own little character, with little regard as to how it connects to the rest of Rain's body. It's almost as if we think the feet and hips are completely separate body parts!

In one sense, this isn't wrong. The ends of an *IK* chain are intended to be posed and animated as independent points in space. The pelvis goes in one place, the foot goes in another place, and the *IK* constraint does the rest of the work for us. The bones for the thigh and shin (which are not posed or animated directly) are completely at the mercy of these start and end points. Rain's legs even stretch so that they always reach their *IK* targets, no matter the distance.

Though convenient, this method can produce peculiar effects in some cases, as with the legs in our walk cycle. They seem to buckle and jitter as Rain walks. As we finalize the animation of the left foot, we can no longer ignore this.

Knee buckling

As we worked on the left foot in this section, you may have noticed that we closed the distance between the ankle and the base of the leg at the hip. When the thigh and shin bones in the *IK* chain no longer need to stretch, they bend at the knee instead, which is generally what we're going for.

The trouble is that, when the *IK* legs are straight or nearly straight, it only takes a very small change to make Rain's knees "buckle":

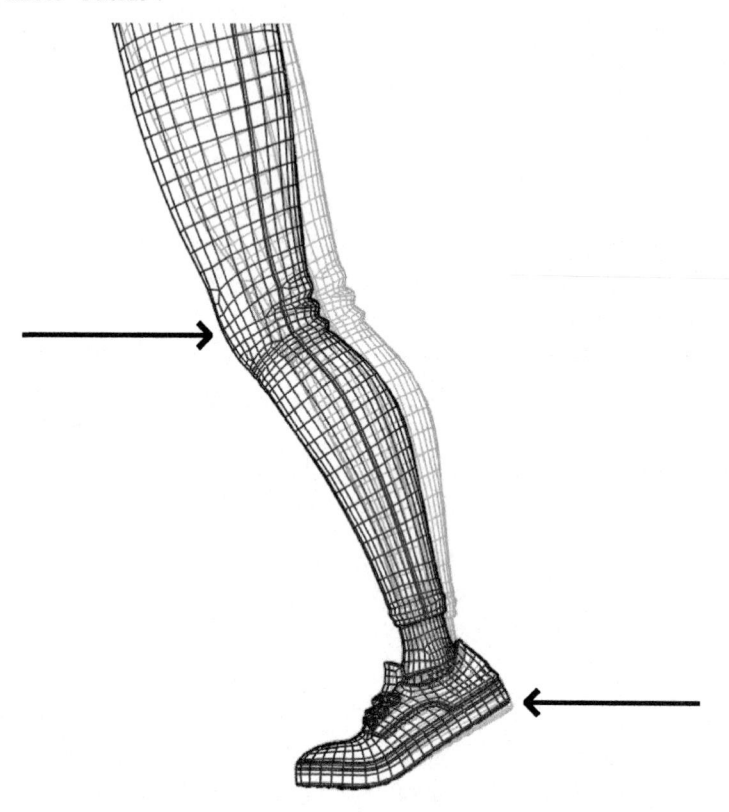

Figure 8.35: A small change in the foot makes a big difference in the knee

The legs in a walk cycle spend a lot of time in this "sweet spot" between stretching and bending. This is what causes the jittery motion of Rain's legs, which is most apparent at the knee.

To diagnose the issue better, we'll take advantage of motion paths, a feature we learned about in *Chapter 3*.

Bone motion paths

Did you know you can view the motion paths of individual bones? The panel for doing so is located in the **Object Data Properties** of the armature object (not object properties).

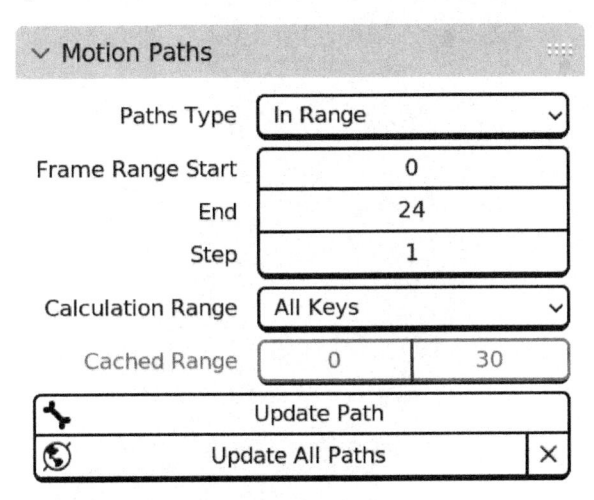

Figure 8.36: Motion Paths panel

We just need to select a bone to use it on. Any bone located at the knee will do. There isn't one in the *IK* layer, but there is one elsewhere:

1. Enable the armature layer **Stretch**.
2. Select the stretch bone in Rain's left knee.
3. Find the **Motion Paths** panel in the **Object Data Properties** tab of the Properties Editor.
4. Generate a motion path for the selected bone. You may need to mess with the **Calculation Range** setting to get all frames to display in the path.

> **Tip**
> Consider making a shortcut for the **Update All Paths** operator. You'll be using it a lot!

Here is my motion path. Note that I've turned on the display of frame numbers and re-hidden the Stretch layer:

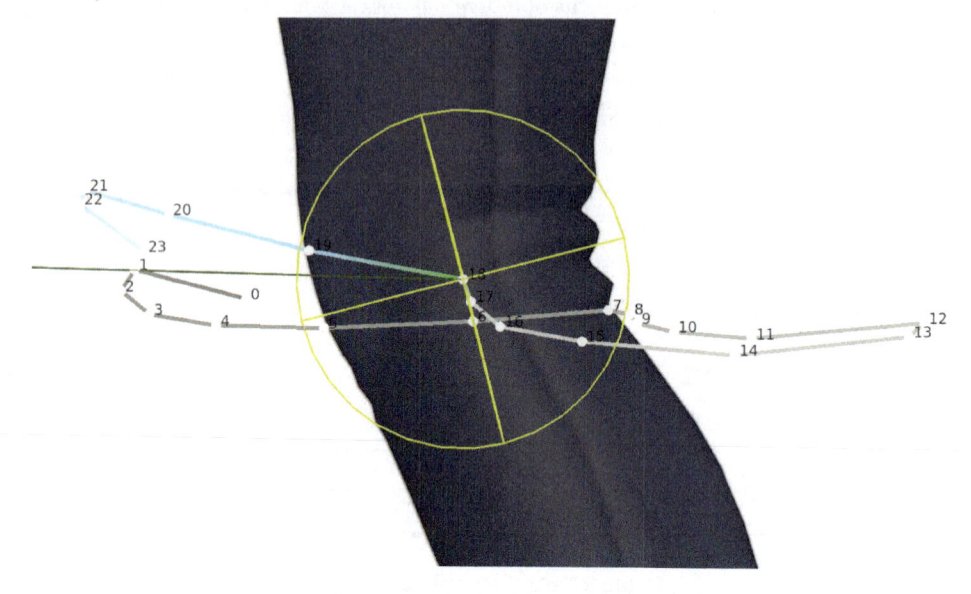

Figure 8.37: Motion path of the knee

That's an ugly-looking path! No wonder the walk cycle looks odd at the knees.

Tweaking the animation to improve the motion path of the knee

By scrubbing the animation and looking at the motion curve of the left knee, we can see on which frames the leg is misbehaving, then focus our attention on tweaking our F-curves at those frames.

For instance, if the motion curve contains an unattractive spike or zig-zag, there's a good chance that Rain's knees are "locked" on one or more of those frames. This can be corrected by editing the animation so that the ankle comes slightly closer to the base of the leg.

Only very small changes are needed to one or more F-curves that affect the *IK* chain. I recommend starting with the F-curves we just made in this section, as they offer the most leniency. Who's to say that the foot can't rise a little faster or slower if it makes the knee look better?

See for yourself:

1. Starting with the F-curves of `MSTR-Foot_Parent.L` and `ROLL-Foot_Control.L` that you just worked on, make adjustments to your animation to smooth out the motion path of the knee.
2. You may also need to tweak the animation of the hips and/or torso as well to close the distance between the ends of the leg *IK* chain so that Rain's leg avoids locking.
3. If all else fails, you can add animation to other bones that affect the *IK* chain, or even directly animate the stretch bone of the knee!

After a little bit of tweaking, my motion path and its associated motion look much better:

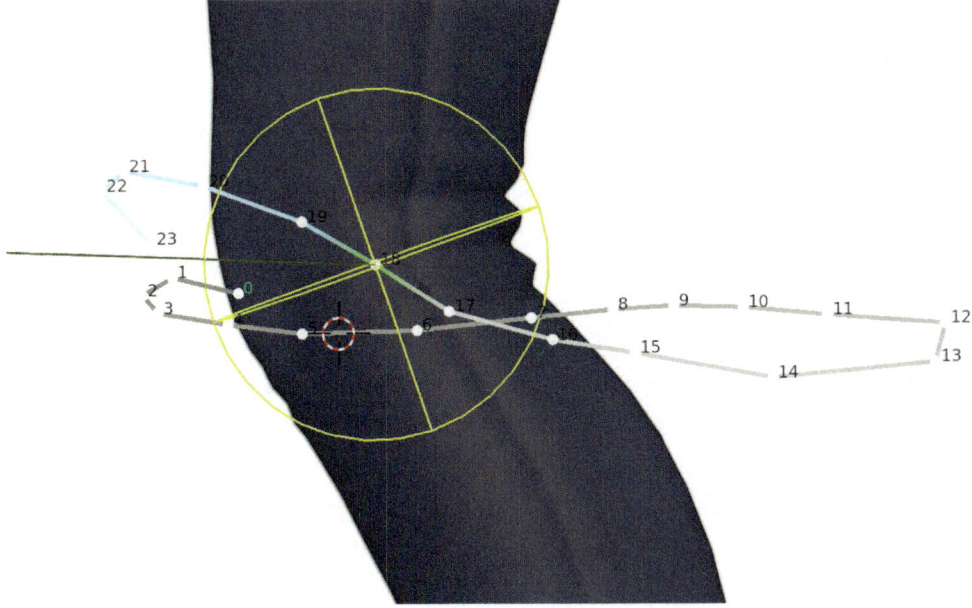

Figure 8.38: Improved motion path of the knee

Once you're satisfied with the complete animation of Rain's left leg, you're ready to copy your work to the right leg.

Copying animation from the left foot to the right foot

The left and right feet in a 24-frame walk cycle period work in 12-frame shifts. When one is in the air swinging forward, the other must be on the ground holding up Rain's body, and vice versa. Every 12 frames, the feet switch roles. We just finalized both these opposing and alternating movements for the bones on a single foot; now it's just a matter of copying what we've done and pasting it to the bones on the other side.

Copying multiple F-curves

You already know how to copy keyframes from one F-curve to another using **Copy** (*Ctrl + C*) and **Paste** (*Ctrl + V*), but did you know we can do so for multiple F-curves at once? When keyframes across multiple animation channels are copied, the paste operator can paste those keyframes to selected animation channels of the same name belonging to other bones or objects. This comes in handy at present, as the animation data we want to copy and paste is that of two F-curves belonging to two different bones.

The Walk Cycle

> **Important note**
>
> The **Y Location** channels of both *IK* foot bones, which we keyed near the beginning, are special. Keyframes from one should not be copied to the other. As usual, be aware of important context such as your selection when you copy, and the current frame when you paste.

Copying and pasting keyframes works in the Graph Editor, the Timeline, and/or the Dope Sheet! Let's try it now so we save a little time:

1. Copy all the keyframes for the F-curves of the left foot that you worked on in this section. These are the **X Euler Rotation** of ROLL-Foot_Control.L and the **Z Location** F-curve of MSTR-Foot_Parent.L.

2. Pasting won't work if the destination F-curve doesn't exist, and we haven't yet keyed the **X Euler Rotation** of ROLL-Foot_Control.R. Go to frame 0 and do so.

3. Select the corresponding animation channels of MSTR-Foot_Parent.R and ROLL-Foot_Control.R and paste your copied keyframes.

Make sure the new keyframes on the right foot match the original ones on the left and watch the animation. If you made a mistake copying and pasting, the animation will look wrong, but if you did everything correctly…

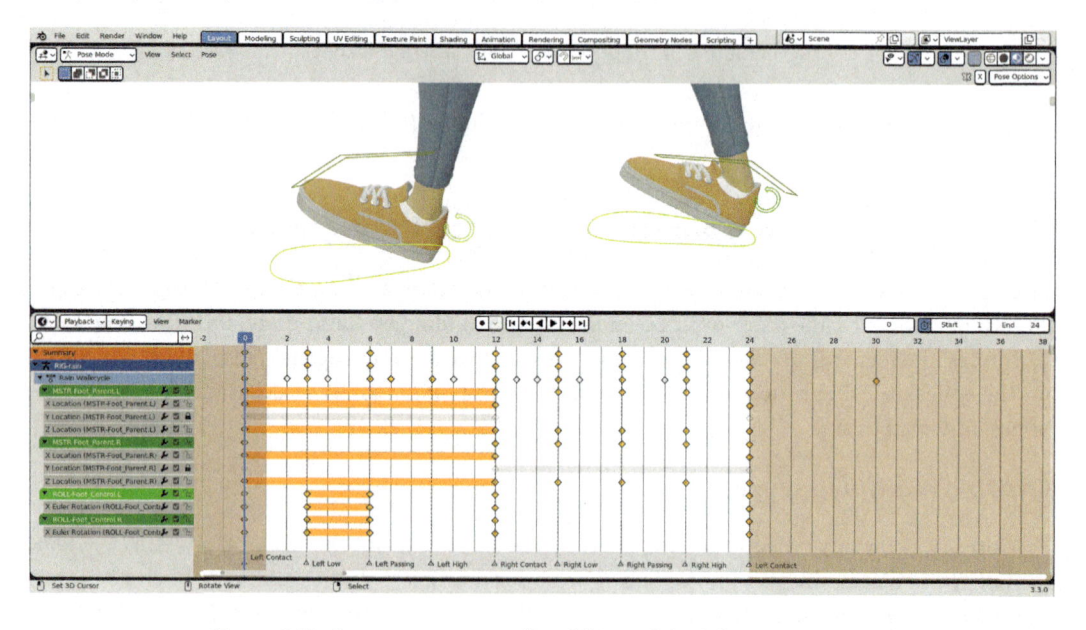

Figure 8.39: Cotemporaneous rolling/lifting of the left and right feet

…the animation will still look wrong. For the moment, it would seem Rain has two left feet, as it were. One more adjustment is needed for the right foot!

Phase shifting

The alternating and opposing movements of the right and left foot must be 12 frames (one-half period) apart. I like to call this a *180° phase-shift*, but you may prefer to call it *moving some keyframes*:

1. Select all the keyframes you just pasted. These are everything belonging to `MSTR-Foot_Parent.R` and `ROLL-Foot_Control.R`, but not any **Y Location** keyframes.
2. Move the selection `12` frames.

You may ask, "12 frames in which direction?" It doesn't matter! The result is the same either way:

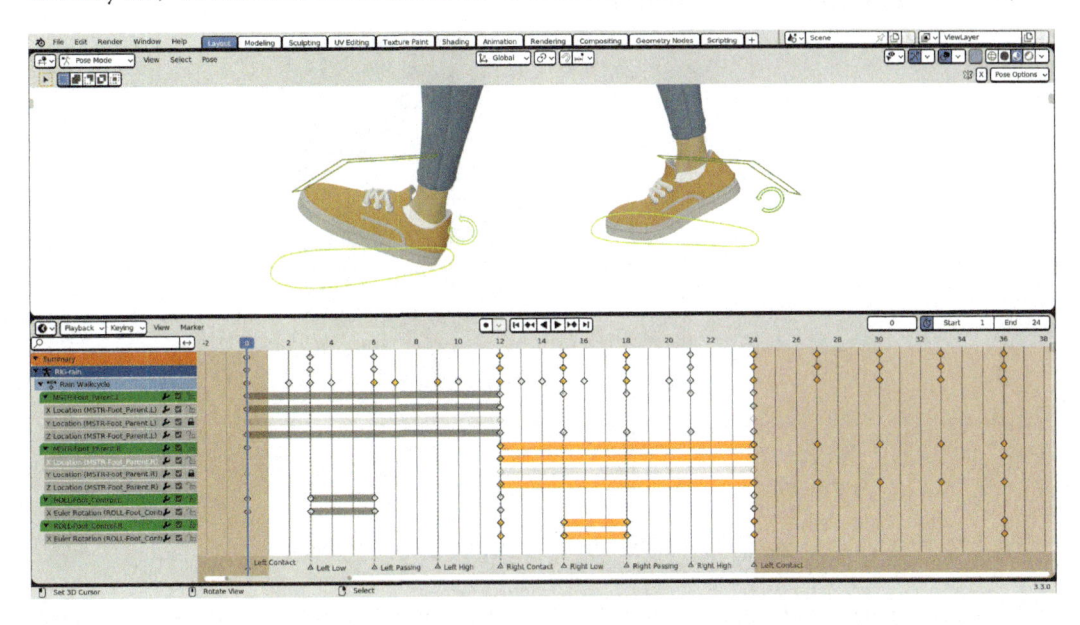

Figure 8.40: Correct rolling/lifting of the left and right feet

> **Important note**
> Similar to when we animated the left foot, you may still see some irregular "shaking" in the right knee, which may require additional tweaking. Sometimes this can't be helped, even if we did everything we could to keep our animation perfectly symmetrical.

Now we can say that Rain is truly walking! We've finished by far the most complicated tasks in a walk cycle; we established independent forward movement of the foot and pelvis bones, added natural rhythm to the torso, then animated the complex rolling and lifting of the feet. There's still more to do, but from here on out, it's plain sailing.

Finishing the walk cycle

We're done with the hardest part of the walk cycle. Now we can relax and animate those less-than-essential limbs so that Rain's walk cycle looks natural and complete. This stage mostly involves animating *FK* bones that are governed by simpler relationships, such as the *FK* bones for Rain's toes and arms.

FK toes

Before we can say Rain's feet are completely animated, we ought to finish by animating the toes. We'll have them extend back as the heel strikes the ground:

Figure 8.41: Toe of front foot extending and flattening

On some later frames, you'll have noticed that Rain's toes automatically bend due to the effects of ball roll. This is nice to have right up until the foot is picked up, after which it looks a bit odd. We can curl the toe bone in the other direction to cancel out this effect after the foot has left the ground:

Figure 8.42: Toes of the rear foot going straight, relative to the rest of the foot

Try it now. The bones for the toes are in the **FK** layer:

1. Enable the **FK** armature layer.
2. Using `FK-Toe.L`, animate Rain's toe flexing and extending over a 24-frame period.
3. Copy the keyframes to the other toe and move them `12` frames, as you did for the feet in the previous section.

Here's my F-curve. Yours may require a bit of extra tweaking to curl the toes without letting them pass through the ground right after:

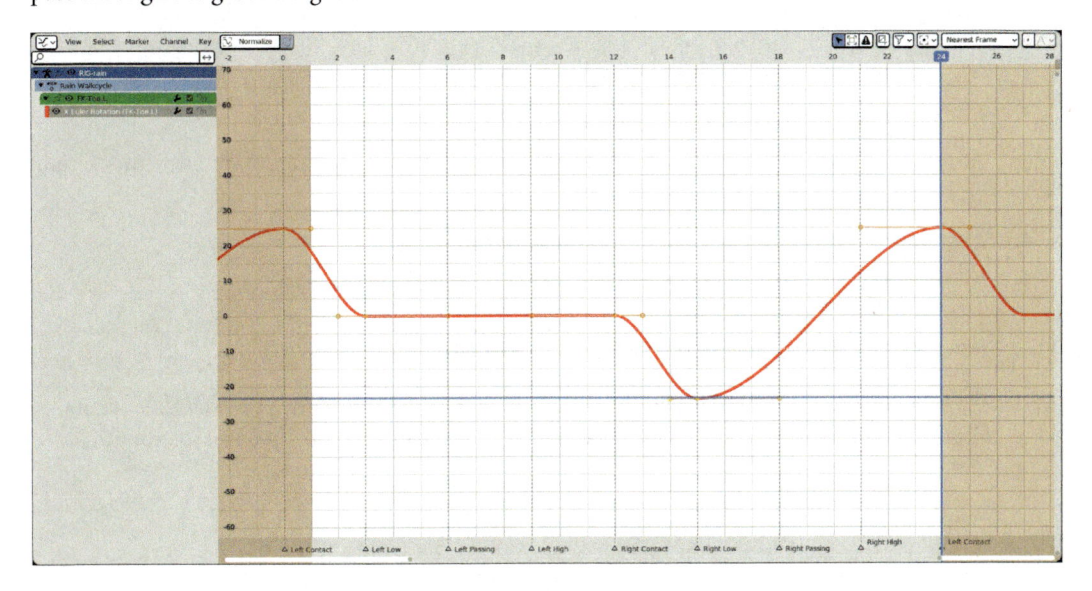

Figure 8.43: X Euler Rotation of FK-Toe.L

With our work on Rain's bottom half concluded, we can tackle the limbs we hid at the beginning of the chapter.

FK arms

In a walk cycle, the arms swing at the sides of the body in opposition to the legs:

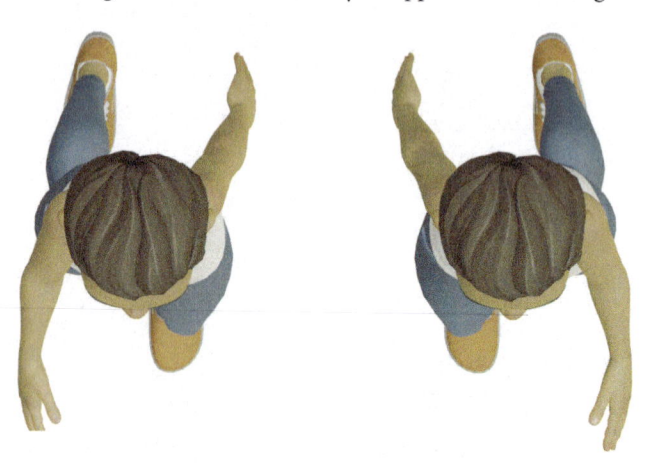

Figure 8.44: Initial key poses of the arms, seen from above

Like many movements using *FK* arms, the timing of the motion should begin at the shoulders and travel down the arms like a delayed signal. Think back to the waving motion we did in the previous chapter.

1. Go to **CloudRig | Outfits** and unhide Rain's arms.
2. In **CloudRig | FK Settings | FK Hinge**, set **Left Arm** and **Right Arm** to `1.0`.
3. At frame 3 (*Left Low*), key the *FK* bones of the arms at their extreme rotations, with the right arm forward and the left arm back.
4. At frame `15` (*Right Low*), key the flipped pose of the arms.
5. Use the Dope Sheet to stagger the motion of the arm bones to your liking.

> **Tip**
> Do Rain's hands pass through her body as they swing? Go to the frame at which this occurs and key one more pose to repel them outward. See if you can keep the F-curves as smooth as possible after the correction.

Final touches?

What else does the walk cycle need? If you're like me, you'll want to relax the pose of Rain's hands, fix her hair and scarf, or maybe add a little 12-frame bounce to her neck and shoulders. You could also explore how her other secondary bones might be useful for layering additional motion without affecting the F-curves you already have.

Perhaps you're still not satisfied with how the legs look or would like to see what a faster or slower walk cycle would look like. If that's the case, keep these rules in mind while editing your animation.

For bone-pairs with .L and .R in their names, edit their keyframes in tandem:

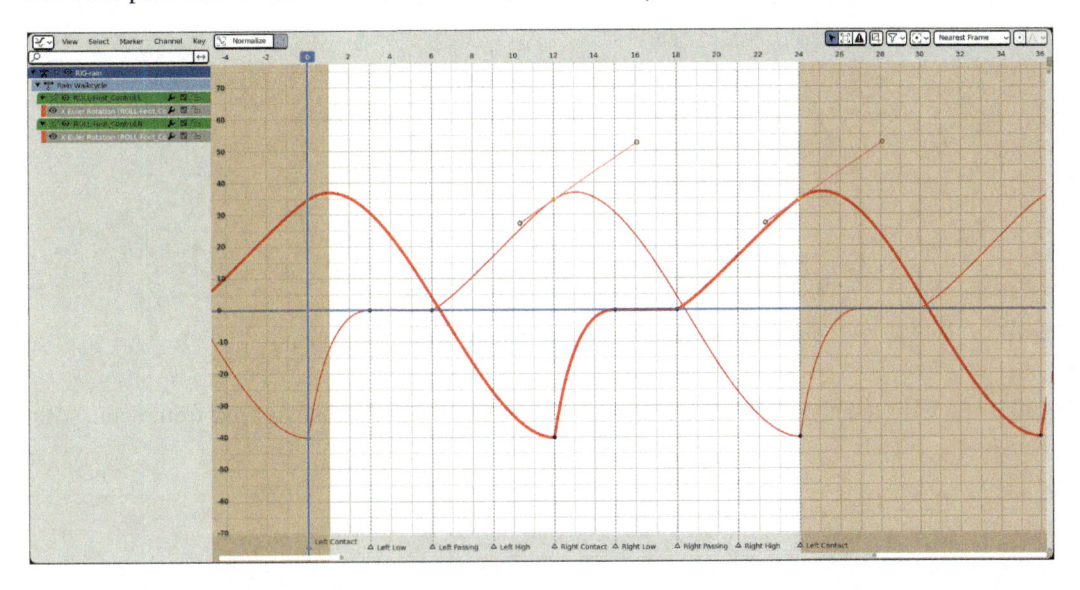

Figure 8.45: Adjusting the Z Location animation for both IK feet

You can alter the stride length, but you'll need to find all the **Y Location** channels we keyed in the initial stage and scale them all together on the *Y* axis of the Graph Editor:

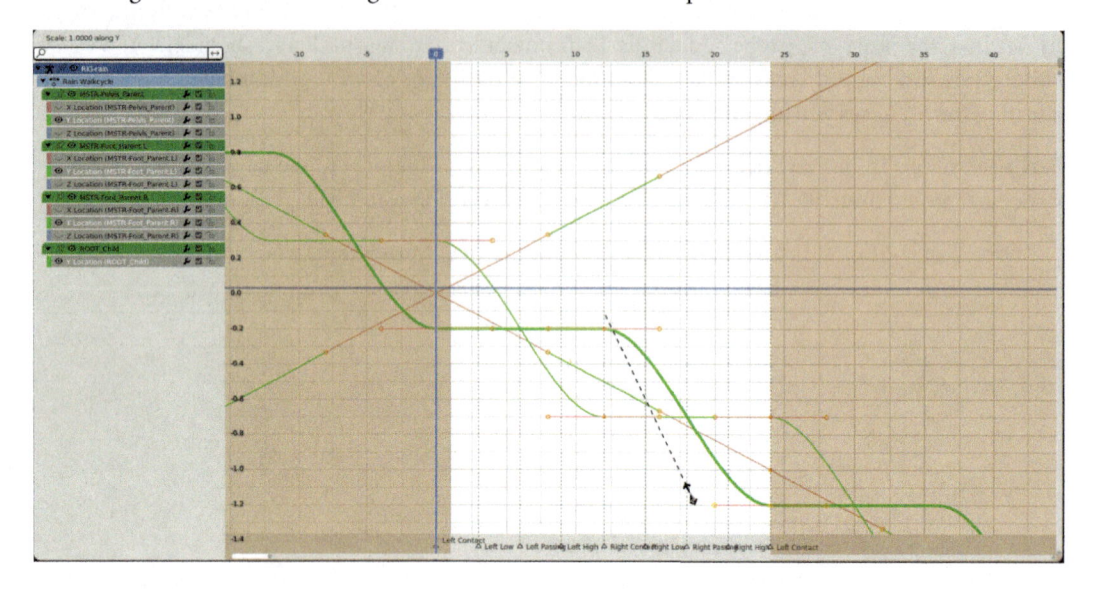

Figure 8.46: Scaling the stride length in the Graph Editor

And if you want to change the period of the whole walk cycle, select all your keyframes and scale them on the *X* axis:

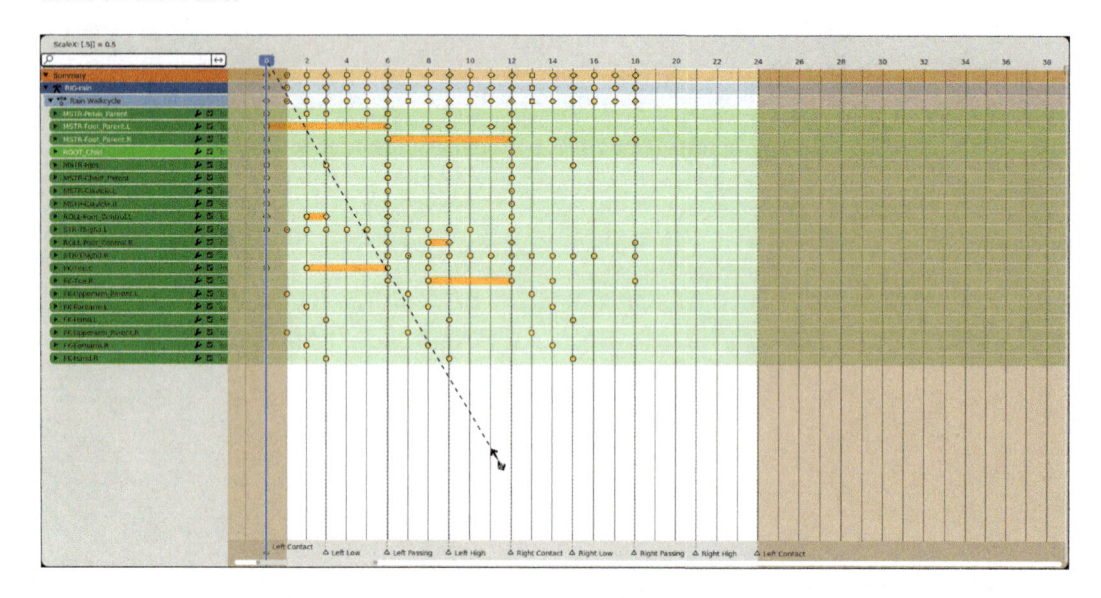

Figure 8.47: Slowing down the walk cycle by scaling everything in the Dope Sheet

One more thing: remember to save your work! Later, I'll show you how to integrate this walk cycle into other animations.

Summary

I hope this exercise went smoothly for you. In the wild, you may create your own cycles – crawl cycles, run cycles, bicycle cycles, and so on – for many different characters in all kinds of scenarios, and your process may differ quite a bit from this one.

No matter how different your own "_____cycles" will be, though, there's one consistent rule you can take away from this lesson: *figure out which bones don't come back*, that is, which bones have location values that will approach infinity as the cycle repeats. Once you figure that out, focus solely on those specific animation channels. After doing the hard part first, everything else will fall into place…

…unless it doesn't. Your own attempts, like mine, will be fraught with mistakes and revisions. You'll have to guess your own "magic numbers" for the stride length and period, then realize later they need changing. This doesn't make you a novice; it makes you a professional!

In the next chapter, we'll set aside all of the bones for walking, and explore another thing most of us take for granted: talking!

Questions

1. If the first pose of our walk cycle is keyed on frame 0, why should our playback range not also begin at frame 0?
2. What makes the number 24 so important?
3. In a normal walk cycle, why would we choose to use *FK* bones for the arms and *IK* bones for the feet? Can you think of animations for which the reverse would be needed?
4. What makes the **Y Location** F-curves so special for those first three bones we keyed?
5. What determines the period of an F-curve?
6. Most F-curves in our walk cycle needed a period of 24 frames, but at least one had a period of 12 frames. Which one, and why?
7. After pasting keyframes to the bones of the right foot, you moved them 12 frames left or right in the animation editor. Why did the direction not matter in this case?
8. In some other character rigs, the *IK* feet have an additional function called "toe roll". What would you guess this does?
9. What makes a walking character like a unicycle?

9
Sound and Lip-Syncing

The visual component of a film or video – be it animated or live-action – is only half of what makes up the finished product. The other half is sound. What the audience hears is no less important than what they see, so I cringe whenever an animator treats the audio as an afterthought in their project; as if sound were just a supplemental sensory layer slapped onto a chiefly visual medium. If anything, it's the other way around!

Whenever applicable, I insist on having a finished soundtrack and/or voiceover before I begin animating, either by obtaining it from the client, working with an audio engineer, or producing the audio myself. Audio is just that important for establishing the pace and timing of an animation, and nowhere is this clearer than in the task of lip-syncing – animating a character's mouth to speak prerecorded lines.

By making Rain lip-sync in this chapter, we'll accustom ourselves to using sound in Blender, practice detailed facial animation, and realize first-hand what makes sound so important to an animation.

We'll learn how to do the following:

- Import and work with audio in Blender's **Video Sequencer**
- Animate Rain's head and face to act in sync with the audio
- Animate Rain's mouth

Technical requirements

As with other chapters in this part of the book, to complete the following exercise we'll need a new scene in Blender with our character Rain in it.

This time, however, we'll also need some audio with which to animate Rain speaking. I've recorded the perfect sound clip to use: a single line of dialogue spoken by a female voice actor – something brief, open to interpretation, and copyright-free.

You can download it here:

https://github.com/PacktPublishing/Realizing-3D-Animation-in-Blender

Instead of using the provided .wav file, you may prefer to furnish one yourself, either by recording your own voice or someone else's or by sampling the sound of someone speaking in a video, film, or podcast. If you know how to do that, that will work as well.

> **Tip**
>
> Blender supports most common sound file formats, such as .mp3, .ogg, .flac, and .wav, and can even extract the audio stream from supported video files. One of the better formats is .wav, as it is lossless and requires little processing to decode.
>
> The one thing Blender can't do is record audio. For that, you'll need an application such as the free and open source Audacity:
>
> https://www.audacityteam.org/

Lastly, make sure you have a working set of speakers or headphones on which to listen to your chosen sound clip. You'll be listening to it repeatedly, so I recommend headphones so as to minimize the number of nearby people this drives insane.

Using sound in Blender

Our first order of business is to get our audio into Blender so that we can hear it when the animation is played. Being able to hear the audio in the same program we use to animate is indispensable, especially for an animation of someone talking.

In the following section, we will learn how to import audio into our scene, then we'll learn how to edit it (though editing may not even be necessary if you've chosen to use the provided voiceover file). Once we're satisfied with the audio, I'll reveal an easily overlooked setting that ensures our audio plays in sync with the animation.

Importing audio files into the Video Sequencer

Let's start by importing our sound file into the scene. Note that this does not require adding a **Speaker** object in 3D space!

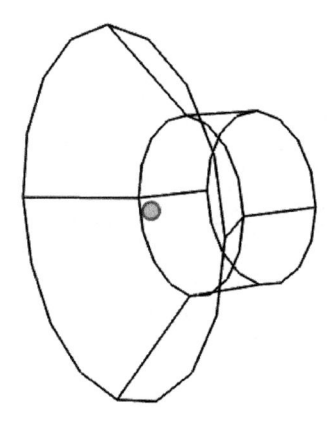

Figure 9.1: An unnecessary Speaker object

Those things are for simulating a particular sound source, panning and fading the audio based on the **Speaker** object's position relative to the active camera. Very cool, but more than what we need.

Instead, let's use the **Video Sequencer**, which doubles as an audio sequencer:

1. Open the **Video Sequencer**.
2. Make sure you're at frame 1, as audio will be inserted at the current frame.
3. Use **Add** (*Shift + A*) | **Sound**.
4. In the invoked file browser, find and select the sound file you want.

This inserts the audio as a sound strip:

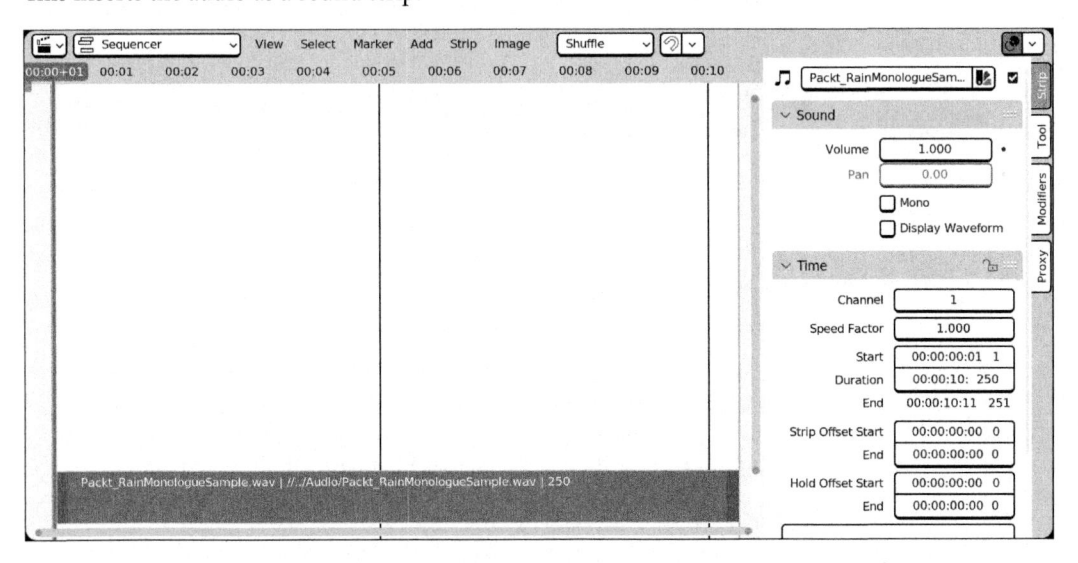

Figure 9.2: Sound strip in the Video Sequencer, with properties to the right

When you hit **Play Animation**, you should be able to hear the audio without needing to adjust any additional parameters.

> **Tip**
> If you hear no sound or very poor-quality sound, and you're certain the issue lies with Blender, check the settings under **Preferences | System | Sound**. It may be an issue with your default **Audio Device**.

Using sound strips

Sound strips can be edited like any other strip in the **Video Sequencer**. Of course, Blender doesn't have anything like the functionality of a real multi-track audio editing suite, but it offers more than what you might expect from a 3D application!

Sound strip properties

Sound strips have some unique properties that can be found in the right-hand sidebar (*N*) of the **Video Sequencer**. Editing a couple of properties here can improve our experience:

1. Select the sound strip and go to its properties in the **Strip** tab of the sidebar.
2. Enable **Sound | Display Waveform**.
3. Enable **Source | Caching**.

Caching makes audio processing go a tiny bit faster (maybe), but the more important thing is enabling **Display Waveform**. With that enabled, we can actually see the peaks of the sound wave like in other audio programs:

Figure 9.3: Visible sound wave in the sound strip

Seeing the waveform in the sound strip makes it much easier to find the exact frame at which a given sound occurs. Among other things, this makes editing the sound strip easier if needed.

> **Tip**
> If you resize your view in the **Video Sequencer** so that one audio strip fills the space, you can customize the interface so that the audio peaks are visible while you work. Try enabling **View | Sync Visible Range** in both the Timeline and the **Video Sequencer** to line them up.

Trimming the audio length

If you choose to use the provided sound clip, you'll hardly need to edit it at all. Just make sure it starts at frame 1. On the other hand, if you've imported your own audio, you may need to trim it down or adjust its position in time.

Here's an example of another sound strip, sourced directly from an entire podcast episode. Note how it goes past the hour mark:

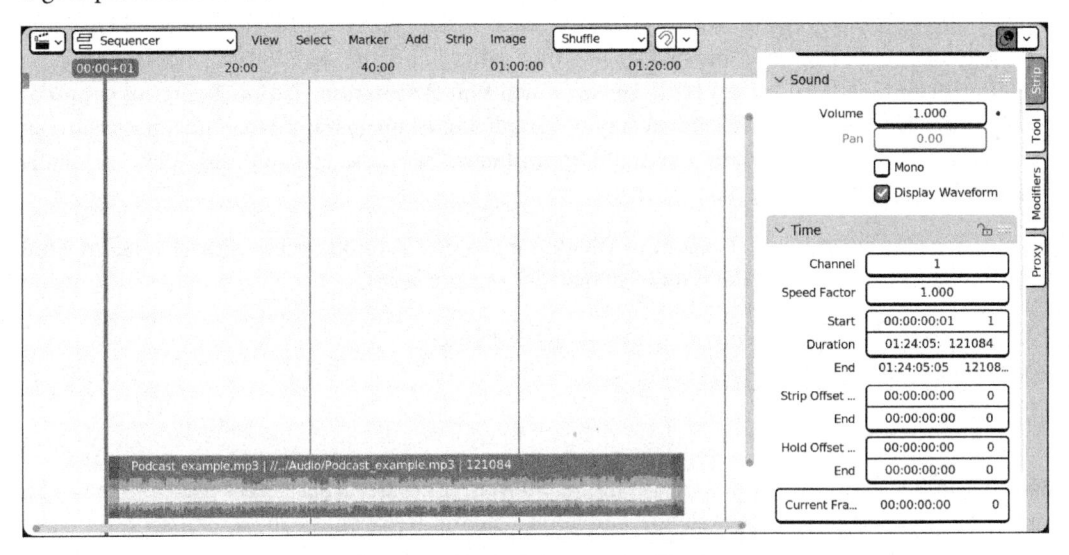

Figure 9.4: A much longer sound strip

If I were to use this audio, I'd need to skip directly to the funny bit I like; no way am I animating the whole thing. I could trim the audio in a dedicated program like Audacity, but Blender can do it as well.

Sound strips can be edited just like any other strip in the **Video Sequencer**. I find that it's easiest to use the **Strip | Time | Hold Offset** properties to quickly get to the section of audio I want:

1. Edit the sound strip so that it includes only the segment of audio you want for the scene.
2. In the Timeline, adjust the frame range of the scene to fit the length of the audio.

Be sure to play back the audio from the start and listen all the way to the end to confirm your choices. What you hear now will be what determines the timing of your animation, and – assuming you don't make any further changes – what you'll end up hearing in the final video.

Timeline settings for working with sound

If you've ever tried to edit audio and video together or watched a poorly encoded TV show episode on some sketchy bootleg website, you'll know how jarring it is to have to watch something in which the audio is out of sync with the video. If we are to animate a character who will appear to be the source of the words being spoken, we must be precise about the frames at which those words occur.

When we hit **Play Animation**, Blender will play back both the animation and the audio simultaneously, but that doesn't necessarily mean the two will be synchronized. By default, Blender is set to **Play Every Frame** in order, even if the frame rate lags. On the other hand, the audio plays smoothly without skipping, beginning from whichever frame on which **Play Animation** was hit. The result is similar to viewing a silent film while listening to a phonograph; there's no guarantee that the timing between video and audio won't drift apart. You might, for instance, see frame `161` in the 3D Viewport while hearing the audio from frame `164`.

Overall, it's a bit difficult to tell exactly in which frame a given sound occurs with Blender's default Timeline settings. Let's make them more suitable for our purposes:

1. Open the **Playback** menu in the header of the Timeline.
2. Set **Sync** to **Sync to Audio**.
3. Enable **Audio Scrubbing**.

Sync to Audio ensures that what we see in the 3D Viewport during playback keeps pace with the audio so that our judgment as to how well our animation synchronizes won't be impaired:

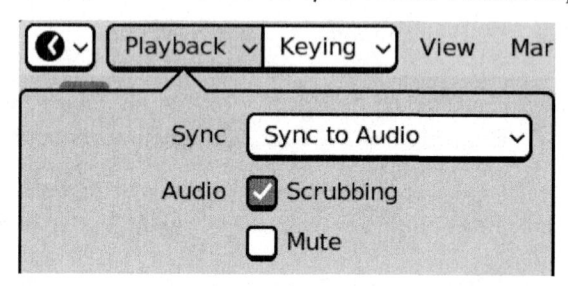

Figure 9.5: Playback settings for audio in the Timeline

On top of that, we've also enabled **Audio Scrubbing**. Now, each time we scrub or change frames, we'll hear the tiny blip of audio play on that frame.

Try it! Annoying, right? But also, kind of helpful. Using this feature while scrubbing, we can hear exactly when each word begins without needing to look at the audio waveform all the time.

> **Tip**
> Another way to stay in sync and keep things organized is to add a marker at the beginning of each word or phrase. I like to rename these markers to reflect the lines being spoken.

This concludes the section on audio! Having ensured our sound is in the right place, we're ready to animate, knowing that our audio will be in sync with our animation. Well, maybe we can't know that just yet – but if it is out of sync, at least we'll know whose fault it is.

Acting without speaking

Using the audio as our guide, we can cast aside all doubt about the timing of our animation. We know exactly what words Rain will say, when she will say those words, and how long it will take to say them.

But does that mean we should begin by animating her mouth? Not necessarily! In fact, it looks kind of weird if we solely animate that part first. All those little phonemes and syllables that the mouth makes are details, and we mustn't start with details. Besides, a character doesn't just speak with their mouth. For this exercise, we'll start by making Rain speak with her whole face.

Key facial expressions

If you've been thinking ahead, you've probably already listened to Rain's lines a few times and mouthed them out yourself at your desk or in a mirror. That's great. Keep doing that. As animators, we can rehearse what we're about to have our characters do by letting the voice actor speak through us, through our own physical bodies, before she possesses her final host body as Rain.

After listening to the audio and animating yourself (so to speak) a few times, try it again without moving your lips so much. This forces you to act with the rest of your face. Where will Rain be looking? Will she nod or shake her head? Will she smile or frown? And what will her eyebrows be doing? These decisions will comprise the first pass of our animation, but try not to think about it – feel it by acting it out!

Here are some key facial poses in my first pass:

Figure 9.6: Facial expressions of Rain talking

Just because we've postponed lip-syncing for a later section doesn't mean we shouldn't include the mouth in our poses. Note, however, that we should avoid keying anything below the neck, as it may conflict with a later exercise in which we combine this animation with our walk cycle from earlier. Follow the next steps:

1. Enable Rain's **Face Primary** armature layer. The **FK** layer should be visible as well, but we only need FK-Head and FK-Neck – you can hide the other *FK* bones.

2. Choose a frame and create a facial pose for it. It doesn't have to be at the beginning but try to get comfortable using lots of available bones to achieve the look you want.

3. As with our first foray into character animation, select all visible bones and key their **Location, Rotation & Scale**. We can always delete unnecessary animation channels later.

4. Now keep going! Continue keying the entire head and face at different frames until you have a nice sequence that vaguely follows the order of facial expressions Rain should make.

5. You may also wish to consolidate the channel groups for individual bones by selecting them in the **Dope Sheet** and using **Channel | Group Channels** (*Ctrl + G*), though I recommend doing this less aggressively than we did back in *Chapter 7*. For instance, we'll want to distinguish the keyframes for the jaw from the lips this time:

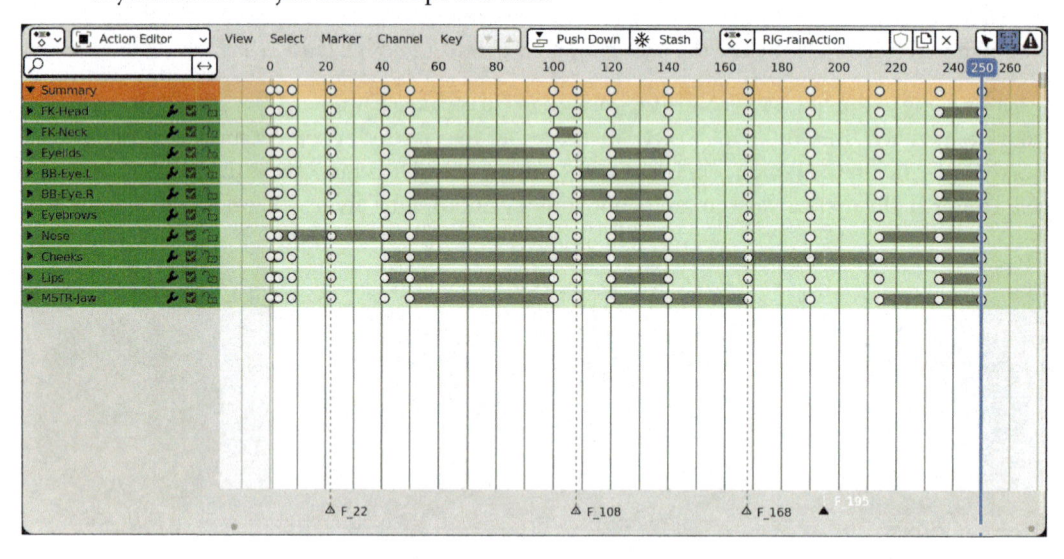

Figure 9.7: Example Action Editor with custom channel groups

When you're done, you should be able to see a kind of coherence forming between Rain and her voice. She's nowhere near speaking, but she's feeling what's being spoken, at least. Don't worry if it's sloppy; at this stage, something is better than nothing.

Automatic keyframing and keying sets

With so many little bones to animate, inserting keyframes gets tedious. After making your pose, you have to remember to select everything and insert keyframes for it, or the pose will reset, and you'll lose your work. These extra clicks and keystrokes add up!

Keying sets

By now, you're probably tired of having to pick which properties to key each time you bring up the **Insert Keyframe** menu (*I*). That's where **Keying Sets** come in.

You can choose an **Active Keying Set** type in the **Keying** menu of the **Timeline**:

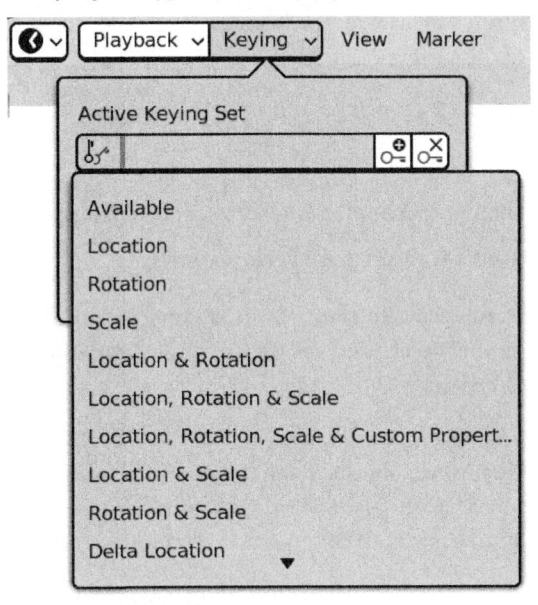

Figure 9.8: Available Keying Sets

You've seen this before – it's the same list that comes up in the **Insert Keyframe** menu (*I*).

While a keying set is chosen, **Insert Keyframe** (*I*) will use that keying set instead of showing you the **Insert Keyframe** menu. For instance, if you select **Location** from this menu, pressing *I* in the 3D Viewport will bypass the usual menu and immediately insert **Location** keyframes for the selection. This is not particularly useful if you want to be discriminating about which properties to key, so for that reason, I almost always select **Available**, a special keying set that only keys existing animation channels of selected bones/objects.

Auto Keying

If you still feel like you're pressing *I* one keystroke too many to insert a keyframe, take a look at the button that lets you insert keyframes automatically. It looks like a record button in the **Timeline** header:

Figure 9.9: Auto Keying

Auto Keying inserts keyframes at the current frame for selected bones or objects every time they are transformed – no need to press *I* afterward. I've been keeping quiet about this feature until now as it can quickly make a mess of things if one isn't careful!

Let's enable **Auto Keying** and then choose an appropriate keying set:

1. Enable **Auto Keying**.
2. Pull up the menu next to the **Auto Keying** button and enable **Only Active Keying Set**.
3. Go to **Keying** | **Active Keying Set** and select **Available**.

With these settings, we no longer have to manually insert keyframes. Additionally, should we choose to delete any superfluous animation channels as we work, the **Available** keying set ensures that they won't be accidentally created again.

Of course, even when **Auto Keying** is enabled, pressing *I* to manually insert keyframes is still necessary in cases where we need to key bones/objects that haven't been transformed. Also, keep in mind that the **Available** keying set cannot create new animation channels – you will raise an error if you try to key a bone that isn't already animated.

One last thing: be careful! One drawback to **Auto Keying** is how easy it is to accidentally overwrite keyframes or clutter up the Dope Sheet.

Using Auto Keying to refine our face poses

Let's try out these new settings for the next pass over our animation:

1. Use the **Dope Sheet** and **Pose** | **In Between** operators to hold poses and create breakdowns in between keyframes you've already made. You may be surprised at how far you get with some fast, "ease-out" style transitions between key poses.
2. Use the **Graph Editor** to finalize the motion of the neck and head.
3. After you're satisfied with the motion of the head, move on to the eyebrows, and finally the eyes.

As you can see, there's a lot of "talking" to be done without using the mouth! When you are satisfied with the range of emotion and feeling in everything north of Rain's nose, you can move on to animating the mouth.

The science of lip-syncing

It's time for the best part of this exercise: animating Rain's mouth. This will make her talk (so to speak).

As with walking, talking is one of those things we see people do every day. As I've mentioned before, this makes it harder to animate, not easier! It will help, then, to begin by deconstructing what it is that our mouths are doing while we're talking.

Phonetics for animators

Fortunately, effective lip-syncing does not require a complete lesson in phonetics. We needn't learn how to speak – just how the act of speaking looks to an observer.

The following are essential elements of speech that we should know – what I'll call mouth poses. When performed in sequence, these positions of the jaw, lips, teeth, and tongue are how we speak, and also how we make a character appear to speak. Most words – even short ones – are comprised of multiple mouth poses, so these poses will proceed more rapidly than any other sequence of poses we've animated so far.

Vowels

Let's begin with vowels: the basic noises we make when our mouths are open. In English, these are commonly known as the sounds signified by the letters *a*, *e*, *i*, *o*, and *u*.

The simple vowel sounds in English, along with the mouth poses that make them, exist on a kind of spectrum, starting with *ee* as in *see*, all the way to *oo* as in *root*:

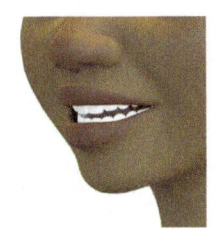

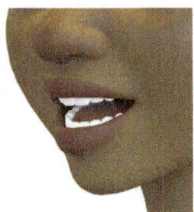

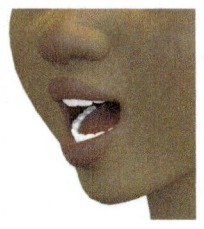

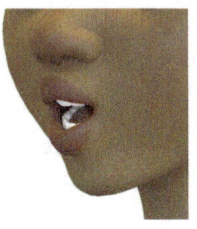

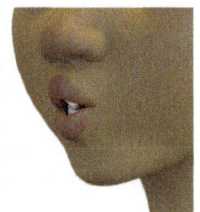

Figure 9.10: ee, eh, ah, oh, oo

Try sounding them out as one word: *eeeeaaaaaaoooooouuuu*.

Notice that the jaw is open wider toward the middle of this spectrum than at the ends; sounds like *ah* as in *hot* and *oh* as in *boat* require a cavernous, resonant space in the mouth. Also, note the corners of the mouth moving steadily inward from *ee* to *oo*.

> **Tip**
>
> The mouth pose for *ee* looks a lot like a smile, doesn't it? They are, in fact, quite similar, and in real life, they use the same muscles. That doesn't mean Rain has to be happy to say cheese, though. A frowning character should only "smile" long enough to make the correct *ee* sound before their mouth settles back into a less happy pose. Likewise, a smiling character can only do the *oo* face long enough to finish their *yous* and *whos* before an *ee*-like smile returns to their lips.

In addition to the vowels shown on the spectrum, there's also the weak *uh* sound at the end of words such as *comma* and *tuna*, which is uttered loosely and looks sort of like how Rain's mouth does when you open her jaw just halfway. Finally, any vowel can be "r-colored" to make the *r* sound; this is done mostly with the tongue, but on the outside, it looks like a slight pursing of the upper lips:

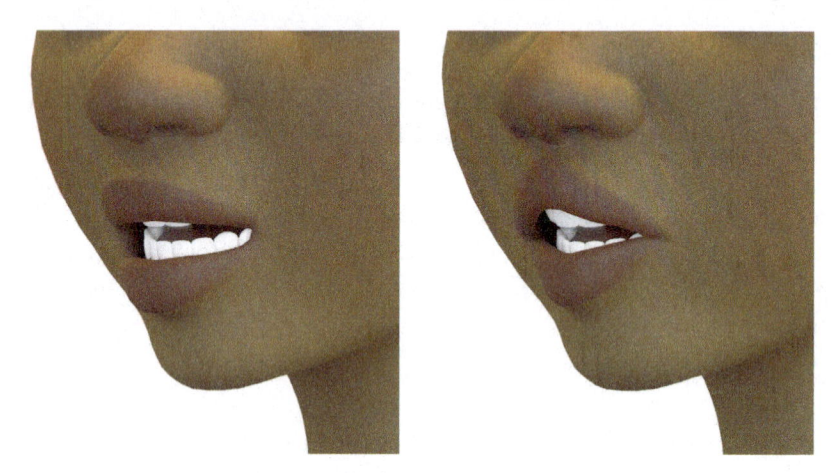

Figure 9.11: "uh" and "er"

Combining vowels

The articulations for these vowel sounds blend together fluidly to make many more sounds. Vowels such as *a* as in *face* and *i* as in *ice* are diphthongs – compounds of *eh* + *ee* and *ah* + *ee*, respectively. This is also true of the "consonants" *w* and *y*, which are really more like vowels if you think about it.

Using just the mouth poses we've seen so far, we can animate words such as *I*, *our*, *way*, *where*, and *you*. These alone aren't enough to make a complete sentence in English, so let's move on to consonants.

Consonants

Consonants are all those other noises in language – the ones between the vowels – that require restricting the flow of air through the mouth in some way. To make these noises, the jaw tends to close a little – though not necessarily all the way – so that some combination of the lips, teeth, and/or tongue can touch.

Lips

Let's start with the consonants *b*, *m*, and *p*. These are important for being the only consonants that require the lips to close completely, which makes them the most conspicuous when it comes to lip-syncing:

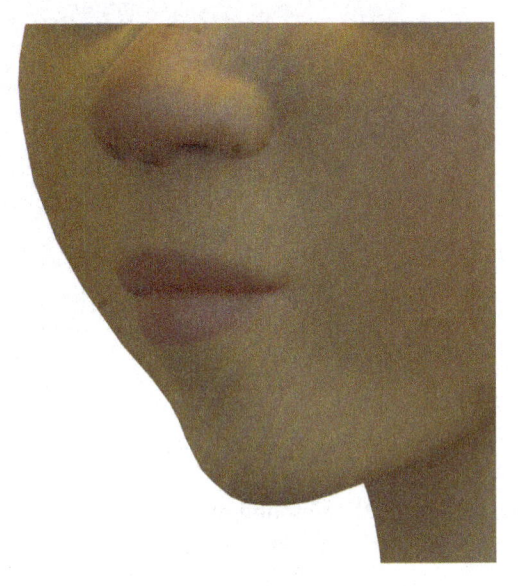

Figure 9.12: The bilabial phoneme

Though they sound different, these consonants look alike from our point of view. For our purposes, the words *mum*, *bum*, and *pub* would all be animated in basically the same way.

> **Tip**
> To make the *b*, *m*, and/or *p* sound, the lips must come together to briefly make an airtight seal. That doesn't mean the whole jaw needs to close, though. Consider as well that this is the only case in which a character's lips must do this. Other times, the mouth often stays open between words and before and after sentences.

Three letters, one mouth pose – easy! Now, let's move on to something harder.

Teeth

The consonants *f* and *v* (as in *five*) also look alike. Making these requires that the lower lip makes contact with the upper teeth:

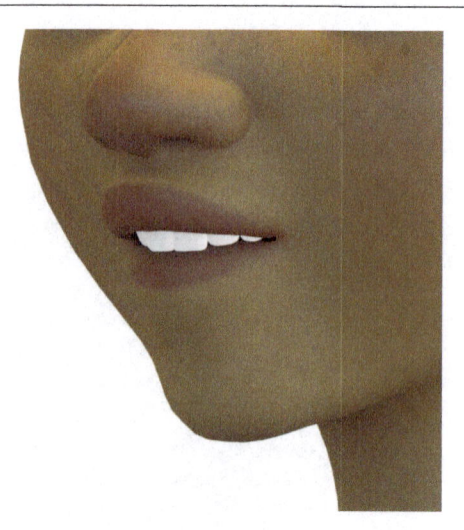

Figure 9.13: The "f" or "v" sound

Tongue

To make things even more difficult, the *th* sound requires that we dig out the bones for the tongue, which, for Rain, are in a whole different armature layer:

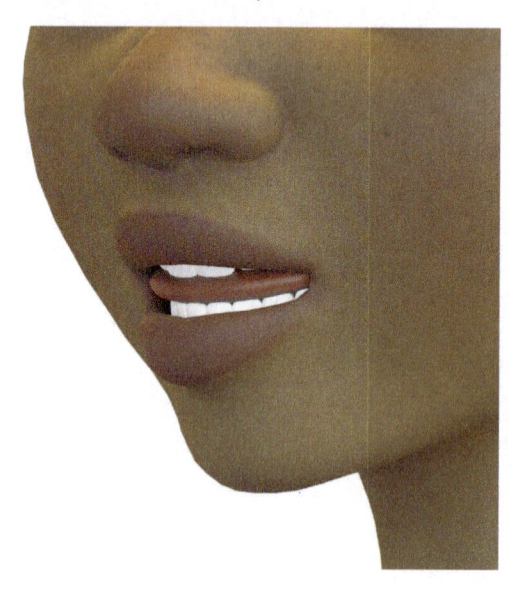

Figure 9.14: Using the tongue bones in Face Extras to make the "th" mouth pose

Another important use of the tongue is for the *l* (lowercase *L*) sound, as in *like*. To make a convincing *l*, the tongue may need to be seen touching the roof of the mouth like so:

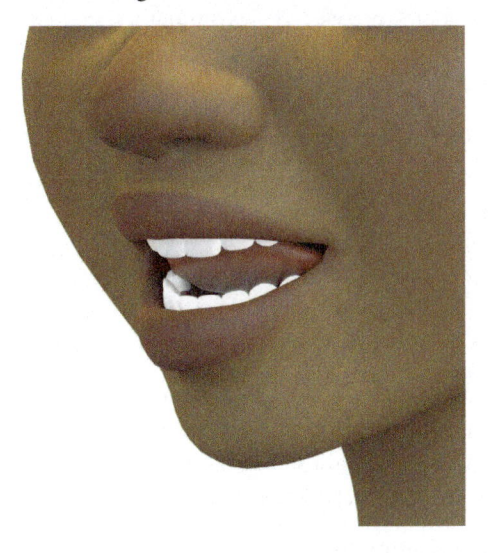

Figure 9.15: The "l" mouth pose

All other sounds

There are so many more phonemes in the English language to cover! Consonants such as *d*, *g*, *j*, *k*, *n*, *s*, *t*, and *z*, as well as *ch* and *sh*...

Anyway, they all kinda look like this:

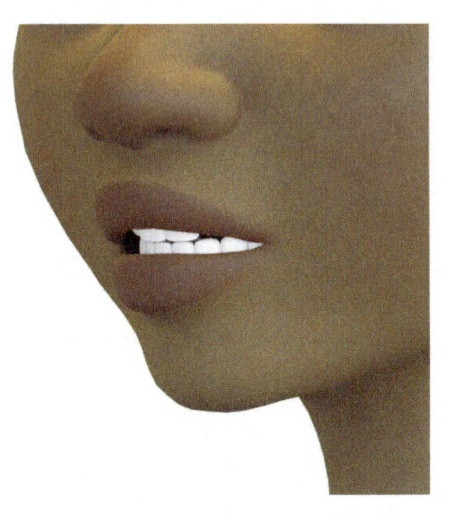

Figure 9.16: All the other phonemes

And that's if they look like anything at all! Complex articulations of the vocal tract are employed in the remainder of these sounds – different parts of the tongue touching different parts of the mouth, and so on – but they're hidden from view. To us animators, therefore, they don't matter that much. In many cases, you can just wiggle the jaw a little to make it look like something's happening, and that's all you need.

We now know enough about phonetics to start lip-syncing!

Animating the mouth

Animating Rain's mouth is not all that different from animating, say, her arms. When animating the arms, you start with the shoulders and elbows, then the hands, and finally the fingers. This *FK* chain is less obvious, but still present in the bones that control Rain's mouth.

Of greatest importance is MSTR-Jaw, the bone that opens and closes Rain's jaw. If Rain intends to speak, she's got to open and close that thing. Next, we have the corners of the mouth and the control bones that move the upper and lower lips, which are nearly as important. Of least importance (but still kind of important) is the tongue, which is sort of like the pinky finger of the mouth.

Note that this matches the order in which we just covered the basic phonemes in human speech! First, the type of vowel determines how far the jawbone should open and roughly how wide the corners of the mouth should be. Next, we have the consonants made by the lips and teeth, and finally, the tongue.

Key the parts of Rain's mouth in roughly that order, listening carefully as you scrub through each frame to make sure that the motion is keyed at just the right time to sync with the sound. Before you know it, you will have animated Rain speaking!

> **Tip**
> Oftentimes, the beginning of a word in the voiceover will sit right between two frames, and you'll wonder when exactly to key the associated action that should appear to be its cause. When faced with such a dilemma, try to err on the side of having the animation *very slightly* precede the sound.
>
> Unlike light, sound has perceptible slowness. We know this from watching loud and distant sight-and-sound events such as lightning and fireworks. At a distance of just 50 feet, the sound of someone's voice will take about 1/24 of a second (1 frame) to reach you.

You now have all the tools and knowledge you need to animate Rain speaking. Try it out!

1. Begin by keying some words, focusing mainly on MSTR-Jaw, the most important bone for opening and closing the mouth, and the corners of the lips.
2. Once you have Rain's jaw flapping in sync with the voiceover, move on to the smaller shapes made by the lips; all those fast little syllables you missed in the first step.
3. Finally, enable the **Face Extras** armature layer and animate the tongue for the remaining sections of speech in which it is (or should be) visible.

4. Using the **Action Editor**, rename the action to something such as `Rain Speaking` and save your work for a later exercise.

After just a few well-placed keyframes, something will "click," and the words we hear will seem to have been spoken by Rain herself!

Summary

When we imported the audio into our scene and played it initially, Rain just stood there motionless while words came out of someone else's mouth. Now, after a lot of work, we can say Rain is the one speaking those lines! It's not unlike making a puppet seem to speak. Even though we're the ones pulling all the strings, there's a giddy satisfaction for animators in letting ourselves be fooled by our own work.

Imagine how hard it would have been to do this animation without a voiceover to work with; how hard it would be to have to animate Rain mouthing out the same lines in silence. Later, a voice actor would have to watch what you made and synchronize their performance with your work instead of the other way around. This process is called dubbing and was employed in a lot of early animations, but in my opinion, it never looks quite right. Always get the audio first, if you can.

As a bonus for completing this exercise, we now have two complementary actions in our little character animation portfolio for Rain: one for talking, and the other for walking. Later, we'll combine these actions using the last, most mysterious animation editor in Blender.

We're nearly done with the character animation part of this book. Continuing our theme of commonplace things being tricky to animate, the next chapter will be on animating the most commonplace action, and therefore one of the trickiest as well: *picking up a thing*.

Questions

1. What can Blender's **Video Sequencer** do besides edit video sequences?
2. What happens to a sound strip when you change the scene frame rate?
3. Blender's default playback setting is **Play Every Frame**. In which cases is this less than ideal?
4. When is **Auto Keying** appropriate?
5. Do you speak a language besides English? Are there any sounds or shapes you make with your mouth that do not occur in English?
6. Which part of the mouth is indispensable for speaking in real life but not as important in animation?
7. Which is faster, sound or light? Why does this matter to an animator?
8. After finishing this animation, imagine you've been told to replace the audio. The director decided they liked another take, with slightly different words and timing. How annoyed are you?

10
Prop Interaction with Dynamic Constraints

Interacting with your environment is an important aspect of... existing. I love touching objects, holding objects, picking them up and putting them down again, rearranging the world around me, and generally having a solid corporeal body. I'd wager you like doing those things as well, and your characters want to do them too!

Animating this can range from being blindingly obvious to devilishly difficult. If we want Rain to, say, wear a hat, we can parent it to a bone in her head and continue as normal; if she is to sit in a chair, we can just animate her sitting down and not let her pass through that chair; and if Rain were to kick a ball, we could animate it flying into the air at just the right moment.

So far, so good – but what if she were to pick up a ball in her hand and toss it? That requires making a *dynamic* constraint – an animated constraint that starts working when Rain touches the ball and ends when it leaves her hand. First, we'll need to put Rain's hand on the ball. Next, we'll line some things up and create our constraint. As far as constraints go, this one is quite easy to understand. The challenging part is animating it...

In this chapter, you'll learn how to do the following:

- Pose Rain grasping an object in her fingers
- "Grab" an object with constraints and special bones
- Key the influence of a constraint
- Apply the effect of a constraint to an object

Technical requirements

No surprises here – to follow along with this character animation exercise, you need three things:

- Blender
- Rain
- A new scene, in Blender, with Rain

These requirements should make sense to you by now. If you don't remember who Rain is or how to use her in Blender, turn back to *Chapter 6*. If you don't remember what Blender is, you might need to go back to *Chapter 1*!

Touching the object

For this animation, Rain will pick up a ball in her right hand, hold it for a moment, and then toss it away. This involves setting up an object relationship between Rain's armature and the ball using constraints, not unlike what we saw in *Chapter 4*, but with some additional complexity.

The first step to having Rain hold a ball in her hand is to make one and put her hand on it. Pretty straightforward! This will be the easiest section of the exercise. After that, things will get a little dicey...

Setting up the shot

We need to model a ball and put it in an easy-to-reach place for Rain. How about right in front of her on a table?

Figure 10.1: Rain, with props

On that note, let's add two new objects: a ball and a table. You may not be a 3D modeler, and this is not a modeling book by a long shot, so "modeling" your ball may involve little more than adding a sphere, and your "table" can just be a box. I think any 3D animator can handle that!

> **Tip**
> If you can't seem to add, select, or edit objects, it might be because you're still in **Pose Mode**. You need to be in **Object Mode** to add new objects and **Edit Mode** to edit them. It's been a while since we used these other modes.

Creating some simple props

Your table can be any old flat surface that comes up to the height of Rain's waist, such as a piano – preferably a concert grand piano:

Figure 10.2: Piano model with 40,000 vertices

Just kidding! Use a cube.

For the ball, any sphere will do, so long as it's small enough to fit in Rain's hand. One-tenth of a meter (`0.1` m) is a good diameter. Make it any color/texture you like.

I've elected to add a material to my ball so that I can see its rotation more easily:

Figure 10.3: Ball

> **Important note**
> Keep an eye on what mode you're in when you move and scale the ball. If you move all the vertices at once in edit mode, you'll displace the ball's geometry from its origin, and if you scale the ball in object mode, you'll have modified its object scale value from [1.0, 1.0, 1.0]. In either case, it could lead to some odd behavior later on.

It's a stretch to even call this modeling, but go ahead and model these and assemble them in a convenient location for Rain:

1. Model a ball that can fit in Rain's hand.
2. Model a simple waist-high table in front of Rain.
3. Put the ball on the table near Rain's right hand so that she won't have to reach too far to grab it.
4. Name these objects `Ball` and `Table`.

Now we have all the objects we need for our shot. As shown in *Figure 10.1*, my table conceals Rain's legs, and the ball is close enough to Rain that I don't even need to animate her bending over to grab it. The task is challenging enough as it is!

With all the objects we need in our scene, we're ready to turn our attention to Rain's rig.

A use for IK arms

In anticipation of the actions she will perform, we will once again adjust some settings in Rain's rig for this scene. As always, our goal is to make Rain easier to animate, and in this case, we'll make things even easier than usual. Things like facial animation and footwork are unimportant details for this chapter.

This exercise focuses on the relationship between Rain's hand and the ball, so the following adjustments will simplify things for us:

1. Use Rain's **CloudRig | Outfits** interface to hide her ponytail and other distracting accessories.
2. Enable the **IK**, **FK**, and **Fingers** layers.
3. In the **FK/IK Switch** settings, set **Left Arm** so that it uses *FK*, but keep **Right Arm** at `1.0` so that it uses *IK*.
4. Under **FK Settings | FK Hinge**, set both **Left Arm** and **Right Arm** to `1.0`.
5. Set **Face Settings | Eye Target Parent** to **Head** (3).
6. You can select and **Hide** (*H*) all of Rain's bones below her hips.

Here's Rain with her superfluous bones and body parts hidden away:

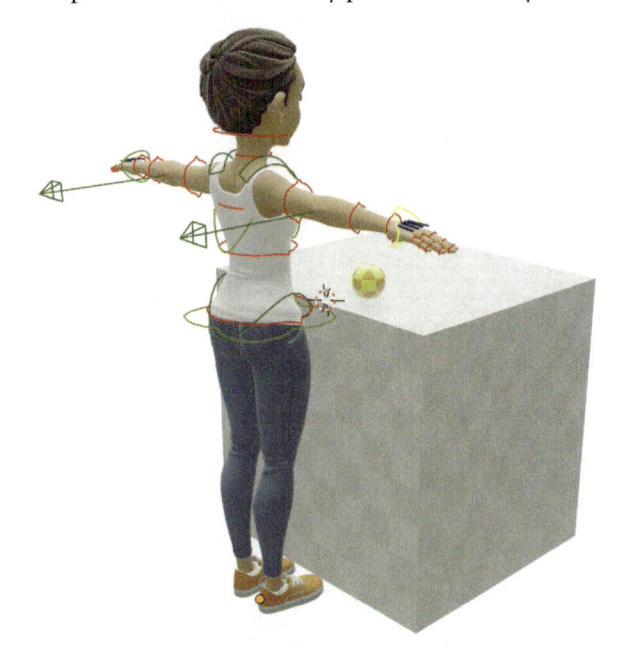

Figure 10.4: Rain with just enough bones to grab a ball

Maybe you can guess why we've made these other changes. For one thing, setting the eye target parent to the head means we can ignore all the face bones – including the eye target – for the rest of this chapter.

The most important decision here was to leave Rain's right arm governed by *IK* and not *FK*. We're ready to begin animating, so we're about to see how much easier that makes our next task.

Reaching for an object

Now we'll implement the first part of our animation from frames 1 to 30:

Figure 10.5: Rain standing versus Rain grasping the ball

Since we can animate in any order that is convenient for us, let's start with the more important pose first.

Hand on the ball

Let's begin by having Rain grab the ball at frame 30. This will be the crucial moment at which the ball makes contact with Rain's skin and we initiate a relationship between the armature and a new object.

One thing that makes this task easier for us is the use of *IK* for the grabbing hand. When we know exactly where the hand needs to be, it's advantageous to only have to move and orient `IK-Hand_Parent.R` instead of the whole *FK* chain of the arm:

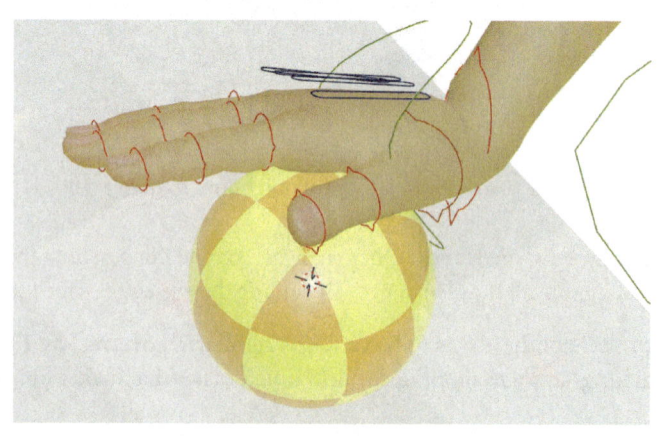

Figure 10.6: Rain's palm on the ball

After that, there's still the matter of getting the fingers on the ball just right. No magic operator in Blender can do this part for us; we just have to put Rain's hand on the ball, zoom in, and look at it closely from many different angles as we tweak her pose:

1. Go to frame 30.
2. Adjust the bones for Rain's torso, neck, and head to have her look at and lean toward the ball. Let her left arm hang down at a comfortable angle (it won't be doing much else in this chapter).
3. Using IK-Hand_Parent.R, put Rain's right hand on the ball so that it fits comfortably in her palm. Adjust the shoulders and *IK* pole target if needed.
4. Pose the finger bones in Rain's right hand so that they grasp the ball. Start with the bones closest to the palm and work your way down the *FK* chain.
5. Key the location and rotation of all visible bones.

There we go – a nice, comfortable grip on the ball:

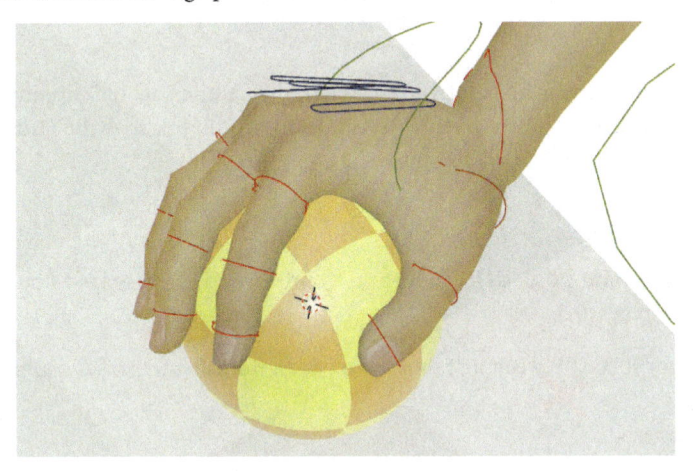

Figure 10.7: Rain's whole hand on the ball

Having a character grasp something believably can be tricky business, right? If you're having trouble here, I'll briefly explain the finer details of making two elements touch.

On making things touch

When posing a character holding something (or really whenever you try to make two 3D objects come into contact with each other), you may find yourself zoomed *way* in – obsessively trying to bring part of the hand closer and closer to the object while never letting the two "touch." If they do, their meshes intersect, which often feels like an unacceptable error somehow. This would seem to make "two things touching" a technical impossibility in 3D. With such a razor-thin margin between "air gap" and "clipping error," what do you do?

In most cases, the answer is that it's preferable to let things intersect just a little bit. In this extreme close-up, you can see the skin on Rain's fingers poking through the surface of the ball from within the ball itself:

Figure 10.8: View from inside the ball

Assuming no one else will see the ball from this view, this subtle sort of "clipping" tends to be less noticeable than a thin layer of air between objects, and may even improve the visual effect. Just don't let any fingers disappear into the ball completely...

Hand OFF the ball

We've keyed the important pose, so let's return to frame 1 and key a simple standing pose like the first one shown in *Figure 10.5*.

Of course, if we interpolate between just those two poses, Rain's hand passes completely through the table and the ball:

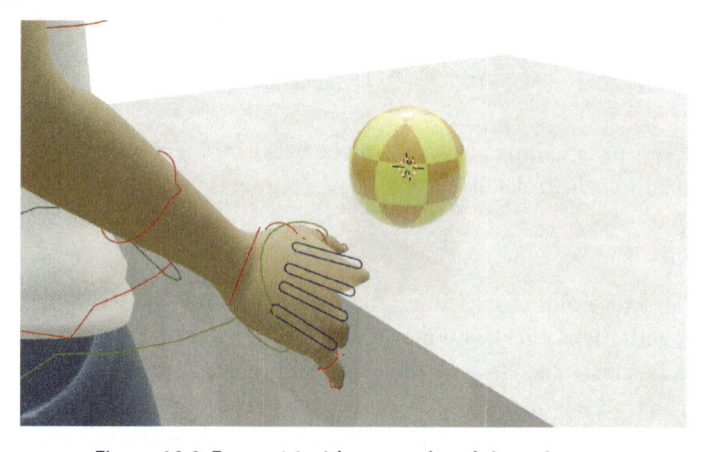

Figure 10.9: Frame 16 without any breakdown keying

So, we'll have to address that too. Here, we want to make sure Rain's fingers don't pass through anything. Character animation may not be our focus here, but let's not be sloppy:

1. Go to frame 1 and key an idle standing pose for before Rain reaches for the ball.
2. Between frames 1 and 30, key one or two additional poses for `IK-Hand_Parent.R` so that Rain's hand doesn't go through the ball or table.
3. Do the same for Rain's right hand so that she extends her fingers, opening her hand before it closes on the ball.

Here's my complete animation of Rain grabbing the ball:

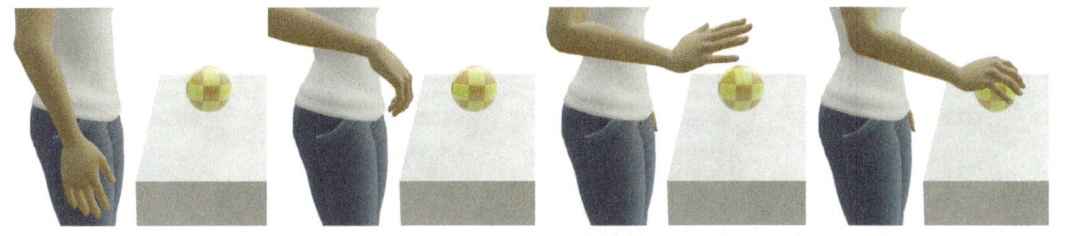

Figure 10.10: Rain on frames 1, 15, 25, and 30

With this movement, our initial phase of character animation is complete. That last pose of the fingers will be important moving forward, and Rain will keep her fingers that way until it's time to release the ball.

Once Rain has a nice firm grip on the ball at frame 30, that's as far as we can get when it comes to animating for now. Before continuing the animation, we need to establish a relationship between the `Ball` object and Rain's armature.

Setting up an object-to-bone relationship

Visually speaking, you might say there's already a relationship between Rain's hand and the ball. I mean, at frame 30, it certainly looks like Rain is holding it (see *Figure 10.7*), but the ball doesn't know that, and if we continued to animate Rain picking up the ball, the ball would stubbornly remain where it is:

Figure 10.11: What does she think she's looking at?

Our goal in this section is to attach that ball to something in Rain's armature so that when Rain picks it up, it actually gets picked up.

"Easy," you might be thinking, "just parent the ball to a bone in Rain's hand." That's how a lot of rigging works, but parenting is a "forever" kind of relationship – one that extends infinitely forward and backward through time. Rain would always be holding the ball. She would never put it down and would have to wear it on her hand like the curl of hair she wears on her forehead. For some scenes, this might be acceptable, but not ours.

No, Rain cannot be this ball's parent - she's too young to be a mother anyway. If the ball is to be picked up and put down again, the ball-hand relationship needs to have a clear beginning and an end. For that, we need a few constraints and one special bone.

Dummy bones – a smarter way to rig

If you look at the **IK Secondary** layer in Rain's armature, you'll find some special bones, some of which are helpfully named "dummy:"

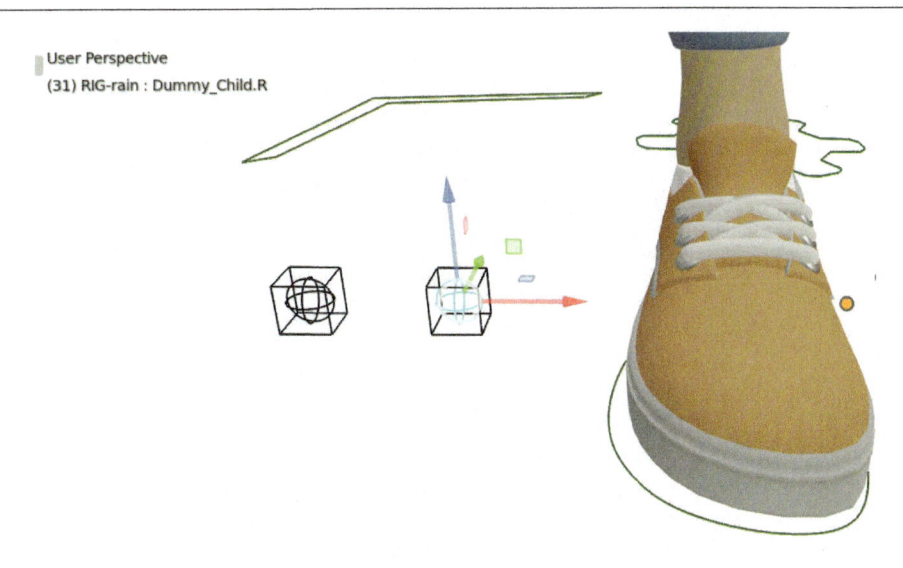

Figure 10.12: Dummy bones at the base of Rain's armature

Want to know what's special about these bones? Nothing! They don't do anything, and that's what makes them so special. **Dummy bones** have no dependents and can be used however the animator pleases. Typically, they are provided so that props may be attached to them and animated as part of the same rig.

> **Tip**
> "Dummy bone" is a practical designation, not a technical one. Any bone can be a dummy bone if, by default, it doesn't make anything happen when you move it. They're a lot like **Empty** objects. If you happen to be working with a rig that doesn't provide dummy bones, you can use an **Empty** object in the place of a dummy bone and it will do the same thing.

The dummy bone we're looking for is by Rain's hand and has "grab" in its name. Can you guess what it might be for?

Finding the grab bone

The bone we want is by Rain's right hand and is named `GRAB-Hand_Child.R`. For our purposes, we'll call this particular dummy bone the *grab bone*:

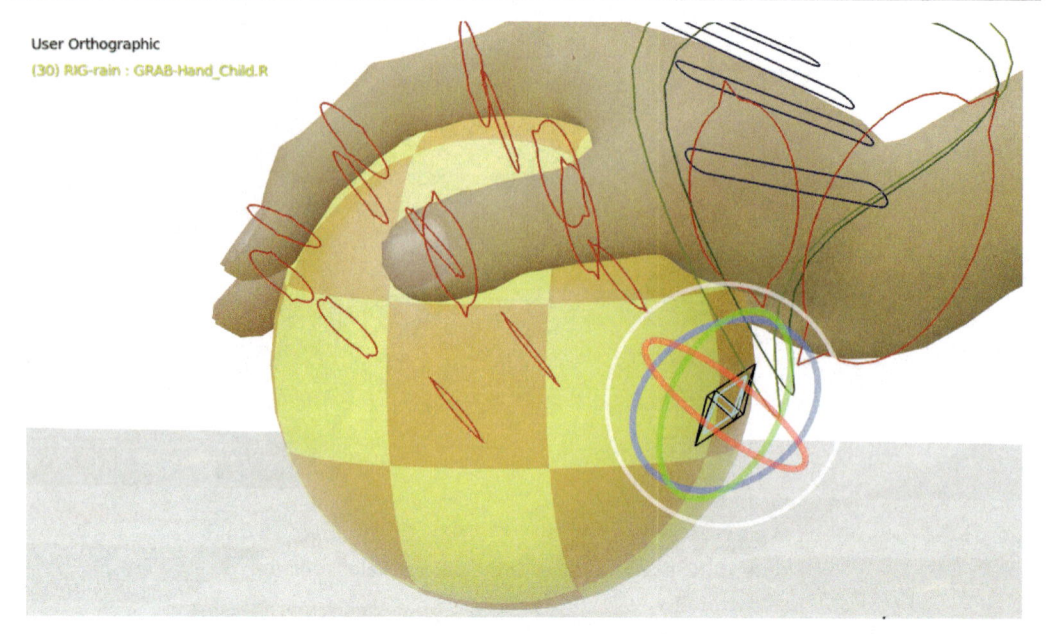

Figure 10.13: "Grab" bones for the right hand

This bone may be difficult to locate if/when it's inside the ball, so we should enable the **Show Bone X-Ray** feature so that we can see and select it more easily. This feature can be enabled by using **Toggle X-Ray** (*Alt + Z*). It can also be found among the viewport drawing options in the header of the 3D Viewport.

Let's select the bone:

1. Enable the **IK Secondary** layer.
2. Use **Toggle X-Ray** (*Alt + Z*) to view those bones that would otherwise be hard to see.
3. Select the bone GRAB-Hand_Child.R, which is just inside its parent, GRAB-Hand.R.
4. You can hide GRAB-Hand.R and all the other bones on the **IK Secondary** layer; we don't need them.

> **Important note**
>
> Make sure you select the child grab bone GRAB-Hand_Child.R, and not its parent, GRAB-Hand.R. The parent has a preexisting constraint on it which confounds our ability to add and apply additional constraints, so we'll just leave it alone and use its child instead. This is another example of why nested parent-child bone relationships can be helpful.

Note the name of this bone, how it floats right in front of the palm, and how it is effectively parented to Rain's hand. It's almost as if the rigger intended for us to use this bone to grab objects! Even though Rain's hand – her fingers, palm, and so on – is the thing that *appears* to pick up the ball, this dummy bone is the thing that will technically do the lifting.

Now that we've got our special bone, let's learn the new constraint we'll be using for it.

The Copy Transforms constraint

Although it calls itself a "grab" bone (and I admit I did call it special), `GRAB-Hand_Child.R` has no special grabbing feature of its own. We've got to add it ourselves using a new constraint.

Simply put, the **Copy Transforms** constraint makes one thing be exactly where another thing is. We want to use it on the the object `Ball`, using the `GRAB-Hand_Child.R` bone as the ball constraint's target:

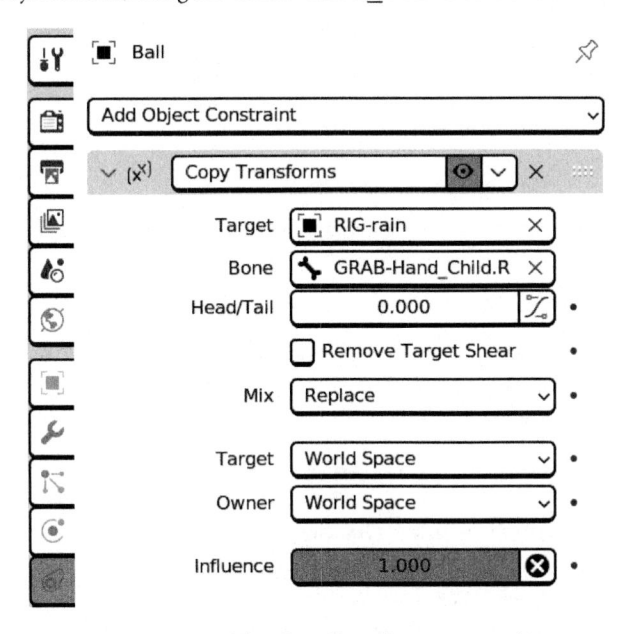

Figure 10.14: The Copy Transforms constraint

It's like **Copy Location**, **Copy Rotation**, and **Copy Scale** all wrapped up in one constraint!

There's just one problem – if we create that constraint right away, the ball will snap away from where it was in Rain's hand:

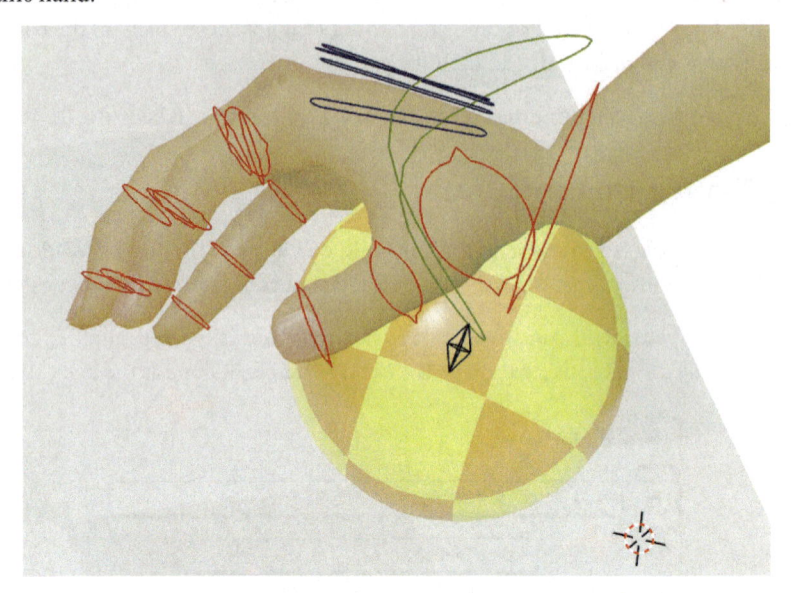

Figure 10.15: Incorrect bone position causes incorrect ball position

...So don't make that constraint just yet!

Our grab bone isn't in quite the right place; we never adjusted it. Before we add a **Copy Transforms** constraint to the ball, the grab bone needs to be in the right place beforehand – *exactly where the ball already is.*

How do we do that? With another **Copy Transforms** constraint, of course!

Snapping the grab bone to where the ball is

Like the other bones in Rain's hand, we must position `GRAB-Hand_Child.R` to account for what's being grabbed. Unlike the other bones, however, our posing of this bone needs to be perfect. Manually transforming it to what looks like the right place isn't good enough.

One effective method is to use a **Copy Transforms** constraint on the bone, and then apply it.

Setting up an object-to-bone relationship

Did you know bones can have **bone constraints**? Well, you do now!

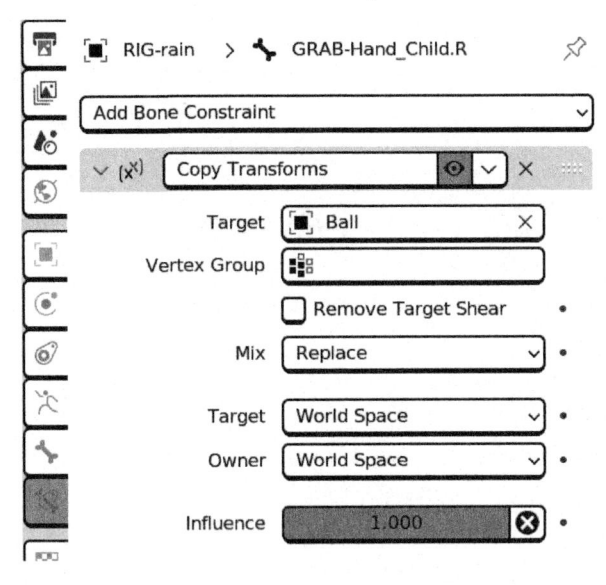

Figure 10.16: Bone constraint for GRAB-Hand_Child.R

Bone constraints work exactly like object constraints but for bones. An advanced armature like Rain's uses lots of bone constraints; they are an indispensable feature in rigging.

> **Important note**
> Make sure you click the **Bone Constraints** tab in the Properties editor (the one with the bone icon in it) and not the regular **Constraints** tab. You'll quickly realize your mistake if you add a constraint to Rain's whole armature object!

Let's add a **Copy Transforms** constraint to our grab bone:

1. Find the **Bone Constraint Properties** area for `GRAB-Hand_Child.R`.
2. Add a **Copy Transforms** constraint.
3. For the constraint **Target**, select the `Ball` object.

With this constraint active, the grab bone occupies the same point in space as the ball and has the same orientation:

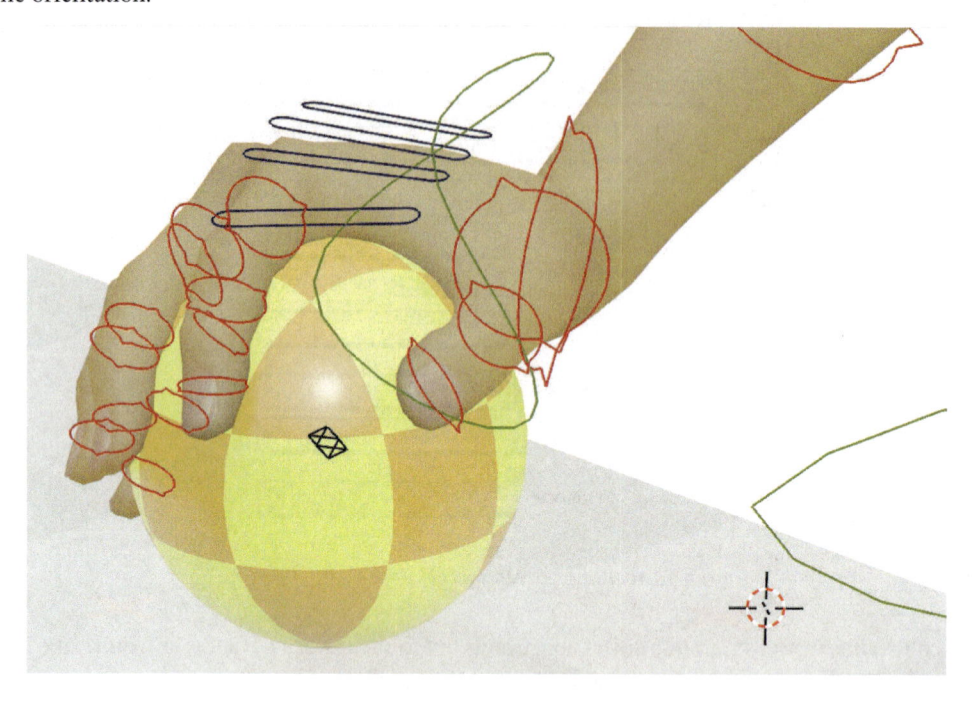

Figure 10.17: The bone is exactly where it should be

This relationship wasn't meant to last, though!

Applying the constraint

The whole purpose of doing all this is to constrain the ball to the grab bone, not the grab bone to the ball. So, before we make *that* constraint, we have to apply the one we have, like so:

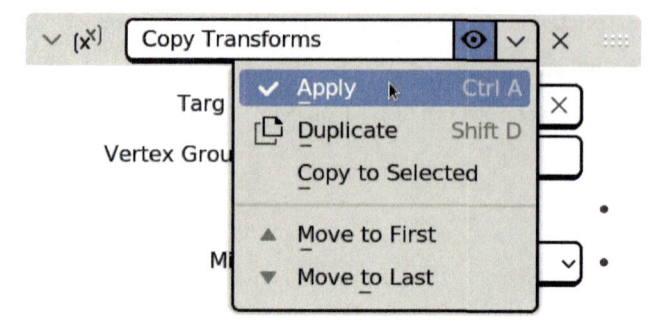

Figure 10.18: Using the Apply operator for a constraint

It doesn't matter what frame you're on when you create a constraint, but it does matter when you apply them, so make sure you're on the right frame when you do this:

1. Go to frame 30.

2. Apply (*Ctrl + A*) the **Copy Transforms** constraint you just made.

The constraint is gone now, but the bone is still in the same place – exactly where the ball is. It's as if we magically knew where to move and rotate the bone, and got it right on the very first try.

> **Important note**
> Two bones/objects cannot be each other's constraint target. If we were to create the next constraint without applying or removing the previous one, it would cause a *cyclic dependency* – an unacceptable error.

We've used a **Copy Transforms** constraint to put the grab bone in exactly the right place, using the ball as a target. For our next **Copy Transforms** constraint, we'll do it again but the other way around!

Adding a constraint to the ball

We just saw a preview of what the **Copy Transforms** constraint can do. Now, it's time for the main event. Let's add one to the ball and use the grab bone we just transformed as its target (see *Figure 10.14*).

> **Tip**
> Switching between selecting the ball and Rain's pose bones requires also switching between **Object Mode** and **Pose Mode**. If you get annoyed having to do this all the time, try disabling **Edit | Lock Object Modes**. You can also select these elements in the Outliner area.

To use a bone as a constraint target, we must first specify the armature object RIG-rain as a target. Doing so will reveal a secondary field where you can specify which bone to use instead of the armature object itself.

> **Important note**
> In the list of objects available as targets, you may see more than one version of RIG-rain. Choose the one that is a **Library Override** (it has an arrow running through the link icon next to it).

Let's go ahead and create our big important constraint:

1. Select the object Ball and go to its **Object Constraint Properties**.

2. Add a **Copy Transforms** constraint.

3. For the constraint's **Target**, select the object `RIG-rain`.
4. Specify the target **Bone** as `GRAB-Hand_Child.R`.

If you're still on frame `30` when you create this constraint, it will appear as if nothing has happened. That's a good thing – it means the target `GRAB-Hand_Child.R` is in the perfect place now. We're about to see the effect when Rain moves her hand.

Seeing the new constraint in action

Ready to continue with the character animation? Let's return to our rig and key the next pose to see what the new constraint does for us:

Figure 10.19: Rain, looking at the ball in her hand

We will also hold this pose for 20 frames, giving Rain a moment to think about it too:

1. Go to frame `40`.
2. Key a pose for Rain picking up the ball.
3. Duplicate all the keyframes for this pose to frame `60`.

Upon playing the animation after frame `30`, we can see the intended effect. Rain lifts her hand, and the ball goes up as well. For the moment, it looks like we parented the ball to Rain's hand.

Congratulations, you got Rain to pick up the ball! But now, it sticks to Rain's hand, and she can't put it down. The ball is too clingy! This relationship needs some work.

Constraints with animated influence

Making Rain grab the ball was our first goal, and we achieved it. You did well! In fact, you did *a little too well*. Our next goal, ironically, is to make Rain *not* grab the ball, and I don't just mean that for when she throws it.

Let's go back to the beginning of our animation. This isn't what we wanted:

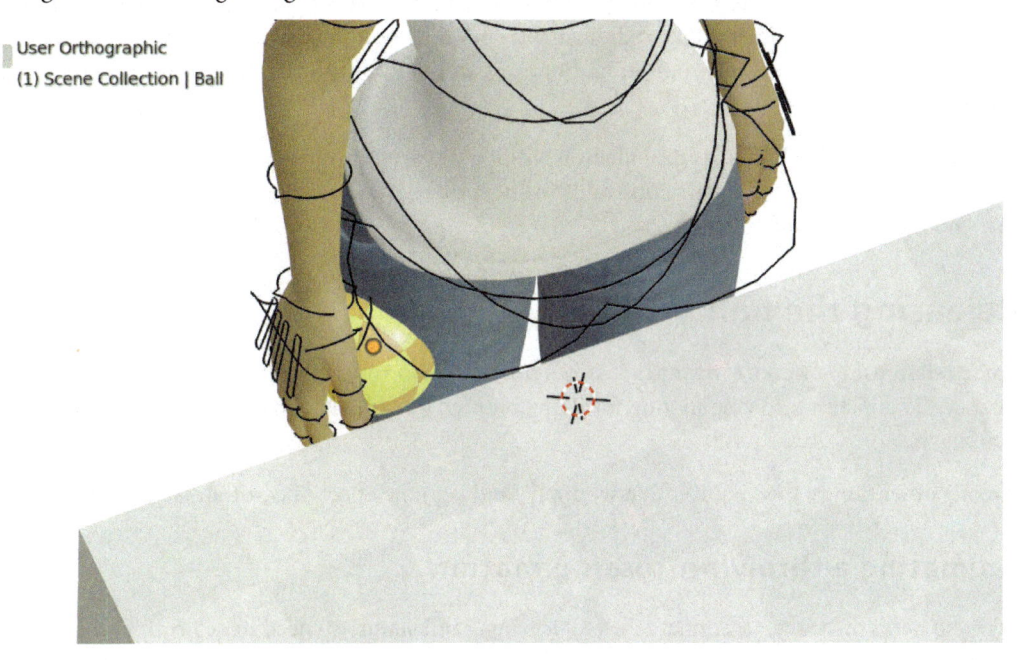

Figure 10.20: The ball stuck to Rain's hand at frame 1

Though the constraint works after Rain grabs the ball, it also works *before* she grabs it; the ball no longer rests on the table like it ought to. We need to be able to turn the constraint off somehow and wait until the right moment in time to turn it on.

It is for this reason that constraints have **Influence** properties, and they can be animated just like anything else.

Keying the influence of a constraint

The **Influence** property of a constraint is pretty self-explanatory. At a value of `1.0`, the constraint is at "full strength," and at `0.0`, it is as if there were no constraint at all.

Therefore, all we need to do to fix our first 30 frames is to key the **Influence** property of the ball's constraint, like so:

1. Find the **Influence** value of the **Copy Transforms** constraint belonging to `Ball`.
2. Key **Influence** to `0.0` on frame `30` and `1.0` on frame `31`.

We've now corrected the ball's behavior by keying one important property. Our animation on those first 30 frames is back to normal, and Rain's hand does not affect the ball until we want it to at frame `31`. Fantastic! When we watch our animation, we can finally see the complete act of Rain picking something up.

Next, we want to have Rain toss the ball away, ending the relationship. As you can guess, that means we will need to animate the ball's constraint **Influence** back down to `0.0` at the right moment, but that's not quite the whole story.

Releasing the ball

Some relationships weren't meant to last. It's time for Rain to let go, and for the ball to move on! First, we'll animate a throwing motion for Rain, followed by the ball leaving Rain's hand as she opens her fingers.

Among other things, this requires that we apply (and key) the effect of constraints on a few things.

Animating a throwing/tossing motion

Okay, so here's the thing: to animate the ball leaving Rain's hand, we need to determine where it will be in global space at the moment when she releases it:

- To do that, we need to animate Rain's arm throwing it.
- To do that, we need to transition from using *IK* instead of *FK* for the right arm by keying the **FK/IK Switch** property for the right arm.
- To do *that*, we have to key the visual rotation of the *FK* bones so that when we switch to them, the arm doesn't go like this:

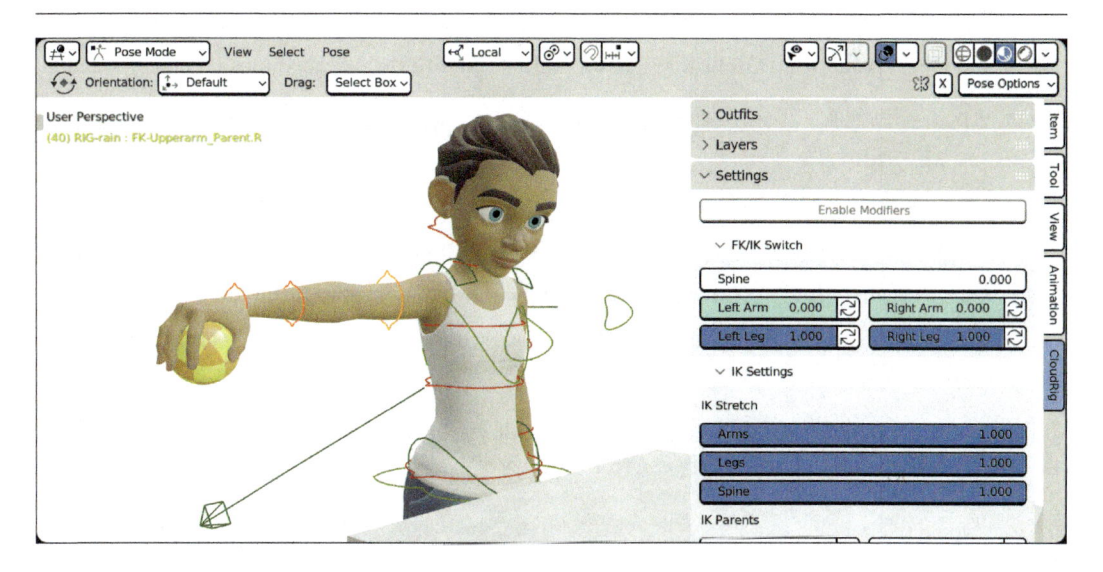

Figure 10.21: FK bones for the right arm, still in their original pose

Phew! Let's start with those *FK* bones.

Introduction to keying visual transforms

Conveniently, we had Rain hold her pose from frame 40 to 60 after she picked up the ball. This gives us a perfect opportunity to key the **FK/IK Switch** property without anybody noticing.

You may recall what happens when we change this value this carelessly, though. Rain's *FK* bones come with constraints of their own, and because we never posed them, the *FK* bones in the right arm want to go back to their original T-pose. To transition seamlessly, we need to key them where they *appear to be from our perspective*, and not where they *want to be*, so to speak.

That's where **visual keying** comes in. The options for visual keying are located near the bottom of the **Insert Keyframe** menu (*I*):

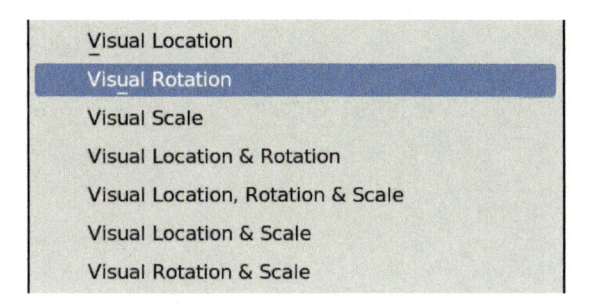

Figure 10.22: Visual keying options in the Insert Keyframe menu

Let's try keying **Visual Rotation** now. Once we do that, the **FK/IK Switch** value can be animated:

1. Select the *FK* bones in Rain's right arm. These are `FK-Upperarm_Parent.R`, `FK-Forearm.R`, and `FK-Hand.R`.
2. Go to frame `40`.
3. Use **Animation | Insert Keyframe** (*I*) **| Visual Rotation**.
4. Do this again at frame `60` (or just duplicate the new keyframes to frame `60`).
5. Between frames `40` and `60`, animate the **FK/IK Switch | Right Arm** value so that it goes from `1.0` to `0.0`.

If you correctly keyed the visual rotation of the *FK* bones, Rain's arm will not appear to move while the **FK/IK Switch** value changes between frames `40` and `60`.

> **Tip**
> Visual keying on an armature works just as if we used **Pose | Apply** (*Ctrl + A*) **| Apply Visual Transform to Pose** before keying the bones like we usually do. The important part is not the keying, but applying the constraint to the keyed properties.

If you're still unsure what's going on here, we'll get another chance to use this feature when we animate the ball.

Keying a throw with two poses

After frame `60`, we can now use the *FK* bones in Rain's right arm to make a throwing/tossing motion.

Here's the trick to animating a convincing throw: start with the "wind up" pose…

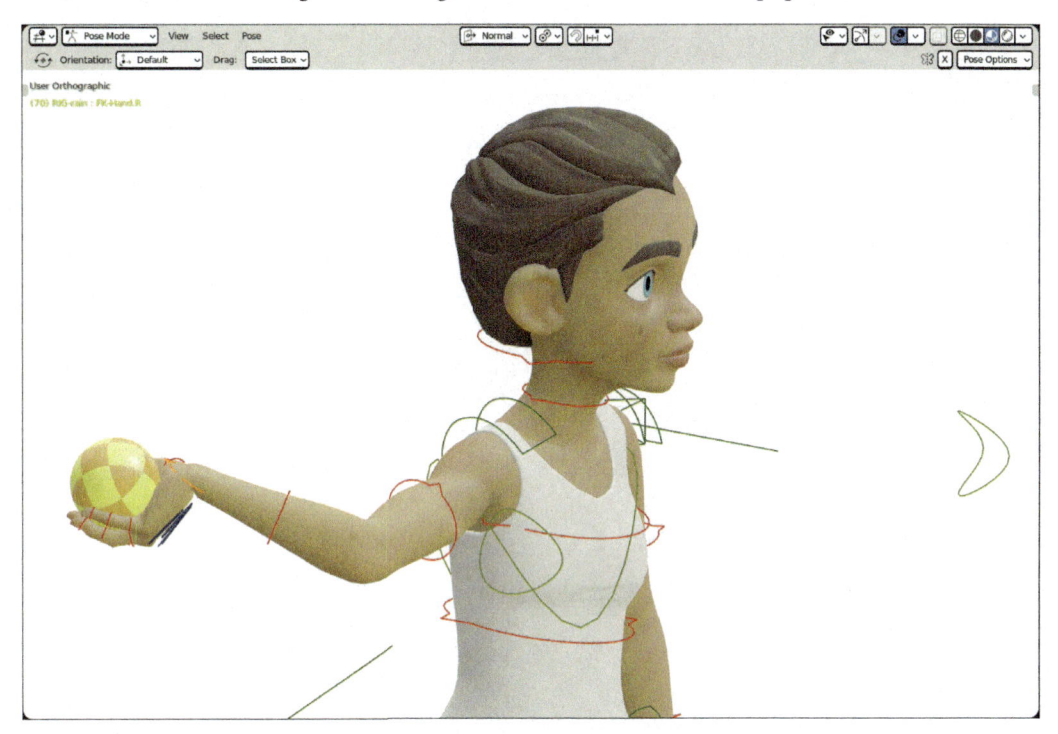

Figure 10.23: Rain winding back to toss the ball at frame 70

...But then, *don't* pose the moment when Rain releases the ball:

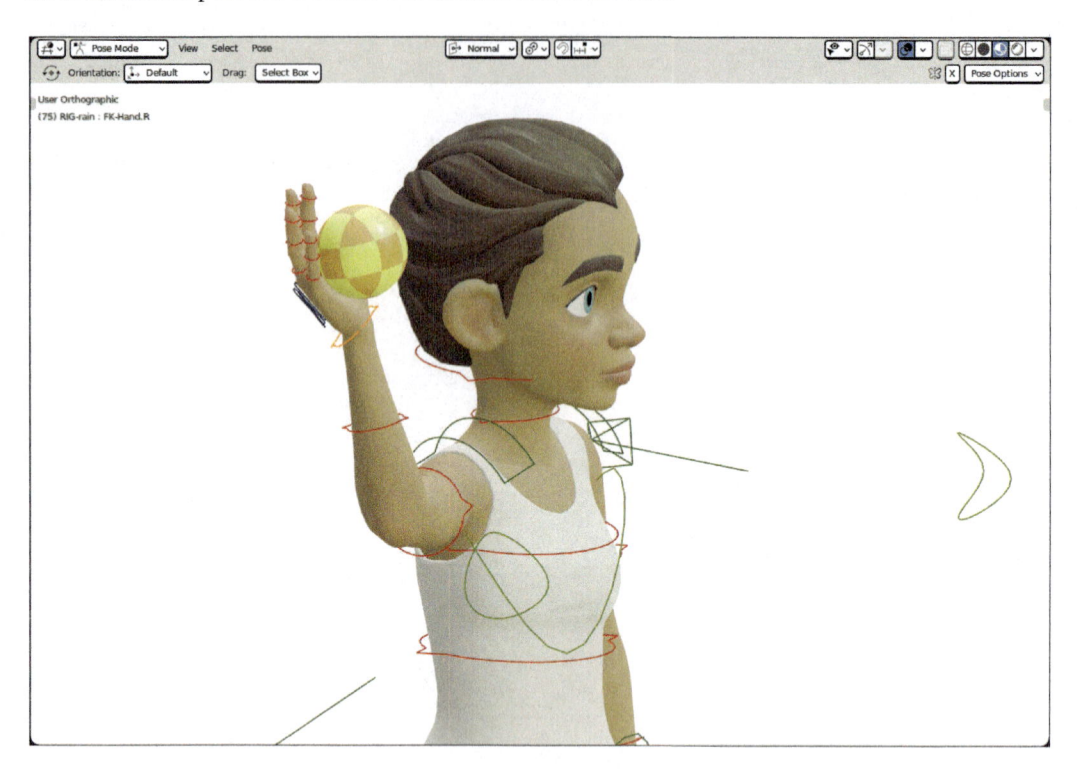

Figure 10.24: Rain releasing the ball at frame 75

This is when the object relationship will end, but it's not when Rain's movement ends. Skip this part and key the "follow through:"

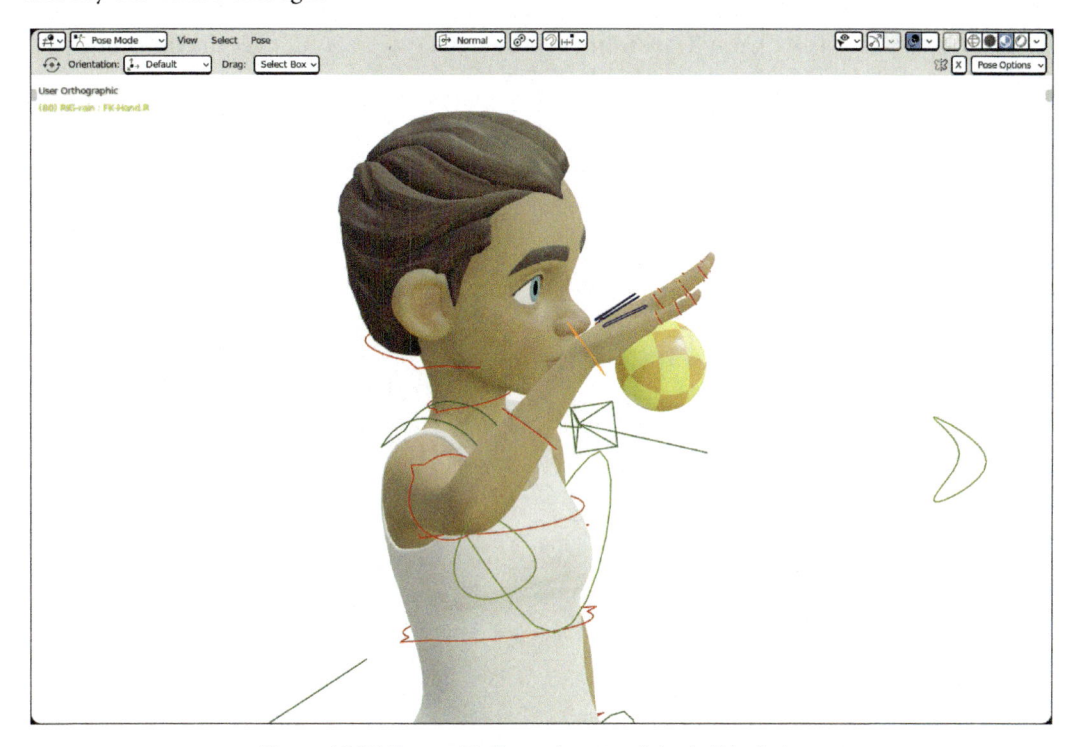

Figure 10.25: Frame 80. Try and pretend the ball isn't there

After keying the "follow through" pose, we can go back to our "release" frame and tweak the hand and fingers as needed:

1. At frame 70, key a "wind up" pose for Rain.
2. At frame 80, key a "follow through" pose for Rain.
3. Key any necessary adjustments to the fingers and other areas to ensure that the ball can leave Rain's hand smoothly after frame 75.

When we're finished with the motion of Rain's arm, we can move on to animating the ball. We're nearly done!

Animating the ball being thrown

We're going to animate the ball leaving Rain's hand around frame 75, and that thing isn't going anywhere by itself until we disable the **Copy Transforms** constraint we gave it. So, just key the **Influence** value from 1.0 back down to 0.0 and we're finished, right?

Almost, but not quite:

Figure 10.26: The ball, at frame 75, is back to where it was at frame 1

Perhaps you expected the constraint to confer its "history" onto the ball's transform properties after we disable its influence – as if the ball will automatically end up in a different place, depending on whether we end the relationship at frame 75, 72, or 80. Not so. If you believe this, then you probably did such a good job at frame 30 that you fell for your own trick!

By setting **Influence** to 0.0, we free the ball as if it never had any constraint to begin with... but where is it supposed to go? Back to where we left it, with its original object transform values that never changed. The ball may have been moving, but those numbers weren't. They didn't feel a thing. With visual keying, we can let the numbers know what happened while they were asleep.

Keying an object's visual transforms

Let's dive a little further into visual keying. We tried some visual keying already with Rain's *FK* arm, but armature bones are rather complicated and we didn't rig Rain ourselves. The ball will serve as a better example.

The ball's location and rotation need to be keyed at two very important frames:

- Frame 30, to determine where it is before it gets picked up.
- Frame 75, to determine where it will be after it is released.

Using the conventional methods of inserting keyframes, keying the transform properties of a bone or object will key only the nominal numeric values we see in that bone/object's **Location**, **Rotation**, or **Scale** properties – that is, whatever numbers happen to appear in the **Transform** panel. Usually, this is fine – we can key the ball at frame 30 as we usually do.

However, when a bone or object is constrained (like the ball currently is at frame 75), those seemingly important numbers are more like polite *suggestions*, which are then rudely ignored:

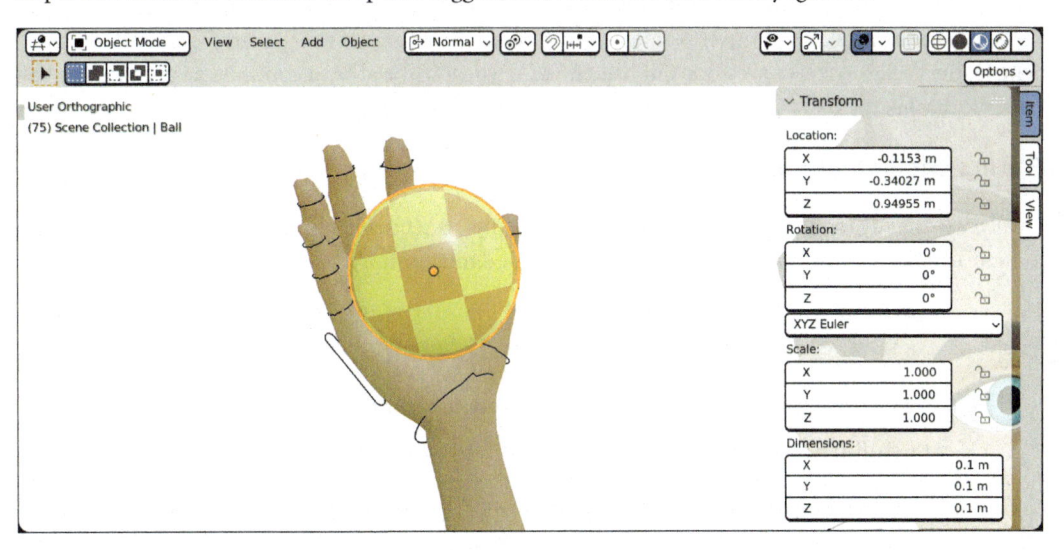

Figure 10.27: These numbers have nothing to do with where the ball is

After frame 30, the constrained ball's nominal **Transform** values here have no effect, nor are they affected by any constraints. They haven't changed at all, so keying them like normal won't do much. What we need to do here instead is key the *visual transforms* – the values for the object's location, rotation, and scale after accounting for the effect of constraints.

> **Important note**
> "Visual" here does not denote a distinct property – for example, objects and bones do not have a **Visual Location** property in addition to a **Location** property. It just means applying the effect of an object's constraints to the transform properties' values before keying them. This is exactly like if we used **Object | Apply** (*Ctrl + A*) **| Visual Transform**, then keyed the location and rotation as usual. Using visual keying conveniently performs these two operations at once.

This time, we'll key **Visual Location & Rotation**:

1. Select the ball.
2. Go to frame 30.
3. Key the ball's **Location & Rotation** (visual or not - it doesn't matter for this frame).
4. Go to frame 75.
5. Key the ball's **Visual Location & Rotation**.

After keying the visual transform properties, nothing about our animation will appear to have changed yet. Nevertheless, we did just insert some very important keyframes – check your f-curves if you don't believe me. Still, those f-curves don't do much yet – we won't be able to continue animating the ball until we disable the ball's **Copy Transforms** constraint. That brings us to our next step…

Ending the object relationship

Finally, we're ready to disable the ball's constraint at frame 75. This will effectively bring the relationship to a close and henceforth allow the ball to be animated like normal.

This part is perfectly straightforward. We'll "disable" the constraint at frame 75 in the same way we "enabled" it at frame 31:

1. One more time, find the **Copy Transforms** constraint for the Ball object.
2. Key the **Influence** to 1.0 at frame 74, and 0.0 at frame 75.

Notice how the ball didn't go anywhere when you turned down the **Influence** value of its constraint. Thanks to visual keying, it remains exactly where it was.

"It was then that I carried you…"

Take a look at the f-curves of the ball, including the f-curve of its **Copy Transforms** constraint's **Influence**:

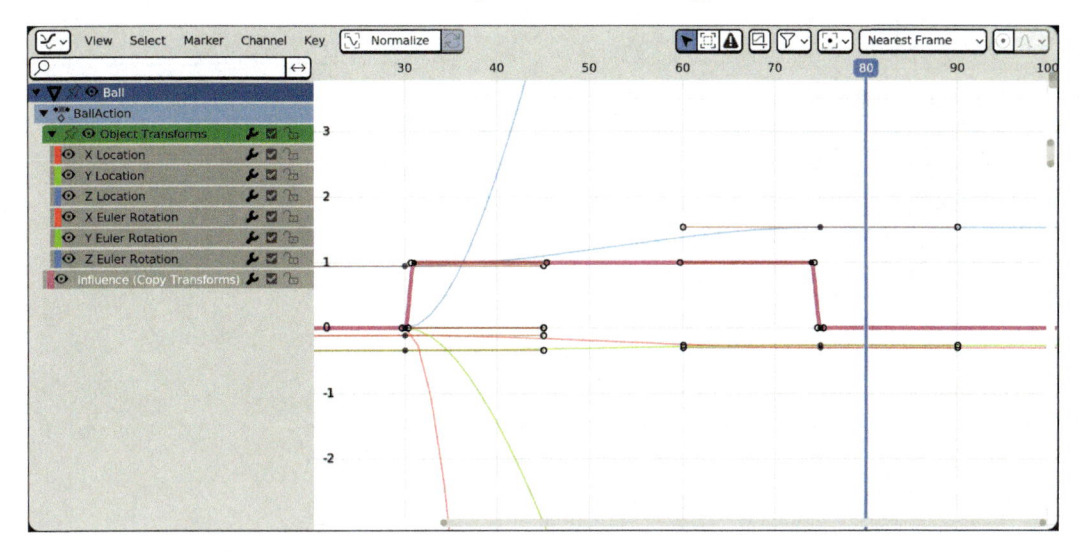

Figure 10.28: F-curves of the ball

As you might have guessed, those f-curves don't tell the whole story of the ball's movement. For all the frames at which the **Influence** value is 1.0, the ball's **Copy Transforms** constraint (and therefore the GRAB-Hand_Child.R bone) was the one in control. Whatever interpolation we use between frames 30 and 75 doesn't matter. But the ball doesn't know that. It's as if it thinks it got up there all by itself. How cute!

After frame 75, the ball is free, but it remains still. Taking the ball the rest of the way is up to us.

Animating a thrown ball

This next part isn't so hard. You've known how to animate a ball since *Chapter 2*! This time, however, we have to consider the hand that threw the ball. How fast was it going right before the ball was released, and in what direction? We want the moment of the ball's release to look as smooth as possible. Any significant visual change in direction or speed will fail to convey the effect of being thrown.

Let me show you a neat technique for capturing this information at the moment of release. We'll key the ball's visual transform one more time – not at frame 75 again, but at frame 74, then key it. This will reveal some valuable insights in the **Graph Editor**:

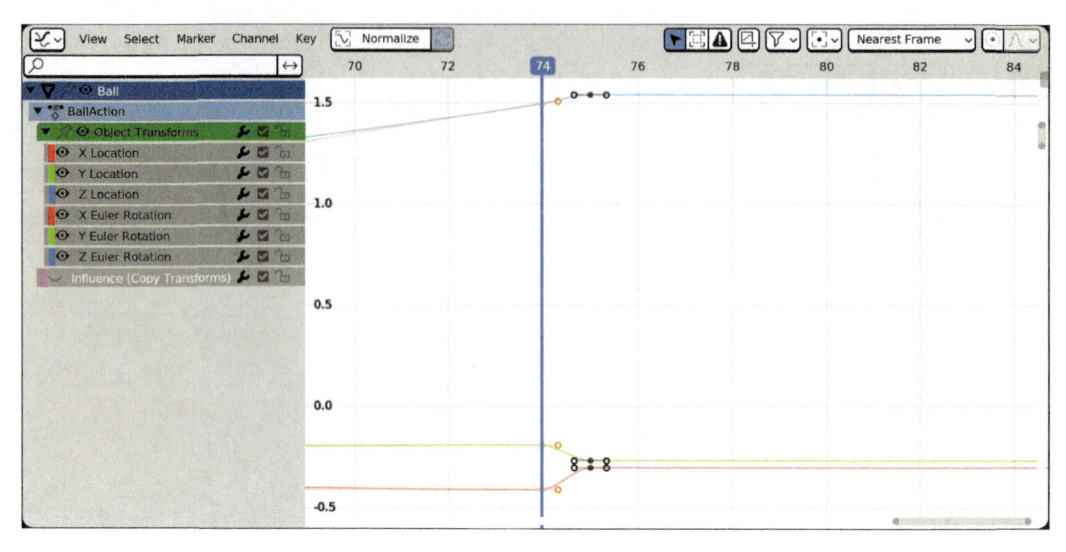

Figure 10.29: F-curves of the ball between frames 74 and 75

That extra "bump" we just created occurs while our ball is still constrained, so it does not affect the ball directly. Instead, we can use it as a reference to determine how to shape the segments of the f-curve that come after.

By keeping the subsequent portion of each f-curve smooth with these segments, we can preserve the speed and heading of the ball and its motion will look nice:

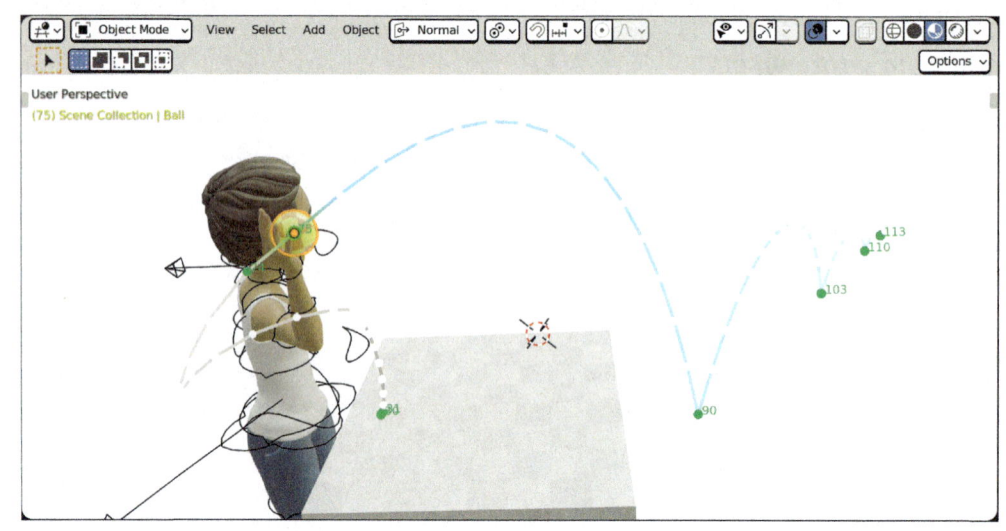

Figure 10.30: F-curves continued after frame 75

Why don't you give it a try?

1. Apply the visual transform of the ball on frame 74 and insert keyframes.
2. With the resulting f-curve segments as your guide, use the **Graph Editor** to continue the motion of the ball after it leaves Rain's hand.
3. Finally, we can inspect our work using a motion path if we like:

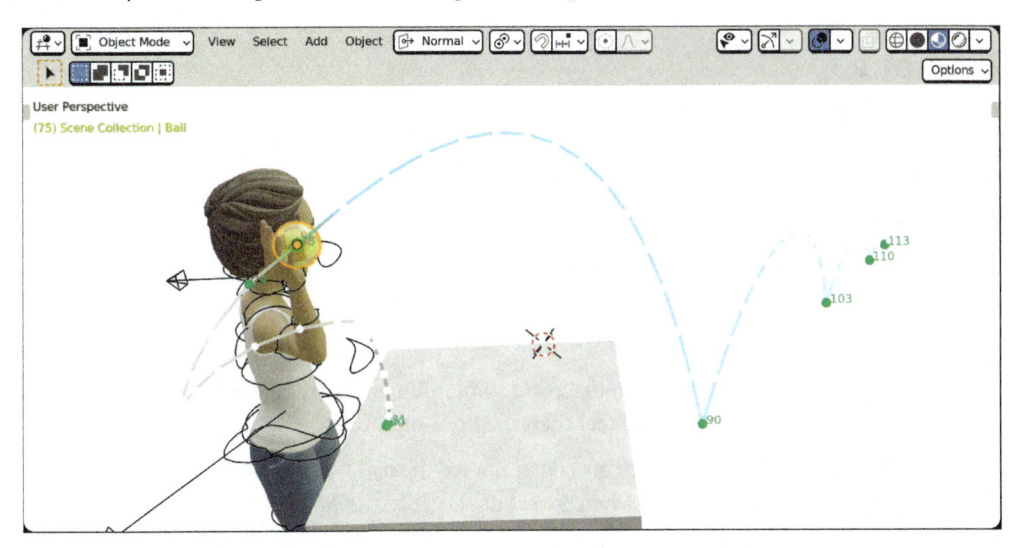

Figure 10.31: The motion path of the ball

It looks good! Just for fun, I've chosen to have my ball bounce away, but you may have another idea. What's most important is not the ball leaving the scene, but those crucial frames at which it leaves the hand from which it was constrained. Once the ball convincingly does this, we can claim victory – our three-part epic battle with constraints is finished!

Summary

It's challenging when we need an object to have different relationships at different frames, but nothing is impossible. We just need to do some careful planning to determine what affects what, and when. Our transitions between these relationships are a bit like stage magic; things change in the blink of an eye, and the audience can't see all the careful planning that went into setting up the shot.

Don't think that the technique we just learned is the only way to do this! For instance, we could do exactly the opposite – that is, parent the ball to the grab bone, then use some **Copy Transforms** constraints targeted to other dummy bones for the frames during which the ball *isn't* in Rain's hand.

In other cases, we might just use two identical balls – only one of them parented to the hand. Then, we could make them appear or disappear at the appropriate times. It all depends on the specific shot and the preferences of the animator.

This chapter concludes the character animation part of our animation journey. If you've made it this far, I'm impressed and truly grateful. You are more than ready to learn some advanced techniques and features in the next few chapters!

Questions

1. Why would it be better to use *IK* instead of *FK* when placing Rain's hand on the ball?
2. Why might *FK* look better than *IK* for throwing the ball?
3. Why is a dummy bone like an empty object?
4. What are visual transforms? In what cases do they differ from nominal transforms?
5. At frame 30, we can key the ball's **Rotation & Location** or its **Visual Location & Rotation** – it doesn't matter which. Why is this?
6. "Visual" denotes perception or simulacrum; something less than reality. So why are they called visual transforms if they're more real than the nominal transforms?
7. When creating the **Copy Transforms** constraint for the ball, how do we make sure that nothing appears to happen at frame 30 when we set its target to the bone `GRAB-Hand_Child.R`
8. After keying the visual location and rotation of the *FK* bones, why does nothing appear to happen when we switch to using them with **FK/IK Switch**?
9. Why do the transform properties of the ball do nothing between frames 31 and 75? Why are they animated during these frames if they do nothing?
10. Why do we keep wanting *nothing* to happen so often? Why is the *happening* of this *nothing* so important to our work?

Part 3: Advanced Tools and Techniques

If you've been reading these chapters in order, congratulations on making it this far! You're already "advanced" as far as I'm concerned.

This final part covers some miscellaneous topics in animation that we weren't able to cover earlier, along with extra features that couldn't quite fit in elsewhere. *Chapter 11*, *12*, and *13* are not as challenging as you might think; feel free to skip ahead and try them out regardless of your current progress. The only chapter that has prerequisites is *Chapter 14*. To follow that last chapter, you'll need to have created two other specific character animations from the exercises in *Part Two*.

This part contains the following chapters:

- *Chapter 11, F-Curve Modifiers*
- *Chapter 12, Rigid Body Physics*
- *Chapter 13, Animating with Multiple Cameras*
- *Chapter 14, Non-Linear Animation*

11
F-Curve Modifiers

With our journey into character animation at an end (mostly), let's get back to the basics – but not too basic! These last few chapters are the *advanced* basics. This time, we're going to visit the **Graph Editor** to learn one more feature: **F-curve modifiers**.

Modifier is a term that appears more than once in Blender. You may be familiar with the more prominent modifiers in the **Properties Editor**, which modify the geometry of a mesh object in your 3D scene. F-curve modifiers are based on a similar idea; they modify an F-curve, conveniently reducing the number of keyframes we need to insert to achieve certain results. In our case, they will even replace the F-curve completely!

In this chapter, you'll learn about the following topics:

- Where F-curve modifiers live
- Periodic movement with F-curve modifiers
- My favorite modifier – **Noise**
- Restricting the frame range of an F-curve modifier

Technical requirements

To begin this exercise, download the following file and open it in Blender:

`https://github.com/PacktPublishing/Realizing-3D-Animation-in-Blender`

It's a grandfather clock!

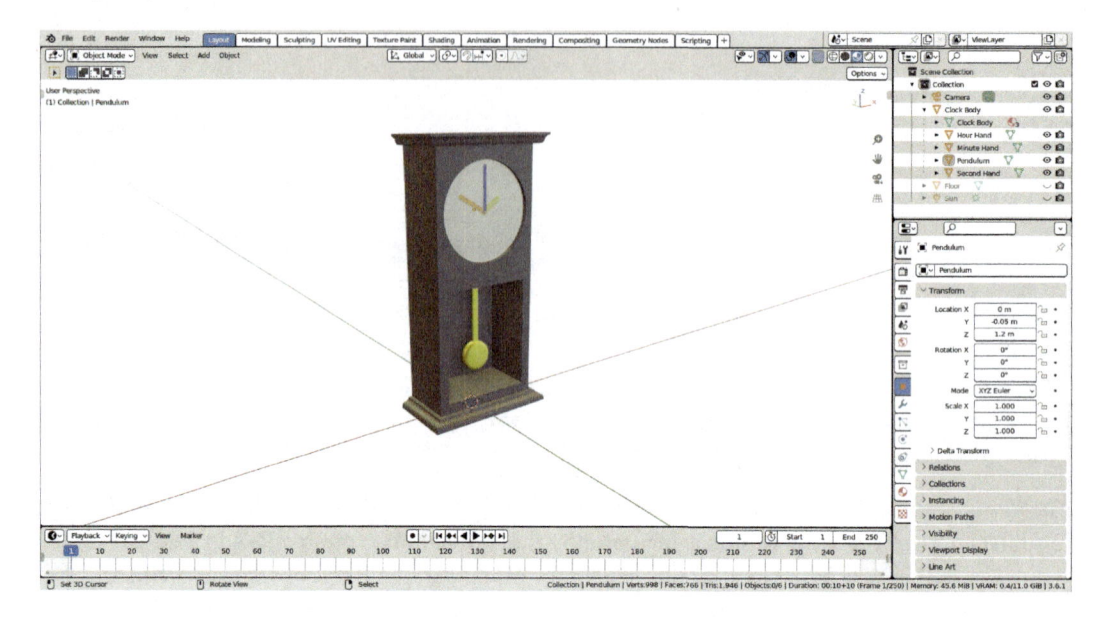

Figure 11.1: Grandfather clock scene

Along with the Camera object, this scene has several things in it that we can animate purely with F-curve modifiers.

Where to find F-curve modifiers

For this exercise, we'll animate everything in this scene using only F-curve modifiers. I wish I could say we didn't need any keyframes at all, but we need some F-curves to work with if we are to modify them, and to create those F-curves, we need to insert at least one keyframe for each of them. On which frame? It doesn't really matter! Once we create F-curves, the modifiers can take over and do the rest of the work.

Our first task is to animate the second hand of the clock, followed by its pendulum. When animated, these two objects will both rotate on the Y axis.

Let's begin by creating the F-curves for that and accessing them:

1. Insert rotation keyframes for the objects Second Hand and Pendulum.
2. Bring up the F-curves for these objects in the Graph Editor.
3. Hide or delete all but the **Y Euler Rotation** F-curves.

Tip

You can insert keyframes for just one transform axis at a time by right-clicking on the property and selecting **Insert Single Keyframe**.

After isolating the **Y Euler Rotation** channels, what we have left are two of the most boring F-curves imaginable:

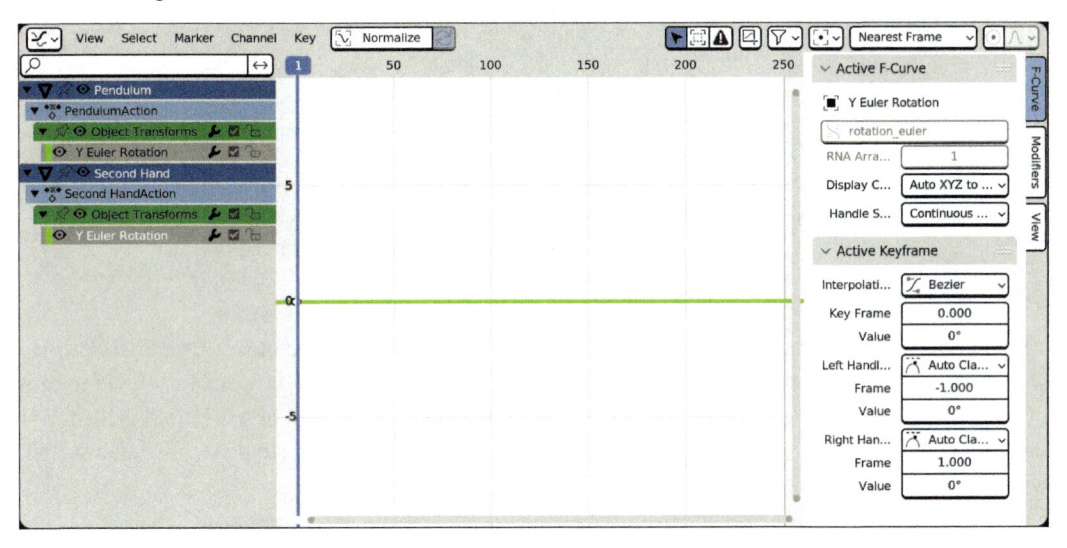

Figure 11.2: Two animation channels; not even worth screen-shotting

If we wanted anything to happen here, we'd normally have to insert at least one more keyframe. That's not the case this time!

Adding our first F-curve modifier

The parts of a clock have simple, precise, predictable motion. This makes their animation perfect for using F-curve modifiers. Modifiers for the selected F-curve can be found in the **Modifiers** tab in the right-hand sidebar:

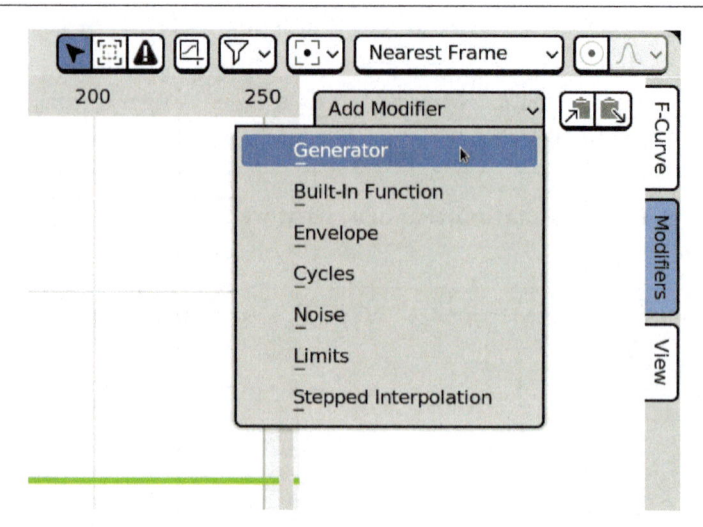

Figure 11.3: Adding a modifier in the sidebar of the Graph Editor

Our first modifier will be added to the **Y Euler Rotation** F-curve of the object `Second Hand`. This part needs to rotate indefinitely according to an exact formula. For that, we can use a **Generator** modifier. This modifier "generates" an F-curve based on a polynomial function, where **X** is the frame number and the editable values are the coefficients. In our case, we want the simplest function available, giving us a rising straight line that never ends.

When we initially add the modifier, it gives us just that, but with one small issue:

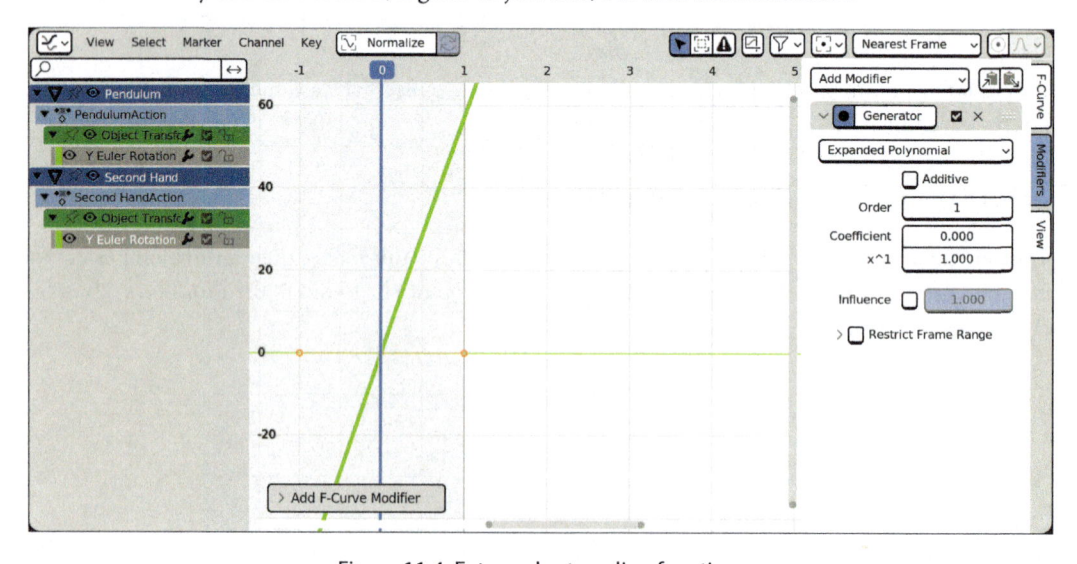

Figure 11.4: Extremely steep line function

As you can see, the default formula of *y = 1x + 0* creates a line that is absurdly steep for most purposes. It's more like the rotation speed of a circular saw! That default value of `1.0` in the formula is the slope of the line, and if it's going to produce the rotation of a second hand, it needs to be a couple orders of magnitude smaller.

Try it out for yourself:

1. Select the **Y Euler Rotation** F-curve for the object `Second Hand`.
2. Find the **Modifiers** tab in the right-hand sidebar of the Graph Editor.
3. Click **Add Modifier | Generator**.
4. For the **x^1** coefficient, enter a value that makes the second hand rotate much slower.

Whatever value you entered for *step 4* may not be exactly correct. That's fine for now. Getting the second hand to make one full rotation exactly once per minute requires a little bit of arithmetic, which I'll explain shortly. Until then, let's continue adding modifiers!

Getting fancy with F-curve modifiers

In this section, we'll take a look at a couple other F-curve modifiers, along with a handy explanation on how to get the parameters exactly right for clock-like periodicity.

The Stepped Interpolation modifier

Our second-hand animation is missing a couple of key features. For one thing, it doesn't "tick" like it ought to. The **Stepped Interpolation** modifier can take care of that:

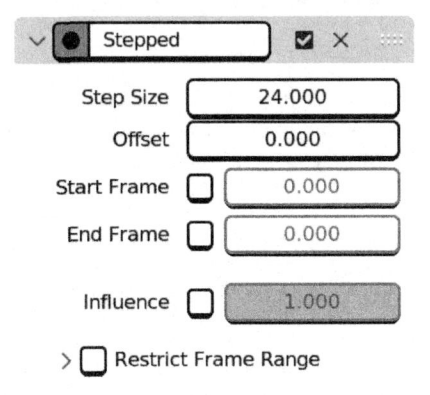

Figure 11.5: Stepped Interpolation modifier

This modifier "steps" the F-curve so that it only produces movement every certain number of frames. If we edit that number of frames to be the same as our frame rate per second (`24`), the second hand of the clock will advance clockwise exactly once every second.

The effect of modifiers "stacks," so we can add the **Stepped Interpolation** modifier to the same F-curve, after the existing **Generator** modifier:

1. For the **Y Euler Rotation** F-curve of `Second Hand`, add a **Stepped Interpolation** modifier.
2. Set the **Step Size** value to `24`.

Easy! The degree of rotation per tick may not work like a real clock just yet, but at least it's ticking like a real clock hand should. Before we tweak the settings to make it perfect, let's show some love to the other F-curve in our editor.

The Built-In Function modifier

The **Built-In Function** modifier modifies or replaces the F-curve with a short selection of mathematical functions. Take a look at the various functions available and guess which two would be useful to animate a swinging pendulum (hint: it's not **Tangent**):

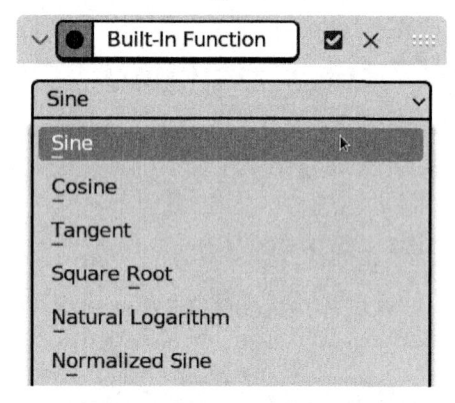

Figure 11.6: Some built-in functions

Initially, we are presented with a sine-wave function by default, which is perfect for pendular movement (technically, you can also use **Cosine** if you want to be cheeky):

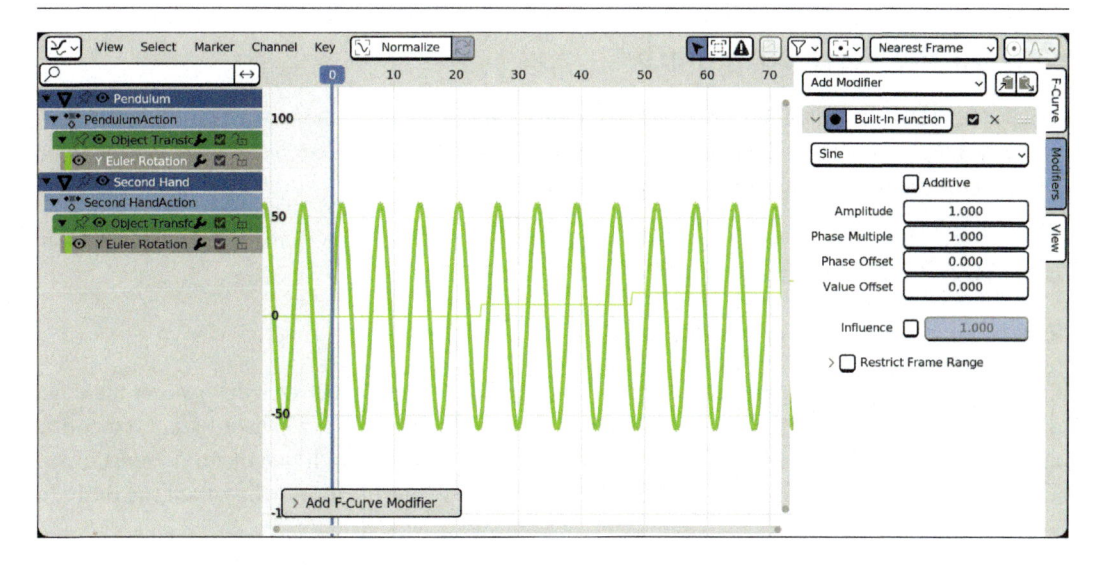

Figure 11.7: Default sine wave created by the modifier

As before, we still need to make some adjustments to the modifier so that the pendulum of the clock swings sensibly inside its box instead of vibrating uncontrollably.

Let's use this modifier to animate the pendulum now:

1. Select the **Y Euler Rotation** F-curve of `Pendulum`.
2. Add a **Built-In Function** modifier.
3. Adjust the **Amplitude** of the modifier's sine function so that the pendulum swings inside the clock.
4. Slow down the wave function by reducing the **Phase Multiple** value.

If you think about it, these modifiers are not very aptly named. After all, the **Generator** modifier itself uses a built-in function, and the **Built-In Function** modifier also "generates" an F-curve. Try not to let it bother you.

> **Tip**
>
> F-curve modifiers can also be used in drivers. This is where those weirder built-in functions (such as **Tangent**) come in handy. When used this way, you can use a mathematical formula to drive a value without needing to use any Python expressions.

After creating and adjusting all the modifiers we've covered so far, you should have a clock that appears to work normally at first glance. Still, there is the matter of making it work like a real clock.

Setting the clock with math

Maybe the second hand of your clock moves a little too fast, or not quite fast enough. Likewise for your pendulum. This may be fine for some shots, but I'm a bit of a perfectionist, so we're going to do a tiny bit of trigonometry to make this clock accurate.

This is much easier than it sounds, as any numeric field in Blender can have a mathematical expression entered into it. We don't even need a calculator!

The periodicity of a pendulum

One neat thing about pendulum clocks is that the swing of the pendulum often determines the exact duration of 1 second. Such is the case with our current pendulum, which will take 1 second to swing to the left, and another second to swing to the right. This leaves us with one burning question: to achieve this, what exact number should be entered into the **Phase Multiple** property of the **Built-In Function** for our pendulum?

For the **Built-In Function** modifier's **Sine**, **Cosine**, and **Tangent** functions, the current frame number is multiplied with the **Phase Multiple** property and then parsed as *radians* by the **Sine/Cosine/Tangent** function. Practically speaking, this means **Phase Multiple** values should be thought of as fractions of *pi* (3.14159). Decide how many frames long a half-cycle of the wave should be (24 in our case). Divide *pi* by that, and we have our answer:

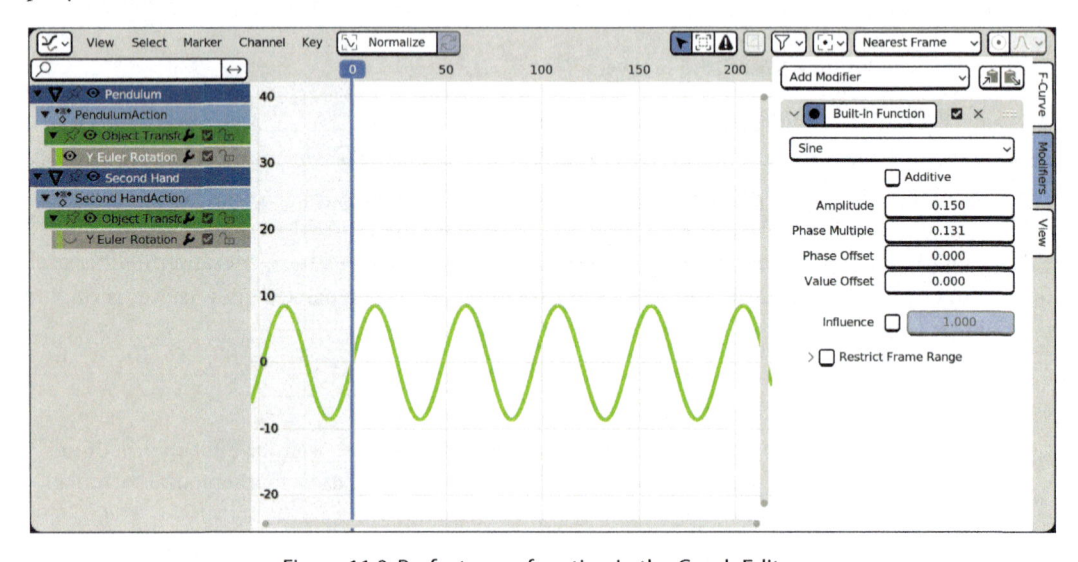

Figure 11.8: Perfect wave function in the Graph Editor

The preceding figure shows the perfect wave function in Graph Editor.

Setting time on the second hand

As with the pendulum, the second hand also has an F-curve modifier for which we require an exact value for one property. The **Generator** modifier's **x^1** coefficient determines the linear slope of the F-curve. If we get that value just right, the clock's second hand will make a full rotation once per minute – a half-rotation every 30 seconds – keeping perfect time.

Also like the pendulum, this requires that we think in terms of radians, even though the **Generator** modifier doesn't use a trigonometric function. This is because **Euler Rotation** values are themselves evaluated as radians, even though they appear to us as degrees in the Graph Editor!

Therefore, we need to calculate the number of frames a half-rotation of the second hand should take. For us, that's 30 seconds times 24 frames per second. Then, divide *pi* by that number:

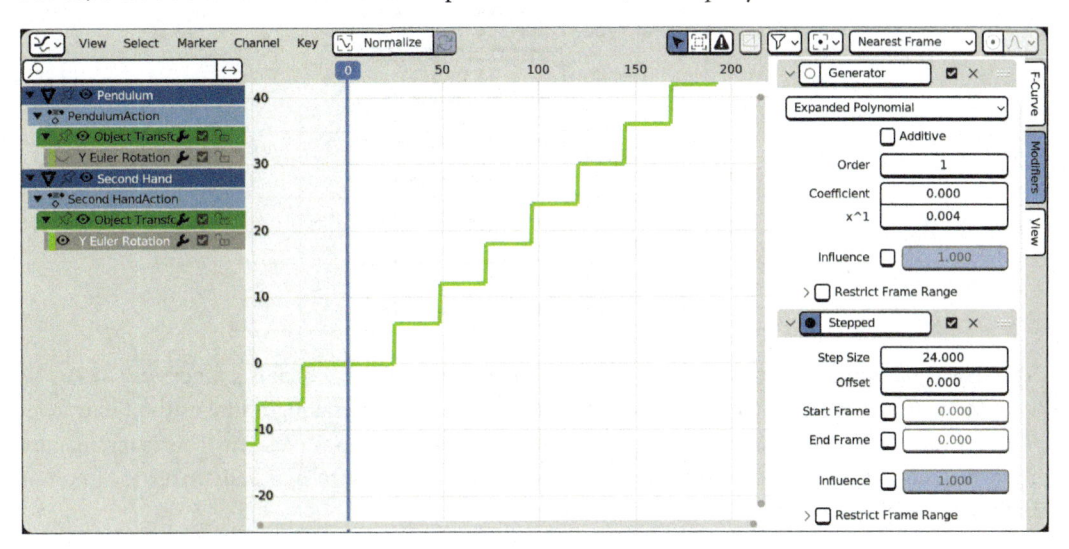

Figure 11.9: Ideal Generator modifier for the rotation of the second hand

The resulting preceding figure shows the Ideal Generator modifier for the rotation of the second hand.

Entering expressions directly into numeric fields

To recap, here are the steps to perfecting our F-curve modifier settings. Note that no calculation is required on our part, as we can simply enter any mathematical expression we like into a number field, and Blender will take care of the rest.

You can even enter *pi* literally as `pi`:

1. Find the **Built-In Function** modifier we created for the **Y Euler Rotation** F-curve of `Pendulum`.
2. Enter `pi/24` into the **Phase Multiple** property field.
3. Find the **Generator** modifier we made for the **Y Euler Rotation** F-curve of `Second Hand`.
4. Enter `pi/(30*24)` into the **x^1** coefficient field.

There you have it: a perfectly accurate grandfather clock. Probably more accurate than the real thing… at least, it would be if we animated the minute and hour hands too…

Don't worry – that'd be way too boring. Who wants to watch a clock for a whole hour? Instead, for the next half of this chapter, I'm going to show you my favorite F-curve modifier and my favorite thing to do with it.

Using the Noise modifier

Here is by far the most useful F-curve modifier in Blender's offering:

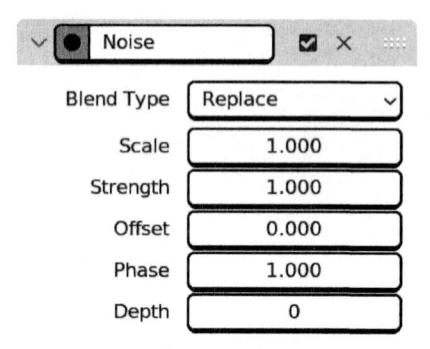

Figure 11.10: The Noise modifier

The **Noise** modifier generates *pseudorandom noise* along an F-curve, which is a fancy way of saying it *deterministically randomizes* the F-curve, which is a fancy way of saying it makes the F-curve *go all wiggly*. It's not all that different from the shape of a "noisy" audio waveform. This is terrific any time we want to create shaky, random movement without needing to manually insert a bunch of random keyframes.

For this exercise, we'll use the **Noise** modifier for its most popular use case: simulating camera shake.

Adding the Noise modifier

When someone operates a video camera without a stand or tripod, their hand will naturally shake a little bit. The effect of this can be seen in the recorded video. In 3D animation, we have to deliberately simulate this to make it look as though our camera is being held by a character or a live person. We can accomplish this in Blender by adding a **Noise** modifier to each **Rotation** and **Location** F-curve for the animated camera.

> **Important note**
> As you work on the camera's F-curves in the Graph Editor, you should also have a 3D Viewport visible in **Camera View** so that you can preview the result through the camera.

Let's begin by creating all the F-curves we need for the camera. As before, it doesn't matter which frame you insert these keyframes on; just make sure the camera is pointing at the clock. Then, we'll add our initial **Noise** modifier:

1. Insert **Location & Rotation** keyframes for the object `Camera`.
2. In the Graph Editor, select the camera's **X Location** F-curve.
3. Add a **Noise** modifier.

We've now got our first **Noise** modifier to work with, but yikes!

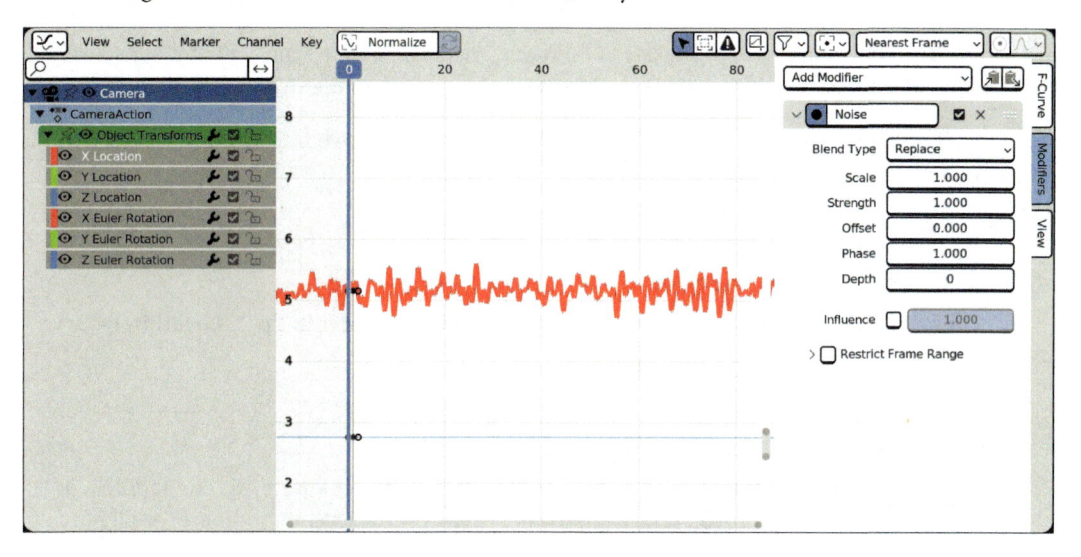

Figure 11.11: A violently noisy F-curve

The initial effect makes the camera look more like it's attached to a paint mixer than someone's hand. It needs adjusting before we can copy and paste it to the next channel.

Adjusting the Noise modifier

As with the F-curve modifiers we added earlier, the default settings for the **Noise** modifier go way too fast. This may be desirable in other cases, but not in ours.

We need to slow down the shakiness using the modifier's **Scale** property and attenuate its overall effect a bit with the **Strength** property. To make up for slowing down the noise so much, we'll also use **Depth** to increase its detail:

1. Turn up the **Scale** of the **Noise** modifier to approximately 50.0.
2. Turn down the **Strength** of the modifier to a much smaller value – something like `0.5`.
3. Increase the **Depth** value to 2 or 3.

Now, our noise looks much more appropriate for the slow, subtle shakiness of a handheld camera. Once we copy this modifier to the other F-curves, the effect will be surprisingly realistic!

> **Tip**
> Though the **Blend Type** setting of the **Noise** modifier says **Replace**, it doesn't actually replace the F-curve or its keyframes. Everything can still be edited as usual.

Copying modifiers

To add noise to our remaining two location F-curves, we don't need to repeat all our steps. Instead, we can copy the **Noise** modifier we just made and paste it onto the other two F-curves.

The **Copy** and **Paste** operators for modifiers can be found in those two little clipboard-icon buttons at the top of the **Modifiers** tab:

1. Click the **Copy F-Modifiers** button to copy the **Noise** modifier.
2. Select the **Y Location** F-curve.
3. Click the **Paste F-Modifiers** button to paste the copied modifier to the **Y Location** F-curve.
4. Do this one more time for the **Z Location** F-curve.

> **Important note**
> The operators **Copy F-Modifiers** and **Paste F-Modifiers** copy and paste all the modifiers in the stack for one F-curve. If you only need to copy/paste one of several modifiers, you'll need to copy/paste them all and delete the ones you don't want later.

We now have three identical **Noise** modifiers with ideal settings, and we didn't need to modify the **Scale**, **Strength**, and **Depth** settings for each one. Unfortunately, we don't want our **Noise** modifiers to be exactly the same! There are one or two more settings we must adjust.

Randomizing the randomization

Having identical noise for each F-curve makes the camera shake along a straight diagonal line, which is kind of pointless. That's the trouble with pseudorandom functions – the randomness can be a little too predictable!

We need each F-curve to be random in a different way. To address this, we'll use the **Phase** property, which smoothly alters the seed of the noise function. The **Offset** property can also help with this by offsetting the wave in time by a given number of frames.

Modifying these properties slightly for each **Noise** modifier has some interesting applications. In our case, though, we just want these values to be *completely* different. Click the property and drag your mouse wildly in one direction or the other, or mash your fists into the keyboard to enter some random number of your own! All that matters is that each F-curve looks different, though it will still have the same **Scale**, **Strength**, and **Depth**.

We'll also add some **Noise** modifiers to the rotation F-curves and do the same to those as well:

1. For each **Noise** modifier, alter the **Phase** and/or **Offset** properties so that no two F-curves look alike.

2. Continue working on the camera-shake effect by creating a similar **Noise** modifier for one of the **Euler Rotation** F-curves.

3. For our camera, the rotation property has a greater "sensitivity" to noise than location, so you'll need to adjust the **Strength** of the new modifiers accordingly so that the camera doesn't shake too much.

4. Copy and paste the modifier to the other **Euler Rotation** F-curves.

5. Finish by altering the **Phase** and/or **Offset** properties of these last three **Noise** modifiers as well so that they bear no resemblance to one another.

And there we have it – six different noisy F-curves!

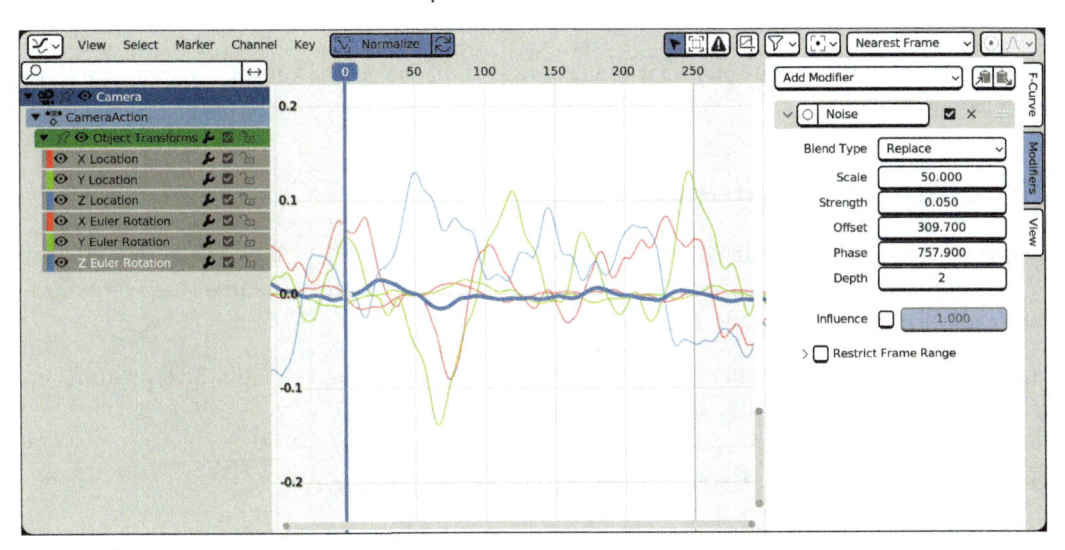

Figure 11.12: Completed camera-shake effect in the F-curves

Play your animation in **Camera View** to see the effect! It should look something like this:

Figure 11.13: Camera View (floor unhidden)

Oh, right – the printed page can't be animated. Just hold up the book in front of you at arm's length, okay? That's the effect we're going for.

If anything looks off, continue playing with the settings until you get the kind of shakiness that looks good to you.

More fun with Noise modifiers

I hope you're learning something from these exercises because I'll admit it – this is a boring animation. Who wants to watch a stupid clock, even for 10 seconds? What is this – some sort of avant-garde media installation? Are we at the *Tate Modern*?!

How about we add some excitement to our little project? Something like… an EXPLOSION just off-camera. That would certainly shake things up a bit.

Using a Noise modifier to simulate an explosion

By default, the **Noise** modifier is very noisy, causing animated objects to behave erratically. That's not necessarily a bad thing! Using additional **Noise** modifiers with different settings, we can cause the camera to shake dramatically as if rocked by an explosion outside the frame.

Go ahead and add a new one now:

1. Add another **Noise** modifier to the camera's **Z Euler Rotation** F-curve.
2. On this new modifier, leave the **Scale** as is, but turn **Strength** down to about 0.2 (that should be plenty strong enough).

There – now, the camera is really shaking! Something crazy must be happening… and happening, and happening, and happening:

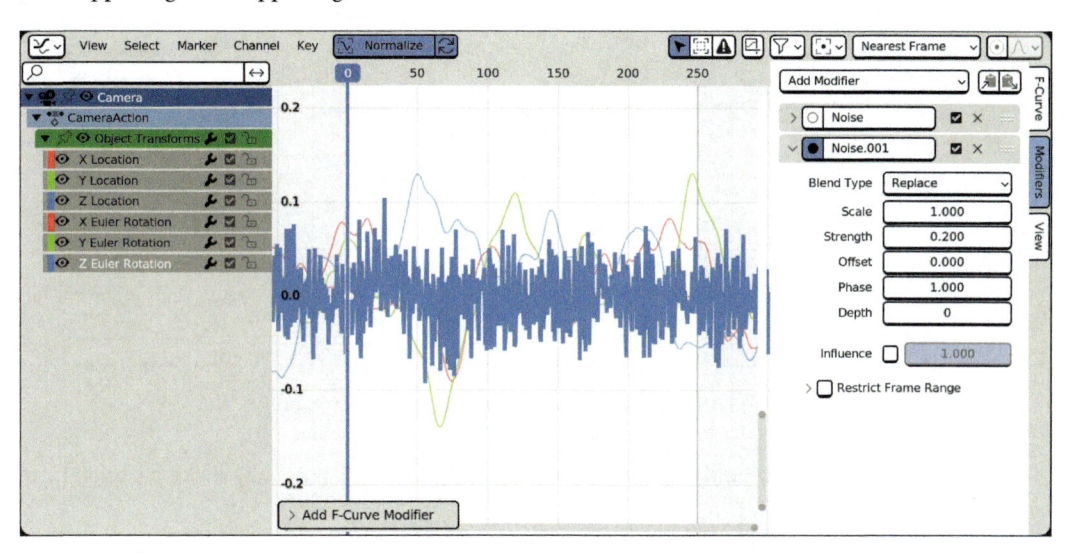

Figure 11.14: Additional Noise modifier

Of course, explosions are meant to be one-time events, not things that linger forever. Next, we'll learn how to time our explosion by giving this modifier a beginning and an end.

Restricting the frame range of a modifier

All F-curve modifiers come with a **Restrict Frame Range** feature. When enabled, this allows us to define when a modifier will begin and/or end. We can also "fade out" the modifier so that it begins with a huge effect before gradually dying out.

Try it now:

1. Enable **Restrict Frame Range** for the new **Noise** modifier.
2. Under the **Restrict Frame Range** parameters, pick a **Start** frame of 50 and an **End** frame of 80.
3. Crank the **Blend Out** value all the way up to 30 (the total duration of the modifier).

Adjust the **Phase** property – or any other properties you like – until the effect looks good to you. You might also consider adding similar modifiers to the **X Location** and **Y Location** F-curves, as I've done in this example:

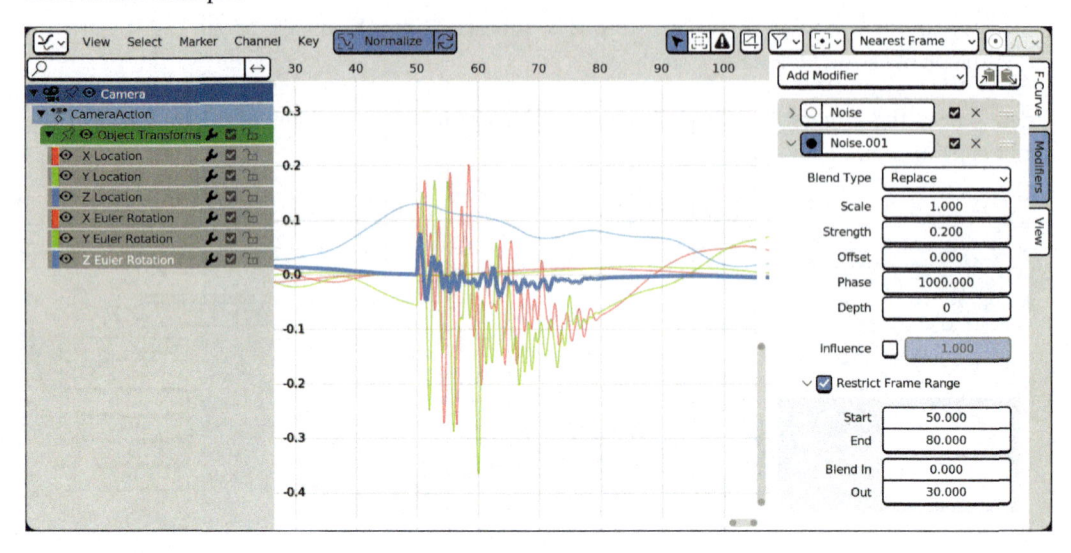

Figure 11.15: Multiple F-curves with frame-restricted noise

To see what the final effect should look like, refer back to *Figure 11.13*, but really shake the book from side to side this time.

Summary

The **Noise** modifier has endless other uses – earthquakes, flickering lights, objects blowing in the wind – in a pinch they can even be used on the bones of a character to make them look more alive while they're just standing there. What a terrific feature! Oh – and those other modifiers we learned about were cool too, I guess.

Another thing that's cool is how much we were able to accomplish with no keyframes except for the mandatory ones we had to insert at the beginning. After adding modifiers, even those keyframes can be deleted, and the F-curve will stick around (don't do that, though). Personally, I enjoy procedural animation techniques that require little to no keying. However, keep in mind that modifiers don't have to replace the regular animation process; they can also work in addition to whatever else we want the F-curves to do.

Sometimes it's fun to let go, add hardly any keyframes, and let Blender procedurally animate things for us, right? If you agree, you're going to have a lot of fun in the next chapter...

Questions

1. If a mesh modifier works in three dimensions, in how many dimensions does an F-curve modifier work?
2. For F-curves that will be modified, why does it (occasionally) not matter where we insert our initial keyframes?
3. The **Generator** modifier can also generate F-curves using quadratic and cubic polynomial functions. What might these be useful for?
4. In what cases is *pi* an important number in F-curve modifiers? Why?
5. Some modifiers have an **Additive** option. What does enabling this allow us to do?
6. What would happen if the **Stepped Interpolation** modifier in our exercise came before the **Generator** modifier in the modifier stack?
7. What happens when you try to animate a property of an F-curve modifier?
8. Why bother trying to simulate camera shake in an animation when so much modern camera and video software tries to eliminate it from live-action footage?

12
Rigid Body Physics

I've spent quite a bit of this book talking about physics – how the objects in our world tend to fall and bounce off of one another. This informs how the objects in our animations ought to behave as well, but as animators, we usually key this behavior deliberately. The ball in *Chapter 2* might look as though it's governed by the laws of physics, but we did all the work to make it look like that – we were the ones in control. But what if we *don't* want to be in control? What if our aim were *chaos and destruction*?

What if, for instance, a character were to flip over a table, or smash through a brick wall? Using conventional techniques, this would require animating a great many things with great effort, but if we don't particularly care where the objects on the table or the bricks in the wall end up, we can simply let the program do the work for us.

Rigid Body Physics is a feature that simulates the physics of rigid bodies moving through space and colliding – rocks, marbles, soup cans – literally anything hard. By designating objects in our scene as rigid bodies, they'll appear to obey many natural laws of physics, such as gravity, inertia, and friction, all without our direct intervention.

In this chapter, we'll explore the following topics:

- Getting started with rigid bodies
- Improving the accuracy and performance of rigid bodies
- Controlling an animated rigid body

Technical requirements

To follow along with this chapter, all you need is the default scene in Blender. You can delete the light and camera, but we'll need that cube. That'll be our first **rigid body**.

Creating a rigid body world

The keyword "rigid" in **Rigid Body** distinguishes the simulation from other kinds of physics simulations such as **Fluid**, **Cloth**, or **Soft Body**. Pick something up and throw it – if it doesn't splatter, bend, or jiggle, you can think of it as a rigid body object.

It may surprise you how easy it is to get started with rigid body physics. We'll begin by creating the simplest rigid body simulation there is.

Our first rigid body simulation

Rigid body physics simulation is automatically enabled when one or more objects in your scene is a rigid body. Any mesh object in your scene can be a rigid body.

The settings for this can be found in the selected mesh object's **Physics Properties** tab:

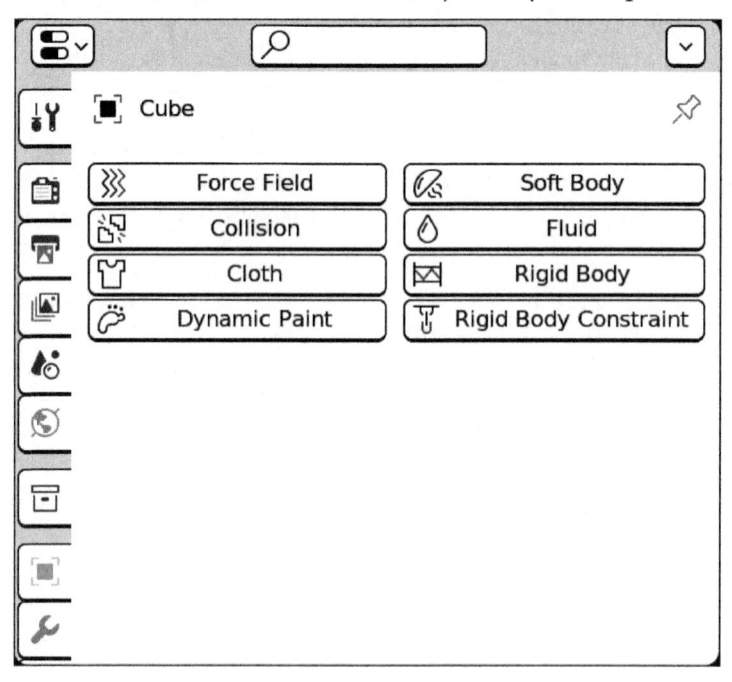

Figure 12.1: Physics Properties

> **Important note**
> Objects don't affect simulations unless they are given specific **Physics Properties** (such as **Rigid Body**).

Clicking **Rigid Body** designates the selected object as such. Try it now:

1. Select the default cube.
2. Go to the cube's physics settings in the **Physics Properties** tab.
3. Click **Rigid Body**.

Ignore the settings that just appeared and play the animation from frame 1. There you have it – a cube falling through empty space!

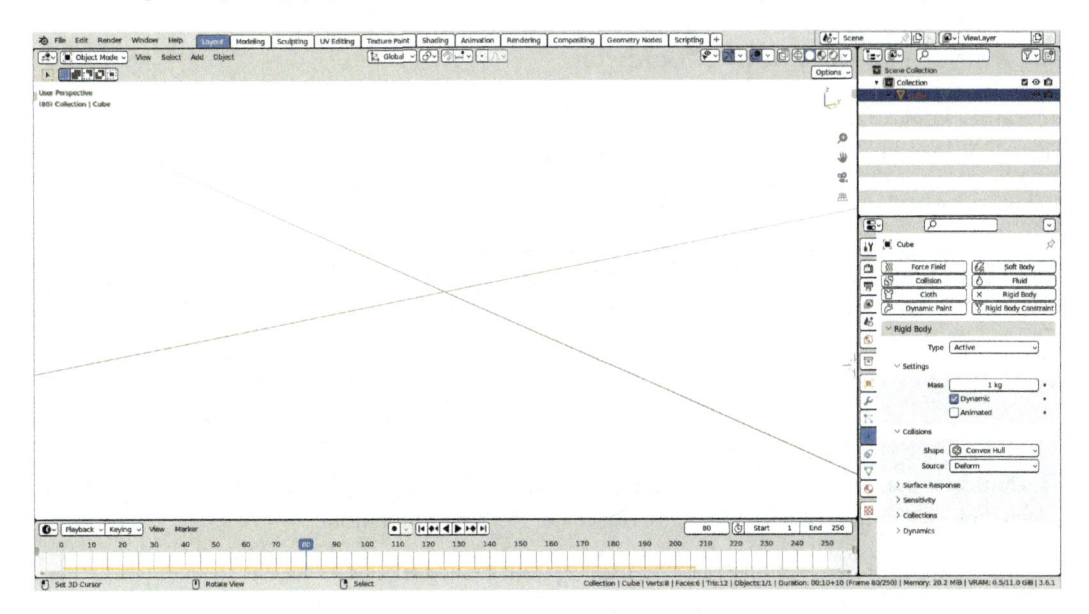

Figure 12.2: It's gone!

Not the most exciting thing to simulate, but bear with me here. To understand what's going on, let's go over some essential things that have changed for your scene and the object you just turned into a rigid body.

Rigid Body

Unlike the objects in a **Fluid**, **Cloth**, or **Soft Body** simulation, the mesh of a **Rigid Body** does not change. Rather, the entire object moves as forces such as gravity and other rigid bodies act upon it (right now we can see the effect of gravity on the cube; the other rigid bodies come later).

By default, we lose control of an object once **Rigid Body** physics are enabled for it. Moving it around determines its initial starting point when the simulation begins, but after that, it's out of our hands.

> **Important note**
> For the reason mentioned previously, you should edit your rigid body objects at or before the starting frame of the simulation (frame `1` by default). Editing things on a frame after the simulation has begun works backward in time, potentially causing unexpected results.

Like any other animation, the simulation result is non-destructive; when we go back to frame `1`, our cube goes back to where it started. That's a good thing – otherwise, we'd have to go and get it ourselves every time it fell!

The frames in a rigid body simulation

Like other kinds of physics in Blender, the rigid body simulation only works when the animation is playing. When the animation is played, the simulation is performed in real time.

Note the thin yellow stripe that has appeared in our **Timeline** area:

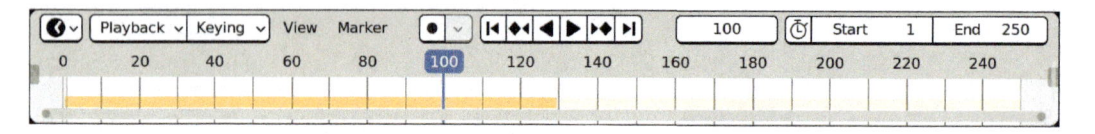

Figure 12.3: The cached frames of the simulation

This indicates the frames for which Blender has stored, or *cached*, the physics simulation result of the selected object, compared with the entire frame range of the simulation.

Caching is done for performance reasons; playing back cached frames is faster than calculating them the first time. The simulation is cached automatically and cleared each time we change something in the simulation.

> **Important note**
> Blender must know the state of the simulation on the first frame before it can calculate what happens on the second frame, and then the third frame, and so on. For this reason, you should allow the animation to play from frame 1 each time you want to view your changes. Don't expect accurate results in the **3D Viewport** if you skip ahead to un-cached frames in the **Timeline**.

Rigid Body World settings

Every rigid body has individual properties that appear when **Rigid Body** is clicked, which we'll get to in a minute. Before we do, you should be aware of the *global* parameters of our **Rigid Body World**, which affect the whole simulation, and are located in **Scene Properties** | **Rigid Body World**:

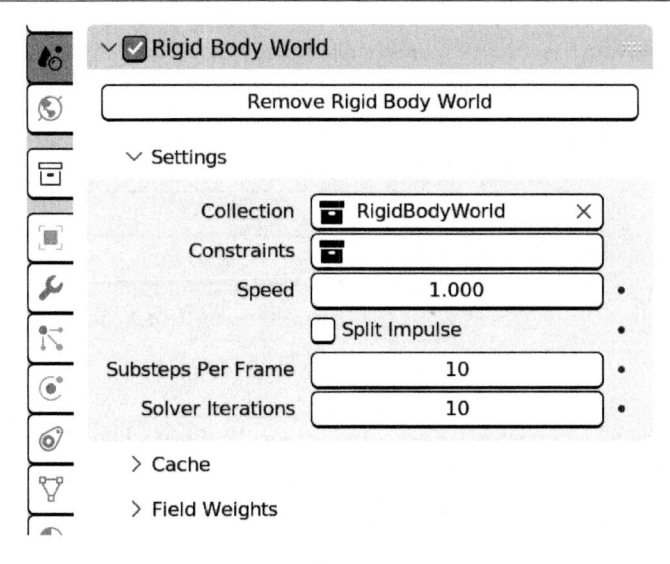

Figure 12.4: Rigid Body World settings

Gravity, for obvious reasons, will affect your rigid bodies as well:

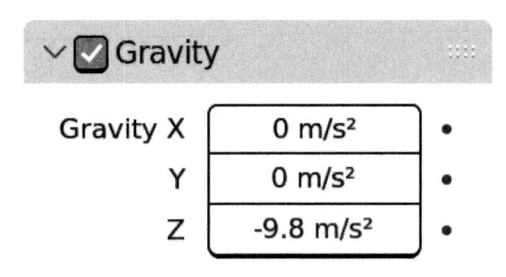

Figure 12.5: Gravity

Most of the defaults you can see here will seldom need to be changed, but it's nice to know we can make things weightless if we like... or even make them fall up or sideways!

> **Tip**
>
> Large things often appear to fall uncharacteristically slowly. The default cube is 2 meters wide, which is quite large compared to the real-world objects we tend to toss around. For accurate-looking simulations, be mindful of the scale of your scene and make sure your objects are realistically sized (and have realistic **Mass** as well). You can also multiply **Gravity** or **Speed** by a given factor, which is effectively the same as scaling the simulation space as a whole.

Also note the **Simulation Start** and **End** properties under **Rigid Body World | Cache**, in case you want the simulation's frame range to be something other than the default 1 to 250:

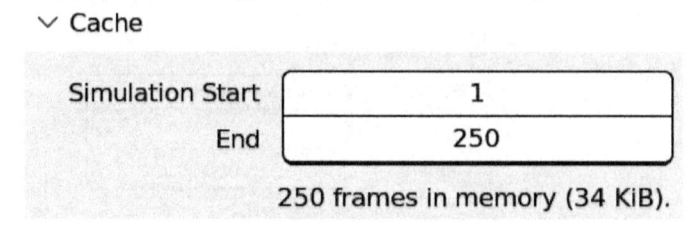

Figure 12.6: Simulation Start and End frames

Now that you know where everything is, we're ready to make this simulation a bit more interesting.

Active and passive rigid bodies

We need a floor in our scene; otherwise, everything will just fall downwards into an infinite void. To repel the rigid bodies that land on it and stop them from falling into an infinite void, our floor must also be a kind of rigid body, but one that doesn't itself fall into the infinite void (infinite voids seem to be the default here).

Let's begin by creating the floor.

Creating the floor

You'd think a plane or grid would suffice as a floor, but not this time. The floor needs to have non-zero thickness; otherwise, other rigid bodies in our simulation may pass right through it. That's not the kind of floor you want in your scene (or in your house for that matter).

The default cube we just turned into a rigid body will serve nicely as a floor:

1. Scale the cube on the *X* and *Y* axes so that it covers a large area.
2. Move the cube down on the *Z* axis by -1.0 so that its top face is aligned with where the "floor" should be.
3. Rename the cube `Floor`.
4. To make such a large object less conspicuous, go to **Object Properties | Viewport Display** and set **Display As** to **Wire**.

Most of these steps are for our convenience; the important thing is that we make the floor nice and big. A few dozen meters in all directions ought to do it:

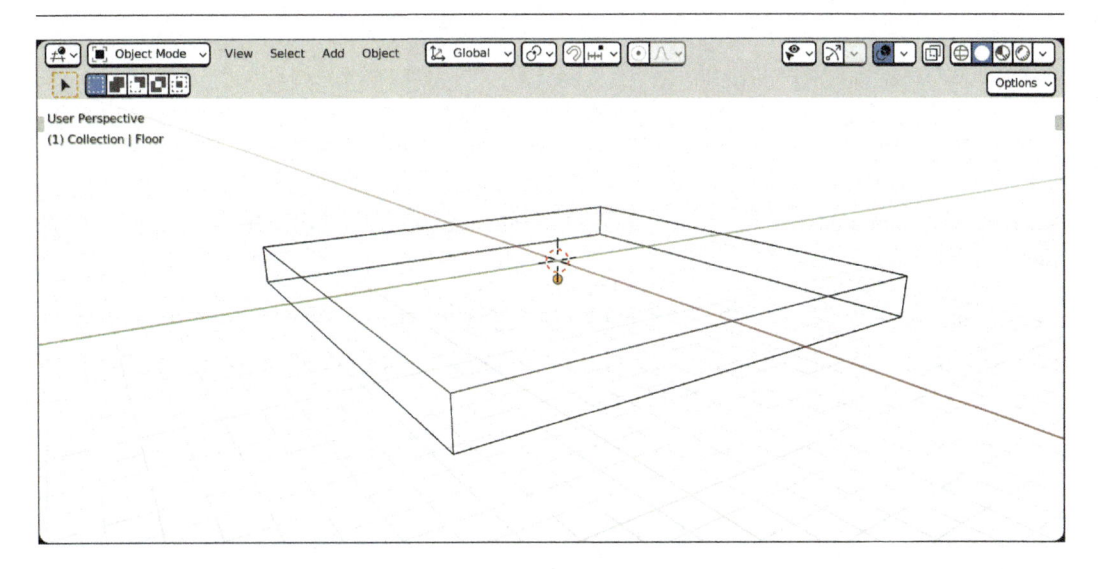

Figure 12.7: Floor

That's a nice floor-sized floor, but it still falls away when we play the simulation. Again, this is not the kind of floor you want in your scene or your house. We'll fix that next as we finally take a look at those **Rigid Body** properties we've been ignoring.

Passive rigid bodies

Make no mistake – our floor does need to be a rigid body, just not an **Active** one.

Rigid bodies come in two types. By default, a rigid body is **Active**, which is a fancy way of saying the physics simulator makes it move around:

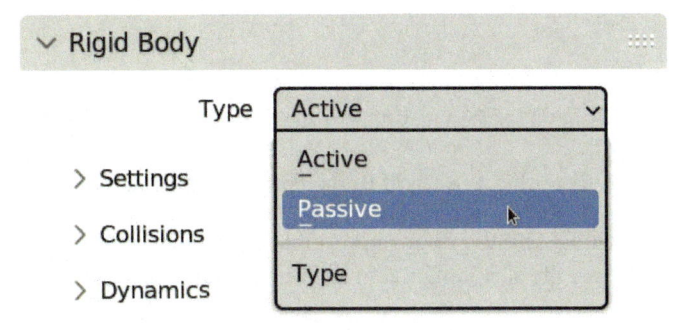

Figure 12.8: Rigid body types

In contrast, a rigid body that is **Passive** remains fixed in space. It will affect other rigid bodies that are **Active** while itself being unaffected by them or anything else in the simulation. That's what we want for our floor.

> **Tip**
> Another way of making an **Active** rigid body effectively passive is to disable **Rigid Body | Settings | Dynamic**. You can animate this property to start and stop individual active rigid bodies.

Let's make our floor a **Passive** rigid body, then add some more **Active** rigid bodies so that we can see what it does:

1. At the top of the Floor object's **Rigid Body** properties, change **Type** from **Active** to **Passive**.

   Our floor now does what a floor ought to do: nothing. But it will stop other rigid bodies! Let's add some to our scene to see this in action.

2. **Add** (*Shift + A*) a few solid **Mesh** objects of your choice to the scene and place them above the floor:

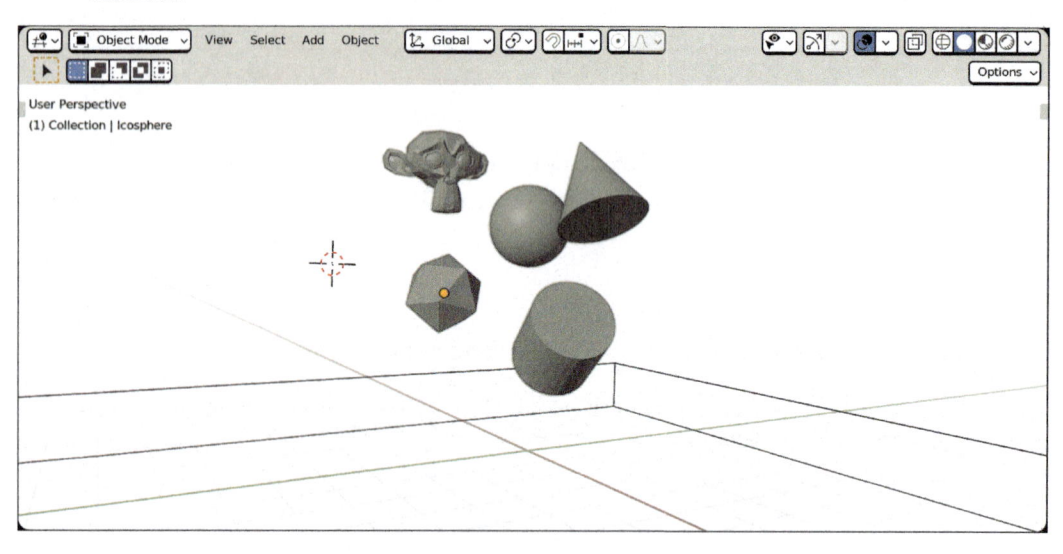

Figure 12.9: Some primitive mesh objects that can be rigid bodies

3. Make each of these new objects a **Rigid Body** like you did the first one.

Your new rigid bodies will fall, hit the floor, and tumble with remarkable realism. Now we can see what rigid body physics is really all about: making a bunch of junk fall down!

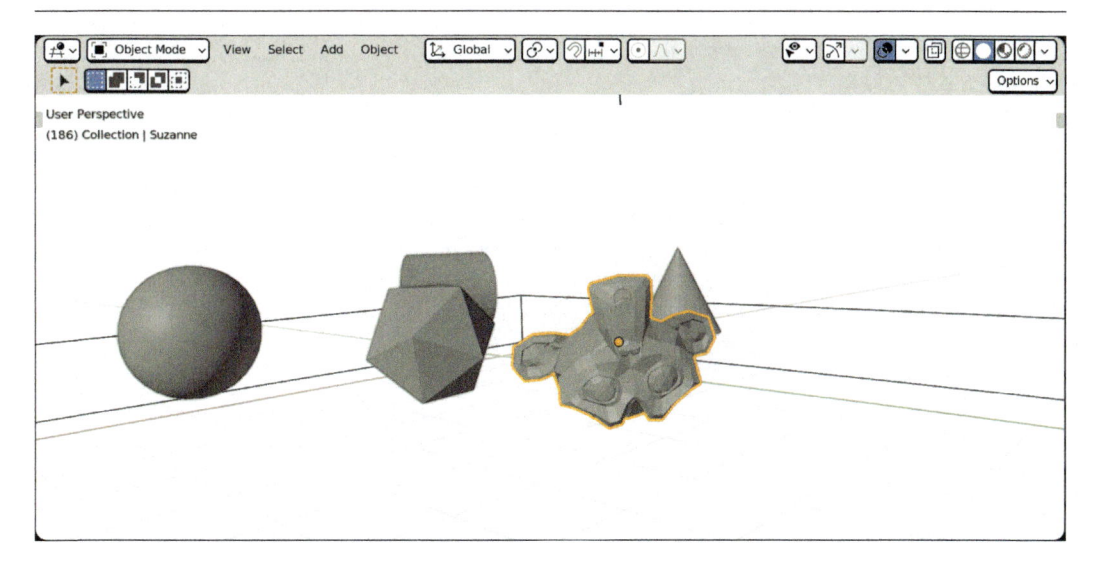

Figure 12.10: Just like dropping a 2-meter monkey head in real life!

I'd estimate at least 60% of the use cases for rigid body physics are just making junk fall down. Go ahead and play around with it; it's terrific fun!

Once you've had enough fun, move on to the next section, where we'll cover *my* idea of fun: learning a bunch of technical details about rigid bodies. Oh boy!

Rigid body collision

Here's the most important thing you need to know about rigid body physics: It's all about **collisions**. You may have noticed your active rigid bodies colliding – crashing into one another and reacting in a realistic way that would be time-consuming to animate. Forces such as gravity are a piece of cake – heck, we can simulate gravity with two keyframes and quadratic interpolation – but collisions? Collisions are where things get interesting.

Take this wall made of bricks, where each brick is an active rigid body. Knocking over brick walls is a fun exercise; we're going to make one of these ourselves soon:

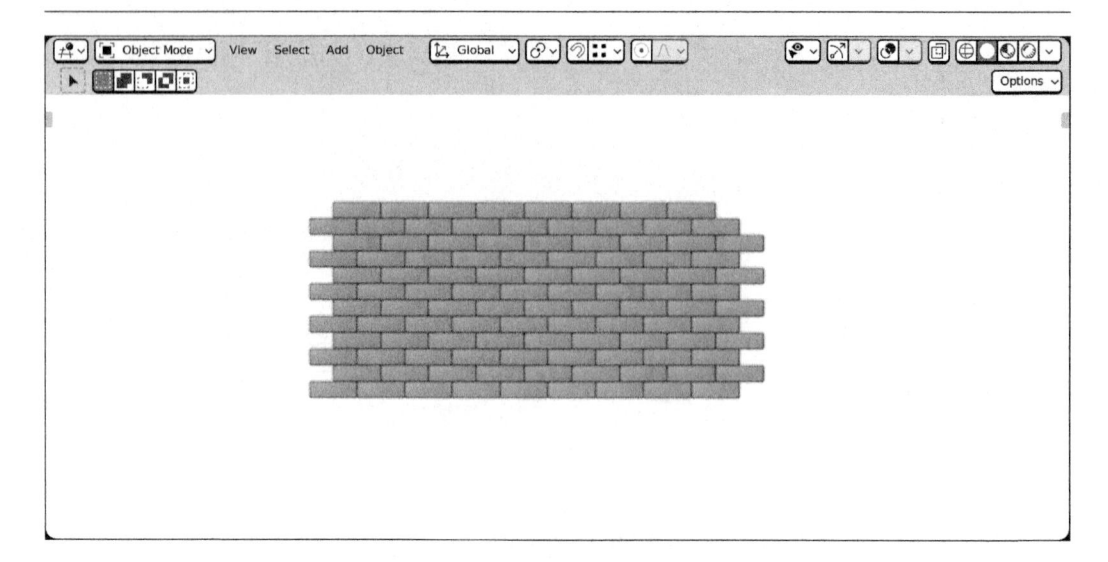

Figure 12.11: A simple wall of bricks on frame 1

Looks decent enough, right? It'll stay upright until we knock it over with something else, right? Wrong! It exploded because you were careless with collisions:

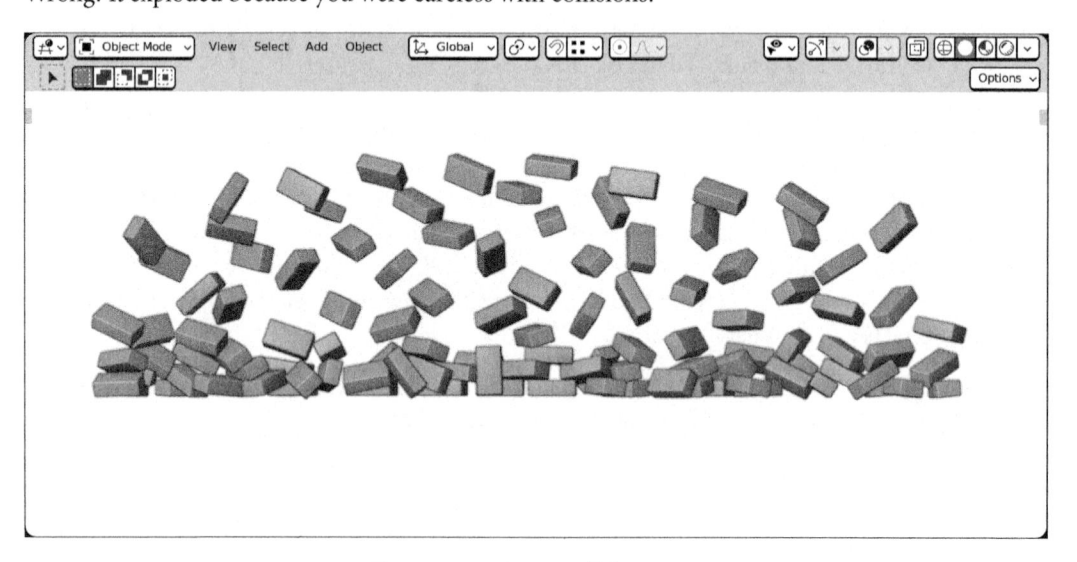

Figure 12.12: Same wall, frame 12

This sort of thing happens more often than you'd think, and it's just one example of one of the many issues you might run into with your simulations. With some knowledge about collisions under our belts, we can avoid a lot of these problems.

The smashing-junk-together algorithm

Rigid body collision works like this: at each frame, the physics engine checks whether an active rigid body is colliding (or is presently to collide) with another rigid body. When this happens, an impulse is applied that changes the motion of the rigid body on the next frame, repelling it away from whatever it collided with. The harder the collision, the harder the impulse.

For instance, take an active rigid body on frame 1 and stick it halfway into the floor:

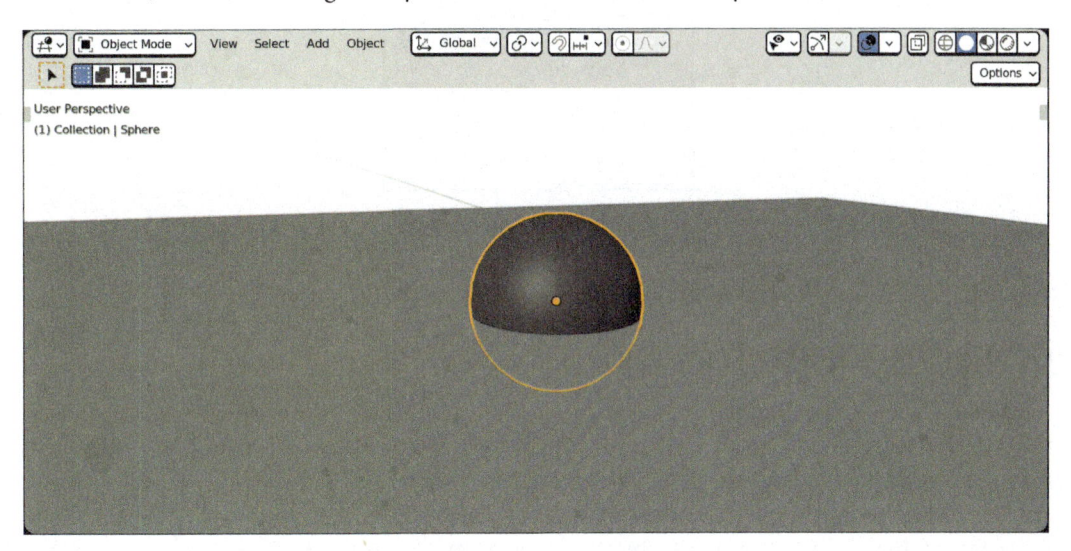

Figure 12.13: A rigid body sphere, stuck into the ground

The engine considers this rigid body to be colliding *really hard* with the floor. When the simulation begins, it will launch into the air as if fired from a cannon. This is why our simulations might "explode" at the beginning if we're not careful.

> Tip
> It doesn't matter if two **Passive** rigid bodies collide, so you can stick them together however you like. They're passive. Where are they gonna go?

So how does the physics engine efficiently detect whether two rigid bodies are colliding? That brings us to our next topic...

Collision shapes

It's not the mesh of a rigid body that's considered in collision detections – it's the **shape**. Note that **Shape** is a specific technical term in this chapter. Every rigid body has a **Shape** property that can be found under **Rigid Body | Collision | Shape**:

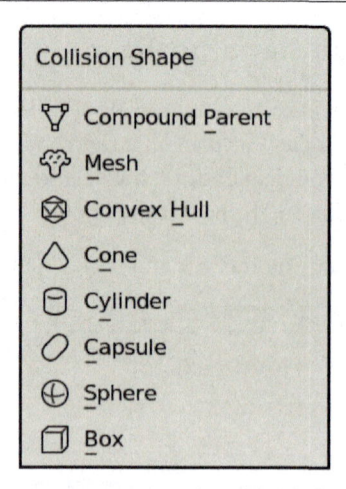

Figure 12.14: Collision Shape

Those shapes are the only shapes the physics engine cares about!

Primitive collision shapes

Rigid bodies' shapes are intended to more or less resemble the object itself, but simplified. **Box**, **Sphere**, **Capsule**, **Cylinder**, and **Cone** are the simplest shapes and should be strongly considered for objects that look like those things. A simpler shape is easier to compute, so it's better for performance and stability, though this comes at the expense of accuracy wherever the **Shape** property of the rigid body deviates from the "shape" of the mesh object we actually see:

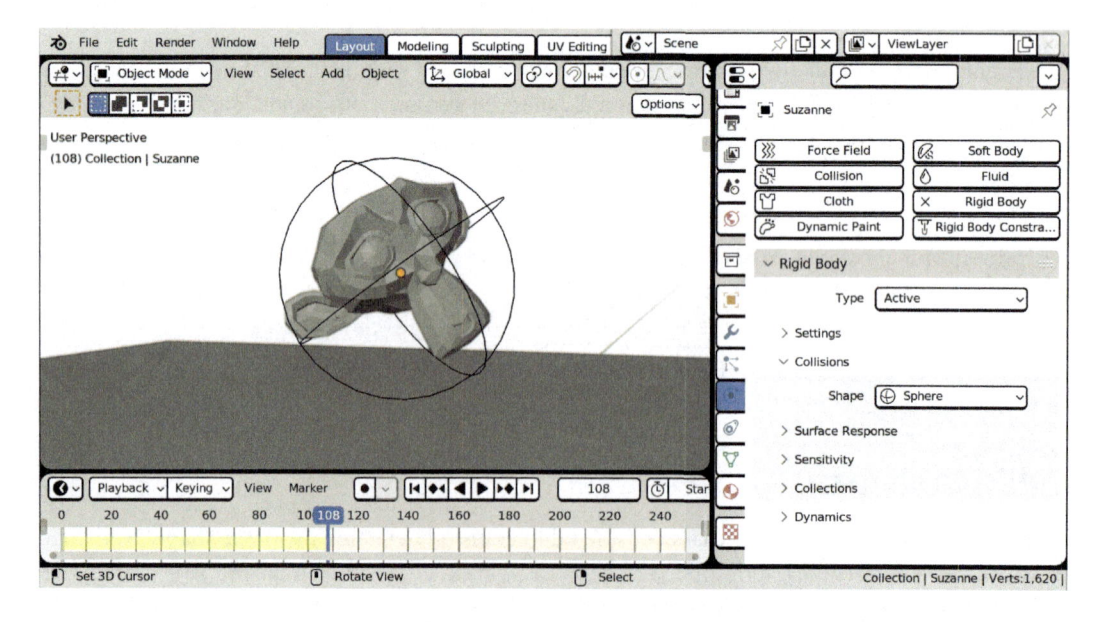

Figure 12.15: A monkey head rolling like a perfect sphere

> **Important note**
>
> When **Box**, **Sphere**, **Capsule**, **Cylinder**, or **Cone** is used, the shape is displayed as a wire in the **3D Viewport** so you can compare it to the object mesh with which it is associated.
>
> The size of the shape is automatically scaled according to the dimensions of the mesh. Some shapes are aligned to the local Z axis, so you may need to edit the object so that its local Z axis aligns with its longer dimension.

Spheres, boxes, capsules, cylinders, and cones are convenient shapes because of the easy geometric formulas needed to test whether they're in collision. What about other shapes, though?

Mesh and Convex Hull

The default shape is **Convex Hull**, a shape copied directly from the mesh with one important difference: it has to be convex, due to computation concerns. If you could see the **Convex Hull** of a rigid body, it would resemble the object covered in shrink wrap. This is a good all-around shape, useful for objects that are mostly convex.

Sometimes, **Convex Hull** just isn't good enough though. Note the "invisible shrink wrap" that seems to cover this bowl:

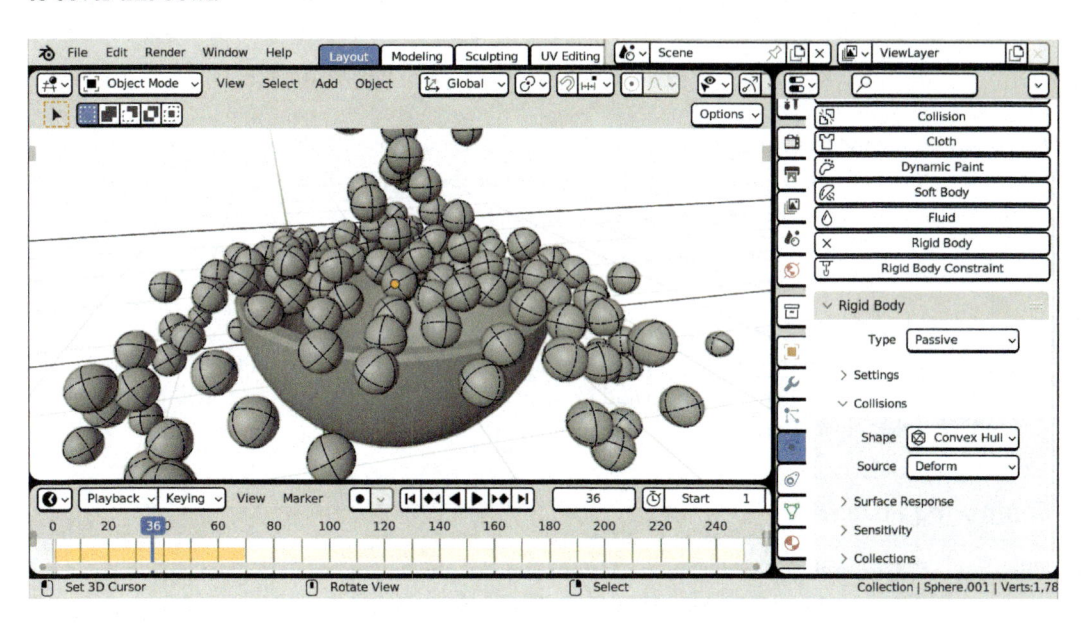

Figure 12.16: Marbles failing to go in a bowl

If you must accurately simulate physics for concave things, there is always the **Mesh** shape, which replicates the mesh itself as faithfully as possible, including all its concave portions:

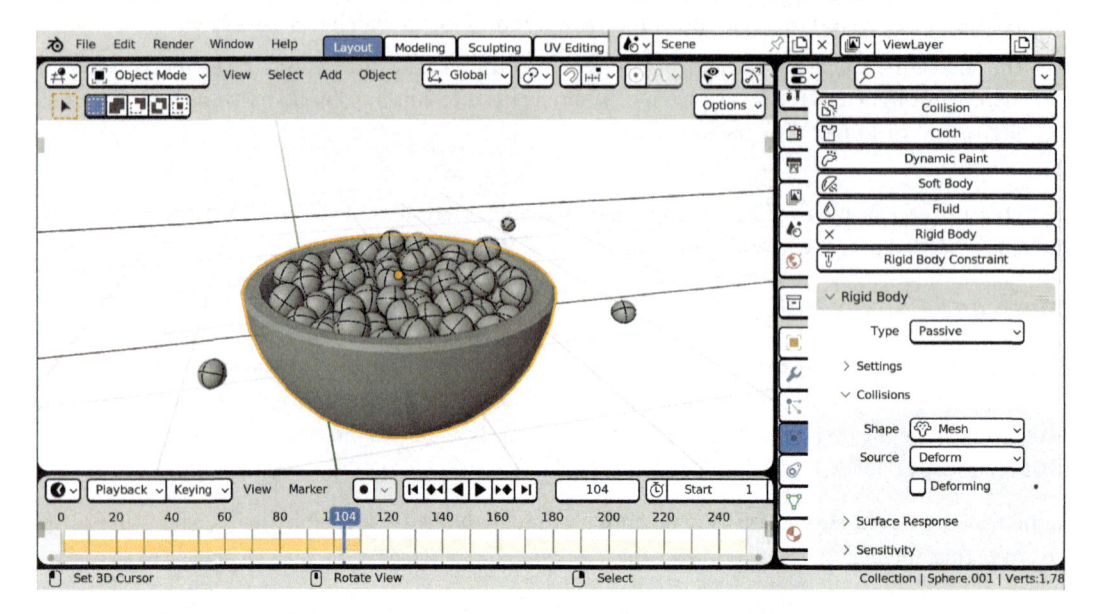

Figure 12.17: Accurate concave collisions with the Mesh shape

This option is the most accurate choice, but also the slowest and least stable. Detecting collisions for concave meshes is more difficult than you'd expect! For this reason, it's best to use the **Mesh** shape sparingly, and only with **Passive** rigid bodies if you can help it.

> **Tip**
>
> **Mesh** or **Convex Hull** shapes with a high level of detail can unnecessarily slow down the simulation. But keep this in mind: an object doesn't need to be its own rigid body. You can instead make a *proxy* – an invisible rigid body of the same basic shape – and then parent the more complex object to it.

Compound Parent

Finally, there's **Compound Parent**, an under-appreciated shape that combines the shapes of all the rigid body's children. Using a combination of simple shapes, you can make all kinds of custom shapes, even concave ones that perform way better than the **Mesh** or **Convex Hull** shape:

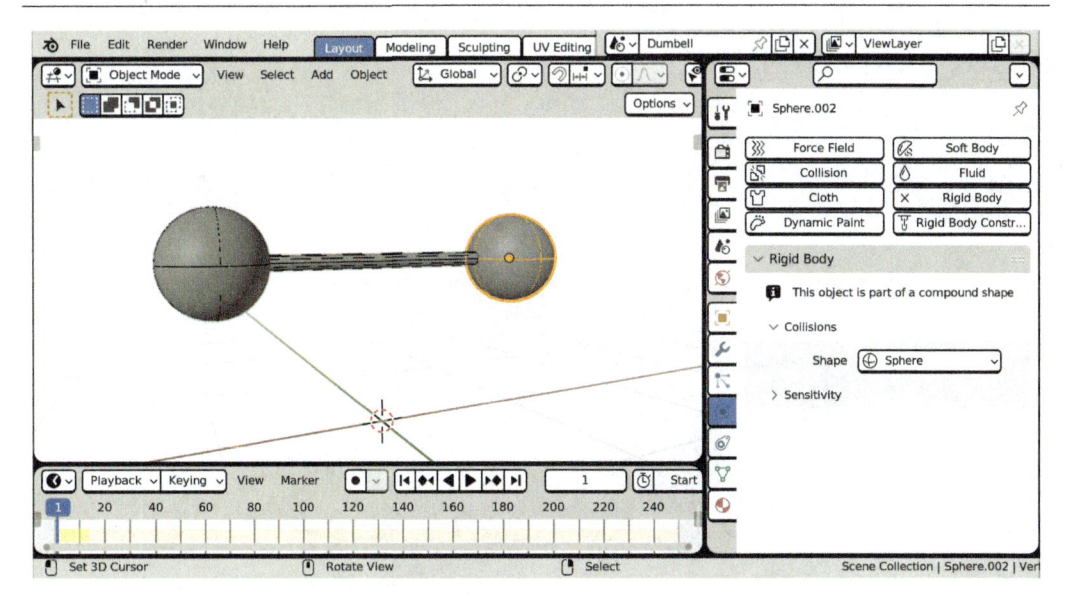

Figure 12.18: Compound shapes used to make a dumbbell

Now that we've seen all the collision shapes available to us, let's see if we can use one or more of them in our simulation.

Selecting rigid body collision shapes

The clearest candidate for treatment is the floor, as it is a **Box** shape. Simple shapes are always better!

1. For the floor, set **Rigid Body | Collisions | Shape** to **Box**.
2. Select the most appropriate collision shape for the rest of your rigid bodies.

A nice, flat shape for our nice, flat floor will help us avoid all sorts of mysterious, unwanted behavior. As for all those other rigid bodies you've been playing with, try out different shapes to see their effect! Moreover, you can check out how properties such as **Settings | Mass**, **Surface Response | Friction**, and **Surface Response | Bounciness** affect the simulation.

Then, after you're done playing around, set your active rigid bodies aside. It's time to put away such childish things… and play with blocks instead!

Destroying a wall

Here comes my favorite part:

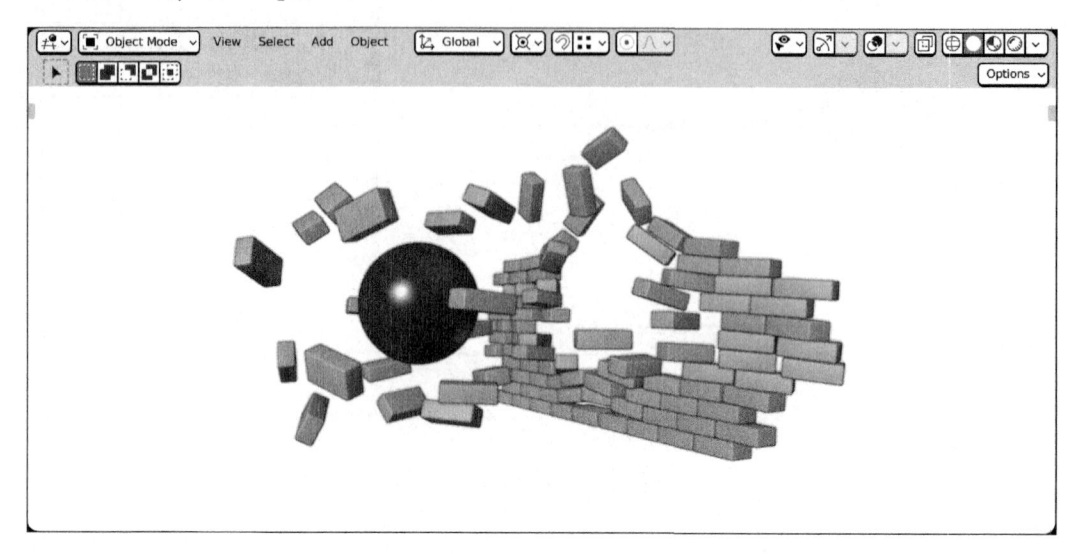

Figure 12.19: Smash!

Need I elaborate further? We're going to build a wall out of rigid body bricks, and then we're going to knock it down!

Building a wall

First, we'll build the wall brick by brick. Each brick will be an individual rigid body, so the trick here is to make sure we stack the bricks right, and that they have the correct **Rigid Body** settings.

The brick

Every wall starts with a single brick, so let's start by making one:

1. **Add** (*Shift + A*) a **Cube** to the scene.
2. In **Edit Mode**, scale your cube down to the approximate dimensions of a brick.
3. Make sure the brick lies flat and does not hover or intersect with the floor.
4. Name the object `Brick`.

> **Important note**
> Active rigid bodies with altered object **Scale** values (that is, scaled in **Object Mode**) will behave incorrectly, as though they are bigger or smaller than they really are. This is another case for always scaling things in **Edit Mode**. You can also use **Apply** (*Ctrl + A*) | **Scale**.

Now we have a brick. I've given my brick a new material and a **Bevel** modifier so I can see each brick better:

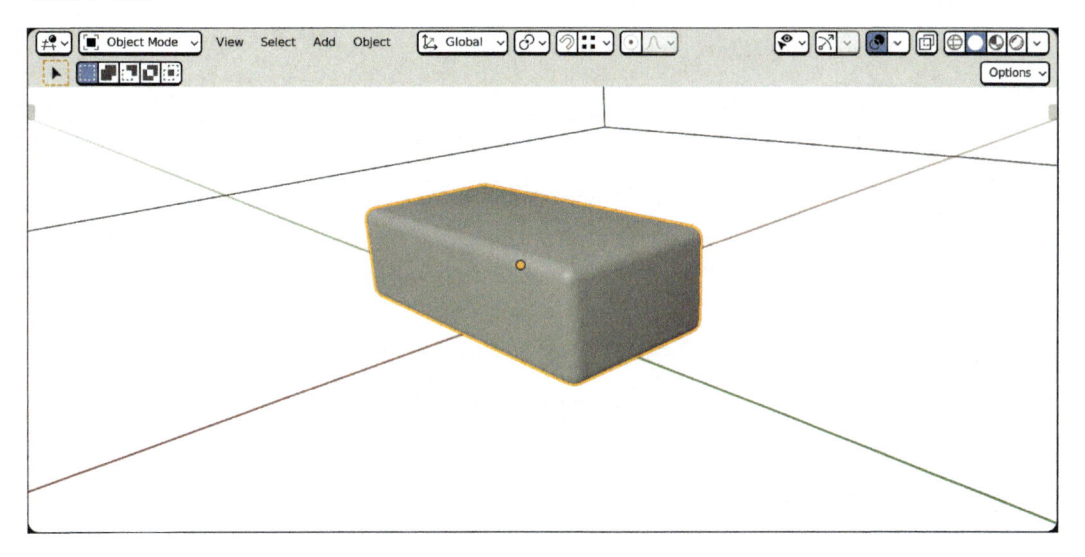

Figure 12.20: A brick

Before we duplicate this brick a bunch of times to make a wall, we should go ahead and make it a rigid body with all the correct parameters.

Rigid Body deactivation

One of the settings we'll need to enable for our bricks includes enabling **Deactivation**, a feature that automatically activates and deactivates the simulation for a rigid body at rest:

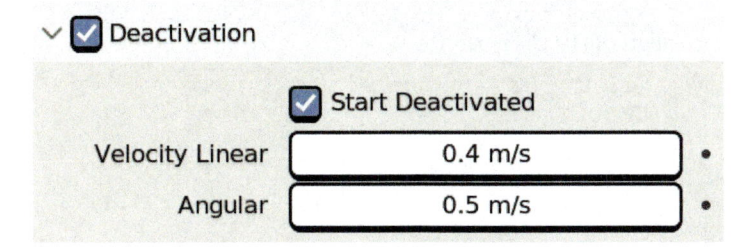

Figure 12.21: Deactivation settings

Not only can this improve performance, it will ensure that the bricks in the wall remain still like bricks ought to and don't start "simulating" until we crash something into them.

Let's take advantage of that feature as we adjust the settings for our brick:

1. Make `Brick` an **Active Rigid Body**.
2. Set the **Collision | Shape** of `Brick` to **Box**.
3. Enable **Dynamics | Deactivation**.
4. Enable **Deactivation | Start Deactivated**.

Now `Brick` is calculated as a **Box** shape, and although it is an **Active Rigid Body** it will not move at the start of the simulation. Not the most exciting thing, but that's bricks for you.

That takes care of all the necessary **Rigid Body** settings for `Brick`. Each copy of `Brick` will have identical **Rigid Body** properties.

> **Tip**
> If you need to adjust the properties of many rigid bodies at once (such as all the bricks *after* you've duplicated them), there's a way to do so: select them all and hold *Alt* while editing a property. This handy trick works for lots of other properties as well!

Building the wall

Now we're ready to duplicate this brick and stack it to make a wall:

1. Select `Brick` and use **Duplicate Linked** (*Alt + D*) several times to make a layer of bricks.
2. Select the layer of bricks, duplicate it, and put the new layer above the old one by one brick-height.
3. Shift the new layer of bricks to one side by half a brick-width.
4. Select both layers, duplicate them, and stack them by the height of two bricks.
5. Repeat *Step 4* until you've got a nice wall. Delete the last overhanging brick.

> **Tip**
> Use **Snapping** to align the bricks perfectly.

Now we have a wall!

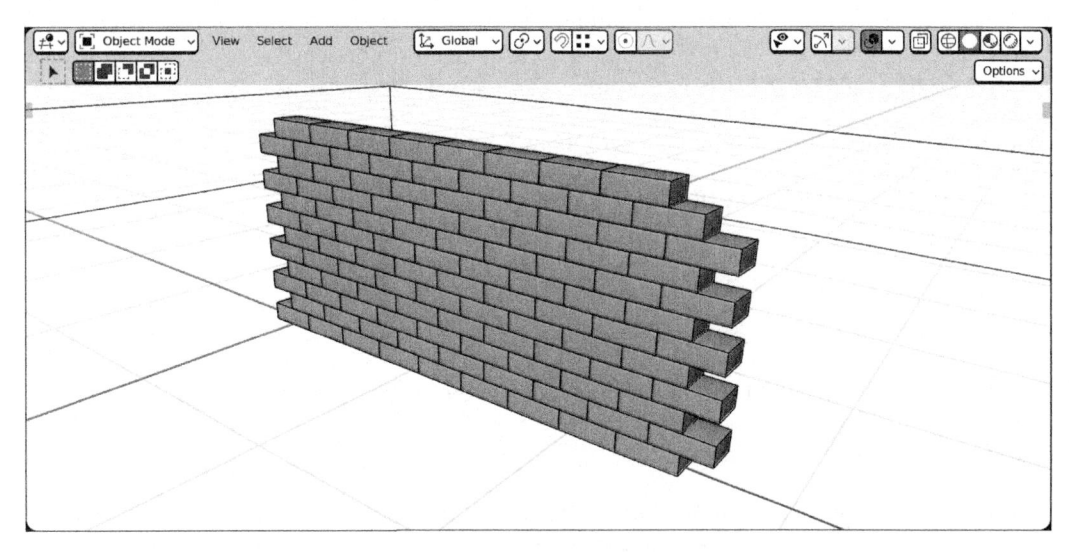

Figure 12.22: Example of a wall

Exactly how big or wide this wall is isn't important. It won't last long anyway...

Destroying the wall

Now for the fun part – destruction and mayhem! We're going to make another rigid body and use it to destroy the wall. So long as you're having fun, you can make your wrecking ball any size and shape you like:

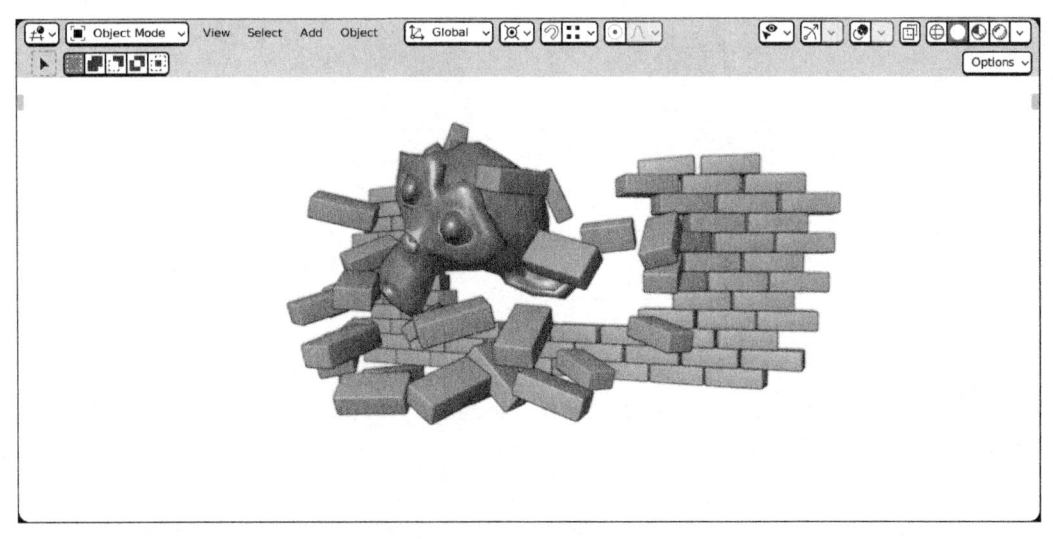

Figure 12.23: A wrecking monkey

Once we've made a big heavy thing, we need to send it crashing into the wall. To do that, we'll learn how to take direct control of it with keyframing.

Creating the wrecking ball

First, let's add our wrecking ball (or cube, or monkey) to the scene:

1. Add a solid mesh object to the scene.
2. Make your new object a **Rigid Body**.
3. Select an appropriate **Collision | Shape**.
4. Enable **Settings | Animated**.

Now that we've got a thing to knock over walls, let's talk about that last setting we enabled.

Controlling rigid bodies directly

How do we make a rigid body do something? This whole time we've been playing around mainly by placing rigid bodies above the floor and watching their potential energy run out as they fall to the ground. To knock over our wall from one side, maybe we could put the wrecking ball at the top of a ramp, like so:

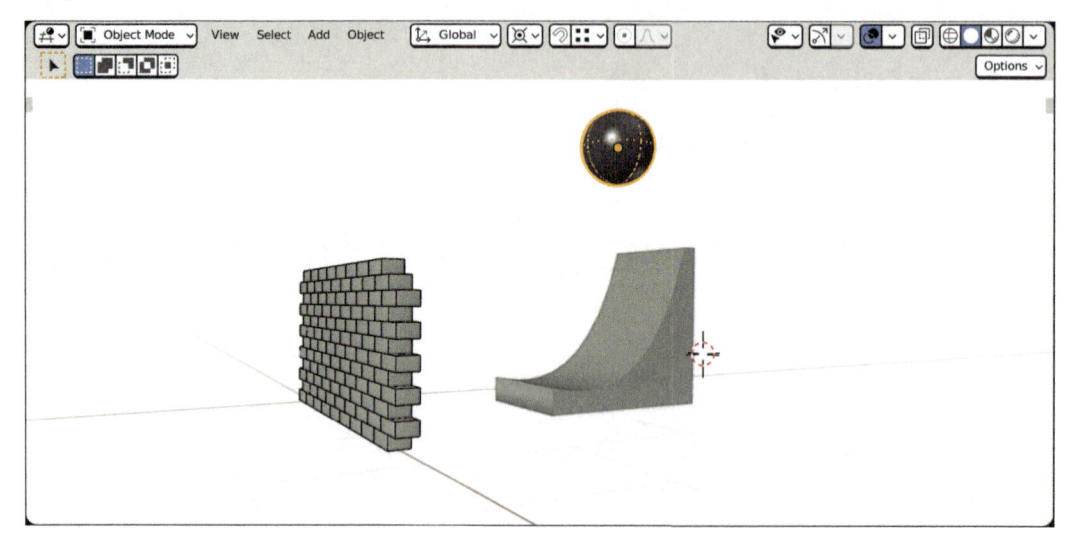

Figure 12.24: A contraption for making the rigid body do what we want

This process of setting things up and watching gravity take care of the rest is fun, but it's not exactly animating, is it?

Rigid Body | Settings | Animated is a crucial property that allows us to directly control a rigid body, be it active or passive. When disabled, the simulation won't respond to the rigid body being animated.

When enabled, however, the rigid body can be animated like any other object, and it will affect the other bodies in the simulation.

Interacting with rigid bodies in realtime

In the case of rigid body physics, **Animated** doesn't strictly mean something *animated* (that is, keyed). It covers any kind of movement not caused within the simulation, such as with constraints, or in this case, manually moving the object as the animation is playing.

Here's something you can try out:

1. Play the animation.
2. While the animation is playing, **Move** (*G*) your wrecking ball into the wall of bricks.

It's almost like a video game… almost. Though it is a lot of fun and has its uses in quick testing, this kind of interactivity functionality is limited. Our little game is just a game, and it only lasts as long as the frame range of the simulation before resetting.

Next, let's do the most obvious thing!

Animating the wrecking ball

We want to call our project here an animation, and not just a weird kind of physics sandbox that's played 250 frames at a time. You've guessed it – it's time to animate the wrecking ball.

What happens when we do so will not surprise you:

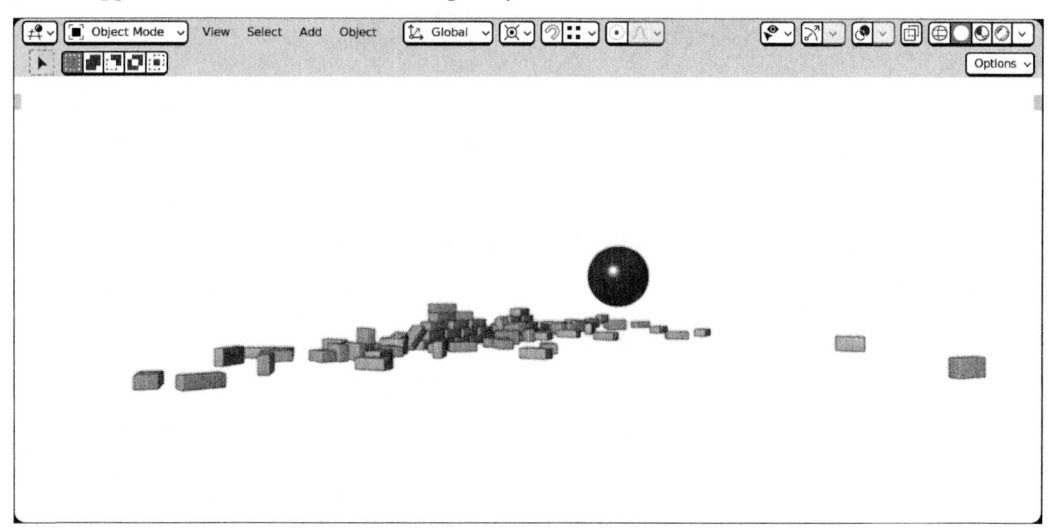

Figure 12.25: A destroyed wall

Something is missing, which is the effect of the simulation on the wrecking ball itself. Look at it just hovering there. Things react to it, but it behaves like a juggernaut, not reacting to anything except where we stupidly tell it to go. Its **Mass** could be 1000 kg or 0.001 kg and it wouldn't matter either way. It'd be nice if it were to land in the rubble with everything else, or perhaps bounce off and roll away after making a dent. But an **Animated** rigid body is always **Passive**, even if it's **Active**.

...Or is it? While it might be true that a rigid body can't be affected by both its **Transform** properties and the simulation at the same time, we can switch between the two by keying the **Animated** property itself.

Here's the last trick I want to show you:

1. **Animate** your wrecking ball so that it bashes through the wall at a satisfying speed.
2. Key the **Animated** property so that it turns off just before the wrecking ball hits the wall.

You can also adjust the **Mass** of your wrecking ball if you're unsatisfied with the effect it has on the wall:

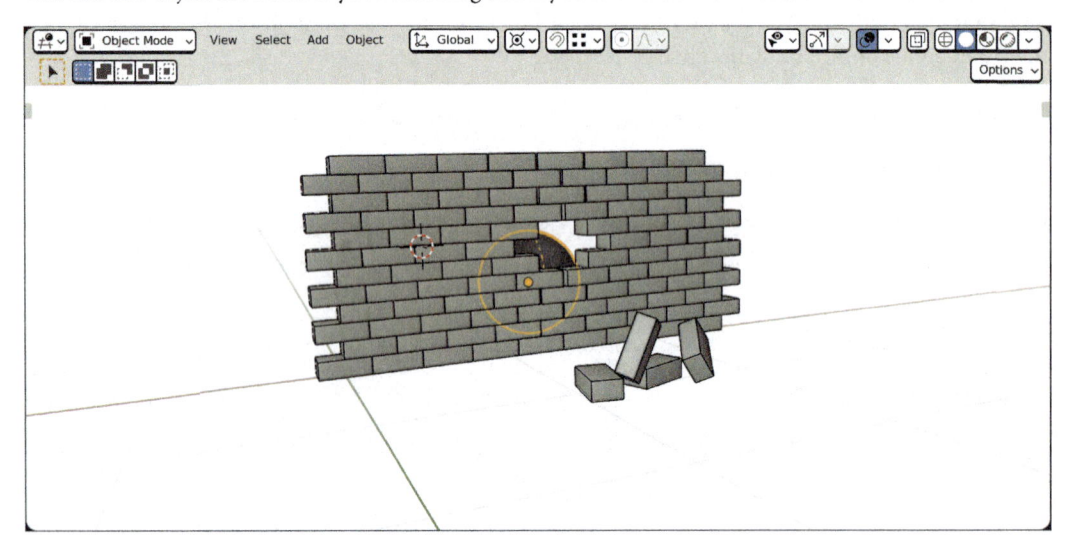

Figure 12.26: The result of a wrecking ball with low mass

That's the last part! Now we've thrown the wrecking ball and allowed it to smash into the wall while behaving like any other rigid body.

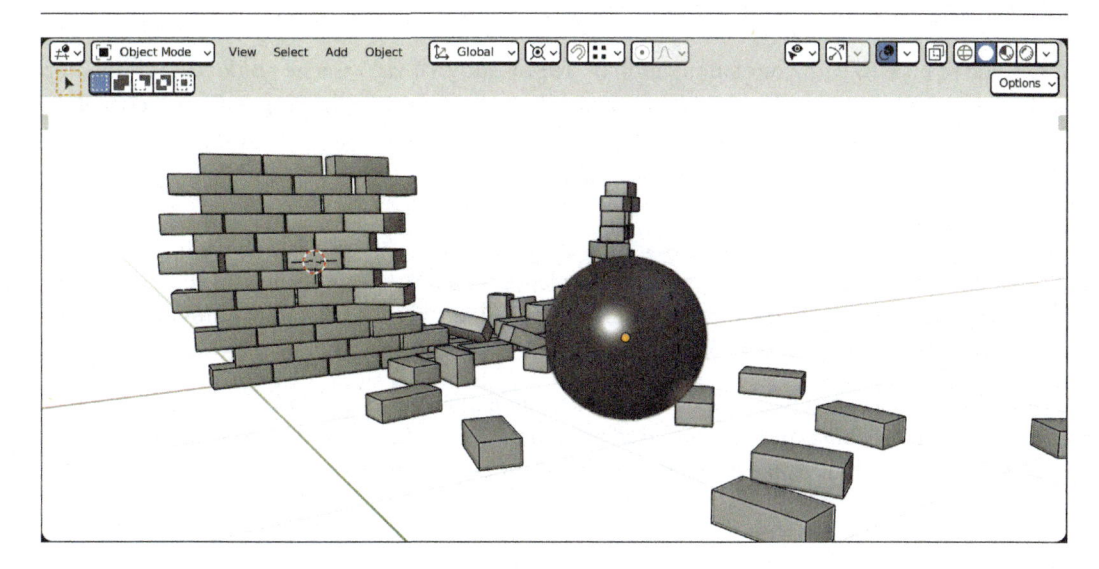

Figure 12.27: Final result

Keep playing with your simulation until you like what you see. Next, we'll learn how to save our work (or, more accurately, the work that Blender has done).

Baking the simulation

So far, we've been simulating "on the fly." With each minor change we make to the scene, the cache automatically clears and the simulation is recalculated so we can see what our changes did. This is fun when our simulations are lightweight and we're continuously experimenting, but eventually, we'll consider ourselves finished. Our simulation results will be perfect, and then we'll want to keep everything the way it is without having to worry about accidentally making a tiny change that clears the cache and changes the result. We certainly wouldn't want to ruin all our destruction!

This is why it's important to **bake** the simulation:

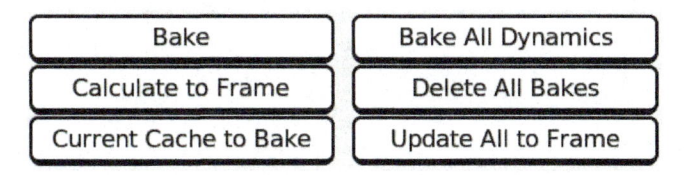

Figure 12.28: Bake, and other operators for updating the cache

Bake is a broad term that appears in many applications and even refers to multiple features in Blender. To bake a simulation is to calculate it in advance and save the result. For simulations such as **Fluid** or **Cloth**, this often takes a long time, and in such cases is the most reliable way to compute a simulation. You can think of baking as kind of like rendering, but for data besides images.

When you're pleased with your simulation, use **Rigid Body World | Cache | Bake**. The simulation data will be saved alongside the `.blend` file and persist after you close the project. Click **Delete Bake** to "unbake" and resume editing the simulation.

Summary

When it comes to Blender's rigid body physics, Blender uses a lot of the same principles and terminology (and potentially the same code in some cases) as for the physics simulation that's provided in many other applications. This includes some game engines.

I wish I could do a chapter on every kind of physics simulation, but that would be a whole book on its own. We have more things to animate and more cameras with which to view them! Specifically, we'll learn how to use multiple cameras in an animation and capture the action from all angles.

Questions

1. Decide whether the following objects are rigid bodies: Raindrop. Pencil. Baseball. Sock. Burrito. Frozen burrito. Horse.
2. What is a rigid body world? Are you in a rigid body world right now? Can you escape?
3. How do you adjust the global scale of a rigid body world?
4. What's the point of rigid bodies that don't move?
5. Picture a mug resting on a table. In the case of both Blender and in real life, is it technically accurate to say the mug is *colliding* with the table?
6. What's the technical reason for why concave shapes are so problematic in rigid body physics?
7. Does **Active** mean simply that a rigid body moves, or does it mean something more specific? Does **Dynamic** mean the same thing? What about **Animated**?
8. What happens when an unstoppable force meets an immovable object? This is not a koan or rhetorical question – seriously, what happens when you do this in Blender?

# 13
Animating with Multiple Cameras

In live-action filmmaking, cameras can be expensive pieces of equipment. No such costs hold us back in the land of computer graphics, however! As animators, we can have as many cameras in a scene as we like. We can render with certain cameras at certain times and view the scene through others. More importantly, we can time the cuts between cameras as easily as one inserts keyframes.

It's hard to think of an animation where this couldn't be useful. Have you ever seen a movie that appeared to be a single take, performed in front of just one camera? Alright, fine, me too, but it's not common! For our animation projects that aren't short clips, exercises from a tutorial, or avant-garde experiments in filmmaking, we'll need to learn how to choose between multiple cameras. In fact, we'll learn how to make *time* itself do the camera selection for us, one camera after the other. Then, we'll throw aside what we just told time to do and render with every camera at once.

In this chapter, you'll explore the following:

- Previewing the scene with multiple cameras
- Switching between cameras using the Timeline
- Switching between cameras in the Video Sequencer

Technical requirements

Having multiple cameras is useful in almost any animation, so this is an open-ended chapter. To follow along, you can use any animation in Blender you like, be it an exercise from this book or anything else you're currently working on.

For my example, I'll use a scene featuring a conversation between two characters:

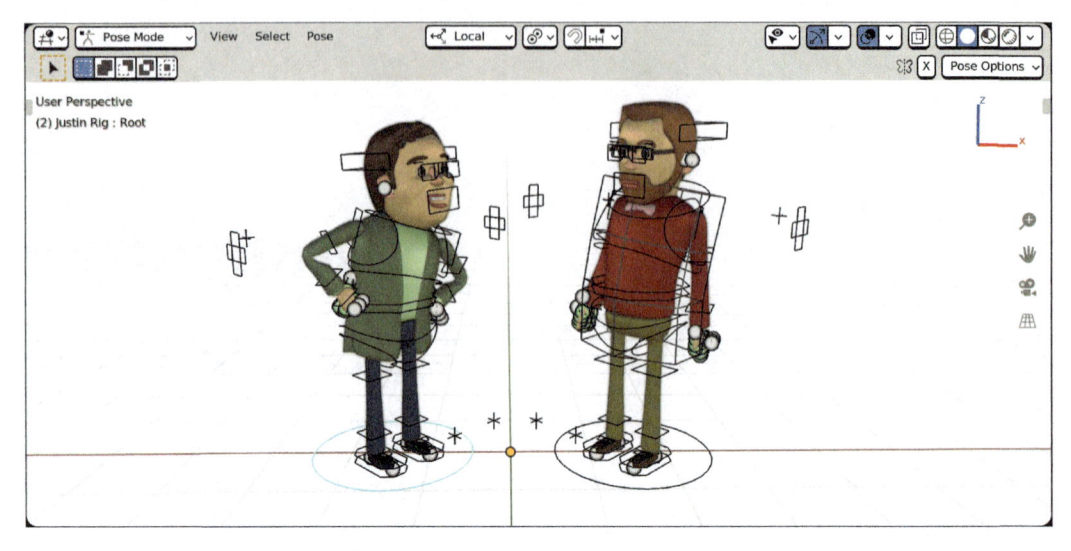

Figure 13.1: A scene with two characters

In live-action productions, scenes such as these are often recorded on a set with two or more cameras. It doesn't need to be so different in Blender.

Ready camera two

If a one-eyed man says, "I've got my eye on you," we know which eye he's talking about. For anyone with more eyes than that, we need them to specify. Which eye are we talking about here? If we think of cameras in Blender as eyes, we'll need to answer a similar question if we've got more than one.

To start, let's make sure our scene has some cameras in it.

Setting up multiple cameras

Adding cameras to your scene is almost too easy. If you know how to add your first camera with **Add** (*Shift* + *A*) | **Camera**, then you know how to add a second camera with **Add** (*Shift* + *A*) | **Camera**. To add the third camera, we use **Add** (*Shift* + *A*) | **Camera** and adding the fourth camera is as easy as using **Add** (*Shift* + *A*) | **Camera**... you get the idea.

Here's my scene with three cameras:

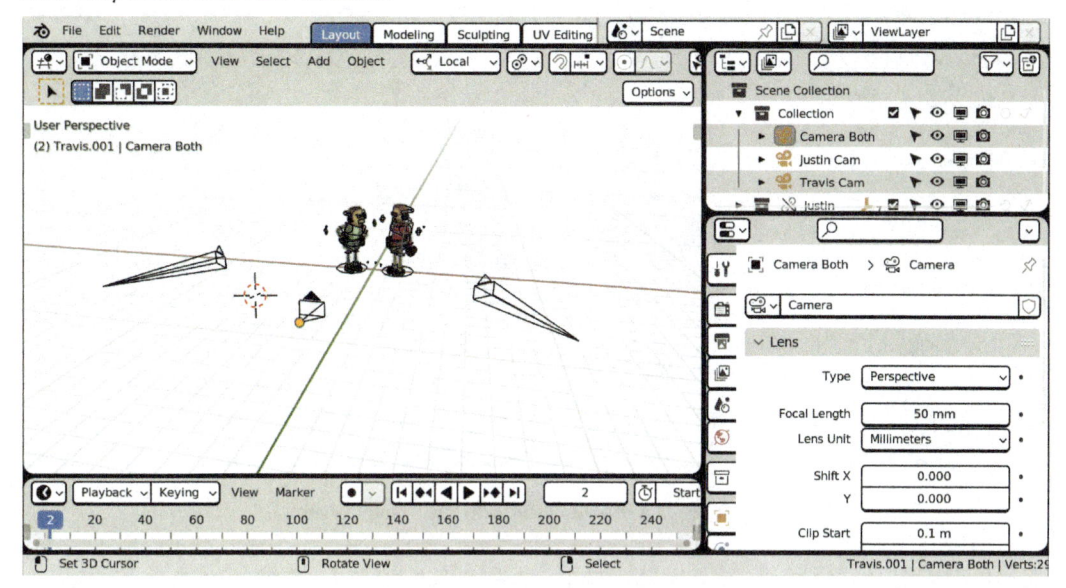

Figure 13.2: A scene with three cameras

By default, each camera object uses its own unique **Camera Data**—properties such as **Focal Length** and **Aperture**. So, in addition to being in different places and pointed at different things, your multiple cameras can have various settings in this regard. As with many other things, it also helps if you give your cameras specific names besides `Camera.001`, `Camera.002`, etc.

Once you've got at least two cameras in your scene, you'll then need to know how to actually look through that second camera or get it to render anything.

The active camera

When using multiple cameras in a scene, our main concern is knowing which camera is the **active camera**—the camera used by default to render and view the scene. By navigating to **View** | **Viewpoint** | **Camera** (*Numpad 0*), you'll be looking through the active camera:

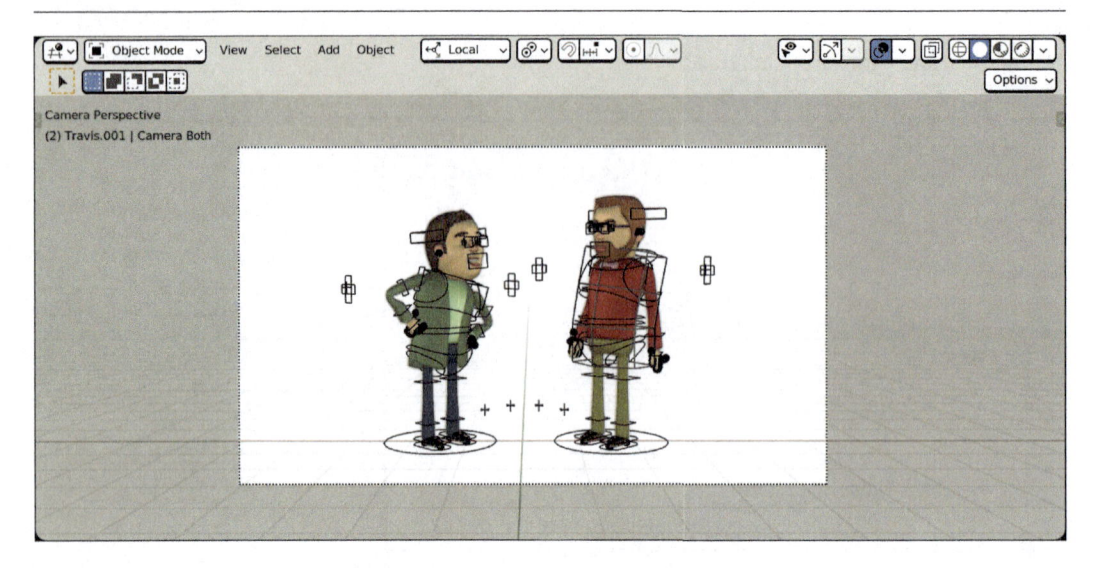

Figure 13.3: Camera view through the active camera

Likewise, for the same result, you can take the **Render | Render Frame** (*F12*) route. If one camera is all you have, that's almost certainly the active one and you don't have to think about it any further. If you start out with zero cameras and add one, it will automatically be made active. There can only be one active camera at a time.

After the first one, each extra camera we add to the scene will be inactive:

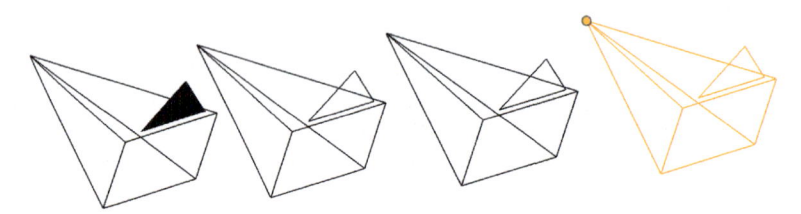

Figure 13.4: One active camera and several non-active cameras

Note the minor difference in how active vs. inactive cameras are drawn in the 3D Viewport. These additional cameras will not view or render anything unless we make one of them active or select them specifically in other contexts that we'll learn about later in this chapter.

Here's how we make an inactive camera active:

1. Select a camera.
2. Click **View | Cameras | Set Active Object as Camera** (*Ctrl + Numpad 0*).

> **Tip**
> The active camera is a property of the **Scene** and can also be accessed via **Scene Properties | Scene | Camera**.

Now I can view and render the scene through another camera:

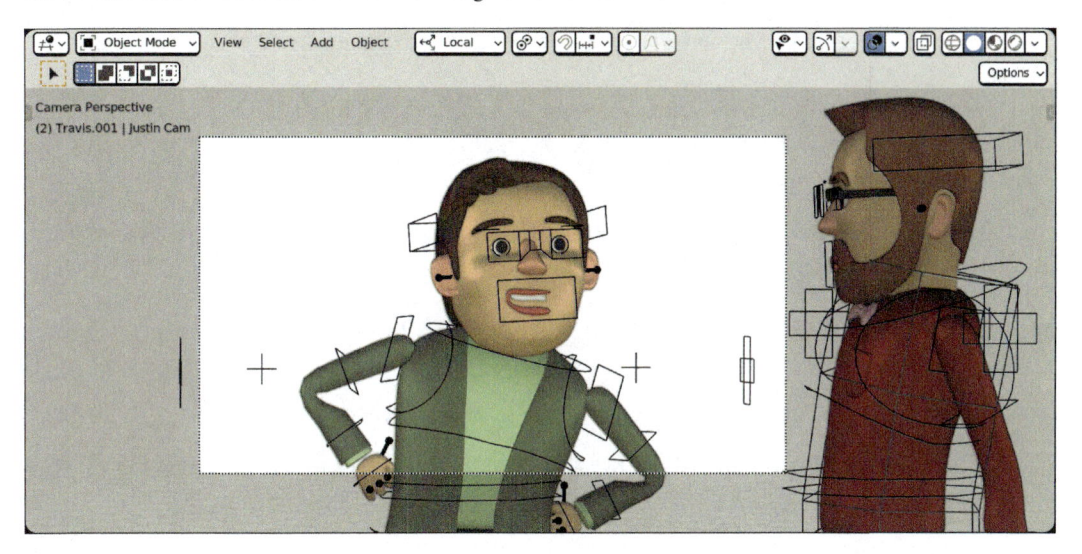

Figure 13.5: Camera view through a second camera

> **Tip**
> You might accidentally discover that any kind of object—not just a camera—can be made an active camera. Though this has limited usefulness, it may occasionally come in handy from time to time, such as when you wish to view the scene from the perspective of a **Spot Light**.

Okay, great, but the first camera, which was just active, is now inactive. Like before, we're still viewing and rendering the scene with one active camera and multiple inactive cameras that don't do anything. This raises a question: how does any of this become useful? Let's find out.

Switching cameras in the Timeline

After all of this talk of keyframes, armatures, and esotericism about object relationships, it's finally time to perform, in our animation, what might be the most basic technique in film editing: cutting from one camera to another.

Recall what I said about there only being one active camera at a time. Using the Timeline, we can establish which camera is to be the active one at any given frame.

We can do this not with keyframes, but with *markers*:

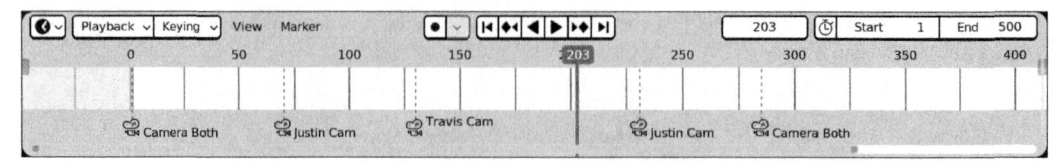

Figure 13.6: Markers in the Timeline bound to different cameras

Markers are funny things. Generally, they're meant to "mark" a frame for the animator's own reference, and we don't need to use them if we don't want to… that is, unless they're the kind that switch active cameras, in which case they're indispensable!

To make a marker in the Timeline that changes the active camera, we must **Bind** that camera to a marker. Here's how to do so:

1. Go to the frame at which you want to change active cameras.
2. Select the camera.
3. In the Timeline, Use **Marker | Bind Camera to Markers** (*Ctrl + B*).

    This inserts a camera-shaped marker at the current frame, to which the camera bearing its name is bound.

4. Repeat these steps for another camera on another frame.

> **Tip**
> It's good practice to use **Bind Camera to Markers** at the first frame of your animation so as to be unambiguous about which camera is the starting active camera.

When a camera is bound to a marker, it will be the active camera for all frames after that marker until another marker that is bound to another camera is reached. The switching of cameras using markers is faithfully obeyed when the animation is rendered, as it is when you play back the animation in **Camera View**.

Since markers can be selected, moved, and duplicated like keyframes, we can easily make lots of cuts and adjust where each one occurs:

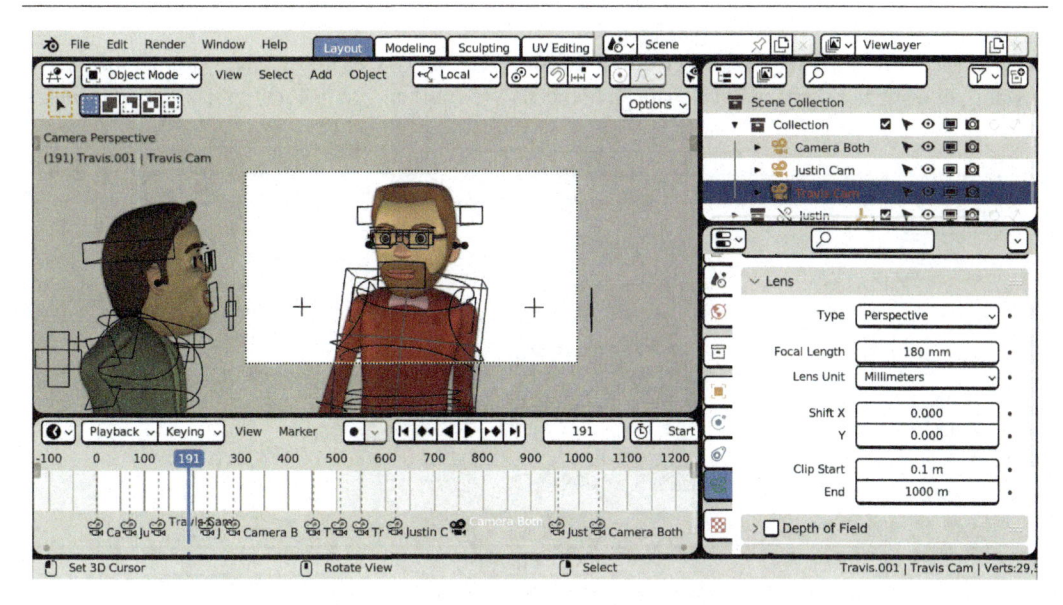

Figure 13.7: Lots of camera switching in the Timeline

Knowing this method of switching cameras gives us access to a technique that is ubiquitous in nearly all films and television shows!

Solely using the active camera to both view and render our scenes has its limitations, however. After all, there can only be one active camera at a time, and sometimes that's not enough. For those cases, we have some extra features at our disposal.

Camera overrides

Knowing what the active camera does and how to change it is not the whole story. What if we want to view or render the scene with something other than the active camera? There are reasons for and methods of doing so.

Viewing with a local camera

When we play the animation in **Camera View**, the played-back animation faithfully switches cameras where it ought to, so we get an idea of how the rendered animation will look in realtime. Depending on the circumstances though, this camera switching might not be what we want to see all the time. Say we've got a camera that is not active, but we want to review a part of the animation through that camera anyway. Or maybe we need to look through that camera in order to figure out exactly when we ought to switch to it.

In such cases, you can always make a camera the **local camera**. To set up a camera as such for a given viewport, open up the right-hand sidebar (*N*) of the 3D Viewport and go to **View** | **View** | **Local Camera**:

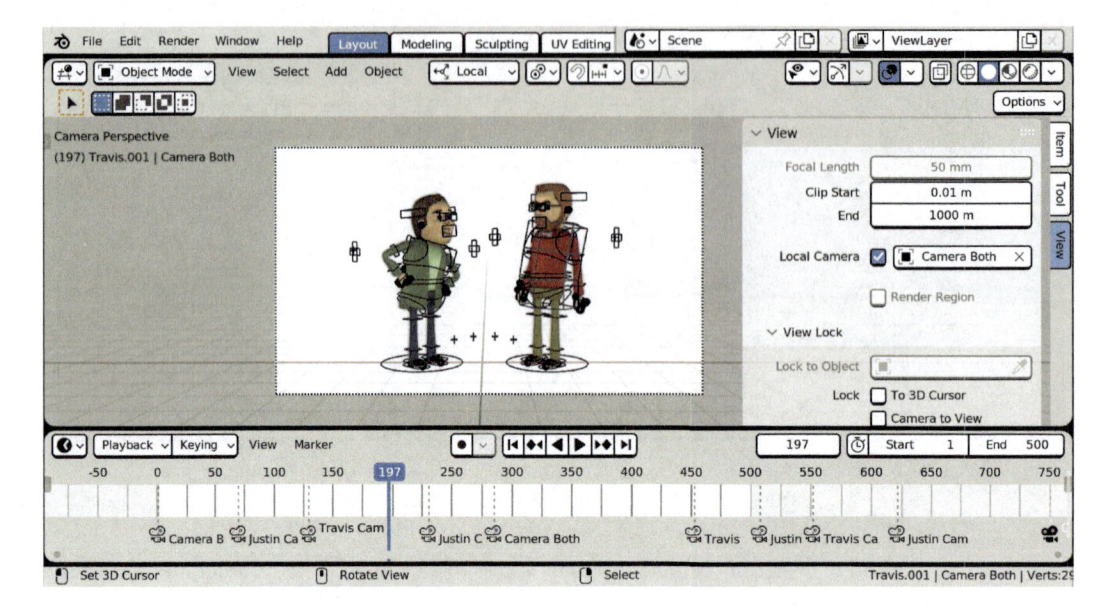

Figure 13.8: The Local Camera feature in the View tab

> **Tip**
> The **Local Camera** property is "local" to each particular 3D Viewport in which it is set. You can customize your user interface to include as many of these viewports as your computer can handle.

We now know a helpful trick for sticking to just one camera in a 3D Viewport. Next, we'll check out a completely different kind of camera override.

Using multiple cameras in the Video Sequencer

We know how to view the scene without the active camera, so now let's consider the other scenario: what if we want to *render* the scene without the active camera? Doing so would let us render the same moment from multiple angles, among other things:

Figure 13.9: A single jumping animation seen from different cameras

To accomplish this, we must turn one more time to our old friend, the Video Sequencer.

Using scene strips

Starting with an animated scene with multiple cameras, let's give ourselves a video sequence that contains that scene as a **scene strip**:

1. Add a new scene to your project (scenes are added and selected using the field in the top-right of your window).
2. Name the scene something such as Sequence so you'll remember what it's for.
3. Open a **Video Sequence** editor in the user interface.
4. In the **Video Sequence** editor, go to **Add** (*Shift + A*) | **Scene** to add, as a **Scene Strip**, the original scene you wish to render.
5. Find the **View Type** setting in the header of the Video Sequencer and set it to **Sequencer & Preview**.

You should now have one scene strip in the sequencer:

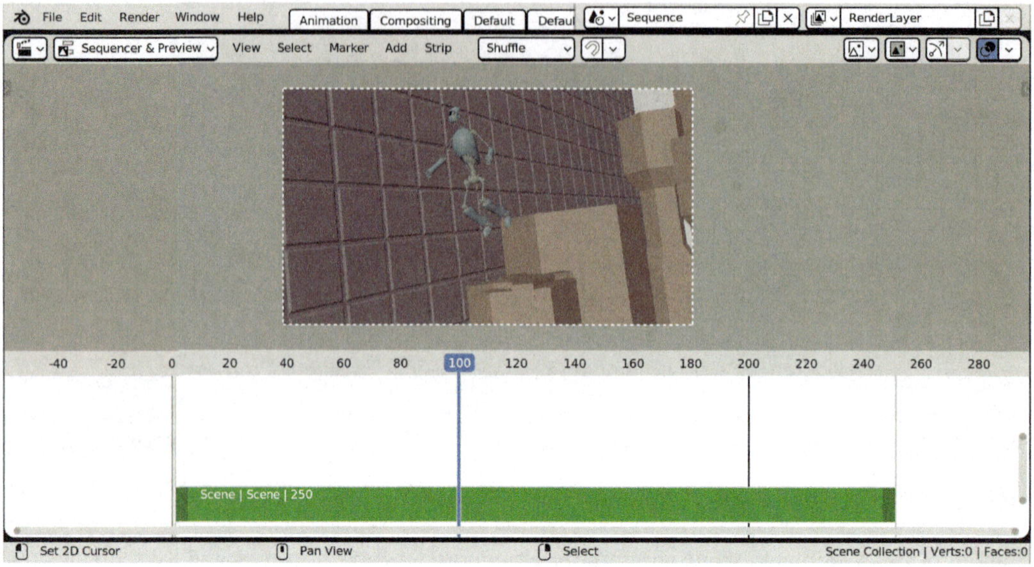

Figure 13.10: A scene strip in the Video Sequencer

Scene strips are a powerful and underrated feature. They represent the frames of a given scene to be rendered and can be edited just like **Movie** or **Image/Sequence** strips, allowing us to perform video editing techniques on and add effects to one or more scenes before they're rendered. The scenes in the scene strips are automatically rendered as needed when the sequence scene is rendered, letting us skip the step where we would otherwise have to render each scene beforehand and import it back into Blender as a **Movie** or **Image/Sequence**. While editing in the **Video Sequencer**, a real time **Camera View** of the scene is used in lieu of a rendered frame to produce what we see in the **Preview** region.

> **Tip**
>
> In the right-hand sidebar (*N*), you can go to **View | Scene Strip Display | Shading** to select how scene strips are previewed in the Video Sequencer. Don't expect **Rendered** to be very fast.

If we have a project with multiple animated scenes, we can sequence those scenes together as scene strips in any order we like, along with transitions and effects, and then render the whole thing in one pass. But even if we have just one scene, we can use the sequencer to take advantage of multiple cameras in a scene.

Selecting a camera for the scene strip

One useful feature of scene strips is located in the right-hand sidebar (*N*) of the Video Sequencer, under **Strip | Scene**:

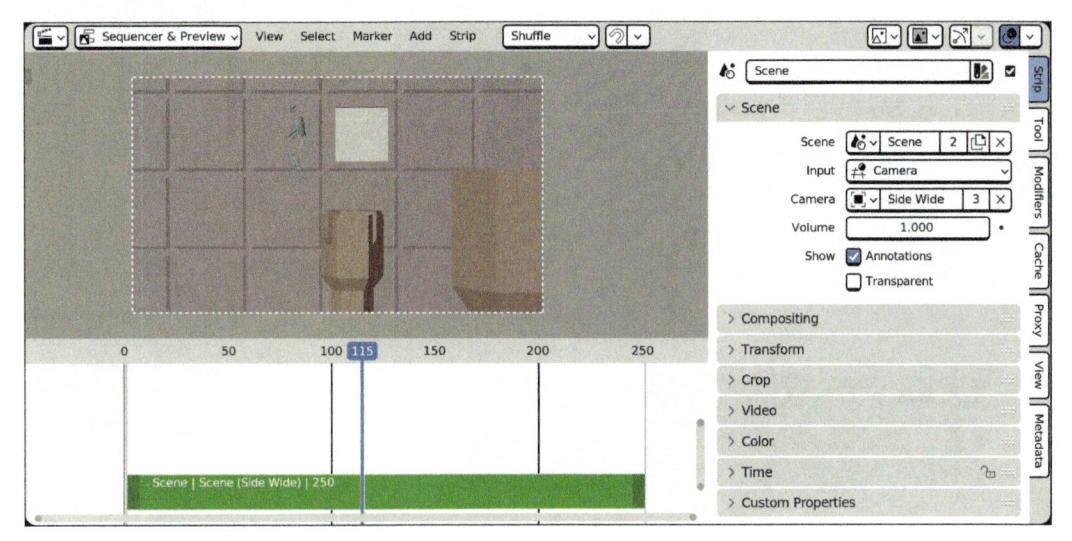

Figure 13.11: Camera property of a scene strip

By default, the scene strip uses the active camera for that scene to render, just as if we rendered the scene within itself like normal. When not blank, however, the **Camera** property of a scene strip overrides the active camera and renders the scene with the chosen camera instead.

No longer constrained by linear time or active camera settings, we can use this feature to render from any camera in the scene, in any order, at any time. To do that, take the following steps:

1. Duplicate (*Shift* + *D*) the scene strip as many times as you have cameras in the scene you wish to use.
2. Open the right-hand sidebar (*N*) of the Video Sequencer and find **Strip | Scene | Camera**.
3. For each strip in your sequence, select the strip and choose a different camera for the **Camera** property.
4. Edit the sequence as desired using **Move** (*G*) or any other tools you like.

Even though there can only be one active camera in a scene at one time, that no longer holds us back. Now we can make instant replays of the same moment in time from multiple camera angles.

And that's only the beginning; the Video Sequencer opens all sorts of possibilities when it comes to layering scene strips together. In this example, a **Wipe** transition is used, not to transition from one strip to the next but to split the frame between two simultaneous strips using two different cameras:

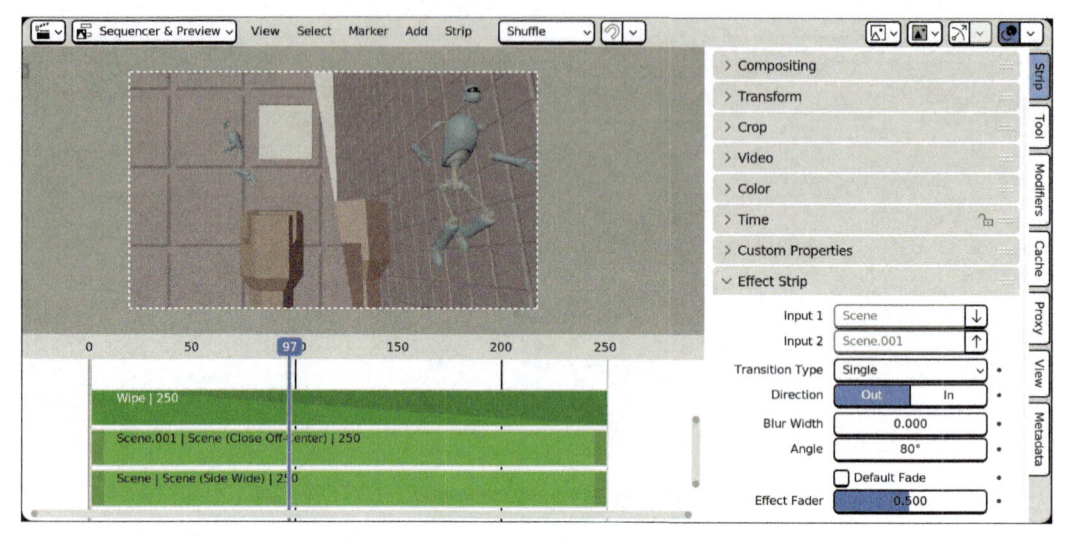

Figure 13.12: Split-screen effect in the Video Sequencer

What effects will you come up with?

Summary

I wasn't kidding about live-action cameras being expensive. The best ones cost thousands of dollars to rent, plus a large deposit. And that's just for the camera itself; you'll also need mounting equipment such as tripods, cranes, dollies, and stabilizers to keep this often very heavy camera upright. Then you've got to hire a specially-trained operator just to use the camera, and he's got to have lunch breaks or he'll get tired and drop the camera and you'll lose your deposit (you do *not* want to lose your deposit).

Good thing that's none of our business! In Blender, cameras are cheaper than dirt and lighter than air, and we don't need to pay anybody union wages to operate them. Incidentally, that last part is a big reason why 3D animation has become so widespread this century, but that's a conversation for another time.

As for the final chapter of this book, you may recall linear time being mentioned earlier, specifically with regard to not needing to be constrained by it. Could this suggest that our animations need not be linear, or even that there might be an animation editor of the non-linear variety? The answer may astound you!

Questions

1. Why might we want multiple cameras in a scene?
2. If we couldn't use multiple cameras, how might we get around this limitation and still animate the effect of switching between cameras? What complications might arise from doing so?
3. Why is the operator called **Bind Camera to Markers** if it creates a marker, and only one marker at that?
4. "The active camera is the camera used to view and render the scene." Is the previous statement always true?
5. How many different ways can you fool a Blender user who thinks they're rendering a frame of the current scene with the active camera?
6. If we wanted to render the same segment of frames with different cameras, but we couldn't use the Video Sequencer, what else could we do?
7. How can you use the `Sequence` scene itself as a scene strip in another sequence?
8. If you render a frame of a sequencer scene containing a sequence of scene strips, one of which is of another sequencer scene containing a sequence of scene strips, can one of the scene strips in that second sequence be of the same scene as a scene strip within the first sequence but of a different frame?
9. What's a segmentation fault? Did you just have one?

14
Nonlinear Animation

Where do keyframes live? In the Timeline? The Graph Editor? The Dope Sheet? Sure, these three editors can access keyframes for editing, but are the keyframes really there? Perhaps the real keyframes are in the slider of an animated property whenever it turns yellow, or maybe they live behind Blender's user interface and scatter like roaches every time you minimize the window. *Maybe there's a keyframe behind you right now.*

The truth is these are all silly answers, but *Where do keyframes live?* is a serious question with a real answer. Keyframes live in F-Curves, which are the same thing as animation channels. Animation channels live in actions, and actions – the ones that directly affect the animation, at least – live in the **Nonlinear Animation editor**.

Also known as the **NLA**, the Nonlinear Animation editor is the executive headquarters of every animation in Blender. With this editor, whole actions can be sped up, slowed down, combined, and overlapped, all while bypassing what appears in the Timeline, Dope Sheet, and Graph Editor. This makes it an excellent tool for character animation at what I'll call a *higher level*, which means animating not with keyframes but with multiple actions at once!

In this chapter, we'll take advantage of the NLA's functionality to make Rain walk and talk at the same time, combining two actions we created previously.

You'll learn how to do the following:

- Import previously made actions into a new animation
- Extend and repeat an action in the NLA
- Layer multiple actions in the NLA
- Dynamically control time for an action

Technical requirements

The Nonlinear Animation editor is well suited for combining multiple actions in a single character animation. To try that out, create a new project featuring our favorite character rig, Rain, as we've done in every character animation exercise since *Chapter 6*.

In addition, we'll need two actions that are suitable for combining. If you completed the exercises in *Chapter 8* and *Chapter 9* and saved your work, then you've already got two such actions, a lip-syncing action, and a walk-cycle action:

Figure 14.1: Rain walking, Rain talking

Using the Nonlinear Animation editor, we will non-destructively combine these actions to have Rain walk and talk at the same time.

Reusing actions

Actions are an interesting type of data block. They store all the animation channels for an object; we've been making them since the start of this book, yet we've scarcely needed to think about them. Actions are created automatically, and there's usually just one action per object for the whole animation. When we first keyed the location of Cube in *Chapter 1*, an action was automatically created called CubeAction. Thenceforth, every keyframe for every property belonging to Cube was stored in the aptly named CubeAction action, and that was that. Blender never prompted us about this. Why would we need it to?

The same goes for all the other animations we worked on, including animations of the character Rain. Every time we animated Rain in a new project, we created an action for her, thinking only of the keyframes in that action and never the action itself as a container of animation data. Sometimes, however, there are actions-qua-actions we do want to think about, as is often the case for character animation, especially particular actions... like a walk cycle.

Appending the walk cycle

A character's walk cycle might be the single most reusable action in a project. We'll begin this exercise by importing the walk cycle we created in *Chapter 8*, which should be called `Rain Walkcycle`, into a new animation.

Let's append the walk cycle from the other `.blend` file into our new project:

1. Use **File | Append** and navigate to the `.blend` file you created for the walk-cycle exercise.
2. Append the `Rain Walkcycle` action.

Using **Append** instead of **Link** avoids creating another dependency between two `.blend` files and makes it easier to edit the walk cycle from within the current `.blend` file. Using **Link** is still a viable and sometimes necessary option, though. As we will see later, the Nonlinear Animation editor allows us to control the animation using appended and/or linked actions alike without altering the action itself.

After using **Append**, you'll see no immediate change, but `Rain Walkcycle` is available for us to assign to our character.

Assigning an action in the Action Editor

Just because we appended the walk cycle doesn't mean Rain will start walking. We've got to assign the action specifically to Rain's armature. Actions can be assigned within the Action Editor, which is basically just like the Dope Sheet, except it edits one action at a time and gives us this very important field in the middle of the header:

Figure 14.2: The Active Action for the active object

This field is blank because Rain is not yet animated. Or perhaps Rain is not yet animated because this field is blank. Either way, let's change that now:

1. Select Rain's armature object `RIG-rain`.
2. Bring up the Action Editor by going to the **Dope Sheet** and changing the **Editing Context** to **Action Editor**.
3. In the header of the **Action Editor**, select the action `Rain Walkcycle`.

Now Rain should be walking exactly as she did before…

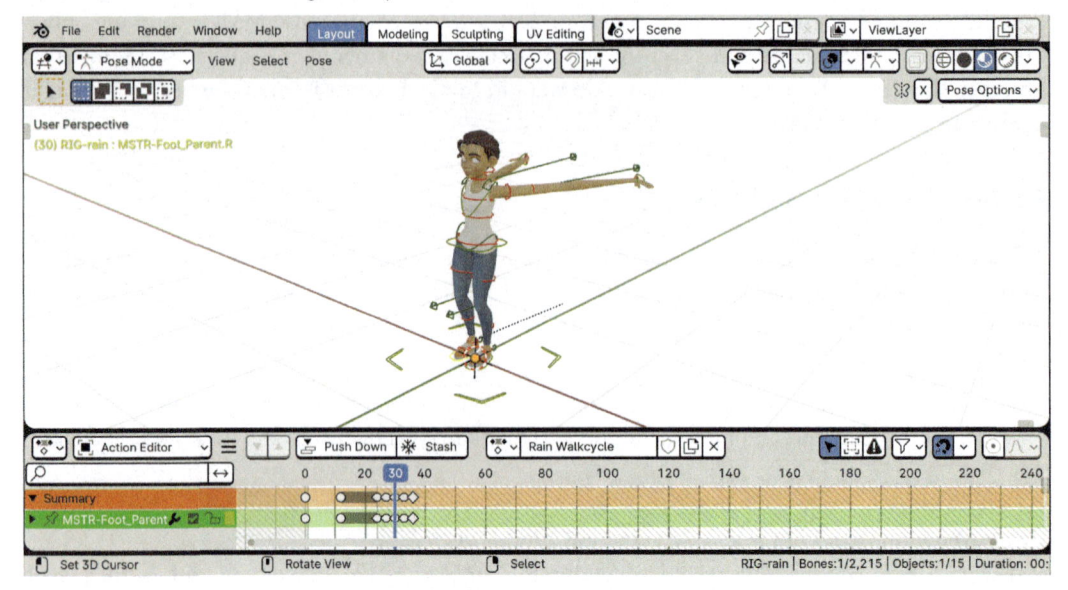

Figure 14.3: A completely normal walk cycle

Well, maybe not exactly. We'll get to fixing that in a minute.

Hidden actions

As you selected `Rain Walkcycle` from the available actions, you may have noticed a whole bunch of other actions cluttering up the list:

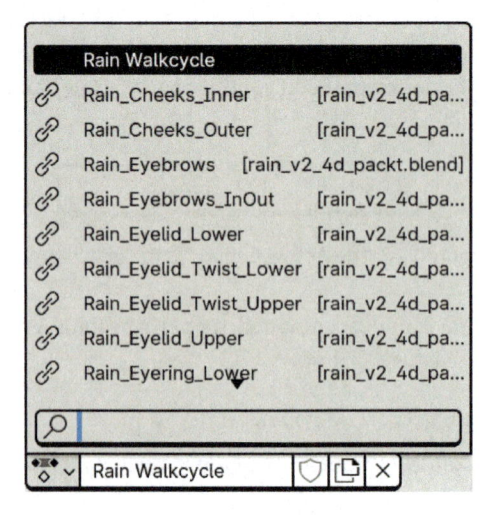

Figure 14.4: List of actions

We don't remember creating these or even appending them!

That's because these other actions were made when Rain was rigged. Not all actions are meant to be used directly in an animation. These additional actions are used by Action Constraints – special constraints that control parts of Rain's armature. The action is "played" by the movement of one or more target bones, enabling those bones to control more complex movements.

I wasn't kidding when I said character rigs are complex! On that note, let's figure out why Rain currently walks all messed up.

A hard lesson in forgotten settings

The issue we're seeing is common when one assigns an action. Recall that, at the start of the walk-cycle exercise, we adjusted some important properties in Rain's rig such as her **FK/IK Switch** settings. But we didn't key those properties, did we? For any bone we posed or value we changed, if we didn't key it, the action has nothing to do with it; whatever we did to that property will not carry over to the new scene. There's no animation data for it, and animation data is the only thing an action has!

That means we'll have to manually fix these left-behind properties ourselves. To do that, follow the next steps:

1. Go to Rain's **CloudRig** settings.

   Under **CloudRig | Settings | FK/IK Switch**, set Rain's arms to use *FK* and her spine to use *IK*.

2. Set **Face Settings | Eye Target Parent** to *Torso_Loc* (2).

Once again, Rain walks like we remember:

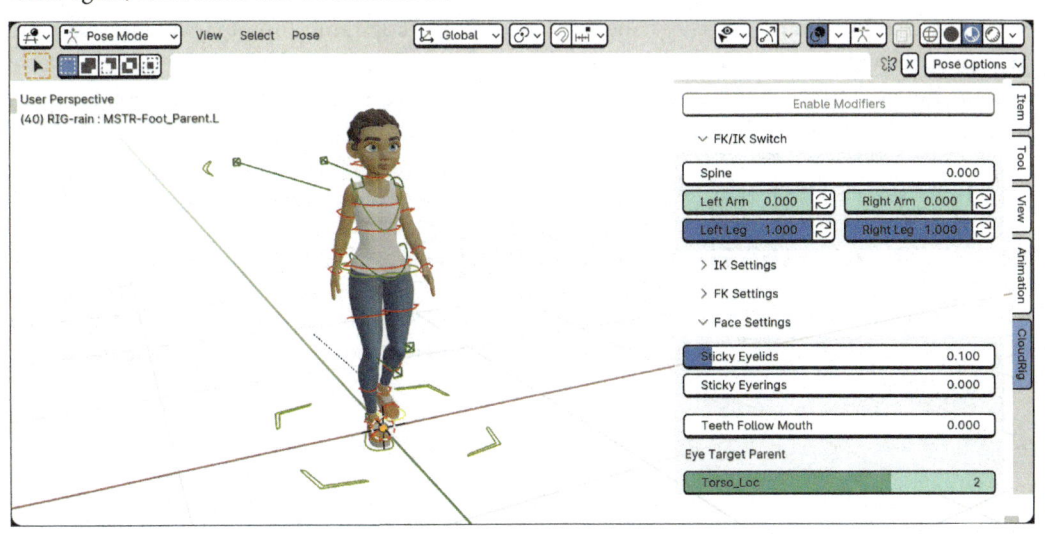

Figure 14.5: Rain, with restored settings

> **Tip**
> To avoid having this issue in the first place, all you need to do is remember to insert just one keyframe for any specific bone that must be posed or property that must to set for the action to work as expected. Keying the pose/property stores it in the action so that it accompanies the rest of the animation data when the action is appended.

Having appended the walk-cycle action and assigned it to Rain, it works the same as any action created automatically when one inserts their first keyframes. And now that we've corrected any remaining settings that straggled behind in the original `.blend` file, it's pretty much as if we had created the walk cycle in the current one. Using the Timeline, the Dope Sheet, or the Graph Editor, we can edit and insert keyframes as normal.

Here's the thing, though – we don't need to edit this action. In fact, we're going to use it in a way that makes it easy to add an additional action and control them both while leaving their data largely unaltered.

The action strip

Consider some basic things we might want to do to Rain's walking animation:

- Offset the walk cycle in time
- Speed up or slow down Rain's pace
- Start/stop the walk cycle (or, put another way, repeat the cycle a finite number of times)

For all these tasks, we already know one solution: edit the keyframes! In other words, select the keyframes, then move them, scale them, or duplicate them as needed. That's often a perfectly good solution, but not always. Editing keyframes means editing the action, which is problematic if you linked that action or if you don't want to duplicate or overwrite it.

That's where the Nonlinear Animation editor comes in.

Introduction to the Nonlinear Animation editor

While you may have thought your animations were controlled solely by the keyframes that appear in the Dope Sheet, the Timeline, and the Graph Editor, another area in Blender was pulling the strings this whole time:

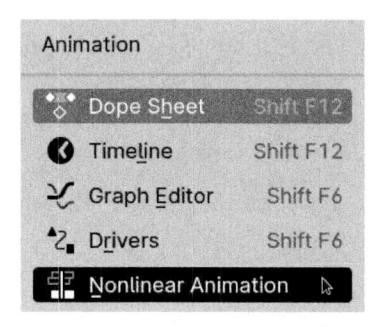

Figure 14.6: All the animation editors

Ever wonder what that last one does? Here's a brief explanation.

When you move a keyframe, you are editing the action, because keyframes live inside actions. This is not only true for the Action Editor; as a matter of fact, the Action Editor is called that only because it edits one action at a time. The Dope Sheet, Graph Editor, and Timeline all edit actions. Everything we've been calling animation so far can be thought of as "action editing," in much the same way that 3D modeling might be called "object editing."

Here's the thing, though: the NLA does not edit the action. Instead, the NLA edits the animation by controlling the action as a discrete element.

Viewing the Nonlinear Animation editor

At first glance, we can see the NLA displays a row for every object with animation data:

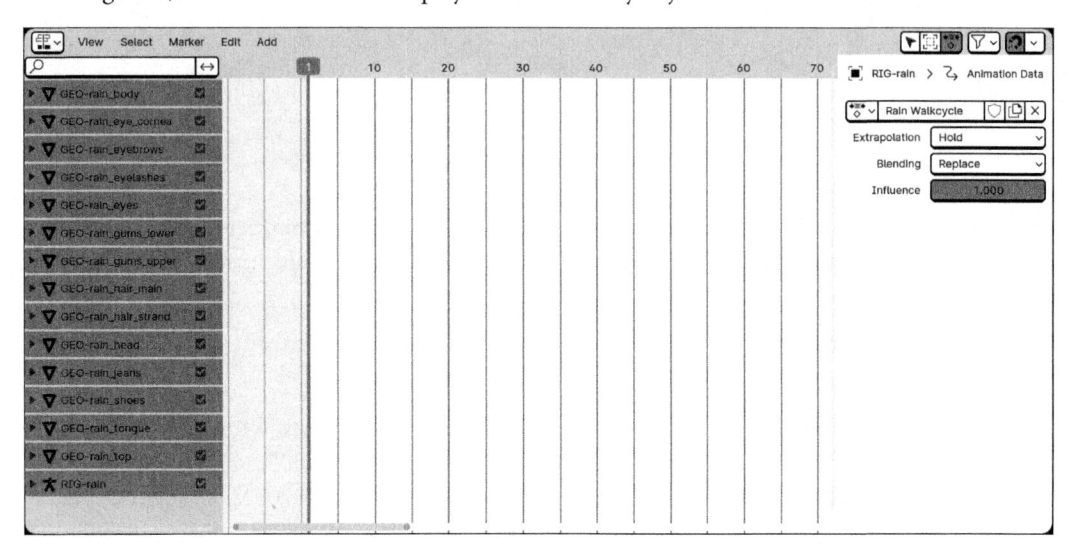

Figure 14.7: The Nonlinear Animation editor, or NLA

As expected, this includes `RIG-rain`, but it also includes some objects we don't remember animating: this is because Rain comes with a lot of drivers, and drivers count as animation data too (though the NLA does not display those drivers). Remember how we also saw a bunch of actions we don't remember creating? When a character rig is linked/appended, it can bring a lot of unexpected data with it.

That doesn't mean we have to look at it, though! We're only concerned with the animation of `RIG-rain`, so let's go to the NLA and hide everything else:

1. Bring up the **Nonlinear Animation** editor.
2. In the header, disable **Include Missing NLA**.

This gets rid of all those empty rows. Now, there's just one for `RIG-rain`, which is all we need to see:

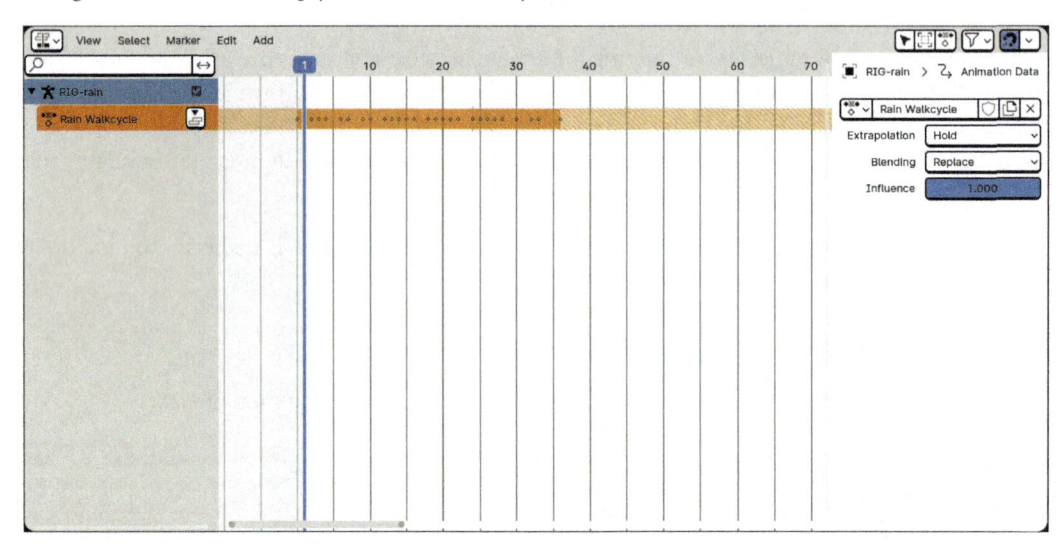

Figure 14.8: A cleaner NLA showing Rain's animation data

Initially, there's not much going on in the NLA except for a row of keyframes that can't be selected and some properties in the right-hand sidebar (*N*) that don't seem to do much. Let's figure out what's going on here.

Actions in the NLA

When you expand the NLA row for `RIG-rain`, you'll see the keyframes in `Rain Walkcycle`, which became the Active Action when we selected it for Rain in the Action Editor. The Active Action is the action for an object that is exposed in all the other animation editors besides the NLA. Every action we've created in this book thus far has been an Active Action; it's another thing in Blender that has always been with us even though we haven't needed to think about it.

There's not much we can do with just the Active Action in the Nonlinear Animation editor. The NLA becomes useful when we turn the Active Action into something called an **action strip**.

"Pushing down" an action

An action strip is an action that can be moved through time and manipulated in the Nonlinear Animation editor, much like the different strips in Blender's Video Sequencer.

It's easier to explain what an action strip does after we create one, which we can do with the present Active Action. All you need to do is go to the left-hand sidebar of the NLA and click the **Push Down Action** button – the little one next to the Active Action's name:

1. In the left-hand sidebar, expand the animation tracks under `RIG-rain`.
2. Click the **Push Down Action** button for the Active Action.

To push down an action is to convert it into an action strip and put it in a new NLA track for the object to which the action belonged.

The `Rain Walkcycle` action is now an action strip:

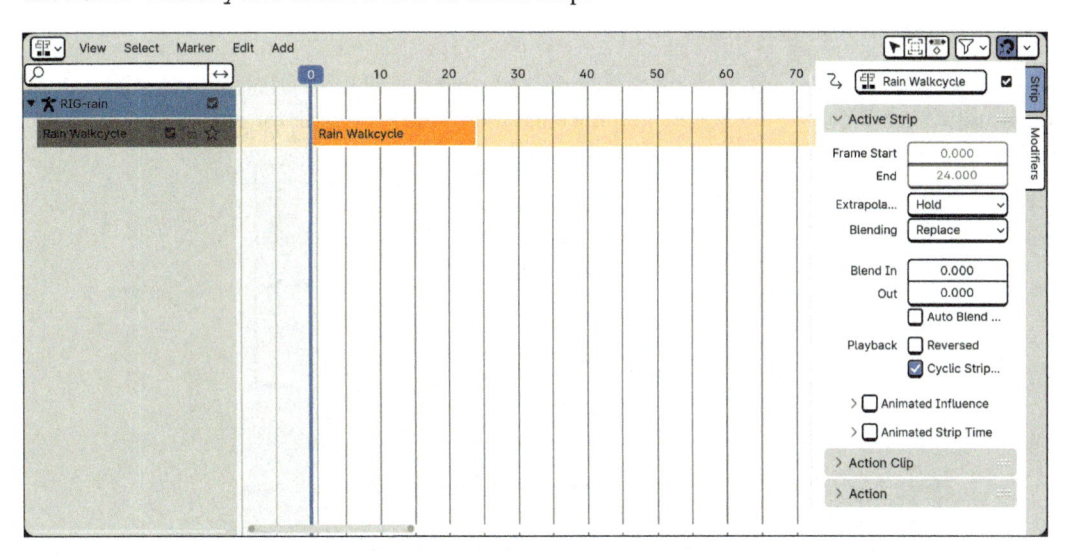

Figure 14.9: An action strip in the NLA

What we just did completely changes how our animation works in a way we haven't seen before. Go to any other animation editor – you'll no longer see keyframes for `Rain Walkcycle` in the Timeline, Graph Editor, or Dope Sheet. It's as if the keyframes are gone… yet Rain is still animated!

What's happening is that the NLA has taken over the animation. From this point onward, if we want to know what's going on with Rain's movement, we must refer to the NLA, which controls our character's animation with one or more action strips.

Next, we'll learn just what this action strip can do.

Using the action strip

What is an action strip, really? Put simply, what you're looking at is the entire action wrapped up as a single discrete object that can be moved in time along the track. Move the action strip in either direction, and Rain begins walking earlier or later.

This is like selecting and moving all our keyframes at once but with one important difference: the action strip moves, and not the individual keyframes. Like passengers seated aboard a moving train, the keyframes stay exactly where they are within the action, and as a data block, the action remains unaltered. It's analogous to moving an object in **Object Mode**; the object moves as a whole, while its data – vertices, edges, and faces – remains fixed to the object.

For our present exercise, we can leave the `Rain Walkcycle` action strip where it is, but we do have one pressing issue: the action strip has a duration of only 24 frames, or one "cycle" of the walk, causing Rain to take 2 steps before stopping. Not exactly an improvement over what we had before, but easily corrected.

Extending the looping action

The action strip also has various properties in the right-hand sidebar (*N*) that, among other things, allow us to extend the strip so that the looping animation continues for as long as we want:

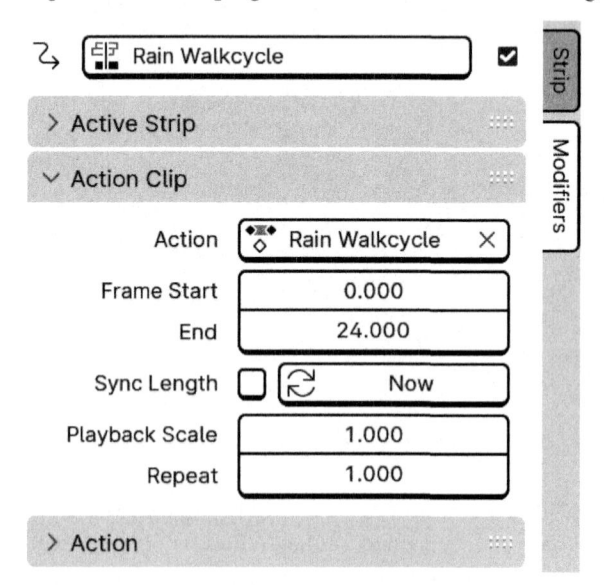

Figure 14.10: Action Clip properties

Normally, we'd use **Strip** | **Action Clip** | **Repeat** to do this, but in the case of `Rain Walkcycle`, it's better to simply increase the **End** frame to fill the length of the whole animation:

1. Select the `Rain Walkcycle` action strip in the Nonlinear Animation editor.
2. In the right-hand sidebar (*N*), find **Strip** | **Action Clip**.
3. Edit the **End** frame to extend the strip to the last frame of your animation.

Though the walk cycle no longer repeats indefinitely, it lasts as long as the animation does, which is effectively the same thing:

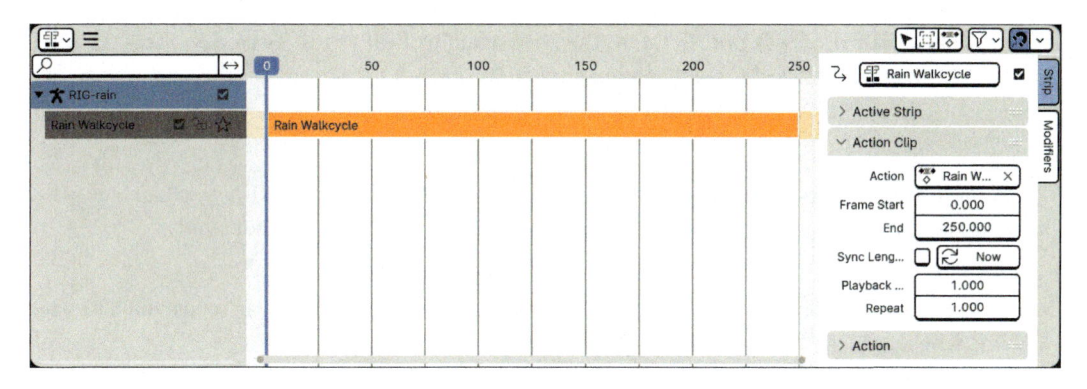

Figure 14.11: Extended action strip

Extending `Rain Walkcycle` this way works because we already made most of the animation channels cyclic, including a few for bones, which have been animated to travel continuously along the *Y* axis. Increasing the **End** frame is preferable as it allows those bones to continue traveling instead of snapping back every 24 frames.

If you haven't done so already, you can mute the **Y Location** channel that makes `ROOT_Child` travel backward, allowing the rest of Rain to travel forward. But that would require editing the action...

Tweaking the action strip

With the action gone from our other animation editors – even as it affects the animation from the NLA – you may be wondering: how do we get it back? Is it so crazy that we might want to go back and edit some keyframes? Not at all! It would be wrong, downright immoral even, if pushing down an action were irreversible.

Editing the action used as an action strip in the NLA is known as *tweaking*. To do this, select the strip and click **Edit** | **Start Tweaking Strip Actions**, or just press *Tab*:

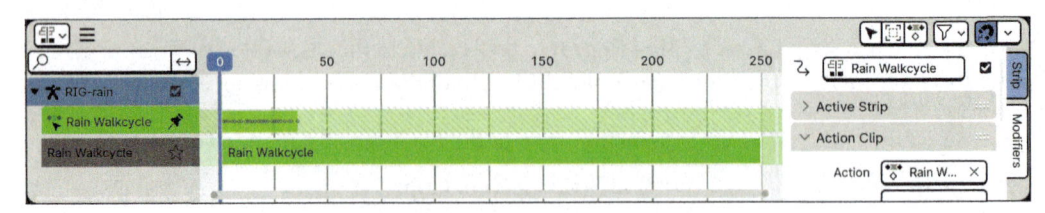

Figure 14.12: action strip being tweaked

This will cause the action in question to reappear in all the lesser animation editors, where keyframes can once again be inserted and edited as normal.

When you're finished, you can press *Tab* in the NLA again or **Edit | Stop Tweaking Strip Actions**. It's a lot like toggling between **Object Mode** and **Edit Mode**, but for actions!

> **Tip**
>
> To completely go back to the way things were before we started using the NLA, you can always delete all the animation tracks and find the action again in the Action Editor.

With action strips, we can think about actions in a brand-new way, but we've yet to see the best part, which is when we bring in more than just one action.

Layering actions

In the previous exercises for *Chapters 8* and *9*, we animated two things: Rain walking, and Rain talking. Working on these two exercises created two actions, one of which we've appended already. Our objective is to append the second action and combine it with the first one so that Rain walks and talks in one shot. This scenario is not uncommon in larger productions; for instance, two animators on a team might work separately on different actions for one character before a third animator combines them. Or, in the case of video game production, a character needs a whole library of pre-made actions (running, jumping, shooting, and so on) that must be tested in combination or tight sequence.

How do we combine two actions? The obvious solution is to copy/paste the keyframes from one action to the other, creating one big *mega* action. Often, this is unavoidable, but it's also destructive and inflexible. What if we expect to change or offset one of the actions later? Or – and this is where the NLA really shines – what if two actions contain animation channels for the same thing?

The Nonlinear Animation editor takes care of these issues. In this section, we'll learn how to use the NLA to non-destructively combine two or more actions as action strips.

Layering actions | 413

Appending the second action

First, we need to find that lip-syncing action we created back in *Chapter 9*:

1. Click **File** | **Append** and navigate to the `.blend` file you made for the lip-syncing exercise.
2. Append the `Rain Lipsync` action.
3. Adjust the length of the animation to suit the new action.
4. If you like, go to the Video Sequencer and add the same audio you used for the lip-syncing exercise as well.

Now we have a second action, the lip-syncing action can be assigned to Rain in the Action Editor, just as we assigned the walk-cycle action before pushing it down in the NLA. But there's more than one way to assign an action...

Adding actions in the NLA

If we select the new action for Rain in the Action Editor, it will be the new Active Action, which we can see when we return to the NLA:

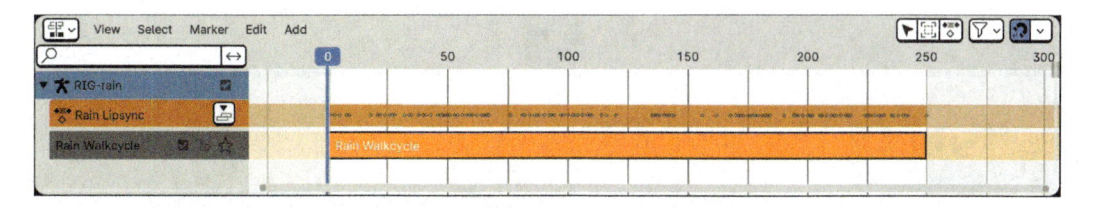

Figure 14.13: Active Action alongside an action strip

Note that this does not replace the existing action strip! More on that in a bit.

We can then push down the second action as we did with the first one, giving us two action strips to work with:

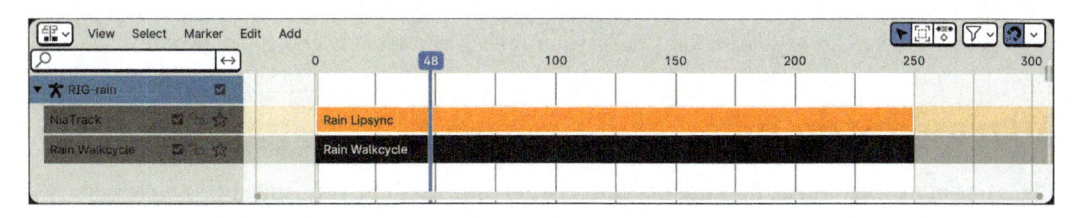

Figure 14.14: Two action strips

We could do that, or we could save ourselves a couple of keystrokes by adding the action as a strip directly in the NLA. To do that, follow the next steps:

1. Go to the Nonlinear Animation editor and make sure `RIG-rain` is selected.
2. Use **Add Action** (*Shift + A*) and choose the lip-syncing action you just appended.
3. If needed, move the new action strip to the correct point in time.

With two action strips influencing Rain at the same time, we can finally see what makes the NLA so special!

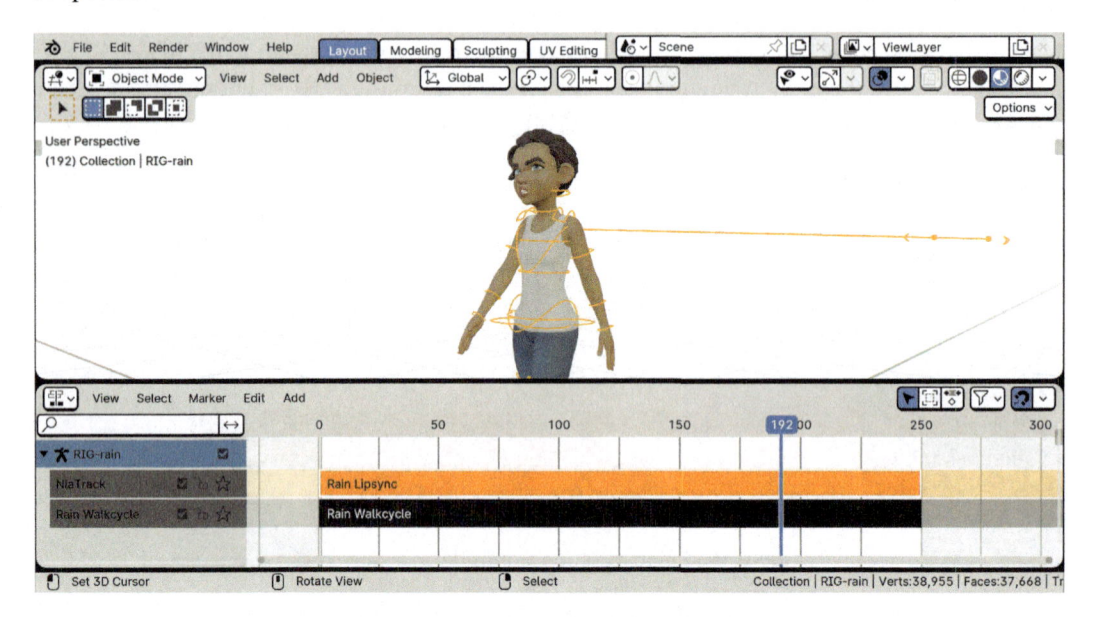

Figure 14.15: Two action strips making Rain walk and talk

Those two actions we made earlier have been combined to make a complete animation, all while keeping the two actions in separate tracks – making them easier to independently control, tweak, or reference as a linked library. Now, Rain can say her lines while actually going somewhere!

Animated Strip Time

Here's one more trick we can do with the NLA: control time itself! By animating one simple value, we can control how time is evaluated for an action strip, allowing us to simulate slow motion or a time lapse, or even to rewind time and make the action go in reverse.

How does it work? Imagine yourself playing with your animation by scrubbing back and forth, making Rain do a little dance as you move the mouse side to side. The result would be a kind of animation in its own right. Essentially, you'd be animating the current frame number, and that's almost exactly what we're about to do in this section.

The Strip Time property

I know what you're thinking: can't we already control time? Just smear around some keyframes until everything moves as quickly or slowly as we want. Isn't that what animation is?

Not anymore! Editing keyframes this way is destructive and sloppy, and besides, we're in the Nonlinear Animation editor now! We've transcended needing to edit all those fiddly little keyframes.

Instead, all we need to do is animate the **Strip Time** property:

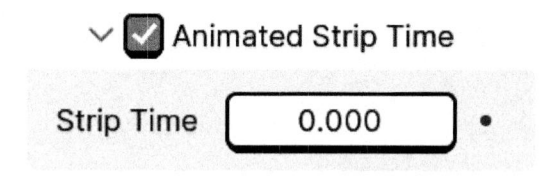

Figure 14.16: The Strip Time property

The **Strip Time** property determines the current frame, not for the scene itself, but just for the action strip. In other words, we might be on frame 50, but which frame of `Rain Walkcycle` in particular do we want to see? That's for us to decide now!

Keying the Strip Time property

Let's start by keying the **Strip Time** property for `Rain Walkcycle`:

1. In the Nonlinear Animation editor, select the action strip for Rain's walk cycle.
2. In the right-hand sidebar (*N*), enable **Strip | Active Strip | Animated Strip Time**.

   Enabling this property initially freezes the action strip. No matter which frame the scene itself is on, the action thinks it's whichever frame is indicated by **Strip Time**. This value must be animated deliberately to make things move again.
3. At frame 0, key the **Strip Time** value.
4. Go to the last frame in your animation, set the **Strip Time** value to a different frame number, and key it.

Animating the **Strip Time** value is now the only way to make time move forward for the action strip, and depending on how you animated the value here, time could be moving very slowly or very quickly for the walk cycle.

Before we start controlling the fabric of time itself, it's often best to have time move ordinarily at first, by animating **Strip Time** to match the current frame. This will help us to understand how the feature works and make it easier to choose exactly when and how we bend the movement of time.

Starting with linear Strip Time

Let's take a look at the F-curve for **Strip Time**. In my case, I keyed a value of 0.0 at frame 0 and a value of 250.0 at frame 250, so I know the **Strip Time** value will match the frame number at those two keyframes:

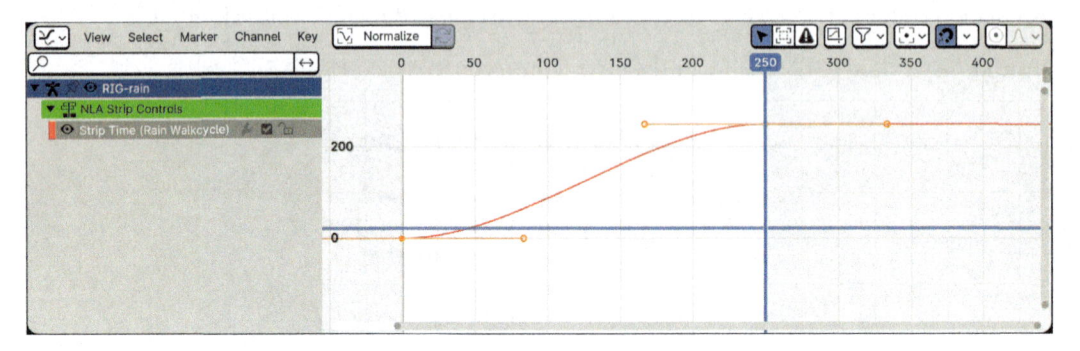

Figure 14.17: Initial animation of Strip Time

But there's still a matter of that interpolation, which has the interesting effect of accelerating and decelerating Rain's walking pace.

Let's try making it completely linear:

1. Go to the **Graph Editor** and find the **Strip Time** animation channel you just keyed.
2. Edit the keyframes of **Strip Time** so that their value equals the frame number.
3. Make the F-curve segment **Linear**.

Now we're back to the most boring line possible, literally $X = Y$:

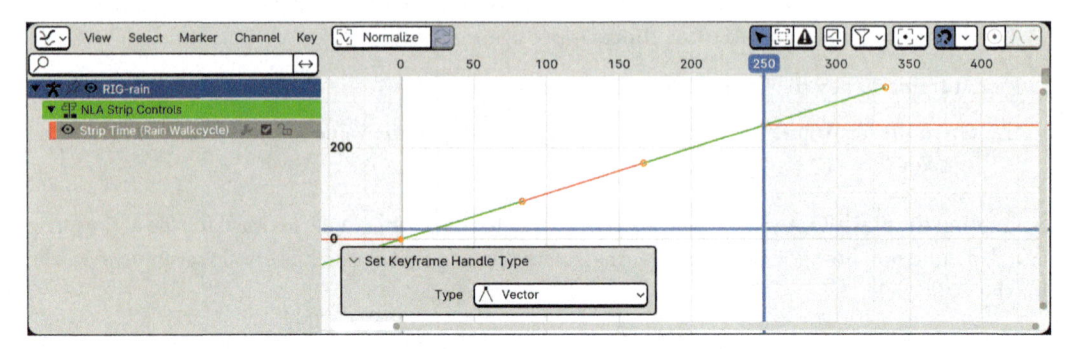

Figure 14.18: A linear function

This 1-to-1 function makes **Strip Time** match the current frame, and the action strip behaves normally again.

I swear there's a reason for doing this. Now, we have a proper starting point from which to deviate, as in this example where Rain walks directly into a slow-motion zone:

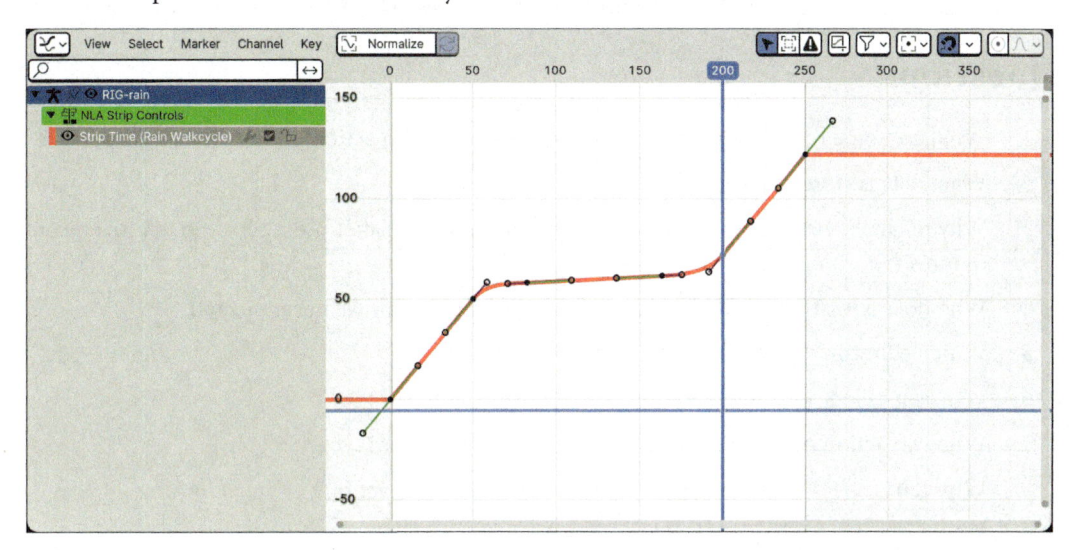

Figure 14.19: Linear time turning into bullet time and back

Not the most exciting thing to do with just a walk cycle, but you get the idea – this is the part where things get truly nonlinear. We can slow Rain down, speed her up, and rewind her all in one shot, without touching the action data itself. We can put Rain in slow motion while everything else moves like a time lapse. If we key the **Strip Time** value of Rain's lip-syncing as well, we can make her talk backward while walking forward or vice versa. Just imagine what you can do when you add some more actions and characters of your own!

Summary

Imagine you're reading a book about Blender that instructs you to model one and only one object in each exercise. Not until the final chapter do you learn what an object is and how you can arrange multiple objects together using something called **Object Mode**. That's what it feels like to teach the Nonlinear Animation editor!

The NLA is a bit of an esoteric tool. As of this writing, not a lot of people really understand how to use it – basically just me, a dozen people in Amsterdam, half a dozen more people in Asia and Australia, and three different guys from South America named Pablo. I'm only half joking. But now that you know what the NLA does and how to use it, you can count yourself as a member of this exclusive elite club!

We began this book learning how to animate a cube, and by the end, we learned how we can animate an animation. Not a bad way to start and end our journey. I'd say you're finally an animator now, but don't you remember? You were already an animator when you finished *Chapter 1* of this book. You're still a student, of course, but that's a good thing – I'm a student too, you know. I'll always be learning and animating, and I hope you'll do the same. Thanks for reading.

Questions

1. What are some reasons an animator would want to link an action instead of using **Append**?
2. What data is stored in an action?
3. Why might you want to insert just one keyframe for a bone after posing it, even if it isn't meant to move?
4. Why does our .blend file for this exercise contain actions we never created?
5. Which editor in Blender is used to edit actions?
6. Why is it called "pushing down"?
7. When an action strip is moved, what happens to the action?
8. Why can't the F-Curve for **Strip Time** be contained in an action?
9. What is "nonlinear" about the Nonlinear Animation editor?
10. How many different technical definitions can you give for the words "animate," "animated," and "animation"?

Index

A

absolute file path 161
    versus relative file path 161, 162
acting, without speaking 299
    Auto Keying 302
    Auto Keying, used for refine
        face poses 302, 303
    automatic keyframing 301
    key facial expressions 299, 300
    keying sets 301
Action Editor 269
    action, assigning 403, 404
    action, establishing as cyclic 271
    action, renaming 270, 271
    Cycle-Aware Keying, enabling 271
    hidden actions 404, 405
action strip 406, 409
    looping action, extending 410, 411
    tweaking 411, 412
    using 410
active camera 389-391
active rigid bodies 369, 379
Aligned handle 63, 64
    Vector handle, combining with 64, 65

animated camera 127
animated constraint 329
    influence property 329
Animated Strip Time
    property 415
    property, keying 415, 416
    working, with linear Strip Time 416, 417
animation channels 26-28
    six keyframes 26
animation, Dope Sheet 218-220
    animation channels 220-222
    channel groups, re-ordering 228, 229
    channels, re-grouping 224
    face bone channels, grouping 227, 228
    finger bone channels, grouping 226, 227
    keyframes, editing 222, 223
    keyframes, in summary 223, 224
    organizing 224
    timeline 220
animation path
    editing 102, 103
appending
    versus linking 159, 160
armature 155
armature layers 169

Asset Browser 195
  poses, adding to 205, 206
  poses, applying from 206, 207
audio files
  importing, into Video Sequencer 294-296
Auto Keying 302
  using, to refine face poses 302, 303

B

ball bounce 36
  bouncing keyframes, adding
    in Graph Editor 37
  linear interpolation for objects, in mid air 36
ball rolling example 22, 23
Bezier handles
  bounces, with Free handles 68-70
  editing 65, 66
  smooth movement, with
    Aligned handles 66-68
Bezier handle, types 57
  Aligned handle 63, 64
  Auto Clamped handles 60-62
  Automatic handles 60-62
  Automatic keyframes, usage
    considerations 62, 63
  keyframe handles, exposing 58
  overview 59, 60
  Vector handle 63, 64
  Vector handle, combining with
    Aligned handles 64, 65
Bezier keyframes 49
Bone Collections 169
bone constraints 325
bones 165-167
bouncing keyframes
  adding, in Graph Editor 37

built-in FFmpeg 149
Built-In Function modifier 350, 351

C

camera
  adding, to scene 123
  animated camera 127
  camera view, toggling 124
  lens 125, 126
  positioning 124, 125
  setting up 122, 123
  switching, in Timeline 391, 392
camera overrides 393
  local camera, viewing 393
  multiple cameras, using in
    Video Sequencer 394
character 155
  linking, into scene 157
character animation 230
  Graph Editor on bones, using 239, 240
  in-between operators 235, 236
  keyframes, inserting in Dope Sheet 232
  keyframes, staggering 238
  key poses, reviewing 217, 218
  library of poses, creating 195
  polishing 238, 239
  pose bones, keying 212
  pose bones, keying guidelines 212-217
  poses, glancing 230, 231
  Rain, linking into new project 204, 205
  Rain, preparing in new scene 204
  Rain's accessories, animating 242, 243
  recognizing 233-235
  two more in-between poses 230
  waving 236, 237

character animation armature
  accessories 193, 194
  facial expressions 189-193
  finger controls 186-188
  fingers 186
  FK bones 181
  IK bones 177, 178
  IK hands 178-180
  Pose Mode 173, 174
  posing 172, 173
  rest position 176, 177
  torso and hips, posing 174-176
character animation, library of poses
  Asset Browser 195
  pose asset, creating 196, 197
  poses, practicing 197-200
character, in scene
  library override, creating 162, 163
  linked libraries 157-159
  linking, versus appending 159, 160
character rig 155
CH-rain 158
clock, setting with math 352
  expressions, entering into numeric fields 353
  periodicity, of pendulum 352
  time, setting on second hand 353
CloudRig interface 163-169
  Rain appearance, preparing in 3D Viewport 170-172
collection 158
  instance 158
collision shapes 373
  Compound Parent 376, 377
  Mesh/Convex Hull shapes 375, 376
  primitive collision shapes 374, 375
Constant Extrapolation 43

constraints 51, 97, 98
  adding 98
  copying 101
  world space, versus local space 99, 100
Copy Transforms constraint 323, 324
  grab bone, snapping 324-326
curve object 102
Cycle-Aware Keying
  enabling 271
cyclic dependency 118
cyclic extrapolation 44-46

D

datablocks 157, 205
dependency loop 118
dependency, parent/child relationship 97
Dope Sheet
  keyframes, inserting in 232
driver 109
  adding 110
  data path, copying 114, 115
  editing 110, 111
  types 112
  variables 112-114
driver F-curves 115
  displaying 116, 117
  editing 117, 118

E

easing
  for bouncing ball 41, 42
easing type
  setting 34, 35
empty object 91
extrapolation 43
eye target 192

F

F-curve 26
  creating 346
  deleting 27
  extrapolation 43
  hiding 27
  locking 27
F-curve modifiers 260, 345, 346
  adding 347-349
  Built-In Function modifier 350, 351
  Stepped Interpolation modifier 349, 350
file dependencies 157
file path 161
FK bones
  connected bones, switching 182
  FK hinge 184
  posing 182, 183
  shoulder bones 185, 186
FK Hinge 184, 185
FK spine 183, 184
floor
  creating 368, 369
Follow Path constraint 101, 104
  adding 104
  path offsets, correcting 105, 106
Forward Kinematics (FK) 181
frames
  in rigid body simulation 366
frames per second (FPS) 6

G

grab bone 321, 322
  constraint, adding 327, 328
  constraint, applying 326, 327
  constraint, viewing 328
  snapping 324-326

Graph Editor 21-24
  bouncing keyframes, adding 37
  keyframes, adding within 38
  keyframes, duplicating 40, 41
  keyframes, inserting in 55-57
  normalized F-curve view 31
  panning 29
  view, adjusting 28, 29
  X and Y axes 24
  X and Y axes, scaling 30
  zooming 29
Graph Editor, on bones
  motion, finessing of torso 240-242
  using 239, 240

H

high dynamic range (HDR) format 142

I

IK bones 177, 178
IK hands 178-180
IK Parents 207-209
IK Pole Target 180, 181
IK solver 180
image sequence conversion, to video
  output settings, for video export 149
  performing 145
  video, outputting 151
  Video Sequence Editor, using 146
image sequence, rendering 139
  animation, rendering 144, 145
  benefits 139
  output file formats 141-143
  Output Path, setting 141

output settings 140
pre-render checklist 143, 144
rendered frames, viewing 145
in-between operators 235
interpolation 12, 32
  for bouncing ball 41, 42
  mode, setting 32-34
Inverse Kinetics (IK) 170

K

keyed property 10, 11
keyframes 3
  adding, within Graph Editor 38
  basic keyframe editing 13
  copying 81
  copying, to another channel 80, 81
  duplicating 14
  duplicating, in Graph Editor 40, 41
  editing, in Timeline 13
  initial location, keying 8
  inserting, in Graph Editor 55-57
  pasting 82
  position, holding 14
  second location, keying 11
  simple movement, creating 8
  single property, keying 81, 82
  timing of animation, editing 15, 16
  values, editing of 38, 39
  values, scaling 83, 84
keying
  material color 17, 18
  methods 17
  principles 12
keying rotation 12, 13
Keying Sets 301

L

library override
  making 162, 163
  Rain, re-booting 163, 164
linear extrapolation 43, 44
linear interpolation
  for objects, in mid-air 36
linear Strip Time 416, 417
linked libraries 157-159
  file path 161, 162
linking
  versus appending 159, 160
lip-syncing
  mouth, animating 308, 309
  phonetics, for animators 303
  science 303
local camera 394

M

markers 392
material color
  keying 17, 18
modifiers
  copying 356
  randomization, randomizing 356, 357
motion path 71
multiple cameras
  scene strip, using 395, 396
  selecting, for scene strip 397, 398
  setting up 388, 389
  using, in Video Sequencer 394
multiple F-curves
  copying 283, 284

N

Noise modifier 358
   adding 354, 355
   adjusting 355, 356
   explosion, simulating 358
   frame range, restricting of 359
   using 354
Nonlinear Animation editor (NLA) 401, 406, 407
   actions, adding in 413, 414
   actions in 408
   actions, layering 412
   actions, reusing 402
   action strip 406, 409
   action strip, tweaking 411, 412
   action strip, using 410
   Animated Strip Time 414
   second action, appending 413
   viewing 407, 408
Nonlinear Animation editor (NLA), actions
   assigning, in Action Editor 403, 404
   hard lesson, in forgotten settings 405, 406
   walk cycle, appending 403
normalized F-curve view 31
Normalize feature 31

O

object origins 88-90
   centering 91, 92
   facts 90, 91
   grabbing 92-94
object relationship
   animation 316
   IK arms, using 314, 315
   props, creating 313, 314
   setting up 312, 313
object relationship, animation
   ball, grabbing 316, 317
   element touch 317, 318
   standing pose 318, 319
object relationship chart 118
objects
   parenting 94, 95
object-to-bone relationship
   Copy Transforms constraint 323, 324
   Dummy bone 320, 321
   setting up 319, 320
output settings, for video export 149
   built-in FFmpeg, using 149
   output path, setting 149

P

parent/child relationship 95, 96
   dependencies 97
parenting 51
passive rigid bodies 369, 370
path, animating 106, 107
   Evaluation Time, keying 107
   points of inflection, along peaks 108, 109
   train speed, refining 107, 108
phonetics for animators 303
   consonants 304
   vowels 303, 304
   vowels, combining 304
phonetics for animators, consonants
   lips 305
   sounds 307
   teeth 305
   tongue 306
points of inflection 78
pose 172
pose asset
   using 205

posing 172
preview playback range
   using 266, 267

R

Rain
   bones, hiding 211, 212
   linking, into new project 204, 205
   preparing, in new scene 204
Rain armature 164
   appearance, preparing in 3D Viewport 170-172
   art, of rigging 165
   bone 165, 167
   CloudRig interface 168, 169
   layers 169, 170
Rain, in scene
   bone relationships, setting for animation 207
   bones, hiding 211, 212
   pose asset, using 205
   poses, adding to asset browser 205, 206
   poses, applying from asset browser 206, 207
Rain's bone, relationship for animation
   IK Parents 207-209
   visual transforms, applying 210, 211
recognizing pose 234
relative file path 162
Rendered Viewport Shading method 129, 130
render engines 128
rendering 127
   basics 127
   controls 130, 131
   operators 131
   scene, setting up for 133
   whole animation render, avoiding 132

render performance
   managing 138, 139
   predicting 138, 139
Repeat with Offset
   using 262
Restrict Frame Range feature 359
rig 165
rigger 165
rigging 165
rigid body 365, 366
   controlling, directly 382
   creating 364
   floor, creating 368, 369
   interacting, in realtime 383
rigid body collision 371, 372
   collision shapes 373
   smashing-junk-together algorithm 373
   shapes, selecting 377
Rigid Body Physics 363
rigid body physics simulation 364, 365
   frames 366
   settings 366-368
rolling 22

S

scene
   Rain, preparing in 204
scene, setting up for rendering
   render resolution 137, 138
   render settings 135-137
   sky and ground, adding 133-135
scene strip
   using 395, 396
smashing-junk-together algorithm 373
sound, in Blender
   audio files, importing into Video Sequencer 294-296

audio length, trimming 297
sound strips, properties 296
sound strips, using 296
timeline, setup for working with 298, 299
using 294

sound strips
audio length, trimming 297
properties 296
using 296

Stepped Interpolation modifier 349, 350

stride length
establishing 254

summary keys 27

T

throwing motion
animating 330-341
object relationship 338, 339
object visual transforms 337, 338
poses, using 332-335

Timeline 3-5
animation playback 7
frame range, setting 6
keyframes, editing 13
moving through time 5, 6
view, adjusting 6

timeline markers 248
adding 249
labeling 249, 250

torso animation
phase shifting 274, 275
rotation, mirroring of 273
twisting, at Contact poses 272, 273
with sine waves 272

torso movement 268
bouncing, down and up 268, 269

tossing motion
animating 330

U

unicycle
animating 50
animation channels, for Seat 70
connected parts 51
course checkpoints, keying 51-55
illusion of balance, completing 79, 80
keyframes, inserting in Graph Editor 55-57
motion paths, as visual guide 71-74
tilting, while turning 74-77
X Euler Rotation channel 77-80

unicycle, animation
keyframes, copying 81
keyframes, copying to another channel 80, 81
keyframes, pasting 82
keyframe values, scaling 83, 84
single property, keying 81, 82

V

Vector handle 63, 64
combining, with Aligned handles 64, 65

Video Sequence Editor 146
example project 146
frame, rendering from 148
image sequence, importing 147
scene, creating for video sequencing 146, 147

Video Sequencer
audio files, importing into 294-296
multiple cameras, using 394

Visual Keying 331, 332

W

walk cycle 246
walk cycle animation
  Action Editor 269
  advanced footwork 276
  final touches 289-291
  FK arms 288
  FK toes 286-288
  focusing, on IK bones 250, 251
  markers, adding 249
  markers, labeling 249, 250
  no bones left behind 251-253
  periodicity 246, 247
  periodic motion, adding 267
  phases 247, 248
  scene, preparing 246
  swaying, from side to side 269
  timeline 246
  timeline markers 248
  torso animation, with sine waves 272
  Torso movement 268
walk cycle animation, advanced footwork
  animation, copying from left foot to right foot 283-285
  feet, picking up 278, 279
  foot, rolling 276, 277
  motion of legs, correcting 279-283
  roll bone, keying 277, 278

walk cycle animation, on Y axis 253, 254
  looping 258-260
  loop, offsetting 260-262
  preview playback range, using 266, 267
  stride length, establishing 254-258
  walking, on treadmill 262-266
wall
  brick, building 378, 379
  building 378-381
  destroying 378, 381
  rigid bodies, controlling directly 382
  Rigid Body deactivation 379, 380
  simulation, baking 385, 386
  wrecking ball, animating 383-385
  wrecking ball, creating 382

X

X Euler Rotation channel 77-80
x-intercept 79
X Location F-curve 66-68

‹packt›

packtpub.com

Subscribe to our online digital library for full access to over 7,000 books and videos, as well as industry leading tools to help you plan your personal development and advance your career. For more information, please visit our website.

Why subscribe?

- Spend less time learning and more time coding with practical eBooks and Videos from over 4,000 industry professionals
- Improve your learning with Skill Plans built especially for you
- Get a free eBook or video every month
- Fully searchable for easy access to vital information
- Copy and paste, print, and bookmark content

Did you know that Packt offers eBook versions of every book published, with PDF and ePub files available? You can upgrade to the eBook version at packtpub.com and as a print book customer, you are entitled to a discount on the eBook copy. Get in touch with us at customercare@packtpub.com for more details.

At www.packtpub.com, you can also read a collection of free technical articles, sign up for a range of free newsletters, and receive exclusive discounts and offers on Packt books and eBooks.

Other Books You May Enjoy

If you enjoyed this book, you may be interested in these other books by Packt:

3D Character Rigging in Blender

Jaime Kelly

ISBN: 978-1-80323-880-7

- Understand the basic terminology of rigging and learn how to create and modify rigs.
- Find out how bones interact with topology.
- Get to grips with weight painting through the mesh.
- Know when and how to add constraints such as Inversion Kinetics, Point To, and Child Of.
- Make rigs visually appealing with advanced techniques such as shape keys and bone drivers.
- Familiarize yourself with advanced techniques used by industry leaders

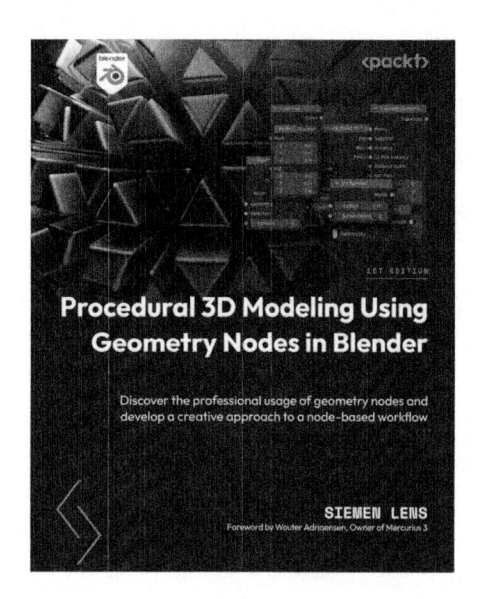

Procedural 3D Modeling Using Geometry Nodes in Blender

Siemen Lens

ISBN: 978-1-80461-255-2

- Discover the different node inputs and outputs that geometry nodes have to offer.
- Get the hang of the flow of the geometry node system.
- Understand the common nodes you'll be using along with their functions in the geometry node editor.
- Modify basic mesh primitives using the node system inside Blender.
- Scatter and modify objects aligned onto a curve.
- Become familiar with the more advanced nodes in the geometry nodes system.
- Link geometry and material nodes editors using named attributes.
- Implement your new-found knowledge of nodes in real-world projects

Packt is searching for authors like you

If you're interested in becoming an author for Packt, please visit `authors.packtpub.com` and apply today. We have worked with thousands of developers and tech professionals, just like you, to help them share their insight with the global tech community. You can make a general application, apply for a specific hot topic that we are recruiting an author for, or submit your own idea.

Hi!

I am Sam Brubaker, author of *Realizing 3D Animation in Blender*. I really hope you enjoyed reading this book and found it useful for increasing your productivity and efficiency.

It would really help me (and other potential readers!) if you could leave a review on Amazon sharing your thoughts on this book.

Go to the link below or scan the QR code to leave your review:

`https://packt.link/r/1801077215`

Your review will help us to understand what's worked well in this book, and what could be improved upon for future editions, so it really is appreciated.

Best wishes,

Sam Brubaker

Download a free PDF copy of this book

Thanks for purchasing this book!

Do you like to read on the go but are unable to carry your print books everywhere?

Is your eBook purchase not compatible with the device of your choice?

Don't worry, now with every Packt book you get a DRM-free PDF version of that book at no cost.

Read anywhere, any place, on any device. Search, copy, and paste code from your favorite technical books directly into your application.

The perks don't stop there, you can get exclusive access to discounts, newsletters, and great free content in your inbox daily

Follow these simple steps to get the benefits:

1. Scan the QR code or visit the link below

`https://packt.link/free-ebook/9781801077217`

2. Submit your proof of purchase
3. That's it! We'll send your free PDF and other benefits to your email directly

Printed in Great Britain
by Amazon